Clara Widenham Hadley
April 18th 1887.

"She lingered at the door before she gathered courage to knock."—PAGE 277.

NOVELS

OF

GEORGE ELIOT.

VOL. IV.

SCENES OF CLERICAL LIFE

AND

SILAS MARNER.

WITH ILLUSTRATIONS.

SHEPPERTON CHURCH, AS IT WAS.

NEW YORK:

HARPER & BROTHERS, PUBLISHERS,

FRANKLIN SQUARE.

SCENES

OF

CLERICAL LIFE.

BY

GEORGE ELIOT.

NEW YORK:

HARPER & BROTHERS, PUBLISHERS,

FRANKLIN SQUARE.

CONTENTS.

THE SAD FORTUNES

OF

THE REV. AMOS BARTON.

CHAPTER I.

SHEPPERTON CHURCH was a very different-looking building five-and-twenty years ago. To be sure, its substantial stone tower looks at you through its intelligent eye, the clock, with the friendly expression of former days; but in every thing else what changes! Now there is a wide span of slated roof flanking the old steeple; the windows are tall and symmetrical; the outer doors are resplendent with oak-graining, the inner doors reverentially noiseless with a garment of red baize; and the walls, you are convinced, no lichen will ever again effect a settlement on—they are smooth and innutrient as the summit of the Rev. Amos Barton's head, after ten years of baldness and supererogatory soap. Pass through the baize doors, and you will see the nave filled with well-shaped benches, understood to be free seats; while in certain eligible corners, less directly under the fire of the clergyman's eye, there are pews reserved for the Shepperton gentility. Ample galleries are supported on iron pillars, and in one of them stands the crowning glory, the very clasp or aigrette of Shepperton church-adornment—namely, an organ, not very much out of repair, on which a collector of small rents, differentiated by the force of circumstances into an organist, will accompany the alacrity of your departure after the blessing, by a sacred minuet or an easy "Gloria."

Immense improvement! says the well-regulated mind, which unintermittingly rejoices in the New Police, the Tithe Commutation Act, the penny-post, and all guaranties of human advancement, and has no moments when conservative-reforming intellect takes a nap, while imagination does a little Toryism by the sly, revelling in regret that dear, old, brown, crumbling, picturesque inefficiency is everywhere giving place to spick-and-span new-painted, new-varnished efficiency, which will yield endless diagrams, plans, elevations, and sections, but alas! no picture. Mine, I fear, is not a well-regulated mind: it has an occasional tenderness for old abuses; it lingers with a certain fondness over the days of nasal clerks and top-booted parsons, and has a sigh for the departed shades of vulgar errors. So it is not surprising that I recall with a fond sadness Shepperton Church as it was in the old days, with its outer coat of rough stucco, its red-tiled roof, its heterogeneous windows patched with desultory bits of painted glass, and its little flight of steps with their wooden rail running up the outer wall, and leading to the school-children's gallery.

Then inside, what dear old quaintnesses! which I began to look at with delight even when I was so crude a member of the congregation that my nurse found it necessary to provide for the re-enforcement of my devotional patience by smuggling bread-and-butter into the sacred edifice. There was the chancel, guarded by two little cherubim looking uncomfortably squeezed between arch and wall, and adorned with the escutcheons of the Oldinport family, which showed me inexhaustible possibilities of meaning in their blood-red hands, their death's-heads and cross-bones, their leopards' paws, and Maltese crosses. There were inscriptions on the panels of the singing-gallery, telling of benefactions to the poor of Shepperton, with an involuted elegance of capitals and final flourishes, which my alphabetic erudition traced with ever-new delight. No benches in those days; but huge roomy pews, round which devout church-goers sat during "lessons," trying to look anywhere else than into each other's eyes. No low partitions allowing you, with a dreary absence of contrast and mystery, to see every thing at all moments; but tall dark panels, under whose shadow I sank with a sense of retirement through the Litany, only to feel with more intensity my burst into the conspicuousness of public life when I was made to stand up on the seat during the psalms or the singing.

And the singing was no mechanical affair of official routine; it had a drama. As the moment of psalmody approached, by some process to me as mysterious and untraceable as the opening of the flowers or the breaking-out of the stars, a slate appeared in front of the gallery, advertising in bold characters the psalm about to be sung, lest the sonorous announcement of the clerk should still leave the bucolic mind in doubt on that head. Then followed the migration of the clerk to the gallery, where, in company with a bassoon, two key-bugles, a carpenter understood to have an amazing power of singing "counter," and two lesser musical stars, he formed a complement of a choir regarded in Shepperton as one of distinguished attraction, occasionally known to draw hearers from the next parish. The innovation of hymn-books was as yet undreamed of; even the New Version was regarded with a sort of melancholy tolerance, as part of the common degeneracy in a time when prices had dwindled, and a cotton gown was no longer stout enough to last a lifetime; for the lyrical taste of the best heads in Shepperton had been formed on Sternhold and Hopkins. But the greatest triumphs of the Shepperton choir were reserved for the Sundays when the slate announced an ANTHEM, with a dignified abstinence from particularization, both words and music lying far beyond the reach of the most ambitious amateur in the congregation:—an anthem in which the key-bugles always ran away at a great pace, while the bassoon every now and then boomed a flying shot after them.

As for the clergyman, Mr. Gilfil, an excellent old gentleman, who smoked very long pipes, and preached very short sermons, I must not speak of him, or I might be tempted to tell the story of his life, which had its little romance, as most lives have between the ages of teetotum and tobacco. And at present I am concerned with quite another sort of clergyman—the Rev. Amos Barton, who did not come to Shepperton until long after Mr. Gilfil had departed this life—until after an interval in which Evangelicalism and the Catholic Question had begun to agitate the rustic mind with controversial debates. A Popish blacksmith had produced a strong Protestant reaction by declaring that, as soon as the Emancipation Bill was passed, he should do a great stroke of business in gridirons; and the disinclination of the Shepperton parishioners generally to dim the unique glory of St. Lawrence, rendered the Church and Constitution an affair of their business and bosoms. A zealous Evangelical preacher had made the old sounding-board vibrate with quite a different sort of elocution from Mr. Gilfil's; the hymn-book had almost superseded the Old and New Versions; and the great square pews were crowded with new faces from distant corners of the parish—perhaps from Dissenting chapels.

You are not imagining, I hope, that Amos Barton was the incumbent of Shepperton. He was no such thing. Those were days when a man could hold three small livings, starve a curate apiece on two of them, and live badly himself on the third. It was so with the Vicar of Shepperton; a vicar given to bricks and mortar, and thereby running into debt far away in a northern county—who executed his vicarial functions towards Shepperton by pocketing the sum of thirty-five pounds ten per annum, the net surplus remaining to him from the proceeds of that living, after the disbursement of eighty pounds as the annual stipend of his curate. And now, pray, can you solve me the following problem? Given a man with a wife and six children: let him be obliged always to exhibit himself when outside his own door in a suit of black broadcloth, such as will not undermine the foundations of the Establishment by a paltry plebeian glossiness or an unseemly whiteness at the edges; in a snowy cravat, which is a serious investment of labor in the hemming, starching, and ironing departments; and in a hat which shows no symptom of taking to the hideous doctrine of expediency, and shaping itself according to circumstances; let him have a parish large enough to create an external necessity for abundant shoe-leather, and an internal necessity for abundant beef and mutton, as well as poor enough to require frequent priestly consolation in the shape of shillings and sixpences; and, lastly, let him be compelled, by his own pride and other people's, to dress his wife and children with gentility from bonnet-strings to shoe-strings. By what process of division can the sum of eighty pounds per annum be made to yield a quotient which will cover that man's weekly expenses? This was the problem presented by the position of the Rev. Amos Barton, as curate of Shepperton, rather more than twenty years ago.

What was thought of this problem, and of the man who had to work it out, by some of the well-to-do inhabitants of Shepperton, two years or more after Mr. Barton's arrival among them, you shall hear, if you will accompany me to Cross Farm, and to the fireside of Mrs. Patten, a childless old lady, who had got rich chiefly by the negative process of spending nothing. Mrs. Patten's passive accumulation of wealth, through all sorts of "bad times," on the farm of which she had been sole tenant since her husband's death, her epigrammatic neighbor, Mrs. Hackit, sarcastically accounted for by supposing that "sixpences grew on the bents of Cross Farm;" while Mr. Hackit, expressing his views more literally, reminded his wife that "money breeds money." Mr. and Mrs. Hackit, from the neighboring farm, are Mrs. Patten's guests this evening; so is Mr. Pilgrim, the doctor from the nearest market-town, who, though occasionally affecting aristocratic airs, and giving late dinners with enigmatic side-dishes and poisonous port, is never so comfortable as when he is relaxing his professional legs in one of those excellent farmhouses where the mice are sleek and the mistress sickly. And he is at this moment in clover.

For the flickering of Mrs. Patten's bright fire is reflected in her bright copper tea-kettle, the home-made muffins glisten with an inviting succulence, and Mrs. Patten's niece, a single lady of fifty, who has refused the most ineligible offers out of devotion to her aged aunt, is pouring the rich cream into the fragrant tea with a discreet liberality.

Reader! *did* you ever taste such a cup of tea as Miss Gibbs is this moment handing to Mr. Pilgrim? Do you know the dulcet strength, the animating blandness of tea sufficiently blended with real farmhouse cream? No—most likely you are a miserable town-bred reader, who thinks of cream as a thinnish white fluid, delivered in infinitesimal pennyworths down area steps; or perhaps, from a presentiment of calves' brains, you refrain from any lacteal addition, and rasp your tongue with unmitigated bohea. You have a vague idea of a milch cow as probably a white-plaster animal standing in a butterman's window, and you know nothing of the sweet history of genuine cream, such as Miss Gibb's: how it was this morning in the udders of the large sleek beasts, as they stood lowing a patient entreaty under the milking-shed; how it fell with a pleasant rhythm into Betty's pail, sending a delicious incense into the cool air; how it was carried into that temple of moist cleanliness, the dairy, where it quietly separated itself from the meaner elements of milk, and lay in mellowed whiteness, ready for the skimming-dish which transferred it to Miss Gibbs's glass cream-jug. If I am right in my conjecture, you are unacquainted with the highest possibilities of tea; and Mr. Pilgrim, who is holding that cup in his hand, has an idea beyond you.

Mrs. Hackit declines cream; she has so long abstained from it with an eye to the weekly butter-money, that abstinence, wedded to habit, has begotten aversion. She is a thin woman with a chronic liver-complaint, which would have secured her Mr. Pilgrim's entire regard and unreserved good word, even if he had not been in awe of her tongue, which was as sharp as his own lancet. She has brought her knitting—no frivolous fancy knitting, but a substantial woollen stocking; the click-click of her knitting-needles is the running accompaniment to all her conversation; and in her utmost enjoyment of spoiling a friend's self-satisfaction, she was never known to spoil a stocking.

Mrs. Patten does not admire this excessive click-clicking activity. Quiescence in an easy-chair, under the sense of compound interest perpetually accumulating, has long seemed an ample function to her, and she does her malevolence gently. She is a pretty little old woman of eighty, with a close cap and tiny flat white curls round her face, as natty and unsoiled and invariable as the waxen image of a little old lady under a glass case; once a lady's-maid, and married for her beauty. She used to adore her husband, and now she adores her money, cherishing a quiet blood-relation's hatred for her niece, Janet Gibbs, who, she knows, expects a large legacy, and whom she is determined to disappoint. Her money shall all go in a lump to a distant relation of her husband's, and Janet shall be saved the trouble of pretending to cry, by finding that she is left with a miserable pittance.

Mrs. Patten has more respect for her neighbor Mr. Hackit than for most people. Mr. Hackit is a shrewd, substantial man, whose advice about crops is always worth listening to, and who is too well off to want to borrow money.

And now that we are snug and warm with this little tea-party, while it is freezing with February bitterness outside, we will listen to what they are talking about.

"So," said Mr. Pilgrim, with his mouth only half empty of muffin, "you had a row in Shepperton Church last Sunday. I was at Jim Hood's, the bassoon-man's, this morning, attending his wife, and he swears he'll be revenged on the parson—a confounded, methodistical, meddlesome chap, who must be putting his finger in every pie. What was it all about?"

"Oh, a passill o' nonsense," said Mr. Hackit, sticking one thumb between the buttons of his capacious waistcoat, and retaining a pinch of snuff with the other—for he was but moderately given to "the cups that cheer but not inebriate," and had already finished his tea; "they began to sing the wedding psalm for a new-married couple, as pretty a psalm an' as pretty a tune as any in the prayer-book. It's been sung for every new-married couple since I was a boy. And what can be better?" Here Mr. Hackit stretched out his left arm, threw back his head, and broke into melody—

"Oh what a happy thing it is,
And joyful for to see
Brethren to dwell together in
Friendship and unity.'

But Mr. Barton is all for the hymns, and a sort o' music as I can't join in at all."

"And so," said Mr. Pilgrim, recalling Mr. Hacket from lyrical reminiscences to narrative, "he called out Silence! did he? when he got into the pulpit; and gave a hymn out himself to some meeting-house tune?"

"Yes," said Mrs. Hackit, stooping towards the candle to pick up a stitch, "and turned as red as a turkey-cock. I often say, when he preaches about meekness, he gives himself a slap in the face. He's like me—he's got a temper of his own."

"Rather a low-bred fellow, I think, Barton," said Mr. Pilgrim, who hated the Reverend Amos for two reasons—because he had called in a new doctor, recently settled in Shepperton; and because, being himself a dabbler in drugs, he had the credit of having cured a patient of Mr. Pilgrim's. "They say his father was a Dissenting shoemaker; and he's half a Dissenter himself. Why, doesn't he preach extempore in that cottage up here, of a Sunday evening?"

"Tchuh!"—this was Mr. Hackit's favorite interjection—"that preaching without book's no good, only when a man has a gift, and has the Bible at his fingers' ends. It was all very well for Parry—he'd a gift; and in my youth I've heard the Ranters out o' doors in Yorkshire go on for an hour or two on end, without ever sticking fast a minute. There was one clever chap, I remember, as used to say, 'You're like the woodpigeon; it says do, do, do all day, and never sets about any work itself.' That's bringing it home to people. But our parson's no gift at all that way; he can preach as good a sermon as need be heard when he writes it down. But when he tries to preach wi'out book, he rambles about, and doesn't stick to his text; and every now and then he flounders about like a sheep as has cast itself, and can't get on its legs again. You wouldn't like that, Mrs. Patten, if you was to go to church now?"

"Eh, dear," said Mrs. Patten, falling back in her chair, and lifting up her little withered hands, "what 'ud Mr. Gilfil say, if he was worthy to know the changes as have come about i' the Church these last ten years? I don't understand these new sort o' doctrines. When Mr. Barton comes to see me, he talks about nothing but my sins and my need o' marcy. Now, Mr. Hackit, I've never been a sinner. From the fust beginning, when I went into service, I al'ys did my duty by my emplyers. I was a good wife as any in the county—never aggravated my husband. The cheese-factor used to say my cheese was al'ys to be depended on. I've known women, as their cheeses swelled a shame to be seen, when their husbands had counted on the cheese-money to make up their rent; and yet they'd three gowns to my one. If I'm not to be saved, I know a many as are in a bad way. But it's well for me as I can't go to church any longer, for if th' old singers are to be done away with, there'll be nothing left as it was in Mr. Patten's time; and what's more, I hear you've settled to pull the church down and build it up new?"

Now the fact was that the Rev. Amos Barton, on his last visit to Mrs. Patten, had urged her to enlarge her promised subscription of twenty pounds, representing to her that she was only a steward of her riches, and that she could not spend them more for the glory of God than by giving a heavy subscription towards the rebuilding of Shepperton Church—a practical precept which was not likely to smooth the way to her acceptance of his theological doctrine. Mr. Hackit, who had more doctrinal enlightenment than Mrs. Patten, had been a little shocked by the heathenism of her speech, and was glad of the new turn given to the subject by this question, addressed to him as church-warden and an authority in all parochial matters.

"Ah," he answered, "the parson's bothered us into it at last, and we're to begin pulling down this spring. But we have'nt got money enough yet. I was for waiting till we'd made up the sum; and, for my part, I think the congregation's fell off o' late, though Mr. Barton says that's because there's been no room for the people when they've come. You see, the congregation got so large in Parry's time, the people stood in the aisles; but there's never any crowd now, as I can see."

"Well," said Mrs. Hackit, whose good-nature began to act, now that it was a little in contradiction with the dominant tone of the conversation, "*I* like Mr. Barton. I think he's a good sort o' man, for all he's not overburden'd i' th' upper story; and his wife's as nice a lady-like woman as I'd wish to see. How nice she keeps her children! and little enough money to do't with; and a delicate creatur'—six children, and another a-coming. I don't know how they make both ends meet, I'm sure, now her aunt has left 'em. But I sent 'em a cheese and a sack o' potatoes last week; that's something towards filling the little mouths."

"Ah!" said Mr. Hackit, "and my wife makes Mr. Barton a good stiff glass o' brandy-and-water, when he comes in to supper after his cottage preaching. The parson likes it; it puts a bit o' color into his face, and makes him look a deal handsomer."

This allusion to brandy-and-water suggested to Miss Gibbs the introduction of the liquor decanters, now that the tea was cleared away; for in bucolic society five-and-twenty years ago, the human animal of the male sex was understood to be perpetually athirst, and "something to drink" was as necessary a "condition of thought" as Time and Space.

"Now, that cottage preaching," said Mr. Pilgrim, mixing

himself a strong glass of "cold without," "I was talking about it to our Parson Ely the other day, and he doesn't approve of it at all. He said it did as much harm as good to give a too familiar aspect to religious teaching. That was what Ely said—it does as much harm as good to give a too familiar aspect to religious teaching."

Mr. Pilgrim generally spoke with an intermittent kind of splutter; indeed, one of his patients had observed that it was a pity such a clever man had a "'pediment" in his speech. But when he came to what he conceived the pith of his argument or the point of his joke, he mouthed out his words with slow emphasis; as a hen, when advertising her accouchement, passes at irregular intervals from pianissimo semiquavers to fortissimo crotchets. He thought this speech of Mr. Ely's particularly metaphysical and profound, and the more decisive of the question because it was a generality which represented no particulars to his mind.

"Well, I don't know about that," said Mrs. Hackit, who had always the courage of her opinion, "but I know, some of our laborers and stockingers as used never to come to church, come to the cottage, and that's better than never hearing any thing good from week's end to week's end. And there's that Track Society as Mr. Barton has begun—I've seen more o' the poor people with going tracking, than all the time I've lived in the parish before. And there'd need be something done among 'em; for the drinking at them Benefit Clubs is shameful. There's hardly a steady man or steady woman either, but what's a Dissenter."

During this speech of Mrs. Hackit's, Mr. Pilgrim had emitted a succession of little snorts, something like the treble grunts of a guinea-pig, which were always with him the sign of suppressed disapproval. But he never contradicted Mrs. Hackit—a woman whose "pot-luck" was always to be relied on, and who on her side had unlimited reliance on bleeding, blistering, and draughts.

Mrs. Patten, however, felt equal disapprobation, and had no reasons for suppressing it.

"Well," she remarked, "I've heard of no good from interfering with one's neighbors, poor or rich. And I hate the sight o' women going about trapesing from house to house in all weathers, wet or dry, and coming in with their petticoats dagged and their shoes all over mud. Janet wanted to join in the tracking, but I told her I'd have nobody tracking out o' my house; when I'm gone, she may do as she likes. I never dagged my petticoats in *my* life, and I've no opinion o' that sort o' religion."

"No," said Mr. Hackit, who was fond of soothing the acerbities of the feminine mind with a jocose compliment, "you held your petticoats so high, to show your tight ankles: it isn't every body as likes to show her ankles."

This joke met with general acceptance, even from the snubbed Janet, whose ankles were only tight in the sense of looking extremely squeezed by her boots. But Janet seemed always to identify herself with her aunt's personality, holding her own under protest.

Under cover of the general laughter the gentlemen replenished their glasses, Mr. Pilgrim attempting to give his the character of a stirrup-cup by observing that he "must be going." Miss Gibbs seized this opportunity of telling Mrs. Hackit that she suspected Betty, the dairymaid, of frying the best bacon for the shepherd, when he sat up with her to "help brew;" whereupon Mrs. Hackit replied that she had always thought Betty false; and Mrs. Patten said there was no bacon stolen when *she* was able to manage. Mr. Hackit, who often complained that he "never saw the like to women with their maids—he never had any trouble with his men," avoided listening to this discussion, by raising the question of vetches with Mr. Pilgrim. The stream of conversation had thus diverged; and no more was said about the Rev. Amos Barton, who is the main object of interest to us just now. So we may leave Cross Farm without waiting till Mrs. Hackit, resolutely donning her clogs and wrappings, renders it incumbent on Mr. Pilgrim also to fulfill his frequent threat of going.

CHAPTER II.

It was happy for the Rev. Amos Barton that he did not, like us, overhear the conversation recorded in the last chapter. Indeed, what mortal is there of us, who would find his satisfaction enhanced by an opportunity of comparing the picture he presents to himself of his own doings, with the picture they make on the mental retina of his neighbors? We are poor plants buoyed up by the air-vessels of our own conceit: alas for us, if we get a few pinches that empty us of that windy self-subsistence! The very capacity for good would go out of us. For, tell the most impassioned orator, suddenly, that his wig is awry, or his shirt-lap hanging out, and that he is tickling people by the oddity of his person, instead of thrilling them by the energy of his periods, and you would infallibly dry up the spring of his eloquence. That is a deep and wide saying, that no miracle can be wrought without faith—without the worker's faith in himself, as well as the recipient's faith in him. And the greater part of the worker's faith in himself is made up of the faith that others believe in him.

Let me be persuaded that my neighbor Jenkins considers me a blockhead, and I shall never shine in conversation with him any more. Let me discover that the lovely Phœbe thinks my squint intolerable, and I shall never be able to fix her blandly with my disengaged eye again.

Thank heaven, then, that a little illusion is left to us, to enable us to be useful and agreeable—that we don't know exactly what our friends think of us—that the world is not made of looking-glass, to show us just the figure we are making, and just what is going on behind our backs! By the help of dear friendly illusion, we are able to dream that we are charming—and our faces wear a becoming air of self-possession; we are able to dream that other men admire our talents—and our benignity is undisturbed; we are able to dream that we are doing much good—and we do a little.

Thus it was with Amos Barton on that very Thursday evening, when he was the subject of the conversation at Cross Farm. He had been dining at Mr. Farquhar's, the secondary squire of the parish, and, stimulated by unwonted gravies and port-wine, had been delivering his opinion on affairs parochial and extra-parochial with considerable animation. And he was now returning home in the moonlight—a little chill, it is true, for he had just now no greatcoat compatible with clerical dignity, and a fur boa round one's neck, with a waterproof cape over one's shoulders, doesn't frighten away the cold from one's legs; but entirely unsuspicious, not only of Mr. Hackit's estimate of his oratorical powers, but also of the critical remarks passed on him by the Misses Farquhar as soon as the drawing-room door had closed behind him. Miss Julia had observed that she *never* heard any one sniff so frightfully as Mr. Barton did—she had a great mind to offer him her pocket-handkerchief; and Miss Arabella wondered why he always said he was going *for* to do a thing. He, excellent man! was meditating fresh pastoral exertions on the morrow; he would set on foot his lending library; in which he had introduced some books that would be a pretty sharp blow to the Dissenters—one especially, purporting to be written by a working man who, out of pure zeal for the welfare of his class, took the trouble to warn them in this way against those hypocritical thieves, the Dissenting preachers. The Rev. Amos Barton profoundly believed in the existence of that working man, and had thoughts of writing to him. Dissent, he considered, would have its head bruised in Shepperton, for did he not attack it in two ways? He preached Low-Church doctrine—as evangelical as any thing to be heard in the Independent Chapel; and he made a High-Church assertion of ecclesiastical powers and functions. Clearly, the Dissenters would feel that "the parson" was too many for them. Nothing like a man who combines shrewdness with energy. The wisdom of the serpent, Mr. Barton considered, was one of his strong points.

Look at him as he winds through the little churchyard! The silver light that falls aslant on church and tomb, enables you to see his slim black figure, made all the slimmer by tight pantaloons, as it flits past the pale gravestones. He walks with a quick step, and is now rapping with sharp decision at the vicarage door. It is opened without delay by the nurse, cook, and housemaid, all at once—that is to say, by the robust maid-of-all-work, Nanny; and as Mr. Barton hangs up his hat in the passage, you see that a narrow face of no particular complexion—even the small-pox that has attacked it seems to have been of a mongrel, indefinite kind—with features of no particular shape, and an eye of no particular expression, is surmounted by a slope of baldness gently rising from brow to crown. You judge him, rightly, to be about forty. The house is quiet, for it is half past ten, and the children have long been gone to bed. He opens the sitting-room door, but instead of seeing his wife, as he expected, stitching with the nimblest of fingers by the light of one candle, he finds her dispensing with the light of a candle altogether. She is softly pacing up and down by the red firelight, holding in her arms little Walter, the year-old baby, who looks over her shoulder with large wide-open eyes, while the patient mother pats his back with her soft hand, and glances with a sigh at the heap of large and small stockings lying unmended on the table.

She was a lovely woman—Mrs. Amos Barton; a large, fair, gentle Madonna, with thick, close chestnut curls beside her well-rounded cheeks, and with large, tender, short-sighted eyes. The flowing lines of her tall figure made the limpest dress look graceful, and her old frayed black silk seemed to repose on her bust and limbs with a placid elegance and sense of distinction, in strong contrast with the uneasy sense of being no fit, that seemed to express itself in the rustling of Mrs. Farquhar's *gros de Naples.* The caps she wore would have been pronounced, when off her head, utterly heavy and hideous—for in those days even fashionable caps were large and floppy; but surmounting her long, arched neck, and mingling their borders of cheap lace and ribbon with her chestnut curls, they seemed miracles of successful millinery. Among strangers she was shy and tremulous as a girl of fifteen; she blushed crimson if any one appealed to her opinion; yet that tall, graceful, substantial presence was so imposing in its mildness, that men spoke to her with an agreeable sensation of timidity.

Soothing, unspeakable charm of gentle womanhood! which supersedes all acquisitions, all accomplishments. You would never have asked, at any period of Mrs. Amos Barton's life, if she sketched or played the piano. You would even perhaps have been rather scandalized if she had descended from the serene dignity of *being* to the assiduous unrest of *doing.* Happy the man, you would have thought, whose eye will rest on her in the pauses of his fireside reading—whose hot aching forehead will be soothed by the contact of her cool, soft hand—who will recover himself from dejection at his mistakes and failures in the loving light of her unreproaching eyes! You would not, perhaps, have anticipated that this bliss would fall to the share of precisely such a man as Amos Barton, whom you have already surmised not to have the refined sensibilities for which you might have imagined Mrs. Barton's qualities to be destined by pre-established harmony. But I, for one, do not grudge Amos Barton his sweet wife. I have all my life had a sympathy for mongrel, ungainly dogs, who are nobody's pets; and I would rather surprise one of them by a pat and a pleasant morsel, than meet the condescending advances of the loveliest Skye-terrier who has his cushion by my lady's chair. That, to be sure, is not the way of the world: if it happens to see a fellow of fine proportions and aristocratic mien, who makes no *faux pas*, and wins golden opinions from all sorts of men, it straightway picks out for him the loveliest of unmarried women, and says, *There* would be a proper match! Not at all, say I: let that successful, well-shapen, discreet and able gentleman put up with something less than the best in the matrimonial department; and let the sweet woman go to make sunshine and a soft pillow for the poor devil whose legs are not models, whose efforts are often blunders, and who in general gets more kicks than halfpence. She—the sweet woman—will like it as well; for her sublime capacity of loving will have all the more scope; and I venture to say, Mrs. Barton's nature would never have grown half so angelic if she had married the man you would perhaps have had in your eye for her—a man with sufficient income and abundant personal éclat. Besides, Amos was an affectionate husband and, in his way, valued his wife as his best treasure.

But now he has shut the door behind him, and said, "Well, Milly!"

"Well, dear!" was the corresponding greeting, made eloquent by a smile.

"So that young rascal won't go to sleep! Can't you give him to Nanny?"

"Why, Nanny has been busy ironing this evening; but I think I'll take him to her now." And Mrs. Barton glided towards the kitchen, while her husband ran up stairs to put on his maize-colored dressing-gown, in which costume he was quietly filling his long pipe when his wife returned to the sitting-room. Maize is a color that decidedly did *not* suit his complexion, and it is one that soon soils; why, then, did Mr. Barton select it for domestic wear? Perhaps because he had a knack of hitting on the wrong thing in garb as well as in grammar.

Mrs. Barton now lighted her candle, and seated herself before her heap of stockings. She had something disagreeable to tell her husband, but she would not enter on it at once.

"Have you had a nice evening, dear?"

"Yes, pretty well. Ely was there to dinner, but went away rather early. Miss Arabella is setting her cap at him with a vengeance. But I don't think he's much smitten. I've a notion Ely's engaged to some one at a distance, and will astonish all the ladies who are languishing for him here, by bringing home his bride one of these days. Ely's a sly dog; he'll like that."

"Did the Farquhars say any thing about the singing last Sunday?"

"Yes; Farquhar said he thought it was time there was some improvement in the choir. But he was rather scandalized at my setting the tune of 'Lydia.' He says he's always hearing it as he passes the Independent meeting." Here Mr. Barton laughed—he had a way of laughing at criticisms that other people thought damaging—and thereby showed the remainder of a set of teeth which, like the remnants of the Old Guard, were few in number, and very much the worse for wear. "But," he continued, "Mrs. Farquhar talked the most about Mr. Bridmain and the Countess. She has taken up all the gossip about them, and wanted to convert me to her opinion, but I told her pretty strongly what I thought."

"Dear me! why will people take so much pains to find out evil about others? I have had a note from the Countess since you went, asking us to dine with them on Friday."

Here Mrs. Barton reached the note from the mantelpiece, and gave it to her husband. We will look over his shoulder while he reads it:

"SWEETEST MILLY,—Bring your lovely face with your husband to dine with us on Friday at seven—do. If not, I will be sulky with you till Sunday, when I shall be obliged to see you, and shall long to kiss you that very moment.—Yours, according to your answer, CAROLINE CZERLASKI."

"Just like her, isn't it?" said Mrs. Barton. "I suppose we can go?"

"Yes; I have no engagement. The Clerical Meeting is to-morrow, you know."

"And, dear, Woods the butcher called, to say he must have some money next week. He has a payment to make up."

This announcement made Mr. Barton thoughtful. He puffed more rapidly, and looked at the fire.

"I think I must ask Hackit to lend me twenty pounds, for it is nearly two months till Lady-day, and we can't give Woods our last shilling."

"I hardly like you to ask Mr. Hackit, dear—he and Mrs. Hackit have been so very kind to us; they have sent us so many things lately."

"Then I must ask Oldinport. I'm going to write to him to-morrow morning, for to tell him the arrangement I've been thinking of about having service in the workhouse while the church is being enlarged. If he agrees to attend service there once or twice, the other people will come. Net the large fish, and you're sure to have the small fry."

"I wish we could do without borrowing money, and yet I don't see how we can. Poor Fred must have some new shoes; I couldn't let him go to Mrs. Bond's yesterday because his toes were peeping out, dear child; and I can't let him walk anywhere except in the garden. He must have a pair before Sunday. Really, boots and shoes are the greatest trouble of my life. Every thing else one can turn and turn about, and make old look like new; but there's no coaxing boots and shoes to look better than they are."

Mrs. Barton was playfully undervaluing her skill in metamorphosing boots and shoes. She had at that moment on her feet a pair of slippers which had long ago lived through the prunella phase of their existence, and were now running a respectable career as black silk slippers, having been neatly covered with that material by Mrs. Barton's own neat fingers. Wonderful fingers those! they were never empty; for if she went to spend a few hours with a friendly parishioner, out came her thimble and a piece of calico or muslin, which, before she left, had become a mysterious little garment with all sorts of hemmed ins and outs. She was even trying to persuade her husband to leave off tight pantaloons, because if he would wear the ordinary gun-cases, she knew she could make them so well that no one would suspect the sex of the tailor.

But by this time Mr. Barton has finished his pipe, the candle begins to burn low, and Mrs. Barton goes to see if Nanny has succeeded in lulling Walter to sleep. Nanny is that moment putting him in the little cot by his mother's bedside; the head, with its thin wavelets of brown hair, indents the little pillow; and a tiny, waxen, dimpled fist hides the rosy lips, for baby is given to the infantine peccadillo of thumb-sucking.

So Nanny could now join in the short evening prayer, and all could go to bed.

Mrs. Barton carried up stairs the remainder of her heap of stockings, and laid them on a table close to her bedside, where also she placed a warm shawl, removing her candle, before she put it out, to a tin socket fixed at the head of her bed. Her body was very weary, but her heart was not heavy, in spite of Mr. Woods the butcher, and the transitory nature of shoe-leather; for her heart so overflowed with love, she felt sure she was near a fountain of love that would care for her husband and babes better than she could foresee; so she was soon asleep. But about half past five o'clock in the morning, if there were any angels watching round her bed—and angels might be glad of such an office—they saw Mrs. Barton rise up quietly, careful not to disturb the slumbering Amos, who was snoring the snore of the just, light her candle, prop herself upright with the pillows, throw the warm shawl round her shoulders, and renew her attack on the heap of undarned stockings. She darned away until she heard Nanny stirring, and then drowsiness came with the dawn; the candle was put out, and she sank into a doze. But at nine o'clock she was at the breakfast-table busy cutting bread-and-butter for five hungry mouths, while Nanny, baby on one arm, in rosy cheeks, fat neck, and night-gown, brought in a jug of hot milk-and-water. Nearest her mother sits the nine-year-old Patty, the eldest child, whose sweet fair face is already rather grave sometimes, and who always wants to run up stairs to save mamma's legs, which get so tired of an evening. Then there are four other blond heads—two boys and two girls, gradually decreasing in size down to Chubby, who is making a round O of her mouth to receive a bit of papa's "baton." Papa's attention was divided between petting Chubby, rebuking the noisy Fred, which he did with a somewhat excessive sharpness, and eating his own breakfast. He did not yet look at Mamma, and did not know that her cheek was paler than usual. But Patty whispered, "Mamma, have you the headache?"

Happily coal was cheap in the neighborhood of Shepperton, and Mr. Hackit would any time let his horses draw a load for "the parson" without charge; so there was a blazing fire in the sitting-room, and not without need, for the vicarage garden, as they looked out on it from the bow-window, was hard with black frost, and the sky had the white, woolly look that portends snow.

Breakfast over, Mr. Barton mounted to his study, and occupied himself in the first place with his letter to Mr. Oldinport. It was very much the same sort of letter as most clergymen would have written under the same circumstances, except that instead of perambulate, the Rev. Amos wrote *pre*ambulate, and instead of "if haply," "if happily," the contingency indicated being the reverse of happy. Mr. Barton had not the gift of perfect accuracy in English orthography and syntax, which was unfortunate, as he was known not to be a Hebrew scholar, and not in the least suspected of being an accomplished Grecian. These lapses, in a man who had gone through the Eleusinian Mysteries of a university education, surprised the young ladies of his parish extremely; especially the Misses Farquhar, whom he had once addressed in a letter as Dear Mads, apparently an abbreviation for Madams. The persons least surprised at the Rev. Amos's deficiencies were his clerical brethren, who had gone through the mysteries themselves.

At eleven o'clock, Mr. Barton walked forth in cape and boa, with the sleet driving in his face, to read prayers at the workhouse, euphuistically called the "College." The College was a huge square stone building, standing on the best apology for an elevation of ground that could be seen for about ten miles round Shepperton. A flat ugly district this; depressing enough to look at even on the brightest days. The roads are black with coal-dust, the brick houses dingy with smoke: and at that time—the time of handloom weavers—every other cottage had a loom at its window, where you might see a pale, sickly-looking man or woman pressing a narrow chest against a board, and doing a sort of treadmill work with legs and arms. A troublesome district for a clergyman; at least to one who, like Amos Barton, understood the "cure of souls" in something more than an official sense; for over and above the rustic stupidity furnished by the farm-laborers, the miners brought obstreperous animalism, and the weavers an acrid Radicalism and Dissent. Indeed, Mrs. Hackit often observed that the colliers, who many of them earned better wages than Mr. Barton, "passed their time in doing nothing but swilling ale and smoking, like the beasts that perish" (speaking, we may presume, in a remotely analogical sense); and in some of the ale-house corners the drink was flavored by a dingy kind of infidelity, something like rinsings of Tom Paine in ditch-water. A certain amount of religious excitement created by the popular preaching of Mr. Parry, Amos's predecessor, had nearly died out, and the religious life of Shepperton was falling back towards low-water mark. Here, you perceive, was a terrible stronghold of Satan; and you may well pity the Rev. Amos Barton, who had to stand single-handed and summon it to surrender. We read, indeed, that the walls of Jericho fell down before the sound of trumpets; but we nowhere hear that those trumpets were hoarse and feeble. Doubtless they were trumpets that gave forth clear ringing tones, and sent a mighty vibration through brick and mortar. But the oratory of the Rev. Amos resembled rather a Belgian railway-horn, which shows praiseworthy intentions inadequately fulfilled. He often missed the right note both in public and private exhortation, and got a little angry in consequence. For though Amos thought himself strong, he did not *feel* himself strong. Nature had given him the opinion, but not the sensation. Without that opinion he would probably never have worn cambric bands, but would have been an excellent cabinetmaker and deacon of an Independent church, as his father was before him (he was not a shoemaker, as Mr. Pilgrim had reported). He might then have sniffed long and loud in the corner of his pew in Gun Street Chapel; he might have indulged in halting rhetoric at prayer-meetings, and have spoken faulty English in private life; and these little infirmities would not have prevented him, honest, faithful man that he was, from being a shining light in the Dissenting circle of Bridgeport. A tallow dip, of the long-eight description, is an excellent thing in the kitchen candlestick, and Betty's nose and eye are not sensitive to the difference between it and the finest wax; it is only when you stick it in the silver candlestick, and introduce it into the drawing-room, that it seems plebeian, dim, and ineffectual. Alas for the worthy man who, like that candle, gets himself into the wrong place! It is only the very largest souls who will be able to appreciate and pity him—who will discern and love sincerity of purpose amid all the bungling feebleness of achievement.

But now Amos Barton has made his way through the sleet as far as the College, has thrown off his hat, cape, and boa, and is reading, in the dreary stone-floored dining-room, a portion of the morning service to the inmates seated on the benches before him. Remember, the New Poor-law had not yet come into operation, and Mr. Barton was not acting as paid chaplain of the Union, but as the pastor who had the care of all souls in his parish, pauper as well as other. After the prayers he always addressed to them a short discourse on some subject suggested by the lesson for the day, striving if by this means some edifying matter might find its way into the pauper mind and conscience—perhaps a task as trying as you could well imagine to the faith and patience of any honest clergyman. For, on the very first bench, these were the faces on which his eye had to rest, watching whether there was any stirring under the stagnant surface.

Right in front of him—probably because he was stone-deaf, and it was deemed more edifying to hear nothing at a short distance than at a long one—sat "Old Maxum," as he was familiarly called, his real patronymic remaining a mystery to most persons. A fine philological sense discerns in this cognomen an indication that the pauper patriarch had once been considered pithy and sententious in his speech; but now the weight of ninety-five years lay heavy on his tongue as well as in his ears, and he sat before the clergyman with protruded chin, and munching mouth, and eyes that seemed to look at emptiness.

Next to him sat Poll Fodge—known to the magistracy of her county as Mary Higgins—a one-eyed woman, with a scarred and seamy face, the most notorious rebel in the workhouse, said to have once thrown her broth over the master's coat-tails, and who, in spite of nature's apparent safeguards against that contingency, had contributed to the perpetuation of the Fodge characteristics in the person of a small boy, who was behaving naughtily on one of the back benches. Miss Fodge fixed her one sore eye on Mr. Barton with a sort of hardy defiance.

Beyond this member of the softer sex, at the end of the bench, sat "Silly Jim," a young man afflicted with hydrocephalus, who rolled his head from side to side, and gazed at the point of his nose. These were the supporters of Old Maxum on his right.

On his left sat Mr. Fitchett, a tall fellow, who had once been a footman in the Oldinport family, and in that giddy elevation had enunciated a contemptuous opinion of boiled beef, which had been traditionally handed down in Shepperton as the direct cause of his ultimate reduction to pauper commons. His calves were now shrunken, and his hair was gray without the aid of powder; but he still carried his chin as if he were conscious of a stiff cravat; he set his dilapidated hat on with a knowing inclination towards the left ear; and when he was on field-work, he carted and uncarted the manure with a sort of flunkey grace, the ghost of that jaunty demeanor with which he used to usher in my lady's morning visitors. The flunkey nature was nowhere completely subdued but in his stomach, and he still divided society into gentry, gentry's flunkeys, and the people who provided for them. A clergyman without a flunkey was an anomaly, belonging to neither of these classes. Mr. Fitchett had an irrepressible tendency to drowsiness under spiritual instruction, and in the recurrent regularity with which he dozed off until he nodded and awaked himself, he looked not unlike a piece of mechanism, ingeniously contrived for measuring the length of Mr. Barton's discourse.

Perfectly wide-awake, on the contrary, was his left-hand neighbor, Mrs. Brick, one of those hard, undying old women, to whom age seems to have given a network of wrinkles, as a coat of magic armor against the attacks of winters, warm or cold. The point on which Mrs. Brick was still sensitive—the theme on which you might possibly excite her hope and fear — was snuff. It seemed to be an embalming powder, helping her soul to do the office of salt.

And now, eke out an audience of which this front benchful was a sample with a certain number of refractory children, over whom Mr. Spratt, the master of the workhouse, exercised an irate surveillance, and I think you will admit that the university-taught clergyman, whose office it is to bring home the gospel to a handful of such souls, has a sufficiently hard task. For, to have any chance of success, short of miraculous intervention, he must bring his geographical, chronological, exegetical mind pretty nearly to the pauper point of view, or of no view; he must have some approximate conception of the mode in which the doctrines that have so much vitality in the plenum of his own brain will comport themselves *in vacuo*—that is to say, in a brain that is neither geographical, chronological, nor exegetical. It is a flexible imagination that can take such a leap as that, and an adroit tongue that can adapt its speech to so unfamiliar a position. The Rev. Amos Barton had neither that flexible imagination, nor that adroit tongue. He talked of Israel and its sins, of chosen vessels, of the Paschal lamb, of blood as a medium of reconciliation; and he strove in this way to convey religious truth within reach of the Fodge and Fitchett mind. This very morning, the first lesson was the twelfth chapter of Exodus, and Mr. Barton's exposition turned on unleavened bread. Nothing in the world more suited to the simple understanding than instruction through familiar types and symbols! But there is always this danger attending it, that the interest or comprehension of your hearers may stop short precisely at the point where your spiritual interpretation begins. And Mr. Barton this morning succeeded in carrying the pauper imagination to the dough-tub, but unfortunately was not able to carry it upward from that well-known object to the unknown truths which it was intended to shadow forth.

Alas! a natural incapacity for teaching, finished by keeping "terms" at Cambridge, where there are able mathematicians, and butter is sold by the yard, is not apparently the medium through which Christian doctrine will distill as welcome dew on withered souls.

And so, while the sleet outside was turning to unquestionable snow, and the stony dining-room looked darker and drearier, and Mr. Fitchett was nodding his lowest, and Mr. Spratt was boxing the boys' ears with a constant *rinforzando*, as he felt more keenly the approach of dinner-time, Mr. Barton wound up his exhortation with something of the February chill at his heart as well as his feet. Mr. Fitchett, thoroughly roused, now the instruction was at an end, obsequiously and gracefully advanced to help Mr. Barton in putting on his cape, while Mrs. Brick rubbed her withered forefinger round and round her little shoe-shaped snuff-box, vainly seeking for the fraction of a pinch. I can't help thinking that if Mr. Barton had shaken into that little box a small portion of Scotch high-dried, he might have produced something more like an amiable emotion in Mrs. Brick's mind than any thing she had felt under his morning's exposition of the unleavened bread. But our good Amos labored under a deficiency of small tact as well as of small cash; and when he observed the action of the old woman's forefinger, he said, in his brusque way, "So your snuff is all gone, eh?"

Mrs. Brick's eyes twinkled with the visionary hope that the parson might be intending to replenish her box, at least mediately, through the present of a small copper.

"Ah, well! you'll soon be going where there is no more

snuff. You'll be in need of mercy then. You must remember that you may have to seek for mercy and not find it, just as you're seeking for snuff."

At the first sentence of this admonition, the twinkle subsided from Mrs. Brick's eyes. The lid of her box went "click!" and her heart was shut up at the same moment.

But now Mr. Barton's attention was called for by Mr. Spratt, who was dragging a small and unwilling boy from the rear. Mr. Spratt was a small-featured, small-statured man, with a remarkable power of language, mitigated by hesitation, who piqued himself on expressing unexceptionable sentiments in unexceptionable language on all occasions.

"Mr. Barton, sir—aw—aw—excuse my trespassing on your time—aw—to beg that you will administer a rebuke to this boy: he is—aw—aw—most inveterate in ill-behavior during service-time."

The inveterate culprit was a boy of seven, vainly contending against "candles" at his nose by feeble sniffing. But no sooner had Mr. Spratt uttered his impeachment, than Miss Fodge rushed forward and placed herself between Mr. Barton and the accused.

"That's *my* child, Muster Barton," she exclaimed, further manifesting her maternal instincts by applying her apron to her offspring's nose. "He's al'ys a-findin' faut wi' him, and a-poundin' him for nothin'. Let him goo an' eat his roost goose as is a-smellin' up in our noses while we're a-swallering them greasy broth, and let my boy alooan."

Mr. Spratt's small eyes flashed, and he was in danger of uttering sentiments not unexceptionable before the clergyman; but Mr. Barton, foreseeing that a prolongation of this episode would not be to edification, said, "Silence!" in his severest tones.

"Let me hear no abuse. Your boy is not likely to behave well, if you set him the example of being saucy." Then stooping down to Master Fodge, and taking him by the shoulder, "Do you like being beaten?"

"No-a."

"Then what a silly boy you are to be naughty. If you were not naughty, you wouldn't be beaten. But if you are naughty, God will be angry, as well as Mr. Spratt; and God can burn you forever. That will be worse than being beaten."

Master Fodge's countenance was neither affirmative nor negative of this proposition.

"But," continued Mr. Barton, "if you will be a good boy, God will love you, and you will grow up to be a good man.

Now, let me hear next Thursday that you have been a good boy."

Master Fodge had no distinct vision of the benefit that would accrue to him from this change of courses. But Mr. Barton, being aware that Miss Fodge had touched on a delicate subject in alluding to the roast goose, was determined to witness no more polemics between her and Mr. Spratt; so, saying good-morning to the latter, he hastily left the College.

The snow was falling in thicker and thicker flakes, and already the vicarage-garden was cloaked in white as he passed through the gate. Mrs. Barton heard him open the door, and ran out of the sitting-room to meet him.

"I'm afraid your feet are very wet, dear. What a terrible morning! Let me take your hat. Your slippers are at the fire."

Mr. Barton was feeling a little cold and cross. It is difficult, when you have been doing disagreeable duties, without praise, on a snowy day, to attend to the very minor morals. So he showed no recognition of Milly's attentions, but simply said, "Fetch me my dressing-gown, will you?"

"It *is* down, dear. I thought you wouldn't go into the study, because you said you would letter and number the books for the Lending Library. Patty and I have been covering them, and they are all ready in the sitting-room."

"Oh, I can't do those this morning," said Mr. Barton, as he took off his boots and put his feet into the slippers Milly had brought him; "you must put them away into the parlor."

The sitting-room was also the day nursery and schoolroom; and while Mamma's back was turned, Dickey, the second boy, had insisted on superseding Chubby in the guidance of a headless horse, of the red-wafered species, which she was drawing round the room, so that when Papa opened the door Chubby was giving tongue energetically.

"Milly, some of these children must go away. I want to be quiet."

"Yes, dear. Hush, Chubby; go with Patty, and see what Nanny is getting for our dinner. Now, Fred and Sophy and Dickey, help me to carry these books into the parlor. There are three for Dickey. Carry them steadily."

Papa meanwhile settled himself in his easy-chair, and took up a work on Episcopacy, which he had from the Clerical Book Society; thinking he would finish it, and return it this afternoon, as he was going to the Clerical Meeting at Milby Vicarage, where the Book Society had its headquarters.

The Clerical Meetings and Book Society, which had been

founded some eight or ten months, had had a noticeable effect on the Rev. Amos Barton. When he first came to Shepperton he was simply an evangelical clergyman, whose Christian experiences had commenced under the teaching of the Rev. Mr. Johns, of Gun Street Chapel, and had been consolidated at Cambridge under the influence of Mr. Simeon. John Newton and Thomas Scott were his doctrinal ideals; he would have taken in the "Christian Observer" and the "Record," if he could have afforded it; his anecdotes were chiefly of the pious-jocose kind, current in Dissenting circles; and he thought an Episcopalian Establishment unobjectionable.

But by this time the effect of the Tractarian agitation was beginning to be felt in backward provincial regions, and the Tractarian satire on the Low-Church party was beginning to tell even on those who disavowed or resisted Tractarian doctrines. The vibration of an intellectual movement was felt from the golden head to the miry toes of the Establishment; and so it came to pass that, in the district round Milby, the market-town close to Shepperton, the clergy had agreed to have a clerical meeting every month, wherein they would exercise their intellects by discussing theological and ecclesiastical questions, and cement their brotherly love by discussing a good dinner. A Book Society naturally suggested itself as an adjunct of this agreeable plan; and thus, you perceive, there was provision made for ample friction of the clerical mind.

Now, the Rev. Amos Barton was one of those men who have a decided will and opinion of their own; he held himself bolt upright, and had no self-distrust. He would march very determinedly along the road he thought best; but then it was wonderfully easy to convince him which *was* the best road. And so a very little unwonted reading and unwonted discussion made him see that an Episcopalian Establishment was much more than unobjectionable, and on many other points he began to feel that he held opinions a little too far-sighted and profound to be crudely and suddenly communicated to ordinary minds. He was like an onion that has been rubbed with spices; the strong original odor was blended with something new and foreign. The Low-Church onion still offended refined High-Church nostrils, and the new spice was unwelcome to the palate of the genuine onion-eater.

We will not accompany him to the Clerical Meeting today, because we shall probably want to go thither some day when he will be absent. And just now I am bent on introducing you to Mr. Bridmain and the Countess Czerlaski, with whom Mr. and Mrs. Barton are invited to dine to-morrow.

CHAPTER III.

Outside, the moon is shedding its cold light on the cold snow, and the white-bearded fir-trees round Camp Villa are casting a blue shadow across the white ground, while the Rev. Amos Barton and his wife are audibly crushing the crisp snow beneath their feet, as, about seven o'clock on Friday evening, they approach the door of the above-named desirable country residence, containing dining, breakfast, and drawing rooms, etc., situated only half a mile from the market-town of Milby.

Inside, there is a bright fire in the drawing-room, casting a pleasant but uncertain light on the delicate silk dress of a lady who is reclining behind a screen in the corner of the sofa, and allowing you to discern that the hair of the gentleman who is seated in the arm-chair opposite, with a newspaper over his knees, is becoming decidedly gray. A little "King Charles," with a crimson ribbon round his neck, who has been lying curled up in the very middle of the hearth-rug, has just discovered that that zone is too hot for him, and is jumping on the sofa, evidently with the intention of accommodating his person on the silk gown. On the table there are two wax-candles, which will be lighted as soon as the expected knock is heard at the door.

The knock is heard, the candles are lighted, and presently Mr. and Mrs. Barton are ushered in—Mr. Barton erect and clerical, in a faultless tie and shining cranium; Mrs. Barton graceful in a newly-turned black silk.

"Now this is charming of you," said the Countess Czerlaski, advancing to meet them, and embracing Milly with careful elegance. "I am really ashamed of my selfishness in asking my friends to come and see me in this frightful weather." Then, giving her hand to Amos, "And you, Mr. Barton, whose time is so precious! But I am doing a good deed in drawing you away from your labors. I have a plot to prevent you from martyrizing yourself."

While this greeting was going forward, Mr. Bridmain and Jet the spaniel looked on with the air of actors who had no idea of by-play. Mr. Bridmain, a stiff and rather thick-set man, gave his welcome with a labored cordiality. It was astonishing how very little he resembled his beautiful sister.

For the Countess Czerlaski was undeniably beautiful. As

she seated herself by Mrs. Barton on the sofa, Milly's eyes, indeed, rested—must it be confessed?—chiefly on the details of the tasteful dress, the rich silk of a pinkish lilac hue (the Countess always wore delicate colors in an evening), the black lace pelerine, and the black lace veil falling at the back of the small, closely-braided head. For Milly had one weakness —don't love her any the less for it, it was a pretty woman's weakness—she was fond of dress; and often, when she was making up her own economical millinery, she had romantic visions how nice it would be to put on really handsome, stylish things—to have very stiff balloon sleeves, for example, without which a woman's dress was naught in those days. You and I, too, reader, have our weakness, have we not? which makes us think foolish things now and then. Perhaps it may lie in an excessive admiration for small hands and feet, a tall, lithe figure, large, dark eyes, and dark silken braided hair. All these the Countess possessed, and she had, moreover, a delicately-formed nose, the least bit curved, and a clear brunette complexion. Her mouth, it must be admitted, receded too much from her nose and chin, and to a prophetic eye threatened "nut-crackers" in advanced age. But by the light of fire and wax candles that age seemed very far off indeed, and you would have said that the Countess was not more than thirty.

Look at the two women on the sofa together! The large, fair, mild-eyed Milly is timid even in friendship; it is not easy to her to speak of the affection of which her heart is full. The lithe, dark, thin-lipped Countess is racking her small brain for caressing words and charming exaggerations.

"And how are all the cherubs at home?" said the Countess, stooping to pick up Jet, and without waiting for an answer. "I have been kept in-doors by a cold ever since Sunday, or I should not have rested without seeing you. What have you done with those wretched singers, Mr. Barton?"

"Oh, we have got a new choir together, which will go on very well with a little practice. I was quite determined that the old set of singers should be dismissed. I had given orders that they should not sing the wedding psalm, as they call it, again, to make a new-married couple look ridiculous, and they sang it in defiance of me. I could put them into the Ecclesiastical Court, if I chose for to do so, for lifting up their voices in church in opposition to the clergyman."

"And a most wholesome discipline that would be," said the Countess; "indeed, you are too patient and forbearing, Mr. Barton. For my part *I* lose *my* temper when I see how far you are from being appreciated in that miserable Shepperton."

If, as is probable, Mr. Barton felt at a loss what to say in reply to the insinuated compliment, it was a relief to him that dinner was announced just then, and that he had to offer his arm to the Countess.

As Mr. Bridmain was leading Mrs. Barton to the dining-room, he observed, "The weather is very severe."

"Very, indeed," said Milly.

Mr. Bridmain studied conversation as an art. To ladies he spoke of the weather, and was accustomed to consider it under three points of view: as a question of climate in general, comparing England with other countries in this respect; as a personal question, inquiring how it affected his lady interlocutor in particular; and as a question of probabilities, discussing whether there would be a change or a continuance of the present atmospheric conditions. To gentlemen he talked politics, and he read two daily papers expressly to qualify himself for this function. Mr. Barton thought him a man of considerable political information, but not of lively parts.

"And so you are always to hold your Clerical Meetings at Mr. Ely's?" said the Countess, between her spoonfuls of soup. (The soup was a little over-spiced. Mrs. Short of Camp Villa, who was in the habit of letting her best apartments, gave only moderate wages to her cook.)

"Yes," said Mr. Barton; "Milby is a central place, and there are many conveniences in having only one point of meeting."

"Well," continued the Countess, "every one seems to agree in giving the precedence to Mr. Ely. For my part, I *can not* admire him. His preaching is too cold for me. It has no fervor—no heart. I often say to my brother, it is a great comfort to me that Shepperton Church is not too far off for us to go to; don't I, Edmund?"

"Yes," answered Mr. Bridmain; "they show us into such a bad pew at Milby—just where there is a draught from that door. I caught a stiff neck the first time I went there."

"Oh, it is the cold in the pulpit that affects me, not the cold in the pew. I was writing to my friend Lady Porter this morning, and telling her all about my feelings. She and I think alike on such matters. She is most anxious that when Sir William has an opportunity of giving away the living at their place, Dippley, they should have a thoroughly zealous, clever man there. I have been describing a certain friend of mine to her, who, I think, would be just to her mind. And there is such a pretty rectory, Milly; shouldn't I like to see you the mistress of it?"

Milly smiled and blushed slightly. The Rev. Amos blushed very red, and gave a little embarrassed laugh—he could rarely keep his muscles within the limits of a smile.

At this moment John, the man-servant, approached Mrs. Barton with a gravy-tureen, and also with a slight odor of the stable, which usually adhered to him throughout his in-door functions. John was rather nervous; and the Countess happening to speak to him at this inopportune moment, the tureen slipped and emptied itself on Mrs. Barton's newly turned black silk.

"Oh, horror! Tell Alice to come directly and rub Mrs. Barton's dress," said the countess to the trembling John, carefully abstaining from approaching the gravy-sprinkled spot on the floor with her own lilac silk. But Mr. Bridmain, who had a strictly private interest in silks, good-naturedly jumped up and applied his napkin at once to Mrs. Barton's gown.

Milly felt a little inward anguish, but no ill-temper, and tried to make light of the matter for the sake of John as well as others. The Countess felt inwardly thankful that her own delicate silk had escaped, but threw out lavish interjections of distress and indignation.

"Dear saint that you are," she said, when Milly laughed, and suggested that, as her silk was not very glossy to begin with, the dim patch would not be much seen; "you don't mind about these things, I know. Just the same sort of thing happened to me at the Princess Wengstein's one day, on a pink satin. I was in an agony. But you are so indifferent to dress; and well you may be. It is you who make dress pretty, and not dress that makes you pretty."

Alice, the buxom lady's-maid, wearing a much better dress than Mrs. Barton's, now appeared to take Mr. Bridmain's place in retrieving the mischief, and after a great amount of supplementary rubbing, composure was restored, and the business of dining was continued.

When John was recounting his accident to the cook in the kitchen, he observed, "Mrs. Barton's a hamable woman; I'd a deal sooner ha' throwed the gravy o'er the Countess's fine gownd. But laws! what tantrums she'd ha' been in arter the visitors was gone."

"You'd a deal sooner not ha' throwed it down at all, *I* should think," responded the unsympathetic cook, to whom John did *not* make love. "Who d'you think's to make gravy anuff, if you're to baste people's gownds wi' it?"

"Well," suggested John, humbly, "you should wet the bottom of the *duree* a bit, to hold it from slippin'."

"Wet your granny!" returned the cook; a retort which she probably regarded in the light of a *reductio ad absurdum*, and which in fact reduced John to silence.

Later on in the evening, while John was removing the tea-things from the drawing-room, and brushing the crumbs from the table-cloth with an accompanying hiss, such as he was wont to encourage himself with in rubbing down Mr. Bridmain's horse, the Rev. Amos Barton drew from his pocket a thin, green-covered pamphlet, and, presenting it to the Countess, said,

"You were pleased, I think, with my sermon on Christmas Day. It has been printed in 'The Pulpit,' and I thought you might like a copy."

"That indeed I shall. I shall quite value the opportunity of reading that sermon. There was such depth in it!—such argument! It was not a sermon to be heard only once. I am delighted that it should become generally known, as it will be, now it is printed in 'The Pulpit.'"

"Yes," said Milly, innocently, "I was so pleased with the editor's letter." And she drew out her little pocket-book, where she carefully treasured the editorial autograph, while Mr. Barton laughed and blushed, and said, "Nonsense, Milly!"

"You see," she said, giving the letter to the Countess, "I am very proud of the praise my husband gets."

The sermon in question, by-the-by, was an extremely argumentative one on the Incarnation; which, as it was preached to a congregation not one of whom had any doubt of that doctrine, and to whom the Socinians therein confuted were as unknown as the Arimaspians, was exceedingly well adapted to trouble and confuse the Sheppertonian mind.

"Ah," said the Countess, returning the editor's letter, "he may well say he will be glad of other sermons from the same source." But I would rather you should publish your sermons in an independent volume, Mr. Barton; it would be so desirable to have them in that shape. For instance, I could send a copy to the Dean of Radborough. And there is Lord Blarney, whom I knew before he was chancellor. I was a special favorite of his, and you can't think what sweet things he used to say to me. I shall not resist the temptation to write to him one of these days *sans façon*, and tell him how he ought to dispose of the next vacant living in his gift."

Whether Jet the spaniel, being a much more knowing dog than was suspected, wished to express his disapproval of the Countess's last speech, as not accordant with his ideas of wisdom and veracity, I can not say; but at this moment he jumped off her lap, and, turning his back upon her, placed one paw on the fender, and held the other up to warm, as if affecting to abstract himself from the current of conversation.

But now Mr. Bridmain brought out the chess-board, and Mr. Barton accepted his challenge to play a game, with immense satisfaction. The Rev. Amos was very fond of chess, as most people are who can continue through many years to create interesting vicissitudes in the game, by taking long-meditated moves with their knights, and subsequently discovering that they have thereby exposed their queen.

Chess is a silent game; and the Countess's chat with Milly is in quite an under-tone—probably relating to women's matters that it would be impertinent for us to listen to; so we will leave Camp Villa and proceed to Milby Vicarage, where Mr. Farquhar has sat out two other guests with whom he has been dining at Mr. Ely's and is now rather wearying that reverend gentleman by his protracted small-talk.

Mr. Ely was a tall, dark-haired, distinguished-looking man of three-and-thirty. By the laity of Milby and its neighborhood he was regarded as a man of quite remarkable powers and learning, who must make a considerable sensation in London pulpits and drawing-rooms on his occasional visits to the metropolis; and by his brother clergy he was regarded as a discreet and agreeable fellow. Mr. Ely never got into a warm discussion; he suggested what might be thought, but rarely said what he thought himself; he never let either men or women see that he was laughing at them, and he never gave any one an opportunity of laughing at *him*. In one thing only he was injudicious. He parted his dark wavy hair down the middle; and as his head was rather flat than otherwise, that style of coiffure was not advantageous to him.

Mr. Farquhar, though not a parishioner of Mr. Ely's, was one of his warmest admirers, and thought he would make an unexceptionable son-in-law, in spite of his being of no particular "family." Mr. Farquhar was susceptible on the point of "blood"—his own circulating fluid, which animated a short and somewhat flabby person, being, he considered, of very superior quality.

"By-the-by," he said, with a certain pomposity counteracted by a lisp, "what an ath Barton makth of himthelf, about that Bridmain and the Counteth, ath she callth herthelf. After you were gone the other evening, Mithith Farquhar wath telling him the general opinion about them in the neighborhood, and he got quite red and angry. Bleth your thoul, he believth the whole thtory about her Polish huthband and hith wonderful ethcapeth; and ath for her—why, he thinkth her perfection, a woman of motht refined feelingth, and no end of thtuff."

Mr. Ely smiled. "Some people would say our friend Barton was not the best judge of refinement. Perhaps the lady flatters him a little, and we men are susceptible. She goes to Shepperton Church every Sunday—drawn there, let us suppose, by Mr. Barton's eloquence."

"Pthaw," said Mr. Farquhar: "now, to my mind, you have only to look at that woman to thee what she ith—throwing her eyth about when she comth into church, and drething in a way to attract attention. I should thay, she'th tired of her brother Bridmain, and looking out for another brother with a thtronger family likeneth. Mithith Farquhar ith very fond of Mithith Barton, and ith quite dithtrethed that she should athothiate with thuch a woman, tho she attacked him on the thubject purpothly. But I tell her it'th of no uthe, with a pig-headed fellow like him. Barton'th well-meaning enough, but *tho* contheited. I've left off giving him my advithe."

Mr. Ely smiled inwardly, and said to himself, "What a punishment!" But to Mr. Farquhar he said, "Barton might be more judicious, it must be confessed." He was getting tired, and did not want to develop the subject.

"Why, nobody vithit-th them but the Bartonth," continued Mr. Farquhar, "and why should thuch people come here, unleth they had particular reathonth for preferring a neighborhood where they are not known? Pooh! it lookth bad on the very fathe of it. *You* called on them, now; how did you find them?"

"Oh!—Mr. Bridmain strikes me as a common sort of man who is making an effort to seem wise and well bred. He comes down on one tremendously with political information, and seems knowing about the King of the French. The Countess is certainly a handsome woman, but she puts on the grand air a little too powerfully. Woodcock was immensely taken with her, and insisted on his wife's calling on her and asking her to dinner; but I think Mrs. Woodcock turned restive after the first visit, and wouldn't invite her again."

"Ha, ha! Woodcock hath alwayth a thoft place in hith heart for a pretty fathe. It'th odd how he came to marry that plain woman, and no fortune either."

"Mysteries of the tender passion," said Mr. Ely. "I am not initiated yet, you know."

Here Mr. Farquhar's carriage was announced, and as we have not found his conversation particularly brilliant under the stimulus of Mr. Ely's exceptional presence, we will not accompany him home to the less exciting atmosphere of domestic life.

Mr. Ely threw himself with a sense of relief into his easiest chair, set his feet on the hobs, and in this attitude of bachelor enjoyment began to read Bishop Jebb's Memoirs.

CHAPTER IV.

I AM by no means sure that if the good people of Milby had known the truth about the Countess Czerlaski, they would not have been considerably disappointed to find that it was very far from being as bad as they imagined. Nice distinctions are troublesome. It is so much easier to say that a thing is black, than to discriminate the particular shade of brown, blue, or green, to which it really belongs. It is so much easier to make up your mind that your neighbor is good for nothing, than to enter into all the circumstances that would oblige you to modify that opinion.

Besides, think of all the virtuous declamation, all the penetrating observations, which had been built up entirely on the fundamental position that the Countess was a very objectionable person indeed, and which would be utterly overturned and nullified by the destruction of that premiss. Mrs. Phipps, the banker's wife, and Mrs. Landor, the attorney's wife, had invested part of their reputation for acuteness in the supposition that Mr. Bridmain was not the Countess's brother. Moreover, Miss Phipps was conscious that if the Countess was not a disreputable person, she, Miss Phipps, had no compensating superiority in virtue to set against the other lady's manifest superiority in personal charms. Miss Phipps's stumpy figure and unsuccessful attire, instead of looking down from a mount of virtue with an aureole round its head, would then be seen on the same level and in the same light as the Countess Czerlaski's Diana-like form and well-chosen drapery. Miss Phipps, for her part, didn't like dressing for effect—she had always avoided that style of appearance which was calculated to create a sensation.

Then what amusing innuendoes of the Milby gentlemen over their wine would have been entirely frustrated and reduced to naught, if you had told them that the Countess had really been guilty of no misdemeanors which demanded her exclusion from strictly respectable society; that her husband had been the veritable Count Czerlaski, who had

had wonderful escapes, as she said, and who, as she did *not* say, but as was said in certain circulars once folded by her fair hands, had subsequently given dancing lessons in the metropolis; that Mr. Bridmain was neither more nor less than her half-brother, who, by unimpeached integrity and industry, had won a partnership in a silk-manufactory, and thereby a moderate fortune, that enabled him to retire, as you see, to study politics, the weather, and the art of conversation at his leisure. Mr. Bridmain, in fact, quadragenarian bachelor as he was, felt extremely well pleased to receive his sister in her widowhood, and to shine in the reflected light of her beauty and title. Every man who is not a monster, a mathematician, or a mad philosopher, is the slave of some woman or other. Mr. Bridmain had put his neck under the yoke of his handsome sister, and though his soul was a very little one—of the smallest description indeed—he would not have ventured to call it his own. He might be slightly recalcitrant now and then, as is the habit of long-eared pachyderms, under the thong of the fair Countess's tongue; but there seemed little probability that he would ever get his neck loose. Still, a bachelor's heart is an outlying fortress that some fair enemy may any day take either by storm or stratagem; and there was always the possibility that Mr. Bridmain's first nuptials might occur before the Countess was quite sure of her second. As it was, however, he submitted to all his sister's caprices, never grumbled because her dress and her maid formed a considerable item beyond her own little income of sixty pounds per annum, and consented to lead with her a migratory life, as personages on the debatable ground between aristocracy and commonalty, instead of settling in some spot where his five hundred a-year might have won him the definite dignity of a parochial magnate.

The Countess had her views in choosing a quiet provincial place like Milby. After three years of widowhood, she had brought her feelings to contemplate giving a successor to her lamented Czerlaski, whose fine whiskers, fine air, and romantic fortunes had won her heart ten years ago, when, as pretty Caroline Bridmain, in full bloom of five-and-twenty, she was governess to Lady Porter's daughters, whom he initiated into the mysteries of the *pas de basque* and the Lancers' quadrilles. She had had seven years of sufficiently happy matrimony with Czerlaski, who had taken her to Paris and Germany, and introduced her there to many of his old friends with large titles and small fortunes. So that the fair Caroline had had considerable experience of life, and had gathered therefrom, not, indeed, any very ripe and comprehensive wisdom, but much external polish, and certain practical conclusions of a very decided kind. One of these conclusions was, that there were things more solid in life than fine whiskers and a title, and that, in accepting a second husband, she would regard these items as quite subordinate to a carriage and a settlement. Now, she had ascertained, by tentative residences, that the kind of bite she was angling for was difficult to be met with at watering-places, which were already preoccupied with abundance of angling beauties, and were chiefly stocked with men whose whiskers might be dyed, and whose incomes were still more problematic; so she had determined on trying a neighborhood where people were extremely well acquainted with each other's affairs, and where the women were mostly ill-dressed and ugly. Mr. Bridmain's slow brain had adopted his sister's views, and it seemed to him that a woman so handsome and distinguished as the Countess must certainly make a match that might lift himself into the region of county celebrities, and give him at least a sort of cousinship to the quarter-sessions.

All this, which was the simple truth, would have seemed extremely flat to the gossips of Milby, who had made up their minds to something much more exciting. There was nothing here so very detestable. It is true, the Countess was a little vain, a little ambitious, a little selfish, a little shallow and frivolous, a little given to white lies.—But who considers such slight blemishes, such moral pimples as these, disqualifications for entering into the most respectable society! Indeed, the severest ladies in Milby would have been perfectly aware that these characteristics would have created no wide distinction between the Countess Czerlaski and themselves; and since it was clear there *was* a wide distinction—why, it must lie in the possession of some vices from which they were undeniably free.

Hence it came to pass that Milby respectability refused to recognize the Countess Czerlaski, in spite of her assiduous church-going, and the deep disgust she was known to have expressed at the extreme paucity of the congregations on Ash-Wednesdays. So she began to feel that she had miscalculated the advantages of a neighborhood where people are well acquainted with each other's private affairs. Under these circumstances, you will imagine how welcome was the perfect credence and admiration she met with from Mr. and Mrs. Barton. She had been especially irritated by Mr. Ely's behavior to her; she felt sure that he was not in the least struck with her beauty, that he quizzed her conversation, and that he spoke of her with a sneer. A woman always knows where she is utterly powerless, and shuns a coldly satirical eye as she would shun a Gorgon. And she was especially eager for clerical notice and friendship, not merely because that is quite the most respectable countenance to be obtained in society, but because she really cared about religious matters, and had an uneasy sense that she was not altogether safe in that quarter. She had serious intentions of becoming *quite* pious—without any reserves—when she had once got her carriage and settlement. Let us do this one sly trick, says Ulysses to Neoptolemus, and we will be perfectly honest ever after—

> *ἀλλ' ἡδὺ γάρ τοι κτῆμα τῆς νίκης λαβεῖν,*
> *τόλμα· δίκαιοι δ' αὖθις ἐκφανούμεθα.*

The Countess did not quote Sophocles, but she said to herself, "Only this little bit of pretense and vanity, and then I will be *quite* good, and make myself quite safe for another world.

And as she had by no means such fine taste and insight in theological teaching as in costume, the Rev. Amos Barton seemed to her a man not only of learning—*that* is always understood with a clergyman—but of much power as a spiritual director. As for Milly, the Countess really loved her as well as the preoccupied state of her affections would allow. For you have already perceived that there was one being to whom the Countess was absorbingly devoted, and to whose desires she made every thing else subservient—namely, Caroline Czerlaski, *née* Bridmain.

Thus there was really not much affectation in her sweet speeches and attentions to Mr. and Mrs. Barton. Still their friendship by no means adequately represented the object she had in view when she came to Milby, and it had been for some time clear to her that she must suggest a new change of residence to her brother.

The thing we look forward to often comes to pass, but never precisely in the way we have imagined to ourselves. The Countess did actually leave Camp Villa before many months were past, but under circumstances which had not at all entered into her contemplation.

CHAPTER V.

THE Rev. Amos Barton, whose sad fortunes I have undertaken to relate, was, you perceive, in no respect an ideal or exceptional character; and perhaps I am doing a bold thing to bespeak your sympathy on behalf of a man who was so very far from remarkable,—a man whose virtues were not heroic, and who had no undetected crime within his breast; who had not the slightest mystery hanging about him, but was palpably and unmistakably commonplace; who was not even in love, but had had that complaint favorably many years ago. "An utterly uninteresting character!" I think I hear a lady reader exclaim—Mrs. Farthingale, for example, who prefers the ideal in fiction; to whom tragedy means ermine tippets, adultery, and murder; and comedy, the adventures of some personage who is quite a "character."

But, my dear madam, it is so very large a majority of your fellow-countrymen that are of this insignificant stamp. At least eighty out of a hundred of your adult male fellow-Britons returned in the last census are neither extraordinarily silly, nor extraordinarily wicked, nor extraordinarily wise; their eyes are neither deep and liquid with sentiment, nor sparkling with suppressed witticisms; they have probably had no hairbreadth escapes or thrilling adventures; their brains are certainly not pregnant with genius, and their passions have not manifested themselves at all after the fashion of a volcano. They are simply men of complexions more or less muddy, whose conversation is more or less bald and disjointed. Yet these commonplace people—many of them—bear a conscience, and have felt the sublime prompting to do the painful right; they have their unspoken sorrows and their sacred joys; their hearts have perhaps gone out towards their first-born, and they have mourned over the irreclaimable dead. Nay, is there not a pathos in their very insignificance—in our comparison of their dim and narrow existence with the glorious possibilities of that human nature which they share.

Depend upon it, you would gain unspeakably if you would learn with me to see some of the poetry and the pathos, the tragedy and the comedy, lying in the experience of a human soul that looks out through dull gray eyes, and that speaks in a voice of quite ordinary tones. In that case, I should have no fear of your not caring to know what further befell the Rev. Amos Barton, or of your thinking the homely details I have to tell at all beneath your attention. As it is, you can, if you please, decline to pursue my story further; and you will easily find reading more to your taste, since I learn from the newspapers that many remarkable novels, full of striking situations, thrilling incidents, and eloquent writing, have appeared only within the last season.

Meanwhile, readers who have begun to feel an interest in the Rev. Amos Barton and his wife, will be glad to learn that Mr. Oldinport lent the twenty pounds. But twenty pounds are soon exhausted when twelve are due as back payment to the butcher, and when the possession of eight extra sovereigns in February weather is an irresistible temptation to order a new greatcoat. And though Mr. Bridmain so far departed from the necessary economy entailed on him by the Countess's elegant toilette and expensive maid, as to choose a handsome black silk, stiff, as his experienced eye discerned, with the genuine strength of its own texture, and not with the factitious strength of gum, and present it to Mrs. Barton, in retrieval of the accident that had occurred at his table, yet, dear me — as every husband has heard — what is the present of a gown when you are deficiently furnished with the et-ceteras of apparel, and when, moreover, there are six children whose wear and tear of clothes is something incredible to the non-maternal mind?

Indeed, the equation of income and expenditure was offering new and constantly accumulating difficulties to Mr. and Mrs. Barton; for shortly after the birth of little Walter, Milly's aunt, who had lived with her ever since her marriage, had withdrawn herself, her furniture, and her yearly income, to the household of another niece; prompted to that step, very probably, by a slight "tiff" with the Rev. Amos, which occurred while Milly was up stairs, and proved one too many for the elderly lady's patience and magnanimity. Mr. Barton's temper was a little warm, but, on the other hand, elderly maiden ladies are known to be susceptible; so we will not suppose that all the blame lay on his side—the less so, as he had every motive for humoring an inmate whose presence kept the wolf from the door. It was now nearly a year since Miss Jackson's departure, and, to a fine ear, the howl of the wolf was audibly approaching.

It was a sad thing, too, that when the last snow had melted, when the purple and yellow crocuses were coming up in the garden, and the old church was already half pulled down, Milly had an illness which made her lips look pale, and rendered it absolutely necessary that she should not exert herself for some time. Mr. Brand, the Shepperton doctor so obnoxious to Mr. Pilgrim, ordered her to drink port-wine, and it was quite necessary to have a charwoman very often to assist Nanny in all the extra work that fell upon her.

Mrs. Hackit, who hardly ever paid a visit to any one but her oldest and nearest neighbor, Mrs. Patten, now took the unusual step of calling at the vicarage one morning; and the tears came into her unsentimental eyes as she saw Milly seated pale and feeble in the parlor, unable to persevere in sewing the pinafore that lay on the table beside her. Little Dickey, a boisterous boy of five, with large pink cheeks and sturdy legs, was having his turn to sit with Mamma, and was squatting quiet as a mouse at her knee, holding her soft white hand between his little red, black-nailed fists. He was a boy whom Mrs. Hackit, in a severe mood, had pronounced "stocky" (a word that etymologically, in all probability, conveys some allusion to an instrument of punishment for the refractory); but seeing him thus subdued into goodness, she smiled at him with her kindest smile, and, stooping down, suggested a kiss—a favor which Dickey resolutely declined.

"Now *do* you take nourishing things enough?" was one of Mrs. Hackit's first questions, and Milly endeavored to make it appear that no woman was ever so much in danger of being over-fed and led into self-indulgent habits as herself. But Mrs. Hackit gathered one fact from her replies, namely, that Mr. Brand had ordered port-wine.

While this conversation was going forward, Dickey had been furtively stroking and kissing the soft white hand; so that at last, when a pause came, his mother said, smilingly, "Why are you kissing my hand, Dickey?"

"It id *to* yovely," answered Dickey, who, you observe, was decidedly backward in his pronunciation.

Mrs. Hackit remembered this little scene in after days, and thought with peculiar tenderness and pity of the "stocky boy."

The next day there came a hamper with Mrs. Hackit's respects; and on being opened it was found to contain half a dozen of port-wine and two couples of fowls. Mrs. Farquhar, too, was very kind; insisted on Mrs. Barton's rejecting all arrow-root but hers, which was genuine Indian, and carried away Sophy and Fred to stay with her a fortnight. These and other good-natured attentions made the trouble of Milly's illness more bearable; but they could not prevent it from swelling expenses, and Mr. Barton began to have serious thoughts of representing his case to a certain charity for the relief of needy curates.

Altogether, as matters stood in Shepperton, the parishioners were more likely to have a strong sense that the clergyman needed their material aid, than that they needed his spiritual aid,—not the best state of things in this age and country, where faith in men solely on the ground of their spiritual gifts has considerably diminished, and especially unfavorable to the influence of the Rev. Amos, whose spiritual gifts would not have had a very commanding power even in an age of faith.

But, you ask, did not the Countess Czerlaski pay any attention to her friends all this time? To be sure she did. She was indefatigable in visiting her "sweet Milly," and sitting with her for hours together. It may seem remarkable to you that she neither thought of taking away any of the children, nor of providing for any of Milly's probable wants; but ladies of rank and of luxurious habits, you know, can not be expected to surmise the details of poverty. She put a great deal of eau-de-Cologne on Mrs. Barton's pocket-handkerchief, re-arranged her pillow and footstool, kissed her cheeks, wrapped her in a soft warm shawl from her own shoulders, and amused her with stories of the life she had seen abroad. When Mr. Barton joined them she talked of Tractarianism, of her determination not to re-enter the vortex of fashionable life, and of her anxiety to see him in a sphere large enough for his talents. Milly thought her sprightliness and affectionate warmth quite charming, and was very fond of her; while the Rev. Amos had a vague consciousness that he had risen into aristocratic life, and only associated with his middle-class parishioners in a pastoral and parenthetic manner.

However, as the days brightened, Milly's cheeks and lips brightened too; and in a few weeks she was almost as active as ever, though watchful eyes might have seen that activity was not easy to her. Mrs. Hackit's eyes were of that kind, and one day, when Mr. and Mrs. Barton had been dining with her for the first time since Milly's illness, she observed to her husband—"That poor thing's dreadful weak an' dilicate; she won't stan' havin' many more children."

Mr. Barton, meanwhile, had been indefatigable in his vocation. He had preached two extemporary sermons every Sunday at the workhouse, where a room had been fitted up for divine service, pending the alterations in the church; and had walked the same evening to a cottage at one or other extremity of his parish to deliver another sermon, still more extemporary, in an atmosphere impregnated with spring-flowers and perspiration. After all these labors you will easily conceive that he was considerably exhausted by half past nine o'clock in the evening, and that a supper at a friendly parishioner's with a glass, or even two glasses, of brandy-and-water after it, was a welcome re-enforcement. Mr. Barton was not at all an ascetic; he thought the benefits of fasting were entirely confined to the Old Testament dispensation; he was fond of relaxing himself with a little gossip; indeed, Miss Bond, and other ladies of enthusiastic views, sometimes regretted that Mr. Barton did not more uninterruptedly exhibit a superiority to the things of the flesh. Thin ladies, who take little exercise, and whose livers are not strong enough to bear stimulants, are so extremely critical about one's personal habits. And, after all, the Rev. Amos never came near the borders of a vice. His very faults were middling—he was not *very* ungrammatical. It was not in his nature to be superlative in any thing; unless, indeed, he was superlatively middling, the quintessential extract of mediocrity. If there was any one point on which he showed an inclination to be excessive, it was confidence in his own shrewdness and ability in practical matters, so that he was very full of plans which were something like his moves in chess—admirably well calculated, supposing the state of the case were otherwise. For example, that notable plan of introducing anti-Dissenting books into his Lending Library did not in the least appear to have bruised the head of Dissent, though it had certainly made Dissent strongly inclined to bite the Rev. Amos's heel. Again, he vexed the souls of his churchwardens and influential parishioners by his fertile suggestiveness as to what it would be well for them to do in the matter of the church repairs, and other ecclesiastical secularities.

"I never saw the like to parsons," Mr. Hackit said one day in conversation with his brother churchwarden, Mr. Bond; "they're al'ys for meddling with business, an' they know no more about it than my black filly."

"Ah!" said Mr. Bond, "they're too high learnt to have much common sense."

"Well," remarked Mr. Hackit, in a modest and dubious tone, as if throwing out an hypothesis which might be considered bold, "I should say that's a bad sort of eddication as makes folks unreasonable."

So that, you perceive, Mr. Barton's popularity was in that precarious condition, in that toppling and contingent state, in which a very slight push from a malignant destiny would utterly upset it. That push was not long in being given, as you shall hear.

One fine May morning, when Amos was out on his parochial visits, and the sunlight was streaming through the bow-window of the sitting-room, where Milly was seated at her sewing, occasionally looking up to glance at the children playing in the garden, there came a loud rap at the door, which she at once recognized as the Countess's, and that well-dressed lady presently entered the sitting-room, with her veil drawn over her face. Milly was not at all surprised or sorry to see her; but when the Countess threw up her veil, and showed that her eyes were red and swollen, she was both surprised and sorry.

"What can be the matter, dear Caroline?"

Caroline threw down Jet, who gave a little yelp; then she threw her arms round Milly's neck, and began to sob; then she threw herself on the sofa, and begged for a glass of water; then she threw off her bonnet and shawl; and by the time Milly's imagination had exhausted itself in conjuring up calamities, she said,

"Dear, how shall I tell you? I am the most wretched woman. To be deceived by a brother to whom I have been so devoted—to see him degrading himself—giving himself utterly to the dogs!"

"What can it be?" said Milly, who began to picture to herself the sober Mr. Bridmain taking to brandy and betting.

"He is going to be married—to marry my own maid, that deceitful Alice, to whom I have been the most indulgent mistress. Did you ever hear of any thing so disgraceful? so mortifying? so disreputable?"

"And has he only just told you of it?" said Milly, who, having really heard of worse conduct, even in her innocent life, avoided a direct answer.

"Told me of it! he had not even the grace to do that. I went into the dining-room suddenly and found him kissing her—disgusting at his time of life, is it not?—and when I reproved her for allowing such liberties, she turned round saucily, and said she was engaged to be married to my brother, and she saw no shame in allowing him to kiss her. Edmund is a miserable coward, you know, and looked frightened; but when she asked him to say whether it was not so, he tried to summon up courage and say yes. I left the room in disgust, and this morning I have been questioning Edmund, and find that he is bent on marrying this woman, and that he has been putting off telling me—because he was ashamed of himself, I suppose. I couldn't possibly stay in the house after this, with my own maid turned mistress. And now, Milly, I am come to throw myself on your charity for a week or two. *Will* you take me in?"

"That we will," said Milly, "if you will only put up with our poor rooms and way of living. It will be delightful to have you."

"It will soothe me to be with you and Mr. Barton a little while. I feel quite unable to go among my other friends just at present. What those two wretched people will do I don't know—leave the neighborhood at once, I hope. I entreated my brother to do so, before he disgraced himself."

When Amos came home, he joined his cordial welcome and sympathy to Milly's. By-and-by the Countess's formidable boxes, which she had carefully packed before her indignation drove her away from Camp Villa, arrived at the vicarage, and were deposited in the spare bedroom, and in two closets, not spare, which Milly emptied for their reception. A week afterwards, the excellent apartments at Camp Villa, comprising dining and drawing-rooms, three bedrooms and a dressing-room, were again to let, and Mr. Bridmain's sudden departure, together with the Countess Czerlaski's installation as a visitor at Shepperton Vicarage, became a topic of general conversation in the neighborhood. The keen-sighted virtue of Milby and Shepperton saw in all this a confirmation of its worst suspicions, and pitied the Rev. Amos Barton's gullibility.

But when week after week, and month after month, slipped by without witnessing the Countess's departure—when summer and harvest had fled, and still left her behind them occupying the spare bedroom and the closets, and also a large proportion of Mrs. Barton's time and attention, new surmises of a very evil kind were added to the old rumors, and began to take the form of settled convictions in the minds even of Mr. Barton's most friendly parishioners.

And now, here is an opportunity for an accomplished writer to apostrophize calumny, to quote Virgil, and to show that he is acquainted with the most ingenious things which have been said on that subject in polite literature.

But what is opportunity to the man who can't use it? An unfecundated egg, which the waves of time wash away into nonentity. So, as my memory is ill-furnished, and my note-book still worse, I am unable to show myself either erudite or eloquent apropos of the calumny whereof the Rev. Amos Barton was the victim. I can only ask my reader,—did you ever upset your inkbottle, and watch, in helpless agony, the rapid spread of Stygian blackness over your fair manuscript or fairer table-cover? With a like inky swiftness did gossip now blacken the reputation of the Rev. Amos

Barton, causing the unfriendly to scorn and even the friendly to stand aloof, at a time when difficulties of another kind were fast thickening around him.

CHAPTER VI.

ONE November morning, at least six months after the Countess Czerlaski had taken up her residence at the vicarage, Mrs. Hackit heard that her neighbor Mrs. Patten had an attack of her old complaint, vaguely called "the spasms." Accordingly, about eleven o'clock, she put on her velvet bonnet and cloth cloak, with a long boa and muff large enough to stow a prize baby in; for Mrs. Hackit regulated her costume by the calendar, and brought out her furs on the first of November, whatever might be the temperature. She was not a woman weakly to accommodate herself to shilly-shally proceedings. If the season didn't know what it ought to do, Mrs. Hackit did. In her best days, it was always sharp weather at "Gunpowder Plot," and she did'nt like new fashions.

And this morning the weather was very rationally in accordance with her costume, for as she made her way through the fields to Cross Farm, the yellow leaves on the hedge-girt elms, which showed bright and golden against the low-hanging purple clouds, were being scattered across the grassy path by the coldest of November winds. "Ah," Mrs. Hackit thought to herself, "I daresay we shall have a sharp pinch this winter, and if we do, I shouldn't wonder if it takes the old lady off. They say a green Yule makes a fat churchyard; but so does a white Yule too, for that matter. When the stool's rotten enough, no matter who sits on it."

However, on her arrival at Cross Farm, the prospect of Mrs. Patten's decease was again thrown into the dim distance in her imagination, for Miss Janet Gibbs met her with the news that Mrs. Patten was much better, and led her, without any preliminary announcement, to the old lady's bedroom. Janet had scarcely reached the end of her circumstantial narrative, how the attack came on and what were her aunt's sensations—a narrative to which Mrs. Patten, in her neatly-plaited nightcap, seemed to listen with a contemptuous resignation to her niece's historical inaccuracy, contenting herself with occasionally confounding Janet by a shake of the head—when the clatter of a horse's hoofs on the yard pavement announced the arrival of Mr. Pilgrim, whose large, top-booted person presently made its appearance up stairs. He found Mrs. Patten going on so well that there was no need to look solemn. He might glide from condolence into gossip without offense, and the temptation of having Mrs. Hackit's ear was irresistible.

"What a disgraceful business this is turning out of your parson's," was the remark with which he made this agreeable transition, throwing himself back in the chair from which he had been leaning towards the patient.

"Eh, dear me!" said Mrs. Hackit, "disgraceful enough. I stuck to Mr. Barton as long as I could, for his wife's sake; but I can't countenance such goings on. It's hateful to see that woman coming with 'em to service of a Sunday, and if Mr. Hackit wasn't churchwarden and I didn't think it wrong to forsake one's own parish, I should go to Knebley Church. There's a many parish'ners as do."

"I used to think Barton was only a fool," observed Mr. Pilgrim, in a tone which implied that he was conscious of having been weakly charitable. "I thought he was imposed upon and led away by those people when they first came. But that's impossible now."

"Oh, it's as plain as the nose in your face," said Mrs. Hackit, unreflectingly, not perceiving the equivoque in her comparison—"comin' to Milby, like a sparrow perchin' on a bough, as I may say, with her brother, as she called him; and then all on a sudden the brother goes off with himself, and she throws herself on the Bartons. Though what could make her take up with a poor notomise of a parson, as hasn't got enough to keep wife and children, there's One above knows —*I* don't."

"Mr. Barton may have attractions we don't know of," said Mr. Pilgrim, who piqued himself on a talent for sarcasm. "The Countess has no maid now, and they say Mr. Barton is handy in assisting at her toilette—laces her boots, and so forth."

"T'ilette be fiddled!" said Mrs. Hackit, with indignant boldness of metaphor; "an' there's that poor thing a-sewing her fingers to the bone for them children—an' another comin' on. What she must have to go through! It goes to my heart to turn my back on her. But she's i' the wrong to let herself be put upon i' that manner."

"Ah! I was talking to Mrs. Farquhar about that the other day. She said, 'I think Mrs. Barton a v-e-r-y w-e-a-k w-o-m-a-n.'" (Mr. Pilgrim gave this quotation with slow emphasis, as if he thought Mrs. Farquhar had uttered a remarkable sentiment.) "They find it impossible to invite her to their house while she has that equivocal person staying with her."

"Well!" remarked Miss Gibbs, "if I was a wife, nothing should induce me to bear what Mrs. Barton does."

"Yes, it's fine talking," said Mrs. Patten, from her pillow; "old maids' husbands are al'ys well-managed. If you was a wife you'd be as foolish as your betters, belike."

"All my wonder is," observed Mrs. Hackit, "how the Bartons make both ends meet. You may depend on it, *she's* got nothing to give 'em; for I understand as he's been having money from some clergy charity. They said at fust as she stuffed Mr. Barton wi' notions about her writing to the Chancellor an' her fine friends, to give him a living. Howiver, I don't know what's true an' what's false. Mr. Barton keeps away from our house now, for I gave him a bit o' my mind one day. Maybe he's ashamed of himself. He seems to me to look dreadful thin an' harassed of a Sunday."

"Oh, he must be aware he's getting into bad odor everywhere. The clergy are quite disgusted with his folly. They say Carpe would be glad to get Barton out of the curacy if he could; but he can't do that without coming to Shepperton himself, as Barton's a licensed curate; and he wouldn't like that, I suppose."

At this moment Mrs. Patten showed signs of uneasiness, which recalled Mr. Pilgrim to professional attentions; and Mrs. Hackit, observing that it was Thursday, and she must see after the butter, said good-bye, promising to look in again soon and bring her knitting.

This Thursday, by-the-by, is the first in the month—the day on which the Clerical Meeting is held at Milby Vicarage; and as the Rev. Amos Barton has reasons for not attending he will very likely be a subject of conversation amongst his clerical brethren. Suppose we go there, and hear whether Mr. Pilgrim has reported their opinion correctly.

There is not a numerous party to-day, for it is a season of sore throats and catarrhs; so that the exegetical and theological discussions, which are the preliminary of dining, have not been quite so spirited as usual; and although a question relative to the Epistle of Jude has not been quite cleared up, the striking of six by the church clock, and the simultaneous announcement of dinner, are sounds that no one feels to be importunate.

Pleasant (when one is not in the least bilious) to enter a comfortable dining-room, where the closely-drawn red curtains glow with the double light of fire and candle, where glass and silver are glittering on the pure damask, and a soup-tureen gives a hint of the fragrance that will presently rush out to inundate your hungry senses, and prepare them, by the delicate visitation of atoms, for the keen gusto of ample contact! Especially if you have confidence in the dinner-giving capacity of your host—if you know that he is not a man who entertains grovelling views of eating and drinking as a mere satisfaction of hunger and thirst, and, dead to all the finer influences of the palate, expects his guest to be brilliant on ill-flavored gravies and the cheapest Marsala. Mr. Ely was particularly worthy of such confidence, and his virtues as an Amphitryon had probably contributed quite as much as the central situation of Milby to the selection of his house as a clerical rendezvous. He looks particularly graceful at the head of his table, and, indeed, on all occasions where he acts as president or moderator: he is a man who seems to listen well, and is an excellent amalgam of dissimilar ingredients.

At the other end of the table, as "Vice," sits Mr. Fellowes, rector and magistrate, a man of imposing appearance, with a mellifluous voice and the readiest of tongues. Mr. Fellowes once obtained a living by the persuasive charms of his conversation, and the fluency with which he interpreted the opinions of an obese and stammering baronet, so as to give that elderly gentleman a very pleasing perception of his own wisdom. Mr. Fellowes is a very successful man, and has the highest character everywhere except in his own parish, where, doubtless because his parishioners happen to be quarrelsome people, he is always at fierce feud with a farmer or two, a colliery proprietor, a grocer who was once churchwarden, and a tailor who formerly officiated as clerk.

At Mr. Ely's right hand you see a very small man with a sallow and somewhat puffy face, whose hair is brushed straight up, evidently with the intention of giving him a height somewhat less disproportionate to his sense of his own importance than the measure of five feet three accorded him by an oversight of nature. This is the Rev. Archibald Duke, a very dyspeptic and evangelical man, who takes the gloomiest view of mankind and their prospects, and thinks the immense sale of the "Pickwick Papers," recently completed, one of the strongest proofs of original sin. Unfortunately, though Mr. Duke was not burdened with a family, his yearly expenditure was apt considerably to exceed his income; and the unpleasant circumstances resulting from this, together with heavy meat-breakfasts, may probably have contributed to his desponding views of the world generally.

Next to him is seated Mr. Furness, a tall young man, with blond hair and whiskers, who was plucked at Cambridge, entirely owing to his genius; at least I know that he soon afterwards published a volume of poems, which were considered remarkably beautiful by many young ladies of his acquaintance. Mr. Furness preached his own sermons, as any one of tolerable critical acumen might have certified by comparing them with his poems; in both, there was an exuberance of metaphor and simile entirely original, and not in the least borrowed from any resemblance in the things compared.

On Mr. Furness's left you see Mr. Pugh, another young curate, of much less marked characteristics. He had not published any poems; he had not even been plucked; he had neat black whiskers and a pale complexion; read prayers and a sermon twice every Sunday, and might be seen any day sallying forth on his parochial duties in a white tie, a well-brushed hat, a perfect suit of black, and well-polished boots—an equipment which he probably supposed hieroglyphically to represent the spirit of Christianity to the parishioners of Whittlecombe.

Mr. Pugh's *vis-à-vis* is the Rev. Martin Cleves, a man about forty—middle-sized, broad-shouldered, with a negligently-tied cravat, large, irregular features, and a large head, thickly covered with lanky brown hair. To a superficial glance, Mr. Cleves is the plainest and least clerical-looking of the party; yet, strange to say, *there* is the true parish priest, the pastor beloved, consulted, relied on by his flock; a clergyman who is not associated with the undertaker, but thought of as the surest helper under a difficulty, as a monitor who is encouraging rather than severe. Mr. Cleves has the wonderful art of preaching sermons which the wheelwright and the blacksmith can understand; not because he talks condescending twaddle, but because he can call a spade a spade, and knows how to disencumber ideas of their wordy frippery. Look at him more attentively and you will see that his face is a very interesting one—that there is a great deal of humor and feeling playing in his gray eyes, and about the corners of his roughly-cut mouth:—a man, you observe, who has most likely sprung from the harder-working section of the middle class, and has hereditary sympathies with the checkered life of the people. He gets together the working-men in his parish on a Monday evening, and gives them a sort of conversational lecture on useful practical matters, telling them stories, or reading some select passages from an agreeable book, and commenting on them; and if you were to ask the first laborer or artisan in Tripplegate what sort of man the parson was, he would say,—"a uncommon knowin', sensable, free-spoken gentleman; very kind an' good-natur'd too." Yet, for all this, he is perhaps the best Grecian of the party, if we except Mr. Baird, the young man on his left.

Mr. Baird has since gained considerable celebrity as an original writer and metropolitan lecturer, but at that time he used to preach in a little church something like a barn, to a congregation consisting of three rich farmers and their servants, about fifteen laborers, and the due proportion of women and children. The rich farmers understood him to be "very high learnt;" but if you had interrogated them for a more precise description, they would have said that he was "a thinnish-faced man, with a sort o' cast in his eye, like."

Seven, altogether: a delightful number for a dinner-party, supposing the units to be delightful, but every thing depends on that. During dinner Mr. Fellowes took the lead in the conversation, which set strongly in the direction of mangold-wurzel and the rotation of crops; for Mr. Fellowes and Mr. Cleves cultivated their own glebes. Mr. Ely, too, had some agricultural notions, and even the Rev. Archibald Duke was made alive to that class of mundane subjects by the possession of some potato-ground. The two young curates talked a little aside during these discussions, which had imperfect interest for their unbeneficed minds; and the transcendental and near-sighted Mr. Baird seemed to listen somewhat abstractedly, knowing little more of potatoes and mangold-wurzel than that they were some form of the "Conditioned."

"What a hobby farming is with Lord Watling!" said Mr. Fellowes, when the cloth was being drawn. "I went over his farm at Tetterley with him last summer. It is really a model farm; first-rate dairy, grazing, and wheat land, and such splendid farm-buildings! An expensive hobby, though. He sinks a good deal of money there, I fancy. He has a great whim for black cattle, and he sends that drunken old Scotch bailiff of his to Scotland every year, with hundreds in his pocket, to buy these beasts."

"By-the-by," said Mr. Ely, "do you know who is the man to whom Lord Watling has given the Bramhill living?"

"A man named Sargent. I knew him at Oxford. His brother is a lawyer, and was very useful to Lord Watling in that ugly Brounsell affair. That's why Sargent got the living."

"Sargent," said Mr. Ely. "I know him. Isn't he a showy, talkative fellow; has written travels in Mesopotamia, or something of that sort?"

"That's the man."

"He was at Witherington once, as Bagshawe's curate.

He got into rather bad odor there, through some scandal about a flirtation, I think."

"Talking of scandal," returned Mr. Fellowes, "have you heard the last story about Barton? Nisbett was telling me the other day that he dines alone with the Countess at six, while Mrs. Barton is in the kitchen acting as cook."

"Rather an apocryphal authority, Nisbett," said Mr. Ely.

"Ah," said Mr. Cleves, with good-natured humor twinkling in his eyes, "depend upon it that is a corrupt version. The original text is, that they all dined together *with* six —meaning six children—and that Mrs. Barton is an excellent cook."

"I wish dining alone together may be the worst of that sad business," said the Rev. Archibald Duke, in a tone implying that his wish was a strong figure of speech.

"Well," said Mr. Fellowes, filling his glass and looking jocose, "Barton is certainly either the greatest gull in existence, or he has some cunning secret,—some philtre or other to make himself charming in the eyes of a fair lady. It isn't all of us that can make conquests when our ugliness is past its bloom."

"The lady seemed to have made a conquest of him at the very outset," said Mr. Ely. "I was immensely amused one night at Granby's when he was telling us her story about her husband's adventures. He said, 'When she told me the tale, I felt I don't know how,—I felt it from the crown of my head to the sole of my feet.'"

Mr. Ely gave these words dramatically, imitating the Rev. Amos's fervor and symbolic action, and every one laughed except Mr. Duke, whose after-dinner view of things was not apt to be jovial. He said,—

"I think some of us ought to remonstrate with Mr. Barton on the scandal he is causing. He is not only imperilling his own soul, but the souls of his flock."

"Depend upon it," said Mr. Cleves, "there is some simple explanation of the whole affair, if we only happened to know it. Barton has always impressed me as a right-minded man, who has the knack of doing himself injustice by his manner."

"Now *I* never liked Barton," said Mr. Fellowes. "He's not a gentleman. Why, he used to be on terms of intimacy with that canting Prior, who died a little while ago;— a fellow who soaked himself with spirits, and talked of the Gospel through an inflamed nose."

"The Countess has given him more refined tastes, I dare say," said Mr. Ely.

"Well," observed Mr. Cleves, "the poor fellow must have

a hard pull to get along, with his small income and large family. Let us hope the Countess does some thing towards making the pot boil."

"Not she," said Mr. Duke; "there are greater signs of poverty about them than ever."

"Well, come," returned Mr. Cleves, who could be caustic sometimes, and who was not at all fond of his reverend brother, Mr. Duke, "that's something in Barton's favor at all events. He might be poor *without* showing signs of poverty."

Mr. Duke turned rather yellow, which was his way of blushing, and Mr. Ely came to his relief by observing,

"They're making a very good piece of work of Shepperton Church. Dolby, the architect, who has it in hand, is a very clever fellow."

"It's he who has been doing Coppleton Church," said Mr. Furness. "They've got it in excellent order for the visitation."

This mention of the visitation suggested the Bishop, and thus opened a wide duct, which entirely diverted the stream of animadversion from that small pipe—that capillary vessel, the Rev. Amos Barton.

The talk of the clergy about their Bishop belongs to the esoteric part of their profession; so we will at once quit the dining-room at Milby Vicarage, lest we should happen to overhear remarks unsuited to the lay understanding, and perhaps dangerous to our repose of mind.

CHAPTER VII.

I DARE say the long residence of the Countess Czerlaski at Shepperton Vicarage is very puzzling to you also, dear reader, as well as to Mr. Barton's clerical brethren; the more so, as I hope you are not in the least inclined to put that very evil interpretation on it which evidently found acceptance with the sallow and dyspeptic Mr. Duke, and with the florid and highly peptic Mr. Fellowes. You have seen enough, I trust, of the Rev. Amos Barton, to be convinced that he was more apt to fall into a blunder than into a sin—more apt to be deceived than to incur a necessity for being deceitful; and if you have a keen eye for physiognomy, you will have detected that the Countess Czerlaski loved herself far too well to get entangled in an unprofitable vice.

How, then, you will say, could this fine lady choose to quarter herself on the establishment of a poor curate, where the carpets were probably falling into holes, where the attendance was limited to a maid-of-all-work, and where six children were running loose from eight o'clock in the morning till eight o'clock in the evening? Surely you must be straining probability.

Heaven forbid! For not having a lofty imagination, as you perceive, and being unable to invent thrilling incidents for your amusement, my only merit must lie in the truth with which I represent to you the humble experience of ordinary fellow-mortals. I wish to stir your sympathy with commonplace troubles—to win your tears for real sorrow: sorrow such as may live next door to you—such as walks neither in rags nor in velvet, but in very ordinary decent apparel.

Therefore, that you may dismiss your suspicions as to the truth of my picture, I will beg you to consider that at the time the Countess Czerlaski left Camp Villa in dudgeon, she had only twenty pounds in her pocket, being about one-third of the income she possessed independently of her brother. You will then perceive that she was in the extremely inconvenient predicament of having quarrelled, not indeed with her bread and cheese, but certainly with her chicken and tart—a predicament all the more inconvenient to her, because the habit of idleness had quite unfitted her for earning those necessary superfluities, and because, with all her fascinations, she had not secured any enthusiastic friends whose houses were open to her, and who were dying to see her. Thus she had completely checkmated herself, unless she could resolve on one unpleasant move—namely, to humble herself to her brother, and recognize his wife. This seemed quite impossible to her as long as she entertained the hope that he would make the first advances; and in this flattering hope she remained month after month at Shepperton Vicarage, gracefully overlooking the deficiencies of accommodation, and feeling that she was really behaving charmingly. "Who indeed," she thought to herself, "could do otherwise, with a lovely, gentle creature like Milly? I shall really be sorry to leave the poor thing."

So, though she lay in bed till ten, and came down to a separate breakfast at eleven, she kindly consented to dine as early as five, when a hot joint was prepared, which coldly furnished forth the children's table the next day; she considerately prevented Milly from devoting herself too closely to the children, by insisting on reading, talking, and walking with her; and she even began to embroider a cap for the next baby, which must certainly be a girl, and be named Caroline.

After the first month or two of her residence at the Vicarage, the Rev. Amos Barton became aware—as, indeed, it was unavoidable that he should—of the strong disapprobation it drew upon him, and the change of feeling towards him which it was producing in his kindest parishioners. But, in the first place, he still believed in the Countess as a charming and influential woman, disposed to befriend him, and, in any case, he could hardly hint departure to a lady guest who had been kind to him and his, and who might any day spontaneously announce the termination of her visit; in the second place, he was conscious of his own innocence, and felt some contemptuous indignation towards people who were ready to imagine evil of him; and, lastly, he had, as I have already intimated, a strong will of his own, so that a certain obstinacy and defiance mingled itself with his other feelings on the subject.

The one unpleasant consequence which was not to be evaded or counteracted by any mere mental state, was the increasing drain on his slender purse for household expenses, to meet which the remittance he had received from the clerical charity threatened to be quite inadequate. Slander may be defeated by equanimity; but courageous thoughts will not pay your baker's bill, and fortitude is nowhere considered legal tender for beef. Month after month the financial aspect of the Rev. Amos's affairs became more and more serious to him, and month after month, too, wore away more and more of that armor of indignation and defiance with which he had at first defended himself from the harsh looks of faces that were once the friendliest.

But quite the heaviest pressure of the trouble fell on Milly—on gentle, uncomplaining Milly—whose delicate body was becoming daily less fit for all the many things that had to be done between rising up and lying down. At first, she thought the Countess's visit would not last long, and she was quite glad to incur extra exertion for the sake of making her friend comfortable. I can hardly bear to think of all the rough work she did with those lovely hands—all by the sly, without letting her husband know any thing about it, and husbands are not clairvoyant: how she salted bacon, ironed shirts and cravats, put patches on patches, and re-darned darns. Then there was the task of mending and eking out baby-linen in prospect, and the problem perpetually suggesting itself how she and Nanny *should* manage when there was another baby, as there would be before very many months were past.

When time glided on, and the Countess's visit did not end, Milly was not blind to any phase of their position. She knew of the slander; she was aware of the keeping aloof of old friends; but these she felt almost entirely on her husband's account. A loving woman's world lies within the four walls of her own home; and it is only through her husband that she is in any electric communication with the world beyond. Mrs. Simpkins may have looked scornfully at her, but baby crows and holds out his little arms none the less blithely; Mrs. Tomkins may have left off calling on her, but her husband comes home none the less to receive her care and caresses; it has been wet and gloomy out of doors to-day, but she has looked well after the shirt-buttons, has cut out baby's pinafores, and half finished Willy's blouse.

So it was with Milly. She was only vexed that her husband should be vexed—only wounded because he was misconceived. But the difficulty about ways and means she felt in quite a different manner. Her rectitude was alarmed lest they should have to make tradesmen wait for their money; her motherly love dreaded the diminution of comforts for the children; and the sense of her own failing health gave exaggerated force to these fears.

Milly could no longer shut her eyes to the fact, that the Countess was inconsiderate, if she did not allow herself to entertain severer thoughts; and she began to feel that it would soon be a duty to tell her frankly that they really could not afford to have her visit further prolonged. But a process was going forward in two other minds, which ultimately saved Milly from having to perform this painful task.

In the first place, the Countess was getting weary of Shepperton—weary of waiting for her brother's overtures which never came; so, one fine morning, she reflected that forgiveness was a Christian duty, that a sister should be placable, that Mr. Bridmain must feel the need of her advice, to which he had been accustomed for three years, and that very likely "that woman" didn't make the poor man happy. In this amiable frame of mind she wrote a very affectionate appeal, and addressed it to Mr. Bridmain, through his banker.

Another mind that was being wrought up to a climax was Nanny's, the maid-of-all-work, who had a warm heart and a still warmer temper. Nanny adored her mistress; she had been heard to say, that she was "ready to kiss the ground as the missis trod on;" and Walter, she considered, was *her* baby, of whom she was as jealous as a lover. But she had, from the first, very slight admiration for the Countess Czerlaski. That lady, from Nanny's point of view, was a personage always "drawed out i' fine clothes," the chief result of whose existence was to cause additional bed-making, carrying of hot water, laying of table-cloths, and cooking of dinners. It was a perpetually heightening "aggravation" to Nanny that she and her mistress had to "slave" more than ever, because there was this fine lady in the house.

"An' she pays nothin' for't neither," observed Nanny to Mr. Jacob Tomms, a young gentleman in the tailoring line, who occasionally—simply out of a taste for dialogue—looked into the vicarage kitchen of an evening. "I know the master's shorter o' money than iver, an' it meks no end o' difference i' th' housekeepin'—her bein' here, besides bein' obliged to have a charwoman constant."

"There's fine stories i' the village about her," said Mr. Tomms. "They say as Muster Barton's great wi' her, or else she'd niver stop here."

"Then they say a passill o' lies, an' you ought to be ashamed to go an' tell 'em o'er again. Do *you* think as the master, as has got a wife like the missis, 'ud go running arter a stuck-up piece o' goods like that Countess, as isn't fit to black the missis's shoes? I'm none so fond o' the master, but I know better on him nor that."

"Well, I didn't b'lieve it," said Mr. Tomms, humbly.

"B'lieve it? you'd ha' been a ninny if yer did. An' she's a nasty, stingy thing, that Countess. She's niver giv me a sixpence nor an old rag neither, sin' here she's been. A lyin' abed an a-comin' down to breakfast when other folks wants their dinner!"

If such was the state of Nanny's mind as early as the end of August, when this dialogue with Mr. Tomms occurred, you may imagine what it must have been by the beginning of November, and that at that time a very slight spark might any day cause the long-smouldering anger to flame forth in open indignation.

That spark happened to fall the very morning that Mrs. Hackit paid the visit to Mrs. Patten, recorded in the last chapter. Nanny's dislike to the Countess extended to the innocent dog Jet, whom she "couldn't a-bear to see made a fuss wi' like a Christian. An' the little ouzel must be washed, too, ivery Saturday, as if there wasn't children enoo to wash, wi'out washin' dogs."

Now this particular morning it happened that Milly was quite too poorly to get up, and Mr. Barton observed to Nanny, on going out, that he would call and tell Mr. Brand to come. These circumstances were already enough to make Nanny anxious and susceptible. But the Countess, comfortably ignorant of them, came down as usual about eleven o'clock to her separate breakfast, which stood ready for her at that hour in the parlor; the kettle singing on the hob that she might make her own tea. There was a little jug of cream, taken according to custom from last night's milk, and specially saved for the Countess's breakfast. Jet always awaited his mistress at her bedroom door, and it was her habit to carry him down stairs.

"Now, my little Jet," she said, putting him down gently on the hearth-rug, "you shall have a nice, nice breakfast."

Jet indicated that he thought that observation extremely pertinent and well-timed, by immediately raising himself on his hind legs, and the Countess emptied the cream-jug into the saucer. Now there was usually a small jug of milk standing on the tray by the side of the cream, and destined for Jet's breakfast, but this morning Nanny, being "moithered," had forgotten that part of the arrangements, so that when the Countess had made her tea, she perceived there was no second jug, and rang the bell. Nanny appeared, looking very red and heated—the fact was, she had been "doing up" the kitchen fire, and that is a sort of work which by no means conduces to blandness of temper.

"Nanny, you have forgotten Jet's milk; will you bring me some more cream, please?"

This was just a little too much for Nanny's forbearance.

"Yes, I dare say. Here am I wi' my hands full o' the children an' the dinner, and missis ill a-bed, and Mr. Brand a-comin'; and I must run o'er the village to get more cream, 'cause you've give it to that nasty little blackamoor."

"Is Mrs. Barton ill?"

"Ill—yes—I should think she *is* ill, an' much you care. She's likely to be ill, moithered as *she* is from mornin' to night, wi' folks as had better be elsewhere."

"What do you mean by behaving in this way?"

"Mean? Why I mean as the missis is a-slavin' her life out an' a-sittin' up o'nights, for folks as are better able to wait of *her*, i'stid o' lyin' a-bed an' doin' nothin' all the blessed day, but mek work."

"Leave the room, and don't be insolent."

"Insolent! I'd better be insolent than like what some folks is,—a-livin' on other folks, an' bringin' a bad name on 'em into the bargain."

Here Nanny flung out of the room, leaving the lady to digest this unexpected breakfast at her leisure.

The Countess was stunned for a few minutes, but when she began to recall Nanny's words, there was no possibility of avoiding very unpleasant conclusions from them, or of failing to see her position at the Vicarage in an entirely new light. The interpretation, too, of Nanny's allusion to a "bad name" did not lie out of the reach of the Countess's imagination, and she saw the necessity of quitting Shepperton without delay. Still, she would like to wait for her brother's letter—no—she would ask Milly to forward it to her—still better, she would go at once to London, inquire her brother's address at his banker's, and go to see him without preliminary.

She went up to Milly's room, and, after kisses and inquiries, said—"I find on consideration, dear Milly, from the letter I had yesterday, that I must bid you good-bye and go up to London at once. But you must not let me leave you ill, you naughty thing."

"Oh no," said Milly, who felt as if a load had been taken off her back, "I shall be very well in an hour or two. Indeed, I'm much better now. You will want me to help you to pack. But you won't go for two or three days?"

"Yes, I must go to-morrow. But I shall not let you help me to pack, so don't entertain any unreasonable projects, but lie still. Mr. Brand is coming, Nanny says."

The news was not an unpleasant surprise to Mr. Barton when he came home, though he was able to express more regret at the idea of parting than Milly could summon to her lips. He retained more of his original feeling for the Countess than Milly did, for women never betray themselves to men as they do to each other; and the Rev. Amos had not a keen instinct for character. But he felt that he was being relieved from a difficulty, and in the way that was easiest for him. Neither he nor Milly suspected that it was Nanny who had cut the knot for them, for the Countess took care to give no sign on that subject. As for Nanny, she was perfectly aware of the relation between cause and effect in the affair, and secretly chuckled over her outburst of "sauce" as the best morning's work she had ever done.

So, on Friday morning, a fly was seen standing at the Vicarage gate with the Countess's boxes packed upon it; and presently that lady herself was seen getting into the vehicle. After a last shake of the hand to Mr. Barton, and last kisses to Milly and the children, the door was closed; and as the fly rolled off, the little party at the Vicarage gate caught a last glimpse of the handsome Countess leaning and waving kisses from the carriage window. Jet's little black phiz was also seen, and doubtless he had his thoughts and feelings on the occasion, but he kept them strictly within his own bosom.

The schoolmistress opposite witnessed this departure, and lost no time in telling it to the schoolmaster, who again communicated the news to the landlord of "The Jolly Colliers," at the close of the morning school-hours. Nanny poured the joyful tidings into the ear of Mr. Farquhar's footman, who happened to call with a letter, and Mr. Brand carried them to all the patients he visited that morning, after calling on Mrs. Barton. So that, before Sunday, it was very generally known in Shepperton parish that the Countess Czerlaski had left the Vicarage.

The Countess had left, but alas, the bills she had contributed to swell still remained; so did the exiguity of the children's clothing, which also was partly an indirect consequence of her presence; and so, too, did the coolness and alienation in the parishioners, which could not at once vanish before the fact of her departure. The Rev. Amos was not exculpated—the past was not expunged. But what was worse than all, Milly's health gave frequent cause for alarm, and the prospect of baby's birth was overshadowed by more than the usual fears. The birth came prematurely, about six weeks after the Countess's departure, but Mr. Brand gave favorable reports to all inquirers on the following day, which was Saturday. On Sunday, after morning service, Mrs. Hackit called at the Vicarage to inquire how Mrs. Barton was, and was invited up stairs to see her. Milly lay placid and lovely in her feebleness, and held out her hand to Mrs. Hackit with a beaming smile. It was very pleasant to her to see her old friend unreserved and cordial once more. The seven months' baby was very tiny and very red, but "handsome is that handsome does"—he was pronounced to be "doing well," and Mrs. Hackit went home gladdened at heart to think that the perilous hour was over.

CHAPTER VIII.

The following Wednesday, when Mr. and Mrs. Hackit were seated comfortably by their bright hearth, enjoying the long afternoon afforded by an early dinner, Rachel, the housemaid, came in and said,

"If you please, 'm, the shepherd says, have you heard as Mrs. Barton's wuss, and not expected to live?"

Mrs. Hackit turned pale, and hurried out to question the shepherd, who, she found, had heard the sad news at an ale-house in the village. Mr. Hackit followed her out and said, "You'd better have the pony-chaise, and go directly."

"Yes," said Mrs. Hackit, too much overcome to utter any exclamations. "Rachel, come and help me on wi' my things." When her husband was wrapping her cloak round her feet in the pony-chaise, she said,

"If I don't come home to-night, I shall send back the pony-chaise, and you'll know I'm wanted there."

"Yes, yes."

It was a bright frosty day, and by the time Mrs. Hackit arrived at the Vicarage, the sun was near its setting. There was a carriage and pair standing at the gate, which she recognized as Dr. Madeley's, the physician from Rotherby. She entered at the kitchen door that she might avoid knocking, and quietly questioned Nanny. No one was in the kitchen, but, passing on, she saw the sitting-room door open, and Nanny, with Walter in her arms, removing the knives and forks, which had been laid for dinner three hours ago.

"Master says he can't eat no dinner," was Nanny's first word. "He's never tasted nothin' sin' yesterday mornin', but a cup o' tea."

"When was your missis took worse?"

"O' Monday night. They sent for Dr. Madeley i' the middle o' the day yisterday, an' he's here again now."

"Is the baby alive?"

"No, it died last night. The children's all at Mrs. Bond's. She come and took 'em away last night, but the master says they must be fetched soon. He's up stairs now, wi' Dr. Madeley and Mr. Brand."

At this moment Mrs. Hackit heard the sound of a heavy, slow foot, in the passage; and presently Amos Barton entered, with dry, despairing eyes, haggard and unshaven. He expected to find the sitting-room as he left it, with nothing to meet his eyes but Milly's work-basket in the corner of the sofa, and the children's toys overturned in the bow-window. But when he saw Mrs. Hackit come towards him with answering sorrow in her face, the pent-up fountain of tears was opened; he threw himself on the sofa, hid his face, and sobbed aloud.

"Bear up, Mr. Barton," Mrs. Hackit ventured to say at last; "bear up, for the sake o' them dear children."

"The children," said Amos, starting up. "They must be sent for. Some one must fetch them. Milly will want to . . ."

He couldn't finish the sentence, but Mrs. Hackit understood him, and said, "I'll send the man with the pony-carriage for 'em."

She went out to give the order, and encountered Dr. Madeley and Mr. Brand, who were just going.

Mr. Brand said: "I am very glad to see you are here, Mrs. Hackit. No time must be lost in sending for the children. Mrs. Barton wants to see them."

"Do you quite give her up, then?"

"She can hardly live through the night. She begged us to tell her how long she had to live; and then asked for the children."

The pony-carriage was sent; and Mrs. Hackit, returning to Mr. Barton, said she would like to go up stairs now. He went up stairs with her and opened the door. The chamber fronted the west; the sun was just setting, and the red light fell full upon the bed, where Milly lay with the hand of death visibly upon her. The feather-bed had been removed, and she lay low on a mattress, with her head slightly raised by pillows. Her long fair neck seemed to be struggling with a painful effort; her features were pallid and pinched, and her eyes were closed. There was no one in the room but the nurse, and the mistress of the free school, who had come to give her help from the beginning of the change.

Amos and Mrs. Hackit stood beside the bed, and Milly opened her eyes.

"My darling, Mrs. Hackit is come to see you."

Milly smiled and looked at her with that strange, far-off look which belongs to ebbing life.

"Are the children coming?" she said painfully.

"Yes, they will be here directly."

She closed her eyes again.

Presently the pony-carriage was heard; and Amos, motioning to Mrs. Hackit to follow him, left the room. On their way down stairs, she suggested that the carriage should remain to take them away again afterwards, and Amos assented.

There they stood in the melancholy sitting-room—the five sweet children, from Patty to Chubby—all, with their mother's eyes—all, except Patty, looking up with a vague fear at their father as he entered. Patty understood the great sorrow that was come upon them, and tried to check her sobs as she heard her papa's footsteps.

"My children," said Amos, taking Chubby in his arms, "God is going to take away your dear mamma from us. She wants to see you to say good-bye. You must try to be very good and not cry."

He could say no more, but turned round to see if Nanny was there with Walter, and then led the way up stairs, leading Dickey with the other hand. Mrs. Hackit followed with Sophy and Patty, and then came Nanny with Walter and Fred.

It seemed as if Milly had heard the little footsteps on the stairs, for when Amos entered her eyes were wide open, eagerly looking towards the door. They all stood by the bedside—Amos nearest to her, holding Chubby and Dickey. But she motioned for Patty to come first, and clasping the poor pale child by the hand, said,

"Patty, I'm going away from you. Love your papa. Comfort him; and take care of your little brothers and sisters. God will help you."

Patty stood perfectly quiet, and said, "Yes, mamma."

The mother motioned with her pallid lips for the dear child to lean towards her and kiss her; and then Patty's great anguish overcame her, and she burst into sobs. Amos drew her towards him and pressed her head gently to him, while Milly beckoned Fred and Sophy, and said to them more faintly,

"Patty will try to be your mamma when I am gone, my darlings. You will be good and not vex her."

They leaned towards her, and she stroked their fair heads, and kissed their tear-stained cheeks. They cried because mamma was ill and papa looked so unhappy; but they thought, perhaps next week things would be as they used to be again.

The little ones were lifted on the bed to kiss her. Little Walter said, "Mamma, mamma," and stretched out his fat arms and smiled; and Chubby seemed gravely wondering; but Dickey, who had been looking fixedly at her, with lip hanging down, ever since he came into the room, now seemed suddenly pierced with the idea that mamma was going away somewhere; his little heart swelled and he cried aloud.

Then Mrs. Hackit and Nanny took them all away. Patty at first begged to stay at home and not go to Mrs. Bond's again; but when Nanny reminded her that she had better go to take care of the younger ones, she submitted at once, and they were all packed in the pony-carriage once more.

Milly kept her eyes shut for some time after the children were gone. Amos had sunk on his knees, and was holding her hand while he watched her face. By-and-by she opened her eyes, and drawing him close to her, whispered slowly,

"My dear—dear—husband—you have been—very—good to me. You—have—made me—very—happy."

She spoke no more for many hours. They watched her breathing becoming more and more difficult, until evening

"*My dear—dear—husband—you have been—very—good to me.*"—PAGE 66.

deepened into night, and until midnight was past. About half past twelve she seemed to be trying to speak, and they leaned to catch her words.

"Music—music—didn't you hear it?"

Amos knelt by the bed and held her hand in his. He did not believe in his sorrow. It was a bad dream. He did not know when she was gone. But Mr. Brand, whom Mrs. Hackit had sent for before twelve o'clock, thinking that Mr. Barton might probably need his help, now came up to him, and said,

"She feels no more pain now. Come, my dear sir, come with me."

"She isn't *dead?*" shrieked the poor desolate man, struggling to shake off Mr. Brand, who had taken him by the arm. But his weary, weakened frame was not equal to resistance, and he was dragged out of the room.

CHAPTER IX.

They laid her in the grave—the sweet mother with her baby in her arms—while the Christmas snow lay thick upon the graves. It was Mr. Cleves who buried her. On the first news of Mr. Barton's calamity, he had ridden over from Tripplegate to beg that he might be made of some use, and his silent grasp of Amos's hand had penetrated like the painful thrill of life-recovering warmth to the poor benumbed heart of the stricken man.

The snow lay thick upon the graves, and the day was cold and dreary; but there was many a sad eye watching that black procession as it passed from the Vicarage to the church, and from the church to the open grave. There were men and women standing in that churchyard who had bandied vulgar jests about their pastor, and who had lightly charged him with sin; but now, when they saw him following the coffin, pale and haggard, he was consecrated anew by his great sorrow, and they looked at him with respectful pity.

All the children were there, for Amos had willed it so, thinking that some dim memory of that sacred moment might remain even with little Walter, and link itself with what he would hear of his sweet mother in after years. He himself led Patty and Dickey; then came Sophy and Fred; Mr. Brand had begged to carry Chubby, and Nanny followed with Walter. They made a circle round the grave while the coffin was being lowered. Patty alone of all the children felt that mamma was in that coffin, and that a new and sadder life had begun for papa and herself. She was pale and trembling, but she clasped his hand more firmly as the coffin went down, and gave no sob. Fred and Sophy, though they were only two and three years younger, and though they had seen mamma in her coffin, seemed to themselves to be looking at some strange show. They had not learned to decipher that terrible handwriting of human destiny, illness and death. Dickey had rebelled against his black clothes, until he was told that it would be naughty to mamma not to put them on, when he at once submitted; and now, though he had heard Nanny say that mamma was in heaven, he had a vague notion that she would come home again to-morrow, and say he had been good boy, and let him empty her work-box. He stood close to his father, with great rosy cheeks, and wide open blue eyes, looking first up at Mr. Cleves and then down at the coffin, and thinking he and Chubby would play at that when they got home.

The burial was over, and Amos turned with his children to re-enter the house—the house where, an hour ago, Milly's dear body lay, where the windows were half-darkened, and sorrow seemed to have a hallowed precinct for itself, shut out from the world. But now she was gone; the broad snow-reflected daylight was in all the rooms; the Vicarage again seemed part of the common working-day world, and Amos, for the first time, felt that he was alone—that day after day, month after month, year after year, would have to be lived through without Milly's love. Spring would come and she would not be there; summer, and she would not be there; and he would never have her again with him by the fireside in the long evenings. The seasons all seemed irksome to his thoughts; and how dreary the sunshiny days that would be sure to come! She was gone from him; and he could never show her his love any more, never make up for omissions in the past by filling future days with tenderness.

Oh the anguish of that thought that we can never atone to our dead for the stinted affection we gave them, for the light answers we returned to their plaints or their pleadings, for the little reverence we showed to that sacred human soul that lived so close to us, and was the divinest thing God had given us to know!

Amos Barton had been an affectionate husband, and while Milly was with him, he was never visited by the thought that perhaps his sympathy with her was not quick and watchful enough; but now he re-lived all their life together, with that terrible keenness of memory and imagination which bereavement gives, and he felt as if his very love needed a pardon for its poverty and selfishness.

No outward solace could counteract the bitterness of this inward woe. But outward solace came. Cold faces looked kind again, and parishioners turned over in their minds what they could best do to help their pastor. Mr. Oldinport wrote to express his sympathy, and enclosed another twenty-pound note, begging that he might be permitted to contribute in this way to the relief of Mr. Barton's mind from pecuniary anxieties, under the pressure of a grief which all his parishioners must share; and offering his interest towards placing the two eldest girls in a school expressly founded for clergymen's daughters. Mr. Cleves succeeded in collecting thirty pounds among his richer clerical brethren, and, adding ten pounds himself, sent the sum to Amos, with the kindest and most delicate words of Christian fellowship and manly friendship. Miss Jackson forgot old grievances, and came to stay some months with Milly's children, bringing such material aid as she could spare from her small income. These were substantial helps, which relieved Amos from the pressure of his money difficulties; and the friendly attentions, the kind pressure of the hand, the cordial looks he met with everywhere in his parish, made him feel that the fatal frost which had settled on his pastoral duties, during the Countess's residence at the Vicarage, was completely thawed, and that the hearts of his parishioners were once more open to him.

No one breathed the Countess's name now; for Milly's memory hallowed her husband, as of old the place was hallowed on which an angel from God had alighted.

When the spring came, Mrs. Hackit begged that she might have Dickey to stay with her, and great was the enlargement of Dickey's experience from that visit. Every morning he was allowed—being well wrapt up as to his chest by Mrs. Hackit's own hands, but very bare and red as to his legs—to run loose in the cow and poultry yard, to persecute the turkey-cock by satirical imitations of his gobble-gobble, and to put difficult questions to the groom as to the reasons why horses had four legs, and other transcendental matters. Then Mr. Hackit would take Dickey up on horseback when he rode round his farm, and Mrs. Hackit had a large plum-cake in cut, ready to meet incidental attacks of hunger. So that Dickey had considerably modified his views as to the desirability of Mrs. Hackit's kisses.

The Misses Farquhar made particular pets of Fred and Sophy, to whom they undertook to give lessons twice a week in writing and geography; and Mrs. Farquhar devised many treats for the little ones. Patty's treat was to stay at home, or walk about with her papa; and when he sat by the fire in an evening, after the other children had gone to bed, she would bring a stool, and, placing it against his feet, would sit down upon it and lean her head against his knee. Then his hand would rest on that fair head, and he would feel that Milly's love was not quite gone out of his life.

So the time wore on till it was May again, and the church was quite finished and reopened in all its new splendor, and Mr. Barton was devoting himself with more vigor than ever to his parochial duties. But one morning—it was a very bright morning, and evil tidings sometimes like to fly in the finest weather—there came a letter for Mr. Barton, addressed in the Vicar's handwriting. Amos opened it with some anxiety—somehow or other he had a presentiment of evil. The letter contained the announcement that Mr. Carpe had resolved on coming to reside at Shepperton, and that, consequently, in six months from that time Mr. Barton's duties as curate in that parish would be closed.

Oh, it was hard! Just when Shepperton had become the place where he most wished to stay—where he had friends who knew his sorrows—where he lived close to Milly's grave. To part from that grave seemed like parting with Milly a second time; for Amos was one who clung to all the material links between his mind and the past. His imagination was not vivid, and required the stimulus of actual perception.

It roused some bitter feeling, too, to think that Mr. Carpe's wish to reside at Shepperton was merely a pretext for removing Mr. Barton, in order that he might ultimately give the curacy of Shepperton to his own brother-in-law, who was known to be wanting a new position.

Still it must be borne; and the painful business of seeking another curacy must be set about without loss of time. After the lapse of some months, Amos was obliged to renounce the hope of getting one at all near Shepperton, and he at length resigned himself to accepting one in a distant county. The parish was in a large manufacturing town, where his walks would lie among noisy streets and dingy alleys, and where the children would have no garden to play in, no pleasant farm-houses to visit.

It was another blow inflicted on the bruised man.

CHAPTER X.

At length the dreaded week was come, when Amos and his children must leave Shepperton. There was general regret among the parishioners at his departure: not that any one of them thought his spiritual gifts pre-eminent, or was conscious of great edification from his ministry. But his recent troubles had called out their better sympathies, and that is always a source of love. Amos failed to touch the spring of goodness by his sermons, but he touched it effectually by his sorrows; and there was now a real bond between him and his flock.

"My heart aches for them poor motherless children," said Mrs. Hackit to her husband, "a-going among strangers, and into a nasty town, where there's no good victuals to be had, and you must pay dear to get bad uns."

Mrs. Hackit had a vague notion of a town life as a combination of dirty backyards, measly pork, and dingy linen.

The same sort of sympathy was strong among the poorer class of parishioners. Old stiff-jointed Mr. Tozer, who was still able to earn a little by gardening "jobs," stopped Mrs. Cramp, the charwoman, on her way home from the Vicarage, where she had been helping Nanny to pack up the day before the departure, and inquired very particularly into Mr. Barton's prospects.

"Ah, poor mon," he was heard to say, "I'm sorry for un. He hedn't much here, but he'll be wuss off theer. Half a loaf's better nor ne'er un."

The sad good-byes had all been said before that last evening; and after all the packing was done and all the arrangements were made, Amos felt the oppression of that blank interval in which one has nothing left to think of but the dreary future—the separation from the loved and familiar, and the chilling entrance on the new and strange. In every parting there is an image of death.

Soon after ten o'clock, when he had sent Nanny to bed, that she might have a good night's rest before the fatigues of the morrow, he stole softly out to pay a last visit to Milly's grave. It was a moonless night, but the sky was thick with stars, and their light was enough to show that the grass had grown long on the grave, and that there was a tombstone telling in bright letters, on a dark ground, that beneath were deposited the remains of Amelia, the beloved wife of Amos Barton, who died in the thirty-fifth year of her age, leaving a husband and six children to lament her loss. The final words of the inscription were, "Thy will be done."

The husband was now advancing towards the dear mound from which he was so soon to be parted, perhaps forever. He stood a few minutes reading over and over again the words on the tombstone, as if to assure himself that all the happy and unhappy past was a reality. For love is frightened at the intervals of insensibility and callousness that encroach by little and little on the dominion of grief, and it makes efforts to recall the keenness of the first anguish.

Gradually, as his eye dwelt on the words, "Amelia, the beloved wife," the waves of feeling swelled within his soul, and he threw himself on the grave, clasping it with his arms, and kissing the cold turf.

"Milly, Milly, dost thou hear me? I didn't love thee enough—I wasn't tender enough to thee—but I think of it all now."

The sobs came and choked his utterance, and the warm tears fell.

CONCLUSION.

ONLY once again in his life has Amos Barton visited Milly's grave. It was in the calm and softened light of an autumnal afternoon, and he was not alone. He held on his arm a young woman, with a sweet, grave face, which strongly recalled the expression of Mrs. Barton's, but was less lovely in form and color. She was about thirty, but there were some premature lines round her mouth and eyes, which told of early anxiety.

Amos himself was much changed. His thin circlet of hair was nearly white, and his walk was no longer firm and upright. But his glance was calm, and even cheerful, and his neat linen told of a woman's care. Milly did not take all her love from the earth when she died. She had left some of it in Patty's heart.

All the other children were now grown up, and had gone their several ways. Dickey, you will be glad to hear, had shown remarkable talents as an engineer. His cheeks are still ruddy, in spite of mixed mathematics, and his eyes are still large and blue; but in other respects his person would present no marks of identification for his friend Mrs. Hackit, if she were to see him; especially now that her eyes must be grown very dim, with the wear of more than twenty additional years. He is nearly six feet high, and has a proportionately broad chest; he wears spectacles, and rubs his large white hands through a mass of shaggy brown hair. But I am sure you have no doubt that Mr. Richard Barton is a thoroughly good fellow, as well as a man of talent, and you will be glad any day to shake hands with him, for his own sake as well as his mother's.

Patty alone remains by her father's side, and makes the evening sunshine of his life.

MR. GILFIL'S LOVE-STORY.

CHAPTER I.

WHEN old Mr. Gilfil died, thirty years ago, there was general sorrow in Shepperton; and if black cloth had not been hung round the pulpit and reading-desk, by order of his nephew and principal legatee, the parishioners would certainly have subscribed the necessary sum out of their own pockets, rather than allow such a tribute of respect to be wanting. All the farmers' wives brought out their black bombazines; and Mrs. Jennings, at the Wharf, by appearing the first Sunday after Mr. Gilfil's death in her salmon-colored ribbons and green shawl, excited the severest remark. To be sure, Mrs. Jennings was a new-comer, and town-bred, so that she could hardly be expected to have very clear notions of what was proper; but, as Mrs. Higgins observed in an undertone to Mrs. Parrot when they were coming out of church, "Her husband, who'd been born i' the parish, might ha' told her better." An unreadiness to put on black on all available occasions, or too great an alacrity in putting it off, argued, in Mrs. Higgins's opinion, a dangerous levity of character, and an unnatural insensibility to the essential fitness of things.

"Some folks can't a-bear to put off their colors," she remarked; "but that was never the way i' *my* family. Why, Mrs. Parrot, from the time I was married, till Mr. Higgins died, nine year ago come Candlemas, I niver was out o' black two years together!"

"Ah," said Mrs. Parrot, who was conscious of inferiority in this respect, "there isn't many families as have had so many deaths as yours, Mrs. Higgins."

Mrs. Higgins, who was an elderly widow, "well left," reflected with complacency that Mrs. Parrot's observation was no more than just, and that Mrs. Jennings very likely belonged to a family which had had no funerals to speak of.

Even dirty Dame Fripp, who was a very rare church-goer, had been to Mrs. Hackit to beg a bit of old crape, and with this sign of grief pinned on her little coal-scuttle bonnet, was seen dropping her courtesy opposite the reading-desk. This manifestation of respect towards Mr. Gilfil's memory on the part of Dame Fripp had no theological bearing whatever. It was due to an event which had occurred some years back, and which, I am sorry to say, had left that grimy old lady as indifferent to the means of grace as ever. Dame Fripp kept leeches, and was understood to have such remarkable influence over those willful animals in inducing them to bite under the most unpromising circumstances, that though her own leeches were usually rejected, from a suspicion that they had lost their appetite, she herself was constantly called in to apply the more lively individuals furnished from Mr. Pilgrim's surgery, when, as was very often the case, one of that clever man's paying patients was attacked with inflammation. Thus Dame Fripp, in addition to "property" supposed to yield her no less than half a crown a week, was in the receipt of professional fees, the gross amount of which was vaguely estimated by her neighbors as "pouns an' pouns." Moreover, she drove a brisk trade in lollipop with epicurean urchins, who recklessly purchased that luxury at the rate of two hundred per cent. Nevertheless, with all these notorious sources of income, the shameless old woman constantly pleaded poverty, and begged for scraps at Mrs. Hackit's, who, though she always said Mrs. Fripp was "as false as two folks," and no better than a miser and a heathen, had yet a leaning towards her as an old neighbor.

"There's that case-hardened old Judy a coming after the tea-leaves again," Mrs. Hackit would say: "an' I'm fool enough to give 'em her, though Sally wants 'em all the while to sweep the floors with!"

Such was Dame Fripp, whom Mr. Gilfil, riding leisurely in top-boots and spurs from doing duty at Knebley one warm Sunday afternoon, observed sitting in the dry ditch near her cottage, and by her side a large pig, who, with that ease and confidence belonging to perfect friendship, was lying with his head in her lap, and making no effort to play the agreeable beyond an occasional grunt.

"Why, Mrs. Fripp," said the Vicar, "I didn't know you had such a fine pig. You'll have some rare flitches at Christmas!"

"Eh, God forbid! My son gev him me two 'ear ago, an' he's been company to me iver sin'. I couldn't find i' my heart to part wi'm, if I niver knowed the taste o' bacon-fat agin."

"Why, he'll eat his head off, and yours too. How can you go on keeping a pig, and making nothing by him?"

"Oh, he picks a bit hisself wi' rootin', and I dooant mind doing wi'out to gi' him summat. A bit o' coompany's meat an' drink too, an' he follers me about, and grunts when I spake to 'm, just like a Christian."

Mr. Gilfil laughed, and I am obliged to admit that he said good-bye to Dame Fripp without asking her why she had not been to church, or making the slightest effort for her spiritual edification. But the next day he ordered his man David to take her a great piece of bacon, with a message, saying, the parson wanted to make sure that Mrs. Fripp would know the taste of bacon-fat again. So, when Mr. Gilfil died, Dame Fripp manifested her gratitude and reverence in the simple dingy fashion I have mentioned.

You already suspect that the Vicar did not shine in the more spiritual functions of his office; and indeed, the utmost I can say for him in this respect is, that he performed those functions with undeviating attention to brevity and dispatch. He had a large heap of short sermons, rather yellow and worn at the edges, from which he took two every Sunday, securing perfect impartiality in the selection by taking them as they came, without reference to topics; and having preached one of these sermons at Shepperton in the morning, he mounted his horse and rode hastily with the other in his pocket to Knebley, where he officiated in a wonderful little church with a checkered pavement which had once rung to the iron tread of military monks, with coats of arms in clusters on the lofty roof, marble warriors and their wives without noses occupying a large proportion of the area, and the twelve apostles with their heads very much on one side, holding didactic ribbons, painted in fresco on the walls. Here, in an absence of mind to which he was prone, Mr. Gilfil would sometimes forget to take off his spurs before putting on his surplice, and only become aware of the omission by feeling something mysteriously tugging at the skirts of that garment as he stepped into the reading-desk. But the Knebley farmers would as soon have thought of criticising the moon as their pastor. He belonged to the course of nature, like markets and toll-gates and dirty bank-notes; and being a vicar, his claim on their veneration had never been counteracted by an exasperating claim on their pockets. Some of them, who did not indulge in the superfluity of a covered cart without springs, had dined half an hour earlier than usual—that is to say, at twelve o'clock—in order to have time for their long walk through miry lanes, and present themselves duly in their places at two o'clock, when Mr. Oldinport and Lady Felicia, to whom Knebley Church was a sort of family temple, made their way among the bows and courtesies of their dependents to a carved and canopied pew in the chancel, diffusing as they went a delicate odor of Indian roses on the unsusceptible nostrils of the congregation.

The farmers' wives and children sat on the dark oaken benches, but the husbands usually chose the distinctive dignity of a stall under one of the twelve apostles, where, when the alternation of prayers and responses had given place to the agreeable monotony of the sermon, Paterfamilias might be seen or heard sinking into a pleasant doze, from which he infallibly woke up at the sound of the concluding doxology. And then they made their way back again through the miry lanes, perhaps almost as much the better for this simple weekly tribute to what they knew of good and right, as many a more wakeful and critical congregation of the present day.

Mr. Gilfil, too, used to make his way home in the later years of his life, for he had given up the habit of dining at Knebley Abbey on a Sunday, having, I am sorry to say, had a very bitter quarrel with Mr. Oldinport, the cousin and predecessor of the Mr. Oldinport who flourished in the Rev. Amos Barton's time. That quarrel was a sad pity, for the two had had many a good day's hunting together when they were younger, and in those friendly times not a few members of the hunt envied Mr. Oldinport the excellent terms he was on with his vicar; for, as Sir Jasper Sitwell observed, "next to a man's wife, there's nobody can be such an infernal plague to you as a parson, always under your nose on your own estate."

I fancy the original difference which led to the rupture was very slight; but Mr. Gilfil was of an extremely caustic turn, his satire having a flavor of originality which was quite wanting in his sermons; and as Mr. Oldinport's armor of conscious virtue presented some considerable and conspicuous gaps, the Vicar's keen-edged retorts probably made a few incisions too deep to be forgiven. Such at least was the view of the case presented by Mr. Hackit, who knew as much of the matter as any third person. For, the very week after the quarrel, when presiding at the annual dinner of the Association for the Prosecution of Felons, held at the Oldinport Arms, he contributed an additional zest to the conviviality on that occasion by informing the company that "the parson had given the squire a lick with the rough side of his tongue." The detection of the person or persons who had driven off Mr. Parrot's heifer, could hardly have been more welcome news to the Shepperton tenantry, with whom Mr. Oldinport was in the worst odor as a landlord, having kept up his rents in spite of falling prices, and not being in the least stung to emulation by paragraphs in the provincial newspapers, stating that the Honorable Augustus Purwell, or Viscount Blethers, had made a return of ten per cent. on their last rent day. The fact was, Mr. Oldinport had not the slightest intention of standing for Parliament, whereas he had the strongest intention of adding to his unentailed estate. Hence, to the Shepperton farmers it was as good as lemon with their grog to know that the vicar had thrown out sarcasms against the Squire's charities, as little better than those of the man who stole a goose, and gave away the giblets in alms. For Shepperton, you observe, was in a state of Attic culture compared with Knebley; it had turnpike roads and a public opinion, whereas, in the Bœotian Knebley, men's minds and wagons alike moved in the deepest of ruts, and the landlord was only grumbled at as a necessary and unalterable evil, like the weather, the weevils, and the turnip-fly.

Thus in Shepperton this breach with Mr. Oldinport tended only to heighten that good understanding which the Vicar had always enjoyed with the rest of his parishioners, from the generation whose children he had christened a quarter of a century before, down to that hopeful generation represented by little Tommy Bond, who had recently quitted frocks and trowsers for the severe simplicity of a tight suit of corduroys, relieved by numerous brass buttons. Tommy was a saucy boy, impervious to all impressions of reverence, and excessively addicted to humming-tops and marbles, with which recreative resources he was in the habit of immoderately distending the pockets of his corduroys. One day, spinning his top on the garden-walk, and seeing the Vicar advance directly towards it, at that exciting moment when it was beginning to "sleep" magnificently, he shouted out with all the force of his lungs—"Stop! don't knock my top down, now!" From that day "little Corduroys" had been an especial favorite with Mr. Gilfil, who delighted to provoke his ready scorn and wonder by putting questions which gave Tommy the meanest opinion of his intellect.

"Well, little Corduroys, have they milked the geese today?"

"Milked the geese! why, they don't milk the geese, you silly!"

"No! dear heart! why, how do the goslings live, then?"

The nutriment of goslings rather transcending Tommy's observations in natural history, he feigned to understand this question in an exclamatory rather than an interrogatory sense, and became absorbed in winding up his top.

"Ah, I see you don't know how the goslings live! But did you notice how it rained sugar-plums yesterday?" (Here Tommy became attentive.) "Why, they fell into my pocket as I rode along. You look in my pocket and see if they didn't."

Tommy, without waiting to discuss the alleged antecedent, lost no time in ascertaining the presence of the agreeable consequent, for he had a well-founded belief in the advantages of diving into the Vicar's pocket. Mr. Gilfil called it his wonderful pocket, because, as he delighted to tell the "young shavers" and "two-shoes"—so he called all little boys and girls—whenever he put pennies into it, they turned into sugar-plums or gingerbread, or some other nice thing. Indeed, little Bessie Parrot, a flaxen-headed "two-shoes," very white and fat as to her neck, always had the admirable directness and sincerity to salute him with the question—"What zoo dot in zoo pottet?"

You can imagine, then, that the christening dinners were none the less merry for the presence of the parson. The farmers relished his society particularly, for he could not only smoke his pipe, and season the details of parish affairs with abundance of caustic jokes and proverbs, but, as Mr. Bond often said, no man knew more than the Vicar about the breed of cows and horses. He had grazing-land of his own about five miles off, which a bailiff, ostensibly a tenant, farmed under his direction; and to ride backward and forward, and look after the buying and selling of stock, was the old gentleman's chief relaxation, now his hunting-days were over. To hear him discussing the respective merits of the Devonshire breed and the short-horns, or the last foolish decision of the magistrates about a pauper, a superficial observer might have seen little difference, beyond his superior shrewdness, between the Vicar and his bucolic parishioners; for it was his habit to approximate his accent and mode of speech to theirs, doubtless because he thought it a mere frustration of the purposes of language to talk of "shear-hogs" and "ewes" to men who habitually said "sharrags" and "yowes." Nevertheless the farmers themselves were perfectly aware of the distinction between them and the parson, and had not at all the less belief in him as a gentleman and a clergyman for his easy speech and familiar manners. Mrs. Parrot smoothed her apron and set her cap right with the utmost solicitude when she saw the Vicar coming, made him her deepest courtesy, and every Christmas had a fat turkey ready to send him with her "duty." And in the most gossiping colloquies with Mr. Gilfil, you might have observed that both men and women "minded their words," and never became indifferent to his approbation.

The same respect attended him in his strictly clerical functions. The benefits of baptism were supposed to be somehow bound up with Mr. Gilfil's personality, so metaphysical a distinction as that between a man and his office being, as yet, quite foreign to the mind of a good Shepperton Churchman, savoring, he would have thought, of Dissent on the very face of it. Miss Selina Parrot put off her marriage a whole month when Mr. Gilfil had an attack of rheumatism, rather than be married in a makeshift manner by the Milby curate.

"We've had a very good sermon this morning," was the frequent remark, after hearing one of the old yellow series, heard with all the more satisfaction because it had been heard for the twentieth time; for to minds on the Shepperton level it is repetition, not novelty, that produces the strongest effect, and phrases, like tunes, are a long time making themselves at home in the brain.

Mr. Gilfil's sermons, as you may imagine, were not of a highly doctrinal, still less of a polemical, cast. They perhaps did not search the conscience very powerfully; for you remember that to Mrs. Patten, who had listened to them thirty years, the announcement that she was a sinner appeared an uncivil heresy; but, on the other hand, they made no unreasonable demand on the Shepperton intellect—amounting, indeed, to little more than an expansion of the concise thesis, that those who do wrong will find it the worse for them, and those who do well will find it the better for them; the nature of wrong-doing being exposed in special sermons against lying, backbiting, anger, slothfulness, and the like; and well-doing being interpreted as honesty, truthfulness, charity, industry, and other common virtues, lying quite on the surface of life, and having very little to do with deep spiritual doctrine. Mrs. Patten understood that if she turned out ill-crushed cheeses, a just retribution awaited her; though, I fear, she made no particular application of the sermon on backbiting. Mrs. Hackit expressed herself greatly edified by the sermon on honesty, the allusion to the unjust weight and deceitful balance having a peculiar lucidity for her, owing to a recent dispute with her grocer; but I am not aware that she ever appeared to be much struck by the sermon on anger.

As to any suspicion that Mr. Gilfil did not dispense the pure Gospel, or any strictures on his doctrine and mode of delivery, such thoughts never visited the minds of the Shepperton parishioners—of those very parishioners who, ten or fifteen years later, showed themselves extremely critical of

4*

Mr. Barton's discourses and demeanor. But in the interim they had tasted that dangerous fruit of the tree of knowledge —innovation, which is well known to open the eyes, even in an uncomfortable manner. At present to find fault with the sermon was regarded as almost equivalent to finding fault with religion itself. One Sunday, Mr. Hackit's nephew, Master Tom Stokes, a flippant town youth, greatly scandalized his excellent relatives by declaring that he could write as good a sermon as Mr. Gilfil's; whereupon Mr. Hackit sought to reduce the presumptuous youth to utter confusion, by offering him a sovereign if he would fulfill his vaunt. The sermon was written, however; and though it was not admitted to be anywhere within reach of Mr. Gilfil's, it was yet so astonishingly like a sermon, having a text, three divisions, and a concluding exhortation beginning "And now, my brethren," that the sovereign, though denied formally, was bestowed informally, and the sermon was pronounced, when Master Stokes's back was turned, to be "an uncommon cliver thing."

The Rev. Mr. Pickard, indeed, of the Independent Meeting, had stated, in a sermon preached at Rotherby, for the reduction of a debt on New Zion, built, with an exuberance of faith and a deficiency of funds, by seceders from the original Zion, that he lived in a parish where the vicar was very "dark;" and in the prayers he addressed to his own congregation, he was in the habit of comprehensively alluding to the parishioners outside the chapel walls, as those who, Gallio-like, "cared for none of these things." But I need hardly say that no church-goer ever came within earshot of Mr. Pickard.

It was not to the Shepperton farmers only that Mr. Gilfil's society was acceptable; he was a welcome guest at some of the best houses in that part of the country. Old Sir Jasper Sitwell would have been glad to see him every week; and if you had seen him conducting Lady Sitwell in to dinner, or had heard him talking to her with quaint yet graceful gallantry, you would have inferred that the earlier period of his life had been past in more stately society than could be found in Shepperton, and that his slipshod chat and homely manners were but like weather-stains on a fine old block of marble, allowing you still to see here and there the fineness of the grain, and the delicacy of the original tint. But in his later years these visits became a little too troublesome to the old gentleman, and he was rarely to be found anywhere of an evening beyond the bounds of his own parish—most frequently, indeed, by the side of his own sitting-room fire, smoking his pipe, and maintaining the pleasing antithesis of dryness and moisture by an occasional sip of gin-and-water.

Here I am aware that I have run the risk of alienating all my refined lady-readers, and utterly annihilating any curiosity they may have felt to know the details of Mr. Gilfil's love-story. "Gin-and-water! foh! you may as well ask us to interest ourselves in the romance of a tallow-chandler, who mingles the image of his beloved with short dips and moulds."

But in the first place, dear ladies, allow me to plead that gin-and-water, like obesity, or baldness, or the gout, does not exclude a vast amount of antecedent romance, any more than the neatly-executed "fronts" which you may some day wear, will exclude your present possession of less expensive braids. Alas, alas! we poor mortals are often little better than wood-ashes—there is small sign of the sap, and the leafy freshness, and the bursting buds that were once there; but wherever we see wood-ashes, we know that all that early fullness of life must have been. I, at least, hardly ever look at a bent old man, or a wizened old woman, but I see also, with my mind's eye, that Past of which they are the shrunken remnant, and the unfinished romance of rosy cheeks and bright eyes seems sometimes of feeble interest and significance, compared with that drama of hope and love which has long ago reached its catastrophe, and left the poor soul, like a dim and dusty stage, with all its sweet garden-scenes and fair perspectives overturned and thrust out of sight.

In the second place, let me assure you that Mr. Gilfil's potations of gin-and-water were quite moderate. His nose was not rubicund; on the contrary, his white hair hung around a pale and venerable face. He drank it chiefly, I believe, because it was cheap: and here I find myself alighting on another of the Vicar's weaknesses, which, if I had cared to paint a flattering portrait rather than a faithful one, I might have chosen to suppress. It is undeniable that, as the years advanced, Mr. Gilfil became, as Mr. Hackit observed, more and more "close-fisted," though the growing propensity showed itself rather in the parsimony of his personal habits, than in withholding help from the needy. He was saving—so he represented the matter to himself—for a nephew, the only son of a sister who had been the dearest object, all but one, in his life. "The lad," he thought, "will have a nice little fortune to begin life with, and will bring his pretty young wife some day to see the spot where his old uncle lies. It will perhaps be all the better for *his* hearth that mine was lonely."

Mr. Gilfil was a bachelor, then?

That is the conclusion to which you would probably have come if you had entered his sitting-room, where the bare tables, the large old-fashioned horse-hair chairs, and the threadbare Turkey carpet, perpetually fumigated with tobacco, seemed to tell a story of wifeless existence that was contradicted by no portrait, no piece of embroidery, no faded bit of pretty triviality, hinting of taper-fingers and small feminine ambitions. And it was here that Mr. Gilfil passed his evenings, seldom with other society than that of Ponto, his old brown setter, who, stretched out at full length on the rug with his nose between his fore paws, would wrinkle his brows and lift up his eyelids every now and then, to exchange a glance of mutual understanding with his master. But there was a chamber in Shepperton Vicarage which told a different story from that bare and cheerless dining-room—a chamber never entered by any one besides Mr. Gilfil and old Martha the housekeeper, who, with David her husband as groom and gardener, formed the Vicar's entire establishment. The blinds of this chamber were always down, except once a quarter, when Martha entered that she might air and clean it. She always asked Mr. Gilfil for the key, which he kept locked up in his bureau, and returned it to him when she had finished her task.

It was a touching sight that the daylight streamed in upon, as Martha drew aside the blinds and thick curtains, and opened the Gothic casement of the oriole window! On the little dressing-table there was a dainty looking-glass in a carved and gilt frame; bits of wax-candle were still in the branched sockets at the sides, and on one of these branches hung a little black lace kerchief; a faded satin pin-cushion, with the pins rusted in it, a scent-bottle, and a large green fan, lay on the table; and on a dressing-box by the side of the glass was a work-basket, and an unfinished baby-cap, yellow with age, lying in it. Two gowns, of a fashion long forgotten, were hanging on nails against the door, and a pair of tiny red slippers, with a bit of tarnished silver embroidery on them, were standing at the foot of the bed. Two or three water-color drawings, views of Naples, hung upon the walls; and over the mantel-piece, above some bits of rare old china, two miniatures in oval frames. One of these miniatures represented a young man about seven-and-twenty, with a sanguine complexion, full lips, and clear, candid gray eyes. The other was the likeness of a girl probably not more than eighteen, with small features, thin cheeks, a pale, southern-looking complexion, and large dark eyes. The gentleman wore powder; the lady had her dark hair gathered away from her face, and a little cap, with a cherry-colored bow, set on the top of her head—a coquettish head-dress, but the eyes spoke of sadness rather than of coquetry.

Such were the things that Martha had dusted and let the air upon four times a-year, ever since she was a blooming lass of twenty; and she was now, in this last decade of Mr. Gilfil's life, unquestionably on the wrong side of fifty. Such was the locked-up chamber in Mr. Gilfil's house: a sort of visible symbol of the secret chamber in his heart, where he had long turned the key on early hopes and early sorrows, shutting up for ever all the passion and the poetry of his life.

There were not many people in the parish, besides Martha, who had any very distinct remembrance of Mr. Gilfil's wife, or indeed who knew any thing of her, beyond the fact that there was a marble tablet, with a Latin inscription in memory of her, over the vicarage pew. The parishioners who were old enough to remember her arrival were not generally gifted with descriptive powers, and the utmost you could gather from them was, that Mrs. Gilfil looked like a "furriner, wi' such eyes, you can't think, an' a voice as went through you when she sung at church." The one exception was Mrs. Patten, whose strong memory and taste for personal narrative made her a great source of oral tradition in Shepperton. Mr. Hackit, who had not come into the parish until ten years after Mrs. Gilfil's death, would often put old questions to Mrs. Patten for the sake of getting the old answers, which pleased him in the same way as passages from a favorite book, or the scenes of a familiar play, please more accomplished people.

"Ah, you remember well the Sunday as Mrs. Gilfil first come to church, eh, Mrs. Patten?"

"To be sure I do. It was a fine bright Sunday as ever was seen, just at the beginnin' o' hay harvest. Mr. Tarbett preached that day, and Mr. Gilfil sat i' the pew with his wife. I think I see him now, a-leading her up the aisle, an' her head not reachin' much above his elber: a little pale woman, with eyes as black as sloes, an' yet lookin' blank-like, as if she see'd nothing with 'em."

"I warrant she had her weddin' clothes on?" said Mr. Hackit.

"Nothin' partickler smart—on'y a white hat tied down under her chin, an' a white Indy muslin gown. But you don't know what Mr. Gilfil was in those times. He was fine an' altered before you come into the parish. He'd a fresh color then, an' a bright look wi' his eyes, as did your heart good to see. He looked rare and happy that Sunday; but somehow, I'd a feelin' as it wouldn't last long. I've no opinion o' furriners, Mr. Hackit, for I've travelled i' their country with my lady in my time, an' seen enough o' their victuals an' their nasty ways."

"Mrs. Gilfil come from It'ly, didn't she?"

"I reckon she did, but I niver could rightly hear about that. Mr. Gilfil was niver to be spoke to about her, and nobody else hereabout knowed any thin'. Howiver, she must ha' come over pretty young, for she spoke English as well as you an' me. It's them Italians as has such fine voices, an' Mrs. Gilfil sung, you never heared the like. He brought her here to have tea with me one afternoon, and says he, in his jovial way, 'Now, Mrs. Patten, I want Mrs. Gilfil to see the neatest house, and drink the best cup o' tea, in all Shepperton; you must show her your dairy and your cheese-room, and then she shall sing you a song.' An' so she did; an' her voice seemed sometimes to fill the room; an' then it went low an' soft, as if it was whisperin' close to your heart like."

"You never heared her again, I reckon?"

"No; she was sickly then, and she died in a few months after. She wasn't in the parish much more nor half a year altogether She didn't seem lively that afternoon, an' I could see she didn't care about the dairy, nor the cheeses, on'y she pretended, to please him. As for him, I never see'd a man so wrapt up in a woman. He looked at her as if he was worshippin' her, an' as if he wanted to lift her off the ground ivery minute to save her the trouble o' walkin'. Poor man, poor man! It had like to ha' killed him when she died, though he niver gev way, but went on ridin' about and preachin'. But he was wore to a shadow, an' his eyes used to look as dead—you wouldn't ha' knowed 'em."

"She brought him no fortin?"

"Not she. All Mr. Gilfil's property come by his mother's side. There was blood an' money too, there. It's a thousand pities as he married i' that way—a fine man like him, as might ha' had the pick o' the county, an' had his grandchildren about him now. An' him so fond o' children, too."

In this manner Mrs. Patten usually wound up her reminiscences of the Vicar's wife, of whom, you perceive, she knew but little. It was clear that the communicative old lady had nothing to tell of Mrs. Gilfil's history previous to her arrival in Shepperton, and that she was unacquainted with Mr. Gilfil's love-story.

But I, dear reader, am quite as communicative as Mrs. Patten, and much better informed; so that, if you care to know more about the Vicar's courtship and marriage, you need only carry your imagination back to the latter end of the last century, and your attention forward into the next chapter.

CHAPTER II.

It is the evening of the 21st of June, 1788. The day has been bright and sultry, and the sun will still be more than an hour above the horizon, but his rays, broken by the leafy fretwork of the elms that border the park, no longer prevent two ladies from carrying out their cushions and embroidery, and seating themselves to work on the lawn in front of Cheverel Manor. The soft turf gives way even under the fairy tread of the younger lady, whose small stature and slim figure rest on the tiniest of full-grown feet. She trips along before the elder, carrying the cushions, which she places in the favorite spot, just on the slope by a clump of laurels, where they can see the sunbeams sparkling among the water-lilies, and can be themselves seen from the dining-room windows. She has deposited the cushions, and now turns round, so that you may have a full view of her as she stands waiting the slower advance of the elder lady. You are at once arrested by her large dark eyes, which, in their inexpressive, unconscious beauty, resemble the eyes of a fawn, and it is only by an effort of attention that you notice the absence of bloom on her young cheek, and the southern yellowish tint of her small neck and face, rising above the little black lace kerchief which prevents the too immediate comparison of her skin with her white muslin gown. Her large eyes seem all the more striking because the dark hair is gathered away from her face, under a little cap set at the top of her head, with a cherry-colored bow on one side.

The elder lady, who is advancing towards the cushions, is cast in a very different mould of womanhood. She is tall, and looks the taller because her powdered hair is turned backward over a toupee, and surmounted by lace and ribbons. She is nearly fifty, but her complexion is still fresh and beautiful, with the beauty of an auburn blonde; her proud pouting lips, and her head thrown a little backward as she walks, give an expression of hauteur which is not contradicted by the cold gray eye. The tucked-in kerchief, rising full over the low tight boddice of her blue dress, sets off the majestic form of her bust, and she treads the lawn as if she were one of Sir Joshua Reynolds's stately ladies, who had suddenly stepped from her frame to enjoy the evening cool.

"*Just on the slope by a clump of laurels, where they can see the sunbeams sparkling among the water-lilies.*"—PAGE 87.

"Put the cushions lower, Caterina, that we may not have so much sun upon us," she called out, in a tone of authority, when still at some distance.

Caterina obeyed, and they sat down, making two bright patches of red and white and blue on the green background of the laurels and the lawn, which would look none the less pretty in a picture because one of the women's hearts was rather cold and the other rather sad.

And a charming picture Cheverel Manor would have made that evening, if some English Watteau had been there to paint it: the castellated house of gray-tinted stone, with the flickering sunbeams sending dashes of golden light across the many-shaped panes in the mullioned windows, and a great beech leaning athwart one of the flanking towers, and breaking, with its dark flattened boughs, the too formal symmetry of the front; the broad gravel-walk winding on the right, by a row of tall pines, alongside the pool — on the left branching out among swelling grassy mounds, surmounted by clumps of trees, where the red trunk of the Scotch fir glows in the descending sunlight against the bright green of limes and acacias; the great pool, where a pair of swans are swimming lazily with one leg tucked under a wing, and where the open water-lilies lie calmly accepting the kisses of the fluttering light-sparkles; the lawn, with its smooth emerald greenness, sloping down to the rougher and browner herbage of the park, from which it is invisibly fenced by a little stream that winds away from the pool, and disappears under a wooden bridge in the distant pleasure-ground; and on this lawn our two ladies, whose part in the landscape the painter, standing at a favorable point of view in the park, would represent with a few little dabs of red and white and blue.

Seen from the great Gothic windows of the dining-room, they had much more definiteness of outline, and were distinctly visible to the three gentlemen sipping their claret there, as two fair women in whom all three had a personal interest. These gentlemen were a group worth considering attentively; but any one entering that dining-room for the first time, would perhaps have had his attention even more strongly arrested by the room itself, which was so bare of furniture that it impressed one with its architectural beauty like a cathedral. A piece of matting stretched from door to door, a bit of worn carpet under the dining-table, and a sideboard in a deep recess, did not detain the eye for a moment from the lofty groined ceiling, with its richly-carved pendants, all of creamy white, relieved here and there by touches of gold. On one side, this lofty ceiling was supported by pillars and arches, beyond which a lower ceiling, a miniature copy of the higher one, covered the square projection which, with its three large pointed windows, formed the central feature of the building. The room looked less like a place to dine in than a piece of space enclosed simply for the sake of beautiful outline; and the small dining-table, with the party round it, seemed an odd and insignificant accident, rather than any thing connected with the original purpose of the apartment.

But, examined closely, that group was far from insignificant; for the eldest, who was reading in the newspaper the last portentous proceedings of the French parliaments, and turning with occasional comments to his young companions, was as fine a specimen of the old English gentleman as could well have been found in those venerable days of cocked-hats and pigtails. His dark eyes sparkled under projecting brows, made more prominent by bushy grizzled eyebrows; but any apprehension of severity excited by these penetrating eyes, and by a somewhat aquiline nose, was allayed by the good-natured lines about the mouth, which retained all its teeth and its vigor of expression in spite of sixty winters. The forehead sloped a little from the projecting brows, and its peaked outline was made conspicuous by the arrangement of the profusely-powdered hair, drawn backward and gathered into a pigtail. He sat in a small hard chair, which did not admit the slightest approach to a lounge, and which showed to advantage the flatness of his back and the breadth of his chest. In fact, Sir Christopher Cheverel was a splendid old gentleman, as any one may see who enters the saloon at Cheverel Manor, where his full-length portrait, taken when he was fifty, hangs side by side with that of his wife, the stately lady seated on the lawn.

Looking at Sir Christopher, you would at once have been inclined to hope that he had a full-grown son and heir; but perhaps you would have wished that it might not prove to be the young man on his right hand, in whom a certain resemblance to the Baronet, in the contour of the nose and brow, seemed to indicate a family relationship. If this young man had been less elegant in his person, he would have been remarked for the elegance of his dress. But the perfections of his slim, well-proportioned figure were so striking that no one but a tailor could notice the perfections of his velvet coat; and his small white hands, with their blue veins and taper fingers, quite eclipsed the beauty of his lace ruffles. The face, however—it was difficult to say why—was certainly not pleasing. Nothing could be more delicate than the blond complexion—its bloom set off by the powdered hair—than the veined over hanging eyelids, which gave an indolent expression to the hazel eyes; nothing more finely cut than the transparent nostril and the short upper-lip. Perhaps the chin and lower jaw were too small for an irreproachable profile, but the defect was on the side of that delicacy and *finesse* which was the distinctive characteristic of the whole person, and which was carried out in the clear brown arch of the eyebrows, and the marble smoothness of the sloping forehead. Impossible to say that this face was not eminently handsome; yet, for the majority both of men and women, it was destitute of charm. Women disliked eyes that seemed to be indolently accepting admiration instead of rendering it; and men, especially if they had a tendency to clumsiness in the nose and ankles, were inclined to think this Antinous in a pigtail a "confounded puppy." I fancy that was frequently the inward interjection of the Rev. Maynard Gilfil, who was seated on the opposite side of the dining-table, though Mr. Gilfil's legs and profile were not at all of a kind to make him peculiarly alive to the impertinence and frivolity of personal advantages. His healthy, open face and robust limbs were after an excellent pattern for everyday wear, and, in the opinion of Mr. Bates, the north-country gardener, would have become regimentals "a fain saight" better than the "peaky" features and slight form of Captain Wybrow, notwithstanding that this young gentleman, as Sir Christopher's nephew and destined heir, had the strongest hereditary claim on the gardener's respect, and was undeniably "clean-limbed." But alas! human longings are perversely obstinate; and to the man whose mouth is watering for a peach, it is of no use to offer the largest vegetable marrow. Mr. Gilfil was not sensitive to Mr. Bates's opinion, whereas he *was* sensitive to the opinion of another person, who by no means shared Mr. Bates's preference.

Who the other person was it would not have required a very keen observer to guess, from a certain eagerness in Mr. Gilfil's glance as that little figure in white tripped along the lawn with the cushions. Captain Wybrow, too, was looking in the same direction, but his handsome face remained handsome—and nothing more.

"Ah," said Sir Christopher, looking up from his paper, "there's my lady. Ring for coffee, Anthony; we'll go and join her, and the little monkey Tina shall give us a song."

The coffee presently appeared, brought—not as usual by the footman, in scarlet and drab, but—by the old butler, in threadbare but well-brushed black, who, as he was placing it on the table said—

"If you please, Sir Christopher, there's the widow Hartopp a-crying i' the still room, and begs leave to see your honor."

"I have given Markham full orders about the widow Hartopp," said Sir Christopher, in a sharp decided tone. "I have nothing to say to her."

"Your honor," pleaded the butler, rubbing his hands, and putting on an additional coating of humility, "the poor woman's dreadful overcome, and says she can't sleep a wink this blessed night without seeing your honor, and she begs you to pardon the great freedom she's took to come at this time. She cries fit to break her heart."

"Ay, ay; water pays no tax. Well, show her into the library."

Coffee dispatched, the two young men walked out through the open window, and joined the ladies on the lawn, while Sir Christopher made his way to the library, solemnly followed by Rupert, his pet bloodhound, who, in his habitual place at the Baronet's right hand, behaved with great urbanity during dinner; but when the cloth was drawn, invariably disappeared under the table, apparently regarding the claret-jug as a mere human weakness, which he winked at but refused to sanction.

The library lay but three steps from the dining-room, on the other side of a cloistered and matted passage. The oriel window was overshadowed by the great beech, and this, with the flat, heavily-carved ceiling and the dark hue of the old books that lined the walls, made the room look sombre, especially on entering it from the dining-room, with its aërial curves and cream-colored fretwork touched with gold. As Sir Christopher opened the door, a jet of brighter light fell on a woman in a widow's dress, who stood in the middle of the room, and made the deepest of courtesies as he entered. She was a buxom woman approaching forty, her eyes red with the tears which had evidently been absorbed by the handkerchief gathered into a damp ball in her right hand.

"Now, Mrs. Hartopp," said Sir Christopher, taking out his gold snuff-box and tapping the lid, "what have you to say to me? Markham has delivered you a notice to quit, I suppose?"

"Oh yis, your honor, an' that's the reason why I've come. I hope your honor'll think better on it, an' not turn me an' my poor children out o' the farm, where my husband al'ys paid his rent as reglar as the day come."

"Nonsense! I should like to know what good it will do

you and your children to stay on a farm and lose every farthing your husband has left you, instead of selling your stock and going into some little place where you can keep your money together. It is very well known to every tenant of mine that I never allow widows to stay on their husbands' farms."

"Oh, Sir Christifer, if you *would* consider—when I've sold the hay, an' corn, an' all the live things, an' paid the debts, an' put the money out to use, I shall have hardly enough to keep our souls an' bodies together. An' how can I rear my boys and put 'em 'prentice? They must go for day-laborers, an' their father a man wi' as good belongings as any on your honor's estate, an' niver threshed his wheat afore it was well i' the rick, nor sold the straw off his farm, nor nothin'. Ask all the farmers round if there was a stiddier, soberer man than my husband as attended Ripstone market. An' he says, 'Bessie,' says he—them was his last words—'you'll mek a shift to manage the farm, if Sir Christifer 'ull let you stay on.'"

"Pooh, pooh!" said Sir Christopher, Mrs. Hartopp's sobs having interrupted her pleadings, "now listen to me, and try to understand a little common-sense. You are about as able to manage the farm as your best milch cow. You'll be obliged to have some managing man, who will either cheat you out of your money or wheedle you into marrying him."

"Oh, your honor, I was never that sort o' woman, an' nobody has known it on me."

"Very likely not, because you were never a widow before. A woman's always silly enough, but she's never quite as great a fool as she can be until she puts on a widow's cap. Now, just ask yourself how much the better you will be for staying on your farm at the end of four years, when you've got through your money, and let your farm run down, and are in arrears for half your rent; or, perhaps, have got some great hulky fellow for a husband, who swears at you and kicks your children."

"Indeed, Sir Christifer, I know a deal o' farmin', an' was brought up i' the thick on it, as you may say. An' there was my husband's great-aunt managed a farm for twenty year, an' left legacies to all her nephys an' nieces, an' even to my husband, as was then a babe unborn."

"Psha! a woman six feet high, with a squint and sharp elbows, I dare say—a man in petticoats. Not a rosy-cheeked widow like you, Mrs. Hartopp."

"Indeed, your honor, I never heard of her squintin', an' they said as she might ha' been married o'er and o'er again, to people as had no call to hanker after her money."

"Ay, ay, that's what you all think. Every man that looks at you wants to marry you, and would like you the better the more children you have and the less money. But it is useless to talk and cry. I have good reasons for my plans, and never alter them. What you have to do is to make the best of your stock, and to look out for some little place to go to, when you leave the Hollows. Now, go back to Mrs. Bellamy's room, and ask her to give you a dish of tea."

Mrs. Hartopp, understanding from Sir Christopher's tone that he was not to be shaken, courtesied low and left the library, while the Baronet, seating himself at his desk in the oriel window, wrote the following letter:

"MR. MARKHAM,—Take no steps about letting Crowsfoot Cottage, as I intend to put in the widow Hartopp when she leaves her farm; and if you will be here at eleven on Saturday morning, I will ride round with you, and settle about making some repairs, and see about adding a bit of land to the take, as she will want to keep a cow and some pigs.

"Yours faithfully, CHRISTOPHER CHEVEREL."

After ringing the bell and ordering this letter to be sent, Sir Christopher walked out to join the party on the lawn. But finding the cushions deserted, he walked on to the eastern front of the building, where, by the side of the grand entrance, was the large bow-window of the saloon, opening on to the gravel-sweep, and looking towards a long vista of undulating turf, bordered by tall trees, which, seeming to unite itself with the green of the meadows and a grassy road through a plantation, only terminated with the Gothic arch of a gateway in the far distance. The bow window was open, and Sir Christopher, stepping in, found the group he sought, examining the progress of the unfinished ceiling. It was in the same style of florid pointed Gothic as the dining-room, but more elaborate in its tracery, which was like petrified lace-work picked out with delicate and varied coloring. About a fourth of it still remained uncolored, and under this part were scaffolding, ladders, and tools; otherwise the spacious saloon was empty of furniture, and seemed to be a grand Gothic canopy for the group of five human figures standing in the centre.

"Francesco has been getting on a little better the last day or two," said Sir Christopher, as he joined the party: "he's a sad lazy dog, and I fancy he has a knack of sleeping as he stands, with his brushes in his hands. But I must spur him on, or we may not have the scaffolding cleared away before the bride comes, if you show dexterous generalship in your wooing, eh, Anthony? and take your Magdeburg quickly."

"Ah, sir, a siege is known to be one of the most tedious operations in war," said Captain Wybrow, with an easy smile.

"Not when there's a traitor within the walls in the shape of a soft heart. And that there will be, if Beatrice has her mother's tenderness as well as her mother's beauty."

"What do you think, Sir Christopher," said Lady Cheverel, who seemed to wince a little under her husband's reminiscences, "of hanging Guercino's 'Sibyl' over that door when we put up the pictures? It is rather lost in my sitting-room."

"Very good, my love," answered Sir Christopher, in a tone of punctiliously polite affection; "if you like to part with the ornament from your own room, it will show admirably here. Our portraits, by Sir Joshua, will hang opposite the window, and the 'Transfiguration' at that end. You see, Anthony, I am leaving no good places on the walls for you and your wife. We shall turn you with your faces to the wall in the gallery, and you may take your revenge on us by-and-by."

While this conversation was going on, Mr. Gilfil turned to Caterina and said,

"I like the view from this window better than any other in the house."

She made no answer, and he saw that her eyes were filling with tears; so he added, "Suppose we walk out a little; Sir Christopher and my lady seem to be occupied."

Caterina complied silently, and they turned down one of the gravel walks that led, after many windings under tall trees and among grassy openings, to a large enclosed flower-garden. Their walk was perfectly silent, for Maynard Gilfil knew that Caterina's thoughts were not with him, and she had been long used to make him endure the weight of those moods which she carefully hid from others.

They reached the flower-garden, and turned mechanically in at the gate that opened, through a high thick hedge, on an expanse of brilliant color, which, after the green shades they had passed through, startled the eye like flames. The effect was assisted by an undulation of the ground, which gradually descended from the entrance-gate, and then rose again towards the opposite end, crowned by an orangery. The flowers were glowing with their evening splendors; verbenas and heliotropes were sending up their finest incense. It seemed a gala where all was happiness and brilliancy, and misery could find no sympathy. This was the effect it had on Caterina. As she wound among the beds of gold and blue and pink, where the flowers seemed to be looking at her with wondering elf-like eyes, knowing nothing of sorrow, the feeling of isolation in her wretchedness overcame her, and the tears, which had been before trickling slowly down her pale cheeks, now gushed forth accompanied with sobs. And yet there was a loving human being close beside her, whose heart was aching for hers, who was possessed by the feeling that she was miserable, and that he was helpless to soothe her. But she was too much irritated by the idea that his wishes were different from hers, that he rather regretted the folly of her hopes than the probability of their disappointment, to take any comfort in his sympathy. Caterina, like the rest of us, turned away from sympathy which she suspected to be mingled with criticism, as the child turns away from the sweetmeat in which it suspects imperceptible medicine.

"Dear Caterina, I think I hear voices," said Mr. Gilfil; "they may be coming this way."

She checked herself like one accustomed to conceal her emotions, and ran rapidly to the other end of the garden, where she seemed occupied in selecting a rose. Presently Lady Cheverel entered, leaning on the arm of Captain Wybrow, and followed by Sir Christopher. The party stopped to admire the tiers of geraniums near the gate; and in the mean time Caterina tripped back with a moss rose-bud in her hand, and, going up to Sir Christopher, said, "There, Padroncello—there is a nice rose for your button-hole."

"Ah, you black-eyed monkey," he said, fondly stroking her cheek; "so you have been running off with Maynard, either to torment or coax him an inch or two deeper into love. Come, come, I want you to sing us '*Ho perduto*' before we sit down to picquet. Anthony goes to-morrow, you know; you must warble him into the right sentimental lover's mood, that he may acquit himself well at Bath." He put her little arm under his, and calling to Lady Cheverel, "Come, Henrietta!" led the way towards the house.

The party entered the drawing-room, which, with its oriel window, corresponded to the library in the other wing, and had also a flat ceiling heavy with carving and blazonry; but the window being unshaded, and the walls hung with full-length portraits of knights and dames in scarlet, white, and gold, it had not the sombre effect of the library. Here hung the portrait of Sir Anthony Cheverel, who in the reign of Charles II. was the renovator of the family splendor, which had suffered some declension from the early brilliancy of that Chevreuil, who came over with the Conqueror. A very imposing personage was this Sir Anthony, standing with one arm akimbo, and one fine leg and foot advanced, evidently with a view to the gratification of his contemporaries and posterity. You might have taken off his splendid peruke, and his scarlet cloak, which was thrown backward from his shoulders, without annihilating the dignity of his appearance. And he had known how to choose a wife, too, for his lady, hanging opposite to him, with her sunny brown hair drawn away in bands from her mild grave face, and falling in two large rich curls on her snowy gently-sloping neck, which shamed the harsher hue and outline of her white satin robe, was a fit mother of "large-acred" heirs.

In this room tea was served; and here, every evening, as regularly as the great clock in the court-yard with deliberate bass tones struck nine, Sir Christopher and Lady Cheverel sat down to picquet until half-past ten, when Mr. Gilfil read prayers to the assembled household in the chapel.

But now it was not near nine, and Caterina must sit down to the harpsichord and sing Sir Christopher's favorite airs, by Gluck and Paesiello, whose operas, for the happiness of that generation, were then to be heard on the London stage. It happened this evening that the sentiment of these airs, "*Che farò senza Eurydice?*" and "*Ho perduto il bel sembiante*," in both of which the singer pours out his yearning after his lost love, came very close to Caterina's own feeling. But her emotion, instead of being a hindrance to her singing, gave her additional power. Her singing was what she could do best; it was her one point of superiority, in which it was probable she would excel the high-born beauty whom Anthony was to woo; and her love, her jealousy, her pride, her rebellion against her destiny, made one stream of passion which welled forth in the deep rich tones of her voice. She had a rare contralto, which Lady Cheverel, who had high musical taste, had been careful to preserve her from straining.

"Excellent, Caterina," said Lady Cheverel, as there was a pause after the wonderful linked sweetness of "*Che farò.*" "I never heard you sing that so well. Once more!"

It was repeated; and then came "*Ho perduto*," which Sir Christopher encored, in spite of the clock, just striking nine. When the last note was dying out, he said—

"There's a clever black-eyed monkey. Now bring out the table for picquet."

Caterina drew out the table and placed the cards; then, with her rapid fairy suddenness of motion, threw herself on her knees, and clasped Sir Christopher's knee. He bent down, stroked her cheek, and smiled.

5

"Caterina, that is foolish," said Lady Cheverel. "I wish you would leave off those stage-players' antics."

She jumped up, arranged the music on the harpsichord, and then, seeing the Baronet and his lady seated at picquet, quietly glided out of the room.

Captain Wybrow had been leaning near the harpsichord during the singing, and the chaplain had thrown himself on a sofa at the end of the room. They both now took up a book. Mr. Gilfil chose the last number of the "Gentleman's Magazine;" Captain Wybrow, stretched on an ottoman near the door, opened "Faublas;" and there was perfect silence in the room which, ten minutes before, was vibrating to the passionate tones of Caterina.

She had made her way along the cloistered passages, now lighted here and there by a small oil-lamp, to the grand staircase, which led directly to a gallery running along the whole eastern side of the building, where it was her habit to walk when she wished to be alone. The bright moonlight was streaming through the windows, throwing into strange light and shadow the heterogeneous objects that lined the long walls: Greek statues and busts of Roman emperors; low cabinets filled with curiosities, natural and antiquarian; tropical birds and huge horns of beasts; Hindoo gods and strange shells; swords and daggers, and bits of chain-armor; Roman lamps and tiny models of Greek temples; and, above all these, queer old family portraits—of little boys and girls, once the hope of the Cheverels with close-shaven heads imprisoned in stiff ruffs—of faded, pink-faced ladies, with rudimentary features and highly-developed head-dresses—of gallant gentlemen, with high hips, high shoulders, and red pointed beards.

Here, on rainy days, Sir Christopher and his lady took their promenade, and here billiards were played; but, in the evening, it was forsaken by all except Caterina—and, sometimes, one other person.

She paced up and down in the moonlight, her pale face and thin white-robed form making her look like the ghost of some former Lady Cheverel come to revisit the glimpses of the moon.

By-and-by she paused opposite the broad window above the portico, and looked out on the long vista of turf and trees now stretching chill and saddened in the moonlight.

Suddenly a breath of warmth and roses seemed to float towards her, and an arm stole gently round her waist, while a soft hand took up her tiny fingers. Caterina felt an electric thrill, and was motionless for one long moment; then she pushed away the arm and hand, and, turning round, lifted up to the face that hung over her eyes full of tenderness and reproach. The fawn-like unconsciousness was gone, and in that one look were the ground tones of poor little Caterina's nature—intense love and fierce jealousy.

"Why do you push me away, Tina?" said Captain Wybrow in a half-whisper; "are you angry with me for what a hard fate puts upon me? Would you have me cross my uncle—who has done so much for us both—in his dearest wish? You know I have duties—we both have duties—before which feeling must be sacrificed."

"Yes, yes," said Caterina, stamping her foot, and turning away her head; "don't tell what I know already."

There was a voice speaking in Caterina's mind to which she had never yet given vent. That voice said continually, "Why did he make me love him—why did he let me know he loved me, if he knew all the while that he couldn't brave every thing for my sake?" Then love answered, "He was led on by the feeling of the moment, as you have been, Caterina; and now you ought to help him to do what is right." Then the voice rejoined, "It was a slight matter to him. He doesn't much mind giving you up. He will soon love that beautiful woman, and forget a poor little pale thing like you."

Thus love, anger, and jealousy were struggling in that young soul.

"Besides, Tina," continued Captain Wybrow in still gentler tones, "I shall not succeed. Miss Assher very likely prefers some one else; and you know I have the best will in the world to fail. I shall come back a hapless bachelor—perhaps to find you already married to the good-looking chaplain, who is over head and ears in love with you. Poor Sir Christopher has made up his mind that you're to have Gilfil."

"Why will you speak so? You speak from your own want of feeling. Go away from me."

"Don't let us part in anger, Tina. All this may pass away. It's as likely as not that I may never marry any one at all. These palpitations may carry me off, and you may have the satisfaction of knowing that I shall never be any body's bridegroom. Who knows what may happen? I may be my own master before I get into the bonds of holy matrimony, and be able to choose my little singing-bird. Why should we distress ourselves before the time?"

"It is easy to talk so when you are not feeling," said Caterina, the tears flowing fast. "It is bad to bear now, whatever may come after. But you don't care about my misery."

"Don't I, Tina?" said Anthony in his tenderest tones, again

stealing his arm around her waist, and drawing her towards him. Poor Tina was the slave of this voice and touch. Grief and resentment, retrospect and foreboding, vanished—all life before and after melted away in the bliss of that moment, as Anthony pressed his lips to hers.

Captain Wybrow thought, "Poor little Tina! it would make her very happy to have me. But she is a mad little thing."

At that moment a loud bell startled Caterina from her trance of bliss. It was the summons to prayers in the chapel, and she hastened away, leaving Captain Wybrow to follow slowly.

It was a pretty sight, that family assembled to worship in the little chapel, where a couple of wax candles threw a mild faint light on the figures kneeling there. In the desk was Mr. Gilfil, with his face a shade graver than usual. On his right hand, kneeling on their red velvet cushions, were the master and mistress of the household, in their elderly dignified beauty. On his left, the youthful grace of Anthony and Caterina, in all the striking contrast of their coloring—he, with his exquisite outline and rounded fairness, like an Olympian god; she, dark and tiny, like a gypsy changeling. Then there were the domestics kneeling on red-covered forms,—the women headed by Mrs. Bellamy, the natty little old housekeeper, in snowy cap and apron, and Mrs. Sharp, my lady's maid, of somewhat vinegar aspect and flaunting attire; the men by Mr. Bellamy the butler, and Mr. Warren, Sir Christopher's venerable valet.

A few collects from the Evening Service was what Mr. Gilfil habitually read, ending with the simple petition, "Lighten our darkness."

And then they all rose, the servants turning to courtesy and bow as they went out. The family returned to the drawing-room, said good-night to each other, and dispersed—all to speedy slumber except two. Caterina only cried herself to sleep after the clock had struck twelve. Mr. Gilfil lay awake still longer, thinking that very likely Caterina was crying.

Captain Wybrow, having dismissed his valet at eleven, was soon in a soft slumber, his face looking like a fine cameo in high relief on the slightly indented pillow.

CHAPTER III.

THE last chapter has given the discerning reader sufficient insight into the state of things at Cheverel Manor in the summer of 1788. In that summer, we know, the great nation of France was agitated by conflicting thoughts and passions, which were but the beginning of sorrows. And in our Caterina's little breast, too, there were terrible struggles. The poor bird was beginning to flutter and vainly dash its soft breast against the hard iron bars of the inevitable, and we see too plainly the danger, if that anguish should go on heightening instead of being allayed, that the palpitating heart may be fatally bruised.

Meanwhile, if, as I hope, you feel some interest in Caterina and her friends at Cheverel Manor, you are perhaps asking, How came she to be there? How was it that this tiny, dark-eyed child of the south, whose face was immediately suggestive of olive-covered hills and taper-lit shrines, came to have her home in that stately English manor-house, by the side of the blonde matron, Lady Cheverel—almost as if a humming-bird were found perched on one of the elm-trees in the park, by the side of her ladyship's handsomest pouter-pigeon? Speaking good English, too, and joining in Protestant prayers! Surely she must have been adopted and brought over to England at a very early age. She was.

During Sir Christopher's last visit to Italy with his lady, fifteen years before, they resided for some time at Milan, where Sir Christopher, who was an enthusiast for Gothic architecture, and was then entertaining the project of metamorphosing his plain brick family mansion into the model of a Gothic manor-house, was bent on studying the details of that marble miracle, the Cathedral. Here Lady Cheverel, as at other Italian cities where she made any protracted stay, engaged a *maestro* to give her lessons in singing, for she had then not only a fine musical taste, but a fine soprano voice. Those were days when very rich people used manuscript music, and many a man who resembled Jean Jacques in nothing else, resembled him in getting a livelihood "à copier la musique à tant la page." Lady Cheverel having need of this service, Maestro Albani told her he would send her a *poveraccio* of his acquaintance, whose manuscript was the neatest and most correct he knew of. Unhappily the *poveraccio* was not always in his best wits, and was sometimes rather slow in consequence; but it would be a work of Christian charity worthy of the beautiful Signora to employ poor Sarti.

The next morning, Mrs. Sharp, then a blooming abigail of three-and-thirty, entered her lady's private room and said, "If you please, my lady, there's the frowiest, shabbiest man you ever saw, outside, and he's told Mr. Warren as the singing-master sent him to see your ladyship. But I think you'll hardly like him to come in here. Belike he's only a beggar."

"Oh, yes, show him in immediately."

Mrs. Sharp retired, muttering something about "fleas and worse." She had the smallest possible admiration for fair Ausonia and its natives, and even her profound deference for Sir Christopher and her lady could not prevent her from expressing her amazement at the infatuation of gentlefolks in choosing to sojourn among "Papises, in countries where there was no getting to air a bit o' linen, and where the people smelt o' garlick fit to knock you down."

However she presently reappeared, ushering in a small, meagre man, sallow and dingy, with a restless, wandering look in his dull eyes, and an excessive timidity about his deep reverences, which gave him the air of a man who had been long a solitary prisoner. Yet through all this squalor and wretchedness there were some traces discernible of comparative youth and former good looks. Lady Cheverel, though not very tender-hearted, still less sentimental, was essentially kind and liked to dispense benefits like a goddess, who looks down benignly on the halt, the maimed, and the blind that approach her shrine. She was smitten with some compassion at the sight of poor Sarti, who struck her as the mere battered wreck of a vessel that might have once floated gayly enough on its outward voyage, to the sound of pipes and tabors. She spoke gently as she pointed out to him the operatic selections she wished him to copy, and he seemed to sun himself in her auburn, radiant presence, so that when he made his exit with the music-books under his arm, his bow, though not less reverent, was less timid.

It was ten years at least since Sarti had seen any thing so bright and stately and beautiful as Lady Cheverel. For the time was far off in which he had trod the stage in satin and feathers, the *primo tenore* of one short season. He had completely lost his voice in the following winter, and had ever since been little better than a cracked fiddle, which is good for nothing but firewood. For, like many Italian singers, he was too ignorant to teach, and if it had not been for his one talent of penmanship, he and his young helpless wife might have starved. Then, just after their third child was born, fever came, swept away the sickly mother and the two eldest children, and attacked Sarti himself, who rose from his sick-bed with enfeebled brain and muscle, and a tiny baby on his hands, scarcely four months old. He lodged over a fruit-shop kept by a stout virago, loud of tongue and irate in temper, but who had had children born to her, and so had taken care of the tiny yellow, black-eyed *bambinetta*, and tended Sarti himself through his sickness. Here he continued to live, earning a meagre subsistence for himself and his little one by the work of copying music, put into his hands chiefly by Maestro Albani. He seemed to exist for nothing but the child: he tended it, he dandled it, he chatted to it, living with it alone in his one room above the fruit-shop, only asking his landlady to take care of the marmoset during his short absences in fetching and carrying home work. Customers frequenting that fruit-shop might often see the tiny Caterina seated on the floor with her legs in a heap of pease, which it was her delight to kick about; or perhaps deposited, like a kitten, in a large basket out of harm's way.

Sometimes, however, Sarti left his little one with another kind of protectress. He was very regular in his devotions, which he paid thrice a week in the great cathedral, carrying Caterina with him. Here, when the high morning sun was warming the myriad glittering pinnacles without, and struggling against the massive gloom within, the shadow of a man with a child on his arm might be seen flitting across the more stationary shadows of pillar and mullion, and making its way towards a little tinsel Madonna hanging in a retired spot near the choir. Amid all the sublimities of the mighty cathedral, poor Sarti had fixed on this tinsel Madonna as the symbol of divine mercy and protection,—just as a child, in the presence of a great landscape, sees none of the glories of wood and sky, but sets its heart on a floating feather or insect that happens to be on a level with its eye. Here, then, Sarti worshipped and prayed, setting Caterina on the floor by his side; and now and then, when the cathedral lay near some place where he had to call, and did not like to take her, he would leave her there in front of the tinsel Madonna, where she would sit, perfectly good, amusing herself with low crowing noises and see-sawings of her tiny body. And when Sarti came back, he always found that the Blessed Mother had taken good care of Caterina.

That was briefly the history of Sarti, who fulfilled so well the orders Lady Cheverel gave him, that she sent him away again with a stock of new work. But this time, week after week passed, and he neither reappeared nor sent home the music intrusted to him. Lady Cheverel began to be anxious, and was thinking of sending Warren to inquire at the address Sarti had given her, when one day, as she was equipped for driving out, the valet brought in a small piece of paper, which, he said, had been left for her ladyship by a man who was carrying fruit. The paper contained only three tremulous lines, in Italian:

"Will the Eccelentissima, for the love of God, have pity on a dying man, and come to him?"

Lady Cheverel recognized the handwriting as Sarti's in spite of its tremulousness, and going down to her carriage, ordered the Milanese coachman to drive to Strada Quinquagesima, Numero 10. The coach stopped in a dirty, narrow street opposite La Pazzini's fruit-shop, and that large specimen of womanhood immediately presented herself at the door, to the extreme disgust of Mrs. Sharp, who remarked privately to Mr. Warren that La Pazzini was a "hijeous porpis." The fruit-woman, however, was all smiles and deep courtesies to the Eccelentissima, who, not very well understanding her Milanese dialect, abbreviated the conversation by asking to be shown at once to Signor Sarti. La Pazzini preceded her up the dark narrow stairs, and opened a door through which she begged her ladyship to enter. Directly opposite the door lay Sarti, on a low miserable bed. His eyes were glazed, and no movement indicated that he was conscious of their entrance.

On the foot of the bed was seated a tiny child, apparently not three years old, her head covered by a linen cap, her feet clothed with leather boots, above which her little yellow legs showed thin and naked. A frock, made of what had once been a gay flowered silk, was her only other garment. Her large dark eyes shone from out her queer little face, like two precious stones in a grotesque image carved in old ivory. She held an empty medicine-bottle in her hand, and was amusing herself by putting the cork in and drawing it out again, to hear how it would pop.

La Pazzini went up to the bed and said, "Ecco la nobilissima donna!" but directly after screamed out, "Holy mother! he is dead!"

It was so. The entreaty had not been sent in time for Sarti to carry out his project of asking the great English lady to take care of his Caterina. That was the thought which haunted his feeble brain as soon as he began to fear that his illness would end in death. She had wealth—she was kind—she would surely do something for the poor orphan. And so, at last, he sent that scrap of paper which won the fulfillment of his prayer, though he did not live to utter it. Lady Cheverel gave La Pazzini money that the last decencies might be paid to the dead man, and carried away Caterina, meaning to consult Sir Christopher as to what should be done with her. Even Mrs. Sharp had been so smitten with pity by the scene she had witnessed when she was summoned up stairs to fetch Caterina, as to shed a small tear, though she was not at all subject to that weakness; indeed, she abstained from it on principle, because, as she often said, it was known to be the worst thing in the world for the eyes.

On the way back to her hotel, Lady Cheverel turned over various projects in her mind regarding Caterina, but at last one gained the preference over all the rest. Why should they not take the child to England, and bring her up there? They had been married twelve years, yet Cheverel Manor was cheered by no children's voices, and the old house would be all the better for a little of that music. Besides, it would be a Christian work to train this little Papist into a good Protestant, and graft as much English fruit as possible on the Italian stem.

Sir Christopher listened to this plan with hearty acquiescence. He loved children, and took at once to the little black-eyed monkey—his name for Caterina all through her short life. But neither he nor Lady Cheverel had any idea of adopting her as their daughter, and giving her their own rank in life. They were much too English and aristocratic to think of any thing so romantic. No! the child would be brought up at Cheverel Manor as a protegée, to be ultimately useful, perhaps, in sorting worsteds, keeping accounts, reading aloud, and otherwise supplying the place of spectacles when her ladyship's eyes should wax dim.

So Mrs. Sharp had to procure new clothes, to replace the linen cap, flowered frock, and leathern boots; and now, strange to say, little Caterina, who had suffered many unconscious evils in her existence of thirty moons, first began to know conscious troubles. "Ignorance," says Ajax, "is a painless evil;" so, I should think, is dirt, considering the merry faces that go along with it. At any rate, cleanliness is sometimes a painful good, as any one can vouch who has had his face washed the wrong way, by a pitiless hand with a gold ring on the third finger. If you, reader, have not known that initiatory anguish, it is idle to expect that you will form any approximate conception of what Caterina endured under Mrs. Sharp's new dispensation of soap-and-wa ter. Happily, this purgatory came presently to be associated in her tiny brain with a passage straightway to a seat of bliss—the sofa in Lady Cheverel's sitting-room, where there were toys to be broken, a ride was to be had on Sir Christopher's knee, and a spaniel of resigned temper was prepared to undergo small tortures without flinching.

CHAPTER IV.

In three months from the time of Caterina's adoption—namely, in the late autumn of 1773—the chimneys of Cheverel Manor were sending up unwonted smoke, and the servants were awaiting in excitement the return of their master and mistress after a two years' absence. Great was the astonisnment of Mrs. Bellamy, the housekeeper, when Mr. Warren lifted a little black-eyed child out of the carriage, and great was Mrs. Sharp's sense of superior information and experience, as she detailed Caterina's history, interspersed with copious comments, to the rest of the upper servants that evening, as they were taking a comfortable glass of grog together in the housekeeper's room.

A pleasant room it was as any party need desire to muster in on a cold November evening. The fireplace alone was a picture: a wide and deep recess with a low brick altar in the middle, where great logs of dry wood sent myriad sparks up the dark chimney-throat; and over the front of this recess a large wooden entablature bearing this motto, finely carved in old English letters, "Fear God and honor the King." And beyond the party, who formed a half-moon with their chairs and well-furnished table round this bright fireplace, what a space of chiaroscuro for the imagination to revel in! Stretching across the far end of the room, what an oak table, high enough surely for Homer's gods, standing on four massive legs, bossed and bulging like sculptured urns! and, lining the distant wall, what vast cupboards, suggestive of inexhaustible apricot jam and promiscuous butler's perquisites! A stray picture or two had found their way down there, and made agreeable patches of dark brown on the buff-colored walls. High over the loud-resounding double door hung one which, from some indications of a face looming out of blackness, might, by a great synthetic effort, be pronounced a Magdalen. Considerably lower down hung the similitude of a hat and feathers, with portions of a ruff, stated by Mrs. Bellamy to represent Sir Francis Bacon, who invented gunpowder, and, in her opinion, "might ha' been better emplyed."

But this evening the mind is but slightly arrested by the great Verulam, and is in the humor to think a dead philosopher less interesting than a living gardener, who sits conspicuous in the half-circle round the fireplace. Mr. Bates is habitually a guest in the housekeeper's room of an evening, preferring the social pleasures there—the feast of gossip and the flow of grog—to a bachelor's chair in his charming thatched cottage on a little island, where every sound is remote but the cawing of rooks and the screaming of wild geese: poetic sounds, doubtless, but, humanly speaking, not convivial.

Mr. Bates was by no means an average person, to be passed without special notice. He was a sturdy Yorkshireman, approaching forty, whose face Nature seemed to have colored when she was in a hurry, and had no time to attend to *nuances*, for every inch of him visible above his neckcloth was of one impartial redness; so that when he was at some distance your imagination was at liberty to place his lips anywhere between his nose and chin. Seen closer, his lips were discerned to be of a peculiar cut, and I fancy this had something to do with the peculiarity of his dialect, which, as we shall see, was individual rather than provincial. Mr. Bates was further distinguished from the common herd by a perpetual blinking of the eyes; and this, together with the red-rose tint of his complexion, and a way he had of hanging his head forward, and rolling it from side to side as he walked, gave him the air of a Bacchus in a blue apron, who, in the present reduced circumstances of Olympus, had taken to the management of his own vines. Yet, as gluttons are often thin, so sober men are often rubicund; and Mr. Bates was sober, with that manly, British, churchman-like sobriety which can carry a few glasses of grog without any perceptible clarification of ideas.

"Dang my boottons!" observed Mr. Bates, who, at the conclusion of Mrs. Sharp's narrative, felt himself urged to his strongest interjection; "it's what I shouldn't ha' looked for from Sir Cristhifer an' my ledy, to bring a furrin child into the coonthry; an' depend on't, whether you an' me lives to see't or noo, it'll coom to soom harm. The first sitiation iver I held—it was a hold hancient habbey, wi' the biggest orchard o' apples an' pears you ever see—there was a French valet, an' he stool silk stoockins, an' shirts, an' rings, an' ivery thin' he could ley his hands on, an' run awey at last wi' th' missis's jewl-box. They're all alaike, them furriners. It roons i' th' blood."

"Well," said Mrs. Sharp, with the air of a person who held liberal views, but knew where to draw the line, "I'm not a-going to defend the furriners, for I've as good reason to know what they are as most folks, an' nobody'll ever hear me say but what they're next door to heathens, and the hile they eat wi' their victuals is enough to turn any Christian's stomach. But for all that—an' for all as the trouble in respect o' washin' and managin' has fell upo' me through the journey—I can't say but what I think as my Lady an' Sir Cristifer's done a right thing by a hinnicent child as doesn't know its right hand from its left, i' bringing it where it'll learn to speak summat better nor gibberish, and be brought up i' the true religion. For as for them furrin churches as Sir Cristifer is so unaccountable mad after, wi' pictures o' men an' women a-showing themselves just for all the world as God made 'em, I think, for my part, as it's almost a sin to go into 'em."

"You're likely to have more foreigners, however," said Mr. Warren, who liked to provoke the gardener, "for Sir Christopher has engaged some Italian workmen to help in the alterations in the house."

"Olterations!" exclaimed Mrs. Bellamy, in alarm. "What olterations?"

"Why," answered Mr. Warren, "Sir Christopher, as I understand, is going to make a new thing of the old Manor-house, both inside and out. And he's got portfolios full of plans and pictures coming. It is to be cased with stone, in the Gothic style—pretty near like the churches, you know, as far as I can make out; and the ceilings are to be beyond any thing that's been seen in the country. Sir Christopher's been giving a deal of study to it."

"Dear heart alive!" said Mrs. Bellamy, "we shall be pisoned wi' lime an' plaster, an' hev the house full o' workmen colloguing wi' the maids, an' makin' no end o' mischief."

"That ye may ley your life on, Mrs. Bellamy," said Mr. Bates. "Howiver, I'll noot denay that the Goothic stayle's prithy anoof, an' it's woonderful how near them stoon-carvers cuts oot the shapes o' the pineapples, an' shamrucks, an' rooses. I dare sey Sir Cristifer'll meck a naice thing o' the Manor, an' there woon't be many gentlemen's houses i' the coonthry as'll coom up to't, wi' sich a garden an' pleasure groons an' wall-fruit as King George maight be prood on."

"Well, I can't think as the house can be better nor it is, Gothic or no Gothic," said Mrs. Bellamy; "an' I've done the picklin' and preservin' in it fourteen year Michaelmas was a three weeks. But what does my lady say to't?"

"My lady knows better than cross Sir Cristifer in what he's set his mind on," said Mr. Bellamy, who objected to the critical tone of the conversation. "Sir Cristifer'll hev his own way, *that* you may tek your oath. An' i' the right on't too. He's a gentleman born, an's got the money. But come, Mester Bates, fill your glass, an' we'll drink health an' happiness to his honor an' my lady, and then you shall give us a song. Sir Cristifer doesn't come hum from Italy ivery night."

This demonstrable position was accepted without hesitation as ground for a toast; but Mr. Bates, apparently thinking that his song was not an equally reasonable sequence, ignored the second part of Mr. Bellamy's proposal. So Mrs. Sharp, who had been heard to say that she had no thoughts at all of marrying Mr. Bates, though he was "a sensable, fresh-colored man as many a woman 'ud snap at for a husband," enforced Mr. Bellamy's appeal.

"Come, Mr. Bates, let us hear 'Roy's Wife.' I'd rether hear a good old song like that, nor all the fine Italian toodlin."

Mr. Bates, urged thus flatteringly, stuck his thumbs into the armholes of his waistcoat, threw himself back in his chair with his head in that position in which he could look directly towards the zenith, and struck up a remarkably *staccato* rendering of "Roy's Wife of Aldivalloch." This melody may certainly be taxed with excessive iteration, but that was precisely its highest recommendation to the present audience, who found it all the easier to swell the chorus. Nor did it at all diminish their pleasure that the only particular concerning "Roy's Wife," which Mr. Bates's enunciation allowed them to gather, was that she "chated" him,—whether in the matter of garden stuff or of some other commodity, or why her name should, in consequence, be repeatedly reiterated with exultation, remaining an agreeable mystery.

Mr. Bates's song formed the climax of the evening's good-fellowship, and the party soon after dispersed—Mrs. Bellamy perhaps to dream of quicklime flying among her preserving-pans, or of love-sick housemaids reckless of unswept corners—and Mrs. Sharp to sink into pleasant visions of independent house-keeping in Mr. Bates's cottage, with no bells to answer, and with fruit and vegetables *ad libitum*.

Caterina soon conquered all prejudices against her foreign blood; for what prejudices will hold out against helplessness and broken prattle? She became the pet of the household, thrusting Sir Christopher's favorite bloodhound of that day,

Mrs. Bellamy's two canaries, and Mr. Bates's largest Dorking hen, into a merely secondary position. The consequence was, that in the space of a summer's day she went through a great cycle of experiences, commencing with the somewhat acidulated good-will of Mrs. Sharp's nursery discipline. Then came the grave luxury of her ladyship's sitting-room, and, perhaps, the dignity of a ride on Sir Christopher's knee, sometimes followed by a visit with him to the stables, where Caterina soon learned to hear without crying the baying of the chained bloodhounds, and say, with ostentatious bravery, clinging to Sir Christopher's leg all the while, "Dey not hurt Tina." Then Mrs. Bellamy would perhaps be going out to gather the rose-leaves and lavender, and Tina was made proud and happy by being allowed to carry a handful in her pinafore; happier still, when they were spread out on sheets to dry, so that she could sit down like a frog among them, and have them poured over her in fragrant showers. Another frequent pleasure was to take a journey with Mr. Bates through the kitchen-gardens and the hothouses, where the rich bunches of green and purple grapes hung from the roof, far out of reach of the tiny yellow hand that could not help stretching itself out towards them; though the hand was sure at last to be satisfied with some delicate-flavored fruit or sweet-scented flower. Indeed, in the long, monotonous leisure of that great country-house, you may be sure there was always some one who had nothing better to do than to play with Tina. So that the little southern bird had its northern nest lined with tenderness, and caresses, and pretty things. A loving sensitive nature was too likely, under such nurture, to have its susceptibility heightened into unfitness for an encounter with any harder experience; all the more, because there were gleams of fierce resistance to any discipline that had a harsh or unloving aspect. For the only thing in which Caterina showed any precocity was a certain ingenuity in vindictiveness. When she was five years old she had revenged herself for an unpleasant prohibition by pouring the ink into Mrs. Sharp's work-basket; and once, when Lady Cheverel took her doll from her, because she was affectionately licking the paint off its face, the little minx straightway climbed on a chair and threw down a flower-vase that stood on a bracket. This was almost the only instance in which her anger overcame her awe of Lady Cheverel, who had the ascendency always belonging to kindness that never melts into caresses, and is severely but uniformly beneficent.

By-and-by the happy monotony of Cheverel Manor was broken in upon in the way Mr. Warren had announced. The roads through the park were cut up by wagons carrying loads of stone from a neighboring quarry, the green court-yard became dusty with lime, and the peaceful house rang with the sound of tools. For the next ten years Sir Christopher was occupied with the architectural metamorphosis of his old family mansion; thus anticipating, through the prompting of his individual taste, that general reaction from the insipid imitation of the Palladian style, towards a restoration of the Gothic, which marked the close of the eighteenth century. This was the object he had set his heart on, with a singleness of determination which was regarded with not a little contempt by his fox-hunting neighbors, who wondered greatly that a man with some of the best blood in England in his veins, should be mean enough to economize in his cellar, and reduce his stud to two old coach-horses and a hack, for the sake of riding a hobby, and playing the architect. Their wives did not see so much to blame in the matter of the cellars and stables, but they were eloquent in pity for poor Lady Cheverel, who had to live in no more than three rooms at once, and who must be distracted with noises, and have her constitution undermined by unhealthy smells. It was as bad as having a husband with an asthma. Why did not Sir Christopher take a house for her at Bath, or, at least, if he must spend his time in overlooking workmen, somewhere in the neighborhood of the Manor? This pity was quite gratuitous, as the most plentiful pity always is; for though Lady Cheverel did not share her husband's architectural enthusiasm, she had too rigorous a view of a wife's duties, and too profound a deference for Sir Christopher, to regard submission as a grievance. As for Sir Christopher, he was perfectly indifferent to criticism. "An obstinate, crotchety man," said his neighbors. But I, who have seen Cheverel Manor, as he bequeathed it to his heirs, rather attribute that unswerving architectural purpose of his, conceived and carried out through long years of systematic personal exertion, to something of the fervor of genius, as well as inflexibility of will; and in walking through those rooms, with their splendid ceilings and their meagre furniture, which tell how all the spare money had been absorbed before personal comfort was thought of, I have felt that there dwelt in this old English baronet some of that sublime spirit which distinguishes art from luxury, and worships beauty apart from self-indulgence.

While Cheverel Manor was growing from ugliness into beauty, Caterina too was growing from a little yellow bantling into a whiter maiden, with no positive beauty indeed, but with a certain light airy grace, which, with her large appealing dark eyes, and a voice that, in its low-toned tenderness, recalled the love-notes of the stock-dove, gave her a more than usual charm. Unlike the building, however, Caterina's development was the result of no systematic or careful appliances. She grew up very much like the primroses, which the gardener is not sorry to see within his enclosure, but takes no pains to cultivate. Lady Cheverel taught her to read and write, and say her catechism; Mr. Warren, being a good accountant, gave her lessons in arithmetic, by her ladyship's desire; and Mrs. Sharp initiated her in all the mysteries of the needle. But, for a long time, there was no thought of giving her any more elaborate education. It is very likely that to her dying day Caterina thought the earth stood still, and that the sun and stars moved round it; but so, for the matter of that, did Helen, and Dido, and Desdemona, and Juliet; whence I hope you will not think my Caterina less worthy to be a heroine on that account. The truth is, that, with one exception, her only talent lay in loving; and there, it is probable, the most astronomical of women could not have surpassed her. Orphan and protegée though she was, this supreme talent of hers found plenty of exercise at Cheverel Manor, and Caterina had more people to love than many a small lady and gentleman affluent in silver mugs and blood relations. I think the first place in her childish heart was given to Sir Christopher, for little girls are apt to attach themselves to the finest looking gentleman at hand, especially as he seldom has any thing to do with discipline. Next to the Baronet, came Dorcas, the merry rosy-cheeked damsel who was Mrs. Sharp's lieutenant in the nursery, and thus played the part of the raisins in a dose of senna. It was a black day for Caterina when Dorcas married the coachman, and went, with a great sense of elevation in the world, to preside over a "public" in the noisy town of Sloppeter. A little china-box, bearing the motto "Though lost to sight, to memory dear," which Dorcas sent her as a remembrance, was among Caterina's treasures ten years after.

The one other exceptional talent, you already guess, was music. When the fact that Caterina had a remarkable ear for music, and a still more remarkable voice, attracted Lady Cheverel's notice, the discovery was very welcome both to her and Sir Christopher. Her musical education became at once an object of interest. Lady Cheverel devoted much time to it; and the rapidity of Tina's progress surpassing all hopes, an Italian singing-master was engaged for several years, to spend some months together at Cheverel Manor. This unexpected gift made a great alteration in Caterina's position. After those first years in which little girls are petted like puppies and kittens, there comes a time when it seems less obvious what they can be good for, especially when, like Caterina, they give no particular promise of cleverness or beauty; and it is not surprising that in that uninteresting period there was no particular plan formed as to her future position. She could always help Mrs. Sharp, supposing she were fit for nothing else, as she grew up; but now this rare gift of song endeared her to Lady Cheverel, who loved music above all things, and it associated her at once with the pleasures of the drawing-room. Insensibly she came to be regarded as one of the family, and the servants began to understand that Miss Sarti was to be a lady, after all.

"And the raight on't too," said Mr. Bates, "for she hasn't the cut of a gell as must work for her bread; she's as nesh an' dilicate as a paich-blossom—welly laike a linnet, wi' on'y joost body anoof to hold her voice."

But long before Tina had reached this stage of her history, a new era had begun for her, in the arrival of a younger companion than any she had hitherto known. When she was no more than seven, a ward of Sir Christopher's—a lad of fifteen, Maynard Gilfil by name—began to spend his vacations at Cheverel Manor, and found there no playfellow so much to his mind as Caterina. Maynard was an affectionate lad, who retained a propensity to white rabbits, pet squirrels, and guinea-pigs, perhaps a little beyond the age at which young gentlemen usually look down on such pleasures as puerile. He was also much given to fishing, and to carpentry, considered as a fine art, without any base view to utility. And in all these pleasures it was his delight to have Caterina as his companion, to call her little pet names, answer her wondering questions, and have her toddling after him as you may have seen a Blenheim spaniel trotting after a large setter. Whenever Maynard went back to school, there was a little scene of parting.

"You won't forget me, Tina, before I come back again? I shall leave you all the whip-cord we've made; and don't you let Guinea die. Come, give me a kiss, and promise not to forget me."

As the years wore on, and Maynard passed from school to college, and from a slim lad to a stalwart young man, their companionship in the vacations necessarily took a different form, but it retained a brotherly and sisterly familiarity. With Maynard the boyish affection had insensibly grown into ardent love. Among all the many kinds of first love, that which begins in childish companionship is the strongest and most enduring: when passion comes to unite its force to long affection, love is at its spring-tide. And Maynard Gilfil's love was of a kind to make him prefer being tormented by Caterina to any pleasure, apart from her, which the most benevolent magician could have devised for him. It is the way with those tall large-limbed men, from Samson downward. As for Tina, the little minx was perfectly well aware that Maynard was her slave; he was the one person in the world whom she did as she pleased with; and I need not tell you that this was a symptom of her being perfectly heart-whole so far as he was concerned: for a passionate woman's love is always overshadowed by fear.

Maynard Gilfil did not deceive himself in his interpretation of Caterina's feelings, but he nursed the hope that some time or other she would at least care enough for him to accept his love. So he waited patiently for the day when he might venture to say, "Caterina, I love you!" You see, he would have been content with very little, being one of those men who pass through life without making the least clamor about themselves; thinking neither the cut of his coat, nor the flavor of his soup, nor the precise depth of a servant's bow, at all momentous. He thought—foolishly enough, as lovers *will* think—that it was a good augury for him when he came to be domesticated at Cheverel Manor in the quality of chaplain there, and curate of a neighboring parish; judging falsely, from his own case, that habit and affection were the likeliest avenues to love. Sir Christopher satisfied several feelings in installing Maynard as chaplain in his house. He liked the old-fashioned dignity of that domestic appendage; he liked his ward's companionship; and, as Maynard had some private fortune, he might take life easily in that agreeable home, keeping his hunter, and observing a mild regimen of clerical duty, until the Cumbermoor living should fall in, when he might be settled for life in the neighborhood of the manor. "With Caterina for a wife, too," Sir Christopher soon began to think; for though the good Baronet was not at all quick to suspect what was unpleasant and opposed to his views of fitness, he was quick to see what would dovetail with his own plans; and he had first guessed, and then ascertained by direct inquiry, the state of Maynard's feelings. He at once leaped to the conclusion that Caterina was of the same mind, or at least would be, when she was old enough. But these were too early days for any thing definite to be said or done.

Meanwhile, new circumstances were arising, which, though they made no change in Sir Christopher's plans and prospects, converted Mr. Gilfil's hopes into anxieties, and made it clear to him not only that Caterina's heart was never likely to be his, but that it was given entirely to another.

Once or twice in Caterina's childhood, there had been another boy-visitor at the manor, younger than Maynard Gilfil—a beautiful boy with brown curls and splendid clothes, on whom Caterina had looked with shy admiration. This was Anthony Wybrow, the son of Sir Christopher's younger sister, and chosen heir of Cheverel Manor. The Baronet had sacrificed a large sum, and even straitened the resources by which he was to carry out his architectural schemes, for the sake of removing the entail from his estate, and making this boy his heir—moved to the step, I am sorry to say, by an implacable quarrel with his elder sister; for a power of forgiveness was not among Sir Christopher's virtues. At length, on the death of Anthony's mother, when he was no longer a curly-headed boy, but a tall young man, with a captain's commission, Cheverel Manor became *his* home too, whenever he was absent from his regiment. Caterina was then a little woman, between sixteen and seventeen, and I need not spend many words in explaining what you perceive to be the most natural thing in the world.

There was little company kept at the Manor, and Captain Wybrow would have been much duller if Caterina had not been there. It was pleasant to pay her attentions—to speak to her in gentle tones, to see her little flutter of pleasure, the blush that just lit up her pale cheek, and the momentary timid glance of her dark eyes, when he praised her singing, leaning at her side over the piano. Pleasant, too, to cut out that chaplain with his large calves! What idle man can withstand the temptation of a woman to fascinate, and another man to eclipse?—especially when it is quite clear to himself that he means no mischief, and shall leave every thing to come right again by-and-by. At the end of eighteen months, however, during which Captain Wybrow had spent much of his time at the Manor, he found that matters had reached a point which he had not at all contemplated. Gentle tones had led to tender words, and tender words had called forth a response of looks which made it impossible not to carry on the *crescendo* of love-making. To find one's self adored by a little, graceful, dark-eyed, sweet-singing woman, whom no one need despise, is an agreeable sensation, comparable to smoking the finest Latakia, and also imposes some return of tenderness as a duty.

Perhaps you think that Captain Wybrow, who knew that it would be ridiculous to dream of his marrying Caterina, must have been a reckless libertine to win her affections in this manner! Not at all. He was a young man of calm passions, who was rarely led into any conduct of which he could not give a plausible account to himself; and the tiny fragile Caterina was a woman who touched the imagination and the affections rather than the senses. He really felt very kindly towards her, and would very likely have loved her—if he had been able to love any one. But nature had not endowed him with that capability. She had given him an admirable figure, the whitest of hands, the most delicate of nostrils, and a large amount of serene self-satisfaction; but, as if to save such a delicate piece of work from any risk of being shattered, she had guarded him from the liability to a strong emotion. There was no list of youthful misdemeanors on record against him, and Sir Christopher and Lady Cheverel thought him the best of nephews, the most satisfactory of heirs, full of grateful deference to themselves, and, above all things, guided by a sense of duty. Captain Wybrow always did the thing easiest and most agreeable to him from a sense of duty: he dressed expensively, because it was a duty he owed to his position; from a sense of duty he adapted himself to Sir Christopher's inflexible will, which it would have been troublesome as well as useless to resist; and, being of a delicate constitution, he took care of his health from a sense of duty. His health was the only point on which he gave anxiety to his friends; and it was owing to this that Sir Christopher wished to see his nephew early married, the more so as a match after the Baronet's own heart appeared immediately attainable. Anthony had seen and admired Miss Assher, the only child of a lady who had been Sir Christopher's earliest love, but who, as things will happen in this world, had married another baronet instead of him. Miss Assher's father was now dead, and she was in possession of a pretty estate. If, as was probable, she should prove susceptible to the merits of Anthony's person and character, nothing could make Sir Christopher so happy as to see a marriage which might be expected to secure the inheritance of Cheverel Manor from getting into the wrong hands. Anthony had already been kindly received by Lady Assher as the nephew of her early friend; why should he not go to Bath, where she and her daughter were then residing, follow up the acquaintance, and win a handsome, well-born, and sufficiently wealthy bride?

Sir Christopher's wishes were communicated to his nephew, who at once intimated his willingness to comply with them—from a sense of duty. Caterina was tenderly informed by her lover of the sacrifice demanded from them both; and three days afterwards occurred the parting scene you have witnessed in the gallery, on the eve of Captain Wybrow's departure for Bath.

CHAPTER V.

THE inexorable ticking of the clock is like the throb of pain to sensations made keen by a sickening fear. And so it is with the great clockwork of nature. Daisies and buttercups give way to the brown waving grasses, tinged with the warm red sorrel; the waving grasses are swept away, and the meadows lie like emeralds set in the bushy hedgerows; the tawny-tipped corn begins to bow with the weight of the full ear; the reapers are bending amongst it, and it soon stands in sheaves; then, presently, the patches of yellow stubble lie side by side with streaks of dark-red earth, which the plough is turning up in preparation for the new-threshed seed. And this passage from beauty to beauty, which to the happy is like the flow of a melody, measures for many a human heart the approach of foreseen anguish—seems hurrying on the moment when the shadow of dread will be followed up by the reality of despair.

How cruelly hasty that summer of 1788 seemed to Caterina! Surely the roses vanished earlier, and the berries on the mountain-ash were more impatient to redden, and bring on the autumn, when she would be face to face with her misery, and witness Anthony giving all his gentle tones, tender words, and soft looks to another.

Before the end of July, Captain Wybrow had written word that Lady Assher and her daughter were about to fly from the heat and gayety of Bath to the shady quiet of their place at Farleigh, and that he was invited to join the party there. His letters implied that he was on an excellent footing with both the ladies, and gave no hint of a rival; so that Sir Christopher was more than usually bright and cheerful after reading them. At length, towards the close of August, came the announcement that Captain Wybrow was an accepted lover, and after much complimentary and congratulatory correspondence between the two families, it was understood that in September Lady Assher and her daughter would pay a visit to Cheverel Manor, when Beatrice would make the acquaintance of her future relatives, and all needful arrangements could be discussed. Captain Wybrow would remain at Farleigh till then, and accompany the ladies on their journey.

In the interval, every one at Cheverel Manor had something to do by way of preparing for the visitors. Sir Christopher was occupied in consultations with his steward and lawyer, and in giving orders to every one else, especially in spurring on Francesco to finish the saloon. Mr. Gilfil had the responsibility of procuring a lady's horse, Miss Assher being a great rider. Lady Cheverel had unwonted calls to make and invitations to deliver. Mr. Bates's turf, and gravel, and flower-beds were always at such a point of neatness and finish that nothing extraordinary could be done in the garden, except a little extraordinary scolding of the under-gardener, and this addition Mr. Bates did not neglect.

Happily for Caterina, she too had her task, to fill up the long dreary daytime: it was to finish a chair-cushion which would complete the set of embroidered covers for the drawing-room, Lady Cheverel's year-long work, and the only noteworthy bit of furniture in the Manor. Over this embroidery she sat with cold lips and a palpitating heart, thankful that this miserable sensation throughout the daytime seemed to counteract the tendency to tears which returned with night and solitude. She was most frightened when Sir Christopher approached her. The Baronet's eye was brighter and his step more elastic than ever, and it seemed to him that only the most leaden or churlish souls could be otherwise than brisk and exulting in a world where every thing went so well. Dear old gentleman! he had gone through life a little flushed with the power of his will, and now his latest plan was succeeding, and Cheverel Manor would be inherited by a grand-nephew, whom he might even yet live to see a fine young fellow with at least the down on his chin. Why not? one is still young at sixty.

Sir Christopher had always something playful to say to Caterina.

"Now, little monkey, you must be in your best voice; you're the minstrel of the Manor, you know, and be sure you have a pretty gown and a new ribbon. You must not be dressed in russet, though you are a singing bird." Or perhaps, "It is your turn to be courted next, Tina. But don't you learn any naughty proud airs. I must have Maynard let off easily."

Caterina's affection for the old Baronet helped her to summon up a smile as he stroked her cheek and looked at her kindly, but that was the moment at which she felt it most difficult not to burst out crying. Lady Cheverel's conversation and presence were less trying; for her ladyship felt no more than calm satisfaction in this family event; and besides, she was further sobered by a little jealousy at Sir Christopher's anticipation of pleasure in seeing Lady Assher, enshrined in his memory as a mild-eyed beauty of sixteen, with whom he had exchanged locks before he went on his first travels. Lady Cheverel would have died rather than confess it, but she couldn't help hoping that he would be disappointed in Lady Assher, and rather ashamed of having called her so charming.

Mr. Gilfil watched Caterina through these days with mixed feelings. Her suffering went to his heart; but, even for her sake, he was glad that a love which could never come to good should be no longer fed by false hopes; and how could he help saying to himself, "Perhaps, after a while, Caterina will be tired of fretting about that cold-hearted puppy, and then . . . ."

At length the much-expected day arrived, and the brightest of September suns was lighting up the yellowing lime-trees, as about five o'clock Lady Assher's carriage drove under the portico. Caterina, seated at work in her own room, heard the rolling of the wheels, followed presently by the opening and shutting of doors, and the sound of voices in the corridors. Remembering that the dinner hour was six, and that Lady Cheverel had desired her to be in the drawing-room early, she started up to dress, and was delighted to find herself feeling suddenly brave and strong. Curiosity to see Miss Assher—the thought that Anthony was in the house—the wish not to look unattractive, were feelings that brought some color to her lips, and made it easy to attend to her toilette. They would ask her to sing this evening, and she would sing well. Miss Assher should not think her utterly insignificant. So she put on her gray silk gown and her cherry-colored ribbon with as much care as if she had been herself the betrothed; not forgetting the pair of round pearl ear-rings which Sir Christopher had told Lady Cheverel to give her, because Tina's little ears were so pretty.

Quick as she had been, she found Sir Christopher and Lady Cheverel in the drawing-room chatting with Mr. Gilfil, and telling him how handsome Miss Assher was, but how entirely unlike her mother—apparently resembling her father only.

"Aha!" said Sir Christopher, as he turned to look at Caterina, "what do you think of this, Maynard? Did you ever see Tina look so pretty before? Why, that little gray gown has been made out of a bit of my lady's, hasn't it? It doesn't take any thing much larger than a pocket-handkerchief to dress the little monkey."

Lady Cheverel, too, serenely radiant in the assurance a single glance had given her of Lady Assher's inferiority, smiled approval, and Caterina was in one of those moods of self-possession and indifference which come as the ebb-tide between the struggles of passion. She retired to the piano, and busied herself with arranging her music, not all insensible to the pleasure of being looked at with admiration the while, and thinking that, the next time the door opened Captain Wybrow would enter, and she would speak to him quite cheerfully. But when she heard him come in, and the scent of roses floated towards her, her heart gave one great leap. She knew nothing till he was pressing her hand, and saying, in the old easy way, "Well, Caterina, how do you do? You look quite blooming."

She felt her cheeks reddening with anger that he could speak and look with such perfect nonchalance. Ah! he was too deeply in love with some one else to remember any thing he had felt for *her*. But the next moment she was conscious of her folly; "as if he could show any feeling then!" This conflict of emotions stretched into a long interval the few moments that elapsed before the door opened again, and her own attention, as well as that of all the rest, was absorbed by the entrance of the two ladies.

The daughter was the more striking, from the contrast she presented to her mother, a round-shouldered, middle-sized woman, who had once had the transient pink-and-white beauty of a blonde, with ill-defined features and early embonpoint. Miss Assher was tall, and gracefully though substantially formed, carrying herself with an air of mingled graciousness and self-confidence; her dark-brown hair, untouched by powder, hanging in bushy curls round her face, and falling behind in long thick ringlets nearly to her waist. The brilliant carmine tint of her well-rounded cheeks, and the finely-cut outline of her straight nose, produced an impression of splendid beauty, in spite of commonplace brown eyes, a narrow forehead, and thin lips. She was in mourning, and the dead black of her crape dress, relieved here and there by jet ornaments, gave the fullest effect to her complexion, and to the rounded whiteness of her arms, bare from the elbow. The first *coup d'œil* was dazzling, and as she stood looking down with a gracious smile on Caterina, whom Lady Cheverel was presenting to her, the poor little thing seemed to herself to feel, for the first time, all the folly of her former dream.

"We are enchanted with your place, Sir Christopher," said Lady Assher, with a feeble kind of pompousness, which she seemed to be copying from some one else; "I'm sure your nephew must have thought Farleigh wretchedly out of order. Poor Sir John was so very careless about keeping up the house and grounds. I often talked to him about it, but he said, 'Pooh, pooh! as long as my friends find a good dinner and a good bottle of wine, they won't care about my ceilings being rather smoky.' He was so very hospitable, was Sir John."

"I think the view of the house from the park, just after we passed the bridge, particularly fine," said Miss Assher, interposing rather eagerly, as if she feared her mother might be making infelicitous speeches, "and the pleasure of the first glimpse was all the greater because Anthony would describe nothing to us beforehand. He would not spoil our first impressions by raising false ideas. I long to go over the house, Sir Christopher, and learn the history of all your architectural designs, which Anthony says have cost you so much time and study."

"Take care how you set an old man talking about the past, my dear," said the Baronet; "I hope we shall find something pleasanter for you to do than turning over my old plans and pictures. Our friend Mr. Gilfil here has found a beautiful mare for you, and you can scour the country to your heart's content. Anthony has sent us word what a horsewoman you are."

Miss Assher turned to Mr. Gilfil with her most beaming smile, and expressed her thanks with the elaborate graciousness of a person who means to be thought charming, and is sure of success.

"Pray do not thank me," said Mr. Gilfil, "till you have tried the mare. She has been ridden by Lady Sara Linter for the last two years; but one lady's taste may not be like another's in horses, any more than in other matters."

While this conversation was passing, Captain Wybrow was leaning against the mantel-piece, contenting himself with responding from under his indolent eyelids to the glances Miss Assher was constantly directing towards him as she spoke. "She is very much in love with him," thought Caterina. But she was relieved that Anthony remained passive in his attentions. She thought, too, that he was looking paler and more languid than usual. "If he didn't love her very much—if he sometimes thought of the past with regret, I think I could bear it all, and be glad to see Sir Christopher made happy."

During dinner there was a little incident which confirmed these thoughts. When the sweets were on the table, there was a mould of jelly just opposite Captain Wybrow, and being inclined to take some himself, he first invited Miss Assher, who colored, and said, in rather a sharper key than usual, "Have you not learned by this time that I never take jelly?"

"Don't you?" said Captain Wybrow, whose perceptions were not acute enough for him to notice the difference of a semitone. "I should have thought you were fond of it. There was always some on the table at Farleigh, I think."

"You don't seem to take much interest in my likes and dislikes."

"I'm too much possessed by the happy thought that you like me," was the *ex officio* reply, in silvery tones.

This little episode was unnoticed by every one but Caterina. Sir Christopher was listening with polite attention to Lady Assher's history of her last man-cook, who was first-rate at gravies, and for that reason pleased Sir John—he was so particular about his gravies, was Sir John: and so they kept the man six years in spite of his bad pastry. Lady Cheverel and Mr. Gilfil were smiling at Rupert the bloodhound, who had pushed his great head under his master's arm, and was taking a survey of the dishes, after snuffing at the contents of the Baronet's plate.

When the ladies were in the drawing-room again, Lady Assher was soon deep in a statement to Lady Cheverel of her views about burying people in woollen.

"To be sure, you must have a woollen dress, because it's the law, you know; but that need hinder no one from putting linen underneath. I always used to say, 'If Sir John died to-morrow, I would bury him in his shirt;' and I did. And let me advise you to do so by Sir Christopher. You never saw Sir John, Lady Cheverel. He was a large tall man with a nose just like Beatrice, and so very particular about his shirts."

Miss Assher, meanwhile, had seated herself by Caterina, and, with that smiling affability which seems to say, 'I am really not at all proud, though you might expect it of me," said,

"Anthony tells me you sing so very beautifully. I hope we shall hear you this evening."

"Oh yes," said Caterina quietly, without smiling; "I always sing when I'm wanted to sing."

"I envy you such a charming talent. Do you know, I have no ear; I can not hum the smallest tune, and I delight in music so. Is it not unfortunate? But I shall have quite a treat while I am here; Captain Wybrow says you will give us some music every day."

"I should have thought you wouldn't care about music if you had no ear," said Caterina, becoming epigrammatic by force of grave simplicity.

"Oh, I assure you I dote on it; and Anthony is so fond of it; it would be so delightful if I could play and sing to him; though he says he likes me best not to sing, because it doesn't belong to his idea of me. What style of music do you like best?"

"I don't know. I like all beautiful music."

"And are you as fond of riding as of music?"

"No; I never ride. I think I should be very frightened."

"Oh no! indeed you would not, after a little practice. I have never been in the least timid. I think Anthony is more afraid for me than I am for myself; and since I have been riding with him, I have been obliged to be more careful, because he is so nervous about me."

Caterina made no reply; but she said to herself, "I wish she would go away and not talk to me. She only wants me to admire her good-nature, and to talk about Anthony."

Miss Assher was thinking at the same time, "This Miss Sarti seems a stupid little thing. Those musical people often are. But she is prettier than I expected; Anthony said she was not pretty."

Happily at this moment Lady Assher called her daughter's attention to the embroidered cushions, and Miss Assher, walking to the opposite sofa, was soon in conversation with Lady Cheverel about tapestry and embroidery in general, while her mother, feeling herself superseded there, came and placed herself beside Caterina.

"I hear you are the most beautiful singer," was of course the opening remark. "All Italians sing so beautifully. I travelled in Italy with Sir John when we were first married, and we went to Venice, where they go about in gondolas, you know. You don't wear powder, I see. No more will Beatrice; though many people think her curls would look all the better for powder. She has so much hair, hasn't she? Our last maid dressed it much better than this; but, do you know, she wore Beatrice's stockings before they went to the wash, and we couldn't keep her after that, could we?"

Caterina, accepting the question as a mere bit of rhetorical effect, thought it superfluous to reply, till Lady Assher repeated, "Could we, now?" as if Tina's sanction were essential to her repose of mind. After a faint "No," she went on.

"Maids are so very troublesome, and Beatrice is so particular, you can't imagine. I often say to her, 'My dear, you can't have perfection.' That very gown she has on—to be sure, it fits her beautifully now—but it has been unmade and made up again twice. But she is like poor Sir John—he was so very particular about his own things, was Sir John. Is Lady Cheverel particular?"

"Rather. But Mrs. Sharp has been her maid twenty years."

"I wish there was any chance of our keeping Griffin twenty years. But I am afraid we shall have to part with her because her health is so delicate; and she is so obstinate, she will not take bitters as I want her. *You* look delicate, now. Let me recommend you to take camomile tea in a morning, fasting. Beatrice is so strong and healthy, she never takes any medicine; but if I had had twenty girls, and they had been delicate, I should have given them all camomile tea. It strengthens the constitution beyond any thing. Now, will you promise me to take camomile tea?"

"Thank you; I'm not at all ill," said Caterina. "I've always been pale and thin."

Lady Assher was sure camomile tea would make all the difference in the world—Caterina must see if it wouldn't—and then went dribbling on like a leaky shower-bath, until the early entrance of the gentlemen created a diversion, and she fastened on Sir Christopher, who probably began to think that, for poetical purposes, it would be better not to meet one's first love again, after a lapse of forty years.

Captain Wybrow, of course, joined his aunt and Miss Assher, and Mr. Gilfil tried to relieve Caterina from the awkwardness of sitting aloof and dumb, by telling her how a friend of his had broken his arm and staked his horse that morning, not at all appearing to heed that she hardly listened, and was looking towards the other side of the room. One of the tortures of jealousy is, that it can never turn away its eyes from the thing that pains it.

By-and-by every one felt the need of a relief from chit-chat—Sir Christopher perhaps the most of all—and it was he who made the acceptable proposition—

"Come, Tina, are we to have no music to-night before we sit down to cards? Your ladyship plays at cards, I think?" he added, recollecting himself, and turning to Lady Assher.

"Oh yes! Poor dear Sir John would have a whist-table every night."

Caterina sat down to the harpischord at once, and had no sooner begun to sing than she perceived with delight that

Captain Wybrow was gliding towards the harpischord, and soon standing in the old place. This consciousness gave fresh strength to her voice; and when she noticed that Miss Assher presently followed him with that air of ostentatious admiration which belongs to the absence of real enjoyment, her closing *bravura* was none the worse for being animated by a little triumphant contempt.

"Why, you are in better voice than ever, Caterina," said Captain Wybrow, when she had ended. "This is rather different from Miss Hibbert's small piping that we used to be glad of at Farleigh, is it not, Beatrice?"

"Indeed it is. You are a most enviable creature, Miss Sarti —Caterina—may I call you Caterina? for I have heard Anthony speak of you so often, I seem to know you quite well. You will let me call you Caterina?"

"Oh yes, every one calls me Caterina, only when they call me Tina."

"Come, come, more singing, more singing, little monkey," Sir Christopher called out from the other side of the room. "We have not had half enough yet."

Caterina was ready enough to obey, for while she was singing she was queen of the room, and Miss Assher was reduced to grimacing admiration. Alas! you see what jealousy was doing in this poor young soul. Caterina, who had passed her life as a little unobtrusive singing-bird, nestling so fondly under the wings that were outstretched for her, her heart beating only to the peaceful rhythm of love, or fluttering with some easily stifled fear, had begun to know the fierce palpitations of triumph and hatred.

When the singing was over, Sir Christopher and Lady Cheverel sat down to whist with Lady Assher and Mr. Gilfil, and Caterina placed herself at the Baronet's elbow, as if to watch the game, that she might not appear to thrust herself on the pair of lovers. At first she was glowing with her little triumph, and felt the strength of pride; but her eye *would* steal to the opposite side of the fireplace, where Captain Wybrow had seated himself close to Miss Assher, and was leaning with his arm over the back of the chair, in the most lover-like position. Caterina began to feel a choking sensation. She could see, almost without looking, that he was taking up her arm to examine her bracelet; their heads were bending close together, her curls touching his cheek—now he was putting his lips to her hand. Caterina felt her cheeks burn—she could sit no longer. She got up, pretended to be gliding about in search of something, and at length slipped out of the room.

Outside, she took a candle, and, hurrying along the passages and up the stairs to her own room, locked the door.

"Oh, I can not bear it, I can not bear it!" the poor thing burst out aloud, clasping her little fingers, and pressing them back against her forehead, as if she wanted to break them.

Then she walked hurriedly up and down the room.

"And this must go on for days and days, and I must see it."

She looked about nervously for something to clutch. There was a muslin kerchief lying on the table; she took it up and tore it into shreds as she walked up and down, and then pressed it into hard balls in her hand.

"And Anthony," she thought, "he can do this without caring for what I feel. Oh, he can forget every thing: how he used to say he loved me—how he used to take my hand in his as we walked—how he used to stand near me in the evenings for the sake of looking into my eyes."

"Oh, it is cruel, it is cruel!" she burst out again aloud, as all those love-moments in the past returned upon her. Then the tears gushed forth, she threw herself on her knees by the bed, and sobbed bitterly.

She did not know how long she had been there, till she was startled by the prayer-bell; when, thinking Lady Cheverel might perhaps send some one to inquire after her, she rose, and began hastily to undress, that there might be no possibility of her going down again. She had hardly unfastened her hair, and thrown a loose gown about her, before there was a knock at the door, and Mrs. Sharp's voice said—"Miss Tina, my lady wants to know if you're ill."

Caterina opened the door and said, "Thank you, dear Mrs. Sharp; I have a bad headache; please tell my lady I felt it come on after singing."

"Then, goodness me! why arn't you in bed, instead o' standing shivering there, fit to catch your death? Come, let me fasten up your hair and tuck you up warm."

"Oh no, thank you; I shall really be in bed very soon. Good-night, dear Sharpy; don't scold; I will be good, and get into bed."

Caterina kissed her old friend coaxingly, but Mrs. Sharp was not to be "come over" in that way, and insisted on seeing her former charge in bed, taking away the candle which the poor child had wanted to keep as a companion.

But it was impossible to lie there long with that beating heart; and the little white figure was soon out of bed again, seeking relief in the very sense of chill and uncomfort. It was light enough for her to see about her room, for the moon, nearly at full, was riding high in the heavens among scattered hurrying clouds. Caterina drew aside the window-curtain; and, sitting with her forehead pressed against the cold pane, looked out on the wide stretch of park and lawn.

How dreary the moonlight is! robbed of all its tenderness and repose by the hard driving wind. The trees are harassed by that tossing motion, when they would like to be at rest; the shivering grass makes her quake with sympathetic cold; and the willows by the pool, bent low and white under that invisible harshness, seem agitated and helpless like herself. But she loves the scene the better for its sadness: there is some pity in it. It is not like that hard unfeeling happiness of lovers, flaunting in the eyes of misery.

She set her teeth tight against the window-frame, and the tears fell thick and fast. She was so thankful she could cry, for the mad passion she had felt when her eyes were dry frightened her. If that dreadful feeling were to come on when Lady Cheverel was present, she should never be able to contain herself.

Then there was Sir Christopher—so good to her—so happy about Anthony's marriage; and all the while she had these wicked feelings.

"Oh, I can not help it, I can not help it!" she said in a loud whisper between her sobs. "O God, have pity upon me!"

In this way Tina wore out the long hours of the windy moonlight, till at last, with weary aching limbs, she lay down in bed again, and slept from mere exhaustion.

While this poor little heart was being bruised with a weight too heavy for it, Nature was holding on her calm inexorable way, in unmoved and terrible beauty. The stars were rushing in their eternal courses; the tides swelled to the level of the last expectant weed; the sun was making brilliant day to busy nations on the other side of the swift earth. The stream of human thought and deed was hurrying and broadening onward. The astronomer was at his telescope; the great ships were laboring over the waves; the toiling eagerness of commerce, the fierce spirit of revolution, were only ebbing in brief rest; and sleepless statesmen were dreading the possible crisis of the morrow. What were our little Tina and her trouble in this mighty torrent, rushing from one awful unknown to another? Lighter than the smallest centre of quivering life in the water-drop, hidden and uncared for as the pulse of anguish in the breast of the tiniest bird that has fluttered down to its nest with the long-sought food, and has found the nest torn and empty.

CHAPTER VI.

The next morning when Caterina was waked from her heavy sleep by Martha bringing in the warm water, the sun was shining, the wind had abated, and those hours of suffering in the night seemed unreal and dreamlike, in spite of weary limbs and aching eyes. She got up and began to dress with a strange feeling of insensibility, as if nothing could make her cry again; and she even felt a sort of longing to be down stairs in the midst of company, that she might get rid of this benumbed condition by contact.

There are few of us that are not rather ashamed of our sins and follies as we look out on the blessed morning sunlight, which comes to us like a bright-winged angel beckoning us to quit the old path of vanity that stretches its dreary length behind us; and Tina, little as she knew about doctrines and theories, seemed to herself to have been both foolish and wicked yesterday. To-day she would try to be good; and when she knelt down to say her short prayer—the very form she had learned by heart when she was ten years old—she added, "O God, help me to bear it!"

That day the prayer seemed to be answered, for after some remarks on her pale looks at breakfast, Caterina passed the morning quietly, Miss Assher and Captain Wybrow being out on a riding excursion. In the evening there was a dinner-party, and after Caterina had sung a little, Lady Cheverel remembering that she was ailing, sent her to bed, where she soon sank into a deep sleep. Body and mind must renew their force to suffer as well as to enjoy.

On the morrow, however, it was rainy, and every one must stay in-doors; so it was resolved that the guests should be taken over the house by Sir Christopher, to hear the story of the architectural alterations, the family portraits, and the family relics. All the party, except Mr. Gilfil, were in the drawing-room when the proposition was made; and when Miss Assher rose to go, she looked towards Captain Wybrow, expecting to see him rise too; but he kept his seat near the fire, turning his eyes towards the newspaper which he had been holding unread in his hand.

"Are you not coming, Anthony?" said Lady Cheverel, noticing Miss Assher's look of expectation.

"I think not, if you'll excuse me," he answered, rising and

opening the door; "I feel a little chilled this morning, and, I am afraid of the cold rooms and draughts."

Miss Assher reddened, but said nothing, and passed on, Lady Cheverel accompanying her.

Caterina was seated at work in the oriel window. It was the first time she and Anthony had been alone together, and she had thought before that he wished to avoid her. But now, surely, he wanted to speak to her—he wanted to say something kind. Presently he rose from his seat near the fire, and placed himself on the ottoman opposite to her.

"Well, Tina, and how have you been all this long time?"

Both the tone and the words were an offense to her; the tone was so different from the old one, the words were so cold and unmeaning. She answered with a little bitterness,

"I think you needn't ask. It doesn't make much difference to you."

"Is that the kindest thing you have to say to me after my long absence?"

"I don't know why you should expect me to say kind things."

Captain Wybrow was silent. He wished very much to avoid allusions to the past or comments on the present. And yet he wished to be well with Caterina. He would have liked to caress her, make her presents, and have her think him very kind to her. But these women are plaguy perverse! There's no bringing them to look rationally at any thing. At last he said, "I hoped you would think all the better of me, Tina, for doing as I have done, instead of bearing malice towards me. I hoped you would see that it is the best thing for every one—the best for your happiness too."

"Oh, pray don't make love to Miss Assher for the sake of my happiness," answered Tina.

At this moment the door opened, and Miss Assher entered, to fetch her reticule, which lay on the harpsichord. She gave a keen glance at Caterina, whose face was flushed, and saying to Captain Wybrow with a slight sneer, "Since you are so chill I wonder you like to sit in the window," left the room again immediately.

The lover did not appear much discomposed, but sat quiet a little longer, and then, seating himself on the music-stool, drew it near to Caterina, and, taking her hand, said, "Come, Tina, look kindly at me, and let us be friends. I shall always be your friend."

"Thank you," said Caterina, drawing away her hand. "You are very generous. But pray move away. Miss Assher may come in again."

6*

"Miss Assher be hanged!" said Anthony, feeling the fascination of old habit returning on him in his proximity to Caterina. He put his arm round her waist, and leaned his cheek down to hers. The lips couldn't help meeting after that; but the next moment, with heart swelling and tears rising, Caterina burst away from him, and rushed out of the room.

CHAPTER VII.

Caterina tore herself from Anthony with the desperate effort of one who has just self-recollection enough left to be conscious that the fumes of charcoal will master his senses unless he bursts a way for himself to the fresh air; but when she reached her own room, she was still too intoxicated with that momentary revival of old emotions, too much agitated by the sudden return of tenderness in her lover, to know whether pain or pleasure predominated. It was as if a miracle had happened in her little world of feeling, and made the future all vague—a dim morning haze of possibilities, instead of the sombre wintry daylight and clear rigid outline of painful certainty.

She felt the need of rapid movement. She must walk out in spite of the rain. Happily, there was a thin place in the curtain of clouds which seemed to promise that now, about noon, the day had a mind to clear up. Caterina thought to herself, "I will walk to the Mosslands, and carry Mr. Bates the comforter I have made for him, and then Lady Cheverel will not wonder so much at my going out." At the hall door she found Rupert, the old bloodhound, stationed on the mat, with the determination that the first person who was sensible enough to take a walk that morning should have the honor of his approbation and society. As he thrust his great black and tawny head under her hand, and wagged his tail with vigorous eloquence, and reached the climax of his welcome by jumping up to lick her face, which was at a convenient licking height for him, Caterina felt quite grateful to the old dog for his friendliness. Animals are such agreeable friends—they ask no questions, they pass no criticisms.

The "Mosslands" was a remote part of the grounds, encircled by the little stream issuing from the pool; and certainly, for a wet day, Caterina could hardly have chosen a less suitable walk, for though the rain was abating, and presently ceased altogether, there was still a smart shower falling from the trees which arched over the greater part of the way. But she found just the desired relief from her feverish excitement in laboring along the wet paths with an umbrella that made her arm ache. This amount of exertion was to her tiny body what a day's hunting often was to Mr. Gilfil, who at times had *his* fits of jealousy and sadness to get rid of, and wisely had recourse to nature's innocent opium—fatigue.

When Caterina reached the pretty arched wooden bridge which formed the only entrance to the Mosslands for any but webbed feet, the sun had mastered the clouds, and was shining through the boughs of the tall elms that made a deep nest for the gardener's cottage—turning the rain-drops into diamonds, and inviting the nasturtium flowers creeping over the porch and low-thatched roof to lift up their flame-colored heads once more. The rooks were cawing with many-voiced monotony, apparently—by a remarkable approximation to human intelligence—finding great conversational resources in the change of weather. The mossy turf, studded with the broad blades of marsh-loving plants, told that Mr. Bates's nest was rather damp in the best of weather; but he was of opinion that a little external moisture would hurt no man who was not perversely neglectful of that obvious and providential antidote, rum-and-water.

Caterina loved this nest. Every object in it, every sound that haunted it, had been familiar to her from the days when she had been carried thither on Mr. Bates's arm, making little cawing noises to imitate the rooks, clapping her hands at the green frogs leaping in the moist grass, and fixing grave eyes on the gardener's fowls cluck-clucking under their pens. And now the spot looked prettier to her than ever; it was so out of the way of Miss Assher, with her brilliant beauty, and personal claims, and small civil remarks. She thought Mr. Bates would not be come into his dinner yet, so she would sit down and wait for him.

But she was mistaken. Mr. Bates was seated in his armchair, with his pocket-handkerchief thrown over his face, as the most eligible mode of passing away those superfluous hours between meals when the weather drives a man in-doors. Roused by the furious barking of his chained bulldog, he descried his little favorite approaching and forthwith presented himself at the doorway, looking disproportionately tall compared with the height of his cottage. The bulldog, meanwhile, unbent from the severity of his official demeanor, and commenced a friendly interchange of ideas with Rupert.

Mr. Bates's hair was now gray, but his frame was none the less stalwart, and his face looked all the redder, making an artistic contrast with the deep blue of his cotton neckerchief, and of his linen apron twisted into a girdle round his waist.

"Why, dang my boottons, Miss Tiny," he exclaimed, "hoo coom ye to coom out dabblin' your faet laike a little Muscovy duck, sich a day as this? Not but what ai'm de-laighted to sae ye. Here, Hesther," he called to his old hump-backed housekeeper, "tek the young ledy's oombrella an' spread it out to dray. Coom, coom in, Miss Tiny, an' set ye doon by the faire an' dray yer faet an' hev summat warm to kape ye from ketchin' coold."

Mr. Bates led the way, stooping under the doorplaces, into his small sitting-room, and, shaking the patchwork cushion in his arm-chair, moved it to within a good roasting distance of the blazing fire.

"Thank you, uncle Bates" (Caterina kept up her childish epithets for her friends, and this was one of them); "not quite so close to the fire, for I am warm with walking."

"Eh, but yer shoes are faine an' wet, an' ye must put up yer faet on the fender. Rare big faet, baint 'em?—aboot the saize of a good big spoon. I woonder ye can mek a shift to stan' on 'em. Now, what'll ye hev to warm yer insaide?—a drop o' hot elder wain, now?"

"No, not any thing to drink, thank you; it isn't very long since breakfast," said Caterina, drawing out the comforter from her deep pocket. Pockets were capacious in those days. "Look here, uncle Bates, here is what I came to bring you. I made it on purpose for you. You must wear it this winter, and give your red one to old Brooks."

"Eh, Miss Tiny, this *is* a beauty. An' ye made it all wi' yer little fingers for an old feller laike mae! I tek it very kaind on ye, an' I belave ye I'll wear it, and be prood on't too. These sthraipes, blue an' whaite, now, they mek it un-common pritty."

"Yes, that will suit your complexion, you know, better than the old scarlet one. I know Mrs. Sharp will be more in love with you than ever when she sees you in the new one."

"My complexion, ye little roogue! ye're a laughin' at me. But talkin' o' complexions, what a beautiful color the bride as is to be has on her cheeks! Dang my boottons! she looks faine and handsome o' hossback—sits as upraight as a dart, wi' a figure like a statty! Misthress Sharp has promised to put me behaind one o' the doors when the ladies are comin' doon to dinner, so as I may sae the young un i' full dress, wi' all her curls an' that. Misthress Sharp says she's almost beau-tifuller nor my ledy was when she was yoong; an' I think ye'll noot faind many i' the counthry as'll coom up to that."

"Yes, Miss Assher is very handsome," said Caterina, rather faintly, feeling the sense of her own insignificance returning at this picture of the impression Miss Assher made on others.

"Well, an' I hope she's good too, an'll mek a good naice to Sir Cristhifer an' my ledy. Misthress Griffin, the maid, says as she's rether tatchy and find-fautin' aboot her cloothes, laike. But she's yoong—she's yoong; that'll wear off when she's got a hoosband, an' children, an' summat else to think on. Sir Cristhifer's fain an' delaighted, I can see. He says to me th'other mornin,' says he, 'Well Bates, what do you think of your young misthress as is to be?' An' I says, 'Whay, yer honor, I think she's as fain a lass as iver I set eyes on; an' I wish the Captain luck in a fain family, an' your honor laife an' health to see't.' Mr. Warren says as the masther's all for forrardin' the weddin', an' it'll very laike be afore the autumn's oot."

As Mr. Bates ran on, Caterina felt something like a painful contraction at her heart. "Yes," she said rising, "I dare say it will. Sir Christopher is very anxious for it. But I must go, uncle Bates; Lady Cheverel will be wanting me, and it is your dinner-time."

"Nay, my dinner doon't sinnify a bit; but I moosn't kaep ye if my ledy wants ye. Though I hevn't thanked ye half anoof for the comfiter—the wrapraskil, as they call't. My feckins, it's a beauty. But ye look very whaite and sadly, Miss Tiny; I doubt ye're poorly; an' this walking i' th' wet isn't good for ye."

"Oh, yes, it is indeed," said Caterina, hastening out, and taking up her umbrella from the kitchen floor. "I must really go now; so, good-bye."

She tripped off, calling Rupert, while the good gardener, his hands thrust deep in his pockets, stood looking after her, and shaking his head with rather a melancholy air.

"She gets moor nesh and dillicat than iver," he said, half to himself and half to Hester. "I shouldn't woonder if she fades away laike them cyclamens as I transplanted. She puts me i' maind on 'em somehow, hangin' on their little thin stalks, so whaite an' tinder."

The poor little thing made her way back, no longer hungering for the cold moist air as a counteractive of inward excitement, but with a chill at her heart which made the outward chill only depressing. The golden sunlight beamed through the dripping boughs like a Shechinah, or visible divine presence, and the birds were chirping and trilling their new autumnal songs so sweetly, it seemed as if their throats, as well as the air, were all the clearer for the rain; but Caterina moved through all this joy and beauty like a poor wounded leveret painfully dragging its little body through the sweet clover-tufts—for it, sweet in vain. Mr. Bates's words about Sir Christopher's joy, Miss Assher's beauty, and the nearness of the wedding, had come upon her like the pressure of a cold hand, rousing her from confused dozing to a perception of hard, familiar realities. It is so with emotional natures, whose thoughts are no more than the fleeting shadows cast by feeling: to them words are facts, and even when known to be false, have a mastery over their smiles and tears. Caterina entered her own room again, with no other change from her former state of despondency and wretchedness than an additional sense of injury from Anthony. His behavior towards her in the morning was a new wrong. To snatch a caress when she justly claimed an expression of penitence, of regret, of sympathy, was to make more light of her than ever.

CHAPTER VIII.

THAT evening Miss Assher seemed to carry herself with unusual haughtiness, and was coldly observant of Caterina. There was unmistakably thunder in the air. Captain Wybrow appeared to take the matter very easily, and was inclined to brave it out by paying more than ordinary attention to Caterina. Mr. Gilfil had induced her to play a game at draughts with him, Lady Assher being seated at picquet with Sir Christopher, and Miss Assher in determined conversation with Lady Cheverel. Anthony, thus left as an odd unit, sauntered up to Caterina's chair, and leaned behind her, watching the game. Tina, with all the remembrances of the morning thick upon her, felt her cheeks becoming more and more crimson, and at last said impatiently, "I wish you would go away."

This happened directly under the view of Miss Assher, who saw Caterina's reddening cheeks, saw that she said something impatiently, and that Captain Wybrow moved away in consequence. There was another person, too, who had noticed this incident with strong interest, and who was moreover aware that Miss Assher not only saw, but keenly observed what was passing. That other person was Mr. Gilfil, and he drew some painful conclusions which heightened his anxiety for Caterina.

The next morning, in spite of the fine weather, Miss Assher declined riding, and Lady Cheverel, perceiving that there was something wrong between the lovers, took care that they should be left together in the drawing-room. Miss Assher, seated on a sofa near the fire, was busy with some fancy-work, in which she seemed bent on making great progress this morning. Captain Wybrow sat opposite with a newspaper in his hand, from which he obligingly read extracts with an elaborately easy air, willfully unconscious of the contemptuous silence with which she pursued her filigree work. At length he put down the paper, which he could no longer pretend not to have exhausted, and Miss Assher then said,

"You seem to be on very intimate terms with Miss Sarti."

"With Tina? oh yes; she has always been the pet of the house, you know. We have been quite brother and sister together."

"Sisters don't generally color so very deeply when their brothers approach them."

"Does she color? I never noticed it. But she's a timid little thing."

"It would be much better if you would not be so hypocritical, Captain Wybrow. I am confident there has been some flirtation between you. Miss Sarti, in her position, would never speak to you with the petulance she did last night, if you had not given her some kind of claim on you."

"My dear Beatrice, now do be reasonable; do ask yourself what earthly probability there is that I should think of flirting with poor little Tina. *Is* there any thing about her to attract that sort of attention? She is more child than woman. One thinks of her as a little girl to be petted and played with."

"Pray, what were you playing at with her yesterday morning, when I came in unexpectedly, and her cheeks were flushed and her hands trembling?"

"Yesterday morning?—Oh, I remember. You know I always tease her about Gilfil, who is over head and ears in love with her; and she is angry at that,—perhaps, because she likes him. They were old play-fellows years before I came here, and Sir Christopher has set his heart on their marrying."

"Captain Wybrow, you are very false. It had nothing to do with Mr. Gilfil that she colored last night when you leaned over her chair. You might just as well be candid. If your own mind is not made up, pray do no violence to yourself. I am quite ready to give way to Miss Sarti's superior attractions. Understand that, so far as I am concerned, you are perfectly at liberty. I decline any share in the affection of a man who forfeits my respect by duplicity."

In saying this Miss Assher rose, and was sweeping haughtily out of the room, when Captain Wybrow placed himself be fore her, and took her hand.

"Dear, dear Beatrice, be patient; do not judge me so rashly. Sit down again, sweet," he added in a pleading voice, pressing both her hands between his, and leading her back to the sofa, where he sat down beside her. Miss Assher was not unwilling to be led back or to listen, but she retained her cold and haughty expression.

"Can you not trust me, Beatrice? Can you not believe me, although there may be things I am unable to explain?"

"Why should there be any thing you are unable to explain? An honorable man will not be placed in circumstances which he can not explain to the woman he seeks to make his wife. He will not ask her to *believe* that he acts properly; he will let her *know* that he does so. Let me go, sir."

She attempted to rise, but he passed his hand round her waist and detained her.

"Now, Beatrice, dear," he said imploringly, "can you not understand that there are things a man doesn't like to talk about—secrets that he must keep for the sake of others, and not for his own sake? Every thing that relates to myself you may ask me, but do not ask me to tell other people's secrets. Don't you understand me?"

"Oh, yes," said Miss Assher scornfully, "I understand. Whenever you make love to a woman—that is her secret, which you are bound to keep for her. But it is folly to be talking in this way, Captain Wybrow. It is very plain that there is some relation more than friendship between you and Miss Sarti. Since you can not explain that relation, there is no more to be said between us."

"Confound it, Beatrice! you'll drive me mad. Can a fellow help a girl's falling in love with him? Such things are always happening, but men don't talk of them. These fancies will spring up without the slightest foundation, especially when a woman sees few people; they die out again when there is no encouragement. If you could like me, you ought not to be surprised that other people can; you ought to think the better of them for it."

"You mean to say, then, that Miss Sarti is in love with you, without your ever having made love to her."

"Do not press me to say such things, dearest. It is enough that you know I love you—that I am devoted to you. You naughty queen you, you know there is no chance for any one else where you are. You are only tormenting me, to prove your power over me. But don't be too cruel; for you know they say I have another heart-disease besides love, and these scenes bring on terrible palpitations."

"But I must have an answer to this one question," said Miss Assher, a little softened: "Has there been, or is there, any love on your side towards Miss Sarti? I have nothing to do with her feelings, but I have a right to know yours."

"I like Tina very much; who would not like such a little simple thing? You would not wish me not to like her? But love—that is a very different affair. One has a brotherly affection for such a woman as Tina; but it is another sort of woman that one loves."

These last words were made doubly significant by a look of tenderness, and a kiss imprinted on the hand Captain Wybrow held in his. Miss Assher was conquered. It was so far from probable that Anthony should love that pale insignificant little thing—so highly probable that he should adore the beautiful Miss Assher. On the whole, it was rather gratifying that other women should be languishing for her handsome lover; he really was an exquisite creature. Poor Miss Sarti! Well, she would get over it.

Captain Wybrow saw his advantage. "Come, sweet love," he continued, "let us talk no more about unpleasant things. You will keep Tina's secret, and be very kind to her—won't you?—for my sake. But you will ride out now? See what a glorious day it is for riding. Let me order the horses. I'm terribly in want of the air. Come, give me one forgiving kiss, and say you will go."

Miss Assher complied with the double request, and then went to equip herself for the ride, while her lover walked to the stables.

CHAPTER IX.

MEANWHILE Mr. Gilfil, who had a heavy weight on his mind, had watched for the moment when, the two elder ladies having driven out, Caterina would probably be alone in Lady Cheverel's sitting-room. He went up and knocked at the door.

"Come in," said the sweet mellow voice, always thrilling to him as the sound of rippling water to the thirsty.

He entered and found Caterina standing in some confusion, as if she had been startled from a reverie. She felt relieved when she saw it was Maynard, but, the next moment, felt a little pettish that he should have come to interrupt and frighten her.

"Oh, it is you, Maynard! Do you want Lady Cheverel?"

"No, Caterina," he answered gravely; "I want you. I have something very particular to say to you. Will you let me sit down with you for half an hour?"

"Yes, dear old preacher," said Caterina, sitting down with an air of weariness; "what is it?"

Mr. Gilfil placed himself opposite to her, and said, "I hope you will not be hurt, Caterina, by what I am going to say to you. I do not speak from any other feelings than real affection and anxiety for you. I put every thing else out of the question. You know you are more to me than all the world; but I will not thrust before you a feeling which you are unable to return. I speak to you as a brother—the old Maynard that used to scold you for getting your fishing-line tangled ten years ago. You will not believe that I have any mean, selfish motive in mentioning things that are painful to you?"

"No; I know you are very good," said Caterina, abstractedly.

"From what I saw yesterday evening," Mr. Gilfil went on, hesitating and coloring slightly, "I am led to fear—pray forgive me if I am wrong, Caterina—that you—that Captain Wybrow is base enough still to trifle with your feelings, that he still allows himself to behave to you as no man ought who is the declared lover of another woman."

"What do you mean, Maynard?" said Caterina, with anger flashing from her eyes. "Do you mean that I let him make love to me? What right have you to think that of me? What do you mean that you saw yesterday evening?"

"Do not be angry, Caterina. I don't suspect you of doing wrong. I only suspect that heartless puppy of behaving so as to keep awake feelings in you that not only destroy your own peace of mind, but may lead to very bad consequences with regard to others. I want to warn you that Miss Assher has her eyes open on what passes between you and Captain Wybrow, and I feel sure she is getting jealous of you. Pray be very careful, Caterina, and try to behave with politeness and indifference to him. You must see by this time that he is not worth the feelings you have given him. He's more disturbed at his pulse beating one too many in a minute, than at all the misery he has caused you by his foolish trifling."

"You ought not to speak so of him, Maynard," said Caterina,

passionately. "He is not what you think. He *did* care for me; he *did* love me; only he wanted to do what his uncle wished."

"Oh, to be sure! I know it is only from the most virtuous motives that he does what is convenient to himself."

Mr. Gilfil paused. He felt that he was getting irritated, and defeating his own object. Presently he continued in a calm and affectionate tone:

"I will say no more about what I think of him, Caterina. But whether he loved you or not, his position now with Miss Assher is such that any love you may cherish for him can bring nothing but misery. God knows, I don't expect you to leave off loving him at a moment's notice. Time and absence, and trying to do what is right, are the only cures. If it were not that Sir Christopher and Lady Cheverel would be displeased and puzzled at your wishing to leave home just now, I would beg you to pay a visit to my sister. She and her husband are good creatures, and would make their house a home to you. But I could not urge the thing just now without giving a special reason; and what is most of all to be dreaded is the raising of any suspicion in Sir Christopher's mind of what has happened in the past, or of your present feelings. You think so too, don't you, Tina?"

Mr. Gilfil paused again, but Caterina said nothing. She was looking away from him, out of the window, and her eyes were filling with tears. He rose, and, advancing a little towards her, held out his hand, and said,

"Forgive me, Caterina, for intruding on your feelings in this way. I was so afraid you might not be aware how Miss Assher watched you. Remember, I entreat you, that the peace of the whole family depends on your power of governing yourself. Only say you forgive me before I go."

"Dear, good Maynard," she said, stretching out her little hand, and taking two of his large fingers in her grasp, while her tears flowed fast; "I am very cross to you. But my heart is breaking. I don't know what I do. Good-bye."

He stooped down, kissed the little hand, and then left the room.

"The cursed scoundrel!" he muttered between his teeth, as he closed the door behind him. "If it were not for Sir Christopher, I should like to pound him into paste to poison puppies like himself."

CHAPTER X.

THAT evening Captain Wybrow, returning from a long ride with Miss Assher, went up to his dressing-room, and seated himself with an air of considerable lassitude before his mirror. The reflection there presented of his exquisite self was certainly paler and more worn than usual, and might excuse the anxiety with which he first felt his pulse and then laid his hand on his heart.

"It's a devil of a position this for a man to be in," was the train of his thought, as he kept his eyes fixed on the glass, while he leaned back in his chair, and crossed his hands behind his head; "between two jealous women, and both of them as ready to take fire as tinder. And in my state of health, too! I should be glad enough to run away from the whole affair, and go off to some lotos-eating place or other where there are no women, or only women who are too sleepy to be jealous. Here am I, doing nothing to please myself, trying to do the best thing for every body else, and all the comfort I get is to have fire shot at me from women's eyes, and venom spirted at me from women's tongues. If Beatrice takes another jealous fit into her head—and it's likely enough, Tina is so unmanageable—I don't know what storm she may raise. And any hitch in this marriage, especially of that sort, might be a fatal business for the old gentleman. I wouldn't have such a blow fall upon him for a great deal. Besides, a man must be married some time in his life, and I could hardly do better than marry Beatrice. She's an uncommonly fine woman, and I'm really very fond of her; and as I shall let her have her own way her temper won't signify much. I wish the wedding was over and done with, for this fuss doesn't suit me at all. I haven't been half so well lately. That scene about Tina this morning quite upset me. Poor little Tina! What a little simpleton it was to set her heart on me in that way! But she ought to see how impossible it is that things should be different. If she would but understand how kindly I feel towards her, and make up her mind to look on me as a friend; but that is what one never can get a woman to do. Beatrice is very good-natured; I'm sure she would be kind to the little thing. It would be a great comfort if Tina would take to Gilfil, if it were only in anger against me. He'd make her a capital husband, and I should like to see the little grasshopper happy. If I had been in a different position I would certainly have married her myself; but that was out of the question with my responsibilities to Sir Christopher. I think a little persuasion from my uncle would bring her to accept Gilfil; I know she would never be able to oppose my uncle's wishes. And if they were once married, she's such a loving little thing, she would soon be billing and cooing with him as if she had never known me. It would certainly be the best thing for her happiness if that marriage were hastened. Heigho! Those are lucky fellows that have no women falling in love with them. It's a confounded responsibility."

At this point in his meditations he turned his head a little, so as to get a three-quarter view of his face. Clearly it was the "*dono infelice della bellezza*" that laid these onerous duties upon him—an idea which naturally suggested that he should ring for his valet.

For the next few days, however, there was such a cessation of threatening symptoms as to allay the anxiety both of Captain Wybrow and Mr. Gilfil. All earthly things have their lull: even on nights when the most unappeasable wind is raging, there will be a moment of stillness before it crashes among the boughs again, and storms against the windows, and howls like a thousand lost demons through the key-holes.

Miss Assher appeared to be in the highest good-humor; Captain Wybrow was more assiduous than usual, and was very circumspect in his behavior to Caterina, on whom Miss Assher bestowed unwonted attentions. The weather was brilliant; there were riding excursions in the mornings and dinner-parties in the evenings. Consultations in the library between Sir Christopher and Lady Assher seemed to be leading to a satisfactory result; and it was understood that this visit at Cheverel Manor would terminate in another fortnight, when the preparations for the wedding would be carried forward with all dispatch at Farleigh. The Baronet seemed every day more radiant. Accustomed to view people who entered into his plans by the pleasant light which his own strong will and bright hopefulness were always casting on the future, he saw nothing but personal charms and promising domestic qualities in Miss Assher, whose quickness of eye and taste in externals formed a real ground of sympathy between her and Sir Christopher. Lady Cheverel's enthusiasm never rose above the temperate mark of calm satisfaction, and, having quite her share of the critical acumen which characterizes the mutual estimates of the fair sex, she had a more moderate opinion of Miss Assher's qualities. She suspected that the fair Beatrice had a sharp and imperious temper; and being herself, on principle and by habitual self-command, the most deferential of wives, she noticed with disapproval Miss Assher's occasional air of authority towards Captain Wybrow. A proud woman who has learned to submit, carries all her pride to the reinforcement of her submission, and looks down with severe superiority on all feminine assumption as "unbecoming." Lady Cheverel, however, confined her criticisms to the privacy of her own thoughts, and, with a reticence which I fear may seem incredible, did not use them as a means of disturbing her husband's complacency.

And Caterina? How did she pass these sunny autumn days, in which the skies seemed to be smiling on the family gladness? To her the change in Miss Assher's manner was unaccountable. Those compassionate attentions, those smiling condescensions, were torture to Caterina, who was constantly tempted to repulse them with anger. She thought, "Perhaps Anthony has told her to be kind to poor Tina." This was an insult. He ought to have known that the mere presence of Miss Assher was painful to her, that Miss Assher's smiles scorched her, that Miss Assher's kind words were like poison-stings inflaming her to madness. And he—Anthony—he was evidently repenting of the tenderness he had been betrayed into that morning in the drawing-room. He was cold and distant and civil to her, to ward off Beatrice's suspicions, and Beatrice could be so gracious now, because she was sure of Anthony's entire devotion. Well! and so it ought to be—and she ought not to wish it otherwise. And yet—oh, he *was* cruel to her. She could never have behaved so to him. To make her love him so—to speak such tender words—to give her such caresses, and then to behave as if such things had never been. He had given her the poison that seemed so sweet while she was drinking it, and now it was in her blood, and she was helpless.

With this tempest pent up in her bosom, the poor child went up to her room every night, and there it all burst forth. There, with loud whispers and sobs, restlessly pacing up and down, lying on the hard floor, courting cold and weariness, she told to the pitiful listening night the anguish which she could pour into no mortal ear. But always sleep came at last, and always in the morning the reactive calm that enabled her to live through the day.

It is amazing how long a young frame will go on battling with this sort of secret wretchedness, and yet show no traces of the conflict for any but sympathetic eyes. The very delicacy of Caterina's usual appearance, her natural paleness and habitually quiet mouse-like ways, made any symptoms of fatigue and suffering less noticeable. And her singing—the one thing in which she ceased to be passive, and became prominent—lost none of its energy. She herself sometimes wondered how it was that, whether she felt sad or angry, crushed with the sense of Anthony's indifference, or burning with impatience under Miss Assher's attentions, it was always a relief to her to sing. Those full deep notes she sent forth seemed to be lifting the pain from her heart—seemed to be carrying away the madness from her brain.

Thus Lady Cheverel noticed no change in Caterina, and it was only Mr. Gilfil who discerned with anxiety the feverish spot that sometimes rose on her cheek, the deepening violet tint under her eyes, and the strange absent glance, the unhealthy glitter of the beautiful eyes themselves.

But those agitated nights were producing a more fatal effect than was represented by these slight outward changes.

CHAPTER XI.

The following Sunday, the morning being rainy, it was determined that the family should not go to Cumbermoor Church as usual, but that Mr. Gilfil, who had only an afternoon service at his curacy, should conduct the morning service in the chapel.

Just before the appointed hour of eleven, Caterina came down into the drawing-room, looking so unusually ill as to call forth an anxious inquiry from Lady Cheverel, who, on learning that she had a severe headache, insisted that she should not attend service, and at once packed her up comfortably on a sofa near the fire, putting a volume of Tillotson's Sermons into her hands—as appropriate reading, if Caterina should feel equal to that means of edification.

Excellent medicine for the mind are the good Archbishop's sermons, but a medicine, unhappily, not suited to Tina's case. She sat with the book open on her knees, her dark eyes fixed vacantly on the portrait of that handsome Lady Cheverel, wife of the notable Sir Anthony. She gazed at the picture without thinking of it, and the fair blonde dame seemed to look down on her with that benignant unconcern, that mild wonder, with which happy self-possessed women are apt to look down on their agitated and weaker sisters.

Caterina was thinking of the near future—of the wedding that was soon to come—of all she would have to live through in the next months.

"I wish I could be very ill, and die before then," she thought. "When people get very ill, they don't mind about things. Poor Patty Richards looked so happy when she was in a decline. She didn't seem to care any more about her lover that she was engaged to be married to, and she liked the smell of the flowers so, that I used to take her. Oh, if I could but like any thing—if I could but think about any thing else! If these dreadful feelings would go away, I wouldn't mind about not being happy. I wouldn't want any thing—and I could do what would please Sir Christopher and Lady Cheverel. But when that rage and anger comes into me, I don't know what to do. I don't feel the ground under me; I only feel my head and heart beating, and it seems as if I must do something dreadful. Oh! I wonder if any one ever felt like me before. I must be very wicked. But God will have pity on me; He knows all I have to bear."

In this way the time wore on till Tina heard the sound of voices along the passage, and became conscious that the volume of Tillotson had slipped on the floor. She had only just picked it up, and seen with alarm that the pages were bent, when Lady Assher, Beatrice, and Captain Wybrow entered, all with that brisk and cheerful air which a sermon is often observed to produce when it is quite finished.

Lady Assher at once came and seated herself by Caterina. Her ladyship had been considerably refreshed by a doze, and was in great force for monologue.

"Well, my dear Miss Sarti, and how do you feel now?—a little better, I see. I thought you would be, sitting quietly here. These headaches, now, are all from weakness. You must not over exert yourself, and you must take bitters. I used to have just the same sort of headaches when I was your age, and old Dr. Samson used to say to my mother, 'Madam, what your daughter suffers from is weakness.' He was such a curious old man, was Dr. Samson. But I wish you could have heard the sermon this morning. Such an excellent sermon! It was about the ten virgins: five of them were foolish, and five were clever, you know; and Mr. Gilfil explained all that. What a very pleasant young man he is! so very quiet and agreeable, and such a good hand at whist. I wish we had him at Farleigh. Sir John would have liked him beyond any thing; he is so good-tempered at cards, and he was such a man for cards, was Sir John. And our rector is a very irritable man; he can't bear to lose his money at cards. I don't think a clergyman ought to mind about losing his money; do you?—do you, now?"

"Oh pray, Lady Assher," interposed Beatrice, in her usual tone of superiority, "do not weary poor Caterina with such uninteresting questions. Your head seems very bad, still, dear," she continued in a condoling tone, to Caterina; "do take my vinaigrette, and keep it in your pocket. It will perhaps refresh you now and then."

"No, thank you," answered Caterina; "I will not take it away from you."

"Indeed, dear, I never use it; you must take it," Miss Assher persisted, holding it close to Tina's hand. Tina colored deeply, pushed the vinaigrette away with some impatience, and said, "Thank you, I never use those things. I don't like vinaigrettes."

Miss Assher returned the vinaigrette to her pocket in surprise and haughty silence, and Captain Wybrow, who had looked on in some alarm, said hastily, "See! it is quite bright out of doors now. There is time for a walk before luncheon. Come, Beatrice, put on your hat and cloak, and let us have half an hour's walk on the gravel."

"Yes, do, my dear," said Lady Assher, "and I will go and see if Sir Christopher is having his walk in the gallery."

As soon as the door had closed behind the two ladies, Captain Wybrow, standing with his back to the fire, turned toward Caterina, and said in a tone of earnest remonstrance, "My dear Caterina, let me beg of you to exercise more control over your feelings; you are really rude to Miss Assher, and I can see that she is quite hurt. Consider how strange your behavior must appear to her. She will wonder what can be the cause of it. Come, dear Tina," he added, approaching her, and attempting to take her hand; "for your own sake let me entreat you to receive her attentions politely. She really feels very kindly towards you, and I should be so happy to see you friends."

Caterina was already in such a state of diseased susceptibility that the most innocent words from Captain Wybrow would have been irritating to her, as the whirr of the most delicate wing will afflict a nervous patient. But this tone of benevolent remonstrance was intolerable. He had inflicted a great and unrepented injury on her, and now he assumed an air of benevolence towards her. This was a new outrage. His profession of good-will was insolence.

Caterina snatched away her hand and said indignantly, "Leave me to myself, Captain Wybrow! I do not disturb you."

"Caterina, why will you be so violent—so unjust to me? It is for you that I feel anxious. Miss Assher has already noticed how strange your behavior is both to her and me, and it puts me into a very difficult position. What can I say to her?"

"Say?" Caterina burst forth with intense bitterness, rising, and moving towards the door; "say that I am a poor silly girl, and have fallen in love with you, and am jealous of her; but that you have never had any feeling but pity for me—you have never behaved with any thing more than friendliness to me. Tell her that, and she will think all the better of you."

Tina uttered this as the bitterest sarcasm her ideas would furnish her with, not having the faintest suspicion that the sarcasm derived any of its bitterness from truth. Underneath all her sense of wrong, which was rather instinctive than reflective—underneath all the madness of her jealousy, and her ungovernable impulses of resentment and vindictiveness—underneath all this scorching passion there were still left some hidden crystal dews of trust, of self-reproof, of belief that Anthony was trying to do the right. Love had not all gone to feed the fires of hatred. Tina still trusted that Anthony felt more for her than he seemed to feel; she was still far from suspecting him of a wrong which a woman resents even more than inconstancy. And she threw out this taunt simply as the most intense expression she could find for the anger of the moment.

As she stood nearly in the middle of the room, her little body trembling under the shock of passions too strong for it, her very lips pale, and her eyes gleaming, the door opened, and Miss Assher appeared, tall, blooming, and splendid, in her walking costume. As she entered, her face wore the smile appropriate to the exits and entrances of a young lady who feels that her presence is an interesting fact; but the next moment she looked at Caterina with grave surprise, and then threw a glance of angry suspicion at Captain Wybrow, who wore an air of weariness and vexation.

"Perhaps you are too much engaged to walk out, Captain Wybrow? I will go alone."

"No, no, I am coming," he answered, hurrying towards her, and leading her out of the room; leaving poor Caterina to feel all the reaction of shame and self-reproach after her outburst of passion.

CHAPTER XII.

"PRAY, what is likely to be the next scene in the drama between you and Miss Sarti?" said Miss Assher to Captain Wybrow as soon as they were out on the gravel. "It would be agreeable to have some idea of what is coming."

Captain Wybrow was silent. He felt out of humor, wearied, annoyed. There come moments when one almost determines never again to oppose any thing but dead silence to an angry woman. "Now then, confound it," he said to himself, "I'm going to be battered on the other flank." He looked resolutely at the horizon, with something more like a frown on his face than Beatrice had ever seen there.

After a pause of two or three minutes, she continued in a still haughtier tone, "I suppose you are aware, Captain Wybrow, that I expect an explanation of what I have just seen."

"I have no explanation, my dear Beatrice," he answered at last, making a strong effort over himself, "except what I have already given you. I hoped you would never recur to the subject."

"Your explanation, however, is very far from satisfactory. I can only say that the airs Miss Sarti thinks herself entitled to put on towards you, are quite incompatible with your position as regards me. And her behavior to me is most insulting. I shall certainly not stay in the house under such circumstances, and mamma must state the reasons to Sir Christopher."

"Beatrice," said Captain Wybrow, his irritation giving way to alarm, "I beseech you to be patient, and exercise your good feelings in this affair. It is very painful, I know, but I am sure you would be grieved to injure poor Caterina—to bring down my uncle's anger upon her. Consider what a poor little dependent thing she is."

"It is very adroit of you to make these evasions, but do not suppose that they deceive me. Miss Sarti would never dare to behave to you as she does, if you had not flirted with her, or made love to her. I suppose she considers your engagement to me a breach of faith to her. I am much obliged to you, certainly, for making me Miss Sarti's rival. You have told me a falsehood, Captain Wybrow."

"Beatrice, I solemnly declare to you that Caterina is nothing more to me than a girl I naturally feel kindly to—as a favorite of my uncle's and a nice little thing enough. I should be glad to see her married to Gilfil to-morrow; that's a good proof that I'm not in love with her, I should think. As to the past, I may have shown her little attentions, which she has exaggerated and misinterpreted. What man is not liable to that sort of thing?"

"But what can she found her behavior on? What had she been saying to you this morning to make her tremble and turn pale in that way?"

"Oh, I don't know. I just said something about her behaving peevishly. With that Italian blood of hers, there's no knowing how she may take what one says. She's a fierce little thing, though she seems so quiet generally."

"But she ought to be made to know how unbecoming and indelicate her conduct is. For my part, I wonder Lady Cheverel has not noticed her short answers and the airs she puts on."

"Let me beg of you, Beatrice, not to hint any thing of the kind to Lady Cheverel. You must have observed how strict my aunt is. It never enters her head that a girl can be in love with a man who has not made her an offer."

"Well, I shall let Miss Sarti know myself that I have observed her conduct. It will be only a charity to her."

"Nay, dear, that will be doing nothing but harm. Caterina's temper is peculiar. The best thing you can do will be to leave her to herself as much as possible. It will all wear off. I've no doubt she'll be married to Gilfil before long. Girls' fancies are easily diverted from one object to another. By Jove, what a rate my heart is galloping at! These confounded palpitations get worse instead of better."

Thus ended the conversation, so far as it concerned Caterina, not without leaving a distinct resolution in Captain Wybrow's mind—a resolution carried into effect the next day when he was in the library with Sir Christopher for the purpose of discussing some arrangements about the approaching marriage.

"By-the-by," he said carelessly, when the business came to a pause, and he was sauntering round the room with his hands in his coat-pockets, surveying the backs of the books that lined the walls, "when is the wedding between Gilfil and Caterina to come off, sir? I've a fellow-feeling for a poor devil so many fathoms deep in love as Maynard. Why shouldn't their marriage happen as soon as ours? I suppose he has come to an understanding with Tina?"

"Why," said Sir Christopher, "I did think of letting the thing be until old Crichley died; he can't hold out very long, poor fellow; and then Maynard might have entered into matrimony and the rectory both at once. But, after all, that really is no good reason for waiting. There is no need for them to leave the Manor when they are married. The little monkey is quite old enough. It would be pretty to see her a matron, with a baby about the size of a kitten in her arms."

"I think that system of waiting is always bad. And if I can further any settlement you would like to make on Caterina, I shall be delighted to carry out your wishes."

"My dear boy, that's very good of you; but Maynard will have enough; and from what I know of him—and I know him well—I think he would rather provide for Caterina himself. However, now you have put this matter into my head, I begin to blame myself for not having thought of it before. I've been so wrapt up in Beatrice and you, you rascal, that I had really forgotten poor Maynard. And he's older than you—it's high time he was settled in life as a family man."

Sir Christopher paused, took snuff in a meditative manner, and presently said, more to himself than to Anthony, who was humming a tune at the far end of the room, "Yes, yes. It will be a capital plan to finish off all our family business at once."

Riding out with Miss Assher the same morning, Captain Wybrow mentioned to her, incidentally, that Sir Christopher was anxious to bring about the wedding between Gilfil and Caterina as soon as possible, and that he, for his part, should do all he could to further the affair. It would be the best thing in the world for Tina, in whose welfare he was really interested.

With Sir Christopher there was never any long interval between purpose and execution. He made up his mind promptly, and he acted promptly. On rising from luncheon, he said to Mr. Gilfil, "Come with me into the library, Maynard. I want to have a word with you."

"Maynard, my boy," he began, as soon as they were seated, tapping his snuff-box, and looking radiant at the idea of the unexpected pleasure he was about to give, "why shouldn't we have two happy couples instead of one, before the autumn is over, eh?

"Eh?" he repeated, after a moment's pause, lengthening out the monosyllable, taking a slow pinch, and looking up at Maynard with a sly smile.

"I'm not quite sure that I understand you, sir," answered Mr. Gilfil, who felt annoyed at the consciousness that he was turning pale.

"Not understand me, you rogue? You know very well whose happiness lies nearest to my heart after Anthony's. You know you let me into your secrets long ago, so there's no confession to make. Tina's quite old enough to be a grave little wife now; and though the Rectory's not ready for you, that's no matter. My lady and I shall feel all the more comfortable for having you with us. We should miss our little singing-bird if we lost her all at once."

Mr. Gilfil felt himself in a painfully difficult position. He dreaded that Sir Christopher should surmise or discover the true state of Caterina's feelings, and yet he was obliged to make those feelings the ground of his reply.

"My dear sir," he at last said with some effort, "you will not suppose that I am not alive to your goodness—that I am not grateful for your fatherly interest in my happiness; but I fear that Caterina's feelings towards me are not such as to warrant the hope that she would accept a proposal of marriage from me."

"Have you ever asked her?"

"No, sir. But we often know these things too well without asking."

"Pooh, pooh! the little monkey *must* love you. Why, you were her first playfellow; and I remember she used to cry if you cut your finger. Besides, she has always silently admitted that you were her lover. You know I have always spoken of you to her in that light. I took it for granted you had settled the business between yourselves; so did Anthony. Anthony thinks she's in love with you, and he has young eyes, which are apt enough to see clearly in these matters. He was talking to me about it this morning, and pleased me very much by the friendly interest he showed in you and Tina."

The blood—more than was wanted—rushed back to Mr. Gilfil's face; he set his teeth and clenched his hands in the effort to repress a burst of indignation. Sir Christopher noticed the flush, but thought it indicated the fluctuation of hope and fear about Caterina. He went on:

"You're too modest by half, Maynard. A fellow who can take a five-barred gate as you can, ought not to be so faint-hearted. If you can't speak to her yourself, leave me to talk to her."

"Sir Christopher," said poor Maynard earnestly, "I shall really feel it the greatest kindness you can possibly show me not to mention this subject to Caterina at present. I think such a proposal, made prematurely, might only alienate her from me."

Sir Christopher was getting a little displeased at this contradiction. His tone became a little sharper as he said, "Have you any grounds to state for this opinion, beyond your general notion that Tina is not enough in love with you?"

"I can state none beyond my own very strong impression that she does not love me well enough to marry me."

"Then I think that ground is worth nothing at all. I am tolerably correct in my judgment of people; and if I am not very much deceived in Tina, she looks forward to nothing else but to your being her husband. Leave me to manage the matter as I think best. You may rely on me that I shall do no harm to your cause, Maynard."

Mr. Gilfil, afraid to say more, yet wretched in the prospect of what might result from Sir Christopher's determination, quitted the library in a state of mingled indignation against Captain Wybrow, and distress for himself and Caterina. What would she think of him? She might suppose that *he* had instigated or sanctioned Sir Christopher's proceeding. He should perhaps not have an opportunity of speaking to her on the subject in time; he would write her a note, and carry it up to her room after the dressing-bell had rung. No; that would agitate her, and unfit her for appearing at dinner, and passing the evening calmly. He would defer it till bed-time. After prayers, he contrived to lead her back to the drawing-room, and to put a letter in her hand. She carried it up to her own room, wondering, and there read—

"DEAR CATERINA,—Do not suspect for a moment that any thing Sir Christopher may say to you about our marriage has been prompted by me. I have done all I dare do to dissuade him from urging the subject, and have only been prevented from speaking more strongly by the dread of provoking questions which I could not answer without causing you fresh misery. I write this, both to prepare you for any thing Sir Christopher may say, and to assure you—but I hope you already believe it—that your feelings are sacred to me. I would rather part with the dearest hope of my life than be the means of adding to your trouble.

"It is Captain Wybrow who has prompted Sir Christopher to take up the subject at this moment. I tell you this, to save you from hearing it suddenly when your are with Sir Christopher. You see now what sort of stuff that dastard's heart is made of. Trust in me always, dearest Caterina, as—whatever may come—your faithful friend and brother, MAYNARD GILFIL."

Caterina was at first too terribly stung by the words about Captain Wybrow to think of the difficulty which threatened her—to think either of what Sir Christopher would say to her, or of what she could say in reply. Bitter sense of injury, fierce resentment, left no room for fear. With the poisoned garment upon him, the victim writhes under the torture—he has no thought of the coming death.

Anthony could do this!—Of this there could be no explanation but the coolest contempt for her feelings, the basest sacrifice of all the consideration and tenderness he owed her to the ease of his position with Miss Assher. No. It was worse than that: it was deliberate, gratuitous cruelty. He wanted to show her how he despised her; he wanted to make her feel her folly in having ever believed that he loved her.

The last crystal drops of trust and tenderness, she thought, were dried up; all was parched, fiery hatred. Now she need no longer check her resentment by the fear of doing him an injustice: he *had* trifled with her, as Maynard had said; he *had* been reckless of her; and now he was base and cruel. She had cause enough for her bitterness and anger; they were not so wicked as they had seemed to her.

As these thoughts were hurrying after each other like so many sharp throbs of fevered pain, she shed no tear. She paced restlessly to and fro, as her habit was—her hands clenched, her eyes gleaming fiercely and wandering uneasily, as if in search of something on which she might throw herself like a tigress.

"If I could speak to him," she whispered, "and tell him I hate him, I despise him, I loathe him!"

Suddenly, as if a new thought had struck her, she drew a key from her pocket, and, unlocking an inlaid desk where she stored up her keepsakes, took from it a small miniature. It was in a very slight gold frame, with a ring to it, as if intended to be worn on a chain; and under the glass at the back were two locks of hair, one dark and the other auburn, arranged in a fantastic knot. It was Anthony's secret present to her a year ago—a copy he had had made specially for her. For the last month she had not taken it from its hiding-place: there was no need to heighten the vividness of the past. But now she clutched it fiercely, and dashed it across the room against the bare hearthstone.

Will she crush it under her feet, and grind it under her high-heeled shoe, till every trace of those false, cruel features is gone?

Ah, no! She rushed across the room; but when she saw the little treasure she had cherished so fondly, so often smothered with kisses, so often laid under her pillow, and remembered with the first return of consciousness in the morning—when she saw this one visible relic of the too happy past lying with the glass shivered, the hair fallen out, the thin ivory cracked, there was a revulsion of the overstrained feeling: relenting came, and she burst into tears.

Look at her stooping down to gather up her treasure, searching for the hair and replacing it, and then mournfully examining the crack that disfigures the once-loved image. There is no glass now to guard either the hair or the portrait; but see how carefully she wraps delicate paper round it, and locks it up again in its old place. Poor child! God send the relenting may always come before the worst irrevocable deed!

This action had quieted her, and she sat down to read Maynard's letter again. She read it two or three times without seeming to take in the sense; her apprehension was dulled by the passion of the last hour, and she found it difficult to call up the ideas suggested by the words. At last she began to have a distinct conception of the impending interview with Sir Christopher. The idea of displeasing the Baronet, of whom every one at the Manor stood in awe, frightened her so much that she thought it would be impossible to resist his wish. He believed that she loved Maynard; he had always spoken as if he were quite sure of it. How could she tell him he was deceived—and what if he were to ask her whether she loved any body else? To have Sir Christopher looking angrily at her, was more than she could bear, even in imagination. He had always been so good to her! Then she began to think of the pain she might give him, and the more selfish distress of fear gave way to the distress of affection. Unselfish tears began to flow, and sorrowful gratitude to Sir Christopher helped to awaken her sensibility to Mr. Gilfil's tenderness and generosity.

"Dear, good Maynard!—what a poor return I make him! If I could but have loved him instead—but I can never love or care for any thing again. My heart is broken."

CHAPTER XIII.

The next morning the dreaded moment came. Caterina, stupefied by the suffering of the previous night, with that dull mental aching which follows on acute anguish, was in

Lady Cheverel's sitting-room, copying out some charity-lists, when her ladyship came in, and said,

"Tina, Sir Christopher wants you; go down into the library."

She went down trembling. As soon as she entered, Sir Christopher, who was seated near his writing-table, said, "Now, little monkey, come and sit down by me; I have something to tell you."

Caterina took a footstool, and seated herself on it at the Baronet's feet. It was her habit to sit on these low stools, and in this way she could hide her face better. She put her little arm round his leg, and leaned her cheek against his knee.

"Why, you seem out of spirits this morning, Tina. What's the matter, eh?"

"Nothing, Padroncello; only my head is bad."

"Poor monkey! Well, now, wouldn't it do the head good if I were to promise you a good husband, and smart little wedding-gowns, and by-and-by a house of your own, where you would be a little mistress, and Padroncello would come and see you sometimes?"

"Oh no, no! I shouldn't like ever to be married. Let me always stay with you!"

"Pooh, pooh, little simpleton. I shall get old and tiresome, and there will be Anthony's children putting your nose out of joint. You will want some one to love you best of all, and you must have children of your own to love. I can't have you withering away into an old maid. I hate old maids; they make me dismal to look at them. I never see Sharp without shuddering. My little black-eyed monkey was never meant for any thing so ugly. And there's Maynard Gilfil, the best man in the county, worth his weight in gold, heavy as he is; he loves you better than his eyes. And you love him too, you silly monkey, whatever you may say about not being married."

"No, no, dear Padroncello, do not say so; I could not marry him."

"Why not, you foolish child? You don't know your own mind. Why, it is plain to every body that you love him. My lady has all along said she was sure you loved him—she has seen what little princess airs you put on to him; and Anthony too, *he* thinks you are in love with Gilfil. Come, what has made you take it into your head that you wouldn't like to marry him?"

Caterina was now sobbing too deeply to make any answer. Sir Christopher patted her on the back and said, "Come,

come; why, Tina, you are not well this morning. Go and rest, little one. You will see things in quite another light when you are well. Think over what I have said, and remember there is nothing, after Anthony's marriage, that I have set my heart on so much as seeing you and Maynard settled for life. I must have no whims and follies—no nonsense." This was said with a slight severity; but he presently added, in a soothing tone, "There, there, stop crying, and be a good little monkey. Go and lie down and get to sleep."

Caterina slipped from the stool on to her knees, took the old Baronet's hand, covered it with tears and kisses, and then ran out of the room.

Before the evening, Captain Wybrow had heard from his uncle the result of the interview with Caterina. He thought, "If I could have a long quiet talk with her, I could perhaps persuade her to look more reasonably at things. But there's no speaking to her in the house without being interrupted, and I can hardly see her anywhere else without Beatrice's finding it out." At last he determined to make it a matter of confidence with Miss Assher—to tell her that he wished to talk to Caterina quietly for the sake of bringing her to a calmer state of mind, and persuade her to listen to Gilfil's affections. He was very much pleased with this judicious and candid plan, and in the course of the evening he had arranged with himself the time and place of meeting, and had communicated his purpose to Miss Assher, who gave her entire approval. Anthony, she thought, would do well to speak plainly and seriously to Miss Sarti. He was really very patient and kind to her, considering how she behaved.

Tina had kept her room all that day, and had been carefully tended as an invalid, Sir Christopher having told her ladyship how matters stood. This tendance was so irksome to Caterina, she felt so uneasy under attentions and kindness that were based on a misconception, that she exerted herself to appear at breakfast the next morning, and declared herself well, though head and heart were throbbing. To be confined in her own room was intolerable; it was wretched enough to be looked at and spoken to, but it was more wretched to be left alone. She was frightened at her own sensations; she was frightened at the imperious vividness with which pictures of the past and future thrust themselves on her imagination. And there was another feeling, too, which made her want to be down stairs and moving about. Perhaps she might have an opportunity of speaking to Captain Wybrow alone—of speaking those words of hatred and scorn that burned on her tongue. That opportunity offered itself in a very unexpected manner.

Lady Cheverel having sent Caterina out of the drawing-room to fetch some patterns of embroidery from her sitting-room, Captain Wybrow presently walked out after her, and met her as she was returning down stairs.

"Caterina," he said, laying his hand on her arm as she was hurrying on without looking at him, "will you meet me in the Rookery at twelve o'clock? I must speak to you, and we shall be in privacy there. I can not speak to you in the house."

To his surprise, there was a flash of pleasure across her face; she answered shortly and decidedly, "Yes," then snatched her arm away from him, and passed down stairs.

Miss Assher was this morning busy winding silks, being bent on emulating Lady Cheverel's embroidery, and Lady Assher chose the passive amusement of holding the skeins. Lady Cheverel had now all her working apparatus about her, and Caterina, thinking she was not wanted, went away and sat down to the harpischord in the sitting-room. It seemed as if playing massive chords—bringing out volumes of sound, would be the easiest way of passing the long feverish moments before twelve o'clock. Handel's "Messiah" stood open on the desk, at the chorus "All we, like sheep," and Caterina threw herself at once into the impetuous intricacies of that magnificent fugue. In her happiest moments she could never have played it so well; for now all the passion that made her misery was hurled by a convulsive effort into her music, just as pain gives new force to the clutch of the sinking wrestler, and as terror gives far-sounding intensity to the shriek of the feeble.

But at half past eleven she was interrupted by Lady Cheverel, who said, "Tina, go down, will you, and hold Miss Assher's silks for her. Lady Assher and I have decided on having our drive before luncheon."

Caterina went down, wondering how she should escape from the drawing-room in time to be in the Rookery at twelve. Nothing should prevent her from going; nothing should rob her of this one precious moment—perhaps the last —when she could speak out the thoughts that were in her. After that, she would be passive; she would bear any thing.

But she had scarcely sat down with a skein of yellow silk on her hands, when Miss Assher said graciously,

"I know you have an engagement with Captain Wybrow this morning. You must not let me detain you beyond the time."

"So he has been talking to her about me," thought Caterina. Her hands began to tremble as she held the skein.

Miss Assher continued, in the same gracious tone: "It is tedious work holding these skeins. I am sure I am very much obliged to you."

"No, you are not obliged to me," said Caterina, completely mastered by her irritation; "I have only done it because Lady Cheverel told me."

The moment was come when Miss Assher could no longer suppress her long latent desire to "let Miss Sarti know the impropriety of her conduct." With the malicious anger that assumes the tone of compassion, she said,

"Miss Sarti, I am really sorry for you that you are not able to control yourself better. This giving way to unwarrantable feelings is lowering you—it is indeed."

"What unwarrantable feelings?" said Caterina, letting her hands fall, and fixing her great dark eyes steadily on Miss Assher.

"It is quite unnecessary for me to say more. You must be conscious what I mean. Only summon a sense of duty to your aid. You are paining Captain Wybrow extremely by your want of self-control."

"Did he tell you I pained him?"

"Yes, indeed, he did. He is very much hurt that you should behave to me as if you had a sort of enmity towards me. He would like you to make a friend of me. I assure you we both feel very kindly towards you, and are sorry you should cherish such feelings."

"He is very good," said Caterina, bitterly. "What feelings did he say I cherished?"

This bitter tone increased Miss Assher's irritation. There was still a lurking suspicion in her mind, though she would not admit it to herself, that Captain Wybrow had told her a falsehood about his conduct and feelings towards Caterina. It was this suspicion, more even than the anger of the moment, which urged her to say something that would test the truth of his statement. That she would be humiliating Caterina at the same time, was only an additional temptation.

"These are things I do not like to talk of, Miss Sarti. I can not even understand how a woman can indulge a passion for a man who has never given her the least ground for it, as Captain Wybrow assures me is the case."

"He told you that, did he?" said Caterina, in clear low tones, her lips turning white as she rose from her chair.

"Yes, indeed, he did. He was bound to tell it me after your strange behavior."

Caterina said nothing, but turned round suddenly and left the room.

See how she rushes noiselessly, like a pale meteor, along the passages and up the gallery stairs! Those gleaming eyes, those bloodless lips, that swift silent tread, make her look like the incarnation of a fierce purpose, rather than a woman. The midday sun is shining on the armor in the gallery, making mimic suns on bossed sword-hilts and the angles of polished breastplates. Yes, there are sharp weapons in the gallery. There is a dagger in that cabinet; she knows it well. And as a dragon-fly wheels in its flight to alight for an instant on a leaf, she darts to the cabinet, takes out the dagger, and thrusts it into her pocket. In three minutes more she is out, in hat and cloak, on the gravel-walk, hurrying along towards the thick shades of the distant Rookery. She threads the windings of the plantations, not feeling the golden leaves that rain upon her, not feeling the earth beneath her feet. Her hand is in her pocket, clenching the handle of the dagger, which she holds half out of its sheath.

She has reached the Rookery, and is under the gloom of the interlacing boughs. Her heart throbs as if it would burst her bosom—as if every next beat must be its last. Wait, wait, O heart!—till she has done this one deed. He will be there—he will be before her in a moment. He will come towards her with that false smile, thinking she does not know his baseness—she will plunge that dagger into his heart.

Poor child! poor child! she who used to cry to have the fish put back into the water—who never willingly killed the smallest living thing—dreams now, in the madness of her passion, that she can kill the man whose very voice unnerves her.

But what is that lying among the dank leaves on the path three yards before her.

Good God! it is he—lying motionless—his hat fallen off. He is ill, then—he has fainted. Her hand lets go the dagger, and she rushes towards him. His eyes are fixed; he does not see her. She sinks down on her knees, takes the dear head in her arms, and kisses the cold forehead.

'Anthony, Anthony! speak to me—it is Tina—speak to me! O God, he is dead!"

"She sinks down on her knees, takes the dear head in her arms, and kisses the cold forehead."—PAGE 158.

CHAPTER XIV.

"Yes, Maynard," said Sir Christopher, chatting with Mr. Gilfil in the library, "it really is a remarkable thing that I never in my life laid a plan, and failed to carry it out. I lay my plans well, and I never swerve from them—that's it. A strong will is the only magic. And next to striking out one's plans, the pleasantest thing in the world is to see them well accomplished. This year, now, will be the happiest of my life, all but the year '53, when I came into possession of the Manor, and married Henrietta. The last touch is given to the old house; Anthony's marriage—the thing I had nearest my heart—is settled to my entire satisfaction; and by-and-by you will be buying a little wedding-ring for Tina's finger. Don't shake your head in that forlorn way;—when I make prophecies they generally come to pass. But there's a quarter after twelve striking. I must be riding to the High Ash to meet Markham about felling some timber. My old oaks will have to groan for this wedding, but—"

The door burst open, and Caterina, ghastly and panting, her eyes distended with terror, rushed in, threw her arms round Sir Christopher's neck, and gasping out—"Anthony . . . the Rookery . . . dead . . . in the Rookery," fell fainting on the floor.

In a moment Sir Christopher was out of the room, and Mr. Gilfil was bending to raise Caterina in his arms. As he lifted her from the ground he felt something hard and heavy in her pocket. What could it be? The weight of it would be enough to hurt her as she lay. He carried her to the sofa, put his hand in her pocket, and drew forth the dagger.

Maynard shuddered. Did she mean to kill herself, then, or . . . or . . . a horrible suspicion forced itself upon him. "Dead—in the Rookery." He hated himself for the thought that prompted him to draw the dagger from its sheath. No! there was no trace of blood, and he was ready to kiss the good steel for its innocence. He thrust the weapon into his own pocket; he would restore it as soon as possible to its well-known place in the gallery. Yet, why had Caterina taken this dagger? What was it that had happened in the Rookery? Was it only a delirious vision of hers?

He was afraid to ring—afraid to summon any one to Caterina's assistance. What might she not say when she awoke from this fainting fit? She might be raving. He could not leave her, and yet he felt as if he were guilty for not following Sir Christopher to see what was the truth. It took but a moment to think and feel all this, but that moment seemed such a long agony to him that he began to reproach himself for letting it pass without seeking some means of reviving Caterina. Happily the decanter of water on Sir Christopher's table was untouched. He would at least try the effect of throwing that water over her. She might revive without his needing to call any one else.

Meanwhile Sir Christopher was hurrying at his utmost speed towards the Rookery; his face, so lately bright and confident, now agitated by a vague dread. The deep alarmed bark of Rupert, who ran by his side, had struck the ear of Mr. Bates, then on his way homeward, as something unwonted, and, hastening in the direction of the sound, he met the Baronet just as he was approaching the entrance of the Rookery. Sir Christopher's look was enough. Mr. Bates said nothing, but hurried along by his side, while Rupert dashed forward among the dead leaves with his nose to the ground. They had scarcely lost sight of him a minute when a change in the tone of his bark told them that he had found something, and in another instant he was leaping back over one of the large planted mounds. They turned aside to ascend the mound, Rupert leading them; the tumultuous cawing of the rooks, the very rustling of the leaves, as their feet plunged among them, falling like an evil omen on the Baronet's ear.

They had reached the summit of the mound, and had begun to descend. Sir Christopher saw something purple down on the path below among the yellow leaves. Rupert was already beside it, but Sir Christopher could not move faster. A tremor had taken hold of the firm limbs. Rupert came back and licked the trembling hand, as if to say "Courage!" and then was down again snuffing the body. Yes, it was a body—Anthony's body. There was the white hand with its diamond-ring clutching the dark leaves. His eyes were half open, but did not heed the gleam of sunlight that darted itself directly on them from between the boughs.

Still he might only have fainted; it might only be a fit. Sir Christopher knelt down, unfastened the cravat, unfastened the waistcoat, and laid his hand on the heart. It might be syncope; it might not—it could not be death. No! that thought must be kept far off.

"Go, Bates, get help; we'll carry him to your cottage. Send some one to the house to tell Mr. Gilfil and Warren.

Bid them send off for Doctor Hart, and break it to my lady and Miss Assher that Anthony is ill."

Mr. Bates hastened away, and the Baronet was left alone kneeling beside the body. The young and supple limbs, the rounded cheeks, the delicate ripe lips, the smooth white hands, were lying cold and rigid; and the aged face was bending over them in silent anguish; the aged deep-veined hands were seeking with tremulous inquiring touches for some symptom that life was not irrevocably gone.

Rupert was there too, waiting and watching; licking first the dead and then the living hands; then running off on Mr. Bates's track as if he would follow and hasten his return, but in a moment turning back again, unable to quit the scene of his master's sorrow.

CHAPTER XV.

It is a wonderful moment, the first time we stand by one who has fainted, and witness the fresh birth of consciousness spreading itself over the blank features, like the rising sunlight on the alpine summits that lay ghastly and dead under the leaden twilight. A slight shudder, and the frost-bound eyes recover their liquid light; for an instant they show the inward semi-consciousness of an infant's; then, with a little start, they open wider and begin to *look;* the present is visible, but only as a strange writing, and the interpreter Memory is not yet there.

Mr. Gilfil felt a trembling joy as this change passed over Caterina's face. He bent over her, rubbing her chill hands, and looking at her with tender pity as her dark eyes opened on him wonderingly. He thought there might be some wine in the dining-room close by. He left the room, and Caterina's eyes turned towards the window—towards Sir Christopher's chair. *There* was the link at which the chain of consciousness had snapped, and the events of the morning were beginning to recur dimly like a half-remembered dream, when Maynard returned with some wine. He raised her, and she drank it; but still she was silent, seeming lost in the attempt to recover the past, when the door opened, and Mr. Warren appeared with looks that announced terrible tidings. Mr. Gilfil, dreading lest he should tell them in Caterina's presence, hurried towards him with his finger on his lips, and drew him away into the dining-room on the opposite side of the passage.

Caterina, revived by the stimulant, was now recovering the full consciousness of the scene in the Rookery. Anthony was lying there dead; she had left him to tell Sir Christopher; she must go and see what they were doing with him; perhaps he was not really dead—only in a trance; people did fall into trances sometimes. While Mr. Gilfil was telling Warren how it would be best to break the news to Lady Cheverel and Miss Assher, anxious himself to return to Caterina, the poor child had made her way feebly to the great entrance-door, which stood open. Her strength increased as she moved and breathed the fresh air, and with every increase of strength came increased vividness of emotion, increased yearning to be where her thought was—in the Rookery with Anthony. She walked more and more swiftly, and at last, gathering the artificial strength of passionate excitement, began to run.

But now she heard the tread of heavy steps, and under the yellow shade near the wooden bridge she saw men slowly carrying something. Soon she was face to face with them. Anthony was no longer in the Rookery: they were carrying him stretched on a door, and there behind him was Sir Christopher, with the firmly-set mouth, the deathly paleness, and the concentrated expression of suffering in the eye, which mark the suppressed grief of the strong man. The sight of this face, on which Caterina had never before beheld the signs of anguish, caused a rush of new feeling which for the moment submerged all the rest. She went gently up to him, put her little hand in his, and walked in silence by his side. Sir Christopher could not tell her to leave him, and so she went on with that sad procession to Mr. Bates's cottage in the Mosslands, and sat there in silence, waiting and watching to know if Anthony were really dead.

She had not yet missed the dagger from her pocket; she had not yet even thought of it. At the sight of Anthony lying dead, her nature had rebounded from its new bias of resentment and hatred to the old sweet habit of love. The earliest and the longest has still the mastery over us; and the only past that linked itself with those glazed unconscious eyes, was the past when they beamed on her with tenderness. She forgot the interval of wrong and jealousy and hatred—all his cruelty, and all her thoughts of revenge—as the exile forgets the stormy passage that lay between home and happiness and the dreary land in which he finds himself desolate.

CHAPTER XVI.

Before night all hope was gone. Dr. Hart had said it was death; Anthony's body had been carried to the house, and every one there knew the calamity that had fallen on them.

Caterina had been questioned by Dr. Hart, and had answered briefly that she found Anthony lying in the Rookery. That she should have been walking there just at that time was not a coincidence to raise conjectures in any one besides Mr. Gilfil. Except in answering this question, she had not broken her silence. She sat mute in a corner of the gardener's kitchen, shaking her head when Maynard entreated her to return with him, and apparently unable to think of any thing but the possibility that Anthony might revive, until she saw them carrying away the body to the house. Then she followed by Sir Christopher's side again, so quietly, that even Dr. Hart did not object to her presence.

It was decided to lay the body in the library until after the coroner's inquest to-morrow; and when Caterina saw the door finally closed, she turned up the gallery stairs on her way to her own room, the place where she felt at home with her sorrows. It was the first time she had been in the gallery since that terrible moment in the morning, and now the spot and the objects around began to reawaken her half-stunned memory. The armor was no longer glittering in the sunlight, but there it hung dead and sombre above the cabinet from which she had taken the dagger. Yes! now it all came back to her—all the wretchedness and all the sin. But where was the dagger now? She felt in her pocket; it was not there. Could it have been her fancy—all that about the dagger? She looked in the cabinet; it was not there. Alas! no; it could not have been her fancy, and she *was* guilty of that wickedness. But where could the dagger be now? Could it have fallen out of her pocket? She heard steps ascending the stairs, and hurried on to her room, where, kneeling by the bed, and burying her face to shut out the hateful light, she tried to recall every feeling and incident of the morning.

It all came back; every thing Anthony had done, and every thing she had felt for the last month—for many months—ever since that June evening when he had last spoken to her in the gallery. She looked back on her storms of passion, her jealusy and hatred of Miss Assher, her thoughts of revenge on nthony. Oh how wicked she had been! It was she who ad been sinning; it was she who had driven him to do and ay those things that had made her so angry. And if he had ronged her, what had she been on the verge of doing to him? he was too wicked ever to be pardoned. She would like to onfess how wicked she had been, that they might punish her; he would like to humble herself to the dust before every one –before Miss Assher even. Sir Christopher would send her way—would never see her again, if he knew all; and she ould be happier to be punished and frowned on, than to be reated tenderly while she had that guilty secret in her breast. But then, if Sir Christopher were to know all, it would add to is sorrow, and make him more wretched than ever. No! he could not confess it—she should have to tell about Anhony. But she could not stay at the Manor; she must go way; she could not bear Sir Christopher's eye, could not bear he sight of all these things that reminded her of Anthony and f her sin. Perhaps she should die soon: she felt very feele; there could not be much life in her. She would go away nd live humbly, and pray to God to pardon her, and let her lie.

The poor child never thought of suicide. No sooner was the storm of anger passed than the tenderness and timidity of her nature returned, and she could do nothing but love and mourn. Her inexperience prevented her from imagining the consequences of her disappearance from the Manor; she foresaw none of the terrible details of alarm and distress and search that must ensue. "They will think I am dead," she said to herself, "and by-and-by they will forget me, and Maynard will get happy again, and love some one else."

She was roused from her absorption by a knock at the door. Mrs. Bellamy was there. She had come by Mr. Gilfil's request to see how Miss Sarti was, and to bring her some food and wine.

"You look sadly, my dear," said the old housekeeper, "an' you're all of a quake wi' cold. Get you to bed, now do. Martha shall come an' warm it, an' light your fire. See now, here's some nice arrowroot, wi' a drop o' wine in it. Take that, an' it'll warm you. I must go down again, for I can't awhile to stay. There's so many things to see to; an' Miss Assher's in hysterics constant, an' her maid's ill i' bed—a poor creachy thing—an' Mrs. Sharp's wanted every minute. But I'll send Martha up, an' do you get ready to go to bed, there's a dear child, an' take care o' yourself."

"Thank you, dear mammy," said Tina, kissing the little old

woman's wrinkled cheek; "I shall eat the arrowroot, and don't trouble about me any more to-night. I shall do very well when Martha has lighted my fire. Tell Mr. Gilfil I'm better. I shall go to bed by-and-by, so don't you come up again, because you may only disturb me."

"Well, well, take care o' yourself, there's a good child, an' God send you may sleep."

Caterina took the arrowroot quite eagerly, while Martha was lighting her fire. She wanted to get strength for her journey, and she kept the plate of biscuits by her that she might put some in her pocket. Her whole mind was now bent on going away from the Manor, and she was thinking of all the ways and means her little life's experience could suggest.

It was dusk now; she must wait till early dawn, for she was too timid to go away in the dark, but she must make her escape before any one was up in the house. There would be people watching Anthony in the library, but she could make her way out of a small door leading into the garden, against the drawing-room on the other side of the house.

She laid her cloak, bonnet, and veil ready; then she lighted a candle, opened her desk, and took out the broken portrait wrapped in paper. She folded it again in two little notes of Anthony's, written in pencil, and placed it in her bosom. There was the little china box, too—Dorcas's present, the pearl ear-rings, and a silk purse, with fifteen seven-shilling pieces in it, the presents Sir Christopher had made her on her birthday, ever since she had been at the Manor. Should she take the ear-rings and the seven-shilling pieces? She could not bear to part with them; it seemed as if they had some of Sir Christopher's love in them. She would like them to be buried with her. She fastened the little round ear-rings in her ears, and put the purse with Dorcas's box in her pocket. She had another purse there, and she took it out to count her money, for she would never spend her seven-shilling pieces. She had a guinea and eight shillings; that would be plenty.

So now she sat down to wait for the morning, afraid to lay herself on the bed lest she should sleep too long. If she could but see Anthony once more and kiss his cold forehead! But that could not be. She did not deserve it. She must go away from him, away from Sir Christopher, and Lady Cheverel, and Maynard, and every body who had been kind to her, and thought her good while she was so wicked.

CHAPTER XVII.

SOME of Mrs. Sharp's earliest thoughts, the next morning, were given to Caterina, whom she had not been able to visit the evening before, and whom, from a nearly equal mixture of affection and self-importance, she did not at all like resigning to Mrs. Bellamy's care. At half past eight o'clock she went up to Tina's room, bent on benevolent dictation as to doses and diet and lying in bed. But on opening the door she found the bed smooth and empty. Evidently it had not been slept in. What could this mean? Had she sat up all night, and was she gone out to walk? The poor thing's head might be touched by what had happened yesterday; it was such a shock—finding Captain Wybrow in that way; she was perhaps gone out of her mind. Mrs. Sharp looked anxiously in the place where Tina kept her hat and cloak; they were not there, so that she had had at least the presence of mind to put them on. Still the good woman felt greatly alarmed, and hastened away to tell Mr. Gilfil, who, she knew, was in his study.

"Mr. Gilfil," she said, as soon as she had closed the door behind her, "my mind misgives me dreadful about Miss Sarti."

"What is it?" said poor Maynard, with a horrible fear that Caterina had betrayed something about the dagger.

"She's not in her room, an' her bed's not been slept in this night, an' her hat an' cloak's gone."

For a minute or two Mr. Gilfil was unable to speak. He felt sure the worst had come: Caterina had destroyed herself. The strong man suddenly looked so ill and helpless that Mrs. Sharp began to be frightened at the effect of her abruptness.

"Oh, sir, I'm grieved to my heart to shock you so; but I didn't know who else to go to."

"No, no, you were quite right."

He gathered some strength from his very despair. It was all over, and he had nothing now to do but to suffer and to help the suffering. He went on in a firmer voice:

"Be sure not to breathe a word about it to any one. We must not alarm Lady Cheverel and Sir Christopher. Miss Sarti may be only walking in the garden. She was terribly excited by what she saw yesterday, and perhaps was unable to lie down from restlessness. Just go quietly through the empty rooms, and see whether she is in the house. I will go and look for her in the grounds."

He went down, and, to avoid giving any alarm in the house, walked at once towards the Mosslands in search of Mr. Bates whom he met returning from his breakfast. To the gardener he confided his fear about Caterina, assigning as a reason for this fear the probability that the shock she had undergone yesterday had unhinged her mind, and begging him to send men in search of her through the gardens and park, and inquire if she had been seen at the lodges; and if she were not found or heard of in this way, to lose no time in dragging the waters round the Manor.

"God forbid it should be so, Bates, but we shall be the easier for having searched everywhere."

"Troost to mae, troost to mae, Mr. Gilfil. Eh! but I'd ha' worked for day-wage all the rest o' my life, rether than any thin' should ha' happened to her."

The good gardener, in deep distress, strode away to the stables that he might send the grooms on horseback through the park.

Mr. Gilfil's next thought was to search the Rookery; she might be haunting the scene of Captain Wybrow's death. He went hastily over every mound, looked round every large tree, and followed every winding of the walks. In reality he had little hope of finding her there; but the bare possibility fenced off for a time the fatal conviction that Caterina's body would be found in the water. When the Rookery had been searched in vain, he walked fast to the border of the little stream that bounded one side of the grounds. The stream was almost everywhere hidden among trees, and there was one place where it was broader and deeper than elsewhere—she would be more likely to come to that spot than to the pool. He hurried along with strained eyes, his imagination continually creating what he dreaded to see.

There is something white behind that overhanging bough. His knees tremble under him. He seems to see part of her dress caught on a branch, and her dear dead face upturned. O God, give strength to thy creature, on whom thou hast laid this great agony! He is nearly up to the bough, and the white object is moving. It is a waterfowl, that spreads its wings and flies away screaming. He hardly knows whether it is a relief or a disappointment that she is not there. The conviction that she is dead presses its cold weight upon him none the less heavily.

As he reached the great pool in front of the Manor, he saw

Mr. Bates, with a group of men already there, preparing for the dreadful search which could only displace his vague despair by a definite horror; for the gardener, in his restless anxiety, had been unable to defer this until other means of search had proved vain. The pool was not now laughing with sparkles among the water-lilies. It looked black and cruel under the sombre sky, as if its cold depths held relentlessly all the murdered hope and joy of Maynard Gilfil's life.

Thoughts of the sad consequences for others as well as himself were crowding on his mind. The blinds and shutters were all closed in front of the Manor, and it was not likely that Sir Christopher would be aware of any thing that was passing outside; but Mr. Gilfil felt that Caterina's disappearance could not long be concealed from him. The coroner's inquest would be held shortly; she would be inquired for, and then it would be inevitable that the Baronet should know all.

CHAPTER XVIII.

At twelve o'clock, when all search and inquiry had been in vain, and the coroner was expected every moment, Mr. Gilfil could no longer defer the hard duty of revealing this fresh calamity to Sir Christopher, who must otherwise have it discovered to him abruptly.

The Baronet was seated in his dressing-room, where the dark window-curtains where drawn so as to admit only a sombre light. It was the first time Mr. Gilfil had had an interview with him this morning, and he was struck to see how a single day and night of grief had aged the fine old man. The lines in his brow and about his mouth were deepened; his complexion looked dull and withered; there was a swollen ridge under his eyes; and the eyes themselves, which used to cast so keen a glance on the present, had the vacant expression which tells that vision is no longer a sense, but a memory.

He held out his hand to Maynard, who pressed it, and sat down beside him in silence. Sir Christopher's heart began to swell at this unspoken sympathy; the tears *would* rise, *would* roll in great drops down his cheeks. The first tears he had shed since boyhood were for Anthony.

Maynard felt as if his tongue were glued to the roof of his mouth. He could not speak first: he must wait until

Sir Christopher said something which might lead on to the cruel words that must be spoken.

At last the Baronet mastered himself enough to say, "I'm very weak, Maynard—God help me! I didn't think any thing would unman me in this way; but I'd built every thing on that lad. Perhaps I've been wrong in not forgiving my sister. She lost one of *her* sons a little while ago. I've been too proud and obstinate."

"We can hardly learn humility and tenderness enough except by suffering," said Maynard; "and God sees we are in need of suffering, for it is falling more and more heavily on us. We have a new trouble this morning."

"Tina?" said Sir Christopher, looking up anxiously—"is Tina ill?"

"I am in dreadful uncertainty about her. She was very much agitated yesterday—and with her delicate health—I am afraid to think what turn the agitation may have taken."

"Is she delirious, poor dear little one!"

"God only knows how she is. We are unable to find her. When Mrs. Sharp went up to her room this morning it was empty. She had not been in bed. Her hat and cloak were gone. I have had search made for her everywhere—in the house and garden, in the park, and—in the water. No one has seen her since Martha went up to light her fire at seven o'clock in the evening."

While Mr. Gilfil was speaking, Sir Christopher's eyes, which were eagerly turned on him, recovered some of their old keenness, and some sudden painful emotion, as at a new thought, flitted rapidly across his already agitated face, like the shadow of a dark cloud over the waves. When the pause came, he laid his hand on Mr. Gilfil's arm, and said in a lower voice.

"Maynard, did that poor thing love Anthony?"

"She did."

Maynard hesitated after these words, struggling between his reluctance to inflict a yet deeper wound on Sir Christopher, and his determination that no injustice should be done to Caterina. Sir Christopher's eyes were still fixed on him in solemn inquiry, and his own sunk towards the ground, while he tried to find the words that would tell the truth least cruelly.

"You must not have any wrong thoughts about Tina," he said, at length. "I must tell you now, for her sake, what nothing but this should ever have caused to pass my lips. Captain Wybrow won her affections by attentions which, in his position, he was bound not to show her. Before his marriage was talked of, he had behaved to her like a lover."

Sir Christopher relaxed his hold of Maynard's arm, and looked away from him. He was silent for some minutes, evdently attempting to master himself, so as to be able to speak calmly.

"I must see Henrietta immediately," he said at last, with something of his old sharp decision; "she must know all; but we must keep it from every one else as far as possible. My dear boy," he continued in a kinder tone, "the heaviest burthen has fallen on you. But we may find her yet; we must not despair: there has not been time enough for us to be certain. Poor dear little one! God help me! I thought I saw every thing, and was stone-blind all the while."

CHAPTER XIX.

THE sad slow week was gone by at last. At the coroner's inquest a verdict of sudden death had been pronounced. Dr. Hart, acquainted with Captain Wybrow's previous state of health, had given his opinion that death had been imminent from long-established disease of the heart, though it had probably been accelerated by some unusual emotion. Miss Assher was the only person who positively knew the motive that led Captain Wybrow to the Rookery; but she had not mentioned Caterina's name, and all painful details or inquiries were studiously kept from her. Mr. Gilfil and Sir Christopher, however, knew enough to conjecture that the fatal agitation was due to an appointed meeting with Caterina.

All search and inquiry after her had been fruitless, and were the more likely to be so because they were carried on under the prepossession that she had committed suicide. No one noticed the absence of the trifles she had taken from her desk; no one knew of the likeness, or that she had hoarded her seven-shilling pieces, and it was not remarkable that she should have happened to be wearing the pearl earrings. She had left the house, they thought, taking nothing with her; it seemed impossible she could have gone far; and she must have been in a state of mental excitement that made it too probable she had only gone to seek relief in death. The same places within three or four miles of the Manor were searched again and again—every pond, every ditch in the neighborhood was examined.

Sometimes Maynard thought that death might have come on unsought, from cold and exhaustion; and not a day passed but he wandered through the neighboring woods, turning up the heaps of dead leaves, as if it were possible her dear body could be hidden there. Then another horrible thought recurred, and before each night came he had been again through all the uninhabited rooms of the house, to satisfy himself once more that she was not hidden behind some cabinet, or door, or curtain—that he should not find her there with madness in her eyes, looking and looking, and yet not seeing him.

But at last those five long days and nights were at an end, the funeral was over, and the carriages were returning through the park. When they had set out, a heavy rain was falling; but now the clouds were breaking up, and a gleam of sunshine was sparkling among the dripping boughs under which they were passing. This gleam fell upon a man on horseback who was jogging slowly along, and whom Mr. Gilfil recognized, in spite of diminished rotundity, as Daniel Knott, the coachman who had married the rosy-cheeked Dorcas ten years before.

Every new incident suggested the same thought to Mr. Gilfil; and his eye no sooner fell on Knott than he said to himself, "Can he be come to tell us any thing about Caterina?" Then he remembered that Caterina had been very fond of Dorcas, and that she always had some present ready to send her when Knott paid an occasional visit to the Manor. Could Tina have gone to Dorcas? But his heart sank again as he thought, very likely Knott had only come because he had heard of Captain Wybrow's death, and wanted to know how his old master had borne the blow.

As soon as the carriage reached the house, he went up to his study and walked about nervously, longing, but afraid, to go down and speak to Knott, lest his faint hope should be dissipated. Any one looking at that face, usually so full of calm good-will, would have seen that the last week's suffering had left deep traces. By day he had been riding or wandering incessantly, either searching for Caterina himself, or directing inquiries to be made by others. By night he had not known sleep—only intermittent dozing, in which he seemed to be finding Caterina dead, and woke up with a start from this unreal agony to the real anguish of believing that he should see her no more. The clear gray eyes looked sunken and restless, the full careless lips had a strange tension about them, and the brow, formerly so smooth and open, was contracted as if with pain. He had not lost the object of a few months' passion; he had lost the being who was bound up with his power of loving, as the brook we played by or the flowers we gathered in childhood are bound up with our sense of beauty. Love meant nothing for him but to love Caterina. For years, the thought of her had been present in every thing, like the air and the light; and now she was gone, it seemed as if all pleasure had lost its vehicle: the sky, the earth, the daily ride, the daily talk might be there, but the loveliness and joy that were in them had gone forever.

Presently, as he still paced backward and forward, he heard steps along the corridor, and there was a knock at his door. His voice trembled as he said "Come in," and the rush of renewed hope was hardly distinguishable from pain when he saw Warren enter with Daniel Knott behind him.

"Knott is come, sir, with news of Miss Sarti. I thought it best to bring him to you first."

Mr. Gilfil could not help going up to the old coachman and wringing his hand; but he was unable to speak, and only motioned to him to take a chair, while Warren left the room. He hung upon Daniel's moon-face, and listened to his small piping voice, with the same solemn yearning expectation with which he would have given ear to the most awful messenger from the land of shades.

"It war Dorkis, sir, would hev me come; but we knowed nothin' o' what's happened at the Manor. She's frightened out on her wits about Miss Sarti, an' she would hev me saddle Blackbird this mornin,' an' leave the ploughin', to come an' let Sir Christifer an' my lady know. P'raps you've heared, sir, we don't keep the Cross Keys at Sloppeter now; a uncle o' mine died three 'ear ago, an' left me a leggicy. He was bailiff to Squire Ramble, as hed them there big farms on his hans; an' so we took a little farm o' forty acres or thereabouts, becos Dorkis didn't like the public when she got moithered wi' children. As pritty a place as iver you see, sir, wi' water at the back convenent for the cattle."

"For God's sake," said Maynard, "tell me what it is about Miss Sarti. Don't stay to tell me any thing else now."

"Well, sir," said Knott, rather frightened by the parson's vehemence, "she come t'our house i' the carrier's cart o' Wednesday, when it was welly nine o'clock at night; and Dorkis run out, for she heared the cart stop, an' Miss Sarti throwed her arms roun' Dorkis's neck an' says, 'Tek me in, Dorkis, tek me in,' an' went off into a swoond, like. An' Dorkis calls out to me,—'Dannel,' she calls—an' I run out and carried the young miss in, an' she come roun' arter a bit, an' opened her eyes, and Dorkis got her to drink a spoon ful o' rum-an'-water—we've got some capital rum as we brought from the Cross Keys, and Dorkis won't let nobody drink it. She says she keeps it for sickness; but for my part, I think it's a pity to drink good rum when your mouth's out o' taste; you may jest as well hev doctor's stuff. However, Dorkis got her to bed, an' there she's lay iver sin', stoopid like, an' niver speaks, an' on'y teks little bits an' sups when Dorkis coaxes her. An' we begun to be frightened, an' couldn't think what had made her come away from the Manor, and Dorkis was afeared there was summat wrong. So this mornin' she could hold no longer, an' would hev no nay but I must come and see; an' so I've rode twenty mile upo' Blackbird, as thinks all the while he's a-ploughin', an' turns sharp roun', every thirty yards, as if he was at the end of a furrow. I've hed a sore time wi' him, I can tell you, sir."

"God bless you, Knott, for coming!" said Mr. Gilfil, wringing the old coachman's hand again. "Now go down and have something and rest yourself. You will stay here to-night, and by-and-by I shall come to you to learn the nearest way to your house. I shall get ready to ride there immediately, when I have spoken to Sir Christopher."

In an hour from that time Mr. Gilfil was galloping on a stout mare towards the little muddy village of Callam, five miles beyond Sloppeter. Once more he saw some gladness in the afternoon sunlight; once more it was a pleasure to see the hedgerow trees flying past him, and to be conscious of a "good seat" while his black Kitty bounded beneath him, and the air whistled to the rhythm of her pace. Caterina was not dead; he had found her; his love and tenderness and long-suffering seemed so strong, they must recall her to life and happiness. After that week of despair, the rebound was so violent that it carried his hopes at once as far as the utmost mark they had ever reached. Caterina would come to love him at last; she would be his. They had been carried through all that dark and weary way that she might know the depth of his love. How he would cherish her—his little bird with the timid bright eye, and the sweet throat that trembled with love and music! She would nestle against him, and the poor little breast which had been so ruffled and bruised should be safe for evermore. In the love of a brave and faithful man there is always a strain of maternal tenderness; he gives out again those beams of protecting fondness which were shed on him as he lay on his mother's knee.

It was twilight as he entered the village of Callam, and, asking a homeward-bound laborer the way to Daniel Knott's, learned that it was by the church, which showed its stumpy ivy-clad spire on a slight elevation of ground; a useful addition to the means of identifying that desirable homestead afforded by Daniel's description—"the prittiest place iver you see"—though a small cow-yard full of excellent manure, and leading right up to the door, without any frivolous interruption from garden or railing, might perhaps have been enough to make that description unmistakably specific.

Mr. Gilfil had no sooner reached the gate leading into the cow-yard, than he was descried by a flaxen-haired lad of nine, prematurely invested with the *toga virilis*, or smock-frock, who ran forward to let in the unusual visitor. In a moment Dorcas was at the door, the roses on her cheeks apparently all the redder for the three pair of cheeks which formed a group round her, and for the very fat baby who stared in her arms, and sucked a long crust with calm relish.

"Is it Mr. Gilfil, sir?" said Dorcas, courtesying low as he made his way through the damp straw, after tying up his horse.

"Yes, Dorcas; I'm grown out of your knowledge. How is Miss Sarti?"

"Just for all the world the same, sir, as I suppose Dannel's told you; for I reckon you've come from the Manor, though you're come uncommon quick, to be sure."

"Yes, he got to the Manor about one o'clock, and I set off as soon as I could. She's not worse, is she?"

"No change, sir, for better or wuss. Will you please to walk in, sir? She lies there takin' no notice o' nothin', no more nor a baby as is on'y a week old, an' looks at me as blank as if she didn't know me. Oh, what can it be, Mr. Gilfil? How come she to leave the Manor? How's his honor an' my lady?"

"In great trouble, Dorcas. Captain Wybrow, Sir Christopher's nephew, you know, has died suddenly. Miss Sarti found him lying dead, and I think the shock has affected her mind."

"Eh, dear! that fine young gentleman as was to be th' heir, as Dannel told me about. I remember seein' him when he was a little un, a-visitin' at the Manor. Well-a-day, what a grief to his honor and my lady. But that poor Miss Tina—an' she found him a-lyin' dead? Oh dear, oh dear!"

Dorcas had led the way into the best kitchen, as charming a room as best kitchens used to be in farmhouses which had no parlors—the fire reflected in a bright row of pewter plates and dishes; the sand-scoured deal tables so clean you longed to stroke them; the salt-coffer in one chimney-corner, and a three-cornered chair in the other, the walls behind handsomely tapestried with flitches of bacon, and the ceiling ornamented with pendent hams.

"Sit ye down, sir—do," said Dorcas, moving the three-cornered chair, "an' let me get you somethin' after your long journey. Here, Becky, come an' tek the baby."

Becky, a red-armed damsel, emerged from the adjoining back-kitchen, and possessed herself of baby, whose feelings or fat made him conveniently apathetic under the transference.

"What'll you please to tek, sir, as I can give you? I'll get you a rasher o' bacon i' no time, an' I've got some tea, or belike you'd tek a glass o' rum-an'-water. I know we've got nothin' as you're used t'eat and drink; but such as I hev, sir, I shall be proud to give you."

"Thank you, Dorcas; I can't eat or drink any thing. I'm not hungry or tired. Let us talk about Tina. Has she spoken at all?"

"Niver since the fust words. 'Dear Dorkis,' says she, 'tek me in;' an' then went off into a faint, an' not a word has she spoken since. I get her t'eat little bits an' sups o' things, but she teks no notice o' nothin'. I've took up Bessie wi' me now an' then"—here Dorcas lifted to her lap a curly-headed little girl of three, who was twisting a corner of her mother's apron, and opening round eyes at the gentleman—"folks'll tek notice o' children sometimes when they won't o' nothin' else. An' we gathered the autumn crocuses out o' th'orchard, and Bessie carried 'em up in her hand, an' put 'em on the bed. I knowed how fond Miss Tina was o' flowers an' them things, when she was a little un. But she looked at Bessie an' the flowers just the same as if she didn't see 'em. It cuts me to th'heart to look at them eyes o' hers; I think they're bigger nor iver, an' they look like my poor baby's as died, when it got so thin—Oh dear, its little hands you could see thro' 'em. But I've great hopes if she was to see you, sir, as come from the Manor, it might bring back her mind, like."

Maynard had that hope too, but he felt cold mists of fear gathering round him after the few bright warm hours of joyful confidence which had passed since he first heard that Caterina was alive. The thought *would* urge itself upon him that her mind and body might never recover the strain that had been put upon them—that her delicate thread of life had already nearly spun itself out.

"Go now, Dorcas, and see how she is, but don't say any thing about my being here. Perhaps it would be better for me to wait till daylight before I see her, and yet it would be very hard to pass another night in this way."

Dorcas set down little Bessie, and went away. The three other children, including young Daniel in his smock-frock, were standing opposite to Mr. Gilfil, watching him still more shyly now they were without their mother's countenance. He drew little Bessie towards him, and set her on his knee. She shook her yellow curls out of her eyes, and looked up at him as she said,

"Zoo tome to tee ze yady? Zoo mek her peak? What zoo do to her? Tiss her?"

"Do you like to be kissed, Bessie?"

"Det," said Bessie, immediately ducking down her head very low, in resistance to the expected rejoinder.

"We've got two pups," said young Daniel, emboldened by observing the gentleman's amenities towards Bessie. "Shall I show 'em yer? One's got white spots."

"Yes, let me see them."

Daniel ran out, and presently reappeared with two blind puppies, eagerly followed by the mother, affectionate though mongrel, and an exciting scene was beginning when Dorcas returned and said,

"There's niver any difference in her hardly. I think you needn't wait, sir. She lies very still, as she al'ys does. I've put two candles i' the room, so as she may see you well. You'll please t' excuse the room, sir, an' the cap as she has on; it's one o' mine."

Mr. Gilfil nodded silently, and rose to follow her up stairs. They turned in at the first door, their footsteps making little noise on the plaster floor. The red-checkered linen curtains were drawn at the head of the bed, and Dorcas had placed the candles on this side of the room, so that the light might not fall oppressively on Caterina's eyes. When she had opened the door, Dorcas whispered, "I'd better leave you, sir, I think?"

Mr. Gilfil motioned assent, and advanced beyond the curtain. Caterina lay with her eyes turned the other way, and seemed unconscious that any one had entered. Her eyes, as Dorcas had said, looked larger than ever, perhaps because her face was thinner and paler, and her hair quite gathered away under one of Dorcas's thick caps. The small hands, too, that lay listlessly on the outside of the bed-clothes were thinner than ever. She looked younger than she really was, and any one seeing the tiny face and hands for the first time might have thought they belonged to a little girl of twelve, who was being taken away from coming instead of past sorrow.

When Mr. Gilfil advanced and stood opposite to her, the light fell full upon his face. A slight startled expression came over Caterina's eyes; she looked at him earnestly for a few moments, then lifted up her hand as if to beckon him to stoop down towards her, and whispered, "Maynard!"

He seated himself on the bed, and stooped down towards her. She whispered again—

"Maynard, did you see the dagger?"

He followed his first impulse in answering her, and it was a wise one.

"Yes," he whispered, "I found it in your pocket, and put it back again in the cabinet."

He took her hand in his and held it gently, awaiting what she would say next. His heart swelled so with thankfulness that she had recognized him, he could hardly repress a sob. Gradually her eyes became softer and less intense in their gaze. The tears were slowly gathering, and presently some large hot drops rolled down her cheek. Then the flood-gates were opened, and the heart-easing stream gushed forth; deep sobs came; and for nearly an hour she lay without speaking, while the heavy icy pressure that withheld her misery from utterance was thus melting away. How precious these tears were to Maynard, who day after day had been shuddering at the continually recurring image of Tina with the dry, scorching stare of insanity!

By degrees the sobs subsided, she began to breathe calmly, and lay quiet with her eyes shut. Patiently Maynard sat, not heeding the flight of the hours, not heeding the old clock that ticked loudly on the landing. But when it was nearly ten, Dorcas, impatiently anxious to know the result of Mr. Gilfil's appearance, could not help stepping in on tiptoe. Without moving, he whispered in her ear to supply him with candles, see that the cow-boy had shaken down his mare, and go to bed—he would watch with Caterina—a great change had come over her.

Before long, Tina's lips began to move. "Maynard," she whispered again. He leaned towards her, and she went on.

"You know how wicked I am, then? You know what I meant to do with the dagger?"

"Did you mean to kill yourself, Tina?"

She shook her head slowly, and then was silent for a long while. At last, looking at him with solemn eyes, she whispered, "To kill *him*."

"Tina, my loved one, you would never have done it. God saw your whole heart; He knows you would never harm a living thing. He watches over His children, and will not let them do things they would pray with their whole hearts not to do. It was the angry thought of a moment, and He forgives you."

She sank into silence again till it was nearly midnight. The weary enfeebled spirit seemed to be making its slow way with difficulty through the windings of thought; and when she began to whisper again, it was in reply to Maynard's words.

"But I had had such wicked feelings for a long while. I was so angry, and I hated Miss Assher so, and I didn't care what came to any body, because I was so miserable myself. I was full of bad passions. No one else was ever so wicked."

"Yes, Tina, many are just as wicked. I often have very wicked feelings, and am tempted to do wrong things; but then my body is stronger than yours, and I can hide my feelings and resist them better. They do not master me so. You have seen the little birds when they are very young and just begin to fly, how all their feathers are ruffled when they are frightened or angry; they have no power over themselves left, and might fall into a pit from mere fright. You were like one of those little birds. Your sorrow and suffering had taken such hold of you, you hardly knew what you did."

He would not speak long, lest he should tire her, and oppress her with too many thoughts. Long pauses seemed needful for her before she could concentrate her feelings in short words.

"But when I meant to do it," was the next thing she whispered, "it was as bad as if I had done it."

"No, my Tina," answered Maynard slowly, waiting a little between each sentence; "we mean to do wicked things that we never could do, just as we mean to do good or clever things that we never could do. Our thoughts are often worse than we are, just as they are often better than we are. And God sees us as we are altogether, not in separate feelings or actions, as our fellow-men see us. We are always doing each other injustice, and thinking better or worse of each other than we deserve, because we only hear and see separate words and actions. We don't see each other's whole nature. But God sees that you could not have committed that crime."

Caterina shook her head slowly, and was silent. After a while,

"I don't know," she said; "I seemed to see him coming towards me, just as he would really have looked, and I meant —I meant to do it."

"But when you saw him—tell me how it was, Tina?"

"I saw him lying on the ground and thought he was ill. I don't know how it was then; I forgot every thing. I knelt down and spoke to him, and—and he took no notice of me, and his eyes were fixed, and I began to think he was dead."

"And you have never felt angry since?"

"Oh no, no; it is I who have been more wicked than any one; it is I who have been wrong all through."

"No, Tina; the fault has not all been yours; *he* was wrong; he gave you provocation. And wrong makes wrong. When people use us ill, we can hardly help having ill feeling towards them. But that second wrong is more excusable. I am more sinful than you, Tina; I have often had very bad feelings towards Captain Wybrow; and if he had provoked me as he did you, I should perhaps have done something more wicked."

"Oh, it was not so wrong in him; he didn't know how he hurt me. How was it likely he could love me as I loved him? And how could he marry a poor little thing like me?"

Maynard made no reply to this, and there was again silence, till Tina said,

"Then I was so deceitful; they didn't know how wicked I was. Padroncello didn't know; his good little monkey he used to call me; and if he had known, oh how naughty he would have thought me!"

"My Tina, we have all our secret sins; and if we knew ourselves, we should not judge each other harshly. Sir Christopher himself has felt, since this trouble came upon him, that he has been too severe and obstinate."

In this way—in these broken confessions and answering words of comfort—the hours wore on, from the deep black night to the chill early twilight, and from early twilight to the first yellow streak of morning parting the purple cloud. Mr. Gilfil felt as if in the long hours of that night the bond that united his love forever and alone to Caterina had acquired fresh strength and sanctity. It is so with the human relations that rest on the deep emotional sympathy of affection; every new day and night of joy or sorrow is a new ground, a new consecration for the love that is nourished by memories as well as hopes—the love to which perpetual repetition is not a weariness but a want, and to which a separated joy is the beginning of pain.

The cocks began to crow; the gate swung; there was a tramp of footsteps in the yard, and Mr. Gilfil heard Dorcas stirring. These sounds seemed to affect Caterina, for she looked anxiously at him and said, "Maynard, are you going away?"

"No, I shall stay here at Callam until you are better, and then you will go away too."

"Never to the Manor again, oh no! I shall live poorly, and get my own bread."

"Well, dearest, you shall do what you would like best.

But I wish you could go to sleep now. Try to rest quietly, and by-and-by you will perhaps sit up a little. God has kept you in life in spite of all this sorrow; it will be sinful not to try and make the best of His gift. Dear Tina, you *will* try;—and little Bessie brought you some crocuses once, you didn't notice the poor little thing; but you will notice her when she comes again, will you not?"

"I will try," whispered Tina humbly, and then closed her eyes.

By the time the sun was above the horizon, scattering the clouds, and shining with pleasant morning warmth through the little leaded window, Caterina was asleep. Maynard gently loosed the tiny hand, cheered Dorcas with the good news, and made his way to the village inn, with a thankful heart that Tina had been so far herself again. Evidently the sight of him had blended naturally with the memories in which her mind was absorbed, and she had been led on to an unburthening of herself that might be the beginning of a complete restoration. But her body was so enfeebled—her soul so bruised—that the utmost tenderness and care would be necessary. The next thing to be done was to send tidings to Sir Christopher and Lady Cheverel; then to write and summon his sister, under whose care he had determined to place Caterina. The Manor, even if she had been wishing to return thither, would, he knew, be the most undesirable home for her at present; every scene, every object there, was associated with still unallayed anguish. If she were domesticated for a time with his mild, gentle sister, who had a peaceful home and a prattling little boy, Tina might attach herself anew to life, and recover, partly at least, the shock that had been given to her constitution. When he had written his letters and taken a hasty breakfast, he was soon in his saddle again, on his way to Sloppeter, where he would post them, and seek out a medical man, to whom he might confide the moral causes of Caterina's enfeebled condition.

CHAPTER XX.

In less than a week from that time, Caterina was persuaded to travel in a comfortable carriage, under the care of Mr. Gilfil and his sister, Mrs. Heron, whose soft blue eyes and mild manners were very soothing to the poor bruised child—the more so as they had an air of sisterly equality which was quite new to her. Under Lady Cheverel's uncaressing authoritative good-will, Tina had always retained a certain constraint and awe; and there was a sweetness before unknown in having a young and gentle woman, like an elder sister, bending over her caressingly, and speaking in low, loving tones.

Maynard was almost angry with himself for feeling happy while Tina's mind and body were still trembling on the verge of irrecoverable decline; but the new delight of acting as her guardian angel, of being with her every hour of the day, of devising every thing for her comfort, of watching for a ray of returning interest in her eyes, was too absorbing to leave room for alarm or regret.

On the third day the carriage drove up to the door of Foxholm Parsonage, where the Rev. Arthur Heron presented himself on the door-step, eager to greet his returning Lucy, and holding by the hand a broad-chested, tawny-haired boy of five, who was smacking a miniature hunting-whip with great vigor.

Nowhere was there a lawn more smooth-shaven, walks better swept, or a porch more prettily festooned with creepers, than at Foxholm Parsonage, standing snugly sheltered by beeches and chestnuts half-way down the pretty green hill which was surmounted by the church, and overlooking a village that straggled at its ease among pastures and meadows, surrounded by wild hedgerows and broad shadowing trees, as yet unthreatened by improved methods of farming.

Brightly the fire shone in the great parlor, and brightly in the little pink bed-room, which was to be Caterina's, because it looked away from the churchyard, and on to a farm homestead, with its little cluster of beehive ricks, and placid groups of cows, and cheerful matin sounds of healthy labor. Mrs. Heron, with the instinct of a delicate, impressible woman, had written to her husband to have this room prepared for Caterina. Contented speckled hens, industriously scratching for the rarely-found corn, may sometimes do more for a sick heart than a grove of nightingales; there is something irresistibly calming in the unsentimental cheeriness of top-knotted pullets, unpetted sheep-dogs, and patient cart-horses enjoying a drink of muddy water.

In such a home as this parsonage, a nest of comfort, without any of the stateliness that would carry a suggestion of Cheverel Manor, Mr. Gilfil was not unreasonable in hoping that Caterina might gradually shake off the haunting vision of the past, and recover from the languor and feebleness which were the physical sign of that vision's blighting presence. The next thing to bed one was to arrange an exchange of duties with Mr. Heron's curate, that Maynard might be constantly near Caterina, and watch over her progress. She seemed to like him to be with her, to look uneasily for his return; and though she seldom spoke to him, she was most contented when he sat by her, and held her tiny hand in his large protecting grasp. But Oswald, *alias* Ozzy, the broad-chested boy, was perhaps her most beneficial companion. With something of his uncle's person, he had inherited also his uncle's early taste for a domestic menagerie, and was very imperative in demanding Tina's sympathy in the welfare of his guinea-pigs, squirrels, and dormice. With him she seemed now and then to have gleams of her childhood coming athwart the leaden clouds, and many hours of winter went by the more easily for being spent in Ozzy's nursery.

Mrs. Heron was not musical, and had no instrument; but one of Mr. Gilfil's cares was to procure a harpsichord, and have it placed in the drawing-room, always open, in the hope that some day the spirit of music would be reawakened in Caterina, and she would be attracted towards the instrument. But the winter was almost gone by, and he had waited in vain. The utmost improvement in Tina had not gone beyond passiveness and acquiescence—a quiet grateful smile, compliance with Oswald's whims, and increasing consciousness of what was being said and done around her. Sometimes she would take up a bit of woman's work, but she seemed too languid to persevere in it; her fingers soon dropped, and she relapsed into motionless reverie.

At last—it was one of those bright days in the end of February, when the sun is shining with a promise of approaching spring. Maynard had been walking with her and Oswald round the garden to look at the snowdrops, and she was resting on the sofa after the walk. Ozzy, roaming about the room in quest of a forbidden pleasure, came to the harpsichord, and struck the handle of his whip on a deep bass note.

The vibration rushed through Caterina like an electric shock: it seemed as if at that instant a new soul were entering into her, and filling her with a deeper, more significant life. She looked round, rose from the sofa, and walked to the harpsichord. In a moment her fingers were wandering with their old sweet method among the keys, and her soul was floating in its true familiar element of delicious sound, as the water-plant that lies withered and shrunken on the ground expands into freedom and beauty when once more bathed in its native flood.

Maynard thanked God. An active power was reawakened, and must make a new epoch in Caterina's recovery.

Presently there were low liquid notes blending themselves with the harder tones of the instrument, and gradually the pure voice swelled into predominance. Little Ozzy stood in the middle of the room, with his mouth open and his legs very wide apart, struck with something like awe at this new power in "Tin-Tin," as he called her, whom he had been accustomed to think of as a playfellow not at all clever, and very much in need of his instruction on many subjects. A genie soaring with broad wings out of his milk-jug would not have been more astonishing.

Caterina was singing the very air from the *Orfeo* which we heard her singing so many months ago at the beginning of her sorrows. It was *Che farò*, Sir Christopher's favorite, and its notes seemed to carry on their wings all the tenderest memories of her life, when Cheverel Manor was still an untroubled home. The long happy days of childhood and girlhood recovered all their rightful predominance over the short interval of sin and sorrow.

She paused, and burst into tears—the first tears she had shed since she had been at Foxholm. Maynard could not help hurrying towards her, putting his arm round her, and leaning down to kiss her hair. She nestled to him, and put up her little mouth to be kissed.

The delicate-tendrilled plant must have something to cling to. The soul that was born anew to music was born anew to love.

CHAPTER XXI.

On the 30th of May, 1790, a very pretty sight was seen by the villagers assembled near the door of Foxholm Church. The sun was bright upon the dewy grass, the air was alive with the murmur of bees and the thrilling of birds, the bushy blossoming chestnuts and the foamy flowering hedgerows seemed to be crowding round to learn why the church-bells were ringing so merrily, as Maynard Gilfil, his face bright with happiness, walked out of the old Gothic doorway with Tina on his arm. The little face was still pale, and there was a subdued melancholy in it, as of one who sups with friends for the last time, and has his ear open for the signal that will call him away. But the tiny hand rested with the pressure of contented affection on Maynard's arm, and the dark eyes met his downward glance with timid answering love.

There was no train of bridesmaids; only pretty Mrs. Heron leaning on the arm of a dark-haired young man hitherto unknown in Foxholm, and holding by the other hand little Ozzy, who exulted less in his new velvet cap and tunic, than in the notion that he was bridesman to Tin-Tin.

Last of all came a couple whom the villagers eyed yet more eagerly than the bride and bridegroom: a fine old gentleman, who looked round with keen glances that cowed the conscious scapegraces among them, and a stately lady in blue-and-white silk robes, who must surely be like Queen Charlotte.

"Well, that theer's whut I call a pictur," said old "Mester" Ford, a true Staffordshire patriarch, who leaned on a stick and held his head very much on one side, with the air of a man who had little hope of the present generation, but would at all events give it the benefit of his criticism. "Th' yoong men noo-a-deys, the're poor squashy things—the' looke well anoof, but the' woon't wear, the' woon't wear. Theer's ne'er un 'll carry his 'ears like that Sir Cris'fer Chuvrell."

"'Ull bet ye two pots," said another of the seniors, "as that yoongster a-walkin' wi' th' parson's wife 'll be Sir Cris'fer's son—he favors him."

"Nay, yae'll bet that wi' as big a fule as yersen; hae's noo son at all. As I oonderstan', hae's the nevey as is t'heir th' esteate. The coochman as puts oop at th' White Hoss tellt me as theer war another nevey, a deal finer chap t' looke at nor this un, as died in a fit, all on a soodden, an' soo this here yoong un's got upo' th' perch istid."

At the church gate Mr. Bates was standing in a new suit, ready to speak words of good omen as the bride and bridegroom approached. He had come all the way from Cheverel Manor on purpose to see Miss Tina happy once more, and would have been in a state of unmixed joy but for the inferiority of the wedding nosegays to what he could have furnished from the garden at the Manor.

"God A'maighty bless ye both, an' send ye long laife an' happiness," were the good gardener's rather tremulous words.

"Thank you, uncle Bates; always remember Tina," said the sweet low voice, which fell on Mr. Bates's ear for the last time.

The wedding journey was to be a circuitous route to Shepperton, where Mr. Gilfil had been for several months inducted as vicar. This small living had been given him through the interest of an old friend who had some claim on the gratitude of the Oldinport family; and it was a satisfaction both to

Maynard and Sir Christopher that a home to which he might take Caterina had thus readily presented itself at a distance from Cheverel Manor. For it had never yet been thought safe that she should revisit the scene of her sufferings, her health continuing too delicate to encourage the slightest risk of painful excitement. In a year or two, perhaps by the time old Mr. Crichley, the rector of Cumbermoor, should have left a world of gout, and when Caterina would very likely be a happy mother, Maynard might safely take up his abode at Cumbermoor, and Tina would feel nothing but content at seeing a new "little black-eyed monkey" running up and down the gallery and gardens of the Manor. A mother dreads no memories—those shadows have all melted away in the dawn of baby's smile.

In these hopes, and in the enjoyment of Tina's nestling affection, Mr. Gilfil tasted a few months of perfect happiness. She had come to lean entirely on his love, and to find life sweet for his sake. Her continual languor and want of active interest was a natural consequence of bodily feebleness, and the prospect of her becoming a mother was a new ground for hoping the best.

But the delicate plant had been too deeply bruised, and in the struggle to put forth a blossom it died.

Tina died, and Maynard Gilfil's love went with her into deep silence for evermore.

EPILOGUE.

This was Mr. Gilfil's love-story, which lay far back from the time when he sat, worn and gray, by his lonely fireside in Shepperton Vicarage. Rich brown locks, passionate love, and deep early sorrow, strangely different as they seem from the scanty white hairs, the apathetic content, and the unexpectant quiescence of old age, are but part of the same life's journey; as the bright Italian plains, with the sweet *Addio* of their beckoning maidens, are part of the same day's travel that brings us to the other side of the mountain, between the sombre rocky walls and among the guttural voices of the Valais.

To those who were familiar only with the gray-haired Vicar, jogging leisurely along on his old chestnut cob, it would perhaps have been hard to believe that he had ever been the Maynard Gilfil who, with a heart full of passion and tenderness, had urged his black Kitty to her swiftest gallop on the way to Callam, or that the old gentleman of caustic tongue, and bucolic tastes, and sparing habits, had known all the deep secrets of devoted love, had struggled through its days and nights of anguish, and trembled under its unspeakable joys. And indeed the Mr. Gilfil of those late Shepperton days had more of the knots and ruggedness of poor human nature than there lay any clear hint of in the open-eyed, loving Maynard. But it is with men as with trees: if you lop off their finest branches, into which they were pouring their young life-juice, the wounds will be healed over with some rough boss, some odd excrescence; and what might have been a grand tree expanding into liberal shade, is but a whimsical, misshapen trunk. Many an irritating fault, many an unlovely oddity, has come of a hard sorrow, which has crushed and maimed the nature just when it was expanding into plenteous beauty; and the trivial erring life which we visit with our harsh blame, may be but as the unsteady motion of a man whose best limb is withered.

And so the dear old Vicar, though he had something of the knotted, whimsical character of the poor lopped oak, had yet been sketched out by nature as a noble tree. The heart of him was sound, the grain was of the finest; and in the gray-haired man who filled his pocket with sugar-plums for the little children, whose most biting words were directed against the evil doing of the rich man, and who, with all his social pipes and slipshod talk, never sank below the highest level of his parishioners' respect, there was the main trunk of the same brave, faithful, tender nature that had poured out the finest, freshest forces of its life-current in a first and only love—the love of Tina.

JANET'S REPENTANCE.

CHAPTER I.

"No!" said lawyer Dempster, in a loud, rasping, oratorical tone, struggling against chronic huskiness, "as long as my Maker grants me power of voice and power of intellect, I will take every legal means to resist the introduction of demoralizing, methodistical doctrine into this parish; I will not supinely suffer an insult to be inflicted on our venerable pastor, who has given us sound instruction for half a century."

It was very warm everywhere that evening, but especially in the bar of the Red Lion at Milby, where Mr. Dempster was seated mixing his third glass of brandy-and-water. He was a tall and rather massive man, and the front half of his large surface was so well dredged with snuff, that the cat, having inadvertently come near him, had been seized with a severe fit of sneezing—an accident which, being cruelly misunderstood, had caused her to be driven contumeliously from the bar. Mr. Dempster habitually held his chin tucked in, and his head hanging forward, weighed down, perhaps, by a preponderant occiput and a bulging forehead, between which his closely-clipped coronal surface lay like a flat and new-mown table-land. The only other observable features were puffy cheeks and a protruding yet lipless mouth. Of his nose I can only say that it was snuffy; and as Mr. Dempster was never caught in the act of looking at any thing in particular, it would have been difficult to swear to the color of his eyes.

"Well! I'll not stick at giving *my*self trouble to put down such hypocritical cant," said Mr. Tomlinson, the rich miller. "I know well enough what your Sunday evening lectures are good for—for wenches to meet their sweethearts, and brew mischief. There's work enough with the servant-maids as it is—such as I never heard the like of in my mother's time, and it's all along o' your schooling and newfangled plans. Give me a servant as can naythar read nor write, I say, and doesn't know the year o' the Lord as she was born in. I should like to know what good those Sunday schools have done, now. Why, the boys used to go a bird's-nesting of a Sunday morning; and a capital thing too—ask any farmer; and very pretty it was to see the strings o' heggs hanging up in poor people's houses. You'll not see 'em nowhere now."

"Pooh!" said Mr. Luke Byles, who piqued himself on his reading, and was in the habit of asking casual acquaintances if they knew any thing of Hobbes; "it is right enough that the lower orders should be instructed. But this sectarianism within the Church ought to be put down. In point of fact, these Evangelicals are not Churchmen at all; they're no better than Presbyterians."

"Presbyterans? what are they?" inquired Mr. Tomlinson, who often said his father had given him "no eddication, and he didn't care who knowed it; he could buy up most o' th' eddicated men he'd ever come across."

"The Presbyterians," said Mr. Dempster, in rather a louder tone than before, holding that every appeal for information must naturally be addressed to him, "are a sect founded in the reign of Charles I., by a man named John Presbyter, who hatched all the brood of Dissenting vermin that crawl about in dirty alleys, and circumvent the lord of the manor in order to get a few yards of ground for their pigeon-house conventicles."

"No, no, Dempster," said Mr. Luke Byles, "you're out there. Presbyterianism is derived from the word presbyter, meaning an elder."

"Don't contradict *me*, sir!" stormed Dempster. "I say the word presbyterian is derived from John Presbyter, a miserable fanatic who wore a suit of leather, and went about from town to village, and from village to hamlet, inoculating the vulgar with the asinine virus of Dissent."

"Come, Byles, that seems a deal more likely," said Mr. Tomlinson, in a conciliatory tone, apparently of opinion that history was a process of ingenious guessing.

"It's not a question of likelihood; it's a known fact. I could fetch you my Encyclopædia, and show it you this moment."

"I don't care a straw, sir, either for you or your Encyclopædia," said Mr. Dempster; "a farrago of false information of which you picked up an imperfect copy in a cargo of waste paper. Will you tell *me*, sir, that I don't know the origin of Presbyterianism? I, sir, a man known through the county intrusted with the affairs of half a score of parishes; while you, sir, are ignored by the very fleas that infest the miserable alley in which you were bred."

A loud and general laugh, with "You'd better let him alone, Byles;" "You'll not get the better of Dempster in a hurry," drowned the retort of the too well informed Mr. Byles, who, white with rage, rose and walked out of the bar.

"A meddlesome, upstart, Jacobinical fellow, gentlemen," continued Mr. Dempster. "I was determined to be rid of him. What does he mean by thrusting himself into our company? A man with about as much principle as he has property, which, to my knowledge, is considerably less than none. An insolvent atheist, gentlemen. A deistical prater, fit to sit in the chimney-corner of a pot-house, and make blasphemous comments on the one greasy newspaper fingered by beer-swilling tinkers. I will not suffer in my company a man who speaks lightly of religion. The signature of a fellow like Byles would be a blot on our protest."

"And how do you get on with your signatures?" said Mr. Pilgrim, the doctor, who had presented his large top-booted person within the bar while Mr. Dempster was speaking. Mr. Pilgrim had just returned from one of his long day's rounds among the farm-houses, in the course of which he had sat down to two hearty meals that might have been mistaken for dinners if he had not declared them to be "snaps;" and as each snap had been followed by a few glasses of "mixture," containing a less liberal proportion of water than the articles he himself labelled with that broadly generic name, he was in that condition which his groom indicated with poetic ambiguity by saying that "master had been in the sunshine." Under these circumstances, after a hard day, in which he had really had no regular meal, it seemed a natural relaxation to step into the bar of the Red Lion, where, as it was Saturday evening, he should be sure to find Dempster, and hear the latest news about the protest against the evening lecture.

"Have you hooked Ben Landor yet?" he continued, as he took two chairs, one for his body, and the other for his right leg.

"No," said Mr. Budd, the churchwarden, shaking his head; "Ben Landor has a way of keeping himself neutral in every thing, and he doesn't like to oppose his father. Old Landor is a regular Tryanite. But we haven't got your name yet, Pilgrim."

"Tut tut, Budd," said Mr. Dempster, sarcastically, "you don't expect Pilgrim to sign? He's got a dozen Tryanite livers under his treatment. Nothing like cant and methodism for producing a superfluity of bile."

"Oh, I thought, as Pratt had declared himself a Tryanite, we should be sure to get Pilgrim on our side."

Mr. Pilgrim was not a man to sit quiet under a sarcasm, nature having endowed him with a considerable share of self-defensive wit. In his most sober moments he had an impediment in his speech, and as copious gin-and-water stimulated not the speech but the impediment, he had time to make his retort sufficiently bitter.

"Why, to tell you the truth, Budd," he spluttered, "there's a report all over the town that Deb Traunter swears you shall take her with you as one of the delegates, and they say there's to be a fine crowd at your door the morning you start, to see the row. Knowing your tenderness for that member of the fair sex, I thought you might find it impossible to deny her. I hang back a little from signing on that account, as Prendergast might not take the protest well if Deb Traunter went with you."

Mr. Budd was a small, sleek-headed bachelor of five-and-forty, whose scandalous life had long furnished his more moral neighbors with an after-dinner joke. He had no other striking characteristic, except that he was a currier of choleric temperament, so that you might wonder why he had been chosen as clergyman's churchwarden, if I did not tell you that he had recently been elected through Mr. Dempster's exertions, in order that his zeal against the threatened evening lecture might be backed by the dignity of office.

"Come, come, Pilgrim," said Mr. Tomlinson, covering Mr. Budd's retreat, "you know you like to wear the crier's coat, green o' one side and red o' the other. You've been to hear Tryan preach at Paddiford Common—you know you have."

"To be sure I have; and a capital sermon too. It's a pity you were not there. It was addressed to those 'void of understanding.'"

"No, no, you'll never catch me there," returned Mr. Tomlinson, not in the least stung; "he preaches without book, they say, just like a Dissenter. It must be a rambling sort of a concern."

"That's not the worst," said Mr. Dempster; "he preaches against good works; says good works are not necessary to salvation—a sectarian, antinomian, anabaptist doctrine. Tell a man he is not to be saved by his works, and you open the flood-gates of all immorality. You see it in all these canting innovators; they're all bad ones by the sly; smooth-faced, drawling, hypocritical fellows, who pretend ginger isn't hot in their mouths, and cry down all innocent pleasures; their hearts are all the blacker for their sanctimonious outsides.

Haven't we been warned against those who make clean the outside of the cup and the platter? There's this Tryan, now, he goes about praying with old women, and singing with charity-children; but what has he really got his eye on all the while? A domineering ambitious Jesuit, gentlemen; all he wants is to get his foot far enough into the parish to step into Crewe's shoes when the old gentleman dies. Depend upon it, whenever you see a man pretending to be better than his neighbors, that man has either some cunning end to serve, or his heart is rotten with spiritual pride."

As if to guarantee himself against this awful sin, Mr. Dempster seized his glass of brandy-and-water, and tossed off the contents with even greater rapidity than usual.

"Have you fixed on your third delegate yet?" said Mr. Pilgrim, whose taste was for detail rather than for dissertation.

"That's the man," answered Dempster, pointing to Mr. Tomlinson. "We start for Elmstoke Rectory on Tuesday morning; so, if you mean to give us your signature, you must make up your mind pretty quickly, Pilgrim."

Mr. Pilgrim did not in the least mean it, so he only said, "I shouldn't wonder if Tryan turns out too many for you, after all. He's got a well-oiled tongue of his own, and has perhaps talked over Prendergast into a determination to stand by him."

"Ve-ry little fear of that," said Dempster, in a confident tone. "I'll soon bring him round. Tryan has got his match. I've plenty of rods in pickle for Tryan."

At this moment Boots entered the bar, and put a letter into the lawyer's hands, saying, "There's Trower's man just come into the yard wi' a gig, sir, an' he's brought this here letter."

Mr. Dempster read the letter and said, "Tell him to turn the gig—I'll be with him in a minute. Here, run to Gruby's and get this snuff-box filled—quick!"

"Trower's worse, I suppose; eh, Dempster? Wants you to alter his will, eh?" said Mr. Pilgrim.

"Business—business—business—I don't know exactly what," answered the cautious Dempster, rising deliberately from his chair, thrusting on his low-crowned hat, and walking with a slow but not unsteady step out of the bar.

"I never see Dempster's equal; if I did I'll be shot," said Mr. Tomlinson, looking after the lawyer admiringly. "Why, he's drunk the best part of a bottle o' brandy since here we've been sitting, and I'll bet a guinea, when he's got to Trower's his head'll be as clear as mine. He knows more about law when he's drunk than all the rest on 'em when they're sober."

"Ay, and other things too, besides law," said Mr. Budd. "Did you notice how he took up Byles about the Presbyterians? Bless your heart, he knows every thing, Dempster does. He studied very hard when he was a young man."

CHAPTER II.

The conversation just recorded is not, I am aware, remarkably refined or witty; but if it had been, it could hardly have taken place in Milby when Mr. Dempster flourished there, and old Mr. Crewe, the curate, was yet alive.

More than a quarter of a century has slipped by since then, and in the interval Milby has advanced at as rapid a pace as other market-towns in her Majesty's dominions. By this time it has a handsome railway station, where the drowsy London traveller may look out by the brilliant gas-light and see perfectly sober papas and husbands alighting with their leather-bags after transacting their day's business at the county town. There is a resident rector, who appeals to the consciences of his hearers with all the immense advantages of a divine who keeps his own carriage; the church is enlarged by at least five hundred sittings; and the grammar-school, conducted on reformed principles, has its upper forms crowded with the genteel youth of Milby. The gentlemen there fall into no other excess at dinner-parties than the perfectly well-bred and virtuous excess of stupidity; and though the ladies are still said sometimes to take too much upon themselves, they are never known to take too much in any other way. The conversation is sometimes quite literary, for there is a flourishing book-club, and many of the younger ladies have carried their studies so far as to have forgotten a little German. In short, Milby is now a refined, moral, and enlightened town; no more resembling the Milby of former days than the huge, long-skirted, drab great-coat that embarrassed the ankles of our grandfathers resembled the light paletot in which we tread jauntily through the muddiest streets, or than the bottle-nosed Britons, rejoicing over a tankard in the old sign of the Two Travellers at Milby, resembled the severe-looking gentleman in straps and high collars whom a modern artist has represented as sipping the imaginary port of that well-known commercial house.

But pray, reader, dismiss from your mind all the refined and fashionable ideas associated with this advanced state of things, and transport your imagination to a time when Milby had no gas-lights; when the mail drove up dusty or bespattered to the door of the Red Lion; when old Mr. Crewe, the curate, in a brown Brutus wig, delivered inaudible sermons on a Sunday, and on a week-day imparted the education of a gentleman—that is to say, an arduous inacquaintance with Latin through the medium of the Eton Grammar—to three pupils in the upper grammar-school.

If you had passed through Milby on the coach at that time, you would have had no idea what important people lived there, and how very high a sense of rank was prevalent among them. It was a dingy-looking town, with a strong smell of tanning up one street and a great shaking of hand-looms up another; and even in that focus of aristocracy, Friar's Gate, the houses would not have seemed very imposing to the hasty and superficial glance of a passenger. You might still less have suspected that the figure in light fustian and large gray whiskers, leaning against the grocer's door-post in High Street, was no less a person than Mr. Lowme, one of the most aristocratic men in Milby, said to have been "brought up a gentleman," and to have had the gay habits accordant with that station, keeping his harriers and other expensive animals. He was now quite an elderly Lothario, reduced to the most economical sins; the prominent form of his gayety being this of lounging at Mr. Gruby's door, embarrassing the servant-maids who came for grocery, and talking scandal with the rare passers-by. Still, it was generally understood that Mr. Lowme belonged to the highest circle of Milby society; his sons and daughters held up their heads very high indeed; and in spite of his condescending way of chatting and drinking with inferior people, he would himself have scorned any closer identification with them. It must be admitted that he was of some service to the town in this station at Mr. Gruby's door, for he and Mr. Landor's Newfoundland dog, who stretched himself and gaped on the opposite causeway, took something from the lifeless air that belonged to the High street on every day except Saturday.

Certainly, in spite of three assemblies and a charity ball in the winter, the occasional advent of a ventriloquist, or a company of itinerant players, some of whom were very highly thought of in London, and the annual three days' fair in June, Milby might be considered dull by people of a hypochondriacal temperament; and perhaps this was one reason why many of the middle-aged inhabitants, male and female, often found it impossible to keep up their spirits without a very abundant supply of stimulants. It is true there were several substantial men who had a reputation for exceptional sobriety, so that Milby habits were really not as bad as possible; and no one is warranted in saying that old Mr. Crewe's flock could not have been worse without any clergyman at all.

The well-dressed parishioners generally were very regular church-goers, and to the young ladies and gentlemen I am inclined to think that the Sunday morning service was the most exciting event of the week; for few places could present a more brilliant show of out-door toilettes than might be seen issuing from Milby church at one o'clock. There were the four tall Miss Pittmans, old lawyer Pittman's daughters, with cannon curls surmounted by large hats, and long, drooping ostrich feathers of parrot green. There was Miss Phipps, with a crimson bonnet, very much tilted up behind, and a cockade of stiff feathers on the summit. There was Miss Landor, the belle of Milby, clad regally in purple and ermine, with a plume of feathers neither drooping nor erect, but maintaining a discreet medium. There were the three Miss Tomlinsons, who imitated Miss Landor, and also wore ermine and feathers; but their beauty was considered of a coarse order, and their square forms were quite unsuited to the round tippet which fell with such remarkable grace on Miss Landor's sloping shoulders. Looking at this plumed procession of ladies, you would have formed rather a high idea of Milby wealth; yet there was only one close carriage in the place, and that was old Mr. Landor's, the banker, who, I think, never drove more than one horse. These sumptuously-attired ladies flashed past the vulgar eye in one-horse chaises, by no means of a superior build.

The young gentlemen, too, were not without their little Sunday displays of costume, of a limited masculine kind. Mr. Eustace Landor, being nearly of age, had recently acquired a diamond ring, together with the habit of rubbing his hand through his hair. He was tall and dark, and thus had an advantage which Mr. Alfred Phipps, who, like his sister, was blond and stumpy, found it difficult to overtake, even by the severest attention to shirt-studs, and the particular shade of brown that was best relieved by gilt buttons.

The respect for the Sabbath, manifested in this attention to costume, was unhappily counterbalanced by considerable levity of behavior during the prayers and sermon; for the young ladies and gentlemen of Milby were of a very satirical turn, Miss Landor especially being considered remarkably clever, and a terrible quiz; and the large congregation necessarily containing many persons inferior in dress and demeanor to the distinguished aristocratic minority, divine service offered irresistible temptations to joking, through the medium of telegraphic communications from the galleries to the aisles and back again. I remember blushing very much, and thinking Miss Landor was laughing at me, because I was appearing in coat-tails for the first time, when I saw her look down slyly towards where I sat, and then turn with a titter to handsome Mr. Bob Lowme, who had such beautiful whiskers meeting under his chin. But perhaps she was not thinking of me, after all; for our pew was near the pulpit, and there was almost always something funny about old Mr. Crewe. His brown wig was hardly ever put on quite right, and he had a way of raising his voice for three or four words, and lowering it again to a mumble, so that we could scarcely make out a word he said; though, as my mother observed, that was of no consequence in the prayer, since every one had a prayer-book; and as for the sermon, she continued with some causticity, we all of us heard more of it than we could remember when we got home.

This youthful generation was not particularly literary. The young ladies who frizzed their hair, and gathered it all into large barricades in front of their heads, leaving their occipital region exposed without ornament, as if that, being a back view, was of no consequence, dreamed as little that their daughters would read a selection of German poetry, and be able to express an admiration for Schiller, as that they would turn all their hair the other way—that instead of threatening us with barricades in front, they would be most killing in retreat,

> "And, like the Parthian, wound us as they fly."

Those charming well-frizzed ladies spoke French indeed with considerable facility, unshackled by any timid regard to idiom, and were in the habit of conducting conversations in that language in the presence of their less instructed elders; for according to the standard of those backward days, their education had been very lavish, such young ladies as Miss Landor, Miss Phipps, and the Miss Pittmans, having been "finished" at distant and expensive schools.

Old lawyer Pittman had once been a very important person indeed, having in his earlier days managed the affairs of several gentlemen in those parts, who had subsequently been obliged to sell every thing and leave the country, in which crisis Mr. Pittman accomodatingly stepped in as a purchaser of their estates, taking on himself the risk and trouble of a more leisurely sale; which, however, happened to turn out very much to his advantage. Such opportunities occur quite unexpectedly in the way of business. But I think Mr. Pittman must have been unlucky in his later speculations, for now, in his old age, he had not the reputation of being very rich; and though he rode slowly to his office in Milby every morning on an old white hackney, he had to resign the chief profits, as well as the active business of the firm, to his younger partner, Dempster. No one in Milby considered old Pittman a virtuous man, and the elder townspeople were not at all backward in narrating the least advantageous portions of his biography in a very round unvarnished manner. Yet I could never observe that they trusted him any the less, or liked him any the worse. Indeed, Pittman and Dempster were the popular lawyers of Milby and its neighborhood, and Mr. Benjamin Landor, whom no one had any thing particular to say against, had a very meagre business in comparison. Hardly a landholder, hardly a farmer, hardly a parish within ten miles of Milby, whose affairs were not under the legal guardianship of Pittman and Dempster; and I think the clients were proud of their lawyers' unscrupulousness, as the patrons of the fancy are proud of their champion's "condition." It was not, to be sure, the thing for ordinary life, but it was the thing to be bet on in a lawyer. Dempster's talent in "bringing through" a client was a very common topic of conversation with the farmers, over an incidental glass of grog at the Red Lion. "He's a long-headed feller, Dempster; why, it shows yer what a head-piece Dempster has, as he can drink a bottle o' brandy at a sittin', an' yit see further through a stone wall when he's done, than other folks'll see through a glass winder." Even Mr. Jerome, chief member of the congregation at Salem Chapel, an elderly man of very strict life, was one of Dempster's clients, and had quite an exceptional indulgence for his attorney's foibles, perhaps attributing them to the inevitable incompatibility of law and gospel.

The standard of morality at Milby, you perceive, was not inconveniently high in those good old times, and an ingenuous vice or two was what every man expected of his neighbor. Old Mr. Crewe, the curate, for example, was allowed to enjoy his avarice in comfort, without fear of sarcastic parish demagogues; and his flock liked him all the better for having scraped together a large fortune out of his school and curacy, and the proceeds of the three thousand pounds he had with his little deaf wife. It was clear he must be a learned man, for he had once had a large private school in connection with the grammar-school, and had even numbered a young nobleman or two among his pupils. The fact that he read nothing at all now, and that his mind seemed absorbed in the commonest matters, was doubtless due to his having exhausted the resources of erudition earlier in life. It is true he was not spoken of in terms of high respect, and old Crewe's stingy housekeeping was a frequent subject of jesting; but this was a good old-fashioned characteristic in a parson who had been part of Milby life for half a century: it was like the dents and disfigurements in an old family tankard, which no one would like to part with for a smart new piece of plate fresh from Birmingham. The parishioners saw no reason at all why it should be desirable to venerate the parson or any one else: they were much more comfortable to look down a little on their fellow-creatures.

Even the Dissent in Milby was then of a lax and indifferent kind. The doctrine of adult baptism, struggling under a heavy load of debt, had let off half its chapel area as a ribbon-shop; and Methodism was only to be detected, as you detect curious larvæ, by diligent search in dirty corners. The Independents were the only Dissenters of whose existence Milby gentility was at all conscious, and it had a vague idea that the salient points of their creed were prayer without book, red brick, and hypocrisy. The Independent chapel, known as Salem, stood red and conspicuous in a broad street; more than one pew-holder kept a brass-bound gig; and Mr. Jerome, a retired corn-factor, and the most eminent member of the congregation, was one of the richest men in the parish. But in spite of this apparent prosperity, together with the usual amount of extemporaneous preaching mitigated by furtive notes, Salem belied its name, and was not always the abode of peace. For some reason or other, it was unfortunate in the choice of its ministers. The Rev. Mr. Horner, elected with brilliant hopes, was discovered to be given to tippling and quarrelling with his wife; the Rev. Mr. Rose's doctrine was a little too "high," verging on antinomianism; the Rev. Mr. Stickney's gift as a preacher was found to be less striking on a more extended acquaintance; and the Rev. Mr. Smith, a distinguished minister much sought after in the iron districts, with a talent for poetry, became objectionable from an inclination to exchange verses with the young ladies of his congregation. It was reasonably argued that such verses as Mr. Smith's must take a long time for their composition, and the habit alluded to might intrench seriously on his pastoral duties. These reverend gentlemen one and all, gave it as their opinion that the Salem church members were among the least enlightened of the Lord's people, and that Milby was a low place, where they would have found it a severe lot to have their lines fall for any long period; though to see the smart and crowded congregation assembled on occasion of the annual charity sermon, any one might have supposed that the minister of Salem had rather a brilliant position in the ranks of Dissent. Several Church families used to attend on that occasion, for Milby, in those uninstructed days, had not yet heard that the schismatic ministers of Salem were obviously typified by Korah, Dathan, and Abiram; and many Church people there were of opinion that Dissent might be a weakness, but, after all, had no great harm in it. These lax Episcopalians were, I believe, chiefly tradespeople, who held that, inasmuch as Congregationalism consumed candles, it ought to be supported, and accordingly made a point of presenting themselves at Salem for the afternoon charity sermon, with the expectation of being asked to hold a plate. Mr. Pilgrim, too, was always there with his half-sovereign; for as there was no Dissenting doctor in Milby, Mr. Pilgrim looked with great tolerance on all shades of religious opinion that did not include a belief in cures by miracle.

On this point he had the concurrence of Mr. Pratt, the only other medical man of the same standing in Milby. Otherwise, it was remarkable how strongly these two clever men were contrasted. Pratt was middle-sized, insinuating, and silvery-voiced; Pilgrim was tall, heavy, rough-mannered, and spluttering. Both were considered to have great powers of conversation, but Pratt's anecdotes were of the fine old crusted quality to be procured only of Joe Miller; Pilgrim's had the full fruity flavor of the most recent scandal. Pratt elegantly referred all diseases to debility, and, with a proper contempt for symptomatic treatment, went to the root of the matter with port-wine and bark; Pilgrim was persuaded that the evil principle in the human system was plethora, and he made war against it with cupping, blistering, and cathartics. They had both been long established in Milby, and as each had a sufficient practice, there was no very malignant rivalry between them; on the contrary, they had that sort of friendly contempt for each other which is always conducive to a good understanding between professional men; and when any new surgeon attempted, in an ill-advised hour, to settle himself in the town, it was strikingly demonstrated how slight and trivial are theoretic differences compared with the broad basis of common human feeling. There was the most perfect unanimity between Pratt and Pilgrim in the determination to drive away the obnoxious and too probably unqualified intruder as soon as possible. Whether the first wonderful cure he effected was on a patient of Pratt's or of Pilgrim's, one was as ready as the other to pull the interloper by the nose, and both alike directed their remarkable powers of conversation towards making the town too hot for him. But by their respective patients these two distinguished men were pitted against each other with great virulence. Mrs. Lowme could not conceal her amazement that Mrs. Phipps should trust her life in the hands of Pratt, who let her feed herself up to that degree, it was really shocking to hear how short her breath was; and Mrs. Phipps had no patience with Mrs. Lowme, living, as she did, on tea and broth, and looking as yellow as any crow-flower, and yet letting Pilgrim bleed and blister her and give her lowering medicine till her clothes hung on her like a scarecrow's. On the whole, perhaps, Mr. Pilgrim's reputation was at the higher pitch, and when any lady under Mr. Pratt's care was doing ill, she was half disposed to think that a little more "active treatment" might suit her better. But without very definite provocation no one would take so serious a step as to part with the family doctor, for in those remote days there were few varieties of human hatred more formidable than the medical. The doctor's estimate, even of a confiding patient, was apt to rise and fall with the entries in the day-book; and I have known Mr. Pilgrim discover the most unexpected virtues in a patient seized with a promising illness. At such times you might have been glad to perceive that there were some of Mr. Pilgrim's fellow-creatures of whom he entertained a high opinion, and that he was liable to the amiable weakness of a too admiring estimate. A good inflammation fired his enthusiasm, and a lingering dropsy dissolved him into charity. Doubtless this *crescendo* of benevolence was partly due to feelings not at all represented by the entries in the day-book; for in Mr. Pilgrim's heart, too, there was a latent store of tenderness and pity which flowed forth at the sight of suffering. Gradually, however, as his patients became convalescent, his view of their characters became more dispassionate; when they could relish mutton-chops, he began to admit that they had foibles, and by the time they had swallowed their last dose of tonic, he was alive to their most inexcusable faults. After this, the thermometer of his regard rested at the moderate point of friendly backbiting, which sufficed to make him agreeable in his morning visits to the amiable and worthy persons who were yet far from convalescent.

Pratt's patients were profoundly uninteresting to Pilgrim; their very diseases were despicable, and he would hardly have thought their bodies worth dissecting. But of all Pratt's patients, Mr. Jerome was the one on whom Mr. Pilgrim heaped the most unmitigated contempt. In spite of the surgeon's wise tolerance, Dissent became odious to him in the person of Mr. Jerome. Perhaps it was because that old gentleman, being rich, and having very large yearly bills for medical attendance on himself and his wife, nevertheless employed Pratt—neglected all the advantages of "active treatment," and paid away his money without getting his system lowered. On any other ground it is hard to explain a feeling of hostility to Mr. Jerome, who was an excellent old gentleman, expressing a great deal of good-will towards his neighbors, not only in imperfect English, but in loans of money to the ostensibly rich, and in sacks of potatoes to the obviously poor.

Assuredly Milby had that salt of goodness which keeps the world together, in greater abundance than was visible on the surface; innocent babes were born there, sweetening their parents' hearts with simple joys; men and women withering in disappointed worldliness, or bloated with sensual ease, had better moments in which they pressed the hand of suffering with sympathy, and were moved to deeds of neighborly kindness. In church and in chapel there were honest-hearted worshippers who strove to keep a conscience void of offense; and even up the dimmest alleys you might have found here and there a Wesleyan to whom Methodism was the vehicle of peace on earth and good-will to men. To a superficial glance, Milby was nothing but dreary prose; a dingy town, surrounded by flat fields, lopped elms, and sprawling manufacturing villages, which crept on and on with their weaving-shops, till they threatened to graft themselves on the town. But the sweet spring came to Milby notwithstanding: the elm-tops were red with buds; the churchyard was starred with daisies; the lark showered his love-music on the flat fields; the rainbows hung over the dingy town, clothing the very roofs and chimneys in a strange transfiguring beauty. And so it was with the human life there, which at first seemed a dismal mixture of griping worldliness, vanity, ostrich feathers, and the fumes of brandy; looking closer, you found some purity, gentleness, and unselfishness, as you may have observed a scented geranium giving forth its wholesome odors amidst blasphemy and gin in a noisy pot-house. Little deaf Mrs. Crewe would often carry half her own spare dinner to the sick and hungry; Miss Phipps, with her cockade of red feathers, had a filial heart, and lighted her father's pipe with a pleasant smile; and there were gray-haired men in drab gaiters, not at all noticeable as you passed them in the street, whose integrity had been the basis of their rich neighbor's wealth.

Such as the place was, the people there were entirely contented with it. They fancied life must be but a dull affair for that large portion of mankind who were necessarily shut out from an acquaintance with Milby families, and that it must be an advantage to London and Liverpool that Milby gentlemen occasionally visited those places on business. But the inhabitants became more intensely conscious of the value they set upon all their advantages, when innovation made its appearance in the person of the Rev. Mr. Tryan, the new curate, at the chapel-of-ease on Paddiford Common. It was soon notorious in Milby that Mr. Tryan held peculiar opinions; that he preached extempore; that he was founding a religious lending-library in his remote corner of the parish; that he expounded the Scriptures in cottages; and that his preaching was attracting the Dissenters, and filling the very aisles of his church. The rumor sprang up that Evangelicalism had invaded Milby parish—a murrain or blight all the more terrible, because its nature was but dimly conjectured. Perhaps Milby was one of the last spots to be reached by the wave of a new movement; and it was only now, when the tide was just on the turn, that the limpets there got a sprinkling. Mr. Tryan was the first Evangelical clergyman who had risen above the Milby horizon: hitherto that obnoxious adjective had been unknown to the townspeople of any gentility; and there were even many Dissenters who considered "evangelical" simply a sort of baptismal name to the magazine which circulated among the congregation of Salem Chapel. But now, at length, the disease had been imported, when the parishioners were expecting it as little as the innocent Red Indians expected small-pox. As long as Mr. Tryan's hearers were confined to Paddiford Common—which, by-the-by, was hardly recognizable as a common at all, but was a dismal district where you heard the rattle of the handloom, and breathed the smoke of coal-pits—the "canting parson" could be treated as a joke. Not so when a number of single ladies in the town appeared to be infected, and even one or two men of substantial property, with old Mr. Landor, the banker, at their head, seemed to be "giving in" to the new movement—when Mr. Tryan was known to be well received in several good houses, where he was in the habit of finishing the evening with exhortation and prayer. Evangelicalism was no longer a nuisance existing merely in by-corners, which any well-clad person could avoid; it was invading the very drawing-rooms, mingling itself with the comfortable fumes of port-wine and brandy, threatening to deaden with its murky breath all the splendor of the ostrich feathers, and to stifle Milby ingenuousness, not pretending to be better than its neighbors, with a cloud of cant and lugubrious hypocrisy. The alarm reached its climax when it was reported that Mr. Tryan was endeavoring to obtain authority from Mr. Prendergast, the non-resident rector, to establish a Sunday evening lecture in the parish church, on the ground that old Mr. Crewe did not preach the Gospel.

It now first appeared how surprisingly high a value Milby in general set on the ministrations of Mr. Crewe; how convinced it was that Mr. Crewe was the model of a parish priest, and his sermons the soundest and most edifying that had ever remained unheard by a church-going population. All allusions to his brown wig were suppressed, and by a rhetorical figure his name was associated with venerable gray hairs; the attempted intrusion of Mr. Tryan was an insult to a man deep in years and learning; moreover, it was an insolent effort to thrust himself forward in a parish where he was clearly distasteful to the superior portion of its inhabitants. The town was divided into two zealous parties, the Tryanites and anti-Tryanites; and by the exertions of the eloquent Dempster, the anti-Tryanite virulence was soon developed into an organized opposition. A protest against the meditated evening lecture was framed by that orthodox attorney, and, after being numerously signed, was to be carried to Mr. Prendergast by three delegates representing the intellect, morality, and wealth of Milby. The intellect, you perceive, was to be personified in Mr. Dempster, the morality in Mr. Budd, and the wealth in Mr. Tomlinson; and the distinguished triad was to set out on its great mission, as we have seen, on the third day from that warm Saturday evening when the conversation recorded in the previous chapter took place in the bar of the Red Lion.

CHAPTER III.

It was quite as warm on the following Thursday evening, when Mr. Dempster and his colleagues were to return from their mission to Elmstoke Rectory; but it was much pleasanter in Mrs. Linnet's parlor than in the bar of the Red Lion.

Through the open window came the scent of mignonnette and honeysuckle; the grass-plot in front of the house was shaded by a little plantation of Gueldres roses, syringas, and laburnums; the noise of looms and carts and unmelodious voices reached the ear simply as an agreeable murmur, for Mrs. Linnet's house was situated quite on the outskirts of Paddiford Common; and the only sound likely to disturb the serenity of the feminine party assembled there, was the occasional buzz of intrusive wasps, apparently mistaking each lady's head for a sugar-basin. No sugar-basin was visible in Mrs. Linnet's parlor, for the time of tea was not yet, and the round table was littered with books which the ladies were covering with black canvas as a reinforcement of the new Paddiford Lending Library. Miss Linnet, whose manuscript was the neatest type of zigzag, was seated at a small table apart, writing on green paper tickets, which were to be pasted on the covers. Miss Linnet had other accomplishments besides that of a neat manuscript, and an index to some of them might be found in the ornaments of the room. She had always combined a love of serious and poetical reading with her skill in fancy-work, and the neatly-bound copies of Dryden's "Virgil," Hannah More's "Sacred Dramas," Falconer's "Shipwreck," Mason "On Self-Knowledge," "Rasselas," and Burke "On the Sublime and Beautiful," which were the chief ornaments of the bookcase, were all inscribed with her name, and had been bought with her pocket-money when she was in her teens. It must have been at least fifteen years since the latest of those purchases, but Miss Linnet's skill in fancy-work appeared to have gone through more numerous phases than her literary taste; for the japanned boxes, the alum and sealing-wax baskets, the fan-dolls, the "transferred" landscapes on the fire-screens, and the recent bouquets of wax-flowers, showed a disparity in freshness which made them referable to widely different periods. Wax-flowers presuppose delicate fingers and robust patience, but there are still many points of mind and person which they leave vague and problematic; so I must tell you that Miss Linnet had dark ringlets, a sallow complexion, and an amiable disposition. As to her features, there was not much to criticise in them, for she had little nose, less lip, and no eyebrow; and as to her intellect, her friend Mrs. Pettifer often said, "She didn't know a more sensible person to talk to than Mary Linnet. There was no one she liked better to come and take a quiet cup of tea with her, and read a little of Klopstock's 'Messiah.' Mary Linnet had often told her a great deal of her mind when they were sitting together; she said there were many things to bear in every condition of life, and nothing should induce her to marry without a prospect of happiness. Once, when Mrs. Pettifer admired her wax-flowers, she said, 'Ah, Mrs. Pettifer, think of the beauties of nature!' She always spoke very prettily, did Mary Linnet; very different, indeed, from Rebecca."

Miss Rebecca Linnet, indeed, was not a general favorite. While most people thought it a pity that a sensible woman like Mary had not found a good husband—and even her female friends said nothing more ill-natured of her than that her face was like a piece of putty with two Scotch pebbles stuck in it—Rebecca was always spoken of sarcastically, and it was a customary kind of banter with young ladies to recommend her as a wife to any gentleman they happened to be flirting with—her fat, her finery, and her thick ankles sufficing to give piquancy to the joke, notwithstanding the absence of novelty. Miss Rebecca, however, possessed the accomplishment of music, and her singing of "Oh no, we never mention her," and "The Soldier's Tear," was so desirable an accession to the pleasures of a tea-party that no one cared to offend her, especially as Rebecca had a high spirit of her own, and, in spite of her expansively rounded contour, had a particularly sharp tongue. Her reading had been more extensive than her sister's, embracing most of the fiction in Mr. Procter's circulating library, and nothing but an acquaintance with the course of her studies could afford a clue to the rapid transitions in her dress, which were suggested by the style of beauty, whether sentimental, sprightly, or severe, possessed by the heroine of the three volumes actually in perusal. A piece of lace, which drooped round the edge of her white bonnet one week, had been rejected by the next; and her cheeks, which, on Whitsunday, loomed through a Turnerian haze of network, were, on Trinity Sunday, seen reposing in distinct red outline on her shelving bust, like the sun on a fog-bank. The black velvet, meeting with a crystal clasp which one evening encircled her head, had on another descended to her neck, and on a third to her wrist, suggesting to an active imagination either a magical contraction of the ornament, or a fearful ratio of expansion in Miss Rebecca's person. With this constant application of art to dress, she could have had little time for fancy-work, even if she had not been destitute of her sister's taste for that delightful and truly feminine occupation. And here, at least, you perceive the justice of the Milby opinion as to the relative suitability of the two Miss Linnets for matrimony. When a man is happy enough to win the affections of a sweet girl, who can soothe his cares with *crochet*, and respond to all his most cherished ideas with beaded urn-rugs and chair-covers in German wool, he has, at least, a guaranty of domestic comfort, whatever trials may await him out of doors. What a resource it is under fatigue and irritation to have your drawing-room well supplied with small mats, which would always be ready if you ever wanted to set any thing on them! And what styptic for a bleeding heart can equal copious squares of *crochet*, which are useful for slipping down the moment you touch them? How our fathers managed without *crochet* is the wonder; but I believe some small and feeble substitute existed in their time under the name of "tatting." Rebecca Linnet, however, had neglected tatting as well as other forms of fancy-work. At school, to be sure, she had spent a great deal of time in acquiring flower-painting, according to the ingenious method then fashionable, of applying the shapes of leaves and flowers cut out in cardboard, and scrubbing a brush over the surface thus conveniently marked out; but even the spill-cases and hand-screens, which were her last half-year's performances in that way, were not considered eminently successful, and had long been consigned to the retirement of the best bed-room. Thus there was a good deal of family unlikeness between Rebecca and her sister, and I am afraid there was also a little family dislike; but Mary's disapproval had usually been kept imprisoned behind her thin lips, for Rebecca was not only of a headstrong disposition, but was her mother's pet; the old lady being herself stout, and preferring a more showy style of cap than she could prevail on her daughter Mary to make up for her.

But I have been describing Miss Rebecca as she was in former days only, for her appearance this evening, as she sits pasting on the green tickets, is in striking contrast with what it was three or four months ago. Her plain gray gingham dress and plain white collar could never have belonged to her wardrobe before that date; and though she is not reduced in size, and her brown hair will do nothing but hang in crisp ringlets down her large cheeks, there is a change in her air and expression which seems to shed a softened light over her person, and make her look like a peony in the shade, instead of the same flower flaunting in a parterre in the hot sunlight.

No one could deny that Evangelicalism had wrought a change for the better in Rebecca Linnet's person—not even Miss Pratt, the thin stiff lady in spectacles, seated opposite to her, who always had a peculiar repulsion for "females with a gross habit of body." Miss Pratt was an old maid; but that is a no more definite description than if I had said she was in the autumn of life. Was it autumn when the orchards are fragrant with apples, or autumn when the oaks are brown, or autumn when the last yellow leaves are fluttering in the chill breeze? The young ladies in Milby would have told you that the Miss Linnets were old maids; but the Miss Linnets were to Miss Pratt what the apple-scented September is to the bare, nipping days of late November. The Miss Linnets were in that temperate zone of old maidism, when a woman will not say but that if a man of suitable years and character were to offer himself, she might be induced to tread the remainder of life's vale in company with him; Miss Pratt was in that arctic region where a woman is confident that at no time of life would she have consented to give up her liberty, and that she has never seen the man whom she would engage to honor and obey. If the Miss Linnets were old maids, they were old maids with natural ringlets and embonpoint, not to say obesity; Miss Pratt was an old maid with a cap, a braided "front," a backbone and appendages. Miss Pratt was the one blue-stocking of Milby, possessing, she said, no less than five hundred volumes, competent, as her brother the doctor often observed, to conduct a conversation on any topic whatever, and occasionally dabbling a little in authorship, though it was understood that she had never put forth the full powers of her mind in print. Her "Letters to a Young Man on his Entrance into Life," and "De Courcy, or the Rash Promise, a Tale for Youth," were mere trifles which she had been induced to publish because they were calculated for popular utility, but they were nothing to what she had for years had by her in manuscript. Her latest production had been Six Stanzas, addressed to the Rev. Edgar Tryan, printed on glazed paper with a neat border, and beginning, "Forward, young wrestler for the truth!"

Miss Pratt having kept her brother's house during his long widowhood, his daughter, Miss Eliza, had had the advantage of being educated by her aunt, and thus of imbibing a very strong antipathy to all that remarkable woman's tastes and opinions. The silent, handsome girl of two-and-twenty, who is covering the "Memoirs of Felix Neff," is Miss Eliza Pratt; and the small elderly lady in dowdy clothing, who is also working diligently, is Mrs. Pettifer, a superior-minded widow, much valued in Milby, being such a very respectable person to have in the house in case of illness, and of quite too good a family to receive any money-payment—you could always send her garden-stuff that would make her ample amends. Miss Pratt has enough to do in commenting on the heap of volumes before her, feeling it a responsibility entailed on her by her great powers of mind to leave nothing without the advantage of her opinion. Whatever was good must be sprinkled with the chrism of her approval; whatever was evil must be blighted by her condemnation.

"Upon my word," she said, in a deliberate high voice, as if she were dictating to an amanuensis, "it is a most admirable selection of works for popular reading, this that our excellent Mr. Tryan has made. I do not know whether, if the task had been confided to me, I could have made a selection combining in a higher degree religious instruction and edification with a due admixture of the purer species of amusement. This story of 'Father Clement' is a library in itself on the errors of Romanism. I have ever considered fiction a suitable form for conveying moral and religious instruction, as I have shown in my little work 'De Courcy,' which, as a very clever writer in the 'Crompton Argus' said at the time of its appearance, is the light vehicle of a weighty moral."

"One 'ud think," said Mrs. Linnet, who also had her spectacles on, but chiefly for the purpose of seeing what the others were doing, "there didn't want much to drive people away from a religion as makes 'em walk barefoot over stone floors, like that girl in 'Father Clement'—sending the blood up to the head frightful. Any body might see that was an unnat'ral creed."

"Yes," said Miss Pratt, "but asceticism is not the root of the error, as Mr. Tryan was telling us the other evening—it is the denial of the great doctrine of justification by faith. Much as I had reflected on all subjects in the course of my life, I am indebted to Mr. Tryan for opening my eyes to the full importance of that cardinal doctrine of the Reformation. From a child I had a deep sense of religion, but in my early days the Gospel light was obscured in the English Church, notwithstanding the possession of our incomparable liturgy, than which I know no human composition more faultless and sublime. As I tell Eliza, I was not blest as she is at the age of two-and-twenty, in knowing a clergyman who unites all that is great and admirable in intellect with the highest spiritual gifts. I am no contemptible judge of a man's acquirements, and I assure you I have tested Mr. Tryan's by questions which are a pretty severe touchstone. It is true, I sometimes carry him a little beyond the depth of the other listeners. Profound learning," continued Miss Pratt, shutting her spectacles, and tapping them on the book before her, "has not many to estimate it in Milby."

"Miss Pratt," said Rebecca, "will you please give me

Scott's Force of Truth?' There—that small book lying against the 'Life of Legh Richmond.'"

"That's a book I'm very fond of—the 'Life of Legh Richmond,'" said Mrs. Linnet. "He found out all about that woman at Tutbury as pretended to live without eating. Stuff and nonsense!"

Mrs. Linnet had become a reader of religious books since Mr. Tryan's advent, and as she was in the habit of confining her perusal to the purely secular portions, which bore a very small proportion to the whole, she could make rapid progress through a large number of volumes. On taking up the biography of a celebrated preacher she immediately turned to the end to see what disease he died of; and if his legs swelled, as her own occasionally did, she felt a stronger interest in ascertaining any earlier facts in the history of the dropsical divine—whether he had ever fallen off a stage-coach, whether he had married more than one wife, and, in general, any adventures or repartees recorded of him previous to the epoch of his conversion. She then glanced over the letters and diary, and wherever there was a predominance of Zion, the River of Life, and notes of exclamation, she turned over to the next page; but any passage in which she saw such promising nouns as "small-pox," "pony," or "boots and shoes," at once arrested her.

"It is half past six now," said Miss Linnet, looking at her watch as the servant appeared with the tea-tray. "I suppose the delegates are come back by this time. If Mr. Tryan had not so kindly promised to call and let us know, I should hardly rest without walking to Milby myself to know what answer they have brought back. It is a great privilege for us, Mr. Tryan living at Mrs. Wagstaff's, for he is often able to take us on his way backward and forward into the town."

"I wonder if there's another man in the world who has been brought up as Mr. Tryan has, that would choose to live in those small close rooms on the common, among heaps of dirty cottages, for the sake of being near the poor people," said Mrs. Pettifer. "I'm afraid he hurts his health by it; he looks to me far from strong."

"Ah," said Miss Pratt, "I understand he is of a highly respectable family indeed, in Huntingdonshire. I heard him myself speak of his father's carriage—quite incidentally, you know—and Eliza tells me what very fine cambric handkerchiefs he uses. My eyes are not good enough to see such things, but I know what breeding is as well as most people, and it is easy to see that Mr. Tryan is quite *comme il faw*, to use a French expression."

"I should like to tell him better nor use fine cambric i' this place, where there's such washing; it's a shame to be seen," said Mrs. Linnet; "he'll get 'em tore to pieces. Good lawn 'ud be far better. I saw what a color his linen looked at the sacrament last Sunday. Mary's making him a black silk case to hold his bands, but I told her she'd more need wash 'em for him."

"Oh, mother!" said Rebecca, with solemn severity, "pray don't think of pocket-handkerchiefs and linen, when we are talking of such a man. And at this moment, too, when he is perhaps having to bear a heavy blow. We don't know but wickedness may have triumphed, and Mr. Prendergast may have consented to forbid the lecture. There have been dispensations quite as mysterious, and Satan is evidently putting forth all his strength to resist the entrance of the Gospel into Milby Church."

"You niver spoke a truer word than that, my dear," said Mrs. Linnet, who accepted all religious phrases, but was extremely rationalistic in her interpretation; "for if iver Old Harry appeared in a human form, it's that Dempster. It was all through him as we got cheated out o' Pye's Croft, making out as the title wasn't good. Such lawyer's villainy! As if paying good money wasn't title enough to any thing. If your father as is dead and gone had been worthy to know it! But he'll have a fall some day, Dempster will. Mark my words."

"Ah, out of his carriage, you mean," said Miss Pratt, who, in the movement occasioned by the clearing of the table, had lost the first part of Mrs. Linnet's speech. "It certainly is alarming to see him driving home from Rotherby, flogging his galloping horse like a madman. My brother has often said he expected every Thursday evening to be called in to set some of Dempster's bones; but I suppose he may drop that expectation now, for we are given to understand from good authority that he has forbidden his wife to call my brother in again either to herself or her mother. He swears no Tryanite doctor shall attend his family. I have reason to believe that Pilgrim was called in to Mrs. Dempster's mother the other day."

"Poor Mrs. Raynor! she's glad to do any thing for the sake of peace and quietness," said Mrs. Pettifer; "but it's no trifle at her time of life to part with a doctor who knows her constitution."

"What trouble that poor woman has to bear in her old age!" said Mary Linnet, "to see her daughter leading such a life!—an only daughter, too, that she doats on."

"Yes, indeed," said Miss Pratt. "We, of course, know

more about it than most people, my brother having attended the family so many years. For my part, I never thought well of the marriage; and I endeavored to dissuade my brother when Mrs. Raynor asked him to give Janet away at the wedding. 'If you will take my advice, Richard,' I said, 'you will have nothing to do with that marriage.' And he has seen the justice of my opinion since. Mrs. Raynor herself was against the connection at first; but she always spoiled Janet; and I fear, too, she was won over by a foolish pride in having her daughter marry a professional man. I fear it was so. No one but myself, I think, foresaw the extent of the evil."

"Well," said Mrs. Pettifer, "Janet had nothing to look to but being a governess; and it was hard for Mrs. Raynor to have to work at millinering—a woman well brought up, and her husband a man who held his head as high as any man in Thurston. And it isn't every body that sees every thing fifteen years beforehand. Robert Dempster was the cleverest man in Milby; and there weren't many young men fit to talk to Janet."

"It is a thousand pities," said Miss Pratt, choosing to ignore Mrs. Pettifer's slight sarcasm, "for I certainly did consider Janet Raynor the most promising young woman of my acquaintance;—a little too much lifted up, perhaps, by her superior education, and too much given to satire, but able to express herself very well indeed about any book I recommended to her perusal. There is no young woman in Milby now who can be compared with what Janet was when she was married, either in mind or person. I consider Miss Landor far, far below her. Indeed, I can not say much for the mental superiority of the young ladies in our first families. They are superficial—very superficial."

"She made the handsomest bride that ever came out of Milby Church, too," said Mrs. Pettifer. "Such a very fine figure! and it showed off her white poplin so well. And what a pretty smile Janet always had! Poor thing, she keeps that now for all her old friends. I never see her but she has something pretty to say to me—living in the same street, you know, I can't help seeing her often, though I've never been to the house since Dempster broke out on me in one of his drunken fits. She comes to me sometimes, poor thing, looking so strange, any body passing her in the street may see plain enough what's the matter; but she's always got some little good-natured plan in her head, for all that. Only last night when I met her, I saw five yards off she wasn't fit to be out; but she had a basin in her hand, full of something she was carrying to Sally Martin, the deformed girl that's in a consumption."

"But she is just as bitter against Mr. Tryan as her husband is, I understand," said Rebecca. "Her heart is very much set against the truth, for I understand she bought Mr. Tryan's sermons on purpose to ridicule them to Mrs. Crewe."

"Well, poor thing," said Mrs. Pettifer, "you know she stands up for every thing her husband says and does. She never will admit to any body that he's not a good husband."

"That is her pride," said Miss Pratt. "She married him in opposition to the advice of her best friends, and now she is not willing to admit that she was wrong. Why, even to my brother—and a medical attendant, you know, can hardly fail to be acquainted with family secrets—she has always pretended to have the highest respect for her husband's qualities. Poor Mrs. Raynor, however, is well aware that every one knows the real state of things. Latterly, she has not even avoided the subject with me. The very last time I called on her she said, 'Have you been to see my poor daughter?' and burst into tears."

"Pride or no pride," said Mrs. Pettifer, "I shall always stand up for Janet Dempster. She sat up with me night after night when I had that attack of rheumatic fever six years ago. There's great excuses for her. When a woman can't think of her husband coming home without trembling, it's enough to make her drink something to blunt her feelings—and no children, either, to keep her from it. You and me might do the same, if we were in her place."

"Speak for yourself, Mrs. Pettifer," said Miss Pratt. "Under no circumstances can I imagine myself resorting to a practice so degrading. A woman should find support in her own strength of mind."

"I think," said Rebecca, who considered Miss Pratt still very blind in spiritual things, notwithstanding her assumption of enlightenment, "she will find poor support if she trusts only to her own strength. She must seek aid elsewhere than in herself."

Happily the removal of the tea-things just then created a little confusion, which aided Miss Pratt to repress her resentment at Rebecca's presumption in correcting her—a person like Rebecca Linnet! who six months ago was as flighty and vain a woman as Miss Pratt had ever known—so very unconscious of her unfortunate person!

The ladies had scarcely been seated at their work another hour, when the sun was sinking, and the clouds that flecked the sky to the very zenith were every moment taking on a brighter gold. The gate of the little garden opened, and Miss Linnet, seated at her small table near the window, saw Mr. Tryan enter.

"There is Mr. Tryan," she said, and her pale cheek was lighted up with a little blush that would have made her look more attractive to almost any one except Miss Eliza Pratt, whose fine gray eyes allowed few things to escape her silent observation. "Mary Linnet gets more and more in love with Mr. Tryan," thought Miss Eliza; "it is really pitiable to see such feelings in a woman of her age, with those old-maidish little ringlets. I dare say she flatters herself Mr. Tryan may fall in love with her, because he makes her useful among the poor." At the same time, Miss Eliza, as she bent her handsome head and large cannon curls with apparent calmness over her work, felt a considerable internal flutter when she heard the knock at the door. Rebecca had less self-command. She felt too much agitated to go on with her pasting, and clutched the leg of the table to counteract the trembling in her hands.

Poor women's hearts! Heaven forbid that I should laugh at you, and make cheap jests on your susceptibility towards the clerical sex, as if it had nothing deeper or more lovely in it than the mere vulgar angling for a husband. Even in these enlightened days, many a curate who, considered abstractedly, is nothing more than a sleek bimanous animal in a white neckcloth, with views more or less Anglican, and furtively addicted to the flute, is adored by a girl who has coarse brothers, or by a solitary woman who would like to be a helpmate in good works beyond her own means, simply because he seems to them the model of refinement and of public usefulness. What wonder, then, that in Milby society, such as I have told you it was a very long while ago, a zealous evangelical clergyman, aged thirty-three, called forth all the little agitations that belong to the divine necessity of loving, implanted in the Miss Linnets, with their seven or eight lustrums and their unfashionable ringlets, no less than in Miss Eliza Pratt, with her youthful bloom and her ample cannon curls.

But Mr. Tryan has entered the room, and the strange light from the golden sky falling on his light-brown hair, which is brushed high up round his head, makes it look almost like an auréole. His gray eyes, too, shine with unwonted brilliancy this evening. They were not remarkable eyes, but they accorded completely in their changing light with the changing expression of his person, which indicated the paradoxical character often observable in a large-limbed sanguine blond; at once mild and irritable, gentle and overbearing, indolent and resolute, self-conscious and dreamy. Except that the well-filled lips had something of the artificially compressed look which is often the sign of a struggle to keep the dragon undermost, and that the complexion was rather pallid, giving the idea of imperfect health, Mr. Tryan's face in repose was that of an ordinary whiskerless blond, and it seemed difficult to refer a certain air of distinction about him to any thing in particular, unless it were his delicate hands and well-shapen feet.

It was a great anomaly to the Milby mind that a canting evangelical parson, who would take tea with tradespeople, and make friends of vulgar women like the Linnets, should have so much the air of a gentleman, and be so little like the splay-footed Mr. Stickney of Salem, to whom he approximated so closely in doctrine. And this want of correspondence between the physique and the creed had excited no less surprise in the larger town of Laxeter, where Mr. Tryan had formerly held a curacy; for of the two other Low Church clergymen in the neighborhood, one was a Welshman of globose figure and unctuous complexion, and the other a man of atrabiliar aspect, with lank black hair, and a redundance of limp cravat—in fact, the sort of thing you might expect in men who distributed the publications of the Religious Tract Society, and introduced Dissenting hymns into the Church.

Mr. Tryan shook hands with Mrs. Linnet, bowed with rather a preoccupied air to the other ladies, and seated himself in the large horse-hair easy-chair which had been drawn forward for him, while the ladies ceased from their work, and fixed their eyes on him, awaiting the news he had to tell them.

"It seems," he began, in a low and silvery tone, "I need a lesson of patience; there has been something wrong in my thought or action about this evening lecture. I have been too much bent on doing good to Milby after my own plan—too reliant on my own wisdom."

Mr. Tryan paused. He was struggling against inward irritation.

"The delegates are come back, then?" "Has Mr. Prendergast given way?" "Has Dempster succeeded?"—were the eager questions of three ladies at once.

"Yes; the town is in an uproar. As we were sitting in Mr. Landor's drawing-room we heard a loud cheering, and presently Mr. Thrupp, the clerk at the bank, who had been waiting at the Red Lion to hear the result, came to let us know. He said Dempster had been making a speech to the mob out the window. They were distributing drink to the people, and hoisting placards in great letters,—'Down with the Tryanites!' 'Down with cant!' They had a hideous caricature of me being tripped-up and pitched head-foremost out of the pulpit. Good old Mr. Landor would insist on sending me round in the carriage; he thought I should not be safe from the mob; but I got down at the Crossways. The row was evidently preconcerted by Dempster before he set out. He made sure of succeeding."

Mr. Tryan's utterance had been getting rather louder and more rapid in the course of this speech, and he now added, in the energetic chest-voice, which, both in and out of the pulpit, alternated continually with his more silvery notes,

"But his triumph will be a short one. If he thinks he can intimidate me by obloquy or threats, he has mistaken the man he has to deal with. Mr. Dempster and his colleagues will find themselves checkmated after all. Mr. Prendergast has been false to his own conscience in this business. He knows as well as I do that he is throwing away the souls of the people by leaving things as they are in the parish. But I shall appeal to the Bishop—I am confident of his sympathy."

"The Bishop will be coming shortly, I suppose," said Miss Pratt, "to hold a confirmation?"

"Yes; but I shall write to him at once, and lay the case before him. Indeed, I must hurry away now, for I have many matters to attend to. You, ladies, have been kindly helping me with your labors, I see," continued Mr. Tryan, politely, glancing at the canvas-covered books as he rose from his seat. Then, turning to Mary Linnet: "Our library is really getting on, I think. You and your sister have quite a heavy task of distribution now."

Poor Rebecca felt it very hard to bear that Mr. Tryan did not turn towards her too. If he knew how much she entered into his feelings about the lecture, and the interest she took in the library. Well! perhaps it was her lot to be overlooked—and it might be a token of mercy. Even a good man might not always know the heart that was most with him. But the next moment poor Mary had a pang, when Mr. Tryan turned to Miss Eliza Pratt, and the preoccupied expression of his face melted into that beaming timidity with which a man almost always addresses a pretty woman.

"I have to thank you, too, Miss Eliza, for seconding me so well in your visits to Joseph Mercer. The old man tells me how precious he finds your reading to him, now he is no longer able to go to church."

Miss Eliza only answered by a blush, which made her look all the handsomer, but her aunt said,

"Yes, Mr. Tryan, I have ever inculcated on my dear Eliza the importance of spending her leisure in being useful to her fellow-creatures. Your example and instruction have been quite in the spirit of the system which I have always pursued, though we are indebted to you for a clearer view of the motives that should actuate us in our pursuit of good works. Not that I can accuse myself of having ever had a self-righteous spirit, but my humility was rather instinctive than based on a firm ground of doctrinal knowledge, such as you so admirably impart to us."

Mrs. Linnet's usual entreaty that Mr. Tryan would "have something — some wine-and-water and a biscuit," was just here a welcome relief from the necessity of answering Miss Pratt's oration.

"Not any thing, my dear Mrs. Linnet, thank you. You forget what a Rechabite I am. By-the-by, when I went this morning to see a poor girl in Butcher's Lane, whom I had heard of as being in a consumption, I found Mrs. Dempster there. I had often met her in the street, but did not know it was Mrs. Dempster. It seems she goes among the poor a good deal. She is really an interesting-looking woman. I was quite surprised, for I have heard the worst account of her habits—that she is almost as bad as her husband. She went out hastily as soon as I entered. But" (apologetically) "I am keeping you all standing, and I must really hurry away. Mrs. Pettifer, I have not had the pleasure of calling on you for some time; I shall take an early opportunity of going your way. Good-evening, good-evening."

CHAPTER IV.

Mr. Tryan was right in saying that the "row" in Milby had been preconcerted by Dempster. The placards and the caricature were prepared before the departure of the delegates; and it had been settled that Mat Paine, Dempster's clerk, should ride out on Thursday morning to meet them at Whitlow, the last place where they would change horses, that he might gallop back and prepare an ovation for the triumvirate in case of their success. Dempster had determined to dine at Whitlow; so that Mat Paine was in Milby again two hours before the entrance of the delegates, and had time to send a whisper up the back streets that there was promise of a "spree" in the Bridge Way, as well as to assemble two knots of picked men—one to feed the flame of orthodox zeal with gin-and-water, at the Green Man, near High Street; the other to solidify their church principles with heady beer at the Bear and Ragged Staff in the Bridge Way.

The Bridge Way was an irregular straggling street, where the town fringed off raggedly into the Whitlow road: rows of new red brick houses, in which ribbon-looms were rattling behind long lines of window, alternating with old, half-thatched, half-tiled cottages—one of those dismal wide streets where dirt and misery have no long shadows thrown on them to soften their ugliness. Here, about half-past five o'clock, Silly Caleb, an idiot well known in Dog Lane, but more of a stranger in the Bridge Way, was seen slouching along with a string of boys hooting at his heels; presently another group, for the most part out at elbows, came briskly in the same direction, looking round them with an air of expectation; and at no long interval, Deb Traunter, in a pink flounced gown and floating ribbons, was observed talking with great affability to two men in seal-skin caps and fustian, who formed her cortège. The Bridge Way began to have a presentiment of something in the wind. Phib Cook left her evening wash-tub and appeared at her door in soap-suds, a bonnet-poke, and general dampness; three narrow-chested ribbon-weavers, in rusty black streaked with shreds of many-colored silk, sauntered out with their hands in their pockets; and Molly Beale, a brawny old virago, descrying wiry Dame Ricketts peeping out from her entry, seized the opportunity of renewing the morning's skirmish. In short, the Bridge Way was in that state of excitement which is understood to announce a "demonstration" on the part of the British public; and the afflux of remote townsmen increasing, there was soon so large a crowd that it was time for Bill Powers, a plethoric Goliath, who presided over the knot of beer-drinkers at the Bear and Ragged Staff, to issue forth with his companions, and, like the enunciator of the ancient myth, make the assemblage distinctly conscious of the common sentiment that had drawn them together. The expectation of the delegates' chaise, added to the fight between Molly Beale and Dame Ricketts, and the ill-advised appearance of a lean bull-terrier, were a sufficient safety-valve to the popular excitement during the remaining quarter of an hour; at the end of which the chaise was seen approaching along the Whitlow road, with oak boughs ornamenting the horses' heads; and, to quote the account of this interesting scene which was sent to the "Rotherby

Guardian," "loud cheers immediately testified to the sympathy of the honest fellows collected there with the public-spirited exertions of their fellow-townsmen." Bill Powers, whose bloodshot eyes, bent hat, and protuberant altitude, marked him out as the natural leader of the assemblage, undertook to interpret the common sentiment by stopping the chaise, advancing to the door with raised hat, and begging to know of Mr. Dempster, whether the Rector had forbidden the "canting lecture."

"Yes, yes," said Mr. Dempster. "Keep up a jolly good hurray."

No public duty could have been more easy and agreeable to Mr. Powers and his associates, and the chorus swelled all the way to the High Street, where, by a mysterious coincidence often observable in these spontaneous "demonstrations," large placards on long poles were observed to shoot upwards from among the crowd, principally in the direction of Tucker's Lane, where the Green Man was situated. One bore, "Down with the Tryanites!" another, "No Cant!" another, "Long live our venerable Curate!" and one in still larger letters, "Sound Church Principles and no Hypocrisy!" But a still more remarkable impromptu was a huge caricature of Mr. Tryan in gown and band, with an enormous auréole of yellow hair and upturned eyes, standing on the pulpit stairs and trying to pull down old Mr. Crewe. Groans, yells, and hisses—hisses, yells, and groans—only stemmed by the appearance of another caricature representing Mr. Tryan being pitched head-foremost from the pulpit stairs by a hand which the artist, either from subtility of intention or want of space, had left unindicated. In the midst of the tremendous cheering that saluted this piece of symbolical art, the chaise had reached the door of the Red Lion, and loud cries of "Dempster forever!" with a feebler cheer now and then for Tomlinson and Budd, were presently responded to by the appearance of the public-spirited attorney at the large upper window, where also were visible a little in the background the small sleek head of Mr. Budd, and the blinking countenance of Mr. Tomlinson.

Mr. Dempster held his hat in his hand, and poked his head forward with a butting motion by way of bow. A storm of cheers subsided at last into dropping sounds of "Silence!" "Hear him!" "Go it, Dempster!" and the lawyer's rasping voice became distinctly audible.

"Fellow-townsmen! It gives us the sincerest pleasure—I speak for my respected colleagues as well as myself—to witness these strong proofs of your attachment to the principles of our excellent Church, and your zeal for the honor of our venerable pastor. But it is no more than I expected of you. I know you well. I've known you for the last twenty years to be as honest and respectable a set of ratepayers as any in this country. Your hearts are sound to the core! No man had better try to thrust his cant and hypocrisy down *your* throats. You're used to wash them with liquor of a better flavor. This is the proudest moment in my own life, and I think I may say in that of my colleagues, in which I have to tell you that our exertions in the cause of sound religion and manly morality have been crowned with success. Yes, my fellow-townsmen! I have the gratification of announcing to you thus formally what you have already learned indirectly. The pulpit from which our venerable pastor has fed us with sound doctrine for half a century is not to be invaded by a fanatical, sectarian, double-faced, Jesuitical interloper! We are not to have our young people demoralized and corrupted by the temptations to vice, notoriously connected with Sunday evening lectures! We are not to have a preacher obtruding himself upon us, who decries good works, and sneaks into our homes perverting the faith of our wives and daughters! We are not to be poisoned with doctrines which damp every innocent enjoyment, and pick a poor man's pocket of the sixpence with which he might buy himself a cheerful glass after a hard day's work, under pretense of paying for Bibles to send to the Chicktaws!

"But I'm not going to waste your valuable time with unnecessary words. I am a man of deeds" ("Ay, damn you, that you are, and you charge well for 'em too," said a voice from the crowd, probably that of a gentleman who was immediately afterwards observed with his hat crushed over his head). "I shall always be at the service of my fellow-townsmen, and whoever dares to hector over you, or interfere with your innocent pleasures, shall have an account to settle with Robert Dempster.

"Now, my boys! you can't do better than disperse and carry the good news to all your fellow-townsmen, whose hearts are as sound as your own. Let some of you go one way and some another, that every man, woman and child in Milby may know what you know yourselves. But before we part, let us have three cheers for True Religion, and down with Cant!"

When the last cheer was dying, Mr. Dempster closed the window, and the judiciously-instructed placards and caricatures moved off in divers directions, followed by larger or smaller divisions of the crowd. The greatest attraction apparently lay in the direction of Dog Lane, the outlet towards Paddiford Common, whither the caricatures were moving; and you foresee, of course, that those works of symbolical art were consumed with a liberal expenditure of dry gorse-bushes and vague shouting.

After these great public exertions, it was natural that Mr. Dempster and his colleagues should feel more in need than usual of a little social relaxation; and a party of their friends was already beginning to assemble in the large parlor of the Red Lion, convened partly by their own curiosity, and partly by the invaluable Mat Paine. The most capacious punch-bowl was put in requisition; and that born gentleman, Mr. Lowme, seated opposite Mr. Dempster as "Vice," undertook to brew the punch, defying the criticisms of the envious men out of office, who, with the readiness of irresponsibility, ignorantly suggested more lemons. The social festivities were continued till long past midnight, when several friends of sound religion were conveyed home with some difficulty, one of them showing a dogged determination to seat himself in the gutter.

Mr. Dempster had done as much justice to the punch as any of the party; and his friend Boots, though aware that the lawyer could "carry his liquor like Old Nick," with whose social demeanor Boots seemed to be particularly well acquainted, nevertheless thought it might be as well to see so good a customer in safety to his own door, and walked quietly behind his elbow out of the inn-yard. Dempster, however, soon became aware of him, stopped short, and, turning slowly round upon him, recognized the well-known drab waistcoat sleeves, conspicuous enough in the starlight.

"You twopenny scoundrel! What do you mean by dogging a professional man's footsteps in this way? I'll break every bone in your skin if you attempt to track me, like a beastly cur sniffing at one's pocket. Do you think a gentleman will make his way home any the better for having the scent of your blacking-bottle thrust up his nostrils?"

Boots slunk back, in more amusement than ill-humor, thinking the lawyer's "rum talk" was doubtless part and parcel of his professional ability; and Mr. Dempster pursued his slow way alone.

His house lay in Orchard Street, which opened on the prettiest outskirt of the town—the church, the parsonage, and a long stretch of green fields. It was an old-fashioned house, with an overhanging upper story; outside it had a face of rough stucco, and casement windows with green frames and shutters; inside, it was full of long passages, and rooms with low ceilings. There was a large heavy knocker on the green door, and though Mr. Dempster carried a latch-key, he sometimes chose to use the knocker. He chose to do so now. The thunder resounded through Orchard Street, and, after a single minute, there was a second clap louder than the first. Another minute, and still the door was not opened; whereupon Mr. Dempster, muttering, took out his latch-key, and, with less difficulty than might have been expected, thrust it into the door. When he opened the door the passage was dark.

"Janet!" in the loudest rasping tone, was the next sound that rang through the house.

"Janet!" again—before a slow step was heard on the stairs, and a distant light began to flicker on the wall of the passage.

"Curse you! you creeping idiot! Come faster, can't you?"

Yet a few seconds, and the figure of a tall woman, holding aslant a heavy-plated drawing-room candlestick, appeared at the turning of the passage that led to the broader entrance.

She had on a light dress which sat loosely about her figure, but did not disguise its liberal, graceful outline. A heavy mass of straight jet-black hair had escaped from its fastening, and hung over her shoulders. Her grandly-cut features, pale, with the natural paleness of a brunette, had premature lines about them, telling that the years had been lengthened by sorrow, and the delicately-curved nostril, which seemed made to quiver with the proud consciousness of power and beauty, must have quivered to the heart-piercing griefs which had given that worn look to the corners of the mouth. Her wide-open black eyes had a strangely fixed, sightless gaze, as she paused at the turning, and stood silent before her husband.

"I'll teach you to keep me waiting in the dark, you pale staring fool!" he said, advancing with his slow drunken step. "What, you've been drinking again, have you? I'll beat you into your senses."

He laid his hand with a firm grip on her shoulder, turned her round, and pushed her slowly before him along the passage and through the dining-room door, which stood open on their left hand.

There was a portrait of Janet's mother, a gray-haired, dark-eyed old woman, in a neatly fluted cap, hanging over the mantel-piece. Surely the aged eyes take on a look of anguish as they see Janet—not trembling, no! it would be better if she trembled—standing stupidly unmoved in her great beauty, while the heavy arm is lifted to strike her. The blow falls—another—and another. Surely the mother hears that cry—"Oh, Robert! pity! pity!"

Poor gray-haired woman! Was it for this you suffered a mother's pangs in your lone widowhood five-and-thirty years ago? Was it for this you kept the little worn morocco shoes Janet had first run in, and kissed them day by day when she was away from you, a tall girl at school? Was it for this you looked proudly at her when she came back to you in her rich pale beauty, like a tall white arum that has just unfolded its grand pure curves to the sun?

The mother lies sleepless and praying in her lonely house, weeping the difficult tears of age, because she dreads this may be a cruel night for her child.

She too has a picture over her mantel-piece, drawn in chalk by Janet long years ago. She looked at it before she went to bed. It is a head bowed beneath a cross, and wearing a crown of thorns.

CHAPTER V.

It was half past nine o'clock in the morning. The midsummer sun was already warm on the roofs and weathercocks of Milby. The church-bells were ringing, and many families were conscious of Sunday sensations, chiefly referable to the fact that the daughters had come down to breakfast in their best frocks, and with their hair particularly well dressed. For it was not Sunday, but Wednesday; and though the Bishop was going to hold a Confirmation, and to decide whether or not there should be a Sunday evening lecture in Milby, the sunbeams had the usual working-day look to the hay-makers already long out in the fields, and to laggard weavers just "setting up" their week's "piece." The notion of its being Sunday was the strongest in young ladies like Miss Phipps, who was going to accompany her younger sister to the confirmation, and to wear a "sweetly pretty" transparent bonnet with marabout feathers on the interesting occasion, thus throwing into relief the suitable simplicity of her sister's attire, who was, of course, to appear in a new white frock; or in the pupils at Miss Townley's, who were absolved from all lessons, and were going to church to see the Bishop, and to hear the Honorable and Reverend Mr. Prendergast, the rector, read prayers—a high intellectual treat, as Miss Townley assured them. It seemed only natural that a rector who was honorable should read better than old Mr. Crewe, who was only a curate, and not honorable; and when little Clara Robins wondered why some clergymen were rectors and others not, Ellen Marriott assured her with great confidence that it was only the clever men who were made rectors. Ellen Marriott was going to be confirmed. She was a short, fair, plump girl, with blue eyes and sandy hair, which was this morning arranged in taller cannon curls than usual, for the reception of the Episcopal benediction, and some of the young ladies thought her the prettiest girl in the school; but others gave the preference to her rival, Maria Gardner, who was much taller, and had a lovely " crop " of dark-brown ringlets, and who, being also about to take upon herself the vows made in her name at her baptism, had oiled and twisted her ringlets with special care. As she seated herself at the breakfast-table before Miss Townley's entrance to dispense the weak coffee, her crop excited so strong a sensation that Ellen Marriott was at length impelled to look at it, and to say with suppressed but bitter sarcasm, "Is that Miss Gardner's head?" "Yes," said Maria, amiable and stuttering, and no match for Ellen in retort; "th—th—this is my head." "Then I don't admire it at all!" was the crushing rejoinder of Ellen, followed by a murmur of approval among her friends. Young ladies, I suppose, exhaust their sac of venom in this way at school. That is the reason why they have such a harmless tooth for each other in after life.

The only other candidate for confirmation at Miss Townley's was Mary Dunn, a draper's daughter in Milby and a distant relation of the Miss Linnets. Her pale lanky hair could never be coaxed into permanent curl, and this morning the heat had brought it down to its natural condition of lankiness earlier than usual. But that was not what made her sit melancholy and apart at the lower end of the form. Her parents were admirers of Mr. Tryan, and had been persuaded, by the Miss Linnets' influence, to insist that their daughter should be prepared for confirmation by him, over and above the preparation given to Miss Townley's pupils by Mr. Crewe. Poor Mary Dunn! I am afraid she thought it too heavy a price to pay for these spiritual advantages, to be excluded from every game at ball, to be obliged to walk with none but little girls—in fact, to be the object of an aversion that nothing short of an incessant supply of plumcakes would have neutralized. And Mrs. Dunn was of opinion that plumcake was unwholesome. The anti-Tryanite spirit, you perceive, was very strong at Miss Townley's, imported probably by day scholars, as well as encouraged by the fact that that clever woman was herself strongly opposed to innovation, and remarked every Sunday that Mr. Crewe had preached an "excellent discourse." Poor Mary Dunn dreaded the moment when school-hours would be over, for then she was sure to be the butt of those very explicit remarks which, in young ladies' as well as young gentlemen's seminaries, constitute the most subtle and delicate form of the innuendo. "I'd never be a Tryanite, would you?" "Oh here comes the lady that knows so much more about religion than we do!" "Some people think themselves so very pious!"

It is really surprising that young ladies should not be thought competent to the same curriculum as young gentlemen. I observe that their powers of sarcasm are quite equal; and if there had been a genteel academy for young gentlemen at Milby, I am inclined to think that, notwithstanding Euclid and the classics, the party spirit there would not have exhibited itself in more pungent irony, or more incisive satire, than was heard in Miss Townley's seminary. But there was no such academy, the existence of the grammar-school under Mr. Crewe's superintendence probably discouraging speculations of that kind; and the genteel youths of Milby were chiefly come home for the midsummer holidays from distant schools. Several of us had just assumed coat-tails, and the assumption of new responsibilities apparently following as a matter of course, we were among the candidates for confirmation. I wish I could say that the solemnity of our feelings was on a level with the solemnity of the occasion; but unimaginative boys find it difficult to recognize apostolical institutions in their developed form, and I fear our chief emotion concerning the ceremony was a sense of sheepishness, and our chief opinion, the speculative and heretical position that it ought to be confined to the girls. It was a pity, you will say; but it is the way with us men in other crises, that come a long while after confirmation. The golden moments in the stream of life rush past us, and we see nothing but sand; the angels come to visit us, and we only know them when they are gone.

But as I said, the morning was sunny, the bells were ringing, the ladies of Milby were dressed in their Sunday garments.

And who is this bright-looking woman walking with hasty step along Orchard Street so early, with a large nosegay in her hand? Can it be Janet Dempster, on whom we looked with such deep pity, one sad midnight, hardly a fortnight ago? Yes; no other woman in Milby has those searching black eyes, that tall, graceful, unconstrained figure, set off by her simple muslin dress and black lace shawl, that massy black hair now so neatly braided in glossy contrast with the white satin ribbons of her modest cap and bonnet. No other woman has that sweet speaking smile, with which she nods to Jonathan Lamb, the old parish clerk. And, ah!—now she comes nearer—there are those sad lines about the mouth and eyes on which that sweet smile plays like sunbeams on the storm-beaten beauty of the full and ripened corn.

She is turning out of Orchard Street, and making her way as fast as she can to her mother's house, a pleasant cottage facing the roadside meadow, from which the hay is being carried. Mrs. Raynor has had her breakfast, and is seated in her arm-chair reading, when Janet opens the door, saying, in her most playful voice,

"Please, mother, I'm come to show myself to you before I go to the Parsonage. Have I put on my pretty cap and bonnet to satisfy you?"

Mrs. Raynor looked over her spectacles, and met her daughter's glance with eyes as dark and loving as her own. She was a much smaller woman than Janet, both in figure and feature, the chief resemblance lying in the eyes and the clear brunette complexion. The mother's hair had long been gray, and was gathered under the neatest of caps, made by her own clever fingers, as all Janet's caps and bonnets were too. They were well-practised fingers, for Mrs. Raynor had supported herself in her widowhood by keeping a millinery establishment, and in this way had earned money enough to give her daughter what was then thought a first-rate education, as well as to save a sum which, eked out by her son-in-law, sufficed to support her in her solitary old age. Always the same clean, neat old lady, dressed in black silk, was Mrs. Raynor: a patient, brave woman, who bowed with resignation under the burden of remembered sorrow, and bore with meek fortitude the new load that the new days brought with them.

"Your bonnet wants pulling a trifle forwarder, my child," she said, smiling, and taking off her spectacles, while Janet at once knelt down before her, and waited to be "set to rights," as she would have done when she was a child. "You're going straight to Mrs. Crewe's, I suppose? Are those flowers to garnish the dishes?"

"No, indeed, mother. This is a nosegay for the middle of the table. I've sent up the dinner-service and the ham we had cooked at our house yesterday, and Betty is coming directly with the garnish and the plate. We shall get our good Mrs. Crewe through her troubles famously. Dear tiny woman! You should have seen her lift up her hands yesterday, and pray heaven to take her before ever she should have another collation to get ready for the Bishop. She said, 'It's bad enough to have the Archdeacon, though he doesn't want half so many jelly-glasses. I wouldn't mind, Janet, if it was to feed all the old hungry cripples in Milby; but so much trouble and expense for people who eat too much every day of their lives!' We had such a cleaning and furbishing up of the sitting-room yesterday! Nothing will ever do away with the smell of Mr. Crewe's pipes, you know; but we have thrown it into the background with yellow soap and dry lavender. And now I must run away. You will come to church, mother?"

"Yes, my dear, I wouldn't lose such a pretty sight. It does my old eyes good to see so many fresh young faces. Is your husband going?"

"Yes, Robert will be there. I've made him as neat as a new pin this morning, and he says the Bishop will think him too buckish by half. I took him into Mammy Dempster's room to show himself. We hear Tryan is making sure of the Bishop's support; but we shall see. I would give my crooked guinea, and all the luck it will ever bring me, to have him beaten, for I can't endure the sight of the man coming to harass dear old Mr. and Mrs. Crewe in their last days. Preaching the Gospel indeed! That is the best Gospel that makes every body happy and comfortable, isn't it, mother?"

"Ah, child, I'm afraid there's no Gospel will do that here below."

"Well, I can do something to comfort Mrs. Crewe, at least; so give me a kiss, and good-bye till church-time."

The mother leaned back in her chair when Janet was gone and sank into a painful reverie. When our life is a continuous trial, the moments of respite seem only to substitute the heaviness of dread for the heaviness of actual suffering: the curtain of cloud seems parted an instant only that we may measure all its horror as it hangs low, black, and imminent, in contrast with the transient brightness; the water-drops that visit the parched lips in the desert bear with them only the keen imagination of thirst. Janet looked glad and tender now —but what scene of misery was coming next? She was too like the cistus-flowers in the little garden before the window, that, with the shades of evening, might lie with the delicate white and glossy dark of their petals trampled in the roadside dust. When the sun had sunk, and the twilight was deepening, Janet might be sitting there, heated, maddened, sobbing out her griefs with selfish passion, and wildly wishing herself dead.

Mrs. Raynor had been reading about the lost sheep, and the joy there is in heaven over the sinner that repenteth. Surely the eternal love she believed in through all the sadness of her lot, would not leave her child to wander farther and farther into the wilderness till there was no turning; the child so lovely, so pitiful to others, so good, till she was goaded into sin by woman's bitterest sorrows! Mrs. Raynor had her faith and her spiritual comforts, though she was not in the least evangelical and knew nothing of doctrinal zeal. I fear most of Mr. Tryan's hearers would have considered her destitute of saving knowledge, and I am quite sure she had no well-defined views on justification. Nevertheless, she read her Bible a great deal, and thought she found divine lessons there—how to bear the cross meekly, and be merciful. Let us hope that there is a saving ignorance, and that Mrs. Raynor was justified without knowing exactly how.

She tried to have hope and trust, though it was hard to believe that the future would be any thing else than the harvest of the seed that was being sown before her eyes. But always there is seed being sown silently and unseen, and everywhere there come sweet flowers without our foresight or labor. We reap what we sow, but Nature has love over and above that justice, and gives us shadow and blossom and fruit that spring from no planting of ours.

CHAPTER VI.

Most people must have agreed with Mrs. Raynor that the Confirmation that day was a pretty sight, at least when those slight girlish forms and fair young faces moved in a white rivulet along the aisles, and flowed into kneeling semicircles under the light of the great chancel window, softened by patches of dark old painted glass; and one would think that to look on while a pair of venerable hands pressed such young heads, and a venerable face looked upward for a blessing on them, would be very likely to make the heart swell gently, and to moisten the eyes. Yet I remember the eyes seemed very dry in Milby Church that day, notwithstanding that the Bishop was an old man, and probably venerable (for though he was not an eminent Grecian, he was the brother of a Whig lord); and I think the eyes must have remained dry because he had small delicate womanish hands adorned with ruffles, and, instead of laying them on the girls' heads, just let them hover

over each in quick succession, as if it were not etiquette to touch them, and as if the laying on of hands were like the theatrical embrace—part of the play, and not to be really believed in. To be sure there were a great many heads, and the Bishop's time was limited. Moreover, a wig can, under no circumstances, be affecting, except in rare cases of illusion; and copious lawn-sleeves can not be expected to go directly to any heart except a washerwoman's.

I know, Ned Phipps, who knelt against me, and I am sure made me behave much worse than I should have done without him, whispered that he thought the Bishop was a "guy," and I certainly remember thinking that Mr. Prendergast looked much more dignified with his plain white surplice and black hair. He was a tall commanding man, and read the Liturgy in a strikingly sonorous and uniform voice, which I tried to imitate the next Sunday at home, until my little sister began to cry, and said I was "yoaring at her."

Mr. Tryan sat in a pew near the pulpit with several other clergymen. He looked pale, and rubbed his hand over his face and pushed back his hair oftener than usual. Standing in the aisle close to him, and repeating the responses with edifying loudness, was Mr. Budd, churchwarden and delegate, with a white staff in his hand and a backward bend of his small head and person, such as, I suppose, he considered suitable to a friend of sound religion. Conspicuous in the gallery, too, was the tall figure of Mr. Dempster, whose professional avocations rarely allowed him to occupy his place at church.

"There's Dempster," said Mrs. Linnet to her daughter Mary, "looking more respectable than usual, I declare. He's got a fine speech by heart to make to the Bishop, I'll answer for it. But he'll be pretty well sprinkled with snuff before service is over, and the Bishop won't be able to listen to him for sneezing, that's one comfort."

At length the last stage in the long ceremony was over, the large assembly streamed warm and weary into the open afternoon sunshine, and the Bishop retired to the Parsonage, where, after honoring Mrs. Crewe's collation, he was to give audience to the delegates and Mr. Tryan on the great question of the evening lecture.

Between five and six o'clock the Parsonage was once more as quiet as usual under the shadow of its tall elms, and the only traces of the Bishop's recent presence there were the wheel-marks on the gravel, and the long table with its garnished dishes awry, its damask sprinkled with crumbs, and its decanters without their stoppers. Mr. Crewe was already calmly smoking his pipe in the opposite sitting-room, and Janet was agreeing with Mrs. Crewe that some of the blanc-mange would be a nice thing to take to Sally Martin, while the little old lady herself had a spoon in her hand ready to gather the crumbs into a plate, that she might scatter them on the gravel for the little birds.

Before that time the Bishop's carriage had been seen driving through the High Street on its way to Lord Trufford's, where he was to dine. The question of the lecture was decided, then?

The nature of the decision may be gathered from the following conversation which took place in the bar of the Red Lion that evening.

"So you're done, eh, Dempster?" was Mr. Pilgrim's observation, uttered with some gusto. He was not glad Mr. Tryan had gained his point, but he was not sorry Dempster was disappointed.

"Done, sir? Not at all. It is what I anticipated. I knew we had nothing else to expect in these days, when the Church is infested by a set of men who are only fit to give out hymns from an empty cask, to tunes set by a journeyman cobbler. But I was not the less to exert myself in the cause of sound Churchmanship for the good of the town. Any coward can fight a battle when he's sure of winning; but give me the man who has pluck to fight when he's sure of losing. That's my way, sir; and there are many victories worse than a defeat, as Mr. Tryan shall learn to his cost."

"He must be a poor shuperannyated sort of a bishop, that's my opinion," said Mr. Tomlinson, "to go along with a sneaking Methodist like Tryan. And, for my part, I think we should be as well wi'out bishops, if they're no wiser than that. Where's the use o' havin' thousands a-year an' livin' in a pallis, if they don't stick to the Church?"

"No. There you're going out of your depth, Tomlinson," said Mr. Dempster. "No one shall hear me say a word against Episcopacy—it is a safeguard of the Church; we must have ranks and dignities there as well as everywhere else. No, sir! Episcopacy is a good thing; but it may happen that a bishop is not a good thing. Just as brandy is a good thing, though this particular brandy is British, and tastes like sugared rain-water caught down the chimney. Here, Ratcliffe, let me have something to drink a little less like a decoction of sugar and soot."

"*I* said nothing again' Episcopacy," returned Mr. Tomlinson. "I only said I thought we should do as well wi'out bishops; and I'll say it again for the matter o' that. Bishops never brought any grist to my mill."

"Do you know when the lectures are to begin?" said Mr. Pilgrim.

"They are to *begin* on Sunday next," said Mr. Dempster, in a significant tone; "but I think it will not take a long-sighted prophet to foresee the end of them. It strikes me Mr. Tryan will be looking out for another curacy shortly."

"He'll not get many Milby people to go and hear his lectures after a while, I'll bet a guinea," observed Mr. Budd. "I know I'll not keep a single workman on my ground who either goes to the lecture himself or lets any body belonging to him go."

"Nor me nayther," said Mr. Tomlinson. "No Tryanite shall touch a sack or drive a wagon o' mine, that you may depend on. An' I know more besides me as are o' the same mind."

"Tryan has a good many friends in the town, though, and friends that are likely to stand by him too," said Mr. Pilgrim. "I should say it would be as well to let him and his lectures alone. If he goes on preaching as he does, with such a constitution as his, he'll get a relapsed throat by-and-by, and you'll be rid of him without any trouble."

"We'll not allow him to do himself that injury," said Mr. Dempster. "Since his health is not good, we'll persuade him to try change of air. Depend upon it, he'll find the climate of Milby too hot for him."

CHAPTER VII.

Mr. Dempster did not stay long at the Red Lion that evening. He was summoned home to meet Mr. Armstrong, a wealthy client, and as he was kept in consultation till a late hour, it happened that this was one of the nights on which Mr. Dempster went to bed tolerably sober. Thus the day, which had been one of Janet's happiest, because it had been spent by her in helping her dear old friend Mrs. Crewe, ended for her with unusual quietude; and as a bright sunset promises a fair morning, so a calm lying down is a good augury for a calm waking. Mr. Dempster, on the Thursday morning, was in one of his best humors, and though perhaps some of the good-humor might result from the prospect of a lucrative and exciting bit of business in Mr. Armstrong's probable lawsuit, the greater part was doubtless due to those stirrings of the more kindly, healthy sap of human feeling, by which goodness tries to get the upper hand in us whenever it seems to have the slightest chance—on Sunday mornings, perhaps, when we are set free from the grinding hurry of the week, and take the little three-year-old on our knee at breakfast to share our egg and muffin; in moments of trouble, when death visits our roof or illness makes us dependent on the tending hand of a slighted wife; in quiet talks with an aged mother, of the days when we stood at her knee with our first picture-book, or wrote her loving letters from school. In the man whose childhood has known caresses there is always a fibre of memory that can be touched to gentle issues, and Mr. Dempster, whom you have hitherto seen only as the orator of the Red Lion, and the drunken tyrant of a dreary midnight home, was the first-born darling son of a fair little mother. That mother was living still, and her own large black easy-chair, where she sat knitting through the livelong day, was now set ready for her at the breakfast-table, by her son's side, a sleek tortoise-shell cat acting as provisional incumbent.

"Good-morning, Mamsey! why, you're looking as fresh as a daisy this morning. You're getting young again," said Mr. Dempster, looking up from his newspaper when the little old lady entered. A very little old lady she was, with a pale, scarcely wrinkled face, hair of that peculiar white which tells that the locks have once been blond, a natty pure white cap on her head, and a white shawl pinned over her shoulders. You saw at a glance that she had been a mignonne blonde, strangely unlike her tall, ugly, dingy-complexioned son; unlike her daughter-in-law, too, whose large-featured brunette beauty seemed always thrown into higher relief by the white presence of little Mamsey. The unlikeness between Janet and her mother-in-law went deeper than outline and complexion, and indeed there was little sympathy between them, for old Mrs. Dempster had not yet learned to believe that her son, Robert, would have gone wrong if he had married the right woman—a meek woman like herself, who would have borne him children and been a deft, orderly housekeeper. In spite of Janet's tenderness and attention to her, she had had little love for her daughter-in-law from the first, and had witnessed the sad growth of home-misery through long years, always with a disposition to lay the blame on the wife rather than on the husband, and to reproach Mrs. Raynor for encouraging her daughter's faults by a too exclusive sympathy. But old Mrs. Dempster had that rare gift of silence and passivity which often supplies the absence of mental strength; and, whatever were her thoughts, she said no word to aggravate the domestic discord. Patient and mute she sat at her knitting through many a scene of quarrel and anguish; resolutely she appeared unconscious of the sounds that reached her ears, and the facts she divined after she had retired to her bed; mutely she witnessed poor Janet's faults, only registering them as a balance of excuse on the side of her son. The hard, astute, domineering attorney was still that little old woman's pet, as he had been when she watched with triumphant pride his first tumbling effort to march alone across the nursery floor. "See what a good son he is to me!" she often thought. "Never gave me a harsh word. And so he might have been a good husband."

Oh, it is piteous—that sorrow of aged women! In early youth, perhaps, they said to themselves, "I shall be happy when I have a husband to love me best of all;" then, when the husband was too careless, "My child will comfort me;" then, through the mother's watching and toil, "My child will repay me all when it grows up." And at last, after the long journey of years has been wearily travelled through, the mother's heart is weighed down by a heavier burden, and no hope remains but the grave.

But this morning old Mrs. Dempster sat down in her easy chair without any painful, suppressed remembrance of the preceding night.

"I declare mammy looks younger than Mrs. Crewe, who is only sixty-five," said Janet. "Mrs. Crewe will come to see you to-day, mammy, and tell you all about her troubles with the Bishop and the collation. She'll bring her knitting, and you'll have a regular gossip together."

"The gossip will be all on one side, then, for Mrs. Crewe gets so very deaf, I can't make her hear a word. And if I motion to her, she always understands me wrong."

"Oh, she will have so much to tell you to-day, you will not want to speak yourself. You, who have patience to knit those wonderful counterpanes, mammy, must not be impatient with dear Mrs. Crewe. Good old lady! I can't bear her to think she's ever tiresome to people, and you know she's very ready to fancy herself in the way. I think she would like to shrink up to the size of a mouse, that she might run about and do people good without their noticing her."

"It isn't patience I want, God knows; it's lungs to speak loud enough. But you'll be at home yourself, I suppose, this morning; and you can talk to her for me."

"No, mammy; I promised poor Mrs. Lowme to go and sit with her. She's confined to her room, and both the Miss Lowmes are out; so I'm going to read the newspaper to her and amuse her."

"Couldn't you go another morning? As Mr. Armstrong and that other gentleman are coming to dinner, I should think it would be better to stay at home. Can you trust Betty to see to every thing? She's new to the place."

"Oh I couldn't disappoint Mrs. Lowme; I promised her. Betty will do very well, no fear."

Old Mrs. Dempster was silent after this, and began to sip her tea. The breakfast went on without further conversation for some time, Mr. Dempster being absorbed in the papers. At length, when he was running over the advertisements, his eye seemed to be caught by something that suggested a new thought to him. He presently thumped the table with an air of exultation, and said, turning to Janet,

"I've a capital idea, Gypsy!" (that was his name for his dark-eyed wife when he was in an extraordinarily good-humor), "and you shall help me. It's just what you're up to."

"What is it?" said Janet, her face beaming at the sound of the pet name, now heard so seldom. "Any thing to do with conveyancing?"

"It's a bit of fun worth a dozen fees—a plan for raising a laugh against Tryan and his gang of hypocrites."

"What is it? Nothing that wants a needle and thread I hope, else I must go and tease mother."

"No, nothing sharper than your wit—except mine. I'll tell you what it is. We'll get up a programme of the Sunday evening lecture, like a play-bill, you know—'Grand Performance of the celebrated Mountebank,' and so on. We'll bring in the Tryanites—old Landor and the rest—in appropriate characters. Proctor shall print it, and we'll circulate it in the town. It will be a capital hit."

"Bravo!" said Janet, clapping her hands. She would just then have pretended to like almost any thing, in her pleasure at being appealed to by her husband, and she really did like to laugh at the Tryanites. "We'll set about it directly, and sketch it out before you go to the office. I've got Tryan's sermons up stairs, but I don't think there's any thing in them we can use. I've only just looked into them; they're not at all what I expected—dull, stupid things—nothing of the roaring fire-and-brimstone sort that I expected."

"Roaring? No; Tryan's as soft as a sucking dove—one of your honey-mouthed hypocrites. Plenty of devil and malice in him, though, I could see that, while he was talking to the Bishop; but as smooth as a snake outside. He's beginning a single-handed fight with me, I can see—persuading my clients away from me. We shall see who will be the first to cry *peccavi*. Milby will do better without Mr. Tryan than without Robert Dempster, I fancy! and Milby shall never be flooded with cant as long as I can raise a breakwater against it. But now, get the breakfast things cleared away, and let us set about the play-bill. Come, mamsey, come and have a walk with me round the garden, and let us see how the cucumbers are getting on. I've never taken you round the garden for an age. Come, you don't want a bonnet. It's like walking in a greenhouse this morning."

"But she will want a parasol," said Janet. "There's one on the stand against the garden-door, Robert."

The little old lady took her son's arm with placid pleasure. She could barely reach it so as to rest upon it, but he inclined a little towards her, and accommodated his heavy long-limbed steps to her feeble pace. The cat chose to sun herself too, and walked close beside them, with tail erect, rubbing her sleek sides against their legs,—too well fed to be excited by the twittering birds. The garden was of the grassy, shady kind, often seen attached to old houses in provincial towns; the apple-trees had had time to spread their branches very wide, the shrubs and hardy perennial plants had grown into a luxuriance that required constant trimming to prevent them from intruding on the space for walking. But the farther end, which united with green fields, was open and sunny.

It was rather sad, and yet pretty, to see that little group passing out of the shadow into the sunshine, and out of the sunshine into the shadow again: sad, because this tenderness of the son for the mother was hardly more than a nucleus of healthy life in an organ hardening by disease, because the man who was linked in this way with an innocent past, had become callous in worldliness, fevered by sensuality, enslaved by chance impulses; pretty, because it showed how hard it is to kill the deep-down fibrous roots of human love and goodness—how the man from whom we make it our pride to shrink, has yet a close brotherhood with us through some of our most sacred feelings.

As they were returning to the house, Janet met them, and said, "Now, Robert, the writing things are ready. I shall be clerk, and Mat Paine can copy it out after."

Mammy once more deposited in her arm-chair, with her knitting in her hand, and the cat purring at her elbow, Janet seated herself at the table, while Mr. Dempster placed himself near her, took out his snuff-box, and plentifully suffusing himself with the inspiring powder, began to dictate.

What he dictated we shall see by-and-by.

CHAPTER VIII.

The next day, Friday, at five o'clock by the sun-dial, the large bow-window of Mrs. Jerome's parlor was open; and that lady herself was seated within its ample semicircle, having a table before her on which her best tea-tray, her best china, and her best urn-rug had already been standing in readiness for half an hour. Mrs. Jerome's best tea-service was of delicate white fluted china, with gold sprigs upon it—as pretty a tea-service as you need wish to see, and quite good enough for chimney ornaments; indeed, as the cups were without handles, most visitors who had the distinction of taking tea out of them, wished that such-charming china had already been promoted to that honorary position. Mrs. Jerome was like her china, handsome and old-fashioned. She was a buxom lady of sixty, in an elaborate lace cap fastened by a frill under her chin, a dark, well-curled front concealing her forehead, a snowy neckerchief exhibiting its ample folds as far as her waist, and a stiff gray silk gown. She had a clean damask napkin pinned before her to guard her dress during the process of tea making; her favorite geraniums in the bow-window were looking as healthy as she could desire; her own handsome portrait, painted when she was twenty years younger, was smiling down on her with agreeable flattery; and altogether she seemed to be in as peaceful and pleasant a position as a buxom, well-dressed elderly lady need desire. But, as in so many other cases, appearances were deceptive. Her mind was greatly perturbed and her temper ruffled by the fact that it was more than a quarter past five even by the losing timepiece, that it was half past by her large gold watch, which she held in her hand as if she were counting the pulse of the afternoon, and that by the kitchen clock, which she felt sure was not an hour too fast, it had already struck six. The lapse of time was rendered the more unendurable to Mrs. Jerome by her wonder that Mr. Jerome could stay out in the garden with Lizzie in that thoughtless way, taking it so easily that tea-time was long past, and that, after all the trouble of getting down the best tea-things, Mr. Tryan would not come.

This honor had been shown to Mr. Tryan, not at all because Mrs. Jerome had any high appreciation of his doctrine or of his exemplary activity as a pastor, but simply because he was a "Church clergyman," and as such was regarded by her with the same sort of exceptional respect that a white woman who had married a native of the Society Islands might be supposed to feel towards a white-skinned visitor from the land of her youth. For Mrs. Jerome had been reared a Churchwoman, and having attained the age of thirty before she was married, had felt the greatest repugnance in the first instance to renouncing the religious forms in which she had been brought up. "You know," she said in confidence to her Church acquaintances, "I wouldn't give no ear at all to Mr. Jerome at fust; but after all, I begun to think as there was a many things worse nor goin' to chapel, an' you'd better do that nor not pay your way. Mr. Jerome had a very pleasant manner with him, an' there was niver another as kept a gig, an' 'ud make a settlement on me like him, chapel or no chapel. It seemed very odd to me for a long while, the preachin' without book, an' the stannin' up to one long prayer, istid o' changin' your postur. But la! there's nothin' as you mayn't get used to i' time; you can al'ys sit down, you know, before the prayer's done. The ministers say pretty nigh the same things as the Church parsons, by what I could iver make out, an' we're out o' chapel i' the mornin' a deal sooner nor they're out o' church. An' as for pews, ours is a deal comfortabler nor any i' Milby Church."

Mrs. Jerome, you perceive, had not a keen susceptibility to shades of doctrine, and it is probable that, after listening to Dissenting eloquence for thirty years, she might safely have re-entered the Establishment without performing any spiritual quarantine. Her mind, apparently, was of that nonporous, flinty character which is not in the least danger from surrounding damp. But on the question of getting start of the sun on the day's business, and clearing her conscience of the necessary sum of meals and the consequent "washing up" as soon as possible, so that the family might be well in bed at nine, Mrs. Jerome *was* susceptible; and the present lingering pace of things, united with Mr. Jerome's unaccountable obliviousness, was not to be borne any longer. So she rang the bell for Sally.

"Goodness me, Sally! go into the garden an' see after your master. Tell him it's goin' on for six, an' Mr. Tryan 'ull niver think o' comin' now, an' it's time we got tea over. An' he's lettin' Lizzie stain her frock, I expect, among them strawberry beds. Make her come in this minute."

No wonder Mr. Jerome was tempted to linger in the garden, for though the house was pretty and well deserved its name—"the White House," the tall damask roses that clustered over the porch being thrown into relief by rough stucco of the most brilliant white, yet the garden and orchards were Mr. Jerome's glory, as well they might be; and there was nothing in which he had a more innocent pride—peace to a good man's memory! all his pride was innocent—than in conducting a hitherto uninitiated visitor over his grounds, and making him in some degree aware of the incomparable advantages possessed by the inhabitants of the White House in the matter of red-streaked apples, russets, northern greens (excellent for baking), swan-egg pears, and early vegetables, to say nothing of flowering "srubs," pink hawthorns, lavender bushes more than ever Mrs. Jerome could use, and, in short, a superabundance of every thing that a person retired from business could desire to possess himself or to share with his friends. The garden was one of those old-fashioned paradises which hardly exist any longer except as memories of our childhood: no finical separation between flower and kitchen garden there; no monotony of enjoyment for one sense to the exclusion of another; but a charming paradisiacal mingling of all that was pleasant to the eyes and good for food. The rich flower-border running along every walk, with its endless succession of spring flowers, anemones, auriculas, wall-flowers, sweet-williams, campanulas, snap dragons, and tiger-lilies, had its taller beauties, such as moss and Provence roses, varied with espalier apple-trees; the crimson of a carnation was carried out in the lurking crimson of the neighboring strawberry-beds; you gathered a moss-rose one moment and a bunch of currants the next; you were in a delicious fluctuation between the scent of jasmine and the juice of gooseberries. Then what a high wall at one end, flanked by a summer-house so lofty, that after ascending its long flight of steps you could see perfectly well there was no view worth looking at; what alcoves and garden-seats in all directions; and along one side, what a hedge, tall, and firm, and unbroken, like a green wall!

It was near this hedge that Mr. Jerome was standing when Sally found him. He had set down the basket of strawberries on the gravel, and had lifted up little Lizzie in his arms to look at a bird's nest. Lizzie peeped, and then looked at her grandpa with round blue eyes, and then peeped again.

"D'ye see it, Lizzie?" he whispered.

"Yes," she whispered in return, putting her lips very near grandpa's face. At this moment Sally appeared.

"Eh, eh, Sally, what's the matter? Is Mr. Tryan come?"

"No, sir, an' Missis says she's sure he won't come now, an'

she wants you to come in an' hev tea. Dear heart, Miss Lizzie, you've stained your pinafore, an' I shouldn't wonder if it's gone through to your frock. There'll be fine work! Come alonk wi' me, do."

"Nay, nay, nay, we've done no harm, we've done no harm, hev we, Lizzie? The wash-tub 'll make all right again."

Sally, regarding the wash-tub from a different point of view, looked sourly serious, and hurried away with Lizzie, who trotted submissively along, her little head in eclipse under a large nankin bonnet, while Mr. Jerome followed leisurely with his full broad shoulders in rather a stooping posture, and his large good-natured features and white locks shaded by a broad-brimmed hat.

"Mr. Jerome, I wonder at you," said Mrs. Jerome, in a tone of indignant remonstrance, evidently sustained by a deep sense of injury, as her husband opened the parlor door. "When will you leave off invitin' people to meals an' not lettin' 'em know the time? I'll answer for't, you niver said a word to Mr. Tryan as we should take tea at five o'clock. It's just like you!"

"Nay, nay, Susan," answered the husband in a soothing tone, "there's nothin' amiss. I told Mr. Tryan as we took tea at five punctial; mayhap summat's a detainin' on him. He's a deal to do, an' to think on, remember."

"Why it's struck six i' the kitchen a'ready. It's nonsense to look for him comin' now. So you may's well ring for th' urn. Now Sally's got th' heater in the fire, we may's well hev th' urn in, though he doesn't come. I niver see'd the like o' you, Mr. Jerome, for axin' people an' givin' me the trouble o' gettin' things down an' hevin' crumpets made, an' after all they don't come. I shall hev to wash every one o' these tea-things myself, for there's no trustin' Sally—she'd break a fortin i' crockery i' no time!"

"But why will you give yourself sich trouble, Susan? Our every-day tea-things would ha' done as well for Mr. Tryan, an' they're a deal convenenter to hold."

"Yes, that's just your way, Mr. Jerome, you're al'ys a-findin' faut wi' my chany, because I bought it myself afore I was married. But let me tell you, I knowed how to choose chany if I didn't know how to choose a husband. An' where's Lizzie? You've niver left her i' the garden by herself, with her white frock on an' clean stockins?"

"Be easy, my dear Susan, be easy; Lizzie's come in wi' Sally. She's hevin' her pinafore took off, I'll be bound. Ah! there's Mr. Tryan a-comin' through the gate."

Mrs. Jerome began hastily to adjust her damask napkin and

the expression of her countenance for the reception of the clergyman, and Mr. Jerome went out to meet his guest, whom he greeted outside the door.

"Mr. Tryan, how do you do, Mr. Tryan? Welcome to the White House! I'm glad to see you, sir—I'm glad to see you."

If you had heard the tone of mingled good-will, veneration, and condolence in which this greeting was uttered, even without seeing the face that completely harmonized with it, you would have no difficulty in inferring the ground-notes of Mr. Jerome's character. To a fine ear that tone said as plainly as possible—"Whatever recommends itself to me, Thomas Jerome, as piety and goodness, shall have my love and honor. Ah friends, this pleasant world is a sad one, too, isn't it? Let us help one another, let us help one another." And it was entirely owing to this basis of character, not at all from any clear and precise doctrinal discrimination, that Mr. Jerome had very early in life become a Dissenter. In his boyish days he had been thrown where Dissent seemed to have the balance of piety, purity, and good works on its side, and to become a Dissenter seemed to him identical with choosing God instead of mammon. That race of Dissenters is extinct in these days, when opinion has got far ahead of feeling, and every chapel-going youth can fill our ears with the advantages of the Voluntary system, the corruptions of a State Church, and the Scriptural evidence that the first Christians were Congregationalists. Mr. Jerome knew nothing of this theoretic basis for Dissent, and in the utmost extent of his polemical discussion he had not gone farther than to question whether a Christian man was bound in conscience to distinguish Christmas and Easter by any peculiar observance beyond the eating of mince-pies and cheese-cakes. It seemed to him that all seasons were alike good for thanking God, departing from evil, and doing well, whereas it might be desirable to restrict the period for indulging in unwholesome forms of pastry. Mr. Jerome's dissent being of this simple, non-polemical kind, it is easy to understand that the report he heard of Mr. Tryan as a good man and a powerful preacher, who was stirring the hearts of the people, had been enough to attract him to the Paddiford Church, and that having felt himself more edified there than he had of late been under Mr. Stickney's discourses at Salem, he had driven thither repeatedly in the Sunday afternoons, and had sought an opportunity of making Mr. Tryan's acquaintance. The evening lecture was a subject of warm interest with him, and the opposition Mr. Tryan met with gave that interest a strong tinge of partisanship; for there was a store of irascibility in Mr. Jerome's nature which must find a vent somewhere, and in so kindly and upright a man could only find it in indignation against those whom he held to be enemies of truth and goodness. Mr. Tryan had not hitherto been to the White House, but yesterday, meeting Mr. Jerome in the street, he had at once accepted the invitation to tea, saying there was something he wished to talk about. He appeared worn and fatigued now, and after shaking hands with Mrs. Jerome, threw himself into a chair and looked out on the pretty garden with an air of relief.

"What a nice place you have here, Mr. Jerome! I've not seen any thing so quiet and pretty since I came to Milby. On Paddiford Common, where I live, you know, the bushes are all sprinkled with soot, and there's never any quiet except in the dead of night."

"Dear heart! dear heart! That's very bad—and for you, too, as hev to study. Wouldn't it be better for you to be somewhere more out i' the country like?"

"Oh no! I should lose so much time in going to and fro, and besides I like to be *among* the people. I've no face to go and preach resignation to those poor things in their smoky air and comfortless homes, when I come straight from every luxury myself. There are many things quite lawful for other men, which a clergyman must forego if he would do any good in a manufacturing population like this."

Here the preparations for tea were crowned by the simultaneous appearance of Lizzie and the crumpet. It is a pretty surprise, when one visits an elderly couple, to see a little figure enter in a white frock with a blond head as smooth as satin, round blue eyes, and a cheek like an apple blossom. A toddling little girl is a centre of common feeling which makes the most dissimilar people understand each other: and Mr. Tryan looked at Lizzie with that quiet pleasure which is always genuine.

"Here we are, here we are!" said proud grandpapa. "You didn't think we'd got such a little gell as this, did you, Mr. Tryan? Why, it seems but th' other day since her mother was just such another. This is our little Lizzie, this is. Come an' shake hands wi' Mr. Tryan, Lizzie; come."

Lizzie advanced without hesitation, and put out one hand, while she fingered her coral necklace with the other, and looked up into Mr. Tryan's face with a reconnoitring gaze. He stroked the satin head, and said in his gentlest voice, "How do you do, Lizzie? will you give me a kiss?" She put up her little bud of a mouth, and then retreating a little and glancing down at her frock, said,

"Lizzie advanced without hesitation, and put out one hand, while she fingered her coral necklace with the other."—PAGE 241.

"Dit id my noo fock. I put it on 'tod you wad toming. Tally taid you wouldn't 'ook at it."

"Hush, hush, Lizzie, little gells must be seen and not heard," said Mrs. Jerome; while grandpapa, winking significantly, and looking radiant with delight at Lizzie's extraordinary promise of cleverness, set her up on her high cane-chair by the side of grandma, who lost no time in shielding the beauties of the new frock with a napkin.

"Well now, Mr. Tryan," said Mr. Jerome, in a very serious tone, when tea had been distributed, "let me hear how you're a-goin' on about the lectur. When I was i' the town yesterday, I heared as there was pessecutin' schemes a-bein' laid again' you. I fear me those raskill's 'll mek things very onpleasant to you."

"I've no doubt they will attempt it; indeed, I quite expect there will be a regular mob got up on Sunday evening, as there was when the delegates returned, on purpose to annoy me and the congregation on our way to church."

"Ah, they're capible o' any thing, such men as Dempster an' Budd; an' Tomlinson backs 'em wi' money, though he can't wi' brains. Howiver, Dempster's lost one client by his wicked doins, an' I'm deceived if he won't lose more nor one. I little thought, Mr. Tryan, when I put my affairs into his hands twenty 'ear ago this Michaelmas, as he was to turn out a pessecutor o' religion. I niver lighted on a cliverer, promisiner young man nor he was then. They talked of his bein' fond of a extry glass now an' then, but niver nothin' like what he's come to since. An' it's head-piece you must look for in a lawyer, Mr. Tryan, it's head-piece. His wife, too, was al'ys an uncommon favorite o' mine—poor thing! I hear sad stories about her now. But she's druv to it, she's druv to it, Mr. Tryan. A tender-hearted woman to the poor, she is, as iver lived; an' as pretty-spoken a woman as you need wish to talk to. Yes! I'd al'ys a likin' for Dempster an' his wife, spite o' ivery thing. But as soon as iver I heared o' that dilegate business, I says, says I, that man shall hev no more to do wi' my affairs. It may put me t' inconvenience, but I'll encourage no man as pessecutes religion."

"He is evidently the brain and hand of the persecution," said Mr. Tryan. "There may be a strong feeling against me in a large number of the inhabitants—it must be so from the great ignorance of spiritual things in this place. But I fancy there would have been no formal opposition to the lecture, if Dempster had not planned it. I am not myself the least alarmed at any thing he can do; he will find I am not to be cowed or driven away by insult or personal danger.

God has sent me to this place, and, by His blessing, I'll not shrink from any thing I may have to encounter in doing His work among the people. But I feel it right to call on all those who know the value of the Gospel, to stand by me publicly. I think—and Mr. Landor agrees with me—that it will be well for my friends to proceed with me in a body to the church on Sunday evening. Dempster, you know, has pretended that almost all the respectable inhabitants are opposed to the lecture. Now, I wish that falsehood to be visibly contradicted. What do you think of the plan? I have to-day been to see several of my friends, who will make a point of being there to accompany me, and will communicate with others on the subject."

"I'll make one, Mr. Tryan, I'll make one. You shall not be wantin' in any support as I can give. Before you come to it, sir, Milby was a dead an' dark place; you are the fust man i' the church to my knowledge as has brought the word o' God home to the people; an' I'll stan' by you, sir, I'll stan' by you. I'm a Dissenter, Mr. Tryan; I've been a Dissenter ever sin' I was fifteen 'ear old; but show me good i' the Church, an' I'm a Churchman too. When I was a boy I lived at Tilston; you mayn't know the place; the best part o' the land there belonged to Squire Sandeman; he'd a club-foot, had Squire Sandeman—lost a deal o' money by canal shares. Well, sir, as I was sayin', I lived at Tilston, an' the rector there was a terrible drinkin', fox-huntin' man; you niver seed such a parish i' your time for wickedness; Milby's nothin' to it. Well, sir, my father was a workin' man, an' couldn't afford to gi' me ony eddication, so I went to a night-school as was kep' by a Dissenter, one Jacob Wright; an' it was from that man, sir, as I got my little schoolin' an' my knowledge o' religion. I went to chapel wi' Jacob—he was a good man was Jacob—an' to chapel I've been iver since. But I'm no enemy o' the Church, sir, when the Church brings light to the ignorant and the sinful; an' that's what you're a-doin', Mr. Tryan. Yes, sir, I'll stan' by you; I'll go to church wi' you o' Sunday evenin'."

"You'd far better stay at home, Mr. Jerome, if I may give *my* opinion," interposed Mrs. Jerome. "It's not as I hevn't ivery respect for you, Mr. Tryan, but Mr. Jerome 'ull do you no good by his interferin'. Dissenters are not at all looked on i' Milby, an' he's as nervous as iver he can be; he'll come back as ill as ill, an' niver let me hev a wink o' sleep all night."

Mrs. Jerome had been frightened at the mention of a mob, and her retrospective regard for the religious communion of her youth by no means inspired her with the temper of a martyr. Her husband looked at her with an expression of tender and grieved remonstrance, which might have been that of the patient patriarch on the memorable occasion when he rebuked *his* wife.

"Susan, Susan, let me beg on you not to oppose me, and put stumblin'-blocks i' the way o' doin' what's right. I can't give up my conscience, let me give up what else I may."

"Perhaps," said Mr. Tryan, feeling slightly uncomfortable, "since you are not very strong, my dear sir, it will be well, as Mrs. Jerome suggests, that you should not run the risk of any excitement."

"Say no more, Mr. Tryan. I'll stan' by you, sir. It's my duty. It's the cause o' God, sir; it's the cause o' God."

Mr. Tryan obeyed his impulse of admiration and gratitude, and put out his hand to the white-haired old man, saying, "Thank you, Mr. Jerome, thank you."

Mr. Jerome grasped the proffered hand in silence, and then threw himself back in his chair, casting a regretful look at his wife, which seemed to say, "Why don't you feel with me, Susan?"

The sympathy of this simple-minded old man was more precious to Mr. Tryan than any mere onlooker could have imagined. To persons possessing a great deal of that facile psychology which prejudges individuals by means of formulæ, and casts them, without further trouble, into duly lettered pigeon-holes, the Evangelical curate might seem to be doing simply what all other men like to do—carrying out objects which were identified not only with his theory, which is but a kind of secondary egoism, but also with the primary egoism of his feelings. Opposition may become sweet to a man when he has christened it persecution: a self-obtrusive, over-hasty reformer complacently disclaiming all merit, while his friends call him a martyr, has not in reality a career the most arduous to the fleshly mind. But Mr. Tryan was not cast in the mould of the gratuitous martyr. With a power of persistence which had been often blamed as obstinacy, he had an acute sensibility to the very hatred or ridicule he did not flinch from provoking. Every form of disapproval jarred him painfully; and, though he fronted his opponents manfully, and often with considerable warmth of temper, he had no pugnacious pleasure in the contest. It was one of the weaknesses of his nature to be too keenly alive to every harsh wind of opinion; to wince under the frowns of the foolish; to be irritated by the injustice of those who could not possibly have the elements indispensable for judging him rightly; and with all this acute sensibility to blame, this dependence on sympathy, he had for years been constrained into a position of antagonism. No wonder, then, that good old Mr. Jerome's cordial words were balm to him. He had often been thankful to an old woman for saying "God bless you;" to a little child for smiling at him; to a dog for submitting to be patted by him.

Tea being over by this time, Mr. Tryan proposed a walk in the garden as a means of dissipating all recollection of the recent conjugal dissidence. Little Lizzie's appeal, "Me go, grandpa!" could not be rejected, so she was duly bonneted and pinafored, and then they turned out into the evening sunshine. Not Mrs. Jerome, however; she had a deeply-meditated plan of retiring *ad interim* to the kitchen and washing up the best tea-things, as a mode of getting forward with the sadly-retarded business of the day."

"This way, Mr. Tryan, this way," said the old gentleman; "I must take you to my pastur fust, an' show you our cow—the best milker i' the county. An' see here at these back-buildin's, how convenent the dairy is; I planned it ivery bit myself. An' here I've got my little carpenter's shop an' my blacksmith's shop; I do no end o' jobs here myself. I niver could bear to be idle, Mr. Tryan; I must al'ys be at somethin' or other. It was time for me to lay by business an' mek room for younger folks. I'd got money enough, wi' only one daughter to leave it to, an' I says to myself, says I, it's time to leave off moitherin' myself wi' this world so much, an' give more time to thinkin' of another. But there's a many hours atween getting up an' lyin' down, an' thoughts are no cumber; you can move about wi' a good many on 'em in your head. See, here's the pastur."

A very pretty pasture it was, where the large-spotted, short-horned cow quietly chewed the cud as she lay and looked sleepily at her admirers—a daintily-trimmed hedge all round, dotted here and there with a mountain-ash or a cherry-tree.

"I've a good bit more land besides this, worth your while to look at, but mayhap it's farther nor you'd like to walk now. Bless you! I've welly an acre o' potato-ground yonders; I've a good big family to supply, you know." (Here Mr. Jerome winked and smiled significantly.) "An' that puts me i' mind, Mr. Tryan, o' summat I wanted to say to you. Clergymen like you, I know, see a deal more poverty an' that, than other folks, an' hev a many claims on 'em more nor they can well meet; an' if you'll mek use o' my purse any time, or let me know where I can be o' any help, I'll tek it very kind on you."

"Thank you, Mr. Jerome, I will do so, I promise you. I saw a sad case yesterday; a collier—a fine broad-chested fellow about thirty—was killed by the falling of a wall in the Paddiford colliery. I was in one of the cottages near, when they brought him home on a door, and the shriek of the wife has been ringing in my ears ever since. There are three little children. Happily the woman has her loom, so she will be able to keep out of the workhouse; but she looks very delicate."

"Give me her name, Mr. Tryan," said Mr. Jerome, drawing out his pocket-book. "I'll call an' see her."

Deep was the fountain of pity in the good old man's heart! He often ate his dinner stintingly, oppressed by the thought that there were men, women, and children, with no dinner to sit down to, and would relieve his mind by going out in the afternoon to look for some need that he could supply, some honest struggle in which he could lend a helping hand. That any living being should want, was his chief sorrow; that any rational being should waste, was the next. Sally, indeed, having been scolded by master for a too lavish use of sticks in lighting the kitchen fire, and various instances of recklessness with regard to candle-ends, considered him "as mean as aeny think;" but he had as kindly a warmth as the morning sunlight, and, like the sunlight, his goodness shone on all that came in his way, from the saucy rosy-cheeked lad whom he delighted to make happy with a Christmas-box, to the pallid sufferers up dim entries, languishing under the tardy death of want and misery.

It was very pleasant to Mr. Tryan to listen to the simple chat of the old man—to walk in the shade of the incomparable orchard, and hear the story of the crops yielded by the red-streaked apple-tree, and the quite embarrassing plentifulness of the summer-pears—to drink in the sweet evening breath of the garden, as they sat in the alcove—and so, for a short interval, to feel the strain of his pastoral task relaxed.

Perhaps he felt the return to that task through the dusty roads all the more painfully, perhaps something in that quiet shady home had reminded him of the time before he had taken on him the yoke of self-denial. The strongest heart will faint sometimes under the feeling that enemies are bitter, and that friends only know half its sorrows. The most resolute soul will now and then cast back a yearning look in treading the rough mountain-path, away from the greensward and laughing voices of the valley. However it was, in the nine o'clock twilight that evening, when Mr. Tryan had entered his small study and turned the key in the door, he threw himself into the chair before his writing-table, and, heedless of the papers there, leaned his face low on his hand, and moaned heavily.

It is apt to be so in this life, I think. While we are coldly discussing a man's career, sneering at his mistakes, blaming his rashness, and labelling his opinions—" Evangelical and narrow," or "Latitudinarian and Pantheistic," or " Anglican and supercilious "—that man, in his solitude, is perhaps shedding hot tears because his sacrifice is a hard one, because strength and patience are failing him to speak the difficult word, and do the difficult deed.

CHAPTER IX.

Mr. Tryan showed no such symptoms of weakness on the critical Sunday. He unhesitatingly rejected the suggestion that he should be taken to church in Mr. Landor's carriage—a proposition which that gentleman made as an amendment on the original plan, when the rumors of meditated insult became alarming. Mr. Tryan declared he would have no precautions taken, but would simply trust in God and his good cause. Some of his more timid friends thought this conduct rather defiant than wise, and reflecting that a mob has great talent for impromptu, and that legal redress is imperfect satisfaction for having one's head broken with a brickbat, were beginning to question their consciences very closely as to whether it was not a duty they owed to their families to stay at home on Sunday evening. These timorous persons, however, were in a small minority, and the generality of Mr. Tryan's friends and hearers rather exulted in an opportunity of braving insult for the sake of a preacher to whom they were attached on personal as well as doctrinal grounds. Miss Pratt spoke of Cranmer, Ridley, and Latimer, and observed that the present crisis afforded an occasion for emulating their heroism even in these degenerate times; while less highly instructed persons, whose memories were not well stored with precedents, simply expressed their determination, as Mr. Jerome had done, to " stan' by " the preacher and his cause, believing it to be the " cause of God."

On Sunday evening, then, at a quarter past six, Mr. Tryan, setting out from Mr. Landor's with a party of his friends who had assembled there, was soon joined by two other groups from Mr. Pratt's and Mr. Dunn's; and stray persons on their way to church naturally falling into rank behind this leading file, by the time they reached the entrance of Orchard Street, Mr. Tryan's friends formed a considerable procession, walking three or four abreast. It was in Orchard Street, and towards the church gates, that the chief crowd was collected; and at Mr. Dempster's drawing-room window, on the upper floor, a more select assembly of Anti-Tryanites were gathered to witness the entertaining spectacle of the Tryanites walking to church amidst the jeers and hootings of the crowd.

To prompt the popular wit with appropriate sobriquets, numerous copies of Mr. Dempster's playbill were posted on the walls, in suitably large and emphatic type. As it is possible that the most industrious collector of mural literature may not have been fortunate enough to possess himself of this production, which ought by all means to be preserved amongst the materials of our provincial religious history, I subjoin a faithful copy.

GRAND ENTERTAINMENT!!!
To be given at Milby on Sunday evening next, by the
FAMOUS COMEDIAN, TRY-IT-ON!
And his first-rate company, including not only an
UNPARALLELED CAST FOR COMEDY!
But a Large Collection of *reclaimed and converted Animals;*
Among the rest
A Bear who used to *dance!*
A Parrot, once given to *swearing!!*
A Polygamous Pig!!!
and
A Monkey who used to *catch fleas on a Sunday!!!!*
Together with a
Pair of *regenerated* LINNETS!
With an entirely new song and *plumage.*
MR. TRY-IT-ON
Will first pass through the streets, in procession, with his unrivalled Company, warranted to have their *eyes turned up higher*, and the *corners of their mouths turned down lower*, than any other company of Mountebanks in this circuit!
AFTER WHICH
The Theatre will be opened, and the entertainment will
COMMENCE AT HALF-PAST SIX,
When will be presented
A piece, never before performed on any stage, entitled,
THE WOLF IN SHEEP'S CLOTHING;
or
THE METHODIST IN A MASK.

Mr. Boanerges Soft Sawder.............................Mr. TRY-IT-ON.
Old Ten-per-cent. Godly...............................Mr. GANDER.
Dr. Feedemup..Mr. TONIC.
Mr. Lime-twig Lady-winner.............................Mr. TRY-IT-ON.
Miss Piety Bait-the-hook..............................Miss TONIC.
Angelica..Miss SERAPHINA TONIC.

After which
A miscellaneous Musical interlude, commencing with
The *Lamentations* of *Jerom-iah!*
In nasal recitative.
To be followed by
The favorite Cackling Quartette,
by
Two Hen-birds who are *no chickens!*
The well-known *counter*-tenor, Mr. Done and a *Gander*,
lineally descended from the *Goose* that laid golden eggs!
To conclude with a
GRAND CHORUS by the
Entire Orchestra of Converted Animals!!

But owing to the unavoidable absence (from illness) of the *Bulldog, who has left off fighting*, Mr. Tonic has kindly undertaken, at a moment's notice, to supply the "*bark!*"

The whole to conclude with a
Screaming Farce of
THE PULPIT SNATCHER.

Mr. Saintly Smooth-face..............................Mr. TRY-IT-ON!
Mr. Worming Sneaker..............................Mr. TRY-IT-ON!!
Mr. All-grace No-works..............................Mr. TRY-IT-ON!!!
Mr. Elect-and-Chosen Apewell......................Mr. TRY-IT-ON!!!!
Mr. Malevolent Prayerful..........................Mr. TRY-IT ON!!!!!
Mr. Foist-himself-everywhere......................Mr. TRY-IT-ON!!!!!!
Mr. Flout-the-aged Upstart........................Mr. TRY-IT-ON!!!!!!!

Admission Free. A *Collection* will be made at the Doors.
Vivat Rex!

This satire, though it presents the keenest edge of Milby wit, does not strike you as lacerating, I imagine. But hatred is like fire—it makes even light rubbish deadly. And Mr. Dempster's sarcasms were not merely visible on the walls; they were reflected in the derisive glances, and audible in the jeering voices of the crowd. Through this pelting shower of nicknames and bad puns, with an *ad libitum* accompaniment of groans, howls, hisses, and hee-haws, but of no heavier missiles, Mr. Tryan walked pale and composed, giving his arm to old Mr. Landor, whose step was feeble. On the other side of him was Mr. Jerome, who still walked firmly though his shoulders were slightly bowed.

Outwardly Mr. Tryan was composed, but inwardly he was suffering acutely from these tones of hatred and scorn. However strong his consciousness of right, he found it no stronger armor against such weapons as derisive glances and virulent words, than against stones and clubs: his conscience was in repose, but his sensibility was bruised.

Once more only did the Evangelical curate pass up Orchard Street followed by a train of friends; once more only was there a crowd assembled to witness his entrance through the church gates. But that second time no voice was heard above a whisper, and the whispers were words of sorrow and blessing. That second time, Janet Dempster was not looking on in scorn and merriment; her eyes were worn with grief and watching, and she was following her beloved friend and pastor to the grave.

CHAPTER X.

History, we know, is apt to repeat itself, and to foist very old incidents upon us with only a slight change of costume. From the time of Xerxes downward, we have seen generals playing the braggadocio at the outset of their campaigns, and conquering the enemy with the greatest ease in after-dinner speeches. But events are apt to be in disgusting discrepancy with the anticipations of the most ingenious tacticians; the difficulties of the expedition are ridiculously at variance with able calculations; the enemy has the impudence not to fall into confusion as had been reasonably expected of him; the mind of the gallant general begins to be distracted by news of intrigues against him at home, and, notwithstanding the handsome compliments he paid to Providence as his undoubted patron before setting out, there seems every probability that the *Te Deums* will be all on the other side.

So it fell out with Mr. Dempster in his memorable campaign against the Anti-Tryanites. After all the premature triumph of the return from Elmstoke, the battle of the Evening Lecture had been lost; the enemy was in possession of the field; and the utmost hope remaining was, that by a harassing guerrilla warfare he might be driven to evacuate the country.

For some time this sort of warfare was kept up with considerable spirit. The shafts of Milby ridicule were made more formidable by being poisoned with calumny; and very ugly stories, narrated with circumstantial minuteness, were soon in circulation concerning Mr. Tryan and his hearers, from which stories it was plainly deducible that Evangelicalism led by a necessary consequence to hypocritical indulgence in vice. Some old friendships were broken asunder, and there were near relations who felt that religious differences, unmitigated by any prospect of a legacy, were a sufficient ground for exhibiting their family antipathy. Mr. Budd harangued his workmen, and threatened them with dismissal if they or their families were known to attend the evening lecture; and Mr. Tomlinson, on discovering that his foreman was a rank Tryanite, blustered to a great extent, and would have cashiered that valuable functionary on the spot, if such a retributive procedure had not been inconvenient.

On the whole, however, at the end of a few months, the balance of substantial loss was on the side of the Anti-Tryanites. Mr. Pratt, indeed, had lost a patient or two besides Mr. Dempster's family; but as it was evident that Evangelicalism had not dried up the stream of his anecdote, or in the least altered his view of any lady's constitution, it is probable that a change accompanied by so few outward and visible signs, was rather the pretext than the ground of his dismissal in those additional cases. Mr. Dunn was threatened with the loss of several good customers, Mrs. Phipps and Mrs. Lowme having set the example of ordering him to send in his bill; and the draper began to look forward to his next stock-taking with an anxiety which was but slightly mitigated by the parallel his wife suggested between his own case and that of Shadrach, Meshech, and Abednego, who were thrust into a burning fiery furnace. For, as he observed to her the next morning, with that perspicacity which belongs to the period of shaving, whereas their deliverance consisted in the fact that their linen and woollen goods were not consumed, his own deliverance lay in precisely the opposite result. But convenience, that admirable branch system from the main line of self-interest, makes us all fellow-helpers in spite of adverse resolutions. It is probable that no speculative or theological hatred would be ultimately strong enough to resist the persuasive power of convenience: that a latitudinarian baker, whose bread was honorably free from alum, would command the custom of any dyspeptic Puseyite; that an Arminian with the toothache would prefer a skillful Calvinistic dentist to a bungler stanch against the doctrines of Election and Final Perseverance, who would be likely to break the tooth in his head; and that a Plymouth Brother, who had a well-furnished grocery shop in a favorable vicinage, would occasionally have the pleasure of furnishing sugar or vinegar to orthodox families that found themselves unexpectedly "out of" those indispensable commodities. In this persuasive power of convenience lay Mr. Dunn's ultimate security from martyrdom. His drapery was the best in Milby; the comfortable use and wont of procuring satisfactory articles at a moment's notice proved too strong for Anti-Tryanite zeal; and the draper could soon look forward to his next stock-taking without the support of a Scriptural parallel.

On the other hand, Mr. Dempster had lost his excellent client, Mr. Jerome—a loss which galled him out of proportion to the mere monetary deficit it represented. The attorney loved money, but he loved power still better. He had always been proud of having early won the confidence of a conventicle-goer, and of being able to "turn the prop of Salem round his thumb." Like most other men, too, he had a certain kindness towards those who had employed him when he was only starting in life; and just as we do not like to part with an old weather-glass from our study, or a two-feet ruler that we have carried in our pocket ever since we began business, so Mr. Dempster did not like having to erase his old client's name from the accustomed drawer in the bureau. Our habitual life is like a wall hung with pictures, which has been shone on by the suns of many years: take one of the pictures away, and it leaves a definite blank space, to which our eyes can never turn without a sensation of discomfort. Nay, the involuntary loss of any familiar object almost always brings a chill as from an evil omen; it seems to be the first finger-shadow of advancing death.

From all these causes combined, Mr. Dempster could never think of his lost client without strong irritation, and the very sight of Mr. Jerome passing in the street was wormwood to him.

One day, when the old gentleman was coming up Orchard Street on his roan mare, shaking the bridle, and tickling her flank with the whip as usual, though there was a perfect mutual understanding that she was not to quicken her pace, Janet happened to be on her own door-step, and he could not resist the temptation of stopping to speak to that "nice little woman," as he always called her, though she was taller than all the rest of his feminine acquaintances. Janet, in spite of her disposition to take her husband's part in all public matters, could bear no malice against her old friend; so they shook hands.

"Well, Mrs. Dempster, I'm sorry to my heart not to see you sometimes, that I am," said Mr. Jerome, in a plaintive tone. "But if you've got any poor people as wants help, and you know's deservin', send 'em to me, send 'em to me, just the same."

"Thank you, Mr. Jerome, that I will. Good-bye."

Janet made the interview as short as she could, but it was not short enough to escape the observation of her husband, who, as she feared, was on his mid-day return from his office at the other end of the street, and this offense of hers, in speaking to Mr. Jerome, was the frequently recurring theme of Mr. Dempster's objurgatory domestic eloquence.

Associating the loss of his old client with Mr. Tryan's influence, Dempster began to know more distinctly why he hated the obnoxious curate. But a passionate hate, as well as a passionate love, demands some leisure and mental freedom. Persecution and revenge, like courtship and toadyism, will not prosper without a considerable expenditure of time and ingenuity, and these are not to spare with a man whose law-business and liver are both beginning to show unpleasant symptoms. Such was the disagreeable turn affairs were taking with Mr. Dempster, and, like the general distracted by home intrigues, he was too much harassed himself to lay ingenious plans for harassing the enemy.

Meanwhile, the evening lecture drew larger and larger congregations; not perhaps attracting many from that select aristocratic circle in which the Lowmes and Pittmans were predominant, but winning the larger proportion of Mr. Crewe's morning and afternoon hearers, and thinning Mr. Stickney's evening audiences at Salem. Evangelicalism was making its way in Milby, and gradually diffusing its subtle odor into chambers that were bolted and barred against it. The movement, like all other religious "revivals," had a mixed effect. Religious ideas have the fate of melodies, which once set afloat in the world, are taken up by all sorts of instruments, some of them woefully coarse, feeble, or out of tune, until people are in danger of crying out that the melody itself is detestable. It may be that some of Mr. Tryan's hearers had gained a religious vocabulary rather than religious experience; that here and there a weaver's wife, who, a few months before had been simply a silly slattern, was converted into that more complex nuisance, a silly and sanctimonious slattern; that the old Adam, with the pertinacity of middle age, continued to tell fibs behind the counter, notwithstanding the new Adam's addiction to Bible-reading and family prayer: that the children in the Paddiford Sunday-school had their memories crammed with phrases about the blood of cleansing, imputed righteousness, and justification by faith alone, which an experience lying principally in chuck-farthing, hop-scotch, parental slappings, and longings after unattainable lollypop, served rather to darken than to illustrate; and that at Milby, in those distant days, as in all other times and places where the mental atmosphere is changing, and men are inhaling the stimulus of new ideas, folly often mistook itself for wisdom, ignorance gave itself airs of knowledge, and selfishness, turning its eyes upward, called itself religion.

Nevertheless, Evangelicalism had brought into palpable existence and operation in Milby society that idea of duty, that recognition of something to be lived for beyond the mere satisfaction of self, which is to the moral life what the addi tion of a great central ganglion is to animal life. No man can begin to mould himself on a faith or an idea without rising to a higher order of experience: a principle of subordination, of self-mastery, has been introduced into his nature; he is no longer a mere bundle of impressions, desires, and impulses. Whatever might be the weaknesses of the ladies who pruned the luxuriance of their lace and ribbons, cut out garments for the poor, distributed tracts, quoted Scripture, and defined the true Gospel, they had learned this—that there was a divine work to be done in life, a rule of goodness higher than the opinion of their neighbors; and if the notion of a heaven in reserve for themselves was a little too prominent, yet the theory of fitness for that heaven consisted in purity of heart, in Christ-like compassion, in the subduing of selfish desires. They might give the name of piety to much that was only puritanic egoism; they might call many things sin that were not sin; but they had at least the feeling that sin was to be avoided and resisted, and color-blindness, which may mistake drab for scarlet, is better than total blindness, which sees no distinction of color at all. Miss Rebecca Linnet, in quiet attire, with a somewhat excessive solemnity of countenance, teaching at the Sunday-school, visiting the poor, and striving after a standard of purity and goodness, had surely more moral loveliness than in those flaunting peony-days, when she had no other model than the costumes of the heroines in the circulating library. Miss Eliza Pratt, listening in rapt attention to Mr. Tryan's evening lecture, no doubt found evangelical channels for vanity and egoism; but she was clearly in moral advance of Miss Phipps giggling under her feathers at old Mr. Crewe's peculiarities of enunciation. And even elderly fathers and mothers, with minds, like Mrs. Linnet's, too tough to imbibe much doctrine, were the better for having their hearts inclined towards the new preacher as a messenger from God. They became ashamed, perhaps, of their evil tempers, ashamed of their worldliness, ashamed of their trivial, futile past. The first condition of human goodness is something to love; the second, something to reverence. And this latter precious gift was brought to Milby by Mr. Tryan and Evangelicalism.

Yes, the movement was good, though it had that mixture of folly and evil which often makes what is good an offense to feeble and fastidious minds, who want human actions and characters riddled through the sieve of their own ideas, before they can accord their sympathy or admiration. Such minds, I dare say, would have found Mr. Tryan's character very much in need of that riddling process. The blessed work of helping the world forward, happily does not wait to be done by perfect men; and I should imagine that neither Luther nor John Bunyan, for example, would have satisfied the modern demand for an ideal hero, who believes nothing but what is true, feels nothing but what is exalted, and does nothing but what is graceful. The real heroes, of God's making, are quite different: they have their natural heritage of love and conscience which they drew in with their mother's milk; they know one or two of those deep spiritual truths which are only to be won by long wrestling with their own sins and their own sorrows; they have earned faith and strength so far as they have done genuine work; but the rest is dry, barren theory, blank prejudice, vague hearsay. Their insight is blended with mere opinion; their sympathy is perhaps confined in narrow conduits of doctrine, instead of flowing forth with the freedom of a stream that blesses every weed in its course; obstinacy or self-assertion will often interfuse itself with their grandest impulses; and their very deeds of self-sacrifice are sometimes only the rebound of a passionate egoism. So it was with Mr. Tryan: and any one looking at him with the bird's-eye glance of a critic might perhaps say that he made the mistake of identifying Christianity with a too narrow doctrinal system; that he saw God's work too exclusively in antagonism to the world, the flesh, and the devil; that his intellectual culture was too limited—and so on; making Mr. Tryan the text for a wise discourse on the characteristics of the Evangelical school in his day.

But I am not poised at that lofty height. I am on the level and in the press with him, as he struggles his way along the stony road through the crowd of unloving fellow-men. He is stumbling, perhaps; his heart now beats fast with dread, now heavily with anguish; his eyes are sometimes dim with tears, which he makes haste to dash away; he pushes manfully on, with fluctuating faith and courage, with a sensitive failing body; at last he falls, the struggle is ended, and the crowd closes over the space he has left.

"One of the Evangelical clergy, a disciple of Venn," says the critic from his bird's-eye station. "Not a remarkable specimen; the anatomy and habits of his species have been determined long ago."

Yet surely, surely the only true knowledge of our fellow-man is that which enables us to feel with him—which gives us a fine ear for the heart-pulses that are beating under the mere clothes of circumstance and opinion. Our subtlest analysis of schools and sects must miss the essential truth, unless it be lit up by the love that sees in all forms of human thought and work the life and death struggles of separate human beings.

CHAPTER XI.

Mr. Tryan's most unfriendly observers were obliged to admit that he gave himself no rest. Three sermons on Sunday, a night-school for young men on Tuesday, a cottage-lecture on Thursday, addresses to school-teachers, and catechising of school-children, with pastoral visits, multiplying as his influence extended beyond his own district of Paddiford Common, would have been enough to tax severely the powers of a much stronger man. Mr. Pratt remonstrated with him on his imprudence, but could not prevail on him so far to economize time and strength as to keep a horse. On some ground or other, which his friends found difficult to explain to themselves, Mr. Tryan seemed bent on wearing himself out. His enemies were at no loss to account for such a course. The Evangelical curate's selfishness was clearly of too bad a kind to exhibit itself after the ordinary manner of a sound, respectable selfishness. "He wants to get the reputation of a saint," said one; "He's eaten up with spiritual pride," said another; "He's got his eye on some fine living, and wants to creep up the Bishop's sleeve," said a third.

Mr. Stickney, of Salem, who considered all voluntary discomfort as a remnant of the legal spirit, pronounced a severe condemnation on this self-neglect, and expressed his fear that Mr. Tryan was still far from having attained true Christian liberty. Good Mr. Jerome eagerly seized this doctrinal view of the subject as a means of enforcing the suggestions of his own benevolence; and one cloudy afternoon, in the end of November, he mounted his roan mare with the determination of riding to Paddiford and "arguying" the point with Mr. Tryan.

The old gentleman's face looked very mournful as he rode along the dismal Paddiford lanes, between rows of grimy houses, darkened with hand-looms, while the black dust was whirled about him by the cold November wind. He was thinking of the object which had brought him on this afternoon ride, and his thoughts, according to his habit when alone, found vent every now and then in audible speech. It seemed to him, as his eyes rested on this scene of Mr. Tryan's labors, that he could understand the clergyman's self-privation without resorting to Mr. Stickney's theory of defective spiritual enlightenment. Do not philosophic doctors tell us that we are unable to discern so much as a tree, except by an unconscious cunning which combines many past and separate sensations; that no one sense is independent of another, so that in the dark we can hardly taste a fricassee, or tell whether our pipe is alight or not, and the most intelligent boy, if accommodated with claws or hoofs instead of fingers, would be likely to remain on the lowest form? If so, it is easy to understand that our discernment of men's motives must depend on the completeness of the elements we can bring from our own susceptibility and our own experience. See to it, friend, before you pronounce a too hasty judgment, that your own moral sensibilities are not of a hoofed or clawed character. The keenest eye will not serve, unless you have the delicate fingers, with their subtle nerve filaments, which elude scientific lenses, and lose themselves in the invisible world of human sensations.

As for Mr. Jerome, he drew the elements of his moral vision from the depths of his veneration and pity. If he himself felt so much for these poor things to whom life was so dim and meagre, what must the clergyman feel who had undertaken before God to be their shepherd?

"Ah!" he whispered, interruptedly, "it's too big a load for his conscience, poor man! He wants to mek himself their brother, like; can't abide to preach to the fastin' on a full stomach. Ah! he's better nor we are, that's it—he's a deal better nor we are."

Here Mr. Jerome shook his bridle violently, and looked up with an air of moral courage, as if Mr. Stickney had been present, and liable to take offense at this conclusion. A few minutes more brought him in front of Mrs. Wagstaff's, where Mr. Tryan lodged. He had often been here before, so that the contrast between this ugly square brick house, with its shabby bit of grass-plot, stared at all round by cottage windows, and his own pretty white home, set in a paradise of orchard and garden and pasture, was not new to him; but he felt it with fresh force to-day, as he slowly fastened his roan by the bridle to the wooden paling, and knocked at the door. Mr. Tryan was at home, and sent to request that Mr. Jerome would walk up into his study, as the fire was out in the parlor below.

At the mention of a clergyman's study, perhaps your too active imagination conjures up a perfect snuggery, where the general air of comfort is rescued from a secular character by strong ecclesiastical suggestions in the shape of the furniture, the pattern of the carpet, and the prints on the wall; where, if a nap is taken, it is in an easy-chair with a Gothic back, and the very feet rest on a warm and velvety simulation of church windows; where the pure art of rigorous English Protestantism smiles above the mantel-piece in the portrait of an eminent bishop, or a refined Anglican taste is indicated by a German print from Overbeck; where the walls are lined with choice divinity in sombre binding, and the light is softened by a screen of boughs with a gray church in the background.

But I must beg you to dismiss all such scenic prettiness, suitable as they may be to a clergyman's character and complexion; for I have to confess that Mr. Tryan's study was a very ugly little room indeed, with an ugly slap-dash pattern on the walls, an ugly carpet on the floor, and an ugly view of cottage roofs and cabbage-gardens from the window. His own person, his writing-table, and his book-case, were the only objects in the room that had the slightest air of refinement; and the sole provision for comfort was a clumsy straight-backed arm-chair, covered with faded chintz. The man who could live in such a room, unconstrained by poverty, must either have his vision fed from within by an intense passion, or he must have chosen that least attractive form of self-mortification which wears no haircloth and has no meagre days, but accepts the vulgar, the commonplace, and the ugly, whenever the highest duty seems to lie among them.

"Mr. Tryan, I hope you'll excuse me disturbin' on you," said Mr. Jerome. "But I'd summat particler to say."

"You don't disturb me at all, Mr. Jerome; I'm very glad to have a visit from you," said Mr. Tryan, shaking him heartily by the hand, and offering him the chintz-covered "easy" chair; "it is some time since I've had an opportunity of seeing you, except on a Sunday."

"Ah, sir! your time's so taken up, I'm well aware o' that; it's not only what you hev to do, but it's goin' about from place to place; an' you don't keep a hoss, Mr. Tryan. You don't take care enough o' yourself—you don't indeed, an' that's what I come to talk to y' about."

"That's very good of you, Mr. Jerome; but I assure you I think walking does me no harm. It is rather a relief to me after speaking or writing. You know I have no great circuit to make. The farthest distance I have to walk is to Milby Church, and if ever I want a horse on a Sunday, I hire Radley's, who lives not many hundred yards from me."

"Well, but now! the winter's comin' on, an' you'll get wet i' your feet, an' Pratt tells me as your constitution's dillicate, as any body may see, for the matter o' that, wi'out bein' a doctor. An' this is the light I look at it in, Mr. Tryan: who's to fill up your place, if you was to be disabled, as I may say? Consider what a valuable life yours is. You've begun a great work i' Milby, and so you might carry it on, if you'd your health and strength. The more care you take o' yourself, the longer you'll live, belike, God willing, to do good to your fellow-creaturs."

"Why, my dear Mr. Jerome, I think I should not be a long-lived man in any case; and if I were to take care of myself under the pretext of doing more good, I should very likely die and leave nothing done after all."

"Well! but keepin' a hoss wouldn't hinder you from workin'. It 'ud help you to do more, though Pratt says as it's usin' your voice so constant as does you the most harm. Now, isn't it—I'm no scholard, Mr. Tryan, an' I'm not a-goin' to dictate to you—but isn't it a'most a-killin' o' yourself, to go on a' that way beyond your strength? We mustn't fling our lives away."

"No, not fling them away lightly, but we are permitted to lay down our lives in a right cause. there are many duties, as you know, Mr. Jerome, which stand before taking care of our own lives."

"Ah! I can't arguy wi' you, Mr. Tryan; but what I wanted to say's this — There's my little chacenut hoss; I should take it quite a kindness if you'd hev him through the winter an' ride him. I've thought o' sellin' him a many times, for Mrs. Jerome can't abide him; and what do I want wi' two nags? But I'm fond o' the little chacenut, an' I shouldn't like to sell him. So if you'll only ride him for me, you'll do me a kindness—you will, indeed, Mr. Tryan."

"Thank you, Mr. Jerome. I promise you to ask for him when I feel that I want a nag. There is no man I would more gladly be indebted to than you; but at present I would rather not have a horse. I should ride him very little, and it would be an inconvenience to me to keep him rather than otherwise."

Mr. Jerome looked troubled and hesitating, as if he had something on his mind that would not readily shape itself into words. At last he said, "You'll excuse me, Mr. Tryan, I wouldn't be takin' a liberty, but I know what great claims you hev on you as a clergyman. Is it the expense, Mr. Tryan? is it the money?"

"No, my dear sir. I have much more than a single man needs. My way of living is quite of my own choosing, and I am doing nothing but what I feel bound to do, quite apart from money considerations. We can not judge for one another, you know; we have each our peculiar weaknesses and temptations. I quite admit that it might be right for another man to allow himself more luxuries, and I assure you I think it no superiority in myself to do without them. On the contrary, if my heart were less rebellious, and if I were less liable to temptation, I should not need that sort of self-denial. But," added Mr. Tryan, holding out his hand to Mr. Jerome, "I understand your kindness, and bless you for it. If I want a horse, I shall ask for the chestnut."

Mr. Jerome was obliged to rest contented with this promise, and rode home sorrowfully, reproaching himself with not having said one thing he meant to say when setting out, and with having "clean forgot" the arguments he had intended to quote from Mr. Stickney.

Mr. Jerome's was not the only mind that was seriously disturbed by the idea that the curate was over-working himself. There were tender women's hearts in which anxiety about the state of his affections was beginning to be merged in anxiety about the state of his health. Miss Eliza Pratt had at one time passed through much sleepless cogitation on the possibility of Mr. Tryan's being attached to some lady at a distance—at Laxeter, perhaps, where he had formerly held a curacy; and her fine eyes kept close watch lest any symptom of engaged affections on his part should escape her. It seemed an alarming fact that his handkerchiefs were beautifully marked with hair, until she reflected that he had an unmarried sister of whom he spoke with much affection as his father's companion and comforter. Besides, Mr. Tryan had never paid any distant visit, except one for a few days to his father, and no hint escaped him of his intending to take a house, or change his mode of living. No! he could not be engaged, though he might have been disappointed. But this latter misfortune is one from which a devoted clergyman has been known to recover, by the aid of a fine pair of gray eyes that beam on him with affectionate reverence. Before Christmas, however, her cogitations began to take another turn. She heard her father say very confidently that "Tryan was consumptive, and if he didn't take more care of himself, his life would not be worth a year's purchase;" and shame at having speculated on suppositions that were likely to prove so false, sent poor Miss Eliza's feelings with all the stronger impetus into the one channel of sorrowful alarm at the prospect of losing the pastor who had opened to her a new life of piety and self-subjection. It is a sad weakness in us, after all, that the thought of a man's death hallows him anew to us; as if life were not sacred too—as if it were comparatively a light thing to fail in love and reverence to the brother who has to climb the whole toilsome steep with us, and all our tears and tenderness were due to the one who is spared that hard journey.

The Miss Linnets, too, were beginning to take a new view of the future, entirely uncolored by jealousy of Miss Eliza Pratt.

"Did you notice," said Mary, one afternoon when Mrs. Pettifer was taking tea with them—"did you notice that short dry cough of Mr. Tryan's yesterday? I think he looks worse and worse every week, and I only wish I knew his sister; I would write to her about him. I'm sure something should be done to make him give up part of his work, and he will listen to no one here."

"Ah," said Mrs. Pettifer, "it's a thousand pities his father and sister can't come and live with him, if he isn't to marry. But I wish with all my heart he could have taken to some nice woman as would have made a comfortable home for him. I used to think he might take to Eliza Pratt; she's a good girl, and very pretty; but I see no likelihood of it now."

"No, indeed," said Rebecca, with some emphasis; "Mr. Tryan's heart is not for any woman to win; it is all given to his work; and I could never wish to see him with a young inexperienced wife who would be a drag on him instead of a helpmate.

"He'd need have somebody, young or old," observed Mrs. Linnet, "to see as he wears a flannel wescoat, an' changes his stockins when he comes in. It's my opinion he's got that cough wi' sittin' i' wet shoes and stockins; an' that Mrs. Wagstaff's a poor addle-headed thing; she doesn't half tek care on him."

"Oh mother!" said Rebecca, "she's a very pious woman. And I'm sure she thinks it too great a privilege to have Mr. Tryan with her, not to do the best she can to make him comfortable. She can't help her rooms being shabby."

"I've nothing to say again' her piety, my dear; but I know very well I shouldn't like her to cook my victual. When a man comes in hungry an' tired, piety won't feed him, I reckon. Hard carrots 'ull lie heavy on his stomach, piety or no piety. I called in one day when she was dishin' up Mr. Tryan's dinner, an' I could see the potatoes was as watery as watery. It's right enough to be speritial—I'm no enemy to that; but I like my potatoes mealy. I don't see as any body 'ull go to heaven the sooner for not digestin' their dinner—

providin' they don't die sooner, as mayhap Mr. Tryan will, poor dear man!"

"It will be a heavy day for us all when that comes to pass," said Mrs. Pettifer. "We shall never get any body to fill up *that* gap. There's the new clergyman that's just come to Shepperton—Mr. Parry; I saw him the other day at Mrs. Bond's. He may be a very good man, and a fine preacher; they say he is; but I thought to myself, What a difference between him and Mr. Tryan! He's a sharp-sort-of-looking man, and hasn't that feeling way with him that Mr. Tryan has. What is so wonderful to me in Mr. Tryan is the way he puts himself on a level with one, and talks to one like a brother. I'm never afraid of telling him any thing. He never seems to look down on any body. He knows how to lift up those that are cast down, if ever man did."

"Yes," said Mary. "And when I see all the faces turned up to him in Paddiford Church, I often think how hard it would be for any clergyman who had to come after him; he has made the people love him so."

CHAPTER XII.

In her occasional visits to her near neighbor Mrs. Pettifer, too old a friend to be shunned because she was a Tryanite, Janet was obliged sometimes to hear allusions to Mr. Tryan, and even to listen to his praises, which she usually met with playful incredulity.

"Ah, well," she answered one day, "I like dear old Mr. Crewe and his pipes a great deal better than your Mr. Tryan and his Gospel. When I was a little toddle, Mr. and Mrs. Crewe used to let me play about in their garden, and have a swing between the great elm-trees, because mother had no garden. I like people who are kind; kindness is my religion; and that's the reason I like you, dear Mrs. Pettifer, though you *are* a Tryanite."

"But that's Mr. Tryan's religion too—at least partly. There's nobody can give himself up more to doing good amongst the poor; and he thinks of their bodies too, as well as their souls."

"Oh yes, yes; but then he talks about faith, and grace, and all that, making people believe they are better than others, and that God loves them more than He does the rest of the world. I know he has put a great deal of that into Sally

Martin's head, and it has done her no good at all. She was as nice, honest, patient a girl as need be before; and now she fancies she has new light and new wisdom. I don't like those notions."

"You mistake him, indeed you do, my dear Mrs. Dempster; I wish you'd go and hear him preach."

"Hear him preach! Why, you wicked woman, you would persuade me to disobey my husband, would you? Oh, shocking! I shall run away from you. Good-bye."

A few days after this conversation, however, Janet went to Sally Martin's about three o'clock in the afternoon. The pudding that had been sent in for herself and "Mammy" struck her as just the sort of delicate morsel the poor consumptive girl would be likely to fancy, and in her usual impulsive way she had started up from the dinner-table at once, put on her bonnet, and set off with a covered plateful to the neighboring street. When she entered the house there was no one to be seen; but in the little side room where Sally lay, Janet heard a voice. It was one she had not heard before, but she immediately guessed it to be Mr. Tryan's. Her first impulse was to set down her plate and go away, but Mrs. Martin might not be in, and then there would be no one to give Sally that delicious bit of pudding. So she stood still, and was obliged to hear what Mr. Tryan was saying. He was interrupted by one of the invalid's violent fits of coughing.

"It is very hard to bear, is it not?" he said when she was still again. "Yet God seems to support you under it wonderfully. Pray for me, Sally, that I may have strength too when the hour of great suffering comes. It is one of my worst weaknesses to shrink from bodily pain, and I think the time is perhaps not far off when I shall have to bear what you are bearing. But now I have tired you. We have talked enough. Good-bye."

Janet was surprised, and forgot her wish not to encounter Mr. Tryan; the tone and the words were so unlike what she had expected to hear. There was none of the self-satisfied unction of the teacher, quoting, or exhorting, or expounding, for the benefit of the hearer, but a simple appeal for help, a confession of weakness. Mr. Tryan had his deeply-felt troubles, then? Mr. Tryan, too, like herself, knew what it was to tremble at a foreseen trial—to shudder at an impending burthen, heavier than he felt able to bear?

The most brilliant deed of virtue could not have inclined Janet's good-will towards Mr. Tryan so much as this fellowship in suffering, and the softening thought was in her eyes when he appeared in the doorway, pale, weary, and depressed.

The sight of Janet standing there with the entire absence of self-consciousness which belongs to a new and vivid impression, made him start and pause a little. Their eyes met, and they looked at each other gravely for a few moments. Then they bowed, and Mr. Tryan passed out.

There is a power in the direct glance of a sincere and loving human soul, which will do more to dissipate prejudice and kindle charity than the most elaborate arguments. The fullest exposition of Mr. Tryan's doctrine might not have sufficed to convince Janet that he had not an odious self-complacency in believing himself a peculiar child of God; but one direct, pathetic look of his had dissociated him with that conception forever.

This happened late in the autumn, not long before Sally Martin died. Janet mentioned her new impression to no one, for she was afraid of arriving at a still more complete contradiction of her former ideas. We have all of us considerable regard for our past self, and are not fond of casting reflections on that respected individual by a total negation of his opinions. Janet could no longer think of Mr. Tryan without sympathy, but she still shrank from the idea of becoming his hearer and admirer. That was a reversal of the past which was as little accordant with her inclination as her circumstances.

And indeed this interview with Mr. Tryan was soon thrust into the background of poor Janet's memory by the daily thickening miseries of her life.

CHAPTER XIII.

The loss of Mr. Jerome as a client proved only the beginning of annoyances to Dempster. That old gentleman had in him the vigorous remnant of an energy and perseverance which had created his own fortune; and being, as I have hinted, given to chewing the cud of a righteous indignation with considerable relish, he was determined to carry on his retributive war against the persecuting attorney. Having some influence with Mr. Pryme, who was one of the most substantial rate-payers in the neighboring parish of Dingley, and who had himself a complex and long-standing private account with Dempster, Mr. Jerome stirred up this gentleman to an investigation of some suspicious points in the attorney's conduct of the parish affairs. The natural consequence was a personal quarrel between Dempster and Mr. Pryme; the client demanded his account, and then followed the old story of an exorbitant lawyer's bill, with the unpleasant anti-climax of taxing.

These disagreeables, extending over many months, ran along side by side with the pressing business of Mr. Armstrong's law-suit, which was threatening to take a turn rather depreciatory of Dempster's professional prevision; and it is not surprising that, being thus kept in a constant state of irritated excitement about his own affairs, he had little time for the further exhibition of his public spirit, or for rallying the forlorn hope of sound churchmanship against cant and hypocrisy. Not a few persons who had a grudge against him began to remark, with satisfaction, that "Dempster's luck was forsaking him;" particularly Mrs. Linnet, who thought she saw distinctly the gradual ripening of a providential scheme, whereby a just retribution would be wrought on the man who had deprived her of Pye's Croft. On the other hand, Dempster's well-satisfied clients, who were of opinion that the punishment of his wickedness might conveniently be deferred to another world, noticed with some concern that he was drinking more than ever, and that both his temper and his driving were becoming more furious. Unhappily those additional glasses of brandy, that exasperation of loud-tongued abuse, had other effects than any that entered into the contemplation of anxious clients: they were the little superadded symbols that were perpetually raising the sum of home misery.

Poor Janet! how heavily the months rolled on for her, laden with fresh sorrows as the summer passed into autumn, the autumn into winter, and the winter into spring again. Every feverish morning, with its blank listlessness and despair, seemed more hateful than the last; every coming night more impossible to brave without arming herself in leaden stupor. The morning light brought no gladness to her: it seemed only to throw its glare on what had happened in the dim candle-light — on the cruel man seated immovable in drunken obstinacy by the dead fire and dying lights in the dining-room, rating her in harsh tones, reiterating old reproaches—or on a hideous blank of something unremembered, something that must have made that dark bruise on her shoulder, which ached as she dressed herself.

Do you wonder how it was that things had come to this pass—what offense Janet had committed in the early years of marriage to rouse the brutal hatred of this man? The seeds of things are very small: the hours that lie between sunrise and the gloom of midnight are travelled through by tiniest markings of the clock: and Janet, looking back along the fifteen years of her married life, hardly knew how or where this total misery began; hardly knew when the sweet wedded love and hope that had set forever had ceased to make a twilight of memory and relenting, before the on-coming of the utter dark.

Old Mrs. Dempster thought she saw the true beginning of it all in Janet's want of housekeeping skill and exactness. "Janet," she said to herself, "was always running about doing things for other people, and neglecting her own house. That provokes a man; what use is it for a woman to be loving, and making a fuss with her husband, if she doesn't take care and keep his home just as he likes it; if she isn't at hand when he wants any thing done; if she doesn't attend to all his wishes, let them be as small as they may? That was what I did when I was a wife, though I didn't make half so much fuss about loving my husband. Then, Janet had no children—" Ah! there Mammy Dempster had touched a true spring, not perhaps of her son's cruelty, but of half Janet's misery. If she had babes to rock to sleep—little ones to kneel in their night-dress and say their prayers at her knees—sweet boys and girls to put their young arms round her neck and kiss away her tears, her poor hungry heart would have been fed with strong love, and might never have needed that fiery poison to still its cravings. Mighty is the force of motherhood! says the great tragic poet to us across the ages, finding, as usual, the simplest words for the sublimest fact—*δεινὸν τὸ τίκτειν ἐστίν.* It transforms all things by its vital heat; it turns timidity into fierce courage, and dreadless defiance into tremulous submission; it turns thoughtlessness into foresight, and yet stills all anxiety into calm content; it makes selfishness become self-denial, and gives even to hard vanity the glance of admiring love. Yes! if Janet had been a mother, she might have been saved from much sin, and therefore from much of her sorrow.

But do not believe that it was any thing either present or wanting in poor Janet that formed the motive of her husband's cruelty. Cruelty, like every other vice, requires no motive outside itself—it only requires opportunity. You do not suppose Dempster had any motive for drinking beyond the craving for drink; the presence of brandy was the only necessary condition. And an unloving, tyrannous, brutal man needs no motive to prompt his cruelty; he needs only the perpetual presence of a woman he can call his own. A whole park full of tame or timid-eyed animals to torment at his will would not serve him so well to glut his lust of torture; they could not *feel* as one woman does; they could not throw out the keen retort which whets the edge of hatred.

Janet's bitterness would overflow in ready words; she was not to be made meek by cruelty; she would repent of nothing in the face of injustice, though she was subdued in a moment by a word or a look that recalled the old days of fondness; and in times of comparative calm would often recover her sweet woman's habit of caressing, playful affection. But such days were become rare, and poor Janet's soul was kept like a vexed sea, tossed by a new storm before the old waves have fallen. Proud, angry resistance and sullen endurance were now almost the only alternations she knew. She would bear it all proudly to the world, but proudly towards him too; her woman's weakness might shriek a cry for pity under a heavy blow, but voluntarily she would do nothing to mollify him, unless he first relented. What had she ever done to him but love him too well—but believe in him too foolishly? He had no pity on her tender flesh; he could strike the soft neck he had once asked to kiss. Yet she would not admit her wretchedness; she had married him blindly, and she would bear it out to the terrible end, whatever that might be. Better this misery than the blank that lay for her outside her married home.

But there was one person who heard all the plaints and all the outbursts of bitterness and despair which Janet was never tempted to pour into any other ear; and alas! in her worst moments, Janet would throw out wild reproaches against that patient listener. For the wrong that rouses our angry passions finds only a medium in us; it passes through us like a vibration, and we inflict what we have suffered.

Mrs. Raynor saw too clearly all through the winter that things were getting worse in Orchard Street. She had evidence enough of it in Janet's visits to her; and, though her own visits to her daughter were so timed that she saw little of Dempster personally, she noticed many indications not only that he was drinking to greater excess, but that he was beginning to lose that physical power of supporting excess which had long been the admiration of such fine spirits as Mr. Tomlinson. It seemed as if Dempster had some consciousness of this—some new distrust of himself; for, before winter was over, it was observed that he had renounced his habit of driving out alone, and was never seen in his gig without a servant by his side.

Nemesis is lame, but she is of colossal stature, like the gods; and sometimes, while her sword is not yet unsheathed, she stretches out her huge left arm and grasps her victim.

The mighty hand is invisible, but the victim totters under the dire clutch.

The various symptoms that things were getting worse with the Dempsters afforded Milby gossip something new to say on an old subject. Mrs. Dempster, every one remarked, looked more miserable than ever, though she kept up the old pretense of being happy and satisfied. She was scarcely ever seen, as she used to be, going about on her good-natured errands; and even old Mrs. Crewe, who had always been willfully blind to any thing wrong in her favorite Janet, was obliged to admit that she had not seemed like herself lately. "The poor thing's out of health," said the kind little old lady, in answer to all gossip about Janet; "her headaches always were bad, and I know what headaches are: why, they make one quite delirious sometimes." Mrs. Phipps, for her part, declared she would never accept an invitation to Dempster's again; it was getting so very disagreeable to go there, Mrs. Dempster was often "so strange." To be sure, there were dreadful stories about the way Dempster used his wife; but in Mrs. Phipps's opinion, it was six of one and half-a-dozen of the other. Mrs. Dempster had never been like other women; she had always a flighty way with her, carrying parcels of snuff to old Mrs. Tooke, and going to drink tea with Mrs. Brinley, the carpenter's wife; and then never taking care of her clothes, always wearing the same things week-day or Sunday. A man has a poor look-out with a wife of that sort. Mr. Phipps, amiable and laconic, wondered how it was women were so fond of running each other down.

Mr. Pratt having been called in provisionally to a patient of Mr. Pilgrim's in a case of compound fracture, observed in a friendly colloquy with his brother surgeon the next day,

"So Dempster has left off driving himself, I see; he won't end with a broken neck after all. You'll have a case of meningitis and delirium tremens instead."

"Ah," said Mr. Pilgrim, "he can hardly stand it much longer at the rate he's going on, one would think. He's been confoundedly cut up about that business of Armstrong's, I fancy. It may do him some harm, perhaps, but Dempster must have feathered his nest pretty well; he can afford to lose a little business."

"His business will outlast him, that's pretty clear," said Pratt; "he'll run down like a watch with a broken spring one of these days."

Another prognostic of evil to Dempster came at the beginning of March. For then little "Mamsey" died—died suddenly. The housemaid found her seated motionless in her arm-chair, her knitting fallen down, and the tortoise-shell cat reposing on it unreproved. The little white old woman had ended her wintry age of patient sorrow, believing to the last that "Robert might have been a good husband as he had been a good son."

When the earth was thrown on Mamsey's coffin, and the son, in crape scarf and hat-band, turned away homeward, his good angel, lingering with outstretched wing on the edge of the grave, cast one despairing look after him, and took flight forever.

CHAPTER XIV.

The last week in March—three weeks after old Mrs. Dempster died—occurred the unpleasant winding-up of affairs between Dempster and Mr. Pryme, and under this additional source of irritation the attorney's diurnal drunkenness had taken on its most ill-tempered and brutal phase. On the Friday morning, before setting out for Rotherby, he told his wife that he had invited "four men" to dinner at half past six that evening. The previous night had been a terrible one for Janet, and when her husband broke his grim morning silence to say these few words, she was looking so blank and listless that he added in a loud, sharp key, "Do you hear what I say? or must I tell the cook?" She started, and said, "Yes, I hear."

"Then mind and have a dinner provided, and don't go mooning about like crazy Jane."

Half an hour afterwards Mrs. Raynor, quietly busy in her kitchen with her household labors—for she had only a little twelve-year-old girl as a servant—heard with trembling the rattling of the garden gate and the opening of the outer door. She knew the step, and in one short moment she lived beforehand through the coming scene. She hurried out of the kitchen, and there in the passage, as she had felt, stood Janet, her eyes worn as if by night-long watching, her dress careless, her step languid. No cheerful morning greeting to her mother—no kiss. She turned into the parlor, and, seating herself on the sofa opposite her mother's chair, looked vacantly at the walls and furniture until the corners of her mouth began to tremble, and her dark eyes filled with tears that fell unwiped down her cheeks. The mother sat silently opposite to her, afraid to speak. She felt sure there was nothing new the matter—sure that the torrent of words would come sooner or later.

"Mother! why don't you speak to me?" Janet burst out at last; "you don't care about my suffering; you are blaming me because I feel—because I am miserable."

"My child, I am not blaming you—my heart is bleeding for you. Your head is bad this morning—you have had a bad night. Let me make you a cup of tea now. Perhaps you didn't like your breakfast."

"Yes, that is what you always think, mother. It is the old story, you think. You don't ask me what it is I have had to bear. You are tired of hearing me. You are cruel, like the rest; every one is cruel in this world. Nothing but blame—blame—blame; never any pity. God is cruel to have sent me into the world to bear all this misery."

"Janet, Janet, don't say so. It is not for us to judge; we must submit; we must be thankful for the gift of life."

"Thankful for life! Why should I be thankful? God has made me with a heart to feel, and He has sent me nothing but misery. How could I help it? How could I know what would come? Why didn't you tell me, mother?—why did you let me marry? You knew what brutes men could be; and there's no help for me—no hope. I can't kill myself; I've tried; but I can't leave this world and go to another. There may be no pity for me there, as there is none here."

"Janet, my child, there *is* pity. Have I ever done any thing but love you? And there is pity in God. Hasn't He put pity into your heart for many a poor sufferer? Where did it come from, if not from Him?"

Janet's nervous irritation now broke out into sobs instead of complainings; and her mother was thankful, for after that crisis there would very likely come relenting, and tenderness, and comparative calm. She went out to make some tea, and when she returned with the tray in her hands, Janet had dried her eyes and now turned them towards her mother with a faint attempt to smile; but the poor face, in its sad blurred beauty, looked all the more piteous.

"Mother will insist upon her tea," she said, "and I really think I can drink a cup. But I must go home directly, for there are people coming to dinner. Could you go with me and help me, mother?"

Mrs. Raynor was always ready to do that. She went to Orchard Street with Janet, and remained with her through the day—comforted, as evening approached, to see her become more cheerful and willing to attend to her toilette.

At half past five every thing was in order; Janet was dressed; and when the mother had kissed her and said good-bye, she could not help pausing a moment in sorrowful admiration at the tall, rich figure, looking all the grander for the plainness of the deep mourning dress, and the noble face with its massy folds of black hair, made matronly by a simple white cap. Janet had that enduring beauty which belongs to pure majestic outline and depth of tint. Sorrow and neglect leave their traces on such beauty, but it thrills us to the last, like a glorious Greek temple, which, for all the loss it has suffered from time and barbarous hands, has gained a solemn history, and fills our imagination the more because it is incomplete to the sense.

It was six o'clock before Dempster returned from Rotherby. He had evidently drunk a great deal, and was in an angry humor; but Janet, who had gathered some little courage and forbearance from the consciousness that she had done her best to-day, was determined to speak pleasantly to him.

"Robert," she said gently, as she saw him seat himself in the dining-room in his dusty, snuffy clothes, and take some documents out of his pocket, "will you not wash and change your dress? It will refresh you."

"Leave me alone, will you?" said Dempster, in his most brutal tone.

"Do change your coat and waistcoat, they are so dusty. I've laid all your things out ready."

"Oh, you have, have you?" After a few minutes he rose very deliberately and walked up stairs into his bedroom. Janet had often been scolded before for not laying out his clothes, and she thought now, not without some wonder, that this attention of hers had brought him to compliance.

Presently, he called out, "Janet!" and she went up stairs.

"Here! Take that!" he said, as soon as she reached the door, flinging at her the coat she had laid out. "Another time, leave me to do as I please, will you?"

The coat, flung with great force, only brushed her shoulder, and fell some distance within the drawing-room, the door of which stood open just opposite. She hastily retreated as she saw the waistcoat coming, and one by one the clothes she had laid out were all flung into the drawing-room.

Janet's face flushed with anger, and for the first time in her life her resentment overcame the long-cherished pride that made her hide her griefs from the world. There are moments when, by some strange impulse, we contradict our past selves—fatal moments, when a fit of passion, like a lava stream, lays low the work of half our lives. Janet thought,

"I will not pick up the clothes; they shall lie there until the visitors come, and he shall be ashamed of himself."

There was a knock at the door, and she made haste to seat herself in the drawing-room, lest the servant should enter and remove the clothes, which were lying half on the table and half on the ground. Mr. Lowme entered with a less familiar visitor, a client of Dempster's, and the next moment Dempster himself came in.

His eye fell at once on the clothes, and then turned for an instant with a devilish glance of concentrated hatred on Janet, who, still flushed and excited, affected unconsciousness. After shaking hands with his visitors he immediately rang the bell.

"Take those clothes away," he said to the servant, not looking at Janet again.

During dinner, she kept up her assumed air of indifference, and tried to seem in high spirits, laughing and talking more than usual. In reality, she felt as if she had defied a wild beast within the four walls of his den, and he was crouching backward in preparation for his deadly spring. Dempster affected to take no notice of her, talked obstreperously, and drank steadily.

About eleven the party dispersed, with the exception of Mr. Budd, who had joined them after dinner, and appeared disposed to stay drinking a little longer. Janet began to hope that he would stay long enough for Dempster to become heavy and stupid, and so to fall asleep down stairs, which was a rare but occasional ending of his nights. She told the servants to sit up no longer, and she herself undressed and went to bed, trying to cheat her imagination into the belief that the day was ended for her. But when she lay down she became more intensely awake than ever. Every thing she had taken this evening seemed only to stimulate her senses and her apprehensions to new vividness. Her heart beat violently, and she heard every sound in the house.

At last, when it was twelve, she heard Mr. Budd go out; she heard the door slam. Dempster had not moved. Was he asleep? Would he forget? The minute seemed long, while, with a quickening pulse, she was on the stretch to catch every sound.

"Janet!" The loud jarring voice seemed to strike her like a hurled weapon.

"Janet!" he called again, moving out of the dining-room to the foot of the stairs.

There was a pause of a minute.

"If you don't come, I'll kill you."

Another pause, and she heard him turn back into the dining-room. He was gone for a light—perhaps for a weapon. Perhaps he *would* kill her. Let him. Life was as hideous as death. For years she had been rushing on to some unknown but certain horror; and now she was close upon it. She was almost glad. She was in a state of flushed, feverish defiance that neutralized her woman's terrors.

She heard his heavy step on the stairs; she saw the slowly advancing light. Then she saw the tall, massive figure, and the heavy face, now fierce with drunken rage. He had nothing but the candle in his hand. He set it down on the table and advanced close to the bed.

"So you think you'll defy me, do you? We'll see how long that will last. Get up, madam; out of bed this instant!"

In the close presence of the dreadful man—of this huge crushing force, armed with savage will—poor Janet's desperate defiance all forsook her, and her terrors came back. Trembling she got up, and stood helpless in her night-dress before her husband.

He seized her with his heavy grasp by the shoulder, and pushed her before him.

"I'll cool your hot spirit for you! I'll teach you to brave me!"

Slowly he pushed her along before him, down stairs and through the passage, where a small oil lamp was still flickering. What was he going to do to her? She thought every moment he was going to dash her before him on the ground. But she gave no scream—she only trembled.

He pushed her on to the entrance and held her firmly in his grasp while he lifted the latch of the door. Then he opened the door a little way, thrust her out, and slammed it behind her.

For a short space it seemed like a deliverance to Janet. The harsh north-east wind that blew through her thin night-dress, and sent her long heavy black hair streaming, seemed like the breath of pity after the grasp of that threatening monster. But soon the sense of release from an overpowering terror gave way before the sense of the fate that had really come upon her.

This, then, was what she had been travelling towards through her long years of misery! Not yet death. Oh! if she had been brave enough for it, death would have been better. The servants slept at the back of the house; it was impossible to make them hear, so that they might let her in again quietly without her husband's knowledge. And she would not have tried. He had thrust her out, and it should be forever.

There would have been dead silence in Orchard Street but for the whistling of the wind and the swirling of the March dust on the pavement. Thick clouds covered the sky; every door was closed; every window was dark. No ray of light fell on the tall white figure that stood in lonely misery on the doorstep; no eye rested on Janet as she sank down on the cold stone, and looked into the dismal night. She seemed to be looking into her own blank future.

CHAPTER XV.

The stony street, the bitter north-east wind and darkness —and in the midst of them a tender woman thrust out from her husband's home in her thin night-dress, the harsh wind cutting her naked feet, and driving her long hair away from her half-clad bosom, where the poor heart is crushed with anguish and despair.

The drowning man, urged by the supreme agony, lives in an instant through all his happy and unhappy past: when the dark flood has fallen like a curtain, memory, in a single moment, sees the drama acted over again. And even in those earlier crises, which are but types of death—when we are cut off abruptly from the life we have known, when we can no longer expect to-morrow to resemble yesterday, and find ourselves by some sudden shock on the confines of the unknown—there is often the same sort of lightning-flash through the dark and unfrequented chambers of memory.

When Janet sat down shivering on the door-stone, with the door shut upon her past life, and the future black and unshapen before her as the night, the scenes of her childhood, her youth, and her painful womanhood, rushed back upon her consciousness, and made one picture with her present desolation. The petted child taking her newest toy to bed with her—the young girl, proud in strength and beauty, dreaming that life was an easy thing, and that it was pitiful weakness to be unhappy—the bride, passing with trembling joy from the outer court to the inner sanctuary of woman's life—the wife, beginning her initiation into sorrow, wounded, resenting, yet still hoping and forgiving—the poor bruised woman, seeking through weary years the one refuge of despair, oblivion:— Janet seemed to herself all these in the same moment that she was conscious of being seated on the cold stone under the shock of a new misery. All her early gladness, all her bright hopes and illusions, all her gifts of beauty and affection, served only to darken the riddle of her life; they were the betraying promises of a cruel destiny which had brought out those sweet blossoms only that the winds and storms might have a greater work of desolation, which had nursed her like a pet fawn into tenderness and fond expectation, only that she might feel a keener terror in the clutch of the panther. Her mother had sometimes said that troubles were sent to make us better and draw us nearer to God. What mockery that seemed to Janet! *Her* troubles had been sinking her lower from year to year, pressing upon her like heavy fever-laden vapors, and perverting the very plenitude of her nature into a deeper source of disease. Her wretchedness had been a perpetually tightening instrument of torture, which had gradually absorbed all the other sensibilities of her nature into the sense of pain and the maddened craving for relief. Oh, if some ray of hope, of pity, of consolation, would pierce through the horrible gloom, she might believe *then* in a Divine love—in a heavenly Father who cared for His children! But now she had no faith, no trust. There was nothing she could lean on in the wide world, for her mother was only a fellow-sufferer in her own lot. The poor patient woman could do little more than mourn with her daughter: she had humble resignation enough to sustain her own soul, but she could no more give comfort and fortitude to Janet, than the withered ivy-covered trunk can bear up its strong, full-boughed offspring crashing down under an Alpine storm. Janet felt she was alone: no human soul had measured her anguish, had understood her self-despair, had entered into her sorrows and her sins with that deep-sighted sympathy which is wiser than all blame, more potent than all reproof—such sympathy as had swelled her own heart for many a sufferer. And if there was any Divine Pity, she could not feel it; it kept aloof from her, it poured no balm into her wounds, it stretched out no hand to bear up her weak resolve, to fortify her fainting courage.

Now, in her utmost loneliness, she shed no tear: she sat staring fixedly into the darkness, while inwardly she gazed at her own past, almost losing the sense that it was her own, or that she was any thing more than a spectator at a strange and dreadful play.

The loud sound of the church clock, striking one, startled her. She had not been there more than half an hour, then? And it seemed to her as if she had been there half the night.

She was getting benumbed with cold. With that strong instinctive dread of pain and death which had made her recoil from suicide, she started up, and the disagreeable sensation of resting on her benumbed feet helped to recall her completely to the sense of the present. The wind was beginning to make rents in the clouds, and there came every now and then a dim light of stars that frightened her more than the darkness; it was like a cruel finger pointing her out in her wretchedness and humiliation; it made her shudder at the thought of the morning twilight. What could she do! Not go to her mother—not rouse her in the dead of night to tell her this. Her mother would think she was a spectre; it would be enough to kill her with horror. And the way there was so long . . . . if she should meet some one . . . . yet she must seek some shelter, somewhere to hide herself. Five doors off there was Mrs. Pettifer's; that kind woman would take her in. It was of no use now to be proud and mind about the world's knowing: she had nothing to wish for, nothing to care about; only she could not help shuddering at the thought of braving the morning light, there in the street —she was frightened at the thought of spending long hours in the cold. Life might mean anguish, might mean despair; but—oh, she must clutch it, though with bleeding fingers; her feet must cling to the firm earth that the sunlight would revisit, not slip into the untried abyss, where she might long even for familiar pains.

Janet trod slowly with her naked feet on the rough pavement, trembling at the fitful gleams of starlight, and supporting herself by the wall, as the gusts of wind drove right against her. The very wind was cruel; it tried to push her back from the door where she wanted to go and knock and ask for pity.

Mrs. Pettifer's house did not look into Orchard Street; it stood a little way up a wide passage which opened into the street through an archway. Janet turned up the archway, and saw a faint light coming from Mrs. Pettifer's bed-room window. The glimmer of a rushlight from a room where a friend was lying, was like a ray of mercy to Janet, after that long, long time of darkness and loneliness; it would not be so dreadful to awake Mrs. Pettifer as she had thought. Yet she lingered some minutes at the door before she gathered courage to knock; she felt as if the sound must betray her to others besides Mrs. Pettifer, though there was no other dwelling that opened into the passage—only warehouses and outbuildings. There was no gravel for her to throw up at the window, nothing but heavy pavement; there was no door-bell; she must knock. Her first rap was very timid—one feeble fall of the knocker; and then she stood still again for many minutes; but presently she rallied her courage and knocked several times together, not loudly, but rapidly, so that Mrs. Pettifer, if she only heard the sound, could not mistake it. And she *had* heard it, for by-and-by the casement of her window was opened, and Janet perceived that she was bending out to try and discern who it was at the door.

"It is I, Mrs. Pettifer; it is Janet Dempster. Take me in, for pity's sake."

"Merciful God! what has happened?"

"Robert has turned me out. I have been in the cold a long while."

Mrs. Pettifer said no more, but hurried away from the window, and was soon at the door with a light in her hand.

"Come in, my poor dear, come in," said the good woman in a tremulous voice, drawing Janet within the door. "Come into my warm bed, and may God in heaven save and comfort you."

The pitying eyes, the tender voice, the warm touch, caused a rush of new feeling in Janet. Her heart swelled, and she burst out suddenly, like a child, into loud, passionate sobs. Mrs. Pettifer could not help crying with her, but she said, "Come up-stairs, my dear, come. Don't linger in the cold."

She drew the poor sobbing thing gently up stairs, and persuaded her to get into the warm bed. But it was long before Janet could lie down. She sat leaning her head on her knees, convulsed by sobs, while the motherly woman covered her with clothes, and held her arms round her to comfort her with warmth. At last the hysterical passion had exhausted itself, and she fell back on the pillow; but her throat was still agitated by piteous after-sobs, such as shake a little child even when it has found a refuge from its alarms on its mother's lap.

Now Janet was getting quieter, Mrs. Pettifer determined to go down and make a cup of tea, the first thing a kind old woman thinks of as a solace and restorative under all calamities. Happily there was no danger of awaking her servant a heavy girl of sixteen, who was snoring blissfully in the attic and might be kept ignorant of the way in which Mrs. Dempster had come in. So Mrs. Pettifer busied herself with rousing the kitchen fire, which was kept in under a huge "raker"—a possibility by which the coal of the midland counties atone for all its slowness and white ashes.

When she carried up the tea, Janet was lying quite still

the spasmodic agitation had ceased, and she seemed lost in thought; her eyes were fixed vacantly on the rushlight shade, and all the lines of sorrow were deepened in her face.

"Now, my dear," said Mrs. Pettifer, "let me persuade you to drink a cup of tea; you'll find it warm you and soothe you very much. Why, dear heart, your feet are like ice still. Now, do drink this tea, and I'll wrap 'em up in flannel, and then they'll get warm."

Janet turned her dark eyes on her old friend and stretched out her arms. She was too much oppressed to say any thing; her suffering lay like a heavy weight on her power of speech; but she wanted to kiss the good kind woman. Mrs. Pettifer, setting down the cup, bent towards the sad, beautiful face, and Janet kissed her with earnest sacramental kisses—such kisses as seal a new and closer bond between the helper and the helped.

She drank the tea obediently. "It *does* warm me," she said. "But now you will get into bed. I shall lie still now."

Mrs. Pettifer felt it was the best thing she could do to lie down quietly and say no more. She hoped Janet might go to sleep. As for herself, with that tendency to wakefulness common to advanced years, she found it impossible to compose herself to sleep again after this agitating surprise. She lay listening to the clock, wondering what had led to this new outrage of Dempster's, praying for the poor thing at her side, and pitying the mother who would have to hear it all to-morrow.

CHAPTER XVI.

Janet lay still, as she had promised; but the tea, which had warmed her and given her a sense of greater bodily ease, had only heightened the previous excitement of her brain. Her ideas had a new vividness, which made her feel as if she had only seen life through a dim haze before; her thoughts, instead of springing from the action of her own mind, were external existences, that thrust themselves imperiously upon her like haunting visions. The future took shape after shape of misery before her, always ending in her being dragged back again to her old life of terror, and stupor, and fevered despair. Her husband had so long overshadowed her life that her imagination could not keep hold of a condition in which that great dread was absent; and even his absence—

what was it? only a dreary, vacant flat, where there was nothing to strive after, nothing to long for.

At last, the light of morning quenched the rushlight, and Janet's thoughts became more and more fragmentary and confused. She was every moment slipping off the level on which she lay thinking, down, down into some depth from which she tried to rise again with a start. Slumber was stealing over her weary brain: that uneasy slumber which is only better than wretched waking, because the life we seemed to live in it determines no wretched future, because the things we do and suffer in it are but hateful shadows, and leave no impress that petrifies into an irrevocable past.

She had scarcely been asleep an hour when her movements became more violent, her mutterings more frequent and agitated, till at last she started up with a smothered cry, and looked wildly round her, shaking with terror.

"Don't be frightened, dear Mrs. Dempster," said Mrs. Pettifer, who was up and dressing, "you are with me, your old friend, Mrs. Pettifer. Nothing will harm you."

Janet sank back again on her pillow, still trembling. After lying silent a little while, she said, "It was a horrible dream. Dear Mrs. Pettifer, don't let any one know I am here. Keep it a secret. If he finds out, he will come and drag me back again."

"No, my dear, depend on me. I've just thought I shall send the servant home on a holiday—I've promised her a good while. I'll send her away as soon as she's had her breakfast, and she'll have no occasion to know you're here. There's no holding servants' tongues, if you let 'em know any thing. What they don't know, they won't tell; you may trust 'em so far. But shouldn't you like me to go and fetch your mother?"

"No, not yet, not yet. I can't bear to see her yet."

"Well, it shall be just as you like. Now try and get to sleep again. I shall leave you for an hour or two, and send off Phœbe, and then bring you some breakfast. I'll lock the door behind me, so that the girl mayn't come in by chance."

The daylight changes the aspect of misery to us, as of every thing else. In the night it presses on our imagination—the forms it takes are false, fitful, exaggerated; in broad day it sickens our sense with the dreary persistence of definite measurable reality. The man who looks with ghastly horror on all his property aflame in the dead of night, has not half the sense of destitution he will have in the morning, when he walks over the ruins lying blackened in the pitiless sunshine. That moment of intensest depression was come to

Janet, when the daylight which showed her the walls, and chairs, and tables, and all the commonplace reality that surrounded her, seemed to lay bare the future too, and bring out into oppressive distinctness all the details of a weary life to be lived from day to day, with no hope to strengthen her against that evil habit, which she loathed in retrospect and yet was powerless to resist. Her husband would never consent to her living away from him: she was become necessary to his tyranny; he would never willingly loosen his grasp on her. She had a vague notion of some protection the law might give her, if she could prove her life in danger from him; but she shrank utterly, as she had always done, from any active, public resistance or vengeance: she felt too crushed, too faulty, too liable to reproach, to have the courage, even if she had had the wish to put herself openly in the position of a wronged woman seeking redress. She had no strength to sustain her in a course of self-defense and independence: there was a darker shadow over her life than the dread of her husband—it was the shadow of self-despair. The easiest thing would be to go away and hide herself from him. But then there was her mother: Robert had all her little property in his hands, and that little was scarcely enough to keep her in comfort without his aid. If Janet went away alone he would be sure to persecute her mother; and if she *did* go away—what then? She must work to maintain herself; she must exert herself, weary and hopeless as she was, to begin life afresh. How hard that seemed to her! Janet's nature did not belie her grand face and form: there was energy, there was strength in it; but it was the strength of the vine, which must have its broad leaves and rich clusters borne up by a firm stay. And now she had nothing to rest on—no faith, no love. If her mother had been very feeble, aged, or sickly, Janet's deep pity and tenderness might have made a daughter's duties an interest and a solace; but Mrs. Raynor had never needed tendance; she had always been giving help to her daughter; she had always been a sort of humble ministering spirit; and it was one of Janet's pangs of memory, that instead of being her mother's comfort, she had been her mother's trial. Everywhere the same sadness! Her life was a sun-dried, barren tract, where there was no shadow and where all the waters were bitter.

No! She suddenly thought—and the thought was like an electric shock—there was one spot in her memory which seemed to promise her an untried spring, where the waters might be sweet. That short interview with Mr. Tryan had come back upon her—his voice, his words, his look, which told her that he knew sorrow. His words had implied that he thought his death was near; yet he had a faith which enabled him to labor—enabled him to give comfort to others. That look of his came back on her with a vividness greater than it had had for her in reality: surely he knew more of the secrets of sorrow than other men; perhaps he had some message of comfort, different from the feeble words she had been used to hear from others. She was tired, she was sick of that barren exhortation—Do right, and keep a clear conscience, and God will reward you, and your troubles will be easier to bear. She wanted *strength* to do right—she wanted something to rely on besides her own resolutions; for was not the path behind her all strewn with *broken* resolutions? How could she trust in new ones? She had often heard Mr. Tryan laughed at for being fond of great sinners. She began to see a new meaning in those words; he would perhaps understand her helplessness, her wants. If she could pour out her heart to him! if she could for the first time in her life unlock all the chambers of her soul!

The impulse to confession almost always requires the presence of a fresh ear and a fresh heart; and in our moments of spiritual need, the man to whom we have no tie but our common nature, seems nearer to us than mother, brother, or friend. Our daily familiar life is but a hiding of ourselves from each other behind a screen of trivial words and deeds, and those who sit with us at the same hearth are often the farthest off from the deep human soul within us, full of unspoken evil and unacted good.

When Mrs. Pettifer came back to her, turning the key and opening the door very gently, Janet, instead of being asleep, as her good friend had hoped, was intensely occupied with her new thought. She longed to ask Mrs. Pettifer if she could see Mr. Tryan; but she was arrested by doubts and timidity. He might not feel for her—he might be shocked at her confession—he might talk to her of doctrines she could not understand or believe. She could not make up her mind yet; but she was too restless under this mental struggle to remain in bed.

"Mrs. Pettifer," she said, "I can't lie here any longer; I must get up. Will you lend me some clothes?"

Wrapt in such drapery as Mrs. Pettifer could find for her tall figure, Janet went down into the little parlor, and tried to take some of the breakfast her friend had prepared for her. But her effort was not a successful one; her cup of tea and bit of toast were only half finished. The leaden weight of discouragement pressed upon her more and more heavily.

The wind had fallen, and a drizzling rain had come on; there was no prospect from Mrs. Pettifer's parlor but a blank wall; and as Janet looked out at the window, the rain and the smoke-blackened bricks seemed to blend themselves in sickening identity with her desolation of spirit and the headachy weariness of her body.

Mrs. Pettifer got through her household work as soon as she could, and sat down with her sewing, hoping that Janet would perhaps be able to talk a little of what had passed, and find some relief by unbosoming herself in that way. But Janet could not speak to her; she was importuned with the longing to see Mr. Tryan, and yet hesitating to express it.

Two hours passed in this way. The rain went on drizzling, and Janet sat still, leaning her aching head on her hand, and looking alternately at the fire and out of the window. She felt this could not last—this motionless, vacant misery. She must determine on something, she must take some step; and yet every thing was so difficult.

It was one o'clock, and Mrs. Pettifer rose from her seat, saying, "I must go and see about dinner."

The movement and the sound startled Janet from her reverie. It seemed as if an opportunity were escaping her, and she said hastily, "Is Mr. Tryan in the town to-day, do you think?"

"No, I should think not, being Saturday, you know," said Mrs. Pettifer, her face lighting up with pleasure; "but he *could* come, if he was sent for. I can send Jesson's boy with a note to him any time. Should you like to see him?"

"Yes, I think I should."

"Then I'll send for him this instant."

CHAPTER XVII.

When Dempster awoke in the morning, he was at no loss to account to himself for the fact that Janet was not by his side. His hours of drunkenness were not cut off from his other hours by any blank wall of oblivion; he remembered what Janet had done to offend him the evening before, he remembered what he had done to her at midnight, just as he would have remembered if he had been consulted about a right of road.

The remembrance gave him a definite ground for the extra ill-humor which had attended his waking every morning this week, but he would not admit to himself that it cost him any anxiety. "Pooh," he said inwardly, "she would go straight to her mother's. She's as timid as a hare; and she'll never let any body know about it. She'll be back again before night."

But it would be as well for the servants not to know any thing of the affair: so he collected the clothes she had taken off the night before, and threw them into a fire-proof closet of which he always kept the key in his pocket. When he went down stairs he said to the housemaid, "Mrs. Dempster is gone to her mother's; bring in the breakfast."

The servants, accustomed to hear domestic broils, and to see their mistress put on her bonnet hastily and go to her mother's, thought it only something a little worse than usual that she should have gone thither in consequence of a violent quarrel, either at midnight, or in the early morning before they were up. The housemaid told the cook what she supposed had happened; the cook shook her head and said, "Eh, dear, dear!" but they both expected to see their mistress back again in an hour or two.

Dempster, on his return home the evening before, had ordered his man, who lived away from the house, to bring up his horse and gig from the stables at ten. After breakfast he said to the housemaid, "No one need sit up for me to-night: I shall not be at home till to-morrow evening;" and then he walked to the office to give some orders, expecting, as he returned, to see the man waiting with his gig. But though the church clock had struck ten, no gig was there. In Dempster's mood this was more than enough to exasperate him. He went in to take his accustomed glass of brandy before setting out, promising himself the satisfaction of presently thundering at Dawes for being a few minutes behind his time. An outbreak of temper towards his man was not common with him; for Dempster, like most tyrannous people, had that dastardly kind of self-restraint which enabled him to control his temper where it suited his own convenience to do so; and feeling the value of Dawes, a steady, punctual fellow, he not only gave him high wages, but usually treated him with exceptional civility. This morning, however, ill-humor got the better of prudence, and Dempster was determined to rate him soundly; a resolution for which Dawes gave him much better ground than he expected. Five minutes, ten minutes, a quarter of an hour, had passed, and Dempster was setting off to the stables in a back street to see what was the cause of the delay, when Dawes appeared with the gig.

"What the devil do you keep me here for?" thundered

Dempster, "kicking my heels like a beggarly tailor waiting for a carrier's cart? I ordered you to be here at ten. We might have driven to Whitlow by this time."

"Why, one o' the traces was welly i' two, an' I had to take it to Brady's to be mended, an' he didn't get it done i' time."

"Then why didn't you take it to him last night? Because of your damned laziness, I suppose. Do you think I give you wages for you to choose your own hours, and come dawdling up a quarter of an hour after my time?"

"Come, give me good words, will yer?" said Dawes, sulkily. "I'm not lazy, nor no man shall call me lazy. I know well anuff what you gi' me wages for; it's for doin' what yer won't find many men as 'ull do."

"What, you impudent scoundrel," said Dempster, getting into the gig, "you think you're necessary to me, do you? As if a beastly bucket-carrying idiot like you wasn't to be got any day. Look out for a new master, then, who'll pay you for not doing as you're bid."

Dawes's blood was now fairly up. "I'll look out for a master as has got a better charicter nor a lyin', bletherin' drunkard, an' I shouldn't hev to go fur."

Dempster, furious, snatched the whip from the socket, and gave Dawes a cut which he meant to fall across his shoulders, saying, "Take that, sir, and go to hell with you!"

Dawes was in the act of turning with the reins in his hand when the lash fell, and the cut went across his face. With white lips, he said, "I'll have the law on yer for that, lawyer as y'are," and threw the reins on the horse's back.

Dempster leaned forward, seized the reins, and drove off.

"Why, there's your friend Dempster driving out without his man again," said Mr. Luke Byles, who was chatting with Mr. Budd in the Bridge Way. "What a fool he is to drive that two-wheeled thing! he'll get pitched on his head one of these days."

"Not he," said Mr. Budd, nodding to Dempster as he passed; "he's got nine lives, Dempster has."

CHAPTER XVIII.

It was dusk, and the candles were lighted before Mr. Tryan knocked at Mrs. Pettifer's door. Her messenger had brought back word that he was not at home, and all afternoon Janet had been agitated by the fear that he would not come; but as soon as that anxiety was removed by the knock at the door, she felt a sudden rush of doubt and timidity: she trembled and turned cold.

Mrs. Pettifer went to open the door, and told Mr. Tryan, in as few words as possible, what had happened in the night. As he laid down his hat and prepared to enter the parlor, she said, "I won't go in with you, for I think perhaps she would rather see you go in alone."

Janet, wrapped up in a large white shawl which threw her dark face into startling relief, was seated with her eyes turned anxiously towards the door when Mr. Tryan entered. He had not seen her since their interview at Sally Martin's, long months ago; and he felt a strong movement of compassion at the sight of the pain-stricken face which seemed to bear written on it the signs of all Janet's intervening misery. Her heart gave a great leap, as her eyes met his once more. No! she had not deceived herself: there was all the sincerity, all the sadness, all the deep pity in them her memory had told her of; more than it had told her, for in proportion as his face had become thinner and more worn, his eyes appeared to have gathered intensity.

He came forward, and, putting out his hand, said, "I am so glad you sent for me—I am so thankful you thought I could be any comfort to you." Janet took his hand in silence. She was unable to utter any words of mere politeness, or even of gratitude; her heart was too full of other words that had welled up the moment she met his pitying glance, and felt her doubts fall away.

They sat down opposite each other, and she said in a low voice, while slow, difficult tears gathered in her aching eyes,

"I want to tell you how unhappy I am—how weak and wicked. I feel no strength to live or die. I thought you could tell me something that would help me." She paused.

"Perhaps I can," Mr. Tryan said, "for in speaking to me you are speaking to a fellow-sinner who has needed just the comfort and help you are needing."

"And you did find it?"

"Yes; and I trust you will find it."

"Oh, I should like to be good and to do right," Janet burst forth; "but indeed, indeed, my lot has been a very hard one. I loved my husband very dearly when we were married, and I meant to make him happy—I wanted nothing else. But he began to be angry with me for little things and . . . . I don't want to accuse him . . . . but he drank and got more and more unkind to me, and then very cruel and he beat me. And that cut me to the heart. It made me almost mad sometimes to think all our love had come to that. . . . I couldn't bear up against it. I had never been used to drink any thing but water. I hated wine and spirits because Robert drank them so; but one day when I was very wretched, and the wine was standing on the table, I suddenly . . . . I can hardly remember how I came to do it. . . . I poured some wine into a large glass and drank it. It blunted my feelings, and made me more indifferent. After that, the temptation was always coming, and it got stronger and stronger. I was ashamed, and I hated what I did; but almost while the thought was passing through my mind that I would never do it again, I did it. It seemed as if there was a demon in me always making me rush to do what I longed not to do. And I thought all the more that God was cruel; for if he had not sent me that dreadful trial, so much worse than other women have to bear, I should not have done wrong in that way. I suppose it is wicked to think so. . . . I feel as if there must be goodness and right above us, but I can't see it, I can't trust in it. And I have gone on in that way for years and years. At one time it used to be better now and then, but every thing has got worse lately: I felt sure it must soon end somehow. And last night he turned me out of doors . . . . I don't know what to do. I will never go back to that life again if I can help it; and yet every thing else seems so miserable. I feel sure that demon will be always urging me to satisfy the craving that comes upon me, and the days will go on as they have done through all those miserable years. I shall always be doing wrong, and hating myself after—sinking lower and lower, and knowing that I am sinking. Oh, can you tell me any way of getting strength? Have you ever known any one like me that got peace of mind and power to do right? Can you give me any comfort—any hope?"

While Janet was speaking, she had forgotten every thing but her misery and her yearning for comfort. Her voice had risen from the low tone of timid distress to an intense pitch of imploring anguish. She clasped her hands tightly, and looked at Mr. Tryan with eager, questioning eyes, with parted, trembling lips, with the deep horizontal lines of overmastering pain on her brow. In this artificial life of ours, it is not often we see a human face with all a heart's agony in it, uncontrolled by self-consciousness; when we do see it, it startles us as if we had suddenly waked into the real world of which this every-day one is but a puppet-show copy. For some moments Mr. Tryan was too deeply moved to speak.

"Yes, dear Mrs. Dempster," he said at last, "there *is* comfort, there *is* hope for you. Believe me there is, for I speak from my own deep and hard experience." He paused, as if he had not made up his mind to utter the words that were urging themselves to his lips. Presently he continued, "Ten years ago, I felt as wretched as you do. I think my wretchedness was even worse than yours, for I had a heavier sin on my conscience. I had suffered no wrong from others as you have, and I had injured another irreparably in body and soul. The image of the wrong I had done pursued me everywhere, and I seemed on the brink of madness. I hated my life, for I thought, just as you do, that I should go on falling into temptation and doing more harm in the world; and I dreaded death, for with that sense of guilt on my soul, I felt that whatever state I entered on must be one of misery. But a dear friend to whom I opened my mind showed me it was just such as I—the helpless who feel themselves helpless—that God specially invites to come to Him, and offers all the riches of His salvation; not forgiveness only; forgiveness would be worth little if it left us under the powers of our evil passions; but strength—that strength which enables us to conquer sin."

"But," said Janet, "I can feel no trust in God. He seems always to have left me to myself. I have sometimes prayed to Him to help me, and yet every thing has been just the same as before. If you felt like me, how did you come to have hope and trust?"

"Do not believe that God has left you to yourself. How can you tell but that the hardest trials you have known have been only the road by which He was leading you to that complete sense of your own sin and helplessness, without which you would never have renounced all other hopes, and trusted in His love alone? I know, dear Mrs. Dempster, I know it is hard to bear. I would not speak lightly of your sorrows. I feel that the mystery of our life is great, and at one time it seemed as dark to me as it does to you." Mr. Tryan hesitated again. He saw that the first thing Janet needed was to be assured of sympathy. She must be made to feel that her anguish was not strange to him; that he entered into the only half-expressed secrets of her spiritual weakness, before any other message of consolation could find its way to her heart. The tale of the Divine Pity was never yet believed from lips that were not felt to be moved by human pity. And Janet's anguish was not strange to Mr. Tryan. He had never been in the presence of a sorrow and a self-despair that had sent so strong a thrill through all the recesses of his saddest experience; and it is because sympathy is but a living again through our own past in a new form, that confession often prompts a response of confession. Mr. Tryan felt this prompting, and his judgment, too, told him that in obeying it he would be taking the best means of administering comfort to Janet. Yet he hesitated; as we tremble to let in the daylight on a chamber of relics which we have never visited except in curtained silence. But the first impulse triumphed, and he went on. "I had lived all my life at a distance from God. My youth was spent in thoughtless self-indulgence, and all my hopes were of a vain, worldly kind. I had no thought of entering the Church; I looked forward to a political career, for my father was private secretary to a man high in the Whig Ministry, and had been promised strong interest in my behalf. At college I lived in intimacy with the gayest men, even adopting follies and vices for which I had no taste, out of mere pliancy and the love of standing well with my companions. You see, I was more guilty even then than you have been, for I threw away all the rich blessings of untroubled youth and health; I had no excuse in my outward lot. But while I was at college that event in my life occurred, which in the end brought on the state of mind I have mentioned to you—the state of self-reproach and despair, which enables me to understand to the full what you are suffering; and I tell you the facts, because I want you to be assured that I am not uttering mere vague words when I say that I have been raised from as low a depth of sin and sorrow as that in which you feel yourself to be. At college I had an attachment to a lovely girl of seventeen; she was very much below my own station in life, and I never contemplated marrying her; but I induced her to leave her father's house. I did not mean to forsake her when I left college, and I quieted all scruples of conscience by promising myself that I would always take care of poor Lucy. But on my return from a vacation spent in travelling, I found that Lucy was gone—gone away with a gentleman, her neighbors said. I was a good deal distressed, but I tried to persuade myself that no harm would come to her. Soon afterwards I had an illness which left my health delicate, and made all dissipation distasteful to me. Life seemed very wearisome and empty, and I looked with envy on every one who had some great and absorbing object—even on my cousin who was preparing to go out as a missionary, and whom I had been used to think a dismal, tedious person, because he was constantly urging religious subjects upon me. We were living in London then; it was three years since I had lost sight of Lucy; and one summer evening, about nine o'clock, as I was walking along Gower Street, I saw a knot of people on the causeway before me. As I came up to them, I heard one woman say, 'I tell you, she is dead.' This awakened my interest, and I pushed my way within the circle. The body of a woman, dressed in fine clothes, was lying against a door-step. Her head was bent on one side, and the long curls had fallen over her cheek. A tremor seized me when I saw the hair: it was light chestnut —the color of Lucy's. I knelt down and turned aside the hair; it was Lucy—dead—with paint on her cheeks. I found out afterwards that she had taken poison—that she was in the power of a wicked woman—that the very clothes on her back were not her own. It was then that my past life burst upon me in all its hideousness. I wished I had never been born. I couldn't look into the future. Lucy's dead painted face would follow me there, as it did when I looked back into the past—as it did when I sat down to table with my friends, when I lay down in my bed, and when I rose up. There was only one thing that could make life tolerable to me; that was, to spend all the rest of it in trying to save others from the ruin I had brought on one. But how was that possible for me? I had no comfort, no strength, no wisdom in my own soul; how could I give them to others? My mind was dark, rebellious, at war with itself and with God."

Mr. Tryan had been looking away from Janet. His face was towards the fire, and he was absorbed in the images his memory was recalling. But now he turned his eyes on her, and they met hers, fixed on him with the look of rapt expectation, with which one clinging to a slippery summit of a rock, while the waves are rising higher and higher, watches the boat that has put from shore to his rescue.

"You see, Mrs. Dempster, how deep my need was. I went on in this way for months. I was convinced that if I ever got health and comfort, it must be from religion. I went to hear celebrated preachers, and I read religious books. But I found nothing that fitted my own need. The faith which puts the sinner in possession of salvation seemed, as I understood it, to be quite out of my reach. I had no faith; I only felt utterly wretched, under the power of habits and dispositions which had wrought hideous evil. At last, as I told you, I found a friend to whom I opened all my feelings—to whom I confessed every thing. He was a man who had gone through very deep experience, and could understand the different wants of different minds. He made it clear to me that the only preparation for coming to Christ and partaking of his salvation, was that very sense of guilt and helplessness which was weighing me down. He said, you are weary and heavy-laden; well, it is you Christ invites to come to him and find rest. He asks you to cling to him, to lean on him; he does not command you to walk alone without stumbling. He does not tell you, as your fellow-men do, that you must first merit his love; he neither condemns nor reproaches you for the past, he only bids you to come to him that you may have life; he bids you stretch out your hands, and take of the fullness of his love. You have only to rest on him as a child rests on its mother's arms, and you will be upborne by his divine strength. That is what is meant by faith. Your evil habits, you feel, are too strong for you; you are unable to wrestle with them; you know beforehand you shall fall. But when once we feel our helplessness in that way, and go to the Saviour, desiring to be freed from the power as well as the punishment of sin, we are no longer left to our own strength. As long as we live in rebellion against God, desiring to have our own will, seeking happiness in the things of this world, it is as if we shut ourselves up in a crowded, stifling room, where we breathe only poisoned air; but we have only to walk out under the infinite heavens, and we breathe the pure free air that gives us health, and strength, and gladness. It is just so with God's spirit: as soon as we submit ourselves to his will, as soon as we desire to be united to him, and made pure and holy, it is as if the walls had fallen down that shut us out from God, and we are fed with his spirit, which gives us new strength."

"That is what I want," said Janet; "I have left off minding about pleasure. I think I could be contented in the midst of hardship, if I felt that God cared for me, and would give me strength to lead a pure life. But tell me, did you soon find peace and strength?"

"Not perfect peace for a long while, but hope and trust, which is strength. No sense of pardon for myself could do away with the pain I had in thinking what I had helped to bring on another. My friend used to urge upon me that my sin against God was greater than my sin against her; but—it may be from want of deeper spiritual feeling—that has remained to this hour the sin which causes me the bitterest pang. I could never rescue Lucy; but by God's blessing I might rescue other weak and falling souls; and that was why I entered the Church. I asked for nothing through the rest of my life but that I might be devoted to God's work, without swerving in search of pleasure either to the right hand or to the left. It has been often a hard struggle—but God has been with me—and perhaps it may not last much longer."

Mr. Tryan paused. For a moment he had forgotten Janet, and for a moment she had forgotten her own sorrows. When she recurred to herself, it was with a new feeling.

"Ah, what a difference between our lives! you have been choosing pain, and working, and denying yourself; and I have been thinking only of myself. I was only angry and discontented because I had pain to bear. You never had that wicked feeling that I have had so often, did you? that God was cruel to send me trials and temptations worse than others have."

"Yes, I had; I had very blasphemous thoughts, and I know that spirit of rebellion must have made the worst part of your lot. You did not feel how impossible it is for us to judge rightly of God's dealings, and you opposed yourself to his will. But what do we know? We can not foretell the working of the smallest event in our own lot; how can we presume to judge of things that are so much too high for us? There is nothing that becomes us but entire submission, perfect resignation. As long as we set up our own will and our own wisdom against God's, we make that wall between us and his love which I have spoken of just now. But as soon as we lay ourselves entirely at his feet, we have enough light given us to guide our own steps; as the foot-soldier who hears nothing of the councils that determine the course of the great battle he is in, hears plainly enough the word of command which he must himself obey. I know, dear Mrs. Dempster, I know it is hard—the hardest thing of all, perhaps—to flesh and blood. But carry that difficulty to the Saviour along with all your other sins and weaknesses, and ask him to pour into you a spirit of submission. He enters into your struggles; he has drunk the cup of our suffering to the dregs; he knows the hard wrestling it costs us to say, 'Not my will, but Thine be done.'"

"Pray with me," said Janet—"pray now that I may have light and strength."

CHAPTER XIX.

Before leaving Janet, Mr. Tryan urged her strongly to send for her mother.

"Do not wound her," he said, "by shutting her out any longer from your troubles. It is right that you should be with her."

"Yes, I will send for her," said Janet. "But I would rather

not go to my mother's yet, because my husband is sure to think I am there, and he might come and fetch me. I can't go back to him . . . . at least, not yet. Ought I to go back to him?"

"No, certainly not, at present. Something should be done to secure you from violence. Your mother, I think, should consult some confidential friend, some man of character and experience, who might mediate between you and your husband."

"Yes, I will send for my mother directly. But I will stay here, with Mrs. Pettifer, till something has been done. I want no one to know where I am, except you. You will come again, will you not? you will not leave me to myself?"

"You will not be left to yourself. God is with you. If I have been able to give you any comfort, it is because his power and love have been present with us. But I am very thankful that he has chosen to work through me. I shall see you again to-morrow—not before evening, for it will be Sunday, you know; but after the evening lecture I shall be at liberty. You will be in my prayers till then. In the mean time, dear Mrs. Dempster, open your heart as much as you can to your mother and Mrs. Pettifer. Cast away from you the pride that makes us shrink from acknowledging our weakness to our friends. Ask them to help you in guarding yourself from the least approach of the sin you most dread. Deprive yourself as far as possible of the very means and opportunity of committing it. Every effort of that kind made in humility and dependence is a prayer. Promise me you will do this."

"Yes, I promise you. I know I have always been too proud; I could never bear to speak to any one about myself. I have been proud towards my mother, even; it has always made me angry when she has seemed to take notice of my faults."

"Ah, dear Mrs. Dempster, you will never say again that life is blank, and that there is nothing to live for, will you? See what work there is to be done in life, both in our own souls and for others. Surely it matters little whether we have more or less of this world's comfort in these short years, when God is training us for the eternal enjoyment of his love. Keep that great end of life before you, and your troubles here will seem only the small hardships of a journey. Now I must go."

Mr. Tryan rose and held out his hand. Janet took it and said, "God has been very good to me in sending you to me. I will trust in him. I will try to do every thing you tell me."

Blessed influence of one true loving human soul on another! Not calculable by algebra, not deducible by logic, but mysterious, effectual, mighty as the hidden process by which the tiny seed is quickened, and bursts forth into tall stem and broad leaf, and glowing tasselled flower. Ideas are often poor ghosts; our sun-filled eyes can not discern them; they pass athwart us in thin vapor, and can not make themselves felt. But sometimes they are made flesh; they breathe upon us with warm breath, they touch us with soft responsive hands, they look at us with sad, sincere eyes, and speak to us in appealing tones; they are clothed in a living human soul, with all its conflicts, its faith, and its love. Then their presence is a power, then they shake us like a passion, and we are drawn after them with gentle compulsion, as flame is drawn to flame.

Janet's dark grand face, still fatigued, had become quite calm, and looked up, as she sat, with a humble, childlike expression at the thin blond face and slightly sunken gray eyes which now shone with hectic brightness. She might have been taken for an image of passionate strength beaten and worn with conflict; and he for an image of the self-renouncing faith which has soothed that conflict into rest. As he looked at the sweet submissive face, he remembered its look of despairing anguish, and his heart was very full as he turned away from her. "Let me only live to see this work confirmed, and then . . . ."

It was nearly ten o'clock when Mr. Tryan left, but Janet was bent on sending for her mother; so Mrs. Pettifer, as the readiest plan, put on her bonnet and went herself to fetch Mrs. Raynor. The mother had been too long used to expect that every fresh week would be more painful than the last, for Mrs. Pettifer's news to come upon her with the shock of a surprise. Quietly, without any show of distress, she made up a bundle of clothes, and, telling her little maid that she should not return home that night, accompanied Mrs. Pettifer back in silence.

When they entered the parlor, Janet, wearied out, had sunk to sleep in the large chair, which stood with its back to the door. The noise of the opening door disturbed her, and she was looking round wonderingly, when Mrs. Raynor came up to her chair, and said, "It's your mother, Janet."

"Mother, dear mother!" Janet cried, clasping her closely. "I have not been a good tender child to you, but I *will* be—I will not grieve you any more."

The calmness which had withstood a new sorrow was overcome by a new joy, and the mother burst into tears.

CHAPTER XX.

On Sunday morning the rain had ceased, and Janet, looking out of the bedroom window, saw, above the house-tops, a shining mass of white cloud rolling under the far-away blue sky. It was going to be a lovely April day. The fresh sky, left clear and calm after the long vexation of wind and rain, mingled its mild influence with Janet's new thoughts and prospects. She felt a buoyant courage that surprised herself, after the cold, crushing weight of despondency which had oppressed her the day before: she could think even of her husband's rage without the old overpowering dread. For a delicious hope—the hope of purification and inward peace—had entered into Janet's soul, and made it spring-time there as well as in the outer world.

While her mother was brushing and coiling up her thick black hair—a favorite task, because it seemed to renew the days of her daughter's girlhood—Janet told how she came to send for Mr. Tryan, how she had remembered their meeting at Sally Martin's in the autumn, and had felt an irresistible desire to see him, and tell him her sins and her troubles.

"I see God's goodness now, mother, in ordering it so that we should meet in that way, to overcome my prejudice against him, and make me feel that he was good, and then bringing it back to my mind in the depth of my trouble. You know what foolish things I used to say about him, knowing nothing of him all the while. And yet he was the man who was to give me comfort and help when every thing else failed me. It is wonderful how I feel able to speak to him as I never have done to any one before; and how every word he says to me enters my heart and has a new meaning for me. I think it must be because he has felt life more deeply than others, and has a deeper faith. I believe every thing he says at once. His words come to me like rain on the parched ground. It has always seemed to me before as if I could see behind people's words, as one sees behind a screen; but in Mr. Tryan it is his very soul that speaks."

"Well, my dear child, I love and bless him for your sake, if he has given you any comfort. I never believed the harm people said of him, though I had no desire to go and hear him, for I am contented with old-fashioned ways. I find more good teaching than I can practise in reading my

Bible at home, and hearing Mr. Crewe at church. But your wants are different, my dear, and we are not all led by the same road. That was certainly good advice of Mr. Tryan's you told me of last night—that we should consult some one that may interfere for you with your husband; and I have been turning it over in my mind while I've been lying awake in the night. I think nobody will do so well as Mr. Benjamin Landor, for we must have a man that knows the law, and that Robert is rather afraid of. And perhaps he could bring about an agreement for you to live apart. Your husband's bound to maintain you, you know; and, if you liked, we could move away from Milby and live somewhere else."

"Oh, mother, we must do nothing yet; I must think about it a little longer. I have a different feeling this morning from what I had yesterday. Something seems to tell me that I must go back to Robert some time—after a little while. I loved him once better than all the world, and I have never had any children to love. There were things in me that were wrong, and I should like to make up for them if I can."

"Well, my dear, I won't persuade you. Think of it a little longer. But something must be done soon."

"How I wish I had my bonnet and shawl and black gown here!" said Janet, after a few minutes' silence. "I should like to go to Paddiford church and hear Mr. Tryan. There would be no fear of my meeting Robert, for he never goes out on a Sunday morning."

"I'm afraid it would not do for me to go to the house and fetch your clothes," said Mrs. Raynor.

"Oh, no, no! I must stay quietly here while you two go to church. I will be Mrs. Pettifer's maid, and get the dinner ready for her by the time she comes back. Dear good woman! She was so tender to me when she took me in, in the night, mother, and all the next day, when I couldn't speak a word to her to thank her."

CHAPTER XXI.

The servants at Dempster's felt some surprise when the morning, noon, and evening of Saturday had passed, and still their mistress did not reappear.

"It's very odd," said Kitty, the housemaid, as she trimmed her next week's cap, while Betty, the middle-aged cook, looked on with folded arms. "Do you think as Mrs. Raynor was ill and sent for the missis afore we was up?"

"Oh," said Betty, "if it had been that, she'd ha' been back'ards an' for'ards three or four times afore now; leastways, she'd ha' sent little Ann to let us know."

"There's summat up more nor usal between her an' the master, that you may depend on," said Kitty. "I know those clothes as was lying i' the drawing-room yesterday, when the company was come, meant summat. I shouldn't wonder if that was what they've had a fresh row about. She's p'raps gone away, an's made up her mind not to come back again."

"An' i' the right on't, too," said Betty. "I'd ha' overrun him long afore now, if it had been me. I wouldn't stan' bein' mauled as she is by no husband, not if he was the biggest lord i' the land. It's poor work bein' a wife at that price: I'd sooner be a cook wi'out perkises, an' hev roast, an' boil, an' fry, an' bake, all to mind at once. She may well do as she does. I know I'm glad enough of a drop o' summat myself when I'm plagued. I feel very low, like, to-night; I think I shall put my beer i' the saucepan an' warm it."

"What a one you are for warmin' your beer, Betty! I couldn't abide it—nasty bitter stuff!"

"It's fine talkin'; if you was a cook you'd know what belongs to bein' a cook. It's none so nice to hev a sinkin' at your stomach, I can tell you. You wouldn't think so much o' fine ribbins i' your cap then."

"Well, well, Betty, don't be grumpy. Liza Thomson, as is at Phipps's, said to me last Sunday, 'I wonder you'll stay at Dempster's,' she says, 'such goins-on as there is.' But I says, 'There's things to put up wi' in ivery place, an' you may change, an' change, an' not better yourself when all's said an' done.' Lors! why, Liza told me herself as Mrs. Phipps was as skinny as skinny i' the kitchen, for all they keep so much company; and as for follyers, she's as cross as a turkey-cock if she finds 'em out. There's nothin' o' that sort i' the missis. How pretty she come an' spoke to Job last Sunday! There isn't a good-natur'der woman i' the world, that's my belief—an' hansome too. I al'ys think there's nobody looks half so well as the missis when she's got her 'air done nice. Lors! I wish I'd got long 'air like her—my 'air's a-comin' off dreadful."

"There'll be fine work to-morrow, I expect," said Betty, "when the master comes home, an' Dawes a-swearin' as he'll niver do a stroke o' work for him again. It'll be good fun if he sets the justice on him for cuttin' him wi' the whip; the master'll p'raps get his comb cut for once in his life!"

"Why, he was in a temper like a fi-end this morning," said Kitty. "I daresay it was along o' what had happened wi' the missis. We shall hev a pretty house wi' him if she doesn't come back—he'll want to be leatherin' *us*, I shouldn't wonder. He must hev somethin' t' ill-use when he's in a passion."

"I'd tek care he didn't leather me—no, not if he was my husban' ten times o'er; I'd pour hot drippin' on him sooner. But the missis hasn't a sperrit like me. He'll mek her come back, you'll see; he'll come round her somehow. There's no likelihood of her coming back to-night, though; so I should think we might fasten the doors and go to bed when we like."

On Sunday morning, however, Kitty's mind became disturbed by more definite and alarming conjectures about her mistress. While Betty, encouraged by the prospect of unwonted leisure, was sitting down to continue a letter which had long lain unfinished between the leaves of her Bible, Kitty came running into the kitchen and said,

"Lor! Betty, I'm all of a tremble; you might knock me down wi' a feather. I've just looked into the missis's wardrobe, an' there's both her bonnets. She must ha' gone wi'out her bonnet. An' then I remember as her night-clothes wasn't on the bed yisterday mornin'; I thought she'd put 'em away to be washed; but she hedn't, for I've been lookin'. It's my belief he's murdered her, and shut her up i' that closet as he keeps locked al'ys. He's capible on't."

"Lors-ha-massy, why you'd better run to Mrs. Raynor's an' see if she's there, arter all. It was p'raps all a lie."

Mrs. Raynor had returned home to give directions to her little maiden, when Kitty, with the elaborate manifestation of alarm which servants delight in, rushed in without knocking, and, holding her hands on her heart as if the consequences to that organ were likely to be very serious, said,

"If you please 'm, is the missis here?"

"No, Kitty; why are you come to ask?"

"Because 'm, she's niver been at home since yesterday mornin', since afore we was up; an' we thought somethin' must ha' happened to her."

"No, don't be frightened, Kitty. Your mistress is quite safe; I know where she is. Is your master at home?"

"No 'm; he went out yesterday mornin', an' said he shouldn't be back afore to-night."

"Well, Kitty, there's nothing the matter with your mistress. You needn't say any thing to any one about her being away from home. I shall call presently and fetch her gown and bonnet. She wants them to put on."

Kitty, perceiving there was a mystery she was not to inquire into, returned to Orchard Street, really glad to know that her mistress was safe, but disappointed nevertheless at being told that she was not to be frightened. She was soon followed by Mrs. Raynor in quest of the gown and bonnet. The good mother, on learning that Dempster was not at home, had at once thought that she could gratify Janet's wish to go to Paddiford Church.

"See, my dear," she said, as she entered Mrs. Pettifer's parlor; "I've brought you your black clothes. Robert's not at home, and is not coming till this evening. I couldn't find your best black gown, but this will do. I wouldn't bring any thing else, you know; but there can't be any objection to my fetching clothes to cover you. You can go to Paddiford Church, now, if you like; and I will go with you."

"That's a dear mother! Then we'll all three go together. Come and help me to get ready. Good little Mrs. Crewe! It will vex her sadly that I should go to hear Mr. Tryan. But I must kiss her, and make it up with her."

Many eyes were turned on Janet with a look of surprise as she walked up the aisle of Paddiford Church. She felt a little tremor at the notice she knew she was exciting, but it was a strong satisfaction to her that she had been able at once to take a step that would let her neighbors know her change of feeling towards Mr. Tryan: she had left herself now no room for proud reluctance or weak hesitation. The walk through the sweet spring air had stimulated all her fresh hopes, all her yearning desires after purity, strength, and peace. She thought she should find a new meaning in the prayers this morning; her full heart, like an overflowing river, wanted those ready-made channels to pour itself into; and then she should hear Mr. Tryan again, and his words would fall on her like precious balm, as they had done last night. There was a liquid brightness in her eyes as they rested on the mere walls, the pews, the weavers and colliers in their Sunday clothes. The commonest things seemed to touch the spring of love within her, just as, when we are suddenly released from an acute absorbing bodily pain, our heart and senses leap out in new freedom; we think even the noise of streets harmonious, and are ready to hug the tradesman who is wrapping up our change. A door had been opened in Janet's cold dark prison of self-despair, and the golden light of morning was pouring in its slanting beams through the blessed opening. There was sunlight in the world; there was a divine love caring for her; it had given her an earnest of good things; it had been preparing comfort for her in the very moment when she had thought herself most forsaken.

Mr. Tryan might well rejoice when his eye rested on her as he entered his desk; but he rejoiced with trembling. He could not look at the sweet hopeful face without remembering its yesterday's look of agony; and there was the possibility that that look might return.

Janet's appearance at church was greeted not only by wondering eyes, but by kind hearts, and after the service several of Mr. Tryan's hearers with whom she had been on cold terms of late, contrived to come up to her and take her by the hand.

"Mother," said Miss Linnet, "do let us go and speak to Mrs. Dempster. I'm sure there's a great change in her mind towards Mr. Tryan. I noticed how eagerly she listened to the sermon, and she's come with Mrs. Pettifer, you see. We ought to go and give her a welcome among us."

"Why, my dear, we've never spoke friendly these five year. You know she's been as haughty as any thing since I quarrelled with her husband. However, let bygones be bygones; I've no grudge again' the poor thing, more particular as she must ha' flew in her husband's face to come and hear Mr. Tryan. Yes, let us go an' speak to her."

The friendly words and looks touched Janet a little too keenly, and Mrs. Pettifer wisely hurried her home by the least-frequented road. When they reached home, a violent fit of weeping, followed by continuous lassitude, showed that the emotions of the morning had overstrained her nerves. She was suffering, too, from the absence of the long-accustomed stimulus which she had promised Mr. Tryan not to touch again. The poor thing was conscious of this, and dreaded her own weakness, as the victim of intermittent insanity dreads the oncoming of the old illusion.

"Mother," she whispered, when Mrs. Raynor urged her to lie down and rest all the afternoon, that she might be the better prepared to see Mr. Tryan in the evening—"mother, don't let me have any thing if I ask for it."

In the mother's mind there was the same anxiety, and in her it was mingled with another fear—the fear lest Janet, in her present excited state of mind, should take some premature step in relation to her husband, which might lead back to all the former troubles. The hint she had thrown out in the morning of her wish to return to him after a time, showed a new eagerness for difficult duties, that only made the long-saddened sober mother tremble.

But as evening approached, Janet's morning heroism all forsook her: her imagination, influenced by physical depression as well as by mental habits, was haunted by the vision of her husband's return home, and she began to shudder with the yesterday's dread. She heard him calling her, she saw him going to her mother's to look for her, she felt sure he would find her out, and burst in upon her.

"Pray, pray, don't leave me, don't go to church," she said to Mrs. Pettifer. "You and mother both stay with me till Mr. Tryan comes."

At twenty minutes past six the church bells were ringing for the evening service, and soon the congregation was streaming along Orchard Street in the mellow sunset. The street opened towards the west. The red half-sunken sun shed a solemn splendor on the every-day houses, and crimsoned the windows of Dempster's projecting upper story.

Suddenly a loud murmur arose and spread along the stream of church-goers, and one group after another paused and looked backward. At the far end of the street, men, accompanied by a miscellaneous group of onlookers, were slowly carrying something—a body stretched on a door. Slowly they passed along the middle of the street, lined all the way with awe-struck faces, till they turned aside and paused in the red sunlight before Dempster's door.

It was Dempster's body. No one knew whether he was alive or dead.

CHAPTER XXII.

It was probably a hard saying to the Pharisees, that "there is more joy in heaven over one sinner that repenteth, than over ninety and nine just persons that need no repentance." And certain ingenious philosophers of our own day must surely take offense at a joy so entirely out of correspondence with arithmetical proportion. But a heart that has been taught by its own sore struggles to bleed for the woes of another—that has "learned pity through suffering"—is likely to find very imperfect satisfaction in the "balance of happiness," "doctrine of compensations," and other short and easy methods of obtaining thorough complacency in the presence of pain; and for such a heart that saying will not be altogether dark. The emotions, I have observed, are but slightly influenced by arithmetical considerations: the mother, when her sweet lisping little ones have all been taken from her one after another, and she is hanging over her last dead babe, finds small consolation in the fact that the tiny dimpled corpse is but one of a necessary average, and that a thousand other babes brought into the world at the same time are doing well, and are likely to live; and if you stood beside that mother—if you knew her pang and shared it—it is probable you would be equally unable to see a ground of complacency in statistics.

Doubtless a complacency resting on that basis is highly rational; but emotion, I fear, is obstinately irrational: it insists on caring for individuals; it absolutely refuses to adopt the quantitative view of human anguish, and to admit that thirteen happy lives are a set off against twelve miserable lives, which leaves a clear balance on the side of satisfaction. This is the inherent imbecility of feeling, and one must be a great philosopher to have got quite clear of all that, and to have emerged into the serene air of pure intellect, in which it is evident that individuals really exist for no other purpose than that abstractions may be drawn from them—abstractions that may rise from heaps of ruined lives like the sweet savor of a sacrifice in the nostrils of philosophers, and of a philosophic Deity. And so it comes to pass that for the man who knows sympathy because he has known sorrow, that old, old saying about the joy of angels over the repentant sinner outweighing their joy over the ninety-nine just, has a meaning which does not jar with the language of his own heart. It only tells him, that for angels too there is a transcendent value in human pain, which refuses to be settled by equations; that the eyes of angels too are turned away from the serene happiness of the righteous to bend with yearning pity on the poor erring soul wandering in the desert where no water is; that for angels too the misery of one casts so tremendous a shadow as to eclipse the bliss of ninety-nine.

Mr. Tryan had gone through the initiation of suffering: it is no wonder, then, that Janet's restoration was the work that lay nearest his heart; and that, weary as he was in body when he entered the vestry after the evening service, he was impatient to fulfill the promise of seeing her. His experience enabled him to divine—what was the fact—that the hopefulness of the morning would be followed by a return of depression and discouragement; and his sense of the inward and outward difficulties in the way of her restoration was so keen, that he could only find relief from the foreboding it excited by lifting up his heart in prayer. There are unseen elements which often frustrate our wisest calculations—which raise up the sufferer from the edge of the grave, contradicting the prophecies of the clear-sighted physician, and fulfilling the blind clinging hopes of affection; such unseen elements Mr. Tryan called the Divine Will, and filled up the margin of ignorance which surrounds all our knowledge with the feelings of trust and resignation. Perhaps the profoundest philosophy could hardly fill it up better.

His mind was occupied in this way as he was absently taking off his gown, when Mr. Landor startled him by entering the vestry and asking abruptly,

"Have you heard the news about Dempster?"

"No," said Mr. Tryan, anxiously; "what is it?"

"He has been thrown out of his gig in the Bridge Way, and he was taken up for dead. They were carrying him home as we were coming to church, and I staid behind to see what I could do. I went in to speak to Mrs. Dempster, and prepare her a little, but she was not at home. Dempster is not dead, however; he was stunned with the fall. Pilgrim came in a few minutes, and he says the right leg is broken in two places. It's likely to be a terrible case, with his state of body. It seems he was more drunk than usual, and they say he came along the Bridge Way flogging his horse like a madman, till at last it gave a sudden wheel, and he was pitched out. The servants said they didn't know where Mrs. Dempster was: she had been away from home since yesterday morning; but Mrs. Raynor knew."

"I know where she is," said Mr. Tryan; "but I think it will be better for her not to be told of this just yet."

"Ah, that was what Pilgrim said, and so I didn't go round to Mrs. Raynor's. He said it would be all the better if Mrs. Dempster could be kept out of the house for the present. Do you know if any thing new has happened between Dempster and his wife lately? I was surprised to hear of her being at Paddiford Church this morning."

"Yes, something has happened; but I believe she is anxious that the particulars of his behavior towards her should not be known. She is at Mrs. Pettifer's—there is no reason for concealing that, since what has happened to her husband; and yesterday, when she was in very deep trouble, she sent for me. I was very thankful she did so: I believe a great change of feeling has begun in her. But she is at present in that excitable state of mind—she has been shaken by so many painful emotions during the last two days, that I think it would be better, for this evening at least, to guard her from a new shock, if possible. But I am going now to call upon her, and I shall see how she is."

"Mr. Tryan," said Mr. Jerome, who had entered during the dialogue, and had been standing by, listening with a distressed face, "I shall take it as a favor if you'll let me know if iver there's any thing I can do for Mrs. Dempster. Eh, dear, what a world this is! I think I see 'em fifteen year ago—as happy a young couple as iver was; and now, what it's all come to! I was in a hurry like, to punish

Dempster for pessecutin', but there was a stronger hand at work nor mine."

"Yes, Mr. Jerome; but don't let us rejoice in punishment, even when the hand of God alone inflicts it. The best of us are but poor wretches just saved from shipwreck: can we feel any thing but awe and pity when we see a fellow-passenger swallowed by the waves?"

"Right, right, Mr. Tryan. I'm over hot and hasty, that I am. But I beg on you to tell Mrs. Dempster—I mean, in course, when you've an opportunity—tell her she's a friend at the White House as she may send for any hour o' the day."

"Yes; I shall have an opportunity, I dare say, and I will remember your wish. I think," continued Mr. Tryan, turning to Mr. Landor, "I had better see Mr. Pilgrim on my way, and learn what is exactly the state of things by this time. What do you think?"

"By all means: if Mrs. Dempster is to know, there's no one can break the news to her so well as you. I'll walk with you to Dempster's door. I dare say Pilgrim is there still. Come, Mr. Jerome, you've got to go our way too, to fetch your horse."

Mr. Pilgrim was in the passage giving some directions to his assistant, when, to his surprise, he saw Mr. Tryan enter. They shook hands; for Mr. Pilgrim, never having joined the party of the Anti-Tryanites, had no ground for resisting the growing conviction that the Evangelical curate was really a good fellow, though he was a fool for not taking better care of himself.

"Why, I didn't expect to see you in your old enemy's quarters," he said to Mr. Tryan. "However, it will be a good while before poor Dempster shows any fight again."

"I came on Mrs. Dempster's account," said Mr. Tryan. "She is staying at Mrs. Pettifer's; she has had a great shock from some severe domestic trouble lately, and I think it will be wise to defer telling her of this dreadful event for a short time."

"Why, what has been up, eh?" said Mr. Pilgrim, whose curiosity was at once awakened. "She used to be no friend of yours. Has there been some split between them? It's a new thing for her to turn round on him."

"Oh, merely an exaggeration of scenes that must often have happened before. But the question now is, whether you think there is any immediate danger of her husband's death; for in that case, I think, from what I have observed of her feelings, she would be pained afterwards to have been kept in ignorance."

"Well, there's no telling in these cases, you know. I don't

apprehend speedy death, and it is not absolutely impossible that we may bring him round again. At present he's in a state of apoplectic stupor; but if that subsides, delirium is almost sure to supervene, and we shall have some painful scenes. It's one of those complicated cases in which the delirium is likely to be of the worst kind—meningitis and delirium tremens together—and we may have a good deal of trouble with him. If Mrs. Dempster were told, I should say it would be desirable to persuade her to remain out of the house at present. She could do no good, you know. I've got nurses."

"Thank you," said Mr. Tryan. "That is what I wanted to know. Good-bye."

When Mrs. Pettifer opened the door for Mr. Tryan, he told her in a few words what had happened, and begged her to take an opportunity of letting Mrs. Raynor know, that they might, if possible, concur in preventing a premature or sudden disclosure of the event to Janet.

"Poor thing?" said Mrs. Pettifer. "She's not fit to hear any bad news; she's very low this evening—worn out with feeling; and she's not had any thing to keep her up, as she's been used to. She seems frightened at the thought of being tempted to take it."

"Thank God for it; that fear is her greatest security."

When Mr. Tryan entered the parlor this time, Janet was again awaiting him eagerly, and her pale sad face was lighted up with a smile as she rose to meet him. But the next moment she said, with a look of anxiety,

"How very ill and tired you look! You have been working so hard all day, and yet you are come to talk to me. Oh, you are wearing yourself out. I must go and ask Mrs. Pettifer to come and make you have some supper. But this is my mother; you have not seen her before, I think."

While Mr. Tryan was speaking to Mrs. Raynor, Janet hurried out, and he, seeing that this good-natured thoughtfulness on his behalf would help to counteract her depression, was not inclined to oppose her wish, but accepted the supper Mrs. Pettifer offered him, quietly talking the while about a clothing club he was going to establish in Paddiford, and the want of provident habits among the poor.

Presently, however, Mrs. Raynor said she must go home for an hour, to see how her little maiden was going on, and Mrs. Pettifer left the room with her to take the opportunity of telling her what had happened to Dempster. When Janet was left alone with Mr. Tryan, she said,

"I feel so uncertain what to do about my husband. I am

so weak—my feelings change so from hour to hour. This morning, when I felt so hopeful and happy, I thought I should like to go back to him, and try to make up for what has been wrong in me. I thought, now God would help me, and I should have you to teach and advise me, and I could bear the troubles that would come. But since then—all this afternoon and evening—I have had the same feelings I used to have, the same dread of his anger and cruelty, and it seems to me as if I should never be able to bear it without falling into the same sins, and doing just what I did before. Yet if it were settled that I should live apart from him, I know it would always be a load on my mind that I had shut myself out from going back to him. It seems a dreadful thing in life, when any one has been so near to one as a husband for fifteen years, to part and be nothing to each other any more. Surely that is a very strong tie, and I feel as if my duty can never lie quite away from it. It is very difficult to know what to do: what ought I to do?"

"I think it will be well not to take any decisive step yet. Wait until your mind is calmer. You might remain with your mother for a little while; I think you have no real ground for fearing any annoyance from your husband at present; he has put himself too much in the wrong; he will very likely leave you unmolested for some time. Dismiss this difficult question from your mind just now, if you can. Every new day may bring you new grounds for decision, and what is most needful for your health of mind is repose from that haunting anxiety about the future which has been preying on you. Cast yourself on God, and trust that he will direct you; he will make your duty clear to you, if you wait submissively on him."

"Yes; I will wait a little, as you tell me. I will go to my mother's to-morrow, and pray to be guided rightly. You will pray for me, too."

CHAPTER XXIII.

The next morning Janet was so much calmer, and at breakfast spoke so decidedly of going to her mother's, that Mrs. Pettifer and Mrs. Raynor agreed it would be wise to let her know by degrees what had befallen her husband, since as soon as she went out there would be danger of her meeting some one who would betray the fact. But Mrs. Raynor thought it would be well first to call at Dempster's, and ascertain how he was: so she said to Janet,

"My dear, I'll go home first, and see to things, and get your room ready. You needn't come yet, you know. I shall be back again in an hour or so, and we can go together."

"Oh no," said Mrs. Pettifer. "Stay with me till evening. I shall be lost without you. You needn't go till quite evening."

Janet had dipped into the "Life of Henry Martyn," which Mrs. Pettifer had from the Paddiford Lending Library, and her interest was so arrested by that pathetic missionary story, that she readily acquiesced in both propositions, and Mrs. Raynor set out.

She had been gone more than an hour, and it was nearly twelve o'clock, when Janet put down her book; and after sitting meditatively for some minutes with her eyes unconsciously fixed on the opposite wall, she rose, went to her bedroom, and, hastily putting on her bonnet and shawl, came down to Mrs. Pettifer, who was busy in the kitchen.

"Mrs. Pettifer," she said, "tell mother, when she comes back, I'm gone to see what has become of those poor Lakins in Butcher Lane. I know they're half starving, and I've neglected them so, lately. And then, I think, I'll go on to Mrs. Crewe. I want to see the dear little woman, and tell her myself about my going to hear Mr. Tryan. She won't feel it half so much if I tell her myself."

"Won't you wait till your mother comes, or put it off till to-morrow?" said Mrs. Pettifer, alarmed. "You'll hardly be back in time for dinner, if you get talking to Mrs. Crewe. And you'll have to pass by your husband's, you know; and yesterday you were so afraid of seeing him."

"Oh, Robert will be shut up at the office now, if he's not gone out of the town. I must go—I feel I must be doing something for some one—not be a mere useless log any longer. I've been reading about that wonderful Henry Martyn; he's just like Mr. Tryan—wearing himself out for other people, and I sit thinking of nothing but myself. I *must* go. Good-bye; I shall be back soon."

She ran off before Mrs. Pettifer could utter another word of dissuasion, leaving the good woman in considerable anxiety lest this new impulse of Janet's should frustrate all precautions to save her from a sudden shock.

Janet having paid her visit in Butcher Lane, turned again into Orchard Street on her way to Mrs. Crewe's, and was thinking, rather sadly, that her mother's economical housekeeping would leave no abundant surplus to be sent to the hungry Lakins, when she saw Mr. Pilgrim in advance of her on the other side of the street. He was walking at a rapid pace, and when he reached Dempster's door he turned and entered without knocking.

Janet was startled. Mr. Pilgrim would never enter in that way unless there was some one very ill in the house. It was her husband; she felt certain of it at once. Something had happened to him. Without a moment's pause, she ran across the street, opened the door, and entered. There was no one in the passage. The dining-room door was wide open—no one was there. Mr. Pilgrim, then, was already up stairs. She rushed up at once to Dempster's room—her own room. The door was open, and she paused in pale horror at the sight before her, which seemed to stand out only with the more appalling distinctness because the noonday light was darkened to twilight in the chamber.

Two strong nurses were using their utmost force to hold Dempster in bed, while the medical assistant was applying a sponge to his head, and Mr. Pilgrim was busy adjusting some apparatus in the background. Dempster's face was purple and swollen, his eyes dilated, and fixed with a look of dire terror on something he seemed to see approaching him from the iron closet. He trembled violently, and struggled as if to jump out of bed.

"Let me go, let me go," he said in a loud, hoarse whisper; "She's coming .... she's cold .... she's dead .... she'll strangle me with her black hair. Ah!" he shrieked aloud, "her hair is all serpents .... they're black serpents .... they hiss .... they hiss .... let me go .... let me go .... she wants to drag me with her cold arms .... her arms are serpents .... they are great white serpents .... they'll twine round me .... she wants to drag me into the cold water .... her bosom is cold .... it is black.... it is all serpents...."

"No, Robert," Janet cried, in tones of yearning pity, rushing to the side of the bed, and stretching out her arms towards him, "no, here is Janet. She is not dead—she forgives you."

Dempster's maddened senses seemed to receive some new impression from her appearance. The terror gave way to rage.

"Ha! you sneaking hypocrite?" he burst out in a grating voice, "you threaten me .... you mean to have your revenge on me, do you? Do your worst! I've got the law on my side.... I know the law.... I'll hunt you down like a hare .... prove it .... prove that I was tampered with .... prove that I took the money .... prove it .... you can prove nothing .... you damned psalm-singing maggots! I'll make a fire under you, and smoke off the whole pack of you.... I'll sweep you up.... I'll grind you to powder .... small powder .... (here his voice dropped to a low tone of shuddering disgust) .... powder on the bed-clothes.... running about .... black lice .... they are coming in swarms.... Janet! come and take them away .... curse you! why don't you come? Janet!"

Poor Janet was kneeling by the bed with her face buried in her hands. She almost wished her worst moment back again rather than this. It seemed as if her husband was already imprisoned in misery, and she could not reach him—his ear deaf forever to the sounds of love and forgiveness. His sins had made a hard crust round his soul; her pitying voice could not pierce it.

"Not there, isn't she?" he went on in a defiant tone. "Why do you ask me where she is? I'll have every drop of yellow blood out of your veins if you come questioning me. Your blood is yellow .... in your purse .... running out of your purse.... What! you're changing it into toads, are you? They're crawling .... they're flying .... they're flying about my head .... the toads are flying about. Ostler! ostler! bring out my gig .... bring it out, you lazy beast .... ha! you'll follow me, will you? .... you'll fly about my head .... you've got fiery tongues.... Ostler! curse you! why don't you come? Janet! come and take the toads away.... Janet!"

This last time he uttered her name with such a shriek of terror, that Janet involuntarily started up from her knees, and stood as if petrified by the horrible vibration. Dempster stared wildly in silence for some moments; then he spoke again in a hoarse whisper:

"Dead .... is she dead? *She* did it, then. She buried herself in the iron chest.... she left her clothes out, though .... she isn't dead .... why do you pretend she's dead? .... she's coming .... she's coming out of the iron closet .... there are the black serpents .... stop her .... let me go .... stop her .... she wants to drag me away into the cold black water .... her bosom is black .... it is all serpents.... they are getting longer .... the great white serpents are getting longer ...."

Here Mr. Pilgrim came forward with the apparatus to bind him, but Dempster's struggles became more and more violent. "Ostler! ostler!" he shouted, "bring out the gig .... give me the whip!"—and bursting loose from the strong hands that held him, he began to flog the bed-clothes furiously with his right arm.

"Get along, you lame brute!—sc — sc — sc! that's it! there you go! They think they've outwitted me, do they? The sneaking idiots! I'll be up with them by-and-by. I'll make them say the Lord's Prayer backwards. . . . I'll pepper them so that the devil shall eat them raw. . . . sc—sc—sc —we shall see who'll be the winner yet . . . . get along, you damned limping beast. . . . I'll lay your back open. . . . I'll . . . ."

He raised himself with a stronger effort than ever to flog the bed-clothes, and fell back in convulsions. Janet gave a scream, and sank on her knees again. She thought he was dead.

As soon as Mr. Pilgrim was able to give her a moment's attention, he came to her, and, taking her by the arm attempted to draw her gently out of the room.

"Now, my dear Mrs. Dempster, let me persuade you not to remain in the room at present. We shall soon relieve these symptoms, I hope; it is nothing but the delirium that ordinarily attends such cases."

"Oh, what is the matter? what brought it on?"

"He fell out of the gig; the right leg is broken. It is a terrible accident, and I don't disguise that there is considerable danger attending it, owing to the state of the brain. But Mr. Dempster has a strong constitution, you know; in a few days these symptoms may be allayed, and he may do well. Let me beg of you to keep out of the room at present: you can do no good until Mr. Dempster is better, and able to know you. But you ought not to be alone; let me advise you to have Mrs. Raynor with you."

"Yes, I will send for mother. But you must not object to my being in the room. I shall be very quiet now, only just at first the shock was so great; I knew nothing about it. I can help the nurses a great deal; I can put the cold things to his head. He may be sensible for a moment and know me. Pray do not say any more against it: my heart is set on being with him."

Mr. Pilgrim gave way, and Janet, having sent for her mother and put off her bonnet and shawl, returned to take her place by the side of her husband's bed.

CHAPTER XXIV.

Day after day, with only short intervals of rest, Janet kept her place in that sad chamber. No wonder the sick-room and the lazaretto have so often been a refuge from the tossings of intellectual doubt—a place of repose for the worn and wounded spirit. Here is a duty about which all creeds and all philosophies are of one; here, at least, the conscience will not be dogged by doubt, the benign impulse will not be checked by adverse theory: here you may begin to act without settling one preliminary question. To moisten the sufferer's parched lips through the long night-watches, to bear up the drooping head, to lift the helpless limbs, to divine the want that can find no utterance beyond the feeble motion of the hand or beseeching glance of the eye—these are offices that demand no self-questionings, no casuistry, no assent to propositions, no weighing of consequences. Within the four walls where the stir and glare of the world are shut out, and every voice is subdued—where a human being lies prostrate, thrown on the tender mercies of his fellow, the moral relation of man to man is reduced to its utmost clearness and simplicity: bigotry can not confuse it, theory can not pervert it, passion, awed into quiescence, can neither pollute nor perturb it. As we bend over the sick-bed, all the forces of our nature rush towards the channels of pity, of patience, and of love, and sweep down the miserable choking drift of our quarrels, our debates, our would-be wisdom, and our clamorous selfish desires. This blessing of serene freedom from the importunities of opinion lies in all simple direct acts of mercy, and is one source of that sweet calm which is often felt by the watcher in the sick-room, even when the duties there are of a hard and terrible kind.

Something of that benign result was felt by Janet during her tendance in her husband's chamber. When the first heart-piercing hours were over—when her horror at his delirium was no longer fresh, she began to be conscious of her relief from the burthen of decision as to her future course. The question that agitated her, about returning to her husband, had been solved in a moment; and this illness, after all, might be the herald of another blessing, just as that dreadful midnight when she stood an outcast in cold and darkness had been followed by the dawn of a new hope.

Robert would get better; this illness might alter him; he would be a long time feeble, needing help, walking with a crutch, perhaps. She would wait on him with such tenderness, such all-forgiving love, that the old harshness and cruelty must melt away forever under the heart-sunshine she would pour around him. Her bosom heaved at the thought, and delicious tears fell. Janet's was a nature in which hatred and revenge could find no place; the long bitter years drew half their bitterness from her ever-living remembrance of the too short years of love that went before; and the thought that her husband would ever put her hand to his lips again, and recall the days when they sat on the grass together, and he laid scarlet poppies on her black hair, and called her his gypsy queen, seemed to send a tide of loving oblivion over all the harsh and stony space they had traversed since. The Divine Love that had already shone upon her would be with her; she would lift up her soul continually for help; Mr. Tryan, she knew, would pray for her. If she felt herself failing, she would confess it to him at once; if her feet began to slip, there was that stay for her to cling to. Oh, she could never be drawn back into that cold damp vault of sin and despair again; she had felt the morning sun, she had tasted the sweet pure air of trust and penitence and submission.

These were the thoughts passing through Janet's mind as she hovered about her husband's bed, and these were the hopes she poured out to Mr. Tryan when he called to see her. It was so evident that they were strengthening her in her new struggle—they shed such a glow of calm enthusiasm over her face as she spoke of them, that Mr. Tryan could not bear to throw on them the chill of premonitory doubts, though a previous conversation he had had with Mr. Pilgrim had convinced him that there was not the faintest probability of Dempster's recovery. Poor Janet did not know the significance of the changing symptoms, and when, after the lapse of a week, the delirium began to lose some of its violence, and to be interrupted by longer and longer intervals of stupor, she tried to think that these might be steps on the way to recovery, and she shrank from questioning Mr. Pilgrim lest he should confirm the fears that began to get predominance in her mind. But before many days were past, he thought it right not to allow her to blind herself any longer. One day—it was just about noon, when bad news always seems most sickening—he led her from her husband's chamber into the opposite drawing-room, where Mrs. Raynor was sitting, and said to her, in that low tone of sympathetic feeling which sometimes gave a sudden air of gentleness to this rough man—

"My dear Mrs. Dempster, it is right in these cases, you know, to be prepared for the worst. I think I shall be saving you pain by preventing you from entertaining any false hopes, and Mr. Dempster's state is now such that I fear we must consider recovery impossible. The affection of the brain might not have been hopeless, but, you see, there is a terrible complication; and I am grieved to say the broken limb is mortifying."

Janet listened with a sinking heart. That future of love and forgiveness would never come, then: he was going out of her sight forever, where her pity could never reach him. She turned cold, and trembled.

"But do you think he will die," she said, "without ever coming to himself? without ever knowing me?"

"One can not say that with certainty. It is not impossible that the cerebral oppression may subside, and that he may become conscious. If there is any thing you would wish to be said or done in that case, it would be well to be prepared. I should think," Mr. Pilgrim continued, turning to Mrs. Raynor, "Mr. Dempster's affairs are likely to be in order—his will is . . . ."

"Oh, I wouldn't have him troubled about those things," interrupted Janet, "he has no relations but quite distant ones —no one but me. I wouldn't take up the time with that. I only want to . . . ."

She was unable to finish; she felt her sobs rising, and left the room. "O God!" she said inwardly, "is not Thy love greater than mine? Have mercy on him! have mercy on him!"

This happened on Wednesday, ten days after the fatal accident. By the following Sunday Dempster was in a state of rapidly increasing prostration; and when Mr. Pilgrim, who, in turn with his assistant, had slept in the house from the beginning, came in, about half past ten, as usual, he scarcely believed that the feebly struggling life would last out till morning. For the last few days he had been administering stimulants to relieve the exhaustion which had succeeded the alternations of delirium and stupor. This slight office was all that now remained to be done for the patient; so at eleven o'clock Mr. Pilgrim went to bed, having given directions to the nurse, and desired her to call him if any change took place, or if Mrs. Dempster desired his presence.

Janet could not be persuaded to leave the room. She was yearning and watching for a moment in which her husband's eyes would rest consciously upon her, and he would know that she had forgiven him.

How changed he was since that terrible Monday, nearly a fortnight ago! He lay motionless, but for the irregular breathing that stirred his broad chest and thick muscular neck. His features were no longer purple and swollen; they were pale, sunken, and haggard. A cold perspiration stood in beads on the protuberant forehead, and on the wasted hands stretched motionless on the bed-clothes. It was better to see the hands so, than convulsively picking the air, as they had been a week ago.

Janet sat on the edge of the bed through the long hours of candle-light, watching the unconscious half-closed eyes, wiping the perspiration from the brow and cheeks, and keeping her left hand on the cold unanswering right hand that lay beside her on the bed-clothes. She was almost as pale as her dying husband, and there were dark lines under her eyes, for this was the third night since she had taken off her clothes; but the eager straining gaze of her dark eyes, and the acute sensibility that lay in every line about her mouth, made a strange contrast with the blank unconsciousness and emaciated animalism of the face she was watching.

There was profound stillness in the house. She heard no sound but her husband's breathing and the ticking of the watch on the mantel-piece. The candle, placed high up, shed a soft light down on the one object she cared to see. There was a smell of brandy in the room; it was given to her husband from time to time; but this smell, which at first had produced in her a faint shuddering sensation, was now becoming indifferent to her: she did not even perceive it; she was too unconscious of herself to feel either temptations or accusations. She only felt that the husband of her youth was dying; far, far out of her reach, as if she were standing helpless on the shore, while he was sinking in the black storm-waves; she only yearned for one moment in which she might satisfy the deep forgiving pity of her soul by one look of love, one word of tenderness.

Her sensations and thoughts were so persistent that she could not measure the hours, and it was a surprise to her when the nurse put out the candle, and let in the faint morning light. Mrs. Raynor, anxious about Janet, was already up, and now brought in some fresh coffee for her; and Mr. Pilgrim having awaked, had hurried on his clothes and was coming in to see how Dempster was.

This change from candle-light to morning, this recommencement of the same round of things that had happened yesterday, was a discouragement rather than a relief to Janet. She was more conscious of her chill weariness; the new light thrown on her husband's face seemed to reveal the still work that death had been doing through the night; she felt her last lingering hope that he would ever know her again forsake her.

But now, Mr. Pilgrim, having felt the pulse, was putting some brandy in a tea-spoon between Dempster's lips; the brandy went down and his breathing became freer. Janet noticed the change, and her heart beat faster as she leaned forward to watch him. Suddenly a slight movement, like the passing away of a shadow, was visible in his face, and he opened his eyes full on Janet.

It was almost like meeting him again on the resurrection morning, after the night of the grave.

"Robert, do you know me?"

He kept his eyes fixed on her, and there was a faintly perceptible motion of the lips, as if he wanted to speak.

But the moment of speech was forever gone—the moment for asking pardon of her, if he wanted to ask it. Could he read the full forgiveness that was written in her eyes? She never knew; for, as she was bending to kiss him, the thick veil of death fell between them, and her lips touched a corpse.

CHAPTER XXV.

The faces looked very hard and unmoved that surrounded Dempster's grave, while old Mr. Crewe read the burial service in his low, broken voice. The pall-bearers were such men as Mr. Pittman, Mr. Lowme, and Mr. Budd—men whom Dempster had called his friends while he was in life; and worldly faces never look so worldly as at a funeral. They have the same effect of grating incongruity as the sound of a coarse voice breaking the solemn silence of night.

The one face that had sorrow in it was covered by a thick crape veil, and the sorrow was suppressed and silent. No one knew how deep it was; for the thought in most of her neighbors' minds was, that Mrs. Dempster could hardly have had better fortune than to lose a bad husband who had left her the compensation of a good income. They found it difficult to conceive that her husband's death could be felt by her otherwise than as a deliverance. The person who was most thoroughly convinced that Janet's grief was deep and real, was Mr. Pilgrim, who in general was not at all weakly given to a belief in disinterested feeling.

"That woman has a tender heart," he was frequently heard to observe in his morning rounds about this time. "I used to think there was a great deal of palaver in her, but you may depend upon it there's no pretense about her. If he'd been the kindest husband in the world she couldn't have felt more. There's a great deal of good in Mrs. Dempster—a great deal of good."

"*I* always said so," was Mrs. Lowme's reply, when he made the observation to her; "she was always so very full of pretty attentions to me when I was ill. But they tell me now she's turned Tryanite; if that's it we sha'n't agree again. It's very inconsistent in her, I think, turning round in that way, after being the foremost to laugh at the Tryanite cant, and especially in a woman of her habits; she should cure herself of *them* before she pretends to be over-religious."

"Well, I think she means to cure herself, do you know," said Mr. Pilgrim, whose good-will towards Janet was just now quite above that temperate point at which he could indulge his feminine patients with a little judicious detraction. "I feel sure she has not taken any stimulants all through her husband's illness; and she has been constantly in the way of them. I can see she sometimes suffers a good deal of depression for want of them—it shows all the more resolution in her. Those cures are rare; but I've known them happen sometimes with people of strong will."

Mrs. Lowme took an opportunity of retailing Mr. Pilgrim's conversation to Mrs. Phipps, who, as a victim of Pratt and plethora, could rarely enjoy that pleasure at first-hand. Mrs. Phipps was a woman of decided opinions, though of wheezy utterance.

"For my part," she remarked, "I'm glad to hear there's any likelihood of improvement in Mrs. Dempster, but I think the way things have turned out seems to show that she was more to blame than people thought she was; else, why should she feel so much about her husband? And Dempster, I understand, has left his wife pretty nearly all his property to do as she likes with; *that* isn't behaving like such a very bad husband. I don't believe Mrs. Dempster can have had so much provocation as they pretended. I've known husbands who've laid plans for tormenting their wives when they're underground—tying up their money and hindering them from marrying again. Not that *I* should ever wish to marry again; I think one husband in one's life is enough in all conscience;"—here she threw a fierce glance at the amiable Mr. Phipps, who was innocently delighting himself with the *facetiæ* in the "Rotherby Guardian," and thinking the editor must be a droll fellow—"but it's aggravating to be tied up in that way. Why, they say Mrs. Dempster will have as good as six hundred a-year at least. A fine thing for her, that was a poor girl without a farthing to her fortune. It's well if she doesn't make ducks and drakes of it somehow."

Mrs. Phipps's view of Janet, however, was far from being the prevalent one in Milby. Even neighbors who had no strong personal interest in her, could hardly see the noble-looking woman in her widow's dress, with a sad sweet gravity in her face, and not be touched with fresh admiration for her—and not feel, at least vaguely, that she had entered on a new life in which it was a sort of desecration to allude to the painful past. And the old friends who had a real regard for her, but whose cordiality had been repelled or chilled of late years, now came round her with hearty demonstrations of affection. Mr. Jerome felt that his happiness had a substantial addition now he could once more call on that "nice little woman Mrs. Dempster," and think of her with rejoicing instead of sorrow. The Pratts lost no time in returning to the footing of old-established friendship with Janet and her mother; and Miss Pratt felt it incumbent on her, on all suitable occasions, to deliver a very emphatic approval of the remarkable strength of mind she understood Mrs. Dempster to be exhibiting. The Miss Linnets were eager to meet Mr. Tryan's wishes by greeting Janet as one who was likely to be a sister in religious feeling and good works; and Mrs. Linnet was so agreeably surprised by the fact that Dempster had left his wife the money "in that handsome way, to do what she liked with it," that she even included Dempster himself, and his villainous discovery of the flaw in her title to Pye's Croft, in her magnanimous oblivion of past offenses. She and Mrs. Jerome agreed over a friendly cup of tea that there were "a many husbands as was very fine spoken an' all that, an' yet all the while kep' a will locked up from you, as tied you up as tight as any thing. I assure *you*," Mrs. Jerome continued, dropping her voice in a confidential manner, "I know no more to this day about Mr. Jerome's will, nor the child as is unborn. I've no fears about a income—I'm well aware Mr. Jerome 'ud niver leave me stret for that; but I should like to hev a thousand or two at my own disposial; it makes a widow a deal more looked on."

Perhaps this ground of respect to widows might not be entirely without its influence on the Milby mind, and might do something towards conciliating those more aristocratic acquaintances of Janet's, who would otherwise have been inclined to take the severest view of her apostasy towards Evangelicalism. Errors look so very ugly in persons of small means—one feels they are taking quite a liberty in going astray; whereas people of fortune may naturally indulge in a few delinquencies. "They've got the money for it," as the girl said of her mistress who had made herself ill with pickled salmon. However it may have been, there was not an acquaintance of Janet's in Milby, that did not offer her civilities in the early days of her widowhood. Even the severe Mrs. Phipps was not an exception; for heaven knows what would become of our sociality if we never visited people we speak ill of: we should live, like Egyptian hermits, in crowded solitude.

Perhaps the attentions most grateful to Janet were those of her old friend Mrs. Crewe, whose attachment to her favorite proved quite too strong for any resentment she might be supposed to feel on the score of Mr. Tryan. The little deaf old lady couldn't do without her accustomed visitor, whom she had seen grow up from child to woman, always so willing to chat with her and tell her all the news, though she was deaf; while other people thought it tiresome to shout in her ear, and irritated her by recommending ear-trumpets of various construction.

All this friendliness was very precious to Janet. She was conscious of the aid it gave her in the self-conquest which was the blessing she prayed for with every fresh morning. The chief strength of her nature lay in her affection, which colored all the rest of her mind: it gave a personal sisterly tenderness to her acts of benevolence; it made her cling with tenacity to every object that had once stirred her kindly emotions. Alas! it was unsatisfied, wounded affection that had made her trouble greater than she could bear. And now there was no check to the full flow of that plenteous current in her nature—no gnawing secret anguish—no overhanging terror—no inward shame. Friendly faces beamed on her; she felt that friendly hearts were approving her, and wishing her well, and that mild sunshine of good-will fell beneficently on her new hopes and efforts, as the clear shining after rain falls on the tender leaf-buds of spring, and wins them from promise to fulfillment.

And she needed these secondary helps, for her wrestling with her past self was not always easy. The strong emotions from which the life of a human being receives a new bias, win their victory as the sea wins his: though their advance may be sure, they will often, after a mightier wave than usual, seem to roll back so far as to lose all the ground they had made. Janet showed the strong bent of her will by taking every outward precaution against the occurrence of a temptation. Her mother was now her constant companion, having shut up her little dwelling and come to reside in Orchard Street; and Janet gave all dangerous keys into her keeping, entreating her to lock them away in some secret place. Whenever the too well known depression and craving threatened her, she would seek a refuge in what had always been her purest enjoyment—in visiting one of her poor neighbors, in carrying some food or comfort to a sick-bed, in cheering with her smile some of the familiar dwellings up the dingy back-lanes. But the great source of courage, the great help to perseverance, was the sense that she had a friend and teacher in Mr. Tryan: she could confess her difficulties to him; she knew he prayed for her; she had always before her the prospect of soon seeing him, and hearing words of admonition and comfort, that came to her charged with a divine power such as she had never found in human words before.

So the time passed, till it was far on in May, nearly a month after her husband's death, when, as she and her mother were seated peacefully at breakfast in the dining-room, looking through the open window at the old-fashioned garden, where the grassplot was now whitened with apple-blossoms, a letter was brought in for Mrs. Raynor.

"Why, there's the Thurston post-mark on it," she said. "It must be about your aunt Anna. Ah, so it is, poor thing! she's been taken worse this last day or two, and has asked them to send for me. That dropsy is carrying her off at last, I daresay. Poor thing! it will be a happy release. I must go, my dear—she's your father's last sister—though I'm sorry to leave you. However, perhaps I shall not have to stay more than a night or two."

Janet looked distressed as she said, "Yes, you must go, mother. But I don't know what I shall do without you. I think I shall run in to Mrs. Pettifer, and ask her to come and stay with me while you're away. I'm sure she will."

At twelve o'clock, Janet, having seen her mother in the coach that was to carry her to Thurston, called, on her way back, at Mrs. Pettifer's, but found, to her great disappointment, that her old friend was gone out for the day. So she wrote on a leaf of her pocket-book an urgent request that Mrs. Pettifer would come and stay with her while her mother was away; and, desiring the servant-girl to give it to her mistress as soon as she came home, walked on to the

Vicarage to sit with Mrs. Crewe, thinking to relieve in this way the feeling of desolateness and undefined fear that was taking possession of her on being left alone for the first time since that great crisis in her life. And Mrs. Crewe, too, was not at home!

Janet, with a sense of discouragement for which she rebuked herself as childish, walked sadly home again; and when she entered the vacant dining-room, she could not help bursting into tears. It is such vague undefinable states of susceptibility as this—states of excitement or depression, half mental, half physical—that determine many a tragedy in women's lives. Janet could scarcely eat any thing at her solitary dinner; she tried to fix her attention on a book in vain; she walked about the garden, and felt the very sunshine melancholy.

Between four and five o'clock, old Mr. Pittman called, and joined her in the garden, where she had been sitting for some time under one of the great apple-trees, thinking how Robert, in his best moods, used to take little Mamsey to look at the cucumbers, or to see the Alderney cow with its calf in the paddock. The tears and sobs had come again at these thoughts; and when Mr. Pittman approached her, she was feeling languid and exhausted. But the old gentleman's sight and sensibility were obtuse, and, to Janet's satisfaction, he showed no consciousness that she was in grief.

"I have a task to impose upon you, Mrs. Dempster," he said, with a certain toothless pomposity habitual to him: "I want you to look over those letters again in Dempster's bureau, and see if you can find one from Poole about the mortgage on those houses at Dingley. It will be worth twenty pounds, if you can find it; and I don't know where it can be, if it isn't among those letters in the bureau. I've looked everywhere at the office for it. I'm going home now, but I'll call again to-morrow, if you'll be good enough to look in the mean time."

Janet said she would look directly, and turned with Mr. Pittman into the house. But the search would take her some time, so he bade her good-bye, and she went at once to a bureau which stood in a small back-room, where Dempster used sometimes to write letters and receive people who came on business out of office-hours. She had looked through the contents of the bureau more than once; but to-day on removing the last bundle of letters from one of the compartments, she saw what she had never seen before, a small nick in the wood, made in the shape of a thumb-nail, evidently intended as a means of pushing aside the movable back of the compartment. In her examination hitherto she had not found such a letter as Mr. Pittman had described—perhaps there might be more letters behind this slide. She pushed it back at once and saw—no letters, but a small spirit-decanter, half full of pale brandy, Dempster's habitual drink.

An impetuous desire shook Janet through all her members; it seemed to master her with the inevitable force of strong fumes that flood our senses before we are aware. Her hand was on the decanter; pale and excited, she was lifting it out of its niche, when, with a start and a shudder, she dashed it to the ground, and the room was filled with the odor of the spirit. Without staying to shut up the bureau, she rushed out of the room, snatched up her bonnet and mantle which lay in the dining-room, and hurried out of the house.

Where should she go? In what place would this demon that had re-entered her be scared back again? She walked rapidly along the street in the direction of the church. She was soon at the gate of the churchyard; she passed through it, and made her way across the graves to a spot she knew—a spot where the turf had been stirred not long before, where a tomb was to be erected soon. It was very near the church wall, on the side which now lay in deep shadow, quite shut out from the rays of the western sun by a projecting buttress.

Janet sat down on the ground. It was a sombre spot. A thick hedge, surmounted by elm-trees, was in front of her; a projecting buttress on each side. But she wanted to shut out even these objects. Her thick crape veil was down; but she closed her eyes behind it, and pressed her hands upon them. She wanted to summon up the vision of the past; she wanted to lash the demon out of her soul with the stinging memories of the bygone misery; she wanted to renew the old horror and the old anguish, that she might throw herself with the more desperate clinging energy at the foot of the cross, where the Divine Sufferer would impart divine strength. She tried to recall those first bitter moments of shame, which were like the shuddering discovery of the leper that the dire taint is upon him; the deeper and deeper lapse; the on-coming of settled despair; the awful moments by the bedside of her self-maddened husband. And then she tried to live through, with a remembrance made more vivid by that contrast, the blessed hours of hope and joy and peace that had come to her of late, since her whole soul had been bent towards the attainment of purity and holiness.

But now, when the paroxysm of temptation was past, dread and despondency began to thrust themselves, like cold heavy mists, between her and the heaven to which she wanted to look for light and guidance. The temptation would come again—that rush of desire might overmaster her the next time—she would slip back again into that deep slimy pit from which she had been once rescued, and there might be no deliverance for her more. Her prayers did not help her, for fear predominated over trust; she had no confidence that the aid she sought would be given; the idea of her future fall had grasped her mind too strongly. Alone, in this way, she was powerless. If she could see Mr. Tryan, if she could confess all to him, she might gather hope again. She *must* see him; she must go to him.

Janet rose from the ground, and walked away with a quick, resolved step. She had been seated there a long while, and the sun had already sunk. It was late for her to walk to Paddiford and go to Mr. Tryan's, where she had never called before; but there was no other way of seeing him that evening, and she could not hesitate about it. She walked towards a footpath through the fields, which would take her to Paddiford without obliging her to go through the town. The way was rather long, but she preferred it, because it left less probability of her meeting acquaintances, and she shrank from having to speak to any one.

The evening red had nearly faded by the time Janet knocked at Mrs. Wagstaff's door. The good woman looked surprised to see her at that hour; but Janet's mourning weeds and the painful agitation of her face quickly brought the second thought, that some urgent trouble had sent her there.

"Mr. Tryan's just come in," she said. "If you'll step into the parlor, I'll go up and tell him you're here. He seemed very tired and poorly."

At another time Janet would have felt distress at the idea that she was disturbing Mr. Tryan when he required rest; but now her need was too great for that: she could feel nothing but a sense of coming relief, when she heard his step on the stair and saw him enter the room.

He went towards her with a look of anxiety, and said, "I fear something is the matter. I fear you are in trouble."

Then poor Janet poured forth her sad tale of temptation and despondency; and even while she was confessing she felt half her burthen removed. The act of confiding in human sympathy, the consciousness that a fellow-being was listening to her with patient pity, prepared her soul for that stronger leap by which faith grasps the idea of the Divine sympathy. When Mr. Tryan spoke words of consolation and encouragement, she could now believe the message of mercy; the water-floods that had threatened to overwhelm her rolled back again, and life once more spread its heaven-covered space before her. She had been unable to pray alone; but now his prayer bore her own soul along with it, as the broad tongue of flame carries upwards in its vigorous leap the little flickering fire that could hardly keep alight by itself.

But Mr. Tryan was anxious that Janet should not linger out at this late hour. When he saw that she was calmed, he said, "I will walk home with you now; we can talk on the way." But Janet's mind was now sufficiently at liberty for her to notice the signs of feverish weariness in his appearance, and she would not hear of causing him any further fatigue.

"No, no," she said, earnestly, "you will pain me very much —indeed you will, by going out again to-night on my account. There is no real reason why I should not go alone." And when he persisted, fearing that for her to be seen out so late alone might excite remark, she said imploringly, with a half sob in her voice, "What should I—what would others like me do, if you went from us? *Why* will you not think more of that, and take care of yourself?"

He had often had that appeal made to him before, but to-night—from Janet's lips—it seemed to have a new force for him, and he gave way. At first, indeed, he only did so on condition that she would let Mrs. Wagstaff go with her; but Janet had determined to walk home alone. She preferred solitude; she wished not to have her present feelings distracted by any conversation.

So she went out into the dewy starlight; and as Mr. Tryan turned away from her, he felt a stronger wish than ever that his fragile life might last out for him to see Janet's restoration thoroughly established—to see her no longer fleeing, struggling, clinging up the steep sides of a precipice whence she might be any moment hurled back into the depths of despair, but walking firmly on the level ground of habit. He inwardly resolved that nothing but a peremptory duty should ever take him from Milby—that he would not cease to watch over her until life forsook him.

Janet walked on quickly till she turned into the fields; then she slackened her pace a little, enjoying the sense of solitude which a few hours before had been intolerable to her. The Divine Presence did not now seem far off, where she had not wings to reach it; prayer itself seemed superfluous in those moments of calm trust. The temptation which had so lately made her shudder before the possibilities of the future, was now a source of confidence; for had she not been delivered from it? Had not rescue come in the extremity of danger? Yes; Infinite Love was caring for her. She felt like a little child whose hand is firmly grasped by its father, as its frail limbs make their way over the rough ground; if it should stumble, the father will not let it go.

That walk in the dewy starlight remained forever in Janet's memory as one of those baptismal epochs, when the soul, dipped in the sacred waters of joy and peace, rises from them with new energies, with more unalterable longings.

When she reached home she found Mrs. Pettifer there, anxious for her return. After thanking her for coming, Janet only said, "I have been to Mr. Tryan's; I wanted to speak to him;" and then remembering how she had left the bureau and papers, she went into the back-room, where, apparently, no one had been since she quitted it; for there lay the fragments of glass, and the room was still full of the hateful odor. How feeble and miserable the temptation seemed to her at this moment! She rang for Kitty to come and pick up the fragments and rub the floor, while she herself replaced the papers and locked up the bureau.

The next morning, when seated at breakfast with Mrs. Pettifer, Janet said,

"What a dreary, unhealthy-looking place that is where Mr. Tryan lives! I'm sure it must be very bad for him to live there. Do you know, all this morning, since I've been awake, I've been turning over a little plan in my mind. I think it a charming one—all the more, because *you* are concerned in it."

"Why, what can that be?"

"You know that house on the Redhill road they call Holly Mount; it is shut up now. That is Robert's house; at least, it is mine now, and it stands on one of the healthiest spots about here. Now, I've been settling in my own mind, that if a dear good woman of my acquaintance, who knows how to make a home as comfortable and cosy as a bird's nest, were to take up her abode there, and have Mr. Tryan as a lodger, she would be doing one of the most useful deeds in all her useful life."

"You've such a way of wrapping up things in pretty words. You must speak plainer."

"In plain words, then, I should like to settle you at Holly Mount. You would not have to pay any more rent than where you are, and it would be twenty times pleasanter for you than living up that passage where you see nothing but a brick wall. And then, as it is not far from Paddiford, I think Mr. Tryan might be persuaded to lodge with you, instead of in that musty house, among dead cabbages and smoky cottages. I know you would like to have him live with you, and you would be such a mother to him."

"To be sure I should like it; it would be the finest thing in the world for me. But there'll be furniture wanted. My little bit of furniture won't fill that house."

"Oh, I can put some in out of this house; it is too full; and we can buy the rest. They tell me I'm to have more money than I shall know what to do with."

"I'm almost afraid," said Mrs. Pettifer, doubtfully, "Mr. Tryan will hardly be persuaded. He's been talked to so much about leaving that place; and he always said he must stay there—he must be among the people, and there was no other place for him in Paddiford. It cuts me to the heart to see him getting thinner and thinner, and I've noticed him quite short o' breath sometimes. Mrs. Linnet will have it, Mrs. Wagstaff half poisons him with bad cooking. I don't know about that, but he can't have many comforts. I expect he'll break down all of a sudden some day, and never be able to preach any more."

"Well, I shall try my skill with him by-and-by. I shall be very cunning, and say nothing to him till all is ready. You and I and mother, when she comes home, will set to work directly and get the house in order, and then we'll get you snugly settled in it. I shall see Mr. Pittman to-day, and I will tell him what I mean to do. I shall say I wish to have you for a tenant. Every body knows I'm very fond of that naughty person, Mrs. Pettifer; so it will seem the most natural thing in the world. And then I shall by-and-by point out to Mr. Tryan that he will be doing you a service as well as himself by taking up his abode with you. I think I can prevail upon him; for last night, when he was quite bent on coming out into the night air, I persuaded him to give it up."

"Well, I only hope you may, my dear. I don't desire any thing better than to do something towards prolonging Mr. Tryan's life, for I've sad fears about him."

"Don't speak of them—I can't bear to think of them. We will only think about getting the house ready. We shall be as busy as bees. How we shall want mother's clever fingers! I know the room up stairs that will just do for Mr. Tryan's study. There shall be no seats in it except a very easy chair and a very easy sofa, so that he shall be obliged to rest himself when he comes home."

CHAPTER XXVI.

THAT was the last terrible crisis of temptation Janet had to pass through. The good-will of her neighbors, the helpful sympathy of the friends who shared her religious feelings, the occupations suggested to her by Mr. Tryan, concurred with her strong spontaneous impulses towards works of love and mercy, to fill up her days with quiet social intercourse and charitable exertion. Besides, her constitution, naturally healthy and strong, was every week tending, with the gathering force of habit, to recover its equipoise, and set her free from those physical solicitations which the smallest habitual vice always leaves behind it. The prisoner feels where the iron has galled him, long after his fetters have been loosed.

There were always neighborly visits to be paid and received; and as the months wore on, increasing familiarity with Janet's present self began to efface, even from minds as rigid as Mrs. Phipps's, the unpleasant impressions that had been left by recent years. Janet was recovering the popularity which her beauty and sweetness of nature had won for her when she was a girl; and popularity, as every one knows, is the most complex and self-multiplying of echoes. Even anti-Tryanite prejudice could not resist the fact that Janet Dempster was a changed woman—changed as the dusty, bruised, and sun-withered plant is changed when the soft rains of heaven have fallen on it—and that this change was due to Mr. Tryan's influence. The last lingering sneers against the Evangelical curate began to die out; and though much of the feeling that had prompted them remained behind, there was an intimidating consciousness that the expression of such feeling would not be effective—jokes of that sort had ceased to tickle the Milby mind. Even Mr. Budd and Mr. Tomlinson, when they saw Mr. Tryan passing pale and worn along the street, had a secret sense that this man was somehow not that very natural and comprehensible thing, a humbug—that, in fact, it was impossible to explain him from the stomach-and-pocket point of view. Twist and stretch their theory as they might, it would not fit Mr. Tryan; and so, with that remarkable resemblance as to mental processes which may frequently be observed to exist between plain men and philosophers, they concluded that the less they said about him the better.

Among all Janet's neighborly pleasures, there was nothing she liked better than to take an early tea at the White House, and to stroll with Mr. Jerome round the old-fashioned garden and orchard. There was endless matter for talk between her and the good old man, for Janet had that genuine delight in human fellowship which gives an interest to all personal details that come warm from truthful lips; and, besides, they had a common interest in good-natured plans for helping their poorer neighbors. One great object of Mr. Jerome's charities was, as he often said, "to keep industrious men an' women off the parish. I'd rether given ten shillin' an' help a man to stand on his own legs, nor pay half-a-crown to buy him a parish crutch; it's the ruination on him if he once goes to the parish. I've see'd many a time, if you help a man wi' a present in a neeborly way, it sweetens his blood —he thinks it kind on you; but the parish shillins turn it sour—he niver thinks 'em enough. In illustration of this opinion Mr. Jerome had a large store of details about such persons as Jim Hardy, the coal-carrier, "as lost his hoss," and Sally Butts, "as hed to sell her mangle, though she was as decent a woman as need to be;" to the hearing of which details Janet seriously inclined; and you would hardly desire to see a prettier picture than the kind-faced, white-haired old man telling these fragments of his simple experience as he walked, with shoulders slightly bent, among the moss-roses and espalier apple-trees, while Janet in her widow's cap, her dark eyes bright with interest, went listening by his side, and little Lizzie, with her nankin bonnet hanging down her back, toddled on before them. Mrs. Jerome usually declined these lingering strolls, and often observed, "I niver see the like to Mr. Jerome when he's got Mrs. Dempster to talk to; it sinnifies nothin' to him whether we've tea at four or at five o'clock; he'd go on till six, if you'd let him alone—he's like off his head." However, Mrs. Jerome herself could not deny that Janet was a very pretty-spoken woman: "She aly's says she niver gets sich pikelets as mine nowhere; I know that very well—other folks buy 'em at shops—thick unwholesome things, you might as well eat a sponge."

The sight of little Lizzie often stirred in Janet's mind a sense of the childlessness which had made a fatal blank in her life. She had fleeting thoughts that perhaps among her husband's distant relatives there might be some children whom she could help to bring up, some little girl whom she might adopt; and she promised herself one day or other to hunt out a second cousin of his—a married woman—of whom he had lost sight for many years.

But at present her hands and heart were too full for her

to carry out that scheme. To her great disappointment, her project of settling Mrs. Pettifer at Holly Mount had been delayed by the discovery that some repairs were necessary in order to make the house habitable, and it was not till September had set in that she had the satisfaction of seeing her old friend comfortably installed, and the rooms destined for Mr. Tryan looking pretty and cosy to her heart's content. She had taken several of his chief friends into her confidence, and they were warmly wishing success to her plan for inducing him to quit poor Mrs. Wagstaff's dingy house and dubious cookery. That he should consent to some such change was becoming more and more a matter of anxiety to his hearers; for though no more decided symptoms were yet observable in him than increasing emaciation, a dry hacking cough, and an occasional shortness of breath, it was felt that the fulfillment of Mr. Pratt's prediction could not long be deferred, and that this obstinate persistence in labor and self-disregard must soon be peremptorily cut short by a total failure of strength. Any hopes that the influence of Mr. Tryan's father and sister would prevail on him to change his mode of life—that they would perhaps come to live with him, or that his sister at least might come to see him, and that the arguments which had failed from other lips might be more persuasive from hers—were now quite dissipated. His father had lately had an attack of paralysis, and could not spare his only daughter's tendance. On Mr. Tryan's return from a visit to his father, Miss Linnet was very anxious to know whether his sister had not urged him to try a change of air. From his answers she gathered that Miss Tryan wished him to give up his curacy and travel, or at least go to the south Devonshire coast.

"And why will you not do so?" Miss Linnet said; "you might come back to us well and strong, and have many years of usefulness before you."

"No," he answered quietly, "I think people attach more importance to such measures than is warranted. I don't see any good end that is to be served by going to die at Nice, instead of dying amongst one's friends and one's work. I can not leave Milby—at least I will not leave it voluntarily."

But though he remained immovable on this point, he had been compelled to give up his afternoon service on the Sunday, and to accept Mr. Parry's offer of aid in the evening service, as well as to curtail his weekday labors; and he had even written to Mr. Prendergast to request that he would appoint another curate to the Paddiford district, on the understanding that the new curate should receive the salary, but that Mr. Tryan should co-operate with him as long as he was able. The hopefulness which is an almost constant attendant on consumption, had not the effect of deceiving him as to the nature of his malady, or of making him look forward to ultimate recovery. He believed himself to be consumptive, and he had not yet felt any desire to escape the early death which he had for some time contemplated as probable. Even diseased hopes will take their direction from the strong habitual bias of the mind, and to Mr. Tryan death had for years seemed nothing else than the laying down of a burthen, under which he sometimes felt himself fainting. He was only sanguine about his powers of work: he flattered himself that what he was unable to do one week he should be equal to the next, and he would not admit that in desisting from any part of his labor he was renouncing it permanently. He had lately delighted Mr. Jerome by accepting his long-proffered loan of the "little chacenut hoss;" and he found so much benefit from substituting constant riding exercise for walking, that he began to think he should soon be able to resume some of the work he had dropped.

That was a happy afternoon for Janet, when, after exerting herself busily for a week with her mother and Mrs. Pettifer, she saw Holly Mount looking orderly and comfortable from attic to cellar. It was an old red-brick house, with two gables in front, and two clipped holly-trees flanking the garden-gate; a simple, homely-looking place, that quiet people might easily get fond of; and now it was scoured and polished and carpeted and furnished so as to look really snug within. When there was nothing more to be done, Janet delighted herself with contemplating Mr. Tryan's study, first sitting down in the easy-chair, and then lying for a moment on the sofa, that she might have a keener sense of the repose he would get from those well-stuffed articles of furniture, which she had gone to Rotherby on purpose to choose.

"Now, mother," she said, when she had finished her survey, "you have done your work as well as any fairy-mother or god-mother that ever turned a pumpkin into a coach and horses. You stay and have tea cosily with Mrs. Pettifer while I go to Mrs. Linnet's. I want to tell Mary and Rebecca the good news, that I've got the exciseman to promise that he will take Mrs. Wagstaff's lodgings when Mr. Tryan leaves. They'll be so pleased to hear it, because they thought he would make her poverty an objection to his leaving her."

"But, my dear child," said Mrs. Raynor, whose face, always calm, was now a happy one, "have a cup of tea with us first. You'll perhaps miss Mrs. Linnet's tea-time."

"No, I feel too excited to take tea yet. I'm like a child with a new baby-house. Walking in the air will do me good."

So she set out. Holly Mount was about a mile from that outskirt of Paddiford Common where Mrs. Linnet's house stood nestled among its laburnums, lilacs, and syringas. Janet's way thither lay for a little while along the high-road, and then led her into a deep-rutted lane, which wound through a flat tract of meadow and pasture, while in front lay smoky Paddiford, and away to the left the mother-town of Milby. There was no line of silvery willows marking the course of a stream—no group of Scotch firs with their trunks reddening in the level sunbeams—nothing to break the flowerless monotony of grass and hedgerow but an occasional oak or elm, and a few cows sprinkled here and there. A very commonplace scene, indeed. But what scene was ever commonplace in the descending sunlight, when color has awakened from its noonday sleep, and the long shadows awe us like a disclosed presence? Above all, what scene is commonplace to the eye that is filled with serene gladness, and brightens all things with its own joy?

And Janet just now was very happy. As she walked along the rough lane with a buoyant step, a half smile of innocent, kindly triumph played about her mouth. She was delighting beforehand in the anticipated success of her persuasive power, and for the time her painful anxiety about Mr. Tryan's health was thrown into abeyance. But she had not gone far along the lane before she heard the sound of a horse advancing at a walking pace behind her. Without looking back, she turned aside to make way for it between the ruts, and did not notice that for a moment it had stopped, and had then come on with a slightly quickened pace. In less than a minute she heard a well-known voice say, "Mrs. Dempster;" and, turning, saw Mr. Tryan close to her, holding his horse by the bridle. It seemed very natural to her that he should be there. Her mind was so full of his presence at that moment, that the actual sight of him was only like a more vivid thought, and she behaved, as we are apt to do when feeling obliges us to be genuine, with a total forgetfulness of polite forms. She only looked at him with a slight deepening of the smile that was already on her face. He said gently, "Take my arm;" and they walked on a little way in silence.

It was he who broke it. "You are going to Paddiford, I suppose?"

The question recalled Janet to the consciousness that this

was an unexpected opportunity for beginning her work of persuasion, and that she was stupidly neglecting it.

"Yes," she said, "I was going to Mrs. Linnet's. I knew Miss Linnet would like to hear that our friend Mrs. Pettifer is quite settled now in her new house. She is as fond of Mrs. Pettifer as I am—almost; I won't admit that any one loves her *quite* as well, for no one else has such good reason as I have. But now the dear woman wants a lodger, for you know she can't afford to live in so large a house by herself. But I knew when I persuaded her to go there that she would be sure to get one—she's such a comfortable creature to live with; and I didn't like her to spend all the rest of her days up that dull passage, being at every one's beck and call who wanted to make use of her."

"Yes," said Mr. Tryan, "I quite understand your feeling; I don't wonder at your strong regard for her."

"Well, but now I want her other friends to second me. There she is, with three rooms to let, ready furnished, every thing in order; and I know some one, who thinks as well of her as I do, and who would be doing good all round—to every one that knows him, as well as to Mrs. Pettifer, if he would go to live with her. He would leave some uncomfortable lodgings, which another person is already coveting and would take immediately; and he would go to breathe pure air at Holly Mount, and gladden Mrs. Pettifer's heart by letting her wait on him; and comfort all his friends, who are quite miserable about him."

Mr. Tryan saw it all in a moment—he saw that it had all been done for his sake. He could not be sorry; he could not say no; he could not resist the sense that life had a new sweetness for him, and that he should like it to be prolonged a little, only a little, for the sake of feeling a stronger security about Janet. When she had finished speaking, she looked at him with a doubtful, inquiring glance. He was not looking at her; his eyes were cast downward; but the expression of his face encouraged her, and she said, in a half-playful tone of entreaty,

"You *will* go and live with her? I know you will. You will come back with me now and see the house."

He looked at her then, and smiled. There is an unspeakable blending of sadness and sweetness in the smile of a face sharpened and paled by slow consumption. That smile of Mr. Tryan's pierced poor Janet's heart: she felt in it at once the assurance of grateful affection and the prophecy of coming death. Her tears rose; they turned round without speaking, and went back again along the lane.

CHAPTER XXVII.

In less than a week Mr. Tryan was settled at Holly Mount, and there was not one of his many attached hearers who did not sincerely rejoice at the event.

The autumn that year was bright and warm, and at the beginning of October, Mr. Walsh, the new curate, came. The mild weather, the relaxation from excessive work, and perhaps another benignant influence, had for a few weeks a visibly favorable effect on Mr. Tryan. At least he began to feel new hopes, which sometimes took the guise of new strength. He thought of the cases in which consumptive patients remain nearly stationary for years, without suffering so as to make their life burthensome to themselves or to others; and he began to struggle with a longing that it might be so with him. He struggled with it, because he felt it to be an indication that earthly affection was beginning to have too strong a hold on him, and he prayed earnestly for more perfect submission, and for a more absorbing delight in the Divine Presence as the chief good. He was conscious that he did not wish for prolonged life solely that he might reclaim the wanderers and sustain the feeble: he was conscious of a new yearning for those pure human joys which he had voluntarily and determinedly banished from his life—for a draught of that deep affection from which he had been cut off by a dark chasm of remorse. For now, that affection was within his reach; he saw it there, like a palm-shadowed well in the desert; he *could* not desire to die in sight of it.

And so the autumn rolled gently by in its "calm decay." Until November, Mr. Tryan continued to preach occasionally, to ride about visiting his flock, and to look in at his schools; but his growing satisfaction in Mr. Walsh as his successor saved him from too eager exertion and from worrying anxieties. Janet was with him a great deal now, for she saw that he liked her to read to him in the lengthening evenings, and it became the rule for her and her mother to have tea at Holly Mount, where, with Mrs. Pettifer, and sometimes another friend or two, they brought Mr. Tryan the unaccustomed enjoyment of companionship by his own fireside.

Janet did not share his new hopes, for she was not only in the habit of hearing Mr. Pratt's opinion that Mr. Tryan could hardly stand out through the winter, but she also knew that

It was shared by Dr. Madely, of Rotherby, whom, at her request, he had consented to call in. It was not necessary or desirable to tell Mr. Tryan what was revealed by the stethoscope, but Janet knew the worst.

She felt no rebellion under this prospect of bereavement, but rather a quiet submissive sorrow. Gratitude that his influence and guidance had been given her, even if only for a little while—gratitude that she was permitted to be with him, to take a deeper and deeper impress from daily communion with him, to be something to him in these last months of his life, was so strong in her that it almost silenced regret. Janet had lived through the great tragedy of woman's life. Her keenest personal emotions had been poured forth in her early love—her wounded affection with its years of anguish—her agony of unavailing pity over that deathbed seven months ago. The thought of Mr. Tryan was associated for her with repose from that conflict of emotion, with trust in the unchangeable, with the influx of a power to subdue self. To have been assured of his sympathy, his teaching, his help, all through her life, would have been to her like a heaven already begun—a deliverance from fear and danger; but the time was not yet come for her to be conscious that the hold he had on her heart was any other than that of the heaven-sent friend who had come to her like the angel in the prison, and loosed her bonds, and led her by the hand till she could look back on the dreadful doors that had once closed her in.

Before November was over, Mr. Tryan had ceased to go out. A new crisis had come on: the cough had changed its character, and the worst symptoms developed themselves so rapidly that Mr. Pratt began to think the end would arrive sooner than he had expected. Janet became a constant attendant on him now, and no one could feel that she was performing any thing but a sacred office. She made Holly Mount her home, and, with her mother and Mrs. Pettifer to help her, she filled the painful days and nights with every soothing influence that care and tenderness could devise. There were many visitors to the sick-room, led thither by venerating affection; and there could hardly be one who did not retain in after years a vivid remembrance of the scene there—of the pale wasted form in the easy-chair (for he sat up to the last), of the gray eyes so full even yet of inquiring kindness, as the thin, almost transparent hand was held out to give the pressure of welcome; and of the sweet woman, too, whose dark watchful eyes detected every want, and who supplied the want with a ready hand.

There were others who would have had the heart and the skill to fill this place by Mr. Tryan's side, and who would have accepted it as an honor; but they could not help feeling that God had given it to Janet by a train of events which were too impressive not to shame all jealousies into silence.

That sad history which most of us know too well, lasted more than three months. He was too feeble and suffering for the last few weeks to see any visitors, but he still sat up through the day. The strange hallucinations of the disease which had seemed to take a more decided hold on him just at the fatal crisis, and had made him think he was perhaps getting better at the very time when death had begun to hurry on with more rapid movement, had now given way and left him calmly conscious of the reality. One afternoon, near the end of February, Janet was moving gently about the room, in the fire-lit dusk, arranging some things that would be wanted in the night. There was no one else in the room, and his eyes followed her as she moved with the firm grace natural to her, while the bright fire every now and then lit up her face, and gave an unusual glow to its dark beauty. Even to follow her in this way with his eyes was an exertion that gave a painful tension to his face, while *she* looked like an image of life and strength.

"Janet," he said presently, in his faint voice—he always called her Janet now. In a moment she was close to him, bending over him. He opened his hand as he looked up at her, and she placed hers within it.

"Janet," he said again, "you will have a long while to live after I am gone."

A sudden pang of fear shot through her. She thought he felt himself dying, and she sank on her knees at his feet, holding his hand, while she looked up at him, almost breathless.

"But you will not feel the need of me as you have done. . . . You have a sure trust in God. . . . I shall not look for you in vain at the last."

"No . . . no. . . . I shall be there. . . . God will not forsake me."

She could hardly utter the words, though she was not weeping. She was waiting with trembling eagerness for any thing else he might have to say.

"Let us kiss each other before we part."

She lifted up her face to his, and the full life-breathing lips met the wasted dying ones in a sacred kiss of promise.

CHAPTER XXVIII.

It soon came—the blessed day of deliverance, the sad day of bereavement; and in the second week of March they carried him to the grave. He was buried as he had desired: there was no hearse, no mourning-coach; his coffin was borne by twelve of his humbler hearers, who relieved each other by turns. But he was followed by a long procession of mourning friends, women as well as men.

Slowly, amid deep silence, the dark stream passed along Orchard Street, where eighteen months before the Evangelical curate had been saluted with hooting and hisses. Mr. Jerome and Mr. Landor were the eldest pall-bearers; and behind the coffin, led by Mr. Tryan's cousin, walked Janet, in quiet submissive sorrow. She could not feel that he was quite gone from her; the unseen world lay so very near her—it held all that had ever stirred the depths of anguish and joy within her.

It was a cloudy morning, and had been raining when they left Holly Mount; but as they walked, the sun broke out, and the clouds were rolling off in large masses when they entered the churchyard, and Mr. Walsh's voice was heard saying, "I am the Resurrection and the Life." The faces were not hard at this funeral; the burial-service was not a hollow form. Every heart there was filled with the memory of a man who, through a self-sacrificing life and in a painful death, had been sustained by the faith which fills that form with breath and substance.

When Janet left the grave, she did not return to Holly Mount; she went to her home in Orchard Street, where her mother was waiting to receive her. She said quite calmly, "Let us walk round the garden, mother." And they walked round in silence, with their hands clasped together, looking at the golden crocuses bright in the spring sunshine. Janet felt a deep stillness within. She thirsted for no pleasure; she craved no worldly good. She saw the years to come stretch before her like an autumn afternoon, filled with resigned memory. Life to her could never more have any eagerness; it was a solemn service of gratitude and patient effort. She walked in the presence of unseen witnesses—of the Divine love that had rescued her, of the human love that waited for its eternal repose until it had seen her endure to the end.

Janet is living still. Her black hair is gray, and her step is no longer buoyant; but the sweetness of her smile remains, the love is not gone from her eyes; and strangers sometimes ask, Who is that noble-looking elderly woman, that walks about holding a little boy by the hand? The little boy is the son of Janet's adopted daughter, and Janet in her old age has children about her knees, and loving young arms round her neck.

There is a simple gravestone in Milby churchyard, telling that in this spot lie the remains of Edgar Tryan, for two years officiating curate at the Paddiford Chapel-of-Ease, in this parish. It is a meagre memorial, and tells you simply that the man who lies there took upon him, faithfully or unfaithfully, the office of guide and instructor to his fellow-men.

But there is another memorial of Edgar Tryan, which bears a fuller record: it is Janet Dempster, rescued from self-despair, strengthened with divine hopes, and now looking back on years of purity and helpful labor. The man who has left such a memorial behind him, must have been one whose heart beat with true compassion, and whose lips were moved by fervent faith.

THE END OF "SCENES OF CLERICAL LIFE."

SILAS MARNER:

THE WEAVER OF RAVELOE.

BY

GEORGE ELIOT.

"A child, more than all other gifts
That earth can offer to declining man,
Brings hope with it, and forward-looking thoughts."
WORDSWORTH.

HARPER'S LIBRARY EDITION.

NEW YORK:
HARPER & BROTHERS, PUBLISHERS,
FRANKLIN SQUARE.

SILAS MARNER:

THE WEAVER OF RAVELOE.

PART I.

CHAPTER I.

In the days when the spinning-wheels hummed busily in the farmhouses—and even great ladies, clothed in silk and thread-lace, had their toy spinning-wheels of polished oak—there might be seen in districts far away among the lanes, or deep in the bosom of the hills, certain pallid undersized men, who, by the side of the brawny country-folk, looked like the remnants of a disinherited race. The shepherd's dog barked fiercely when one of these alien-looking men appeared on the upland, dark against the early winter sunset; for what dog likes a figure bent under a heavy bag?—and these pale men rarely stirred abroad without that mysterious burden. The shepherd himself, though he had good reason to believe that the bag held nothing but flaxen thread, or else the long rolls of strong linen spun from that thread, was not quite sure that this trade of weaving, indispensable though it was, could be carried on entirely without the help of the Evil One. In that far-off time superstition clung easily round every person or thing that was at all unwonted, or even intermittent and occasional merely, like the visits of the peddler or the knife-grinder. No one knew where wandering men had their homes or their origin; and how was a man to be explained unless you at least knew somebody who knew his father and mother? To the peasants of old times, the world outside their own direct experience was a region of vagueness and mystery: to their untravelled thought a state of wandering was a conception as dim as the winter life of the swallows that came back with the spring; and even a settler, if he came from distant parts, hardly ever ceased to be viewed with a remnant of distrust, which would have prevented any surprise if a long course of inoffensive conduct on his part had ended in the commission of a crime; especially if he had any reputation for knowledge, or showed any skill in handicraft. All cleverness, whether in the rapid use of that difficult instrument the tongue, or in some other art unfamiliar to villagers, was in itself suspicious: honest folks, born and bred in a visible manner, were mostly not over-wise or clever —at least not beyond such a matter as knowing the signs of the weather; and the process by which rapidity and dexterity of any kind were acquired was so wholly hidden, that they partook of the nature of conjuring. In this way it came to pass that those scattered linen-weavers—emigrants from the town into the country—were to the last regarded as aliens by their rustic neighbors, and usually contracted the eccentric habits which belong to a state of loneliness.

In the early years of this century, such a linen-weaver, named Silas Marner, worked at his vocation in a stone cottage that stood among the nutty hedgerows near the village of Raveloe, and not far from the edge of a deserted stone-pit. The questionable sound of Silas's loom, so unlike the natural cheerful trotting of the winnowing machine, or the simpler rhythm of the flail, had a half-fearful fascination for the Raveloe boys, who would often leave off their nutting or birds'-nesting to peep in at the window of the stone cottage, counterbalancing a certain awe at the mysterious action of the loom, by a pleasant sense of scornful superiority, drawn from the mockery of its alternating noises, along with the bent, tread-mill attitude of the weaver. But sometimes it happened that Marner, pausing to adjust an irregularity in his thread, became aware of the small scoundrels, and, though chary of his time, he liked their intrusion so ill that he would descend from his loom, and, opening the door, would fix on them a gaze that was always enough to make them take to their legs in terror. For how was it possible to believe that those large brown protuberant eyes in Silas Marner's pale face really saw nothing very distinctly that was not close to them and not rather that their dreadful stare could dart cramp, or rickets, or a wry mouth at any boy who happened to be in the rear? They had, perhaps, heard their fathers and mothers hint that Silas Marner could cure folks' rheumatism if he had a mind, and add, still more darkly, that if you could only speak the devil fair enough, he might save you the cost of the doctor. Such strange lingering echoes of the old demon-worship might perhaps even now be caught by the diligent listener among the gray-haired peasantry; for the rude mind with difficulty associates the ideas of power and benignity. A shadowy conception of power that by much persuasion can be induced to refrain from inflicting harm, is the shape most easily taken by the sense of the Invisible in the minds of men who have always been pressed close by primitive wants, and to whom a life of hard toil has never been illuminated by any enthusiastic religious faith. To them pain and mishap present a far wider range of possibilities than gladness and enjoyment: their imagination is almost barren of the images that feed desire and hope, but is all overgrown by recollections that are a perpetual pasture to fear. "Is there any thing you can fancy that you would like to eat?" I once said to an old laboring man, who was in his last illness, and who had refused all the food his wife had offered him. "No," he answered, "I've never been used to nothing but common victual, and I can't eat that." Experience had bred no fancies in him that could raise the phantasm of appetite.

And Raveloe was a village where many of the old echoes lingered, undrowned by new voices. Not that it was one of those barren parishes lying on the outskirts of civilization —inhabited by meagre sheep and thinly-scattered shepherds; on the contrary, it lay in the rich central plain of what we are pleased to call Merry England, and held farms which, speaking from a spiritual point of view, paid highly-desirable tithes. But it was nestled in a snug well-wooded hollow, quite an hour's journey on horseback from any turnpike, where it was never reached by the vibrations of the coach-horn, or of public opinion. It was an important-looking village, with a fine old church and large churchyard in the heart of it, and two or three large brick-and-stone homesteads, with well-walled orchards and ornamental weathercocks, standing close upon the road, and lifting more imposing fronts than the rectory, which peeped from among the trees on the other side of the churchyard; a village which showed at once the summits of its social life, and told the practised eye that there was no great park and manor-house in the vicinity, but that there were several chiefs in Raveloe who could farm badly quite at their ease, drawing enough money from their bad farming, in those war times, to live in a rollicking fashion, and keep a jolly Christmas, Whitsun, and Easter tide.

It was fifteen years since Silas Marner had first come to Raveloe; he was then simply a pallid young man, with prominent, short-sighted brown eyes, whose appearance would have had nothing strange for people of average culture and experience, but for the villagers near whom he had come to settle it had mysterious peculiarities which corresponded with the exceptional nature of his occupation, and his advent from an unknown region called "North'ard." So had his way of life: he invited no comer to step across his door-sill, and he never strolled into the village to drink a pint at the Rainbow, or to gossip at the wheelwright's: he sought no man or woman, save for the purposes of his calling, or in order to supply himself with necessaries; and it was soon clear to the Raveloe lasses that he would never urge one of them to accept him against her will—quite as if he had heard them declare that they would never marry a dead man come to life again. This view of Marner's personality was not without another ground than his pale face and unexampled eyes; for Jem Rodney, the mole-catcher, averred that, one evening as he was returning homeward, he saw Silas Marner leaning against a stile with a heavy bag on his back, instead of resting the bag on the stile as a man in his senses would have done; and that, on coming up to him, he saw that Marner's eyes were set like a dead man's, and he spoke to him, and shook him, and his limbs were stiff, and his hands clutched the bag as if they'd been made of iron; but just as he had made up his mind that the weaver was dead, he came all right again, like, as you might say, in the winking of an eye, and said "Good-night," and walked off. All this Jem swore he had seen, more by token that it was the very day he had been mole-catching on Squire Cass's land, down by the old saw-pit. Some said Marner must have been in a "fit," a word which seemed to explain things otherwise incredible; but the argumentative Mr. Macey, clerk of the parish, shook his head, and asked if any body was ever known to go off in a fit and not fall down. A fit was a stroke, wasn't it? and it was in the nature of a stroke to partly take away the use of a man's limbs and throw him on the parish, if he'd got no children to look to. No, no; it was no stroke that would let a man stand on his legs, like a horse between the shafts, and then walk off as soon as you can say "Gee!" But there might be such a thing as a man's soul being loose from his body, and going out and in, like a bird out of its nest and back; and that was how folks got over-wise, for they went to school in this shell-less state to those who could teach them more than their neighbors could learn with their five senses and the parson. And where did Master Marner get his knowledge of herbs from—and charms too, if he liked to give them away? Jem Rodney's story was no more than what might have been expected by any body who had seen how Marner had cured Sally Oates, and made her sleep like a baby, when her heart had been beating enough to burst her body, for two months and more, while she had been under the doctor's care. He might cure more folks if he would; but he was worth speaking fair, if it was only to keep him from doing you a mischief.

It was partly to this vague fear that Marner was indebted for protecting him from the persecution that his singularities might have drawn upon him, but still more to the fact that, the old linen-weaver in the neighboring parish of Tarley being dead, his handicraft made him a highly welcome settler to the richer housewives of the district, and even to the more provident cottagers, who had their little stock of yarn at the year's end; and their sense of his usefulness would have counteracted any repugnance or suspicion which was not confirmed by a deficiency in the quality or the tale of the cloth he wove for them. And the years had rolled on without producing any change in the impressions of the neighbors concerning Marner, except the change from novelty to habit. At the end of fifteen years the Raveloe men said just the same things about Silas Marner as at the beginning: they did not say them quite so often, but they believed them much more strongly when they did say them. There was only one important addition which the years had brought: it was, that Master Marner had laid by a fine sight of money somewhere, and that he could buy up "bigger men" than himself.

But while opinion concerning him had remained nearly

stationary, and his daily habits had presented scarcely any visible change, Marner's inward life had been a history and a metamorphosis, as that of every fervid nature must be when it has fled, or been condemned to solitude. His life, before he came to Raveloe, had been filled with the movement, the mental activity, and the close fellowship which, in that day as in this, marked the life of an artisan early incorporated in a narrow religious sect, where the poorest layman has the chance of distinguishing himself by gifts of speech, and has, at the very least, the weight of a silent voter in the government of his community. Marner was highly thought of in that little hidden world, known to itself as the church assembling in Lantern Yard; he was believed to be a young man of exemplary life and ardent faith; and a peculiar interest had been centred in him ever since he had fallen, at a prayer-meeting, into a mysterious rigidity and suspension of consciousness, which, lasting for an hour or more, had been mistaken for death. To have sought a medical explanation for this phenomenon would have been held by Silas himself, as well as by his minister and fellow-members, a willful self-exclusion from the spiritual significance that might lie therein. Silas was evidently a brother selected for a peculiar discipline, and though the effort to interpret this discipline was discouraged by the absence, on his part, of any spiritual vision during his outward trance, yet it was believed by himself and others that its effect was seen in an accession of light and fervor. A less truthful man than him might have been tempted into the subsequent creation of a vision in the form of resurgent memory; a less sane man might have believed in such a creation; but Silas was both sane and honest, though, as with many honest and fervent men, culture had not defined any channels for his sense of mystery, and so it spread itself over the proper pathway of inquiry and knowledge. He had inherited from his mother some acquaintance with medicinal herbs and their preparation—a little store of wisdom which she had imparted to him as a solemn bequest—but of late years he had had doubts about the lawfulness of applying this knowledge, believing that herbs could have no efficacy without prayer, and that prayer might suffice without herbs; so that the inherited delight he had in wandering in the fields in search of foxglove and dandelion and coltsfoot, began to wear to him the character of a temptation.

Among the members of his church there was one young man, a little older than himself, with whom he had long lived in such close friendship that it was the custom of their Lantern Yard brethren to call them David and Jonathan. The real name of the friend was William Dane, and he, too, was regarded as a shining instance of youthful piety, though somewhat given to over-severity towards weaker brethren, and to be so dazzled by his own light as to hold himself wiser than his teachers. But whatever blemishes others might discern in William, to his friend's mind he was faultless; for Marner had one of those impressible self-doubting natures which, at an inexperienced age, admire imperativeness and lean on contradiction. The expression of trusting simplicity in Marner's face, heightened by that absence of special observation, that defenseless, deer-like gaze which belongs to large prominent eyes, was strongly contrasted by the self-complacent suppression of inward triumph that lurked in the narrow slanting eyes and compressed lips of William Dane. One of the most frequent topics of conversation between the two friends was Assurance of salvation: Silas confessed that he could never arrive at any thing higher than hope mingled with fear, and listened with longing wonder when William declared that he had possessed unshaken assurance ever since, in the period of his conversion, he had dreamed that he saw the words "calling and election sure" standing by themselves on a white page in the open Bible. Such colloquies have occupied many a pair of pale-faced weavers, whose unnurtured souls have been like young winged things, fluttering forsaken in the twilight.

It had seemed to the unsuspecting Silas that the friendship had suffered no chill even from his formation of another attachment of a closer kind. For some months he had been engaged to a young servant-woman, waiting only for a little increase to their mutual savings in order to their marriage; and it was a great delight to him that Sarah did not object to William's occasional presence in their Sunday interviews. It was at this point in their history that Silas's cataleptic fit occurred during the prayer-meeting; and amidst the various queries and expressions of interest addressed to him by his fellow-members, William's suggestion alone jarred with the general sympathy towards a brother thus singled out for special dealings. He observed that, to him, this trance looked more like a visitation of Satan than a proof of divine favor, and exhorted his friend to see that he hid no accursed thing within his soul. Silas, feeling bound to accept rebuke and admonition as a brotherly office, felt no resentment, but only pain, at his friend's doubts concerning him; and to this was soon added some anxiety at the perception that Sarah's manner towards him began to exhibit a strange fluctuation between an effort at an increased manifestation of regard and involuntary signs of shrinking and dislike. He asked her if she wished to break off their engagement; but she denied this: their engagement was known to the church, and had been recognized in the prayer-meetings; it could not be broken off without strict investigation, and Sarah could render no reason that would be sanctioned by the feeling of the community. At this time the senior deacon was taken dangerously ill, and, being a childless widower, he was tended night and day by some of the younger brethren or sisters. Silas frequently took his turn in the night-watching with William, the one relieving the other at two in the morning. The old man, contrary to expectation, seemed to be on the way to recovery, when one night Silas, sitting up by his bedside, observed that his usual audible breathing had ceased. The candle was burning low, and he had to lift it to see the patient's face distinctly. Examination convinced him that the deacon was dead—had been dead some time, for the limbs were rigid. Silas asked himself if he had been asleep, and looked at the clock: it was already four in the morning. How was it that William had not come? In much anxiety he went to seek for help, and soon there were several friends assembled in the house, the minister among them, while Silas went away to his work, wishing he could have met William to know the reason of his non-appearance. But at six o'clock, as he was thinking of going to seek his friend, William came, and with him the minister. They came to summon him to Lantern Yard, to meet the church members there; and to his inquiry concerning the cause of the summons the only reply was, "You will hear." Nothing further was said until Silas was seated in the vestry, in front of the minister, with the eyes of those who to him represented God's people fixed solemnly upon him. Then the minister, taking out a pocket-knife, showed it to Silas, and asked him if he knew where he had left that knife? Silas said, he did not know that he had left it anywhere out of his own pocket—but he was trembling at this strange interrogation. He was then exhorted not to hide his sin, but to confess and repent. The knife had been found in the bureau by the departed deacon's bedside—found in the place where the little bag of church money had lain, which the minister himself had seen the day before. Some hand had removed that bag; and whose hand could it be, if not that of the man to whom the knife belonged? For some time Silas was mute with astonishment: then he said, "God will clear me: I know nothing about the knife being there, or the money being gone. Search me and my dwelling; you will find nothing but three pound five of my own savings, which William Dane knows I have had these six months." At this William groaned, but the minister said, "The proof is heavy against you, brother Marner. The money was taken in the night last past, and no man was with our departed brother but you, for William Dane declares to us that he was hindered by sudden sickness from going to take his place as usual, and you yourself said that he had not come; and, moreover, you neglected the dead body."

' I must have slept," said Silas. Then, after a pause, he added, " Or I must have had another visitation like that which you have all seen me under, so that the thief must have come and gone while I was not in the body, but out of the body. But, I say again, search me and my dwelling, for I have been nowhere else."

The search was made, and it ended—in William Dane's finding the well-known bag, empty, tucked behind the chest of drawers in Silas's chamber! On this William exhorted his friend to confess, and not to hide his sin any longer. Silas turned a look of keen reproach on him, and said, " William, for nine years that we have gone in and out together, have you ever known me tell a lie? But God will clear me."

" Brother," said William, " how do I know what you may have done in the secret chambers of your heart, to give Satan an advantage over you?"

Silas was still looking at his friend. Suddenly a deep flush came over his face, and he was about to speak impetuously, when he seemed checked again by some inward shock, that sent the flush back and made him tremble. But at last he spoke feebly, looking at William.

" I remember now—the knife wasn't in my pocket."

William said, " I know nothing of what you mean." The other persons present, however, began to inquire where Silas meant to say that the knife was, but he would give no further explanation: he only said, " I am sore stricken; I can say nothing. God will clear me."

On their return to the vestry there was further deliberation. Any resort to legal measures for ascertaining the culprit was contrary to the principles of the Church: prosecution was held by them to be forbidden to Christians, even if it had been a case in which there was no scandal to the community. But they were bound to take other measures for finding out the truth, and they resolved on praying and drawing lots. This resolution can be a ground of surprise only to those who are unacquainted with that obscure religious life which has gone on in the alleys of our towns. Silas knelt with his brethren, relying on his own innocence being certified by immediate divine interference, but feeling that there was sorrow and mourning behind for him even then—that his trust in man had been cruelly bruised. *The lots declared that Silas Marner was guilty.* He was solemnly suspended from church-membership, and called upon to render up the stolen money: only on confession, as the sign of repentance, could he be received once more within the fold of the church. Marner listened in silence. At last, when every one rose to depart, he went towards William Dane and said, in a voice shaken by agitation—

"The last time I remember using my knife, was when I took it out to cut a strap for you. I don't remember putting it in my pocket again. *You* stole the money, and you have woven a plot to lay the sin at my door. But you may prosper, for all that: there is no just God that governs the earth righteously, but a God of lies, that bears witness against the innocent."

There was a general shudder at this blasphemy.

William said meekly, "I leave our brethren to judge whether this is the voice of Satan or not. I can do nothing but pray for you, Silas."

Poor Marner went out with that despair in his soul—that shaken trust in God and man, which is little short of madness to a loving nature. In the bitterness of his wounded spirit, he said to himself, "*She* will cast me off too." And he reflected that, if she did not believe the testimony against him, her whole faith must be upset as his was. To people accustomed to reason about the forms in which their religious feeling has incorporated itself, it is difficult to enter into that simple, untaught state of mind in which the form and the feeling have never been severed by an act of reflection. We are apt to think it inevitable that a man in Marner's position should have begun to question the validity of an appeal to the divine judgment by drawing lots; but to him this would have been an effort of independent thought such as he had never known; and he must have made the effort at a moment when all his energies were turned into the anguish of disappointed faith. If there is an angel who records the sorrows of men as well as their sins, he knows how many and deep are the sorrows that spring from false ideas for which no man is culpable.

Marner went home, and for a whole day sat alone, stunned by despair, without any impulse to go to Sarah and attempt to win her belief in his innocence. The second day he took refuge from benumbing unbelief, by getting into his loom and working away as usual; and before many hours were past, the minister and one of the deacons came to him with the message from Sarah, that she held her engagement to him at an end.

Silas received the message mutely, and then turned away from the messengers to work at his loom again. In little more than a month from that time, Sarah was married to William Dane; and not long afterwards it was known to the brethren in Lantern Yard that Silas Marner had departed from the town.

CHAPTER II.

EVEN people whose lives have been made various by learning, sometimes find it hard to keep a fast hold on their habitual views of life, on their faith in the Invisible—nay, on the sense that their past joys and sorrows are a real experience, when they are suddenly transported to a new land, where the beings around them know nothing of their history, and share none of their ideas—where their mother earth shows another lap, and human life has other forms than those on which their souls have been nourished. Minds that have been unhinged from their old faith and love, have perhaps sought this Lethean influence of exile, in which the past becomes dreamy because its symbols have all vanished, and the present too is dreamy because it is linked with no memories. But even *their* experience may hardly enable them thoroughly to imagine what was the effect on a simple weaver like Silas Marner, when he left his own country and people and came to settle in Raveloe. Nothing could be more unlike his native town, set within sight of the wide-spread hillsides, than this low, wooded region, where he felt hidden even from the heavens by the screening trees and hedge-rows. There was nothing here, when he rose in the deep morning quiet and looked out on the dewy brambles and rank tufted grass, that seemed to have any relation with that life centring in Lantern Yard, which had once been to him the altar-place of high dispensations. The white-washed walls; the little pews where well-known figures entered with a subdued rustling, and where first one well-known voice and then another, pitched in a peculiar key of petition, uttered phrases at once occult and familiar, like the amulet worn on the heart; the pulpit where the minister delivered unquestioned doctrine, and swayed to and fro, and handled the book in a long accustomed manner; the very pauses between the couplets of the hymn, as it was given out, and the recurrent swell of voices in song; these things had been the channel of divine influences to Marner—they were the fostering home of his religious emotions—they were Christianity and God's kingdom upon earth. A weaver who finds hard words in his hymn-book knows nothing of abstractions; as the little child knows nothing of parental love, but only knows one face and one lap towards which it stretches its arms for refuge and nurture.

And what could be more unlike that Lantern Yard world than the world in Raveloe?—orchards looking lazy with neglected plenty; the large church in the wide churchyard; which men gazed at lounging at their own doors in service-time; the purple-faced farmers jogging along the lanes or turning in at the Rainbow; homesteads, where men supped heavily and slept in the light of the evening hearth, and where women seemed to be laying up a stock of linen for the life to come. There were no lips in Raveloe from which a word could fall that would stir Silas Marner's benumbed faith to a sense of pain. In the early ages of the world, we know, it was believed that each territory was inhabited and ruled by its own divinities, so that a man could cross the bordering heights and be out of the reach of his native gods, whose presence was confined to the streams and the groves and the hills among which he had lived from his birth. And poor Silas was vaguely conscious of something not unlike the feeling of primitive men, when they fled thus, in fear or in sullenness, from the face of an unpropitious deity. It seemed to him that the Power in which he had vainly trusted among the streets and in the prayer-meetings, was very far away from this land in which he had taken refuge, where men lived in careless abundance, knowing and needing nothing of that trust, which, for him, had been turned to bitterness. The little light he possessed spread its beams so narrowly, that frustrated belief was a curtain broad enough to create for him the blackness of night.

His first movement after the shock had been to work in his loom; and he went on with this unremittingly, never asking himself why, now he was come to Raveloe, he worked far on into the night to finish the tale of Mrs. Osgood's table-linen sooner than she expected—without contemplating beforehand the money she would put into his hand for the work. He seemed to weave, like the spider, from pure impulse, without reflection. Every man's work, pursued steadily, tends in this way to become an end in itself, and so to bridge over the loveless chasms of his life. Silas's hand satisfied itself with throwing the shuttle, and his eye with seeing the little squares in the cloth complete themselves under his effort. Then there were the calls of hunger; and Silas, in his solitude, had to provide his own breakfast, dinner, and supper, to fetch his own water from the well, and put his own kettle on the fire; and all these immediate promptings helped, along with the weaving, to reduce his life to the unquestioning activity of a spinning insect. He hated the thought of the past; there was nothing that called out his love and fellowship towards the strangers he had come amongst; and the future was all dark, for there was no Unseen Love that cared for him. Thought was arrested by utter bewilderment, now its old narrow pathway was closed, and affection seemed to have died under the bruise that had fallen on its keenest nerves.

But at last Mrs. Osgood's table-linen was finished, and Silas was paid in gold. His earnings in his native town, where he worked for a wholesale dealer, had been after a lower rate; he had been paid weekly, and of his weekly earnings a large proportion had gone to objects of piety and charity. Now, for the first time in his life, he had five bright guineas put into his hand; no man expected a share of them, and he loved no man that he should offer him a share. But what were the guineas to him who saw no vista beyond countless days of weaving? It was needless for him to ask that, for it was pleasant to him to feel them in his palm, and look at their bright faces, which were all his own: it was another element of life, like the weaving and the satisfaction of hunger, subsisting quite aloof from the life of belief and love from which he had been cut off. The weaver's hand had known the touch of hard-won money even before the palm had grown to its full breadth; for twenty years, mysterious money had stood to him as the symbol of earthly good, and the immediate object of toil. He had seemed to love it little in the years when every penny had its purpose for him; for he loved the *purpose* then. But now, when all purpose was gone, that habit of looking towards the money and grasping it with a sense of fulfilled effort made a loam that was deep enough for the seeds of desire; and as Silas walked homeward across the fields in the twilight, he drew out the money, and thought it was brighter in the gathering gloom.

About this time an incident happened which seemed to open a possibility of some fellowship with his neighbors. One day, taking a pair of shoes to be mended, he saw the cobbler's wife seated by the fire, suffering from the terrible symptoms of heart-disease and dropsy, which he had witnessed as the precursors of his mother's death. He felt a rush of pity at the mingled sight and remembrance, and, recalling the relief his mother had found from a simple preparation of foxglove, he promised Sally Oates to bring her something that would ease her, since the doctor did her no good. In this office of charity, Silas felt, for the first time since he had come to Raveloe, a sense of unity between his past and present life, which might have been the beginning of his rescue from the insect-like existence into which his nature had shrunk. But Sally Oates's disease had raised her into a personage of much interest and importance among the neighbors, and the fact of her having found relief from drinking Silas Marner's "stuff" became a matter of general discourse. When Doctor Kimble gave physic, it was natural that it should have an effect; but when a weaver, who came from nobody knew where, worked wonders with a bottle of brown waters, the occult character of the process was evident. Such a sort of thing had not been known since the Wise Woman at Tarley died; and she had charms as well as "stuff:" every body went to her when their children had fits. Silas Marner must be a person of the same sort, for how did he know what would bring back Sally Oates's breath, if he didn't know a fine sight more than that? The Wise Woman had words that she muttered to herself, so that you couldn't hear what they were, and if she tied a bit of red thread round the child's toe the while, it would keep off the water in the head. There were women in Raveloe, at that present time, who had worn one of the Wise Woman's little bags round their necks, and, in consequence, had never had an idiot child, as Ann Coulter had. Silas Marner could very likely do as much, and more; and now it was all clear how he should have come from unknown parts, and be so "comical-looking." But Sally Oates must mind and not tell the doctor, for he would be sure to set his face against Marner; he was always angry about the Wise Woman, and used to threaten those who went to her that they should have none of his help any more.

Silas now found himself and his cottage suddenly beset by mothers who wanted him to charm away the whooping-cough, or bring back the milk, and by men who wanted stuff against the rheumatics or the knots in the hands; and, to secure themselves against a refusal, the applicants brought silver in their palms. Silas might have driven a profitable trade in charms as well as in his small list of drugs; but money on this condition was no temptation to him: he had never known an impulse towards falsity, and he drove one after another away with growing irritation, for the news of him as a wise man had spread even to Tarley, and it was long before people ceased to take long walks for the sake of asking his aid. But the hope in his wisdom was at length changed into dread, for no one believed him when he said he knew no charms and could work no cures, and every man and woman who had an accident or a new attack after applying to him, set the misfortune down to Master Marner's ill-will and irritated glances. Thus it came to pass that his movement of pity towards Sally Oates, which had given him a transient sense of brotherhood, heightened the repulsion between him and his neighbors, and made his isolation more complete.

Gradually the guineas, the crowns, and the half-crowns, grew to a heap, and Marner drew less and less for his own wants, trying to solve the problem of keeping himself strong enough to work sixteen hours a day on as small an outlay as possible. Have not men, shut up in solitary imprisonment, found an interest in marking the moments by straight strokes of a certain length on the wall, until the growth of the sum of straight strokes, arranged in triangles, has become a mastering purpose? Do we not while away moments of inanity or fatigued waiting by repeating some trivial movement or sound, until the repetition has bred a want, which is incipient habit? That will help us to understand how the love of accumulating money grows an absorbing passion in men whose imaginations, even in the very beginning of their hoard, showed them no purpose beyond it. Marner wanted the heaps of ten to grow into a square, and then into a larger square; and every added guinea, while it was itself a satisfaction, bred a new desire. In this strange world, made a hopeless riddle to him, he might, if he had had a less intense nature, have sat weaving, weaving—looking towards the end of his pattern, or towards the end of his web, till he forgot the riddle, and every thing else but his immediate sensations: but the money had come to mark off his weaving into periods, and the money not only grew, but it remained with him. He began to think it was conscious of him, as his loom was, and he would on no account have exchanged those coins, which had become his familiars, for other coins with unknown faces. He handled them, he counted them, till their form and color were like the satisfaction of a thirst to him: but it was only in the night, when his work was done, that he drew them out to enjoy their companionship. He had taken up some bricks in his floor underneath his loom, and here he had made a hole in which he set the iron pot that contained his guineas and silver coins, covering the bricks with sand whenever he replaced them. Not that the idea of being robbed presented itself often or strongly to his mind: hoarding was common in country districts in those days; there were old laborers in the parish of Raveloe who were known to have their savings by them, probably inside their flock-beds; but their rustic neighbors, though not all of them as honest as their ancestors in the days of King Alfred, had not imaginations bold enough to lay a plan of burglary. How could they have spent the money in their own village without betraying themselves? They would be obliged to "run away"—a course as dark and dubious as a balloon journey.

So, year after year, Silas Marner had lived in this solitude, his guineas rising in the iron pot, and his life narrowing and hardening itself more and more into a mere pulsation of desire and satisfaction that had no relation to any other being. His life had reduced itself to the mere functions of weaving and hoarding, without any contemplation of an end towards which the functions tended. The same sort of process has perhaps been undergone by wiser men, when they have been cut off from faith and love—only, instead of a loom and a heap of guineas, they have had some erudite research, some ingenious project, or some well-knit theory. Strangely Marner's face and figure shrank and bent themselves into a constant mechanical relation to the objects of his life, so that he produced the same sort of impression as a handle or a crooked tube, which has no meaning standing apart. The prominent eyes that used to look trusting and dreamy, now looked as if they had been made to see only one kind of thing that was very small, like tiny grain, for which they hunted everywhere: and he was so withered and yellow, that, though he was not yet forty, the children always called him "Old Master Marner."

Yet even in this stage of withering a little incident happened which showed that the sap of affection was not all gone. It was one of his daily tasks to fetch his water from a well a couple of fields off, and for this purpose, ever since he came to Raveloe, he had had a brown earthenware pot, which he held as his most precious utensil, among the very few conveniences he had granted himself. It had been his companion for twelve years, always standing on the same spot, always lending its handle to him in the early morning, so that its form had an expression for him of willing helpfulness, and the impress of its handle on his palm gave a satisfaction mingled with that of having the fresh clear water. One day as he was returning from the well, he stumbled against the step of the stile, and his brown pot, falling with force against the stones that overarched the ditch below him, was broken in three pieces. Silas picked up the pieces and carried them home with grief in his heart. The brown pot could never be of use to him any more, but he stuck the bits together and propped the ruin in its old place for a memorial.

This is the history of Silas Marner until the fifteenth year after he came to Raveloe. The livelong day he sat in his loom, his ear filled with its monotony, his eyes bent close down on the slow growth of sameness in the brownish web, his muscles moving with such even repetition that their pause seemed almost as much a constraint as the holding of his breath. But at night came his revelry; at night he closed his shutters, and made fast his doors, and drew out his gold. Long ago the heap of coins had become too large for the iron pot to hold them, and he had made for them two thick leather bags, which wasted no room in their resting-place, but lent themselves flexibly to every corner. How the guineas shone as they came pouring out of the dark leather mouths! The silver bore no large proportion in amount to the gold, because the long pieces of linen which formed his chief work were always partly paid for in gold, and out of the silver he supplied his own bodily wants, choosing always the shillings and sixpences to spend in this way. He loved the guineas best, but he would not change the silver—the crowns and half-crowns that were his own earnings, begotten by his labor; he loved them all. He spread them out in heaps and bathed his hands in them; then he counted them and set them up in regular piles, and felt their rounded outline between his thumb and fingers, and thought fondly of the guineas that were only half-earned by the work in his loom, as if they had been unborn children—thought of the guineas that were coming slowly through the coming years, through all his life, which spread far away before him, the end quite hidden by countless days of weaving. No wonder his thoughts were still with his loom and his money when he made his journeys through the fields and the lanes to fetch and carry home his work, so that his steps never wandered to the hedge-banks and the lane-side in search of the once familiar herbs: these too belonged to the past, from which his life had shrunk away, like a rivulet that has sunk far down from the grassy fringe of its old breadth into a little shivering thread, that cuts a groove for itself in the barren sand.

But about the Christmas of that fifteenth year, a second great change came over Marner's life, and his history became blent in a singular manner with the life of his neighbors.

CHAPTER III.

THE greatest man in Raveloe was Squire Cass, who lived in the large red house with the handsome flight of stone steps in front and the high stables behind it, nearly opposite the church. He was only one among several landed parishioners, but he alone was honored with the title of Squire: for though Mr. Osgood's family was also understood to be of timeless origin—the Raveloe imagination having never ventured back to that fearful blank when there were no Osgoods—still, he merely owned the farm he occupied; whereas Squire Cass had a tenant or two, who complained of the game to him quite as if he had been a lord.

It was still that glorious war-time which was felt to be a peculiar favor of Providence towards the landed interest, and the fall of prices had not yet come to carry the race of small squires and yeomen down that road to ruin for which extravagant habits and bad husbandry were plentifully anointing their wheels. I am speaking now in relation to Raveloe and the parishes that resembled it; for our old-fashioned country life had many different aspects, as all life must have when it is spread over a various surface, and breathed on variously by multitudinous currents, from the winds of heaven to the thoughts of men, which are forever moving and crossing each other with incalculable results. Raveloe lay low among the bushy trees and the rutted lanes, aloof from the currents of industrial energy and Puritan earnestness; the rich ate and drank freely, and accepted gout and apoplexy as things that ran mysteriously in respectable families, and the poor thought that the rich were entirely in the right of it to lead a jolly life; besides, their feasting caused a multiplication of orts, which were the heirlooms of the poor. Betty Jay scented the boiling of Squire Cass's hams, but her longing was arrested by the unctuous liquor in which they were boiled; and when the seasons brought round the great merry-makings, they were regarded on all hands as a fine thing for the poor. For the Raveloe feasts were like the rounds of beef and the barrels of ale—they were on a large scale, and lasted a good while, especially in the winter-time. After ladies had packed up their best gowns and top-knots in bandboxes, and had incurred the risk of fording streams on pillions with the precious burden in rainy or snowy weather, when there was no knowing how high the water would rise, it was not to be supposed that they looked forward to a brief pleasure. On this ground it was always contrived in the dark seasons, when there was little work to be done, and the hours were long, that several neighbors should keep open house in succession. So soon as Squire Cass's standing dishes diminished in plenty and freshness, his guests had nothing to do but to walk a little higher up the village to Mr. Osgood's, at the Orchards, and they found hams and chines uncut, pork-pies with the scent of the fire in them, spun butter in all its freshness—every thing, in fact, that appetites at leisure could desire, in perhaps greater perfection, though not in greater abundance, than at Squire Cass's.

For the Squire's wife had died long ago, and the Red House was without that presence of the wife and mother which is the fountain of wholesome love and fear in parlor and kitchen; and this helped to account not only for there being more profusion than finished excellence in the holiday provisions, but also for the frequency with which the proud Squire condescended to preside in the parlor of the Rainbow rather than under the shadow of his own dark wainscot; perhaps, also, for the fact that his sons had turned out rather ill. Raveloe was not a place where moral censure was severe, but it was thought a weakness in the Squire that he had kept all his sons at home in idleness; and though some license was to be allowed to young men whose fathers could afford it, people shook their heads at the courses of the second son, Dunstan, commonly called Dunsey Cass, whose taste for swopping and betting might turn out to be a sowing of something worse than wild oats. To be sure, the neighbors said, it was no matter what became of Dunsey—a spiteful jeering fellow, who seemed to enjoy his drink the more when other people went dry—always provided that his doings did not bring trouble on a family like Squire Cass's, with a monument in the church and tankards older than King George. But it would be a thousand pities if Mr. Godfrey, the eldest, a fine, open-faced, good-natured young man, who was to come into the land some day, should take to going along the same road as his brother, as he had seemed to do of late. If he went on in that way, he would lose Miss Nancy Lammeter; for it was well-known that she had looked very shyly on him ever since last Whitsuntide twelvemonth, when there was so much talk about his being away from home days and days together. There was something wrong, more than common—that was quite clear; for Mr. Godfrey didn't look half so fresh-colored and open as he used to do. At one time every body was saying, What a handsome couple he and Miss Nancy Lammeter would make! and if she could come to be mistress at the Red House, there would be a fine change, for the Lammeters had been brought up in that way, that they never suffered a pinch of salt to be wasted, and yet every body in their household had of the best, according to his place. Such a daughter-in-law would be a saving to the old Squire, if she never brought a penny to her fortune, for it was to be feared that, notwithstanding his incomings, there were more holes in his pocket than the one where he put his own hand in. But if Mr. Godfrey didn't turn over a new leaf, he might say "Good-bye" to Miss Nancy Lammeter.

It was the once hopeful Godfrey who was standing, with his hands in his side-pockets and his back to the fire, in the dark wainscoted parlor, one late November afternoon, in that fifteenth year of Silas Marner's life at Raveloe. The fading gray light fell dimly on the walls decorated with guns, whips, and foxes' brushes, on coats and hats flung on the chairs, on tankards sending forth a scent of flat ale, and on a half-choked fire, with pipes propped up in the chimney-corners: signs of a domestic life destitute of any hallowing charm, with which the look of gloomy vexation on Godfrey's blond face was in sad accordance. He seemed to be waiting and listening for some one's approach, and presently the sound of a heavy step, with an accompanying whistle, was heard across the large empty entrance-hall.

The door opened, and a thick-set, heavy-looking young man entered, with the flushed face and the gratuitously elated bearing which mark the first stage of intoxication. It was Dunsey, and at the sight of him Godfrey's face parted with some of its gloom to take on the more active expression of hatred. The handsome brown spaniel that lay on the hearth retreated under the chair in the chimney-corner.

"Well, Master Godfrey, what do you want with me?" said Dunsey, in a mocking tone. "You're my elders and betters, you know; I was obliged to come when you sent for me."

"Why, this is what I want—and just shake yourself sober and listen, will you?" said Godfrey, savagely. He had himself been drinking more than was good for him, trying to turn his gloom into uncalculating anger. "I want to tell you, I must hand over that rent of Fowler's to the Squire, or else tell him I gave it you; for he's threatening to distrain for it, and it'll all be out soon, whether I tell him or not. He said just now, before he went out, he should send word to Cox to distrain, if Fowler didn't come and pay up his arrears this week. The

Squire's short o' cash, and in no humor to stand any nonsense; and you know what he threatened, if ever he found you making away with his money again. So, see and get the money, and pretty quickly, will you?"

"Oh!" said Dunsey, sneeringly, coming nearer to his brother, and looking in his face. "Suppose, now, you get the money yourself, and save me the trouble, eh? Since you was so kind as to hand it over to me, you'll not refuse me the kindness to pay it back for me: it was your brotherly love made you do it, you know."

Godfrey bit his lips and clenched his fist. "Don't come near me with that look, else I'll knock you down."

"Oh, no, you won't," said Dunsey, turning away on his heel, however. "Because I'm such a good-natured brother, you know. I might get you turned out of house and home, and cut off with a shilling any day. I might tell the Squire how his handsome son was married to that nice young woman, Molly Farran, and was very unhappy because he couldn't live with his drunken wife, and I should slip into your place as comfortable as could be. But you see, I don't do it—I'm so easy and good-natured. You'll take any trouble for me. You'll get the hundred pounds for me—I know you will."

"How can I get the money?" said Godfrey, quivering. "I haven't a shilling to bless myself with. And it's a lie that you'd slip into my place: you'd get yourself turned out too, that's all. For if you begin telling tales I'll follow. Bob's my father's favorite—you know that very well. He'd only think himself well rid of you."

"Never mind," said Dunsey, nodding his head sideways as he looked out of the window. "It' ud be very pleasant to me to go in your company—you're such a handsome brother, and we've always been so fond of quarrelling with one another I shouldn't know what to do without you. But you'd like better for us both to stay at home together; I know you would. So you'll manage to get that little sum o' money, and I'll bid you good-bye, though I'm sorry to part."

Dunstan was moving off, but Godfrey rushed after him and seized him by the arm, saying, with an oath,

"I tell you I have no money: I can get no money."

"Borrow of old Kimble."

"I tell you, he won't lend me any more, and I sha'n't ask him."

"Well then, sell Wildfire."

"Yes, that's easy talking. I must have the money directly."

"Well, you've only got to ride him to the hunt to-morrow.

There'll be Bryce and Keating there, for sure. You'll get more bids than one."

"I dare say, and get back home at eight o'clock, splashed up to the chin. I'm going to Mrs. Osgood's birthday dance."

"Oho!" said Dunsey, turning his head on one side, and trying to speak in a small mincing treble. "And there's sweet Miss Nancy coming; and we shall dance with her and promise never to be naughty again, and be taken into favor, and—"

"Hold your tongue about Miss Nancy, you fool," said Godfrey, turning very red, "else I'll throttle you."

"What for?" said Dunsey, still in an artificial tone, but taking a whip from the table and beating the butt-end of it on his palm. "You've a very good chance. I'd advise you to creep up her sleeve again: it 'ud be saving time, if Molly should happen to take a drop too much laudanum some day, and make a widower of you. Miss Nancy wouldn't mind being a second, if she didn't know it. And you've got a good-natured brother, who'll keep your secret well, because you'll be so very obliging to him."

"I'll tell you what it is," said Godfrey, quivering, and pale again. "My patience is pretty near at an end. If you'd a little more sharpness in you, you might know that you may urge a man a bit too far, and make one leap as easy as another. I don't know but what it is so now: I may as well tell the Squire every thing myself—I should get you off my back, if I got nothing else. And, after all, he'll know some time. She's been threatening to come herself and tell him. So, don't flatter yourself that your secrecy's worth any price you choose to ask. You drain me of money till I have got nothing to pacify *her* with, and she'll do as she threatens some day. It's all one. I'll tell my father every thing myself, and you may go to the devil."

Dunsey perceived that he had overshot his mark, and that there was a point at which even the hesitating Godfrey might be driven into decision. But he said with an air of unconcern,

"As you please; but I'll have a draught of ale first." And ringing the bell, he threw himself across two chairs, and began to rap the window-seat with the handle of his whip.

Godfrey stood still with his back to the fire, uneasily moving his fingers among the contents of his side-pockets, and looking at the floor. That big muscular frame of his held plenty of animal courage, but helped him to no decision when the dangers to be braved were such as could neither be knocked down nor throttled. His natural irresolution and moral cowardice were exaggerated by a position in which dreaded consequences seemed to press equally on all sides, and his irritation had no sooner provoked him to defy Dunstan and anticipate all possible betrayals, than the miseries he must bring on himself by such a step seemed more unendurable to him than the present evil. The results of confession were not contingent, they were certain; whereas betrayal was not certain. From the near vision of that certainty he fell back on suspense and vacillation with a sense of repose. The disinherited son of a small squire, equally disinclined to dig and to beg, was almost as helpless as an uprooted tree, which, by the favor of earth and sky, has grown to a handsome bulk on the spot where it first shot upward. Perhaps it would have been possible to think of digging with some cheerfulness if Nancy Lammeter were to be won on those terms; but since he must irrevocably lose *her* as well as the inheritance, and must break every tie but the one that degraded him and left him without motive for trying to recover his better self, he could imagine no future for himself on the other side of confession but that of "'listing for a soldier"—the most desperate step short of suicide, in the eyes of respectable families. No! he would rather trust to casualties than to his own resolve—rather go on sitting at the feast and sipping the wine he loved, though with the sword hanging over him and terror in his heart, than rush away into the cold darkness where there was no pleasure left. The utmost concession to Dunstan about the horse began to seem easy, compared with the fulfillment of his own threat. But his pride would not let him recommence the conversation otherwise than by continuing the quarrel. Dunstan was waiting for this, and took his ale in shorter draughts than usual.

"It's just like you," Godfrey burst out in a bitter tone, "to talk about my selling Wildfire in that cool way—the last thing I've got to call my own, and the best bit of horse-flesh I ever had in my life. And if you'd got a spark of pride in you, you'd be ashamed to see the stables emptied, and every body sneering about it. But it's my belief you'd sell yourself, if it was only for the pleasure of making somebody feel he'd got a bad bargain."

"Ay, ay," said Dunstan, very placably, "you do me justice, I see. You know I'm a jewel for 'ticing people into bargains. For which reason I advise you to let *me* sell Wildfire. I'd ride him to the hunt to-morrow for you with pleasure. I shouldn't look so handsome as you in the saddle, but it's the horse they'll bid for, and not the rider."

"Yes, I dare say—trust my horse to you!"

"As you please," said Dunstan, rapping the window-seat again with an air of great unconcern. "It's *you* have got to pay Fowler's money; it's none of my business. You received the money from him when you went to Bramcote, and *you* told the Squire it wasn't paid. I'd nothing to do with that; you chose to be so obliging as give it me, that was all. If you don't want to pay the money, let it alone; it's all one to me. But I was willing to accommodate you by undertaking to sell the horse, seeing it's not convenient to you to go so far to-morrow."

Godfrey was silent for some moments. He would have liked to spring on Dunstan, wrench the whip from his hand, and flog him to within an inch of his life; and no bodily fear could have deterred him; but he was mastered by another sort of fear, which was fed by feelings stronger even than his resentment. When he spoke again, it was in a half-conciliatory tone.

"Well, you mean no nonsense about the horse, eh? You'll sell him all fair, and hand over the money? If you don't, you know, every thing 'ull go to smash, for I've got nothing else to trust to. And you'll have less pleasure in pulling the house over my head, when your own skull's to be broken too."

"Ay, ay," said Dunstan, rising, "all right. I thought you'd come round. I'm the fellow to bring old Bryce up to the scratch. I'll get you a hundred and twenty for him, if I get you a penny."

"But it'll perhaps rain cats and dogs to-morrow, as it did yesterday, and then you can't go," said Godfrey, hardly knowing whether he wished for that obstacle or not.

"Not *it*," said Dunstan. "I'm always lucky in my weather. It might rain if you wanted to go yourself. You never hold trumps, you know—I always do. You've got the beauty, you see, and I've got the luck, so you must keep me by you for your crooked sixpence; you'll *ne*-ver get along without me."

"Confound you, hold your tongue!" said Godfrey, impetuously. "And take care to keep sober to-morrow, else you'll get pitched on your head coming home, and Wildfire might be the worse for it."

"Make your tender heart easy," said Dunstan, opening the door. "You never knew me see double when I'd got a bargain to make; it 'ud spoil the fun. Besides, whenever I fall, I'm warranted to fall on my legs."

With that, Dunstan slammed the door behind him, and left Godfrey to that bitter rumination on his personal circumstances which was now unbroken from day to day save by the excitement of sporting, drinking, card-playing, or the rarer and less oblivious pleasure of seeing Miss Nancy Lammeter. The subtle and varied pains springing from the higher sensibility that accompanies higher culture are perhaps less pitiable than that dreary absence of impersonal enjoyment and consolation which leaves ruder minds to the perpetual urgent companionship of their own griefs and discontents. The lives of those rural forefathers, whom we are apt to think very prosaic figures—men whose only work was to ride round their land, getting heavier and heavier in their saddles, and who passed the rest of their days in the half-listless gratification of senses dulled by monotony—had a certain pathos in them nevertheless. Calamities came to *them* too, and their early errors carried hard consequences: perhaps the love of some sweet maiden, the image of purity, order, and calm, had opened their eyes to the vision of a life in which the days would not seem too long, even without rioting; but the maiden was lost, and the vision passed away, and then what was left to them, especially when they had become too heavy for the hunt, or for carrying a gun over the furrows, but to drink and get merry, or to drink and get angry, so that they might be independent of variety, and say over again with eager emphasis the things they had said already any time that twelvemonth? Assuredly, among these flushed and dull-eyed men there were some whom—thanks to their native human kindness—even riot could never drive into brutality; men who, when their cheeks were fresh, had felt the keen point of sorrow or remorse, had been pierced by the reeds they leaned on, or had lightly put their limbs in fetters from which no struggle could loose them; and under these sad circumstances, common to us all, their thoughts could find no resting-place outside the ever-trodden round of their own petty history.

That, at least, was the condition of Godfrey Cass in this six-and-twentieth year of his life. A movement of compunction, helped by those small indefinable influences which every personal relation exerts on a pliant nature, had urged him into a secret marriage, which was a blight on his life. It was an ugly story of low passion, delusion, and waking from delusion, which needs not to be dragged from the privacy of Godfrey's bitter memory. He had long known that the delusion was partly due to a trap laid for him by Dunstan, who saw in his brother's degrading marriage the means of gratifying at once his jealous hate and his cupidity. And if Godfrey could have felt himself simply a victim, the iron bit that destiny had put into his mouth would have chafed him less intolerably. If the curses he muttered half aloud when he was alone had had no other object than Dunstan's diabolical cunning, he might have shrunk less from the consequences of avowal. But he had something else to curse —his own vicious folly, which now seemed as mad and unaccountable to him as almost all our follies and vices do when their promptings have long passed away. For four years he had thought of Nancy Lammeter, and wooed her with tacit, patient worship, as the woman who made him think of the future with joy: she would be his wife, and would make home lovely to him, as his father's home had never been; and it would be easy, when she was always near, to shake off those foolish habits that were no pleasures, but only a feverish way of annulling vacancy. Godfrey's was an essentially domestic nature, bred up in a home where the hearth had no smiles, and where the daily habits were not chastised by the presence of household order; his easy disposition made him fall in unresistingly with the family courses, but the need of some tender, permanent affection, the longing for some influence that would make the good he preferred easy to pursue, caused the neatness, purity, and liberal orderliness of the Lammeter household, sunned by the smile of Nancy, to seem like those fresh bright hours of the morning, when temptations go to sleep, and leave the ear open to the voice of the good angel, inviting to industry, sobriety, and peace. And yet the hope of this paradise had not been enough to save him from a course which shut him out of it forever. Instead of keeping fast hold of the strong silken rope by which Nancy would have drawn him safe to the green banks, where it was easy to step firmly, he had let himself be dragged back into mud and slime, in which it was useless to struggle. He had made ties for himself which robbed him of all wholesome motive, and were a constant exasperation.

Still, there was one position worse than the present; it was the position he would be in when the ugly secret was disclosed; and the desire that continually triumphed over every other was that of warding off the evil day, when he would have to bear the consequences of his father's violent resentment for the wound inflicted on his family pride— would have, perhaps, to turn his back on that hereditary ease and dignity which, after all, was a sort of reason for living, and would carry with him the certainty that he was banished forever from the sight and esteem of Nancy Lammeter. The longer the interval, the more chance there was of deliverance from some, at least, of the hateful consequences to which he had sold himself—the more opportunities remained for him to snatch the strange gratification of seeing Nancy, and gathering some faint indications of her lingering regard. Towards this gratification he was impelled fitfully, every now and then, after having passed weeks in which he had avoided her as the far-off bright-winged prize, that only made him spring forward, and find his chain all the more galling. One of those fits of yearning was on him now, and it would have been strong enough to have persuaded him to trust Wildfire to Dunstan rather than disappoint the yearning, even if he had not had another reason for his disinclination towards the morrow's hunt. That other reason was the fact that the morning's meet was near Batherley, the market-town where the unhappy woman lived, whose image became more odious to him every day; and to his thought the whole vicinage was haunted by her. The yoke a man creates for himself by wrong-doing will breed hate in the kindliest nature; and the good-humored, affectionate-hearted Godfrey Cass was fast becoming a bitter man, visited by cruel wishes, that seemed to enter, and depart, and enter again, like demons who had found in him a ready-garnished home.

What was he to do this evening to pass the time? He might as well go to the Rainbow, and hear the talk about the cock-fighting: every body was there, and what else was there to be done? Though, for his own part, he did not care a button for cock-fighting. Snuff, the brown spaniel, who had placed herself in front of him, and had been watching him for some time, now jumped up in impatience for the expected caress. But Godfrey thrust her away without looking at her, and left the room, followed humbly by the unresenting Snuff—perhaps because she saw no other career open to her.

CHAPTER IV.

Dunstan Cass, setting off in the raw morning, at the judiciously quiet pace of a man who is obliged to ride to cover on his hunter, had to take his way along the lane which, at its farther extremity, passed by the piece of unenclosed ground called the Stonepit, where stood the cottage, once a stone-cutter's shed, now for fifteen years inhabited by Silas Marner. The spot looked very dreary at this season, with the moist trodden clay about it, and the red muddy water high up in the deserted quarry. That was Dunstan's first thought as he approached it; the second was, that the old fool of a weaver, whose loom he heard rattling already, had a great deal of money hidden somewhere. How was it that he, Dunstan Cass, who had often heard talk of Marner's miserliness, had never thought of suggesting to Godfrey that he should frighten or persuade the old fellow into lending the money on the excellent security of the young Squire's prospects? The resource occurred to him now as so easy and agreeable, especially as Marner's hoard was likely to be large enough to leave Godfrey a handsome surplus beyond his immediate needs, and enable him to accommodate his faithful brother, that he had almost turned the horse's head towards home again. Godfrey would be ready enough to accept the suggestion: he would snatch eagerly at a plan that might save him from parting with Wildfire. But when Dunstan's meditation reached this point, the inclination to go on grew strong and prevailed. He didn't want to give Godfrey that pleasure: he preferred that Master Godfrey should be vexed. Moreover, Dunstan enjoyed the self-important consciousness of having a horse to sell, and the opportunity of driving a bargain, swaggering, and, possibly, taking somebody in. He might have all the satisfaction attendant on selling his brother's horse, and not the less have the further satisfaction of setting Godfrey to borrow Marner's money. So he rode on to cover.

Bryce and Keating were there, as Dunstan was quite sure they would be—he was such a lucky fellow.

"Hey-day," said Bryce, who had long had his eye on Wildfire, "you're on your brother's horse to-day; how's that?"

"Oh, I've swapped with him," said Dunstan, whose delight in lying, grandly independent of utility, was not to be diminished by the likelihood that his hearer would not believe him—"Wildfire's mine now."

"What! has he swopped with you for that big-boned hack of yours?" said Bryce, quite aware that he should get another lie in answer.

"Oh, there was a little account between us," said Dunstan, carelessly, "and Wildfire made it even. I accommodated him by taking the horse, though it was against my will, for I'd got an itch for a mare o' Jortin's—as rare a bit o' blood as ever you threw your leg across. But I shall keep Wildfire, now I've got him, though I'd a bid of a hundred and fifty for him the other day from a man over at Flitton—he's buying for Lord Cromleck—a fellow with a cast in his eye, and a green waistcoat. But I mean to stick to Wildfire: I sha'n't get a better at a fence in a hurry. The mare's got more blood, but she's a bit too weak in the hind quarters."

Bryce of course divined that Dunstan wanted to sell the horse, and Dunstan knew that he divined it (horse-dealing is only one of many human transactions carried on in this ingenious manner); and they both considered that the bargain was in its first stage, when Bryce replied ironically—

"I wonder at that now; I wonder you mean to keep him; for I never heard of a man who didn't want to sell his horse getting a bid of half as much again as the horse was worth. You'll be lucky if you get a hundred."

Keating rode up now, and the transaction became more complicated. It ended in the purchase of the horse by Bryce for a hundred and twenty, to be paid on the delivery of Wildfire, safe and sound, at the Batherley stables. It did occur to Dunsey that it might be wise for him to give up the day's hunting, proceed at once to Batherley, and, having waited for Bryce's return, hire a horse to carry him home with the money in his pocket. But the inclination for a run, encouraged by confidence in his luck, and by a draught of brandy from his pocket-pistol at the conclusion of the bargain, was not easy to overcome, especially with a horse under him that would take the fences to the admiration of the field. Dunstan, however, took one fence too many, and "staked" his horse. His own ill-favored person, which was quite unmarketable, escaped without injury, but poor Wildfire, unconscious of his price, turned on his flank, and painfully panted his last. It happened that Dunstan, a short time before, having had to get down to arrange his stirrup, had muttered a good many curses at this interruption, which had thrown him in the rear of the hunt near the moment of glory, and under this exasperation had taken the fences more blindly. He would soon have been up with the hounds again, when the fatal accident happened; and hence he was between eager riders in advance, not troubling themselves about what happened behind them, and far-off stragglers, who were as likely as not to pass quite aloof from the line of road in which Wildfire had fallen. Dunstan, whose nature it was to care more for immediate annoyances than for remote consequences, no sooner recovered his legs, and saw that it was all over with Wildfire, than he felt a satisfaction at the absence of witnesses to a position which no swaggering could make enviable. Reinforcing himself, after his shake, with a little brandy and much swearing, he walked as fast as he could to a coppice on his right hand, through which it occurred to him that he could make his way to Batherley without danger of encountering any member of the hunt. His first intention was to hire a horse there and ride home forthwith, for to walk many miles without a gun in his hand, and along an ordinary road, was as much out of the question to him as to other spirited young men of his kind. He did not much mind about taking the bad news to Godfrey, for he had to offer him at the same time the resource of Marner's money; and if Godfrey kicked, as he always did, at the notion of making a fresh debt, from which he himself got the smallest share of advantage, why, he wouldn't kick long: Dunstan felt sure he could worry Godfrey into any thing. The idea of Marner's money kept growing in vividness, now the want of it had become immediate; the prospect of having to make his appearance with the muddy boots of a pedestrian at Batherley, and encounter the grinning queries of stablemen, stood unpleasantly in the way of his impatience to be back at Raveloe and carry out his felicitous plan; and a casual visitation of his waistcoat-pocket, as he was ruminating, awakened his memory to the fact that the two or three small coins his fore-finger encountered there were of too pale a color to cover that small debt, without payment of which Jennings had declared he would never do any more business with Dunsey Cass. After all, according to the direction in which the run had brought him, he was not so very much farther from home than he was from Batherley; but Dunsey, not being remarkable for clearness of head, was only led to this conclusion by the gradual perception that there were other reasons for choosing the unprecedented course of walking home. It was now nearly four o'clock, and a mist was gathering: the sooner he got into the road the better. He remembered having crossed the road and seen the finger-post only a little while before Wildfire broke down; so, buttoning his coat, twisting the lash of his hunting-whip compactly round the handle, and rapping the tops of his boots with a self-possessed air, as if to assure himself that he was not at all taken by surprise, he set off with the sense that he was undertaking a remarkable feat of bodily exertion, which somehow, and at some time, he should be able to dress up and magnify to the admiration of a select circle at the Rainbow. When a young gentleman like Dunsey is reduced to so exceptional a mode of locomotion as walking, a whip in his hand is a desirable corrective to a too bewildering dreamy sense of unwontedness in his position; and Dunstan, as he went along through the gathering mist, was always rapping his whip somewhere. It was Godfrey's whip, which he had chosen to take without leave because it had a gold handle;

of course no one could see, when Dunstan held it, that the name *Godfrey Cass* was cut in deep letters on that gold handle—they could only see that it was a very handsome whip. Dunsey was not without fear that he might meet some acquaintance in whose eyes he would cut a pitiable figure, for mist is no screen where people get close to each other; but when he at last found himself in the well-known Raveloe lanes without having met a soul, he silently remarked that that was part of his usual good-luck. But now the mist, helped by the evening darkness, was more of a screen than he desired, for it hid the ruts into which his feet were liable to slip—hid every thing, so that he had to guide his steps by dragging his whip along the low bushes in advance of the hedgerow. He must soon, he thought, be getting near the opening at the Stone-pits: he should find it out by the break in the hedgerow. He found it out, however, by another circumstance which he had not expected—namely, by certain gleams of light, which he presently guessed to proceed from Silas Marner's cottage. That cottage and the money hidden within it had been in his mind continually during his walk, and he had been imagining ways of cajoling and tempting the weaver to part with the immediate possession of his money for the sake of receiving interest. Dunstan felt as if there must be a little frightening added to the cajolery, for his own arithmetical convictions were not clear enough to afford him any forcible demonstration as to the advantages of interest; and as for security, he regarded it vaguely as a means of cheating a man, by making him believe that he would be paid. Altogether, the operation on the miser's mind was a task that Godfrey would be sure to hand over to his more daring and cunning brother: Dunstan had made up his mind to that; and by the time he saw the light gleaming through the chinks of Marner's shutters, the idea of a dialogue with the weaver had become so familiar to him, that it occurred to him as quite a natural thing to make the acquaintance forthwith. There might be several conveniences attending this course; the weaver had possibly got a lantern, and Dunstan was tired of feeling his way. He was still nearly three-quarters of a mile from home, and the lane was becoming unpleasantly slippery, for the mist was passing into rain. He turned up the bank, not without some fear lest he might miss the right way, since he was not certain whether the light were in front or on the side of the cottage. But he felt the ground before him cautiously with his whip-handle, and at last arrived safely at the door. He knocked loudly, rather enjoying the idea that the old fellow would be frightened at the sudden noise.

He heard no movement in reply: all was silence in the cottage. Was the weaver gone to bed, then? If so, why had he left a light? That was a strange forgetfulness in a miser. Dunstan knocked still more loudly, and, without pausing for a reply, pushed his fingers through the latch-hole, intending to shake the door and pull the latch-string up and down, not doubting that the door was fastened. But, to his surprise, at this double motion the door opened, and he found himself in front of a bright fire, which lit up every corner of the cottage—the bed, the loom, the three chairs, and the table—and showed him that Marner was not there.

Nothing at that moment could be much more inviting to Dunsey than the bright fire on the brick hearth; he walked in and seated himself by it at once. There was something in front of the fire, too, that would have been inviting to a hungry man, if it had been in a different stage of cooking. It was a small bit of pork suspended from the kettle-hanger by a string passed through a large door-key, in a way known to primitive housekeepers unpossessed of jacks. But the pork had been hung at the farthest extremity of the hanger, apparently to prevent the roasting from proceeding too rapidly during the owner's absence. The old staring simpleton had hot meat for his supper, then? thought Dunstan. People had always said he lived on mouldy bread, on purpose to check his appetite. But where could he be at this time, and on such an evening, leaving his supper in this stage of preparation, and his door unfastened? Dunstan's own recent difficulty in making his way suggested to him that the weaver had perhaps gone outside his cottage to fetch in fuel, or for some such brief purpose, and had slipped into the Stone-pit. That was an interesting idea to Dunston, carrying consequences of entire novelty. If the weaver was dead, who had a right to his money? Who would know where his money was hidden? *Who would know that any body had come to take it away?* He went no farther into the subtleties of evidence: the pressing question, "Where *is* the money?" now took such entire possession of him as to make him quite forget that the weaver's death was not a certainty. A dull mind, once arriving at an inference that flatters a desire, is rarely able to retain the impression that the notion from which the inference started was purely problematic. And Dunstan's mind was as dull as the mind of a possible felon usually is. There were only three hiding-places where he had ever heard of cottagers' hoards being found; the thatch, the bed, and a hole in the floor. Marner's cottage had no thatch; and Dunstan's first act, after a train of thought made rapid by the stimulus of cupidity, was to go up to the bed; but while he did so, his eyes travelled eagerly over the floor, where the bricks, distinct in the fire-light, were discernible under the sprinkling of sand. But not everywhere; for there was one spot, and one only, which was quite covered with sand, and sand showing the marks of fingers, which had apparently been careful to spread it over a given space. It was near the treddles of the loom. In an instant Dunstan darted to that spot, swept away the sand with his whip, and, inserting the thin end of the hook between the bricks, found that they were loose. In haste he lifted up two bricks, and saw what he had no doubt was the object of his search; for what could there be but money in those two leathern bags? And, from their weight, they must be filled with guineas. Dunstan felt round the hole, to be certain that it held no more; then hastily replaced the bricks, and spread the sand over them. Hardly more than five minutes had passed since he entered the cottage, but it seemed to Dunstan like a long while; and though he was without any distinct recognition of the possibility that Marner might be alive, and might re-enter the cottage at any moment, he felt an undefinable dread laying hold on him, as he rose to his feet with the bags in his hand. He would hasten out into the darkness, and then consider what he should do with the bags. He closed the door behind him immediately, that he might shut in the stream of light; a few steps would be enough to carry him beyond betrayal by the gleams from the shutter-chinks and the latch-hole. The rain and darkness had got thicker, and he was glad of it; though it was awkward walking with both hands filled, so that it was as much as he could do to grasp his whip along with one of the bags. But when he had gone a yard or two, he might take his time. So he stepped forward into the darkness.

CHAPTER V.

WHEN Dunstan Cass turned his back on the cottage, Silas Marner was not more than a hundred yards away from it, plodding along from the village with a sack thrown round his shoulders as an over-coat, and with a horn lantern in his hand. His legs were weary, but his mind was at ease, free from the presentiment of change. The sense of security more frequently springs from habit than from conviction, and for this reason it often subsists after such a change in the conditions as might have been expected to suggest alarm. The lapse of time during which a given event has not happened, is, in this logic of habit, constantly alleged as a reason why the event should never happen, even when the lapse of time is precisely the added condition which makes the event imminent. A man will tell you that he has worked in a mine for forty years unhurt by an accident as a reason why he should apprehend no danger, though the roof is beginning to sink; and it is often observable, that the older a man gets, the more difficult it is to him to retain a believing conception of his own death. This influence of habit was necessarily strong in a man whose life was so monotonous as Marner's—who saw no new people and heard of no new events to keep alive in him the idea of the unexpected and the changeful; and it explains, simply enough, why his mind could be at ease, though he had left his house and his treasure more defenseless than usual. Silas was thinking with double complacency of his supper: first, because it would be hot and savory; and secondly, because it would cost him nothing. For the little bit of pork was a present from that excellent housewife, Miss Priscilla Lammeter, to whom he had this day carried home a handsome piece of linen; and it was only on occasion of a present like this, that Silas indulged himself with roast-meat. Supper was his favorite meal, because it came at his time of revelry, when his heart warmed over his gold; whenever he had roast-meat, he always chose to have it for supper. But this evening, he had no sooner ingeniously knotted his string fast round his bit of pork, twisted the string according to rule over his door-key, passed it through the handle, and made it fast on the hanger, than he remembered that a piece of very fine twine was indispensable to his "setting up" a new piece of work in his loom early in the morning. It had slipped his memory, because, in coming from Mr. Lammeter's, he had not had to pass through the village; but to lose time by going on errands in the morning was out of the question. It was a nasty fog to turn out into, but there were things Silas loved better than his own comfort; so, drawing his pork to the extremity of the hanger, and arming himself with his lantern and his old sack, he set out on what, in ordinary weather, would have been a twenty minutes' errand. He could not have locked his door without undoing his well-knotted string and retarding his supper; it was not worth his while to make that sacrifice. What thief would find his way to the Stone-pits on such a night as this? and why should he come on this particular night, when he had never come through all the fifteen years before? These questions were not distinctly pres ent in Silas's mind; they merely serve to represent the vaguely-felt foundation of his freedom from anxiety.

He reached his door in much satisfaction that his errand was done: he opened it, and to his short-sighted eyes every thing remained as he had left it, except that the fire sent out a welcome increase of heat. He trod about the floor while putting by his lantern and throwing aside his hat and sack, so as to merge the marks of Dunstan's feet on the sand in the marks of his own nailed boots. Then he moved his pork nearer to the fire, and sat down to the agreeable business of tending the meat and warming himself at the same time.

Any one who had looked at him as the red light shone upon his pale face, strange straining eyes, and meagre form, would perhaps have understood the mixture of contemptuous pity, dread, and suspicion with which he was regarded by his neighbors in Raveloe. Yet few men could be more harmless than poor Marner. In his truthful simple soul, not even the growing greed and worship of gold could beget any vice directly injurious to others. The light of his faith quite put out, and his affections made desolate, he had clung with all the force of his nature to his work and his money; and like all objects to which a man devotes himself, they had fashioned him into correspondence with themselves. His loom, as he wrought in it without ceasing, had in its turn wrought on him, and confirmed more and more the monotonous craving for its monotonous response. His gold, as he hung over it and saw it grow, gathered his power of loving together into a hard isolation like its own.

As soon as he was warm he began to think it would be a long while to wait till after supper before he drew out his guineas, and it would be pleasant to see them on the table before him as he ate his unwonted feast. For joy is the best of wine, and Silas's guineas were a golden wine of that sort.

He rose and placed his candle unsuspectingly on the floor near his loom, swept away the sand without noticing any change, and removed the bricks. The sight of the empty hole made his heart leap violently, but the belief that his gold was gone could not come at once—only terror, and the eager effort to put an end to the terror. He passed his trembling hand all about the hole, trying to think it possible that his eyes had deceived him; then he held the candle in the hole and examined it curiously, trembling more and more. At last he shook so violently that he let fall the candle, and lifted his hands to his head, trying to steady himself, that he might think. Had he put his gold somewhere else, by a sudden resolution last night, and then forgotten it? A man falling into dark waters seeks a momentary footing even on sliding stones; and Silas, by acting as if he believed in false hopes, warded off the moment of despair. He searched in every corner, he turned his bed over, and shook it, and kneaded it; he looked in his brick oven where he laid his sticks. When there was no other place to be searched, he kneeled down again and felt once more all round the hole. There was no untried refuge left for a moment's shelter from the terrible truth.

Yes, there was a sort of refuge which always comes with the prostration of thought under an overpowering passion: it was that expectation of impossibilities, that belief in contradictory images, which is still distinct from madness, because it is capable of being dissipated by the external fact. Silas got up from his knees trembling, and looked round at the table: didn't the gold lie there after all? The table was bare. Then he turned and looked behind him—looked all round his dwelling, seeming to strain his brown eyes after some possible appearance of the bags where he had already sought them in vain. He could see every object in his cottage—and his gold was not there.

Again he put his trembling hands to his head, and gave a wild ringing scream, the cry of desolation. For a few moments after, he stood motionless; but the cry had relieved him from the first maddening pressure of the truth. He turned, and tottered towards his loom, and got into the seat where he worked, instinctively seeking this as the strongest assurance of reality.

And now that all the false hopes had vanished, and the first shock of certainty was past, the idea of a thief began to present itself, and he entertained it eagerly, because a thief might be caught and made to restore the gold. The thought brought some new strength with it, and he started from his loom to the door. As he opened it the rain beat in upon him, for it was falling more and more heavily. There were no footsteps to be tracked on such a night—footsteps? When had the thief come? During Silas's absence in the day-time the door had been locked, and there had been no marks of any inroad on his return by day-light. And in the evening, too, he said to himself, every thing was the same as when he had left it. The sand and bricks looked as if they had not been moved. *Was* it a thief who had taken the bags? or was it a cruel power that no hands could reach, which had delighted in making him a second time desolate? He shrank from this vaguer dread, and fixed his mind with struggling effort on the robber with hands, who could be reached by hands.

His thoughts glanced at all the neighbors who had made any remarks, or asked any questions which he might now regard as a ground of suspicion. There was Jem Rodney, a known poacher, and otherwise disreputable: he had often met Marner in his journeys across the fields, and had said something jestingly about the weaver's money; nay, he had once irritated Marner, by lingering at the fire when he called to light his pipe, instead of going about his business. Jem Rodney was the man—there was ease in the thought. Jem could be found and made to restore the money: Marner did not want to punish him, but only to get back his gold which had gone from him, and left his soul like a forlorn traveller on an unknown desert. The robber must be laid hold of. Marner's ideas of legal authority were confused, but he felt that he must go and proclaim his loss; and the great people in the village—the clergyman, the constable, and Squire Cass—would make Jem Rodney, or somebody else, deliver up the stolen money. He rushed out in the rain, under the stimulus of this hope, forgetting to cover his head, not caring to fasten his door; for he felt as if he had nothing left to lose. He ran swiftly, till want of breath compelled him to slacken his pace as he was entering the village at the turning close to the Rainbow.

The Rainbow, in Marner's view, was a place of luxurious resort for rich and stout husbands, whose wives had superfluous stores of linen; it was the place where he was likely to find the powers and dignities of Raveloe, and where he could most speedily make his loss public. He lifted the latch, and turned into the bright bar or kitchen on the right hand, where the less lofty customers of the house were in the habit of assembling, the parlor on the left being reserved for the more select society in which Squire Cass frequently enjoyed the double pleasure of conviviality and condescension. But the parlor was dark to-night, the chief personages who ornamented its circle being all at Mrs. Osgood's birthday dance, as Godfrey Cass was. And in consequence of this, the party on the high-screened seats in the kitchen was more numerous than usual; several personages, who would otherwise have been admitted into the parlor and enlarged the opportunity of hectoring and condescension for their betters, being content this evening to vary their enjoyment by taking their spirits-and-water where they could themselves hector and condescend in company that called for beer.

CHAPTER VI.

The conversation, which was at a high pitch of animation when Silas approached the door of the Rainbow, had, as usual, been slow and intermittent when the company first assembled. The pipes began to be puffed in a silence which had an air of severity; the more important customers, who drank spirits and sat nearest the fire, staring at each other as if a bet were depending on the first man who winked; while the beer-drinkers, chiefly men in fustian jackets and smock-frocks, kept their eyelids down and rubbed their hands across their mouths, as if their draughts of beer were a funereal duty attended with embarrassing sadness. At last, Mr. Snell, the landlord, a man of a neutral disposition, accustomed to stand aloof from human differences, as those of beings who were all alike in need of liquor, broke silence, by saying in a doubtful tone to his cousin the butcher—

"Some folks 'ud say that was a fine beast you druv in yesterday, Bob?"

The butcher, a jolly, smiling, red-haired man, was not disposed to answer rashly. He gave a few puffs before he spat and replied, "And they wouldn't be fur wrong, John."

After this feeble delusive thaw, the silence set in as severely as before.

"Was it a red Durham?" said the farrier, taking up the thread of discourse after the lapse of a few minutes.

The farrier looked at the landlord, and the landlord looked at the butcher, as the person who must take the responsibility of answering.

"Red it was," said the butcher, in his good-humored husky treble—"and a Durham it was."

"Then you needn't tell *me* who you bought it of," said the farrier, looking round with some triumph; "I know who it is has got the red Durhams o' this country-side. And she'd a white star on her brow, I'll bet a penny?" The farrier leaned forward with his hands on his knees as he put this question, and his eyes twinkled knowingly.

"Well; yes—she might," said the butcher, slowly, considering that he was giving a decided affirmative. "I don't say contrairy."

"I knew that very well," said the farrier, throwing himself backward again, and speaking defiantly; "if *I* don't know Mr.

Lammeter's cows, I should like to know who does—that's all. And as for the cow you've bought, bargain or no bargain, I've been at the drenching of her—contradick me who will."

The farrier looked fierce, and the mild butcher's conversational spirit was roused a little.

"I'm not for contradicking no man," he said; "I'm for peace and quietness. Some are for cutting long ribs—I'm for cutting 'em short myself; but *I* don't quarrel with 'em. All I say is, it's a lovely carkiss—and any body as was reasonable, it 'ud bring tears into their eyes to look at it."

"Well, it's the cow as I drenched, whatever it is," pursued the farrier, angrily; "and it was Mr. Lammeter's cow, else you told a lie when you said it was a red Durham."

"I tell no lies," said the butcher, with the same mild huskiness as before, "and I contradick none—not if a man was to swear himself black: he's no meat o' mine, or none o' my bargains. All I say is, it's a lovely carkiss. And what I say I'll stick to; but I'll quarrel wi' no man."

"No," said the farrier, with bitter sarcasm, looking at the company generally; "and p'raps you aren't pig-headed; and p'raps you didn't say the cow was a red Durham; and p'raps you didn't say she'd got a star on her brow—stick to that, now you're at it."

"Come, come," said the landlord; "let the cow alone. The truth lies atween you: you're both right and both wrong, as I allays say. And as for the cow's being Mr. Lammeter's, I say nothing to that; but this I say, as the Rainbow's the Rainbow. And for the matter o' that, if the talk is to be o' the Lammeters, *you* know the most upo' that head, eh, Mr. Macey? You remember when first Mr. Lammeter's father came into these parts, and took the Warrens?"

Mr. Macey, tailor and parish-clerk, the latter of which functions rheumatism had of late obliged him to share with a small-featured young man who sat opposite him, held his white head on one side, and twirled his thumbs with an air of complacency, slightly seasoned with criticism. He smiled pityingly, in answer to the landlord's appeal, and said—

"Ay, ay; I know, I know; but I let other folks talk. I've laid by now, and gev up to the young uns. Ask them as have been to school at Tarley: they've learnt pernouncing; that's come up since my day."

"If you're pointing at me, Mr. Macey," said the deputy-clerk, with an air of anxious propriety, "I'm nowise a man to speak out of my place. As the psalm says—

'I know what's right, nor only so,
But also practise what I know.'"

"Well, then, I wish you'd keep hold o' the tune, when it's set for you; if you're for prac*tis*ing, I wish you'd prac*tise* that," said a large jocose-looking man, an excellent wheelwright in his week-day capacity, but on Sundays leader of the choir. He winked, as he spoke, at two of the company, who were known officially as the "bassoon" and the "key-bugle," in the confidence that he was expressing the sense of the musical profession in Raveloe.

Mr. Tookey, the deputy-clerk, who shared the unpopularity common to deputies, turned very red, but replied, with careful moderation—"Mr. Winthrop, if you'll bring me any proof as I'm in the wrong, I'm not the man to say I won't alter. But there's people set up their own ears for a standard, and expect the whole choir to follow 'em. There may be two opinions, I hope."

"Ay, ay," said Mr. Macey, who felt very well satisfied with this attack on youthful presumption; "you're right there, Tookey: there's allays two 'pinions; there's the 'pinion a man has of himsen, and there's the 'pinion other folks have on him. There'd be two 'pinions about a cracked bell, if the bell could hear itself."

"Well, Mr. Macey," said poor Tookey, serious amidst the general laughter, "I undertook to partially fill up the office of parish-clerk by Mr. Crackenthorp's desire, whenever your infirmities should make you unfitting; and it's one of the rights thereof to sing in the choir—else why have you done the same yourself?"

"Ah! but the old gentleman and you are two folks," said Ben Winthrop. "The old gentleman's got a gift. Why the Squire used to invite him to take a glass, only to hear him sing the 'Red Rovier;' didn't he, Mr. Macey? It's a nat'ral gift. There's my little lad Aaron, he's got a gift—he can sing a tune off straight, like a throstle. But as for you, Master Tookey, you'd better stick to your 'Amens:' your voice is well enough when you keep it up in your nose. It's your inside as isn't right made for music: it's no better nor a hollow stalk."

This kind of unflinching frankness was the most piquant form of joke to the company at the Rainbow, and Ben Winthrop's insult was felt by every body to have capped Mr. Macey's epigram.

"I see what it is plain enough," said Mr. Tookey, unable to keep cool any longer. "There's a consperacy to turn me out o' the choir, as I shouldn't share the Christmas money—that's where it is. But I shall speak to Mr. Crackenthorp; I'll not be put upon by no man."

"Nay, nay, Tookey," said Ben Winthrop. "We'll pay you your share to keep out of it—that's what we'll do. There's things folks 'ud pay to be rid on, besides varmin."

"Come, come," said the landlord, who felt that paying people for their absence was a principle dangerous to society; "a joke's a joke. We're all good friends here, I hope. We must give and take. You're both right and you're both wrong, as I say. I agree with Mr. Macey here, as there's two opinions; and if mine was asked, I should say they're both right. Tookey's right and Winthrop's right, and they've only got to split the difference and make themselves even."

The farrier was puffing his pipe rather fiercely, in some contempt at this trivial discussion. He had no ear for music himself, and never went to church, as being of the medical profession, and likely to be in requisition for delicate cows. But the butcher, having music in his soul, had listened with a divided desire for Tookey's defeat, and for the preservation of the peace.

"To be sure," he said, following up the landlord's conciliatory view, "we're fond of our old clerk; it's nat'ral, and him used to be such a singer, and got a brother as is known for the first fiddler in this country-side. Eh, it's a pity but what Solomon lived in our village, and could give us a tune when we liked; eh, Mr. Macey? I'd keep him in liver and lights for nothing—that I would."

"Ay, ay," said Mr. Macey, in the height of complacency; "our family's been known for musicianers as far back as any body can tell. But them things are dying out, as I tell Solomon every time he comes round; there's no voices like what there used to be, and there's nobody remembers what we remember, if it isn't the old crows."

"Ay, you remember when first Mr. Lammeter's father come into these parts, don't you, Mr. Macey?" said the landlord.

"I should think I did," said the old man, who had now gone through that complimentary process necessary to bring him up to the point of narration; "and a fine old gentleman he was—as fine, and finer nor the Mr. Lammeter as now is. He came from a bit north'ard, so far as I could ever make out. But there's nobody rightly knows about those parts: only it couldn't be far north'ard, nor much different from this country, for he brought a fine breed o' sheep with him, so there must be pastures there, and every thing reasonable. We heared tell as he'd sold his own land to come and take the Warrens, and that seemed odd for a man as had land of his own, to come and rent a farm in a strange place. But they said it was along of his wife's dying; though there's reasons in things as nobody knows on—that's pretty much what I've made out; though some folks are so wise, they'll find you fifty reasons straight off, and all the while the real reason's winking at 'em in the corner, and they niver see't. Howsomever, it was soon seen as we'd got a new parish'ner as know'd the rights and customs o' things, and kep a good house, and was well looked on by every body. And the young man—that's the Mr. Lammeter as now is, for he'd niver a sister—soon begun to court Miss Osgood, that's the sister o' the Mr. Osgood as now is, and a fine handsome lass she was—eh, you can't think—they pretend this young lass is like her, but that's the way wi' people as don't know what come before 'em. *I* should know, for I helped the old rector, Mr. Drumlow as was, I helped him marry 'em."

Here Mr. Macey paused; he always gave his narrative in instalments, expecting to be questioned according to precedent.

"Ay, and a partic'lar thing happened, didn't it, Mr. Macey, so as you were likely to remember that marriage?" said the landlord, in a congratulatory tone.

"I should think there did—a *very* partic'lar thing," said Mr. Macey, nodding sideways. "For Mr. Drumlow—poor old gentleman, I was fond on him, though he'd got a bit confused in his head, what wi' age and wi' taking a drop o' summat warm when the service come of a cold morning. And young Mr. Lammeter, he'd have no way but he must be married in Janiwary, which, to be sure, 's a unreasonable time to be married in, for it isn't like a christening or a burying, as you can't help; and so Mr. Drumlow—poor old gentleman, I was fond on him—but when he come to put the questions, he put 'em by the rule o' contrairy, like, and he says, 'Wilt thou have this man to thy wedded wife?' says he, and then he says, 'Wilt thou have this woman to thy wedded husband?' says he. But the partic'larest thing of all is, as nobody took any notice on it but me, and they answered straight off 'yes,' like as if it had been me saying 'Amen' i' the right place, without listening to what went before."

"But *you* knew what was going on well enough, didn't you, Mr. Macey? You were live enough, eh?" said the butcher.

"Lor bless you!" said Mr. Macey, pausing, and smiling in pity at the impotence of his hearer's imagination—"why, I was all of a tremble; it was as if I'd been a coat pulled by the two tails, like; for I couldn't stop the parson, I couldn't take upon me to do that; and yet I said to myself, I says,

'Suppose they shouldn't be fast married, 'cause the words are contrairy?' and my head went working like a mill, for I was allays uncommon for turning things over and seeing all round 'em; and I says to myself, 'Is't the meanin' or the words as makes folks fast i' wedlock?' For the parson meant right, and the bride and bridegroom meant right. But then, when I come to think on it, meanin' goes but a little way i' most things, for you may mean to stick things together and your glue may be bad, and then where are you? And so I says to mysen, 'It isn't the meanin', it's the glue.' And I was worreted as if I'd got three bells to pull at once, when we got into the vestry, and they begun to sign their names. But where's the use o' talking? you can't think what goes on in a 'cute man's inside."

"But you held in, for all that, didn't you, Mr. Macey?" said the landlord.

"Ay, I held in tight till I was by mysen wi' Mr. Drumlow, and then I out wi' every thing, but respectful, as I allays did. And he made light on it, and he says, 'Pooh, pooh, Macey, make yourself easy,' he says; 'it's neither the meaning nor the words—it's the re*gester* does it—that's the glue.' So you see he settled it easy; for parsons and doctors know every thing by heart, like, so as they aren't worreted wi' thinking what's the rights and wrongs o' things, as I'n been many and many's the time. And sure enough the wedding turned out all right, on'y poor Mrs. Lammeter—that's Miss Osgood as was—died afore the lasses were growed up; but for prosperity and every thing respectable, there's no family more looked on."

Every one of Mr. Macey's audience had heard this story many times, but it was listened to as if it had been a favorite tune, and at certain points the puffing of the pipes was momentarily suspended, that the listeners might give their whole minds to the expected words. But there was more to come; and Mr. Snell, the landlord, duly put the leading question.

"Why, old Mr. Lammeter had a pretty fortin, didn't they say, when he come into these parts?"

"Well, yes," said Mr. Macey; "but I dare say it's as much as this Mr. Lammeter has done to keep it whole. For there was allays a talk as nobody could get rich on the Warrens: though he holds it cheap, for it's what they call Charity Land."

"Ay, and there's few folks know so well as you how it come to be Charity Land, eh, Mr. Macey?" said the butcher.

"How should they?" said the old clerk, with some contempt. "Why, my grandfather made the grooms' livery for that Mr. Cliff as came and built the big stables at the Warrens. Why, they're stables four times as big as Squire Cass's, for he thought o' nothing but hosses and hunting, Cliff didn't—a Lunnon tailor, some folks said, as had gone mad wi' cheating. For he couldn't ride; lor bless you! they said he'd got no more grip o' the hoss than if his legs had been cross sticks; my grandfather heared old Squire Cass say so many and many a time. But ride he would as if Old Harry had been a-driving him; and he'd a son, a lad o' sixteen; and nothing would his father have him do, but he must ride and ride—though the lad was frighted, they said. And it was a common saying as the father wanted to ride the tailor out o' the lad, and make a gentleman on him—not but what I'm a tailor myself, but in respect as God made me such, I'm proud on it, for 'Macey, tailor,' 's been wrote up over our door since afore the Queen's heads went out on the shillings. But Cliff, he was ashamed o' being called a tailor, and he was sore vexed as his riding was laughed at, and nobody o' the gentlefolks hereabouts could abide him. Howsomever, the poor lad got sickly and died, and the father didn't live long after him, for he got queerer nor ever, and they said he used to go out i' the dead o' the night, wi' a lantern in his hand, to the stables, and set a lot o' lights burning, for he got as he couldn't sleep; and there he'd stand, cracking his whip and looking at his hosses; and they said it was a mercy as the stables didn't get burnt down wi' the poor dumb creaturs in 'em. But at last he died raving, and they found as he'd left all his property, Warrens and all, to a Lunnon Charity, and that's how the Warrens come to be Charity Land; though, as for the stables, Mr. Lammeter never uses 'em—they're out o' all charicter—lor bless you! if you was to set the doors a-banging in 'em, it 'ud sound like thunder half o'er the parish."

"Ay, but there's more going on in the stables than what folks see by daylight, eh, Mr. Macey?" said the landlord.

"Ay, ay; go that way of a dark night, that's all," said Mr. Macey, winking mysteriously, "and then make believe, if you like, as you didn't see lights i' the stables, nor hear the stamping o' the hosses, nor the cracking o' the whips, and howling, too, if it's tow'rt daybreak. 'Cliff's Holiday' has been the name of it ever sin' I were a boy; that's to say, some said as it was the holiday Old Harry gev him from roasting, like. That's what my father told me, and he was a reasonable man, though there's folks nowadays know what happened afore they were born better nor they know their own business."

"What do you say to that, eh, Dowlas?" said the landlord, turning to the farrier, who was swelling with impatience for his cue. "There's a nut for *you* to crack."

Mr. Dowlas was the negative spirit in the company, and was proud of his position.

"Say? I say what a man *should* say as doesn't shut his eyes to look at a finger-post. I say, as I'm ready to wager any man ten pound, if he'll stand out wi' me any dry night in the pasture before the Warren stables, as we shall neither see lights nor hear noises, if it isn't the blowing of our own noses. That's what I say, and I've said it many a time; but there's nobody 'ull ventur a ten-pun' note on their ghos'es as they make so sure of."

"Why, Dowlas, that's easy betting, that is," said Ben Winthrop. "You might as well bet a man as he wouldn't catch the rheumatise if he stood up to 's neck in the pool of a frosty night. It 'ud be fine fun for a man to win his bet as he'd catch the rheumatise. Folks as believe in Cliff's Holiday aren't a-going to ventur near it for a matter o' ten pound."

"If Master Dowlas wants to know the truth on it," said Mr. Macey, with a sarcastic smile, tapping his thumbs together, "he's no call to lay any bet—let him go and stan' by himself—there's nobody 'ull hinder him; and then he can let the parish'ners know if they're wrong."

"Thank you! I'm obliged to you," said the farrier, with a snort of scorn. "If folks are fools, it's no business o' mine. *I* don't want to make out the truth about ghos'es: I know it a'ready. But I'm not against a bet—every thing fair and open. Let any man bet me ten pound as I shall see Cliff's Holiday, and I'll go and stand by myself. I want no company. I'd as lief do it as I'd fill this pipe."

"Ah, but who's to watch you, Dowlas, and see you do it? That's no fair bet," said the butcher.

"No fair bet?" replied Mr. Dowlas, angrily. "I should like to hear any man stand up and say I want to bet unfair. Come now, Master Lundy, I should like to hear you say it."

"Very like you would," said the butcher. "But it's no business o' mine. You're none o' my bargains, and I aren't agoing to try and 'bate your price. If any body'll bid for you at your own vallying, let him. I'm for peace and quietness, I am."

"Yes, that's what every yapping cur is, when you hold a stick up at him," said the farrier. "But I'm afraid o' neither man nor ghost, and I'm ready to lay a fair bet—*I* aren't a turn-tail cur."

"Ay, but there's this in it, Dowlas," said the landlord, speaking in a tone of much candor and tolerance. "There's folks, i' my opinion, they can't see ghos'es, not if they stood as plain as a pike-staff before 'em. And there's reason i' that. For there's my wife now, can't smell, not if she'd the strongest o' cheese under her nose. I never see'd a ghost myself; but then I says to myself, 'Very like I haven't got the smell for 'em.' I mean, putting a ghost for a smell, or else contrairiways. And so, I'm for holding with both sides; for, as I say, the truth lies between 'em. And if Dowlas was to go and stand, and say he'd never seen a wink o' Cliff's Holiday all the night through, I'd back him; and if any body said as Cliff's Holiday was certain sure for all that, I'd back *him* too. For the smell's what I go by."

The landlord's analogical argument was not well received by the farrier—a man intensely opposed to compromise.

"Tut, tut," he said, setting down his glass with refreshed irritation; "what's the smell got to do with it? Did ever a ghost give a man a black eye? That's what I should like to know. If ghos'es want me to believe in 'em, let 'em leave off skulking i' the dark and i' lone places—let 'em come where there's company and candles."

"As if ghos'es 'ud want to be believed in by any body so ignirant!" said Mr. Macey, in deep disgust at the farrier's crass incompetence to apprehend the conditions of ghostly phenomena.

CHAPTER VII.

Yet the next moment there seemed to be some evidence that ghosts had a more condescending disposition than Mr. Macey attributed to them; for the pale thin figure of Silas Marner was suddenly seen standing in the warm light, uttering no word, but looking round at the company with his strange unearthly eyes. The long pipes gave a simultaneous movement, like the antennæ of startled insects, and every man present, not excepting even the skeptical farrier, had an impression that he saw, not Silas Marner in the flesh, but an apparition; for the door by which Silas had entered was hidden by the high-screened seats, and no one had noticed his approach. Mr. Macey, sitting a long way off the ghost, might be supposed to have felt an argumentative triumph, which would tend to neutralize his share of the general alarm. Had he not always said that when Silas Marner was in that strange trance of his, his soul went loose from his body? Here was the demonstration: nevertheless, on the whole, he would have been as well contented without it. For a few moments there was a dead silence, Marner's want of breath and agitation not allowing him to speak. The landlord, under the habitual sense that he was bound to keep his house open to all company, and confident in the protection of his unbroken neutrality, at last took on himself the task of adjuring the ghost.

"Master Marner," he said, in a conciliatory tone, "what's lacking to you? What's your business here?"

"Robbed!" said Silas, gaspingly. "I've been robbed! I want the constable—and the Justice—and Squire Cass—and Mr. Crackenthorp."

"Lay hold on him, Jem Rodney," said the landlord, the idea of a ghost subsiding; "he's off his head, I doubt. He's wet through."

Jem Rodney was the outermost man, and sat conveniently near Marner's standing-place; but he declined to give his services.

"Come and lay hold on him yourself, Mr. Snell, if you've a a mind," said Jem, rather sullenly. "He's been robbed, and murdered too, for what I know," he added, in a muttering tone.

"Jem Rodney!" said Silas, turning and fixing his strange eyes on the suspected man.

"Ay, Master Marner, what do ye want wi' me?" said Jem, trembling a little, and seizing his drinking-can as a defensive weapon.

"If it was you stole my money," said Silas, clasping his hands entreatingly, and raising his voice to a cry, "give it me back,—and I won't meddle with you. I won't set the constable on you. Give it me back, and I'll let you—I'll let you have a guinea."

"Me stole your money!" said Jem, angrily. "I'll pitch this can at your eye if you talk o' *my* stealing your money."

"Come, come, Master Marner," said the landlord, now rising resolutely, and seizing Marner by the shoulder, "if you've got any information to lay, speak it out sensible, and show as you're in your right mind, if you expect any body to listen to you. You're as wet as a drownded rat. Sit down and dry yourself, and speak straight forrard."

"Ah, to be sure, man," said the farrier, who began to feel that he had not been quite on a par with himself and the occasion. "Let's have no more staring and screaming, else we'll have you strapped for a madman. That was why I didn't speak at the first—thinks I, the man's run mad."

"Ay, ay, make him sit down," said several voices at once, well pleased that the reality of ghosts remained still an open question.

The landlord forced Marner to take off his coat, and then to sit down on a chair aloof from every one else in the centre of the circle, and in the direct rays of the fire. The weaver, too feeble to have any distinct purpose beyond that of getting help to recover his money, submitted unresistingly. The transient fears of the company were now forgotten in their strong curiosity, and all faces were turned towards Silas, when the landlord, having seated himself again, said—

"Now then, Master Marner, what's this you've got to say, as you've been robbed? Speak out."

"He'd better not say again as it was me robbed him," cried Jem Rodney, hastily. "What could I ha' done with his money? I could as easy steal the parson's surplice, and wear it."

"Hold your tongue, Jem, and let's hear what he's got to say," said the landlord. "Now then, Master Marner."

Silas now told his story under frequent questioning, as the mysterious character of the robbery became evident.

This strangely novel situation of opening his trouble to his Raveloe neighbors, of sitting in the warmth of a hearth not his own, and feeling the presence of faces and voices which were his nearest promise of help, had doubtless its influence on Marner, in spite of his passionate preoccupation with his loss. Our consciousness rarely registers the beginning of a growth within us any more than without us: there have been many circulations of the sap before we detect the smallest sign of the bud.

The slight suspicion with which his hearers at first listened to him, gradually melted away before the convincing simplicity of his distress: it was impossible for the neighbors to doubt that Marner was telling the truth, not because they were capable of arguing at once from the nature of his statements to the absence of any motive for making them falsely, but because, as Mr. Macey observed, "Folks as had the devil to back 'em were not likely to be so mushed" as poor Silas was. Rather, from the strange fact that the robber had left no traces, and had happened to know the nick of time, utterly incalculable by mortal agents, when Silas would go away from home without locking his door, the more probable conclusion seemed to be that his disreputable intimacy in that quarter, if it ever existed, had been broken up, and that, in consequence, this ill turn had been done to Marner by somebody it was quite in vain to set the constable after. Why this preternatural felon should be obliged to wait till the door was left unlocked, was a question which did not present itself.

"It isn't Jem Rodney as has done this work, Master Marner," said the landlord. "You mustn't be a-casting your eye at poor Jem. There may be a bit of a reckoning against Jem for the matter of a hare or so, if any body was bound to keep their eyes staring open, and niver to wink—but Jem's been a-sitting here drinking his can, like the decentest man i' the parish, since before you left your house, Master Marner, by your own account."

"Ay, ay," said Mr. Macey; "let's have no accusing o' the innicent. That isn't the law. There must be folks to swear again' a man before he can be ta'en up. Let's have no accusing o' the innicent, Master Marner."

Memory was not so utterly torpid in Silas that it could not be wakened by these words. With a movement of compunction as new and strange to him as every thing else within the last hour, he started from his chair and went close up to Jem, looking at him as if he wanted to assure himself of the expression in his face.

"I was wrong," he said—"yes, yes—I ought to have thought. There's nothing to witness against you, Jem. Only you'd been into my house oftener than any body else, and so you came into my head. I don't accuse you—I won't accuse any body—only," he added, lifting up his hands to his head, and turning away with bewildered misery, "I try—I try to think where my money can be."

"Ay, ay, they're gone where it's hot enough to melt 'em, I doubt," said Mr. Macey.

"Tchuh!" said the farrier. And then he asked, with a cross-examining air, "How much money might there be in the bags, Master Marner?"

"Two hundred and seventy-two pounds, twelve and sixpence, last night when I counted it," said Silas, seating himself again, with a groan.

"Pooh! why, they'd be none so heavy to carry. Some tramp's been in, that's all; and as for the no footmarks, and the bricks and the sand being all right—why, your eyes are pretty much like a insect's, Master Marner; they're obliged to look so close, you can't see much at a time. It's my opinion as, if I'd been you, or you'd been me—for it comes to the same thing—you wouldn't have thought you'd found every thing as you left it. But what I vote is, as two of the sensiblest o' the company should go with you to Master Kench, the constable's—he's ill i' bed, I know that much—and get him to appoint one of us his deppity; for that's the law, and I don't think any body 'ull take upon him to contradick me there. It isn't much of a walk to Kench's; and then if it's me as is deppity, I'll go back with you, Master Marner, and examine your primises; and if any body's got any fault to find with that, I'll thank him to stand up and say it out like a man."

By this pregnant speech the farrier had re-established his self-complacency, and waited with confidence to hear himself named as one of the superlatively sensible men.

"Let us see how the night is, though," said the landlord, who also considered himself personally concerned in this proposition. "Why it rains heavy still," he said, returning from the door.

"Well, I'm not the man to be afraid o' the rain," said the farrier. "For it'll look bad when Justice Malam hears as respectable men like us had a information laid before 'em and took no steps."

The landlord agreed with this view, and after taking the sense of the company, and duly rehearsing a small ceremony known in high ecclesiastical life as the *nolo episcopari*, he consented to take on himself the chill dignity of going to Kench's. But to the farrier's strong disgust, Mr. Macey now started an objection to his proposing himself as a deputy-constable; for that oracular old gentleman, claiming to know the law, stated, as a fact delivered to him by his father, that no doctor could be a constable.

"And you're a doctor, I reckon, though you're only a cow-doctor—for a fly's a fly, though it may be a hoss-fly," concluded Mr. Macey, wondering a little at his own "'cuteness."

There was a hot debate upon this, the farrier being of course indisposed to renounce the quality of doctor, but contending that a doctor could be a constable if he liked—the law meant, he needn't be one if he didn't like. Mr. Macey thought this was nonsense, since the law was not likely to be fonder of doctors more than of other folks. Moreover, if it was in the nature of doctors more than of other men not to like being constables, how came Mr. Dowlas to be so eager to act in that capacity?

"*I* don't want to act the constable," said the farrier, driven into a corner by this merciless reasoning; "and there's no man can say it of me, if he'd tell the truth. But if there's to be any jealousy and en*vy*ing about going to Kench's in the rain, let them go as like it—you won't get me to go, I can tell you."

By the landlord's intervention, however, the dispute was accommodated. Mr. Dowlas consented to go as a second person disinclined to act officially; and so poor Silas, furnished with some old coverings, turned out with his two companions into the rain again, thinking of the long night-hours before him, not as those do who long to rest, but as those who expect to "watch for the morning."

CHAPTER VIII.

When Godfrey Cass returned from Mrs. Osgood's party at midnight, he was not much surprised to learn that Dunsey had not come home. Perhaps he had not sold Wildfire, and was waiting for another chance—perhaps, on that foggy afternoon, he had preferred housing himself at the Red Lion at Batherley for the night, if the run had kept him in that neighborhood; for he was not likely to feel much concern about leaving his brother in suspense. Godfrey's mind was too full of Nancy Lammeter's looks and behavior, too full of the exasperation against himself and his lot, which the sight of her always produced in him, for him to give much thought to Wildfire, or to the probabilities of Dunstan's conduct.

The next morning the whole village was excited by the story of the robbery, and Godfrey, like every one else, was occupied in gathering and discussing news about it, and in visiting the Stone-pits. The rain had washed away all possibility of distinguishing footmarks, but a close investigation of the spot had disclosed, in the direction opposite to the village, a tinder-box, with a flint and steel, half sunk in the mud. It was not Silas's tinder-box, for the only one he had ever had was still standing on his shelf; and the inference generally accepted was, that the tinder-box in the ditch was somehow connected with the robbery. A small minority shook their heads, and intimated their opinion that it was not a robbery to have much light thrown on it by tinder-boxes, that Master Marner's tale had a queer look with it, and that such things had been known as a man's doing himself a mischief, and then setting the justice to look for the doer. But when questioned closely as to their grounds for this opinion, and what Master Marner had to gain by such false pretenses, they only shook their heads as before, and observed that there was no knowing what some folks counted gain; moreover, that every body had a right to their own opinions, grounds or no grounds, and that the weaver, as every body knew, was partly crazy. Mr. Macey, though he joined in the defense of Marner against all suspicions of deceit, also pooh-poohed the tinder-box; indeed, repudiated it as a rather impious suggestion, tending to imply that every thing must be done by human hands, and that there was no power which could make away with the guineas without moving the bricks. Nevertheless, he turned round rather sharply on Mr. Tookey, when the zealous deputy, feeling that this was a view of the case peculiarly suited to a parish-clerk, carried it still farther, and doubted whether it was right to inquire into a robbery at all when the circumstances were so mysterious.

"As if," concluded Mr. Tookey—"as if there was nothing but what could be made out by justices and constables."

"Now, don't you be for overshooting the mark, Tookey," said Mr. Macey, nodding his head aside admonishingly. "That's what your allays at; if I throw a stone and hit, you think there's summat better than hitting, and you try to throw a stone beyond. What I said was against the tinder-box: I said nothing against justices and constables, for they're o' King George's making, and it 'ud be ill-becoming a man in a parish office to fly out again' King George."

While these discussions were going on amongst the group outside the Rainbow, a higher consultation was being carried on within, under the presidency of Mr. Crackenthorp, the rector, assisted by Squire Cass, and other substantial parishioners. It had just occurred to Mr. Snell, the landlord—he being, as he observed, a man accustomed to put two and two together—to connect with the tinder-box, which, as deputy constable, he himself had had the honorable distinction of finding, certain recollections of a peddler who had called to drink at the house about a month before, and had actually stated that he carried a tinder-box about with him to light his pipe. Here, surely, was a clue to be followed out. And as memory, when duly impregnated with ascertained facts, is sometimes surprisingly fertile, Mr. Snell gradually recovered a vivid impression of the effect produced on him by the peddler's countenance and conversation. He had a "look with his eye" which fell unpleasantly on Mr. Snell's sensitive organism. To be sure, he didn't say any thing particular—no, except that about the tinder-box—but it isn't what a man says, it's the way he says it. Moreover, he had a swarthy foreignness of complexion, which boded little honesty.

"Did he wear ear-rings?" Mr. Crackenthorp wished to know, having some acquaintance with foreign customs.

"Well—stay—let me see," said Mr. Snell, like a docile clairvoyante, who would really not make a mistake if she could help it. After stretching the corners of his mouth and contracting his eyes, as if he were trying to see the ear-rings, he appeared to give up the effort, and said, "Well, he'd got ear-rings in his box to sell, so it's nat'ral to suppose he might wear 'em. But he called at every house, a'most, in the village: there's somebody else, mayhap, saw 'em in his ears, though I can't take upon me rightly to say."

Mr. Snell was correct in his surmise, that somebody else would remember the peddler's ear-rings. For, on the spread of inquiry among the villagers, it was stated with gathering emphasis, that the parson had wanted to know whether the peddler wore ear-rings in his ears, and an impression was created that a great deal depended on the eliciting of this fact. Of course, every one who heard the question, not having any distinct image of the peddler as *without* ear-rings, immediately had an image of him *with* ear-rings, larger or smaller, as the case might be; and the image was presently taken for a vivid recollection, so that the glazier's wife, a well-intentioned woman, not given to lying, and whose house was among the cleanest in the village, was ready to declare, as sure as ever she meant to take the sacrament the very next Christmas that was ever coming, that she had seen big ear-rings, in the shape of the young moon, in the peddler's two ears; while Jinny Oates, the cobbler's daughter, being a more imaginative person, stated not only that she had seen them too, but that they had made her blood creep, as it did at that very moment while there she stood.

Also, by way of throwing further light on this clue of the tinder-box, a collection was made of all the articles purchased from the peddler at various houses, and carried to the Rainbow to be exhibited there. In fact, there was a general feeling in the village, that for the clearing-up of this robbery there must be a great deal done at the Rainbow, and that no man need offer his wife an excuse for going there while it was the scene of severe public duties.

Some disappointment was felt, and perhaps a little indignation also, when it became known that Silas Marner, on being questioned by the Squire and the parson, had retained no other recollection of the peddler than that he had called at his door, but had not entered his house, having turned away at once when Silas, holding the door ajar, had said that he wanted nothing. This had been Silas's testimony, though he clutched strongly at the idea of the peddler's being the culprit, if only because it gave him a definite image of a whereabout for his gold, after it had been taken away from its hiding-place: he could see it now in the peddler's box. But it was observed with some irritation in the village, that any body but a "blind creatur" like Marner would have seen the man prowling about, for how came he to leave his tinder-box in the ditch close by, if he hadn't been lingering there? Doubtless, he had made his observations when he saw Marner at the door. Any body might know—and only look at him—that the weaver was a half-crazy miser. It was a wonder the peddler hadn't murdered him; men of that sort, with rings in their ears, had been known for murderers often and often; there had been one tried at the 'sizes, not so long ago but what there were people living who remembered it.

Godfrey Cass, indeed, entering the Rainbow during one of Mr. Snell's frequently repeated recitals of his testimony, had treated it lightly, stating that he himself had bought a penknife of the peddler, and thought him a merry grinning fellow enough; it was all nonsense, he said, about the man's evil looks. But this was spoken of in the village as the random talk of youth, "as if it was only Mr. Snell who had seen something odd about the peddler!" On the contrary, there were at least half a dozen who were ready to go before Justice Malam, and give in much more striking testimony than any the landlord could furnish. It was to be hoped Mr. Godfrey would not go to Tarley and throw cold water on what Mr. Snell said there, and so prevent the justice from drawing up a warrant. He was suspected of intending this, when, after mid-day, he was seen setting off on horseback in the direction of Tarley.

But by this time Godfrey's interest in the robbery had faded before his growing anxiety about Dunstan and Wildfire, and he was going, not to Tarley, but to Batherley, unable to rest in uncertainty about them any longer. The possibility that Dunstan had played him the ugly trick of riding away with Wildfire, to return at the end of a month, when he had gambled away or otherwise squandered the price of the horse, was a fear that urged itself upon him more, even, then the thought of an accidental injury; and now that the dance at Mrs. Osgood's was past, he was irritated with himself that he had trusted his horse to Dunstan. Instead of trying to still his fears, he encouraged them, with that superstitious impression which clings to us all, that if we expect evil very strongly it is the less likely to come; and when he heard a horse approaching at a trot, and saw a hat rising above a hedge beyond an angle of the lane, he felt as if his conjuration had succeeded. But no sooner did the horse come within sight, than his heart sank again. It was not Wildfire; and in a few moments more he discerned that the rider was not Dunstan, but Bryce, who pulled up to speak, with a face that implied something disagreeable.

"Well, Mr. Godfrey, that's a lucky brother of yours, that Master Dunsey, isn't he?"

"What do you mean?" said Godfrey, hastily.

"Why, hasn't he been home yet?" said Bryce.

"Home? no. What has happened? Be quick. What has he done with my horse?"

"Ah, I thought it was yours, though he pretended you had parted with it to him."

"Has he thrown him down and broken his knees?" said Godfrey, flushed with exasperation.

"Worse than that," said Bryce. "You see, I'd made a bargain with him to buy the horse for a hundred and twenty—a swinging price, but I always liked the horse. And what does he do but go and stake him—fly at a hedge with stakes in it, atop of a bank with a ditch before it. The horse had been dead a pretty good while when he was found. So he hasn't been home since, has he?"

"Home? no," said Godfrey, "and he'd better keep away. Confound me for a fool! I might have known this would be the end of it."

"Well, to tell you the truth," said Bryce, "after I'd bargained for the horse, it did come into my head that he might be riding and selling the horse without your knowledge, for I didn't believe it was his own. I knew Master Dunsey was up to his tricks sometimes. But where can he be gone? He's never been seen at Batherley. He couldn't have been hurt, for he must have walked off."

"Hurt?" said Godfrey, bitterly. "He'll never be hurt—he's made to hurt other people."

"And so you *did* give him leave to sell the horse, eh?" said Bryce.

"Yes; I wanted to part with the horse—he was always a little too hard in the mouth for me," said Godfrey; his pride making him wince under the idea that Bryce guessed the sale to be a matter of necessity. "I was going to see after him—I thought some mischief had happened. I'll go back now," he added, turning the horse's head, and wishing he could get rid of Bryce; for he felt that the long-dreaded crisis in his life was close upon him. "You're coming on to Raveloe, aren't you?"

"Well, no, not now," said Bryce. "I *was* coming round there, for I had to go to Flitton, and I thought I might as well take you in my way, and just let you know all I knew myself about the horse. I suppose Master Dunsey didn't like to show himself till the ill news had blown over a bit. He's perhaps gone to pay a visit at the Three Crowns, by Whitbridge—I know he's fond of the house."

"Perhaps he is," said Godfrey, rather absently. Then rousing himself, he said, with an effort at carelessness, "We shall hear of him soon enough, I'll be bound."

"Well, here's my turning," said Bryce, not surprised to perceive that Godfrey was rather 'down;' "so I'll bid you good-day, and wish I may bring you better news another time."

Godfrey rode along slowly, representing to himself the scene of confession to his father from which he felt that there was now no longer any escape. The revelation about the money must be made the very next morning; and if he withheld the rest, Dunstan would be sure to come back shortly, and, finding that he must bear the brunt of his father's anger, would tell the whole story out of spite, even though he had nothing to gain by it. There was one step, perhaps, by which he might still win Dunstan's silence and put off the evil day: he might tell his father that he had himself spent the money paid to him by Fowler; and as he had never been guilty of such an offense before, the affair would blow over after a little storming. But Godfrey could not bend himself to this. He felt that in letting Dunstan have the money, he had already been guilty of a breach of trust hardly less culpable than that of spending the money directly for his own behoof; and yet there was a distinction between the two acts which made him feel that the one was so much more blackening than the other as to be intolerable to him.

"I don't pretend to be a good fellow," he said to himself; "but I'm not a scoundrel—at least, I'll stop short somewhere. I'll bear the consequences of what I *have* done, sooner than make believe I've done what I never would have done. I'd never have spent the money for my own pleasure—I was tortured into it."

Through the remainder of this day Godfrey, with only occasional fluctuations, kept his will bent in the direction of a complete avowal to his father, and he withheld the story of Wildfire's loss till the next morning, that it might serve him as an introduction to heavier matter. The old Squire was accustomed to his son's frequent absence from home, and thought neither Dunstan's nor Wildfire's non-appearance a matter calling for remark. Godfrey said to himself again and again, that if he let slip this one opportunity of confession, he might never have another; the revelation might be made even in a more odious way than by Dunstan's malignity: *she* might come as she had threatened to do. And then he tried to make the scene easier to himself by rehearsal: he made up his mind how he would pass from the admission of his weakness in letting Dunstan have the money to the fact that Dunstan had a hold on him which he had been unable to shake off, and how he would work up his father to expect something very bad before he told him the fact. The old Squire was an implacable man: he made resolutions in violent anger, but he was not to be moved from them after his anger had subsided—as fiery volcanic matters cool and harden into rock. Like many violent and implacable men, he allowed evils to grow under favor of his own heedlessness, till they pressed upon him with exasperating force, and then he turned round with fierce severity and became unrelentingly hard. This was his system with his tenants: he allowed them to get into arrears, neglect their fences, reduce their stock, sell their straw, and otherwise go the wrong way,—and then, when he became short of money in consequence of this indulgence, he took the hardest measures and would listen to no appeal. Godfrey knew all this, and felt it with the greater force because he had constantly suffered annoyance from witnessing his father's sudden fits of unrelentingness, for which his own habitual irresolution deprived him of all sympathy. (He was not critical on the faulty indulgence which preceded these fits; *that* seemed to him natural enough.) Still there was just the chance, Godfrey thought, that his father's pride might see this marriage in a light that would induce him to hush it up, rather than turn his son out and make the family the talk of the country for ten miles round.

This was the view of the case that Godfrey managed to keep before him pretty closely till midnight, and he went to sleep thinking that he had done with inward debating. But when he awoke in the still morning darkness he found it impossible to re-awaken his evening thoughts; it was as if they had been tired out and were not to be roused to further work. Instead of arguments for confession, he could now feel the presence of nothing but its evil consequences: the old dread of disgrace came back—the old shrinking from the thought of raising a hopeless barrier between himself and Nancy—the old disposition to rely on chances which might be favorable to him, and save him from betrayal. Why, after all, should he cut off the hope of them by his own act? He had seen the matter in a wrong light yesterday. He had been in a rage with Dunstan, and had thought of nothing but a thorough break-up of their mutual understanding; but what it would be really wisest for him to do, was to try and soften his father's anger against Dunsey, and keep things as nearly as possible in their old condition. If Dunsey did not come back for a few days (and Godfrey did not know but that the rascal had enough money in his pocket to enable him to keep away still longer), every thing might blow over.

CHAPTER IX.

GODFREY rose and took his own breakfast earlier than usual, but lingered in the wainscoted parlor till his younger brothers had finished their meal and gone out, awaiting his father, who always went out and had a walk with his managing-man before breakfast. Every one breakfasted at a different hour in the Red House, and the Squire was always the latest, giving a long chance to a rather feeble morning appetite before he tried it. The table had been spread with substantial eatables nearly two hours before he presented himself—a tall, stout man of sixty, with a face in which the knit brow and rather hard glance seemed contradicted by the slack and feeble mouth. His person showed marks of habitual neglect, his dress was slovenly; and yet there was something in the presence of the old Squire distinguishable from that of the ordinary farmers in the parish, who were perhaps every whit as refined as he, but, having slouched their way through life with a consciousness of being in the vicinity of their "betters," wanted that self-possession and authoritativeness of voice and carriage which belonged to a man who thought of superiors as remote existences, with whom he had personally little more to do than with America or the stars. The Squire had been used to parish homage all his life, used to the presupposition that his family, his tankards, and every thing that was his, were the oldest and best; and as he never associated with any gentry higher than himself, his opinion was not disturbed by comparison.

He glanced at his son as he entered the room, and said, "What, sir! haven't *you* had your breakfast yet?" but there was no pleasant morning greeting between them; not because of any unfriendliness, but because the sweet flower of courtesy is not a growth of such homes as the Red House.

"Yes, sir," said Godfrey, "I've had my breakfast, but I was waiting to speak to you."

"Ah! well," said the Squire, throwing himself indifferently into his chair, and speaking in a ponderous coughing fashion, which was felt in Raveloe to be a sort of privilege of his rank, while he cut a piece of beef, and held it up before the deer-hound that had come in with him. "Ring the bell for my ale, will you? You youngsters' business is your own pleasure, mostly. There's no hurry about it for any body but yourselves."

The Squire's life was quite as idle as his sons', but it was a fiction kept up by himself and his contemporaries in Raveloe that youth was exclusively the period of folly, and that their aged wisdom was constantly in a state of endurance mitigated by sarcasm. Godfrey waited, before he spoke again, until the ale had been brought and the door closed— an interval during which Fleet, the deer-hound, had consumed enough bits of beef to make a poor man's holiday dinner.

"There's been a cursed piece of ill-luck with Wildfire," he began; "happened the day before yesterday."

"What! broke his knees?" said the Squire, after taking a draught of ale. "I thought you knew how to ride better than that, sir. I never threw a horse down in my life. If I had, I might ha' whistled for another, for *my* father wasn't quite so ready to unstring as some other fathers I know of. But they must turn over a new leaf—*they* must. What with mortgages and arrears, I'm as short o' cash as a roadside pauper. And that fool Kimble says the newspaper's talking about peace. Why, the country wouldn't have a leg to stand on. Prices 'ud run down like a jack, and I should never get my arrears, not if I sold all the fellows up. And there's that damned Fowler, I won't put up with him any longer; I've told Winthrop to go to Cox this very day. The lying scoundrel told me he'd be sure to pay me a hundred last month. He takes advantage because he's on that outlying farm, and thinks I shall forget him."

The squire had delivered this speech in a coughing and interrupted manner, but with no pause long enough for Godfrey to make it a pretext for taking up the word again. He felt that his father meant to ward off any request for money on the ground of the misfortune with Wildfire, and that the emphasis he had thus been led to lay on his shortness of cash and his arrears was likely to produce an attitude of mind the most unfavorable for his own disclosure. But he must go on, now he had begun.

"It's worse than breaking the horse's knees — he's been staked and killed," he said, as soon as his father was silent.

and had begun to cut his meat. "But I wasn't thinking of asking you to buy me another horse; I was only thinking I'd lost the means of paying you with the price of Wildfire, as I'd meant to do. Dunsey took him to the hunt to sell him for me the other day, and after he'd made a bargain for a hundred and twenty with Bryce, he went after the hounds, and took some fool's leap or other, that did for the horse at once. If it hadn't been for that, I should have paid you a hundred pounds this morning."

The Squire had laid down his knife and fork, and was staring at his son in amazement, not being sufficiently quick of brain to form a probable guess as to what could have caused so strange an inversion of the paternal and filial relations as this proposition of his son to pay him a hundred pounds.

"The truth is, sir—I'm very sorry—I was quite to blame," said Godfrey. "Fowler did pay that hundred pounds. He paid it to me, when I was over there one day last month. And Dunsey bothered me for the money, and I let him have it, because I hoped I should be able to pay it you before this."

The Squire was purple with anger before his son had done speaking, and found utterance difficult. "You let Dunsey have it, sir? And how long have you been so thick with Dunsey that you must *collogue* with him to embezzle my money? Are you turning out a scamp? I tell you I won't have it. I'll turn the whole pack of you out of the house together, and marry again. I'd have you to remember, sir, my property's got no entail on it;—since my grandfather's time the Casses can do as they like with their land. Remember that, sir. Let Dunsey have the money! Why should you let Dunsey have the money? There's some lie at the bottom of it."

"There's no lie, sir," said Godfrey. "I wouldn't have spent the money myself, but Dunsey bothered me, and I was a fool, and let him have it. But I meant to pay it, whether he did or not. That's the whole story. I never meant to embezzle money, and I'm not the man to do it. You never knew me do a dishonest trick, sir."

"Where's Dunsey, then? What do you stand talking there for? Go and fetch Dunsey, as I tell you, and let him give account of what he wanted the money for, and what he's done with it. He shall repent it. I'll turn him out. I said I would, and I'll do it. He sha'n't brave me. Go and fetch him."

"Dunsey isn't come back, sir."

"What! did he break his own neck, then?" said the

Squire, with some disgust at the idea that, in that case, he could not fulfill his threat.

"No, he wasn't hurt, I believe, for the horse was found dead, and Dunsey must have walked off. I dare say we shall see him again by-and-by. I don't know where he is."

"And what must you be letting him have my money for? Answer me that," said the Squire, attacking Godfrey again, since Dunsey was not within reach.

"Well, sir, I don't know," said Godfrey hesitatingly. That was a feeble evasion, but Godfrey was not fond of lying, and, not being sufficiently aware that no sort of duplicity can long flourish without the help of vocal falsehoods, he was quite unprepared with invented motives.

"You don't know? I tell you what it is, sir. You've been up to some trick, and you've been bribing him not to tell," said the Squire, with a sudden acuteness which startled Godfrey, who felt his heart beat violently at the nearness of his father's guess. The sudden alarm pushed him on to take the next step—a very slight impulse suffices for that on a downward road.

"Why, sir," he said, trying to speak with careless ease, "it was a little affair between me and Dunsey; it's no matter to any body else. It's hardly worth while to pry into young men's fooleries: it wouldn't have made any difference to you, sir, if I'd not had the bad luck to lose Wildfire. I should have paid you the money."

"Fooleries! Pshaw! it's time you'd done with fooleries. And I'd have you know, sir, you *must* ha' done with 'em," said the Squire, frowning and casting an angry glance at his son. "Your goings-on are not what I shall find money for any longer. There's my grandfather had his stables full o' horses, and kept a good house, too, and in worse times, by what I can make out; and so might I, if I hadn't four good-for-nothing fellows to hang on me like horse-leeches. I've been too good a father to you all—that's what it is. But I shall pull up, sir."

Godfrey was silent. He was not likely to be very penetrating in his judgments, but he had always had a sense that his father's indulgence had not been kindness, and had had a vague looking for some discipline that would have checked his own errant weakness, and helped his better will. The Squire ate his bread and meat hastily, took a deep draught of ale, then turned his chair from the table, and began to speak again.

"It'll be all the worse for you, you know—you'd need try and help me keep things together."

"Well, sir, I've often offered to take the management of things, but you know you've taken it ill always, and seemed to think I wanted to push you out of your place."

"I know nothing o' your offering or o' my taking it ill," said the Squire, whose memory consisted in certain strong impressions unmodified by detail; "but I know, one while you seemed to be thinking o' marrying, and I didn't offer to put any obstacles in your way, as some fathers would. I'd as lieve you married Lammeter's daughter as any body. I suppose, if I'd said you nay you'd ha' kept on with it; but, for want o' contradiction, you've changed your mind. You're a shilly-shally fellow: you take after your poor mother. She never had a will of her own; a woman has no call for one, if she's got a proper man for a husband. But *your* wife had need have one, for you hardly know your own mind enough to make both your legs walk one way. The lass hasn't said downright she won't have you, has she?"

"No," said Godfrey, feeling very hot and uncomfortable; "but I don't think she will."

"Think! why haven't you the courage to ask her? Do you stick to it, you want to have *her*—that's the thing?"

"There's no other woman I want to marry," said Godfrey, evasively.

"Well, then, let me make the offer for you, that's all, if you haven't the pluck to do it yourself. Lammeter isn't likely to be loath for his daughter to marry into *my* family, I should think. And as for the pretty lass, she wouldn't have her cousin—and there's nobody else, as I see, could ha' stood in your way."

"I'd rather let it be, please sir, at present," said Godfrey, in alarm. "I think she's a little offended with me just now, and I should like to speak for myself. A man must manage these things for himself."

"Well, speak, then, and manage it, and see if you can't turn over a new leaf. That's what a man must do when he thinks o' marrying."

"I don't see how I can think of it at present, sir. You wouldn't like to settle me on one of the farms, I suppose, and I don't think she'd come to live in this house with all my brothers. It's a different sort of life to what she's been used to."

"Not come to live in this house? Don't tell me. You ask her, that's all," said the Squire, with a short, scornful laugh.

"I'd rather let the thing be, at present, sir," said Godfrey. "I hope you won't try to hurry it on by saying any thing."

"I shall do what I choose," said the Squire, "and I shall let you know I'm master; else you may turn out, and find an estate to drop into somewhere else. Go out and tell Winthrop not to go to Cox's, but wait for me. And tell 'em to get my horse saddled. And stop: look out and get that hack o' Dunsey's sold, and hand me the money, will you? He'll keep no more hacks at my expense. And if you know where he's sneaking—I daresay you do—you may tell him to spare himself the journey o' coming back home. Let him turn ostler, and keep himself. He sha'n't hang on me any more."

"I don't know where he is, sir; and if I did, it isn't my place to tell him to keep away," said Godfrey, moving towards the door.

"Confound it, sir, don't stay arguing, but go and order my horse," said the Squire, taking up a pipe.

Godfrey left the room, hardly knowing whether he were more relieved by the sense that the interview was ended without having made any change in his position, or more uneasy that he had entangled himself still further in prevarication and deceit. What had passed about his proposing to Nancy had raised a new alarm, lest by some after-dinner words of his father's to Mr. Lammeter he should be thrown into the embarrassment of being obliged absolutely to decline her when she seemed to be within his reach. He fled to his usual refuge, that of hoping for some unforeseen turn of fortune, some favorable chance which would save him from unpleasant consequences—perhaps even justify his insincerity by manifesting its prudence. And in this point of trusting to some throw of fortune's dice, Godfrey can hardly be called specially old-fashioned. Favorable Chance, I fancy, is the god of all men who follow their own devices instead of obeying a law they believe in. Let even a polished man of these days get into a position he is ashamed to avow, and his mind will be bent on all the possible issues that may deliver him from the calculable results of that position. Let him live outside his income, or shirk the resolute honest work that brings wages, and he will presently find himself dreaming of a possible benefactor, a possible simpleton who may be cajoled into using his interest, a possible state of mind in some possible person not yet forthcoming. Let him neglect the responsibilities of his office, and he will inevitably anchor himself on the chance that the thing left undone may turn out not to be of the supposed importance. Let him betray his friend's confidence, and he will adore that same cunning complexity called Chance, which gives him the hope that his friend will never know. Let him forsake a decent craft that he may pursue the gentilities of a profession to which nature never called him, and his religion will infallibly be the worship of blessed Chance, which he will believe in as the mighty creator of success. The evil principle deprecated in that religion, is the orderly sequence by which the seed brings forth a crop after its kind.

CHAPTER X.

Justice Malam was naturally regarded in Tarley and Raveloe as a man of capacious mind, seeing that he could draw much wider conclusions without evidence than could be expected of his neighbors who were not on the Commission of the Peace. Such a man was not likely to neglect the clue of the tinder-box, and an inquiry was set on foot concerning a peddler, name unknown, with curly black hair and a foreign complexion, carrying a box of cutlery and jewelry, and wearing large rings in his ears. But either because inquiry was too slow-footed to overtake him, or because the description applied to so many peddlers that inquiry did not know how to choose among them, weeks passed away, and there was no other result concerning the robbery than a gradual cessation of the excitement it had caused in Raveloe. Dunstan Cass's absence was hardly a subject of remark: he had once before had a quarrel with his father, and had gone off, nobody knew whither, to return at the end of six weeks, take up his old quarters unforbidden, and swagger as usual. His own family, who equally expected this issue, with the sole difference that the Squire was determined this time to forbid him the old quarters, never mentioned his absence; and when his uncle Kimble or Mr. Osgood noticed it, the story of his having killed Wildfire, and committed some offense against his father, was enough to prevent surprise. To connect the fact of Dunsey's disappearance with that of the robbery occurring on the same day, lay quite away from the track of every one's thought—even Godfrey's, who had better reason than any one else to know what his brother was capable of. He remembered no mention of the weaver between them since the time, twelve years ago, when it was their boyish sport to deride him; and, besides, his imagination constantly created an *alibi* for Dunstan: he saw him continually in some congenial haunt, to which he had walked off on leaving Wildfire—saw him sponging on chance acquaintances, and meditating a return home to the old amusement of tormenting his elder brother. Even if any brain in Raveloe had put the said two facts together, I doubt whether a combination so injurious to the prescriptive respectability of a family with a mural monument and venerable tankards, would not have been suppressed as of unsound tendency. But Christmas puddings, brawn, and abundance of spirituous liquors, throwing the mental originality into the channel of nightmare, are great preservatives against a dangerous spontaneity of waking thought.

When the robbery was talked of at the Rainbow and elsewhere, in good company, the balance continued to waver between the rational explanation founded on the tinder-box, and the theory of an impenetrable mystery that mocked investigation. The advocates of the tinder-box-and-peddler view considered the other side a muddle-headed and credulous set, who, because they themselves were wall-eyed, supposed every body else to have the same blank outlook; and the adherents of the inexplicable more than hinted that their antagonists were animals inclined to crow before they had found any corn—mere skimming-dishes in point of depth—whose clear-sightedness consisted in supposing there was nothing behind a barn-door because they couldn't see through it; so that, though their controversy did not serve to elicit the fact concerning the robbery, it elicited some true opinions of collateral importance.

But while poor Silas's loss served thus to brush the slow current of Raveloe conversation, Silas himself was feeling the withering desolation of that bereavement, about which his neighbors were arguing at their ease. To any one who had observed him before he lost his gold, it might have seemed that so withered and shrunken a life as his could hardly be susceptible of a bruise, could hardly endure any subtraction but such as would put an end to it altogether. But in reality it had been an eager life, filled with immediate purpose, which fenced him in from the wide, cheerless unknown. It had been a clinging life; and though the object round which its fibres had clung was a dead disrupted thing, it satisfied the need for clinging. But now the fence was broken down—the support was snatched away. Marner's thoughts could no longer move in their old round, and were baffled by a blank like that which meets a plodding ant when the earth has broken away on its homeward path. The loom was there, and the weaving, and the growing pattern in the cloth; but the bright treasure in the hole under his feet was gone; the prospect of handling and counting it was gone: the evening had no phantasm of delight to still the poor soul's craving. The thought of the money he would get by his actual work could bring no joy, for its meagre image was only a fresh reminder of his loss; and hope was too heavily crushed by the sudden blow for his imagination to dwell on the growth of a new hoard from that small beginning.

He filled up the blank with grief. As he sat weaving, he every now and then moaned low, like one in pain: it was the sign that his thoughts had come round again to the sudden chasm—to the empty evening time. And all the evening, as he sat in his loneliness by his dull fire, he leaned his elbows on his knees, and clasped his head with his hands, and moaned very low—not as one who seeks to be heard.

And yet he was not utterly forsaken in his trouble. The repulsion Marner had always created in his neighbors was partly dissipated by the new light in which this misfortune had shown him. Instead of a man who had more cunning than honest folks could come by, and, what was worse, had not the inclination to use that cunning in a neighborly way, it was now apparent that Silas had not cunning enough to keep his own. He was generally spoken of as a "poor mushed creatur;" and that avoidance of his neighbors, which had before been referred to his ill-will, and to a probable addiction to worse company, was now considered mere craziness.

This change to a kindlier feeling was shown in various ways. The odor of Christmas cooking being on the wind, it was the season when superfluous pork and black puddings are suggestive of charity in well-to-do families; and Silas's misfortune had brought him uppermost in the memory of housekeepers like Mrs. Osgood. Mr. Crackenthorp, too, while he admonished Silas that his money had probably been taken from him because he thought too much of it, and never came to church, enforced the doctrine by a present of pigs' pettitoes, well calculated to dissipate unfounded prejudices against the clerical character. Neighbors, who had nothing but verbal consolation to give, showed a disposition not only to greet Silas, and discuss his misfortune at some length when they encountered him in the village, but also to take the trouble of calling at his cottage, and getting him to repeat all the details on the very spot; and then they would try to cheer him by saying, "Well, Master Marner, you're no worse off nor other poor folks, after all; and if you was to be crippled, the parish 'ud give you a 'lowance."

I suppose one reason why we are seldom able to comfort our neighbors with our words is, that our good-will gets adulterated, in spite of ourselves, before it can pass our lips. We can send black puddings and pettitoes without giving them a flavor or our own egoism; but language is a stream that is almost sure to smack of a mingled soil. There was a fair proportion of kindness in Raveloe; but it was often of a beery and bungling sort, and took the shape least allied to the complimentary and hypocritical.

Mr. Macey, for example, coming one evening expressly to let Silas know that recent events had given him the advantage of standing more favorably in the opinion of a man whose judgment was not formed lightly, opened the conversation by saying, as soon as he had seated himself and adjusted his thumbs—

"Come, Master Marner, why, you've no call to sit a-moaning. You're a deal better off to ha' lost your money, nor to ha' kep it by foul means. I used to think, when you first come into these parts, as you were no better nor you should be; you were younger a deal than what you are now; but you were allays a staring, white-faced creatur, partly like a bald-faced calf, as I may say. But there's no knowing; it isn't every queer-looksed thing as Old Harry's had the making of—I mean, speaking o' toads and such; for they're often harmless, and useful against varmin. And it's pretty much the same wi' you, as fur as I can see. Though as to the yarbs and stuff to cure the breathing, if you brought that sort o' knowledge from distant parts, you might ha' been a bit freer of it. And if the knowledge wasn't well come by, why, you might ha' made up for it by coming to church reg'lar; for, as for the children as the Wise Woman charmed, I've been at the christening of 'em again and again, and they took the water just as well. And that's reasonable; for if Old Harry's a mind to do a bit o' kindness for a holiday, like, who's got any thing against it? That's my thinking; and I've been clerk o' this parish forty year, and I know, when the parson and me does the cussing of a Ash Wednesday, there's no cussing o' folks as have a mind to be cured without a doctor, let Kimble say what he will. And so, Master Marner, as I was saying—for there's windings i' things as they may carry you to the fur end o' the prayer-book afore you get back to 'em—my advice is, as you keep up your sperrits; for as for thinking you're a deep un, and ha' got more inside you nor 'ull bear daylight, I'm not o' that opinion at all, and so I tell the neighbors. For, says I, you talk o' Master Marner making out a tale—why, it's nonsense, that is: it 'ud take a 'cute man to make a tale like that; and, says I, he looked as scared as a rabbit."

During this discursive address Silas had continued motionless in his previous attitude, leaning his elbows on his knees, and pressing his hands against his head. Mr. Macey, not doubting that he had been listened to, paused, in the expectation of some appreciatory reply, but Marner remained silent. He had a sense that the old man meant to be good-natured and neighborly; but the kindness fell on him as sunshine falls on the wretched—he had no heart to taste it, and felt that it was very far off him.

"Come, Master Marner, have you got nothing to say to that?" said Mr. Macey, at last, with a slight accent of impatience.

"Oh," said Marner, slowly, shaking his head between his hands, "I thank you—thank you—kindly."

"Ay, ay, to be sure: I thought you would," said Mr. Macey; "and my advice is—have you got a Sunday suit?"

"No," said Marner.

"I doubted it was so," said Mr. Macey. "Now, let me advise you to get a Sunday suit: there's Tookey, he's a poor creatur, but he's got my tailoring business, and some o' my money in it, and he shall make a suit at a low price, and give you trust, and then you can come to church, and be a bit neighborly. Why, you've never heared me say 'Amen' since you come into these parts, and I recommend you to lose no time, for it'll be poor work when Tookey has it all to himself, for I mayn't be equil to stand i' the desk at all, come another winter." Here Mr. Macey paused, perhaps expecting some sign of emotion in his hearer; but not observing any, he went on. "And as for the money for the suit o' clothes, why, you get a matter of a pound a-week at your weaving, Master Marner, and you're a young man, eh, for all you look so mushed. Why, you couldn't ha' been five-and-twenty when you come into these parts, eh?"

Silas started a little at the change to a questioning tone, and answered mildly, "I don't know; I can't rightly say—it's a long while since."

After receiving such an answer as this, it is not surprising that Mr. Macey observed, later on in the evening at the Rainbow, that Marner's head was "all of a muddle," and that it was to be doubted if he ever knew when Sunday came around, which showed him a worse heathen than many a dog.

Another of Silas's comforters, besides Mr. Macey, came to him with a mind highly charged on the same topic. This was Mrs. Winthrop, the wheelwright's wife. The inhabitants of Raveloe were not severely regular in their church-going, and perhaps there was hardly a person in the parish who would not have held that to go to church every Sunday in the calendar would have shown a greedy desire to stand well with Heaven, and get an undue advantage over their neighbors—a wish to be better than the "common run," that would have implied a reflection on those who had had godfathers and godmothers as well as themselves, and had an equal right to the burying-service. At the same time, it was understood to be requisite for all who were not household servants, or young men, to take the sacrament at one of the great festivals: Squire Cass himself took it on Christmas-day; while those who were held to be "good livers" went to church with greater, though still with moderate, frequency.

Mrs. Winthrop was one of these: she was in all respects a woman of scrupulous conscience, so eager for duties, that life seemed to offer them too scantily unless she rose at half-past four, though this threw a scarcity of work over the more advanced hours of the morning, which it was a constant problem with her to remove. Yet she had not the vixenish temper which is sometimes supposed to be a necessary condition of such habits: she was a very mild, patient woman, whose nature it was to seek out all the sadder and more serious elements of life, and pasture her mind upon them. She was the person always first thought of in Raveloe when there was illness or death in a family, when leeches were to be applied, or there was a sudden disappointment in a monthly nurse. She was a "comfortable woman"—good-looking, fresh-complexioned, having her lips always slightly screwed, as if she felt herself in a sick-room with the doctor or the clergyman present. But she was never whimpering; no one had seen her shed tears; she was simply grave and inclined to shake her head and sigh, almost imperceptibly, like a funereal mourner who is not a relation. It seemed surprising that Ben Winthrop, who loved his quart-pot and his joke, got along so well with Dolly; but she took her husband's jokes and joviality as patiently as every thing else, considering that "men *would* be so," and viewing the stronger sex in the light of animals whom it had pleased Heaven to make naturally troublesome, like bulls and turkey-cocks.

This good wholesome woman could hardly fail to have her mind drawn strongly towards Silas Marner, now that he appeared in the light of a sufferer; and one Sunday afternoon she took her little boy Aaron with her, and went to call on Silas, carrying in her hand some small lard-cakes, flat paste-like articles, much esteemed in Raveloe. Aaron, an apple-cheeked youngster of seven, with a clean starched frill, which looked like a plate for the apples, needed all his adventurous curiosity to embolden him against the possibility that the big-eyed weaver might do him some bodily injury; and his dubiety was much increased when, on arriving at the Stone pits, they heard the mysterious sound of the loom.

"Ah, it is as I thought," said Mrs. Winthrop, sadly.

They had to knock loudly before Silas heard them; but when he did come to the door, he showed no impatience, as he would once have done, at a visit that had been unasked for and unexpected. Formerly, his heart had been as a locked casket with its treasure inside; but now the casket was empty, and the lock was broken. Left groping in darkness, with his prop utterly gone, Silas had inevitably a sense, though a dull and half-despairing one, that if any help came to him it must come from without; and there was a slight stirring of expectation at the sight of his fellow-men, a faint consciousness of dependence on their good-will. He opened the door wide to admit Dolly, but without otherwise returning her greeting than by moving the arm-chair a few inches as a sign that she was to sit down in it. Dolly, as soon as she was seated, removed the white cloth that covered her lard-cakes, and said in her gravest way—

"I'd a baking yisterday, Master Marner, and the lard-cakes turned out better nor common, and I'd ha' asked you to accept some, if you'd thought well. I don't eat such things myself, for a bit o' bread's what I like from one year's end to the other; but men's stomichs are made so comical, they want a change—they do, I know, God help 'em."

Dolly sighed gently as she held out the cakes to Silas, who thanked her kindly, and looked very close at them, absently, being accustomed to look so at every thing he took into his hand—eyed all the while by the wondering bright orbs of the small Aaron, who had made an outwork of his mother's chair, and was peeping round from behind it.

"There's letters pricked on 'em," said Dolly. "I can't read 'em myself, and there's nobody, not Mr. Macey himself, rightly knows what they mean; but they've a good meaning, for they're the same as is on the pulpit-cloth at church. What are they, Aaron, my dear?"

Aaron retreated completely behind his outwork.

"Oh go, that's naughty," said his mother, mildly. "Well, whativer the letters are, they've a good meaning; and it's a stamp as has been in our house, Ben says, ever since he was a little un, and his mother used to put it on the cakes, and I've allays put it on too; for if there's any good, we've need of it i' this world."

"It's I. H. S.," said Silas, at which proof of learning Aaron peeped round the chair again.

"Well, to be sure, you can read 'em off," said Dolly.

"Ben's read 'em to me many and many a time, but they slip out o' my mind again; the more's the pity, for they're good letters, else they wouldn't be in the church; and so I prick 'em on all the loaves and all the cakes, though sometimes they won't hold, because o' the rising—for, as I said, if there's any good to be got, we've need on it i' this world—that we have; and I hope they'll bring good to you, Master Marner, for it's wi' that will I brought you the cakes; and you see the letters have held better nor common."

Silas was as unable to interpret the letters as Dolly, but there was no possibility of misunderstanding the desire to give comfort that made itself heard in her quiet tones. He said, with more feeling than before—"Thank you—thank you kindly." But he laid down the cakes and seated himself absently—drearily unconscious of any distinct benefit towards which the cakes and the letters, or even Dolly's kindness, could tend for him.

"Ah, if there's good anywhere, we've need of it," repeated Dolly, who did not lightly forsake a serviceable phrase. She looked at Silas pityingly as she went on. "But you didn't hear the church-bells this morning, Master Marner? I doubt you didn't know it was Sunday. Living so lone here, you lose your count, I daresay; and then, when your loom makes a noise, you can't hear the bells, more partic'lar now the frost kills the sound."

"Yes, I did; I heard 'em," said Silas, to whom Sunday bells were a mere accident of the day, and not part of its sacredness. There had been no bells in Lantern Yard.

"Dear heart!" said Dolly, pausing before she spoke again. "But what a pity it is you should work of a Sunday, and not clean yourself—if you *didn't* go to church; for if you'd a roasting bit, it might be as you couldn't leave it, being a lone man. But there's the bakehus, if you could make up your mind to spend a twopence on the oven now and then, not every week, in course—I shouldn't like to do that myself,—you might carry your bit o' dinner there, for it's nothing but right to have a bit o' summat hot of a Sunday, and not to make it as you can't know your dinner from Saturday. But now, upo' Christmas-day, this blessed Christmas as is ever coming, if you was to take your dinner to the bakehus, and go to church, and see the holly and the yew, and hear the anthim, and then take the sacramen', you'd be a deal the better, and you'd know which end you stood on, and you could put your trust i' Them as knows better nor we do, seein' you'd ha' done what it lies on us all to do."

Dolly's exhortation, which was an unusually long effort of

speech for her, was uttered in the soothing persuasive tone with which she would have tried to prevail on a sick man to take his medicine, or a basin of gruel for which he had no appetite. Silas had never before been closely urged on the point of his absence from church, which had only been thought of as a part of his general queerness; and he was too direct and simple to evade Dolly's appeal.

"Nay, nay," he said, "I know nothing o' church. I've never been to church."

"No!" said Dolly, in a low tone of wonderment. Then bethinking herself of Silas's advent from an unknown country, she said, "Could it ha' been as they'd no church where you was born?"

"Oh yes," said Silas, meditatively, sitting in his usual posture of leaning on his knees, and supporting his head. "There was churches—a many—it was a big town. But I knew nothing of 'em—I went to chapel."

Dolly was much puzzled at this new word, but she was rather afraid of inquiring further, lest "chapel" might mean some haunt of wickedness. After a little thought, she said—

"Well, Master Marner, it's niver too late to turn over a new leaf, and if you've never had no church, there's no telling the good it'll do you. For I feel so set up and comfortable as niver was, when I've been and heard the prayers, and the singing to the praise and glory o' God, as Mr. Macey gives out—and Mr. Crackenthorp saying good words, and more partic'ler on Sacramen' Day; and if a bit o trouble comes, I feel as I can put up wi' it, for I've looked for help i' the right quarter, and gev myself up to them as we must all give ourselves up to at the last; and if we'n done our part, it isn't to be believed as Them as are above us 'ull be worse nor we are, and come short o' Theirn."

Poor Dolly's exposition of her simple Raveloe theology fell rather unmeaningly on Silas's ears, for there was no word in it that could rouse a memory of what he had known as religion, and his comprehension was quite baffled by the plural pronoun, which was no heresy of Dolly's, but only her way of avoiding a presumptuous familiarity. He remained silent, not feeling inclined to assent to the part of Dolly's speech which he fully understood—her recommendation that he should go to church. Indeed, Silas was so unaccustomed to talk beyond the brief questions and answers necessary for the transaction of his simple business, that words did not easily come to him without the urgency of a distinct purpose.

But now, little Aaron, having become used to the weaver's awful presence, had advanced to his mother's side, and Silas, seeming to notice him for the first time, tried to return Dolly's signs of good-will by offering the lad a bit of lard-cake. Aaron shrank back a little, and rubbed his head against his mother's shoulder, but still thought the piece of cake worth the risk of putting his hand out for it.

"Oh, for shame, Aaron," said his mother, taking him on her lap, however; "why, you don't want cake again yet awhile. He's wonderful hearty," she went on, with a little sigh—"that he is, God knows. He's my youngest, and we spoil him sadly, for either me or the father must allays hev him in our sight—that we must."

She stroked Aaron's brown head, and thought it must do Master Marner good to see such a "pictur of a child." But Marner, on the other side of the hearth, saw the neat-featured rosy face as a mere dim round, with two dark spots in it.

"And he's got a voice like a bird—you wouldn't think," Dolly went on; "he can sing a Christmas carril as his father's taught him: and I take it for a token as he'll come to good, as he can learn the good tunes so quick. Come, Aaron, stan' up and sing the carril to Master Marner, come."

Aaron replied by rubbing his forehead against his mother's shoulder.

"Oh, that's naughty," said Dolly, gently. "Stan' up, when mother tells you, and let me hold the cake till you've done."

Aaron was not indisposed to display his talents, even to an ogre, under protecting circumstances; and after a few more signs of coyness, consisting chiefly in rubbing the backs of his hands over his eyes, and then peeping between them at Master Marner, to see if he looked anxious for the "carril," he at length allowed his head to be duly adjusted, and standing behind the table, which let him appear above it only as far as his broad frill, so that he looked like a cherubic head untroubled with a body, he began with a clear chirp, and in a melody that had the rhythm of an industrious hammer,—

"God rest you, merry gentlemen,
Let nothing you dismay,
For Jesus Christ our Saviour
Was born on Christmas-day."

Dolly listened with a devout look, glancing at Marner in some confidence that this strain would help to allure him to church.

"That's Christmas music," she said, when Aaron had ended, and had secured his piece of cake again. "There's no other music equil to the Christmas music—'Hark the erol angils sing.' And you may judge what it is at church, Master Marner, with the bassoon and the voices, as you can't help thinking you've got to a better place a'ready—for I wouldn't speak ill o' this world, seeing as Them put us in it as knows best; but what wi' the drink, and the quarrelling, and the bad illnesses, and the hard dying, as I've seen times and times, one's thankful to hear of a better. The boy sings pretty, don't he, Master Marner?"

"Yes," said Silas, absently, "very pretty."

The Christmas carol, with its hammer-like rhythm, had fallen on his ears as strange music, quite unlike a hymn, and could have none of the effect Dolly contemplated. But he wanted to show her that he was grateful, and the only mode that occurred to him was to offer Aaron a bit more cake.

"Oh, no, thank you, Master Marner," said Dolly, holding down Aaron's willing hands. "We must be going home now. And so I wish you good-bye, Master Marner; and if you ever feel anyways bad in your inside, as you can't fend for yourself, I'll come and clean up for you, and get you a bit o' victual, and willing. But I beg and pray of you to leave off weaving of a Sunday, for it's bad for soul and body—and the money as comes i' that way 'ull be a bad bed to lie down on at the last, if it doesn't fly away, nobody knows where, like the white frost. And you'll excuse me being that free with you, Master Marner, for I wish you well—I do. Make your bow, Aaron."

Silas said "Good-bye, and thank you kindly," as he opened the door for Dolly, but he couldn't help feeling relieved when she was gone—relieved that he might weave again and moan at his ease. Her simple view of life and its comforts, by which she had tried to cheer him, was only like a report of unknown objects, which his imagination could not fashion. The fountains of human love and divine faith had not yet been unlocked, and his soul was still the shrunken rivulet, with only this difference, that its little groove of sand was blocked up, and it wandered confusedly against dark obstruction.

And so, notwithstanding the honest persuasions of Mr. Macey and Dolly Winthrop, Silas spent his Christmas-day in loneliness, eating his meat in sadness of heart, though the meat had come to him as a neighborly present. In the morning he looked out on the black frost that seemed to press cruelly on every blade of grass, while the half-icy red pool shivered under the bitter wind; but towards evening the snow began to fall, and curtained from him even that dreary outlook, shutting him close up with his narrow grief. And he sat in his robbed home through the livelong evening, not caring to close his shutters or lock his door, pressing his head between his hands and moaning, till the cold grasped him and told him that his fire was gray.

Nobody in this world but himself knew that he was the same Silas Marner who had once loved his fellow with tender love, and trusted in an unseen goodness. Even to himself that past experience had become dim.

But in Raveloe village the bells rang merrily, and the church was fuller than all through the rest of the year, with red faces among the abundant dark-green boughs—faces prepared for a longer service than usual by an odorous breakfast of toast and ale. Those green boughs, the hymn and anthem never heard but at Christmas—even the Athanasian Creed, which was discriminated from the others only as being longer and of exceptional virtue, since it was only read on rare occasions—brought a vague exulting sense, for which the grown men could as little have found words as the children, that something great and mysterious had been done for them in heaven above, and in earth below, which they were appropriating by their presence. And then the red faces made their way through the black biting frost to their own homes, feeling themselves free for the rest of the day to eat, drink, and be merry, and using that Christian freedom without diffidence.

At Squire Cass's family party that day nobody mentioned Dunstan—nobody was sorry for his absence, or feared it would be too long. The doctor and his wife, uncle and aunt Kimble, were there, and the annual Christmas talk was carried through without any omissions, rising to the climax of Mr. Kimble's experience when he walked the London hospitals thirty years back, together with striking professional anecdotes then gathered. Whereupon cards followed, with Aunt Kimble's annual failure to follow suit, and Uncle Kimble's irascibility concerning the odd trick which was rarely explicable to him, when it was not on his side, without a general visitation of tricks to see that they were formed on sound principles: the whole being accompanied by a strong steaming odor of spirits-and-water.

But the party on Christmas-day, being a strictly family party, was not the pre-eminently brilliant celebration of the season at the Red House. It was the great dance on New Year's Eve that made the glory of Squire Cass's hospitality, as of his forefathers', time out of mind. This was the occasion when all the society of Raveloe and Tarley, whether old acquaintances separated by long rutty distances, or cooled acquaintances separated by misunderstandings concerning runaway calves, or acquaintances founded on intermittent condescension, counted on meeting and on comporting themselves with mutual appropriateness. This was the occasion on which fair dames who came on pillions sent their bandboxes before them, supplied with more than their evening costume; for the feast was not to end with a single evening, like a paltry town entertainment, where the whole supply of eatables is put on the table at once, and bedding is scanty. The Red House was provisioned as if for a siege; and as for the spare feather-beds ready to be laid on floors, they were as plentiful as might naturally be expected in a family that had killed its own geese for many generations.

Godfrey Cass was looking forward to this New Year's Eve with a foolish reckless longing, that made him half deaf to his importunate companion, Anxiety.

"Dunsey will be coming home soon: there will be a great blow-up, and how will you bribe his spite to silence?" said Anxiety.

"Oh, he won't come home before New Year's Eve, perhaps," said Godfrey; "and I shall sit by Nancy then, and dance with her, and get a kind look from her in spite of herself."

"But money is wanted in another quarter," said Anxiety, in a louder voice, "and how will you get it without selling your mother's diamond pin? And if you don't get it. . . .?"

"Well, but something may happen to make things easier. At any rate, there's one pleasure for me close at hand: Nancy is coming."

"Yes, and suppose your father should bring matters to a pass that will oblige you to decline marrying her—and to give your reasons?"

"Hold your tongue, and don't worry me. I can see Nancy's eyes, just as they will look at me, and feel her hand in mine already."

But Anxiety went on, though in noisy Christmas company; refusing to be utterly quieted even by much drinking.

CHAPTER XI.

SOME women, I grant, would not appear to advantage seated on a pillion, and attired in a drab joseph and a drab beaver-bonnet, with a crown resembling a small stew-pan; for a garment suggesting a coachman's great-coat, cut out under an exiguity of cloth that would only allow of miniature capes, is not well adapted to conceal deficiencies of contour, nor is drab a color that will throw sallow cheeks into lively contrast. It was all the greater triumph to Miss Nancy Lammeter's beauty that she looked thoroughly bewitching in that costume, as, seated on the pillion behind her tall, erect father, she held one arm round him, and looked down, with open-eyed anxiety, at the treacherous snow-covered pools and puddles, which sent up formidable splashings of mud under the stamp of Dobbin's foot. A painter would, perhaps, have preferred her in those moments when she was free from self-consciousness; but certainly the bloom on her cheeks was at its highest point of contrast with the surrounding drab when she arrived at the door of the Red House, and saw Mr. Godfrey Cass ready to lift her from the pillion. She wished her sister Priscilla had come up at the same time with the servant, for then she would have contrived that Mr. Godfrey should have lifted off Priscilla first, and, in the mean time, she would have persuaded her father to go round to the horse-block instead of alighting at the door-steps. It was very painful, when you had made it quite clear to a young man that you were determined not to marry him, however much he might wish it, that he would still continue to pay you marked attentions; besides, why didn't he always show the same attentions, if he meant them sincerely, instead of being so strange as Mr. Godfrey Cass was, sometimes behaving as if he didn't want to speak to her, and taking no notice of her for weeks and weeks, and then, all on a sudden, almost making love again? Moreover, it was quite plain he had no real love for her, else he would not let people have *that* to say of him which they did say. Did he suppose that Miss Nancy Lammeter was to be won by any man, squire or no squire, who led a bad life? That was not what she had been used to see in her own father, who was the soberest and best man in that country-side, only a little hot and hasty now and then, if things were not done to the minute.

All these thoughts rushed through Miss Nancy's mind, in their habitual succession, in the moments between her first sight of Mr. Godfrey Cass standing at the door and her own arrival there. Happily, the Squire came out too, and gave a loud greeting to her father, so that, somehow, under cover of this noise, she seemed to find concealment for her confusion and neglect of any suitably formal behavior, while she was being lifted from the pillion by strong arms, which seemed to find her ridiculously small and light. And there was the best reason for hastening into the house at once, since the snow was beginning to fall again, threatening an unpleasant journey for such guests as were still on the road. These were a small minority; for already the afternoon was beginning to decline, and there would not be too much time for the ladies who came from a distance to attire themselves in readiness for the early tea which was to inspirit them for the dance.

There was a buzz of voices through the house, as Miss Nancy entered, mingled with the scrape of a fiddle preluding in the kitchen; but the Lammeters were guests whose arrival had evidently been thought of so much that it had been watched for from the windows, for Mrs. Kimble, who did the honors at the Red House on these great occasions, came forward to meet Miss Nancy in the hall, and conduct her up stairs. Mrs. Kimble was the Squire's sister, as well as the doctor's wife—a double dignity, with which her diameter was in direct proportion; so that, a journey up stairs being rather fatiguing to her, she did not oppose Miss Nancy's request to be allowed to find her way alone to the Blue Room, where the Miss Lammeters' bandboxes had been deposited on their arrival in the morning.

There was hardly a bedroom in the house where feminine compliments were not passing and feminine toilettes going forward, in various stages, in space made scanty by extra beds spread upon the floor; and Miss Nancy, as she entered the Blue Room, had to make her little formal courtesy to a group of six. On the one hand, there were ladies no less important than the two Miss Gunns, the wine merchant's daughters from Lytherly, dressed in the height of fashion, with the tightest skirts and the shortest waists, and gazed at by Miss Ladbrook (of the Old Pastures) with a shyness not unsustained by inward criticism. Partly, Miss Ladbrook felt that her own skirt must be regarded as unduly lax by the Miss Gunns, and partly, that it was a pity the Miss Gunns did not show that judgment which she herself would show if she were in their place, by stopping a little on this side of the fashion. On the other hand, Mrs. Ladbrook was standing in skull-cap and front, with her turban in her hand, courtesying and smiling blandly and saying, "After you, ma'am," to another lady in similar circumstances, who had politely offered the precedence at the looking-glass.

But Miss Nancy had no sooner made her courtesy than an elderly lady came forward, whose full white muslin kerchief, and mob-cab round her curls of smooth gray hair, were in daring contrast with the puffed yellow satins and top-knotted caps of her neighbors. She approached Miss Nancy with much primness, and said, with a slow, treble suavity,

"Niece, I hope I see you well in health." Miss Nancy kissed her aunt's cheek dutifully, and answered, with the same sort of amiable primness, "Quite well, I thank you, aunt; and I hope I see you the same."

"Thank you, niece; I keep my health for the present. And how is my brother-in-law?"

These dutiful questions and answers were continued until it was ascertained in detail that the Lammeters were all as well as usual, and the Osgoods likewise, also that niece Priscilla, must certainly arrive shortly, and that travelling on pillions in snowy weather was unpleasant, though a joseph was a great protection. Then Nancy was formally introduced to her aunt's visitors, the Miss Gunns, as being the daughters of a mother known to *their* mother, though now for the first time induced to make a journey in these parts; and these ladies were so taken by surprise at finding such a lovely face and figure in an out-of-the-way country place, that they began to feel some curiosity about the dress she would put on when she took off her joseph. Miss Nancy, whose thoughts were always conducted with the propriety and moderation conspicuous in her manners, remarked to herself that the Miss Gunns were rather hard-featured than otherwise, and that such very low dresses as they wore might have been attributed to vanity if their shoulders had been pretty, but that, being as they were, it was not reasonable to suppose that they showed their necks from a love of display, but rather from some obligation not inconsistent with sense and modesty. She felt convinced, as she opened her box, that this must be her aunt Osgood's opinion, for Miss Nancy's mind resembled her aunt's to a degree that every body said was surprising, considering the kinship was on Mr. Osgood's side; and though you might not have supposed it from the formality of their greeting, there was a devoted attachment and mutual admiration between aunt and niece. Even Miss Nancy's refusal of her cousin Gilbert Osgood (on the ground solely that he was her cousin), though it had grieved her aunt greatly, had not in the least cooled the preference which had determined her to leave Nancy several of her hereditary ornaments, let Gilbert's future wife be whom she might.

Three of the ladies quickly retired, but the Miss Gunns were quite content that Mrs. Osgood's inclination to remain with her niece gave them also a reason for staying to see the rustic beauty's toilette. And it was really a pleasure—from the first opening of the bandbox, where every thing smelt of lavender and rose-leaves, to the clasping of the small coral necklace that fitted closely round her little white neck. Every thing belonging to Miss Nancy was of delicate purity and nattiness: not a crease was where it had no business to be, not a bit of her linen professed whiteness without fulfilling its profession; the very pins on her pincushion were stuck in after a pattern from which she was careful to allow no aberration; and as for her own person, it gave the same idea of perfect unvarying neatness as the body of a little bird. It is true that her light-brown hair was cropped behind like a boy's, and was dressed in front in a number of flat rings, that lay quite away from her face; but there was no sort of coiffure that could make Miss Nancy's cheek and neck look otherwise than pretty; and when at last she stood complete in her silvery twilled silk, her lace tucker, her coral necklace, and coral ear-drops, the Miss Gunns could see nothing to criticise except her hands, which bore the traces of butter-making, cheese-crushing, and even still coarser work. But Miss Nancy was not ashamed of that, for while she was dressing she narrated to her aunt how she and Priscilla had packed their boxes yesterday, because this morning was baking morning, and since they were leaving home, it was desirable to make a good supply of meat-pies for the kitchen; and as she concluded this judicious remark, she turned to the Miss Gunns that she might not commit the rudeness of not including them in the conversation. The Miss Gunns smiled stiffly, and thought what a pity it was that these rich country people, who could afford to buy such good clothes (really Miss Nancy's lace and silk were very costly), should be brought up in utter ignorance and vulgarity. She actually said "mate" for "meat," "'appen" for "perhaps," and "oss" for "horse," which, to young ladies living in good Lytherly society, who habitually said 'orse, even in domestic privacy, and only said 'appen on the right occasions, was necessarily shocking. Miss Nancy, indeed, had never been to any school higher than Dame Tedman's: her acquaintance with profane literature hardly went beyond the rhymes she had worked in her large sampler under the lamb and the shepherdess; and in order to balance an account, she was obliged to effect her subtraction by removing visible metallic shillings and sixpences from a visible metallic total. There is hardly a servant-maid in these days who is not better informed than Miss Nancy; yet she had the essential attributes of a lady—high veracity, delicate honor in her dealings, deference to others, and refined personal habits,—and lest these should not suffice to convince grammatical fair ones that her feelings can at all resemble theirs, I will add that she was slightly proud and exacting, and as constant in her affection towards a baseless opinion as towards an erring lover.

The anxiety about sister Priscilla, which had grown rather active by the time the coral necklace was clasped, was happily ended by the entrance of that cheerful-looking lady herself, with a face made blowsy by cold and damp. After the first questions and greetings, she turned to Nancy, and surveyed her from head to foot—then wheeled her round, to ascertain that the back view was equally faultless.

"What do you think o' *these* gowns, aunt Osgood?" said Priscilla, while Nancy helped her to unrobe.

"Very handsome indeed, niece," said Mrs. Osgood, with a slight increase of formality. She always thought niece Priscilla too rough.

"I'm obliged to have the same as Nancy, you know, for all I'm five years older, and it makes me look yallow; for she never *will* have any thing without I have mine just like it, because she wants us to look like sisters. And I tell her, folks 'ull think it's my weakness makes me fancy as I shall look pretty in what she looks pretty in. For I *am* ugly—there's no denying that: I feature my father's family. But, law! I don't mind, do you?" Priscilla here turned to the Miss Gunns, rattling on in too much preoccupation with the delight of talking, to notice that her candor was not appreciated. "The pretty uns do for fly-catchers—they keep the men off us. I've no opinion o' the men, Miss Gunn—I don't know what *you* have. And as for fretting and stewing about what *they*'ll think of you from morning till night, and making your life uneasy about what they're doing when they're out o' your sight—as I tell Nancy, it's a folly no woman need be guilty of, if she's got a good father and a good home: let her leave it to them as have got no fortin, and can't help themselves. As I say, Mr. Have-your-own-way is the best husband, and the only one I'd ever promise to obey. I know it isn't pleasant, when you've been used to living in a big way, and managing hogsheads and all that, to go and put your nose in by somebody's else's fireside, or to sit down by yourself to a scrag or a knuckle; but, thank God! my father's a sober man and likely to live; and if you've got a man by the chimney-corner, it doesn't matter if he's childish—the business needn't be broke up."

The delicate process of getting her narrow gown over her head without injury to her smooth curls, obliged Miss Priscilla to pause in this rapid survey of life, and Mrs. Osgood seized the opportunity of rising and saying,

"Well, niece, you'll follow us. The Miss Gunns will like to go down."

"Sister," said Nancy, when they were alone, "you've offended the Miss Gunns, I'm sure."

"What have I done, child?" said Priscilla, in some alarm.

"Why, you asked them if they minded about being ugly—you're so very blunt."

"Law, did I? Well, it popped out: it's a mercy I said no more, for I'm a bad un to live with folks when they don't like the truth. But as for being ugly, look at me, child, in this silver-colored silk—I told you how it 'ud be—I look as yallow as a daffodil. Any body 'ud say you wanted to make a mawkin of me."

"No, Priscy, don't say so. I begged and prayed of you not to let us have this silk if you'd like another better. I was willing to have *your* choice, you know I was," said Nancy, in anxious self-vindication.

"Nonsense, child, you know you'd set your heart on this: and reason good, for you're the color o' cream. It 'ud be fine doings for you to dress yourself to suit *my* skin. What I find fault with, is that notion o' yours as I must dress myself just like you. But you do as you like with me—you always did, from when first you begun to walk. If you wanted to go the field's length, the field's length you'd go; and there was no whipping you, for you looked as prim and innicent as a daisy all the while."

"Priscy," said Nancy, gently, as she fastened a coral necklace, exactly like her own, round Priscilla's neck, which was very far from being like her own, "I'm sure I'm willing to give way as far as is right, but who shouldn't dress alike if it isn't sisters? Would you have us go about looking as if we were no kin to one another—us that have got no mother and not another sister in the world? I'd do what was right, if I dressed in a gown dyed with cheese-coloring; and I'd rather you'd choose, and let me wear what pleases you."

"There you go again! You'd come round to the same thing if one talked to you from Saturday night till Saturday morning. It will be fine fun to see how you'll master your husband and never raise your voice above the singing o' the kettle all the while. I like to see the men mastered!"

"Don't talk *so*, Priscy," said Nancy, blushing. "You know I don't mean ever to be married."

"Oh, you never mean a fiddlestick's end!" said Priscilla, as she arranged her discarded dress, and closed her bandbox. "Who shall *I* have to work for when father's gone, if you are to go and take notions in your head and be an old maid, because some folks are no better than they should be? I haven't a bit o' patience with you—sitting on an addled egg forever, as if there was never a fresh un in the world. One old maid's enough out o' two sisters; and I shall do credit to a single life, for God A'mighty meant me for it. Come, we can go down now. I'm as ready as a mawkin *can* be—there's nothing awanting to frighten the crows, now I've got my ear-droppers in."

As the two Miss Lammeters walked into the large parlor together, any one who did not know the character of both, might certainly have supposed that the reason why the square-shouldered, clumsy, high-featured Priscilla wore a dress the fac-simile of her pretty sister's, was either the mistaken vanity of the one, or the malicious contrivance of the other in order to set off her own rare beauty. But the good-natured self-forgetful cheeriness and common-sense of Priscilla would soon have dissipated the one suspicion; and the modest calm of Nancy's speech and manners told clearly of a mind free from all disavowed devices.

Places of honor had been kept for the Miss Lammeters near the head of the principal tea-table in the wainscoted parlor, now looking fresh and pleasant with handsome branches of holly, yew, and laurel, from the abundant growths of the old garden; and Nancy felt an inward flutter, that no firmness of purpose could prevent, when she saw Mr. Godfrey Cass advancing to lead her to a seat between himself and Mr. Crackenthorp, while Priscilla was called to the opposite side between her father and the Squire. It certainly did make some difference to Nancy that the lover she had given up was the young man of quite the highest consequence in the parish—at home in a venerable and unique parlor, which was the extremity of grandeur in her experience, a parlor, where *she* might one day have been mistress, with the consciousness that she was spoken of as "Madam Cass," the Squire's wife. These circumstances exalted her inward drama in her own eyes, and deepened the emphasis with which she declared to herself that not the most dazzling rank should induce her to marry a man whose conduct showed him careless of his character, but that, "love once, love always," was the motto of a true and pure woman, and no man should ever have any right over her which would be a call on her to destroy the dried flowers that she treasured, and always would treasure, for Godfrey Cass's sake. And Nancy was capable of keeping her word to herself under very trying conditions. Nothing but a becoming blush betrayed the moving thoughts that urged themselves upon her as she accepted the seat next to Mr. Crackenthorp; for she was so instinctively neat and adroit in all her actions, and her pretty lips met each other with such quiet firmness, that it would have been difficult for her to appear agitated.

It was not the rector's practice to let a charming blush pass without an appropriate compliment. He was not in the least lofty or aristocratic, but simply a merry-eyed, small-featured, gray-haired man, with his chin propped by an ample, many-creased white neckcloth, which seemed to predominate over every other point in his person, and somehow to impress its peculiar character on his remarks; so that to have considered his amenities apart from his cravat, would have been a severe, and perhaps a dangerous, effort of abstraction.

"Ha, Miss Nancy," he said, turning his head within his cravat, and smiling down pleasantly upon her, "when any body pretends this has been a severe winter, I shall tell them I saw the roses blooming on New Year's Eve—eh, Godfrey, what do *you* say?"

Godfrey made no reply, and avoided looking at Nancy very markedly; for though these complimentary personalities were held to be in excellent taste in old-fashioned Raveloe society, reverent love has a politeness of its own which it teaches to men otherwise of small schooling. But the Squire was rather impatient at Godfrey's showing himself a dull spark in this way. By this advanced hour of the day, the Squire was always in higher spirits than we have seen him in at the breakfast-table, and felt it quite pleasant to fulfill the hereditary duty of being noisily jovial and patronizing: the large silver snuff-box was in active service, and was offered without fail to all neighbors from time to time, however often they might have declined the favor. At present the Squire had only given an express welcome to the heads of families as they appeared; but always as the evening deepened, his hospitality rayed out more widely, till he had tapped the youngest guests on the back, and shown a peculiar fondness for their presence, in the full belief that they must feel their lives made happy by their belonging to a parish where there was such a hearty man as Squire Cass to invite them and wish them well. Even in this early stage of the jovial mood, it was natural that he should wish to supply his son's deficiencies by looking and speaking for him.

"Ay, ay," he began, offering his snuff-box to Mr. Lammeter, who for the second time bowed his head and waved his hand in stiff rejection of the offer, "us old fellows may wish ourselves young to-night, when we see the mistletoe-bough in the White Parlor. It's true, most things are gone back'ard in these last thirty years—the country's going down since the old king fell ill. But when I look at Miss Nancy here, I begin to think the lasses keep up their quality;—ding me if I remember a sample to match her, not when I was a fine young fellow, and thought a deal about my pigtail. No offense to you, madam," he added, bending to Mrs. Crackenthorp, who sat by him, "I didn't know *you* when you were as young as Miss Nancy here."

Mrs. Crackenthorp—a small blinking woman, who fidgeted incessantly with her lace, ribbons, and gold chain, turning her head about and making subdued noises, very much like a guinea-pig, that twitches its nose and soliloquizes in all company indiscriminately—now blinked and fidgeted towards the Squire, and said, "Oh no—no offense."

This emphatic compliment of the Squire's to Nancy was felt by others besides Godfrey to have a diplomatic significance; and her father gave a slight additional erectness to his back, as he looked across the table at her with complacent gravity. That grave and orderly senior was not going to bate a jot of his dignity by seeming elated at the notion of a match between his family and the Squire's: he was gratified by any honor paid to his daughter; but he must see an alteration in several ways before his consent would be vouchsafed. His spare but healthy person, and high-featured, firm face, that looked as if it had never been flushed by excess, was in strong contrast, not only with the Squire's, but with the appearance of the Raveloe farmers generally—in accordance with a favorite saying of his own, that "breed was stronger than pasture."

"Miss Nancy's wonderful like what her mother was, though; isn't she, Kimble?" said the stout lady of that name, looking round for her husband.

But Doctor Kimble (country apothecaries in old days enjoyed that title without authority of diploma), being a thin and agile man, was flitting about the room with his hands in his pockets, making himself agreeable to his feminine patients, with medical impartiality, and being welcomed everywhere as a doctor by hereditary right—not one of those miserable apothecaries who canvass for practice in strange neighborhoods, and spend all their income in starving their one horse, but a man of substance, able to keep an extravagant table like the best of his patients. Time out of mind the Raveloe doctor had been a Kimble; Kimble was inherently a doctor's name; and it was difficult to contemplate firmly the melancholy fact that the actual Kimble had no son, so that his practice might one day be handed over to a successor, with the incongruous name of Taylor or Johnson. But in that case the wiser people in Raveloe would employ Dr. Blick of Flitton—as less unnatural.

"Did you speak to me, my dear?" said the authentic doctor, coming quickly to his wife's side; but, as if foreseeing that she would be too much out of breath to repeat her remark, he went on immediately—"Ha, Miss Priscilla, the sight of you revives the taste of that super-excellent pork-pie. I hope the batch isn't near an end."

"Yes, indeed, it is, doctor," said Priscilla; "but I'll answer for it the next shall be as good. My pork-pies don't turn out well by chance."

"Not as your doctoring does, eh, Kimble?—because folks forget to take your physic, eh?" said the Squire, who regarded physic and doctors as many loyal churchmen regard the church and the clergy—tasting a joke against them when he was in health, but impatiently eager for their aid when any thing was the matter with him. He tapped his box, and looked round with a triumphant laugh.

"Ah, she has a quick wit, my friend Priscilla has," said the doctor, choosing to attribute the epigram to a lady rather than allow a brother-in-law that advantage over him. "She saves a little pepper to sprinkle over her talk—that's the reason why she never puts too much into her pies. There's my wife, now, she never has an answer at her tongue's end; but if I offend her, she's sure to scarify my throat with black pepper the next day, or else give me the colic with watery greens. That's an awful tit-for-tat." Here the vivacious doctor made a pathetic grimace.

"Did you ever hear the like?" said Mrs. Kimble, laughing above her double chin with much good-humor, aside to Mrs. Crackenthorp, who blinked and nodded, and seemed to intend a smile, which, by the correlation of forces, went off in small twitchings and noises.

"I suppose that's the sort of tit-for-tat adopted in your profession, Kimble, if you've a grudge against a patient," said the rector.

"Never do have a grudge against our patients," said Mr. Kimble, "except when they leave us: and then, you see, we haven't a chance of prescribing for 'em. Ha, Miss Nancy," he continued, suddenly skipping to Nancy's side, "you won't forget your promise? You're to save a dance for me, you know."

"Come, come, Kimble, don't you be too for'ard," said the Squire. "Give the young uns fair-play. There's my son Godfrey 'll be wanting to have a round with you if you run off with Miss Nancy. He's bespoke her for the first dance, I'll be bound. Eh, sir! what do you say?" he continued throwing himself backward, and looking at Godfrey. "Haven't you asked Miss Nancy to open the dance with you?"

Godfrey, sorely uncomfortable under this significant insistance about Nancy, and afraid to think where it would end by the time his father had set his usual hospitable example of drinking before and after supper, saw no course open but to turn to Nancy and say, with as little awkwardness as possible—

"No; I've not asked her yet, but I hope she'll consent—if somebody else hasn't been before me."

"No, I've not engaged myself," said Nancy, quietly, though blushingly. (If Mr. Godfrey founded any hopes on her consenting to dance with him, he would soon be undeceived; but there was no need for her to be uncivil.)

"Then I hope you've no objections to dancing with me," said Godfrey, beginning to lose the sense that there was any thing uncomfortable in this arrangement.

"No, no objections," said Nancy, in a cold tone.

"Ah, well, you're a lucky fellow, Godfrey," said uncle Kimble; "but you're my godson, so I won't stand in your way. Else I'm not so very old, eh, my dear?" he went on, skipping to his wife's side again. "You wouldn't mind my having a second after you were gone—not if I cried a good deal first."

"Come, come, take a cup o' tea and stop your tongue, do," said good-humored Mrs. Kimble, feeling some pride in a husband who must be regarded as so clever and amusing by the company generally. If he had only not been irritable at cards!

While safe, well-tested personalities were enlivening the tea in this way, the sound of the fiddle approaching within a distance at which it could be heard distinctly, made the young people look at each other with sympathetic impatience for the end of the meal.

"Why, there's Solomon in the hall," said the Squire, "and playing my fav'rite tune, *I* believe—'The flaxen-headed plough-boy'—he's for giving us a hint as we aren't enough in a hurry to hear him play. Bob," he called out to his third long-legged son, who was at the other end of the room, "open the door, and tell Solomon to come in. He shall give us a tune here."

Bob obeyed, and Solomon walked in, fiddling as he walked, for he would on no account break off in the middle of a tune.

"Here, Solomon," said the Squire with loud patronage. "Round here, my man. Ah, I knew it was 'The flaxen-headed plough-boy:' there's no finer tune."

Solomon Macey, a small, hale old man with an abundant crop of long white hair reaching nearly to his shoulders, advanced to the indicated spot, bowing reverently while he fiddled, as much as to say that he respected the company, though he respected the key-note more. As soon as he had repeated the tune and lowered his fiddle, he bowed again to the Squire and the rector, and said, "I hope I see your honor and your reverence well, and wishing you health and long life and a happy New Year. And wishing the same to you, Mr. Lammeter, sir; and to the other gentlemen, and the madams, and the young lasses."

As Solomon uttered the last words, he bowed in all directions solicitously, lest he should be wanting in due respect. But thereupon he immediately began to prelude, and fell into the tune which he knew would be taken as a special compliment by Mr. Lammeter.

"Thank ye, Solomon, thank ye," said Mr. Lammeter when the fiddle paused again. "That's 'Over the hills and far away,' that is. My father used say to me, whenever we heard that tune, 'Ah, lad, *I* come from over the hills and far away.' There's a many tunes I don't make head or tail of; but that speaks to me like the blackbird's whistle. I suppose it's the name: there's a deal in the name of a tune."

But Solomon was already impatient to prelude again, and presently broke with much spirit into "Sir Roger de Coverly," at which there was a sound of chairs pushed back, and laughing voices.

"Ay, ay, Solomon, we know what that means," said the Squire, rising. "It's time to begin the dance, eh? Lead the way, then, and we'll all follow you."

So Solomon, holding his white head on one side, and playing vigorously, marched forward at the head of the gay procession into the White Parlor, where the mistletoe-bough was hung, and multitudinous tallow candles made rather a brilliant effect, gleaming from among the berried holly-boughs, and reflected in the old-fashioned oval mirrors fastened in the panels of the white wainscot. A quaint procession! Old Solomon, in his seedy clothes and long white locks, seemed to be luring that decent company by the magic scream of his fiddle—luring discreet matrons in turban-shaped caps, nay, Mrs. Crackenthorp herself, the summit of whose perpendicular feather was on a level with the Squire's shoulder—luring fair lasses complacently conscious of very short waists and skirts blameless of front folds—luring burly fathers in large variegated waistcoats, and ruddy sons, for the most part shy and sheepish, in short nether garments and very long coat-tails.

Already Mr. Macey and a few other privileged villagers, who were allowed to be spectators on these great occasions, were seated on benches placed for them near the door; and great was the admiration and satisfaction in that quarter when the couples had formed themselves for the dance, and the Squire led off with Mrs. Crackenthorp, joining hands with the rector and Mrs. Osgood. That was as it should be—that was what every body had been used to—and the charter of Raveloe seemed to be renewed by the ceremony. It was not thought of as an unbecoming levity for the old and middle-aged people to dance a little before sitting down to cards, but rather as part of their social duties. For what were these if not to be merry at appropriate times, interchanging visits and poultry with due frequency, paying each other old-established compliments in sound traditional phrases, passing well-tried personal jokes, urging your guests to eat and drink too much out of hospitality, and eating and drinking too much in your neighbor's house to show that you liked your cheer? And the parson naturally set an example in these social duties. For it would not have been possible for the Raveloe mind, without a peculiar revelation, to know that a clergyman should be a pale-faced memento of solemnities, instead of a reasonably faulty man, whose exclusive authority to read prayers and preach, to christen, marry, and bury you, necessarily co-existed with the right to sell you the ground to be buried in, and to take tithe in kind; on which last point, of course, there was a little grumbling, but not to the extent of irreligion—not of deeper significance than the grumbling at the rain, which was by no means accompanied with a spirit of impious defiance, but with a desire that the prayer for fine weather might be read forthwith.

There was no reason, then, why the rector's dancing should not be received as part of the fitness of things quite as much as the Squire's, or why, on the other hand, Mr. Macey's official respect should restrain him from subjecting the parson's performance to that criticism with which minds of extraordinary acuteness must necessarily contemplate the doings of their fallible fellow-men.

"The Squire's pretty springy, considering his weight," said Mr. Macey, "and he stamps uncommon well. But Mr. Lammeter beats 'em all for shapes: you see he holds his head like a sodger, and he isn't so cushiony as most o' the oldish gentlefolks—they run fat in general; and he's got a fine leg. The parson's nimble enough, but he hasn't got much of a leg: it's a bit too thick down'ard, and his knees might be a bit nearer wi'out damage; but he might do worse, he might do worse. Though he hasn't that grand way o' waving his hand as the Squire has."

"Talk o' nimbleness, look at Mrs. Osgood," said Ben Winthrop, who was holding his son Aaron between his knees. "She trips along with her little steps, so as nobody can see how she goes—it's like as if she had little wheels to her feet. She doesn't look a day older nor last year: she's the finest-made woman as is, let the next be where she will."

"I don't heed how the women are made," said Mr. Macey, with some contempt. "They wear nayther coat nor breeches you can't make much out o' their shapes."

"Fayder," said Aaron, whose feet were busy beating out the tune, "how does that big cock's-feather stick in Mrs. Crackenthorp's yead? Is there a little hole for it, like in my shuttlecock?"

"Hush, lad, hush; that's the way the ladies dress theirselves, that is," said the father, adding, however, in an undertone to Mr. Macey, "It does make her look funny, though—partly like a short-necked bottle wi' a long quill in it. Hey, by jingo, there's the young Squire leading off now, wi' Miss Nancy for partners. There's a lass for you!—like a pink-and-white posy—there's nobody 'ud think as any body could be so pritty. I shouldn't wonder if she's Madam Cass some day, arter all—and nobody more rightfuller, for they'd make a fine match. You can find nothing against Master Godfrey's shapes, Macey, *I*'ll bet a penny."

Mr. Macey screwed up his mouth, leaned his head farther on one side, and twirled his thumbs with a presto movement as his eyes followed Godfrey up the dance. At last he summed up his opinion.

"Pretty well down'ard, but a bit too round i' the shoulder-blades. And as for them coats as he gets from the Flitton tailor, they're a poor cut to pay double money for."

"Ah, Mr. Macey, you and me are two folks," said Ben, slightly indignant at this carping. "When I've got a pot of good ale, I like to swaller it, and do my inside good, i'stead o' smelling and staring at it to see if I can't find faut wi' the brewing. I should like you to pick me out a finer-limbed young fellow nor Master Godfrey—one as 'ud knock you down easier, or's more pleasanter looksed when he's piert and merry."

"Tchuh!" said Mr. Macey, provoked to increased severity, "he isn't come to his right color yet; he's partly like a slack-baked pie. And I doubt he's got a soft place in his head, else why should he be turned round the finger by that offal Dunsey as nobody's seen o' late, and let him kill that fine hunting hoss as was the talk o' the country? And one while he was allays after Miss Nancy, and then it all went off again, like a smell o' hot porridge, as I may say. That wasn't my way when *I* went a-coorting."

"Ah, but mayhap, Miss Nancy hung off, like, and your lass didn't," said Ben.

"I should say she didn't," said Mr. Macey, significantly. "Before I said 'sniff,' I took care to know as she'd say 'snaff,' and pretty quick too. I wasn't a-going to open *my* mouth, like a dog at a fly, and snap it to again, wi' nothing to swaller."

"Well, I think Miss Nancy's a-coming round again," said Ben, "for Master Godfrey doesn't look so down-hearted tonight. And I see he's for taking her away to sit down, now they're at the end o' the dance: that looks like sweethearting, that does."

The reason why Godfrey and Nancy had left the dance was not so tender as Ben imagined. In the close press of couples a slight accident had happened to Nancy's dress, which, while it was short enough to show her neat ankle in front, was long enough behind to be caught under the stately stamp of the Squire's foot, so as to rend certain stiches at the waist, and cause much sisterly agitation in Priscilla's mind, as well as serious concern in Nancy's. One's thoughts may be much occupied with love-struggles, but hardly so as to be insensible to a disorder in the general framework of things. Nancy had no sooner completed her duty in the figure they were dancing than she said to Godfrey, with a deep blush, that she must go and sit down till Priscilla could come to her; for the sisters had already exchanged a short whisper and an open-eyed glance full of meaning. No reason less urgent than this could have prevailed on Nancy to give Godfrey this opportunity of sitting apart with her. As for Godfrey, he was feeling so happy and oblivious under the long charm of the country-dance with Nancy, that he got rather bold on the strength of her confusion, and was capable of leading her straight away, without leave asked, into the adjoining small parlor, where the card-tables were set.

"Oh, no, thank you," said Nancy, coldly, as soon as she perceived where he was going, "not in there. I'll wait here till Priscilla's ready to come to me. I'm sorry to bring you out of the dance and make myself troublesome."

"Why, you'll be more comfortable here by yourself," said

the artful Godfrey: "I'll leave you here till your sister can come." He spoke in an indifferent tone.

That was an agreeable proposition, and just what Nancy desired; why, then, was she a little hurt that Mr. Godfrey should make it? They entered, and she seated herself on a chair against one of the card-tables, as the stiffest and most unapproachable position she could choose.

"Thank you, sir," she said immediately. "I needn't give you any more trouble. I'm sorry you've had such an unlucky partner."

"That's very ill-natured of you," said Godfrey, standing by her without any sign of intended departure, "to be sorry you've danced with me."

"Oh, no, sir, I don't mean to say what's ill-natured at all," said Nancy, looking distractingly prim and pretty. "When gentlemen have so many pleasures, one dance can matter but very little."

"You know that isn't true. You know one dance with you matters more to me than all the other pleasures in the world."

It was a long, long while since Godfrey had said any thing so direct as that, and Nancy was startled. But her instinctive dignity and repugnance to any show of emotion made her sit perfectly still, and only throw a little more decision into her voice as she said—

"No, indeed, Mr. Godfrey, that's not known to me, and I have very good reasons for thinking different. But if it's true, I don't wish to hear it."

"Would you never forgive me, then, Nancy—never think well of me, let what would happen—would you never think the present made amends for the past? Not if I turned a good fellow, and gave up every thing you didn't like?"

Godfrey was half conscious that this sudden opportunity of speaking to Nancy alone had driven him beside himself, but blind feeling had got the mastery of his tongue. Nancy really felt much agitated by the possibility Godfrey's words suggested, but this very pressure of emotion that she was in danger of finding too strong for her, roused all her power of self-command.

"I should be glad to see a good change in any body, Mr. Godfrey," she answered, with the slightest discernible difference of tone, "but it 'ud be better if no change was wanted."

"You're very hard-hearted, Nancy," said Godfrey, pettishly. "You might encourage me to be a better fellow. I'm very miserable—but you've no feeling."

"I think those have the least feeling that act wrong, to begin with," said Nancy, sending out a flash in spite of herself. Godfrey was delighted with that little flash, and would have liked to go on and make her quarrel with him; Nancy was so exasperatingly quiet and firm. But she was not indifferent to him *yet.*

The entrance of Priscilla, bustling forward and saying, "Dear heart alive, child, let us look at this gown," cut off Godfrey's hopes of a quarrel.

"I suppose I must go now," he said to Priscilla.

"It's no matter to me whether you go or stay," said that frank lady, searching for something in her pocket, with a preoccupied brow.

"Do *you* want me to go?" said Godfrey, looking at Nancy, who was now standing up by Priscilla's order.

"As you like," said Nancy, trying to recover all her former coldness, and looking down carefully at the hem of her gown.

"Then I like to stay," said Godfrey, with a reckless determination to get as much of this joy as he could to-night, and think nothing of the morrow.

CHAPTER XII.

WHILE Godfrey Cass was taking draughts of forgetfulness from the sweet presence of Nancy, willingly losing all sense of that hidden bond which at other moments galled and fretted him so as to mingle irritation with the very sunshine, Godfrey's wife was walking with slow, uncertain steps through the snow-covered Raveloe lanes, carrying her child in her arms.

This journey on New Year's Eve was a premeditated act of vengeance which she had kept in her heart ever since Godfrey, in a fit of passion, had told her he would sooner die than acknowledge her as his wife. There would be a great party at the Red House on New Year's Eve, she knew: her husband would be smiling and smiled upon, hiding *her* existence in the darkest corner of his heart. But she would mar his pleasure: she would go in her dingy rags, with her faded face, once as handsome as the best, with her little child that had its father's hair and eyes, and disclose herself to the Squire as his eldest son's wife. It is seldom that the miserable can help regarding their misery as a wrong inflicted by those who are less miserable. Molly knew that the cause of her dingy rags was not her husband's neglect, but the demon

Opium to whom she was enslaved, body and soul, except in the lingering mother's tenderness that refused to give him her hungry child. She knew this well; and yet, in the moments of wretched unbenumbed consciousness, the sense of her want and degradation transformed itself continually into bitterness towards Godfrey. *He* was well off; and if she had her rights she would be well off too. The belief that he repented his marriage, and suffered from it, only aggravated her vindictiveness. Just and self-reproving thoughts do not come to us too thickly, even in the purest air, and with the best lessons of heaven and earth; how should those white winged delicate messengers make their way to Molly's poisoned chamber, inhabited by no higher memories than those of a bar-maid's paradise of pink ribbons and gentlemen's jokes?

She had set out at an early hour, but had lingered on the road, inclined by her indolence to believe that if she waited under a warm shed the snow would cease to fall. She had waited longer than she knew, and now that she found herself belated in the snow-hidden ruggedness of the long lanes, even the animation of a vindictive purpose could not keep her spirit from failing. It was seven o'clock, and by this time she was not very far from Raveloe, but she was not familiar enough with those monotonous lanes to know how near she was to her journey's end. She needed comfort, and she knew but one comforter—the familiar demon in her bosom; but she hesitated a moment, after drawing out the black remnant, before she raised it to her lips. In that moment the mother's love pleaded for painful consciousness rather than oblivion—pleaded to be left in aching weariness, rather than to have the encircling arms benumbed so that they could not feel the dear burden. In another moment Molly had flung something away, but it was not the black remnant—it was an empty vial. And she walked on again under the breaking cloud, from which there came now and then the light of a quickly-veiled star, for a freezing wind had sprung up since the snowing had ceased. But she walked always more and more drowsily, and clutched more and more automatically the sleeping child at her bosom.

Slowly the demon was working his will, and cold and weariness were his helpers. Soon she felt nothing but a supreme immediate longing that curtained off all futurity—the longing to lie down and sleep. She had arrived at a spot where her footsteps were no longer checked by a hedgerow, and she had wandered vaguely, unable to distinguish any objects, notwithstanding the wide whiteness around her, and the growing starlight. She sank down against a straggling furze bush, an easy pillow enough; and the bed of snow, too, was soft. She did not feel that the bed was cold, and did not heed whether the child would wake and cry for her. But her arms had not yet relaxed their instinctive clutch; and the little one slumbered on as gently as if it had been rocked in a lace-trimmed cradle.

But the complete torpor came at last: the fingers lost their tension, the arms unbent; then the little head fell away from the bosom, and the blue eyes opened wide on the cold starlight. At first there was a little peevish cry of "mammy," and an effort to regain the pillowing arm and bosom; but mammy's ear was deaf, and the pillow seemed to be slipping away backward. Suddenly, as the child rolled downward on its mother's knees, all wet with snow, its eyes were caught by a bright glancing light on the white ground, and, with the ready transition of infancy, it was immediately absorbed in watching the bright living thing running towards it, yet never arriving. That bright living thing must be caught; and in an instant the child had slipped on all fours, and held out one little hand to catch the gleam. But the gleam would not be caught in that way, and now the head was held up to see where the cunning gleam came from. It came from a very bright place; and the little one, rising on its legs, toddled through the snow, the old grimy shawl in which it was wrapped trailing behind it, and the queer little bonnet dangling at its back—toddled on to the open door of Silas Marner's cottage, and right up to the warm hearth, where there was a bright fire of logs and sticks, which had thoroughly warmed the old sack (Silas's great-coat) spread out on the bricks to dry. The little one, accustomed to be left to itself for long hours without notice from its mother, squatted down on the sack, and spread its tiny hands towards the blaze, in perfect contentment, gurgling and making many inarticulate communications to the cheerful fire, like a new-hatched gosling beginning to find itself comfortable. But presently the warmth had a lulling effect, and the little golden head sank down on the old sack, and the blue eyes were veiled by their delicate half-transparent lids.

But where was Silas Marner while this strange visitor had come to his hearth? He was in the cottage, but he did not see the child. During the last few weeks, since he had lost his money, he had contracted the habit of opening his door and looking out from time to time, as if he thought that his money might be somehow coming back to him, or that some trace, some news of it, might be mysteriously on the road, and be caught by the listening ear or the straining eye. It was chiefly at night, when he was not occupied in his loom, that he fell into this repetition of an act for which he could have assigned no definite purpose, and which can hardly be understood except by those who have undergone a bewildering separation from a supremely loved object. In the evening twilight, and later whenever the night was not dark, Silas looked out on that narrow prospect round the Stone-pits, listening and gazing, not with hope, but with mere yearning and unrest.

This morning he had been told by some of his neighbors that it was New Year's Eve, and that he must sit up and hear the old year rung out and the new rung in, because that was good luck, and might bring his money back again. This was only a friendly Raveloe-way of jesting with the half-crazy oddities of a miser, but it had perhaps helped to throw Silas into a more than usually excited state. Since the on-coming of twilight he had opened his door again and again, though only to shut it immediately at seeing all distance veiled by the falling snow. But the last time he opened it the snow had ceased, and the clouds were parting here and there. He stood and listened, and gazed for a long while—there was really something on the road coming towards him then, but he caught no sign of it; and the stillness and the wide trackless snow seemed to narrow his solitude, and touched his yearning with the chill of despair. He went in again, and put his right hand on the latch of the door to close it—but he did not close it: he was arrested, as he had been already since his loss, by the invisible wand of catalepsy, and stood like a graven image, with wide but sightless eyes, holding open his door, powerless to resist either the good or evil that might enter there.

When Marner's sensibility returned, he continued the action which had been arrested, and closed his door, unaware of the chasm in his consciousness, unaware of any intermediate change, except that the light had grown dim, and that he was chilled and faint. He thought he had been too long standing at the door and looking out. Turning towards the hearth, where the two logs had fallen apart, and sent forth only a red uncertain glimmer, he seated himself on his fireside chair, and was stooping to push his logs together, when, to his blurred vision, it seemed as if there were gold on the floor in front of the hearth. Gold!—his own gold—brought back to him as mysteriously as it had been taken away! He felt his heart begin to beat violently, and for a few moments he was unable to stretch out his hand and

"He felt his heart begin to beat violently, and for a few moments he was unable to stretch out his hand and grasp the restored treasure."—PAGE 434.

grasp the restored treasure. The heap of gold seemed to glow and get larger beneath his agitated gaze. He leaned forward at last, and stretched forth his hand; but instead of the hard coin with the familiar resisting outline, his fingers encountered soft warm curls. In utter amazement, Silas fell on his knees and bent his head low to examine the marvel: it was a sleeping child—a round, fair thing, with soft yellow rings all over its head. Could this be his little sister come back to him in a dream—his little sister whom he had carried about in his arms for a year before she died, when he was a small boy without shoes or stockings? That was the first thought that darted across Silas's blank wonderment. *Was* it a dream? He rose to his feet again, pushed his logs together, and, throwing on some dried leaves and sticks, raised a flame; but the flame did not disperse the vision—it only lit up more distinctly the little round form of the child, and its shabby clothing. It was very much like his little sister. Silas sank into his chair powerless, under the double presence of an inexplicable surprise and a hurrying influx of memories. How and when had the child come in without his knowledge? He had never been beyond the door. But along with that question, and almost thrusting it away, there was a vision of the old home and the old streets leading to Lantern Yard—and within that vision another, of the thoughts which had been present with him in those far-off scenes. The thoughts were strange to him now, like old friendships impossible to revive; and yet he had a dreamy feeling that this child was somehow a message come to him from that far-off life: it stirred fibres that had never been moved in Raveloe—old quiverings of tenderness—old impressions of awe at the presentiment of some Power presiding over his life; for his imagination had not yet extricated itself from the sense of mystery in the child's sudden presence, and had formed no conjectures of ordinary natural means by which the event could have been brought about.

But there was a cry on the hearth: the child had awaked, and Marner stooped to lift it on his knee. It clung round his neck, and burst louder and louder into that mingling of inarticulate cries with "mammy" by which little children express the bewilderment of waking. Silas pressed it to him, and almost unconsciously uttered sounds of hushing tenderness, while he bethought himself that some of his porridge, which had got cool by the dying fire, would do to feed the child with if it were only warmed up a little.

He had plenty to do through the next hour. The porridge, sweetened with some dry brown sugar from an old store which he had refrained from using for himself, stopped the cries of the little one, and made her lift her blue eyes with a wide quiet gaze at Silas, as he put the spoon into her mouth. Presently she slipped from his knee and began to toddle about, but with a pretty stagger that made Silas jump up and follow her lest she should fall against any thing that would hurt her. But she only fell in a sitting posture on the ground, and began to pull at her boots, looking up at him with a crying face as if the boots hurt her. He took her on his knee again, but it was some time before it occurred to Silas's dull bachelor mind that the wet boots were the grievance, pressing on her warm ankles. He got them off with difficulty, and baby was at once happily occupied with the primary mystery of her own toes, inviting Silas, with much chuckling, to consider the mystery too. But the wet boots had at last suggested to Silas that the child had been walking on the snow, and this roused him from his entire oblivion of any ordinary means by which it could have entered or been brought into his house. Under the prompting of this new idea, and without waiting to form conjectures, he raised the child in his arms, and went to the door. As soon as he had opened it, there was the cry of "mammy" again, which Silas had not heard since the child's first hungry waking. Bending forward, he could just discern the marks made by the little feet on the virgin snow, and he followed their track to the furze bushes. "Mammy!" the little one cried again and again, stretching itself forward so as almost to escape from Silas's arms, before he himself was aware that there was something more than the bush before him—that there was a human body, with the head sunk low in the furze, and half-covered with the shaken snow.

CHAPTER XIII.

It was after the early supper-time at the Red House, and the entertainment was in that stage when bashfulness itself had passed into easy jollity, when gentlemen, conscious of unusual accomplishments, could at length be prevailed on to dance a hornpipe, and when the Squire preferred talking loudly, scattering snuff, and patting his visitors' backs, to sitting longer at the whist-table—a choice exasperating to uncle Kimble, who, being always volatile in sober business hours, became intense and bitter over cards and brandy, shuffled before his adversary's deal with a glare of suspicion, and turned up a mean trump-card with an air of inexpressible disgust, as if in a world where such things could happen one might as well enter on a course of reckless profligacy. When the evening had advanced to this pitch of freedom and enjoyment, it was usual for the servants, the heavy duties of supper being well over, to get their share of amusement by coming to look on at the dancing; so that the back regions of the house were left in solitude.

There were two doors by which the White Parlor was entered from the hall, and they were both standing open for the sake of air; but the lower one was crowded with the servants and villagers, and only the upper doorway was left free. Bob Cass was figuring in a hornpipe, and his father, very proud of this lithe son, whom he repeatedly declared to be just like himself in his young days, in a tone that implied this to be the very highest stamp of juvenile merit, was the centre of a group who had placed themselves opposite the performer, not far from the upper door. Godfrey was standing a little way off, not to admire his brother's dancing, but to keep sight of Nancy, who was seated in the group, near her father. He stood aloof, because he wished to avoid suggesting himself as a subject for the Squire's fatherly jokes in connection with matrimony and Miss Nancy Lammeter's beauty, which were likely to become more and more explicit. But he had the prospect of dancing with her again when the hornpipe was concluded, and in the mean while it was very pleasant to get long glances at her quite unobserved.

But when Godfrey was lifting his eyes from one of those long glances, they encountered an object as startling to him at that moment as if it had been an apparition from the dead. It *was* an apparition from that hidden life which lies, like a dark by-street, behind the goodly ornamented façade that meets the sunlight and the gaze of respectable admirers. It was his own child carried in Silas Marner's arms. That was his instantaneous impression, unaccompanied by doubt, though he had not seen the child for months past; and when the hope was rising that he might possibly be mistaken, Mr. Crackenthorp and Mr. Lammeter had already advanced to Silas, in astonishment at this strange advent. Godfrey joined them immediately, unable to rest without hearing every word—trying to control himself, but conscious that if any one noticed him, they must see that he was white-lipped and trembling.

But now all eyes at that end of the room were bent on Silas Marner; the Squire himself had risen, and asked angrily,

"How's this?—what's this?—what do you do coming in here in this way?"

"I'm come for the doctor—I want the doctor," Silas had said, in the first moment, to Mr. Crackenthorp.

"Why, what's the matter, Marner?" said the rector. "The doctor's here; but say quietly what you want him for."

"It's a woman," said Silas, speaking low, and half-breathlessly, just as Godfrey came up. "She's dead, I think—dead in the snow at the Stone-pits—not far from my door."

Godfrey felt a great throb: there was one terror in his mind at that moment: it was, that the woman might *not* be dead. That was an evil terror—an ugly inmate to have found a nestling-place in Godfrey's kindly disposition; but no disposition is a security from evil wishes to a man whose happiness hangs on duplicity.

"Hush, hush!" said Mr. Crackenthorp. "Go out into the hall there. I'll fetch the doctor to you. Found a woman in the snow—and thinks she's dead," he added, speaking low, to the Squire. "Better say as little about it as possible: it will shock the ladies. Just tell them a poor woman is ill from cold and hunger. I'll go and fetch Kimble."

By this time, however, the ladies had pressed forward, curious to know what could have brought the solitary linen-weaver there under such strange circumstances, and interested in the pretty child, who, half alarmed and half attracted by the brightness and the numerous company, now frowned and hid her face, now lifted up her head again and looked round placably, until a touch or a coaxing word brought back the frown, and made her bury her face with new determination.

"What child is it?" said several ladies at once, and, among the rest, Nancy Lammeter, addressing Godfrey.

"I don't know—some poor woman's who has been found in the snow, I believe," was the answer Godfrey wrung from himself with a terrible effort. ("After all, *am* I certain?" he hastened to add, silently, in anticipation of his own conscience.)

"Why, you'd better leave the child here, then, Master Marner," said good-natured Mrs. Kimble, hesitating, however, to take those dingy clothes into contact with her own ornamented satin boddice. "I'll tell one o' the girls to fetch it."

"No—no—I can't part with it, I can't let it go," said Silas, abruptly. "It's come to me—I've a right to keep it."

The proposition to take the child from him had come to Silas quite unexpectedly, and his speech, uttered under a strong sudden impulse, was almost like a revelation to himself: a minute before, he had no distinct intention about the child.

"Did you ever hear the like?" said Mrs. Kimble, in mild surprise to her neighbor.

"Now, ladies, I must trouble you to stand aside," said Mr. Kimble, coming from the card-room in some bitterness at the interruption, but drilled by the long habit of his profession into obedience to unpleasant calls, even when he was hardly sober.

"It's a nasty business turning out now, eh, Kimble?" said the Squire. "He might ha' gone for your young fellow—the 'prentice there—what's his name?"

"Might? ay—what's the use of talking about might?" growled uncle Kimble, hastening out with Marner, and followed by Mr. Crackenthorp and Godfrey. "Get me a pair of thick boots, Godfrey, will you? And stay, let somebody run to Winthrop's and fetch Dolly—she's the best woman to get. Ben was here himself before supper: is he gone?"

"Yes, sir, I met him," said Marner; "but I couldn't stop to tell him any thing, only I said I was going for the doctor, and he said the doctor was at the Squire's. And I made haste and ran, and there was nobody to be seen at the back o' the house, and so I went in to where the company was."

The child, no longer distracted by the bright light and the smiling women's faces, began to cry and call for "mammy," though always clinging to Marner, who had apparently won her thorough confidence. Godfrey had come back with the boots, and felt the cry as if some fibre were drawn tight within him.

"I'll go," he said, hastily, eager for some movement; "I'll go and fetch the woman—Mrs. Winthrop."

"Oh, pooh—send somebody else," said uncle Kimble, hurrying away with Marner.

"You'll let me know if I can be of any use, Kimble," said Mr. Crackenthorp. But the doctor was out of hearing.

Godfrey, too, had disappeared: he was gone to snatch his hat and coat, having just reflection enough to remember that he must not look like a madman; but he rushed out of the house into the snow without heeding his thin shoes.

In a few minutes he was on his rapid way to the Stone-pits by the side of Dolly, who, though feeling that she was entirely in her place in encountering cold and snow on an errand of mercy, was much concerned at a young gentleman's getting his feet wet under a like impulse.

"You'd a deal better go back, sir," said Dolly, with respectful compassion. "You've no call to catch cold; and

I'd ask you if you'd be so good as tell my husband to come, on your way back—he's at the Rainbow, I doubt—if you found him any way sober enough to be o' use. Or else, there's Mrs. Snell 'ud happen send the boy up to fetch and carry, for there may be things wanted from the doctor's."

"No, I'll stay, now I'm once out—I'll stay outside here," said Godfrey, when they came opposite Marner's cottage. "You can come and tell me if I can do any thing."

"Well, sir, you're very good: you've a tender heart," said Dolly, going to the door.

Godfrey was too painfully preoccupied to feel a twinge of self-reproach at this undeserved praise. He walked up and down, unconscious that he was plunging ankle-deep in snow, unconscious of every thing but trembling suspense about what was going on in the cottage, and the effect of each alternative on his future lot. No, not quite unconscious of every thing else. Deeper down, and half-smothered by passionate desire and dread, there was the sense that he ought not to be waiting on these alternatives; that he ought to accept the consequences of his deeds, own the miserable wife, and fulfill the claims of the helpless child. But he had not moral courage enough to contemplate that active renunciation of Nancy as possible for him: he had only conscience and heart enough to make him forever uneasy under the weakness that forbade the renunciation. And at this moment his mind leaped away from all restraint towards the sudden prospect of deliverance from his long bondage.

"Is she dead?" said the voice that predominated over every other within him. "If she is, I may marry Nancy; and then I shall be a good fellow in future, and have no secrets, and the child—shall be taken care of somehow." But across that vision came the other possibility—"She may live, and then it's all up with me."

Godfrey never knew how long it was before the door of the cottage opened and Mr. Kimble came out. He went forward to meet his uncle, prepared to suppress the agitation he must feel, whatever news he was to hear.

"I waited for you, as I'd come so far," he said, speaking first.

"Pooh, it was nonsense for you to come out: why didn't you send one of the men? There's nothing to be done. She's dead—has been dead for hours, I should say."

"What sort of a woman is she?" said Godfrey, feeling the blood rush to his face.

"A young woman, but emaciated, with long black hair. Some vagrant—quite in rags. She's got a wedding-ring on, however. They must fetch her away to the workhouse to-morrow. Come, come along."

"I want to look at her," said Godfrey. "I think I saw such a woman yesterday. I'll overtake you in a minute or two."

Mr. Kimble went on, and Godfrey turned back to the cottage. He cast only one glance at the dead face on the pillow, which Dolly had smoothed with decent care; but he remembered that last look at his unhappy hated wife so well, that at the end of sixteen years every line in the worn face was present to him when he told the full story of this night.

He turned immediately towards the hearth, where Silas Marner sat lulling the child. She was perfectly quiet now, but not asleep—only soothed by sweet porridge and warmth into that wide-gazing calm which makes us older human beings, with our inward turmoil, feel a certain awe in the presence of a little child, such as we feel before some quiet majesty or beauty in the earth or sky—before a steady glowing planet, or a full-flowered eglantine, or the bending trees over a silent pathway. The wide-open blue eyes looked up at Godfrey's without any uneasiness or sign of recognition: the child could make no visible audible claim on its father; and the father felt a strange mixture of feelings, a conflict of regret and joy, that the pulse of that little heart had no response for the half-jealous yearning in his own, when the blue eyes turned away from him slowly, and fixed themselves on the weaver's queer face, which was bent low down to look at them, while the small hand began to pull Marner's withered cheek with loving disfiguration.

"You'll take the child to the parish to-morrow?" asked Godfrey, speaking as indifferently as he could.

"Who says so?" said Marner, sharply. "Will they make me take her?"

"Why, you wouldn't like to keep her, should you—an old bachelor like you?"

"Till any body shows they've a right to take her away from me," said Marner. "The mother's dead, and I reckon it's got no father: it's a lone thing—and I'm a lone thing. My money's gone, I don't know where—and this is come from I don't know where. I know nothing—I'm partly mazed."

"Poor little thing!" said Godfrey. "Let me give something towards finding it clothes."

He had put his hand in his pocket and found half a guinea, and, thrusting it into Silas's hand, he hurried out of the cottage to overtake Mr. Kimble.

"Ah, I see it's not the same woman I saw," he said, as he

came up. "It's a pretty little child: the old fellow seems to want to keep it; that's strange for a miser like him. But I gave him a trifle to help him out: the parish isn't likely to quarrel with him for the right to keep the child."

"No; but I've seen the time when I might have quarrelled with him for it myself. It's too late now, though. If the child ran into the fire, your aunt's too fat to overtake it: she could only sit and grunt like an alarmed sow. But what a fool you are, Godfrey, to come out in your dancing shoes and stockings in this way—and you one of the beaux of the evening, and at your own house! What do you mean by such freaks, young fellow? Has Miss Nancy been cruel, and do you want to spite her by spoiling your pumps?"

"Oh, every thing has been disagreeable to-night. I was tired to death of jigging and gallanting, and that bother about the hornpipes. And I'd got to dance with the other Miss Gunn," said Godfrey, glad of the subterfuge his uncle had suggested to him.

The prevarication and white lies which a mind that keeps itself ambitiously pure is as uneasy under as a great artist under the false touches that no eye detects but his own, are worn as lightly as mere trimmings when once the actions have become a lie.

Godfrey reappeared in the White Parlor with dry feet, and, since the truth must be told, with a sense of relief and gladness that was too strong for painful thoughts to struggle with. For could he not venture now, whenever opportunity offered, to say the tenderest things to Nancy Lammeter—to promise her and himself that he would always be just what she would desire to see him? There was no danger that his dead wife would be recognized: those were not days of active inquiry and wide report; and as for the registry of their marriage, that was a long way off, buried in unturned pages, away from every one's interest but his own. Dunsey might betray him if he came back; but Dunsey might be won to silence.

And when events turn out so much better for a man than he has had reason to dread, is it not a proof that his conduct has been less foolish and blameworthy than it might otherwise have appeared? When we are treated well, we naturally begin to think that we are not altogether unmeritorious, and that it is only just we should treat ourselves well, and not mar our own good fortune. Where, after all, would be the use of his confessing the past to Nancy Lammeter, and throwing away his happiness?—nay, hers? for he felt some confidence that she loved him. As for the child, he would see that it was cared for: he would never forsake it; he would do every thing but own it. Perhaps it would be just as happy in life without being owned by its father, seeing that nobody could tell how things would turn out, and that—is there any other reason wanted?—well, then, that the father would be much happier without owning the child.

CHAPTER XIV.

THERE was a pauper's burial that week in Raveloe, and up Kench Yard at Batherley it was known that the dark-haired woman with the fair child, who had lately come to lodge there, was gone away again. That was all the express note taken that Molly had disappeared from the eyes of men. But the unwept death which, to the general lot, seemed as trivial as the summer-shed leaf, was charged with the force of destiny to certain human lives that we know of, shaping their joys and sorrows even to the end.

Silas Marner's determination to keep the "tramp's child" was matter of hardly less surprise and iterated talk in the village than the robbery of his money. That softening of feeling towards him which dated from his misfortune, that merging of suspicion and dislike in a rather contemptuous pity for him as lone and crazy, was now accompanied with a more active sympathy, especially amongst the women. Notable mothers, who knew what it was to keep children "whole and sweet;" lazy mothers, who knew what it was to be interrupted in folding their arms and scratching their elbows by the mischievous propensities of children just firm on their legs, were equally interested in conjecturing how a lone man would manage with a two-year-old child on his hands, and were equally ready with their suggestions; the notable chiefly telling him what he had better do, and the lazy ones being emphatic in telling him what he would never be able to do.

Among the notable mothers, Dolly Winthrop was the one whose neighborly offices were the most acceptable to Marner, for they were rendered without any show of bustling instruction. Silas had shown her the half guinea given to him by Godfrey, and had asked her what he should do about getting some clothes for the child.

"Eh, Master Marner," said Dolly, "there's no call to buy, no more nor a pair o' shoes; for I've got the little petticoats as Aaron wore five years ago, and it's ill spending the money on them baby-clothes, for the child 'ull grow like grass i' May, bless it—that it will."

And the same day Dolly brought her bundle, and displayed to Marner, one by one, the tiny garments in their due order of succession, most of them patched and darned, but clean and neat as fresh-sprung herbs. This was the introduction to a great ceremony with soap and water, from which baby came out in new beauty, and sat on Dolly's knee, handling her toes and chuckling and patting her palms together with an air of having made several discoveries about herself, which she communicated by alternate sounds of "gug-gug-gug," and "mammy." The "mammy" was not a cry of need or uneasiness; Baby had been used to utter it without expecting either tender sound or touch to follow.

"Any body 'ud think the angils in heaven couldn't be prettier," said Dolly, rubbing the golden curls and kissing them. "And to think of its being covered wi' them dirty rags—and the poor mother—froze to death; but there's Them as took care of it, and brought it to your door, Master Marner. The door was open, and it walked in over the snow, like as if it had been a little starved robin. Didn't you say the door was open?"

"Yes," said Silas, meditatively. "Yes—the door was open. The money's gone I don't know where, and this is come from I don't know where."

He had not mentioned to any one his unconsciousness of the child's entrance, shrinking from questions which might lead to the fact he himself suspected—namely, that he had been in one of his trances.

"Ah," said Dolly, with soothing gravity, "it's like the night and the morning, and the sleeping and the waking, and the rain and the harvest—one goes and the other comes, and we know nothing how nor where. We may strive and scrat and fend, but it's little we can do arter all—the big things come and go wi' no striving o' our'n—they do, that they do; and I think you're in the right on it to keep the little un, Master Marner, seeing as it's been sent to you, though there's folks as thinks different. You'll happen be a bit moithered with it while it's so little; but I'll come, and welcome, and see to it for you: I've a bit o' time to spare most days, for when one gets up betimes i' the morning, the clock seems to stan' still tow'rt ten, afore it's time to go about the victual. So, as I say, I'll come and see to the child for you, and welcome."

"Thank you . . . kindly," said Silas, hesitating a little. "I'll be glad if you'll tell me things. But," he added, uneasily, leaning forward to look at baby with some jealousy, as she was resting her head backward against Dolly's arm, and eying him contentedly from a distance—"But I want to do things for it myself, else it may get fond o' somebody else, and not fond o' me. I've been used to fending for myself in the house—I can learn, I can learn."

"Eh, to be sure," said Dolly, gently. "I've seen men as are wonderful handy wi' children. The men are awk'ard and contrary mostly, God help 'em—but when the drink's out of 'em, they aren't unsensible, though they're bad for leeching and bandaging—so fiery and impatient. You see this goes first, next the skin," proceeded Dolly, taking up the little shirt, and putting it on.

"Yes," said Marner, docilely, bringing his eyes very close, that they might be initiated in the mysteries; whereupon Baby seized his head with both her small arms, and put her lips against his face with purring noises.

"See there," said Dolly, with a woman's tender tact, "she's fondest o' you. She want's to go o' your lap, I'll be bound. Go, then: take her, Master Marner; you can put the things on, and then you can say as you've done for her from the first of her coming to you."

Marner took her on his lap, trembling with an emotion mysterious to himself, at something unknown dawning on his life. Thought and feeling were so confused within him, that if he had tried to give them utterance, he could only have said that the child was come instead of the gold—that the gold had turned into the child. He took the garments from Dolly, and put them on under her teaching; interrupted, of course, by Baby's gymnastics.

"There, then! why, you take to it quite easy, Master Marner," said Dolly; "but what shall you do when you're forced to sit in your loom? For she'll get busier and mischievouser every day—she will, bless her. It's lucky as you've got that high hearth i'stead of a grate, for that keeps the fire more out of her reach: but if you've got any thing as can be spilt or broke, or as is fit to cut her fingers off, she'll be at it—and it is but right you should know."

Silas meditated a little while in some perplexity. "I'll tie her to the leg o' the loom," he said at last—"tie her with a good long strip o' something."

"Well, mayhap that'll do, as it's a little gell, for they're easier persuaded to sit i' one place nor the lads. I know what the lads are; for I've had four—four I've had, God knows—and if you was to take and tie 'em up, they'd make a fighting and a crying as if you was ringing the pigs. But

I'll bring you my little chair, and some bits o' red rag and things for her to play wi'; an' she'll sit and chatter to 'em as if they was alive. Eh, if it wasn't a sin to the lads to wish 'em made different, bless 'em, I should ha' been glad for one of 'em to be a little gell; and to think as I could ha' taught her to scour, and mend, and the knitting, and every thing. But I can teach 'em this little un, Master Marner, when she gets old enough."

"But she'll be *my* little un," said Marner, rather hastily. "She'll be nobody else's."

"No, to be sure; you'll have a right to her, if you're a father to her, and bring her up according. But," added Dolly, coming to a point which she had determined beforehand to touch upon, "you must bring her up like christened folks's children, and take her to church, and let her learn her catechise, as my little Aaron can say off—the 'I believe,' and every thing, and 'hurt nobody by word or deed,'—as well as if he was the clerk. That's what you must do, Master Marner, if you'd do the right thing by the orphan child."

Marner's pale face flushed suddenly under a new anxiety. His mind was too busy trying to give some definite bearing to Dolly's words for him to think of answering her.

"And it's my belief," she went on, "as the poor little creature has never been christened, and it's nothing but right as the parson should be spoke to; and if you was noways unwilling, I'd talk to Mr. Macey about it this very day. For if the child ever went anyways wrong, and you hadn't done your part by it, Master Marner—'noculation, and every thing to save it from harm—it 'ud be a thorn i' your bed forever o' this side the grave; and I can't think as it 'ud be easy lying down for any body when they'd got to another world, if they hadn't done their part by the helpless children as come wi'out their own asking."

Dolly herself was disposed to be silent for some time now, for she had spoken from the depths of her own simple belief, and was much concerned to know whether her words would produce the desired effect on Silas. He was puzzled and anxious, for Dolly's word "christened" conveyed no distinct meaning to him. He had only heard of baptism, and had only seen the baptism of grown-up men and women.

"What is it as you mean by 'christened?'" he said at last, timidly. "Won't folks be good to her without it?"

"Dear, dear! Master Marner," said Dolly, with gentle distress and compassion. "Had you never no father nor mother as taught you to say your prayers, and as there's good words and good things to keep us from harm?"

"Yes," said Silas, in a low voice; "I know a deal about that—used to, used to. But your ways are different: my country was a good way off." He paused a few moments, and then added, more decidedly, "But I want to do every thing as can be done for the child. And whatever's right for it i' this country, and you think 'ull do it good, I'll act according, if you'll tell me."

"Well, then, Master Marner," said Dolly, inwardly rejoiced, "I'll ask Mr. Macey to speak to the parson about it; and you must fix on a name for it, because it must have a name giv' it when it's christened."

"My mother's name was Hephzibah," said Silas, "and my little sister was named after her."

"Eh, that's a hard name," said Dolly. "I partly think it isn't a christened name."

"It's a Bible name," said Silas, old ideas recurring.

"Then I've no call to speak again' it," said Dolly, rather startled by Silas's knowledge on this head; "but you see I'm no scholard, and I'm slow at catching the words. My husband says I'm allays like as if I was putting the haft for the handle—that's what he says—for he's very sharp, God help him. But it was awk'ard calling your little sister by such a hard name, when you'd got nothing big to say, like—wasn't it, Master Marner?"

"We called her Eppie," said Silas.

"Well, if it was noways wrong to shorten the name, it 'ud be a deal handier. And so I'll go now, Master Marner, and I'll speak about the christening afore dark; and I wish you the best o' luck, and it's my belief as it'll come to you, if you do what's right by the orphan child;—and there's the 'noculation to be seen to; and as to washing its bits o' things, you need look to nobody but me, for I can do 'em wi' one hand when I've got my suds about. Eh, the blessed angil! You'll let me bring my Aaron one o' these days, and he'll show her his little cart as his father's made for him, and the black-and-white pup as he's got a-rearing."

Baby *was* christened, the rector deciding that a double baptism was the lesser risk to incur; and on this occasion Silas, making himself as clean and tidy as he could, appeared for the first time within the church, and shared in the observances held sacred by his neighbors. He was quite unable, by means of any thing he heard or saw, to identify the Raveloe religion with his old faith; if he could at any time in his previous life have done so, it must have been by the aid of a strong feeling ready to vibrate with sympathy, rather than by a comparison of phrases and ideas: and now for long years that feeling had been dormant. He had no distinct idea about the baptism and the church-going, except that Dolly had said it was for the good of the child; and in this way, as the weeks grew to months, the child created fresh and fresh links between his life and the lives from which he had hitherto shrunk continually into narrower isolation. Unlike the gold which needed nothing, and must be worshipped in close-locked solitude—which was hidden away from the daylight, was deaf to the song of birds, and started to no human tones—Eppie was a creature of endless claims and ever-growing desires, seeking and loving sunshine, and living sounds, and living movements; making trial of every thing, with trust in new joy, and stirring the human kindness in all eyes that looked on her. The gold had kept his thoughts in an ever-repeated circle, leading to nothing beyond itself; but Eppie was an object compacted of changes and hopes that forced his thoughts onward, and carried them far away from their old eager pacing towards the same blank limit—carried them away to the new things that would come with the coming years, when Eppie would have learned to understand how her father Silas cared for her; and made him look for images of that time in the ties and charities that bound together the families of his neighbors. The gold had asked that he should sit weaving longer and longer, deafened and blinded more and more to all things except the monotony of his loom and the repetition of his web; but Eppie called him away from his weaving, and made him think all its pauses a holiday, re-awakening his senses with her fresh life, even to the old winter-flies that came crawling forth in the early spring sunshine, and warming him into joy because *she* had joy.

And when the sunshine grew strong and lasting, so that the buttercups were thick in the meadows, Silas might be seen in the sunny mid-day, or in the late afternoon when the shadows were lengthening under the hedgerows, strolling out with uncovered head to carry Eppie beyond the Stone-pits to where the flowers grew, till they reached some favorite bank where he could sit down, while Eppie toddled to pluck the flowers, and make remarks to the winged things that murmured happily above the bright petals, calling "Dad-dad's" attention continually by bringing him the flowers. Then she would turn her ear to some sudden bird-note, and Silas learned to please her by making signs of hushed stillness, that they might listen for the note to come again: so that when it came, she set up her small back and laughed with gurgling triumph. Sitting on the banks in this way, Silas began to look for the once familiar herbs again; and as the leaves, with their unchanged outline and markings, lay on his palm, there was a sense of crowding remembrances from which he turned away timidly, taking refuge in Eppie's little world, that lay lightly on his enfeebled spirit.

As the child's mind was growing into knowledge, his mind was growing into memory: as her life unfolded, his soul, long stupefied in a cold, narrow prison, was unfolding too, and trembling gradually into full consciousness.

It was an influence which must gather force with every new year: the tones that stirred Silas's heart grew articulate, and called for more distinct answers; shapes and sounds grew clearer for Eppie's eyes and ears, and there was more that "Dad-dad" was imperatively required to notice and account for. Also, by the time Eppie was three years old, she developed a fine capacity for mischief, and for devising ingenious ways of being troublesome, which found much exercise, not only for Silas's patience, but for his watchfulness and penetration. Sorely was poor Silas puzzled on such occasions by the incompatible demands of love. Dolly Winthrop told him punishment was good for Eppie, and that, as for rearing a child without making it tingle a little in soft and safe places now and then, it was not to be done.

"To be sure, there's another thing you might do, Master Marner," added Dolly, meditatively: "you might shut her up once i' the coal-hole. That was what I did wi' Aaron; for I was that silly wi' the youngest lad, as I could never bear to smack him. Not as I could find i' my heart to let him stay i' the coal-hole more nor a minute, but it was enough to colly him all over, so as he must be new washed and dressed, and it was as good as a rod to him—that was. But I put it upo' your conscience, Master Marner, as there's one of 'em you must choose—ayther smacking or the coal-hole—else she'll get so masterful, there'll be no holding her."

Silas was impressed with the melancholy truth of this last remark; but his force of mind failed before the only two penal methods open to him, not only because it was painful to him to hurt Eppie, but because he trembled at a moment's contention with her, lest she should love him the less for it. Let even an affectionate Goliath get himself tied to a small tender thing, dreading to hurt it by pulling, and dreading still more to snap the cord, and which of the two, pray, will be master? It was clear that Eppie, with her short toddling steps, must lead father Silas a pretty dance on any fine morning when circumstances favored mischief.

For example. He had wisely chosen a broad strip of linen as a means of fastening her to his loom when he was busy:

it made a broad belt round her waist, and was long enough to allow of her reaching the truckle-bed and sitting down on it, but not long enough for her to attempt any dangerous climbing. One bright summer's morning Silas had been more engrossed than usual in "setting up" a new piece of work, an occasion on which his scissors were in requisition. These scissors, owing to an especial warning of Dolly's, had been kept carefully out of Eppie's reach; but the click of them had had a peculiar attraction for her ear, and, watching the results of that click, she had derived the philosophic lesson that the same cause would produce the same effect. Silas had seated himself in his loom, and the noise of weaving had begun; but he had left his scissors on a ledge which Eppie's arm was long enough to reach; and now, like a small mouse, watching her opportunity, she stole quietly from her corner, secured the scissors, and toddled to the bed again, setting up her back as a mode of concealing the fact. She had a distinct intention as to the use of the scissors; and having cut the linen strip in a jagged but effectual manner, in two moments she had run out at the open door where the sunshine was inviting her, while poor Silas believed her to be a better child than usual. It was not until he happened to need his scissors that the terrible fact burst upon him: Eppie had run out by herself—had perhaps fallen into the Stone-pit. Silas, shaken by the worst fear that could have befallen him, rushed out, calling "Eppie!" and ran eagerly about the unenclosed space, exploring the dry cavities into which she might have fallen, and then gazing with questioning dread at the smooth red surface of the water. The cold drops stood on his brow. How long had she been out? There was one hope—that she had crept through the stile and got into the fields, where he habitually took her to stroll. But the grass was high in the meadow, and there was no descrying her, if she were there, except by a close search that would be a trespass on Mr. Osgood's crop. Still, that misdemeanor must be committed; and poor Silas, after peering all round the hedgerows, traversed the grass, beginning with perturbed vision to see Eppie behind every group of red sorrel, and to see her moving always farther off as he approached. The meadow was searched in vain; and he got over the stile into the next field, looking with dying hope towards a small pond which was now reduced to its summer shallowness, so as to leave a wide margin of good adhesive mud. Here, however, sat Eppie, discoursing cheerfully to her own small boot, which she was using as a bucket to convey the water into a deep hoof-mark, while her little naked foot was planted comfortably on a cushion of olive-green mud. A red-headed calf was observing her with alarmed doubt through the opposite hedge.

Here was clearly a case of aberration in a christened child which demanded severe treatment; but Silas, overcome with convulsive joy at finding his treasure again, could do nothing but snatch her up, and cover her with half-sobbing kisses. It was not until he had carried her home, and had begun to think of the necessary washing, that he recollected the need that he should punish Eppie, and "make her remember." The idea that she might run away again and come to harm, gave him unusual resolution, and for the first time he determined to try the coal-hole—a small closet near the hearth.

"Naughty, naughty Eppie," he suddenly began, holding her on his knee, and pointing to her muddy feet and clothes —"naughty to cut with the scissors and run away. Eppie must go into the coal-hole for being naughty. Daddy must put her in the coal-hole."

He half expected that this would be shock enough, and that Eppie would begin to cry. But instead of that, she began to shake herself on his knee, as if the proposition opened a pleasing novelty. Seeing that he must proceed to extremities, he put her into the coal-hole, and held the door closed, with a trembling sense that he was using a strong measure. For a moment there was silence, but then came a little cry, "Opy, opy!" and Silas let her out again, saying, "Now Eppie 'ull never be naughty again, else she must go in the coal-hole—a black naughty place."

The weaving must stand still a long while this morning, for now Eppie must be washed, and have clean clothes on; but it was to be hoped that this punishment would have a lasting effect, and save time in future—though, perhaps, it would have been better if Eppie had cried more.

In half an hour she was clean again, and Silas having turned his back to see what he could do with the linen band, threw it down again, with the reflection that Eppie would be good without fastening for the rest of the morning. He turned round again, and was going to place her in her little chair near the loom, when she peeped out at him with black face and hands again, and said, "Eppie in de toal-hole!"

This total failure of the coal-hole discipline shook Silas's belief in the efficacy of punishment. "She'd take it all for fun," he observed to Dolly, "if I didn't hurt her, and that I can't do, Mrs. Winthrop. If she makes me a bit o' trouble, I can bear it. And she's got no tricks but what she'll grow out of."

"Well, that's partly true, Master Marner," said Dolly, sympathetically; "and if you can't bring your mind to frighten her off touching things, you must do what you can to keep 'em out of her way. That's what I do wi' the pups as the lads are allays a-rearing. They *will* worry and gnaw—worry and gnaw they will, if it was one's Sunday cap as hung anywhere so as they could drag it. They know no difference, God help 'em: it's the pushing o' the teeth as sets 'em on, that's what it is."

So Eppie was reared without punishment, the burden of her misdeeds being borne vicariously by father Silas. The stone hut was made a soft nest for her, lined with downy patience: and also in the world that lay beyond the stone hut she knew nothing of frowns and denials.

Notwithstanding the difficulty of carrying her and his yarn or linen at the same time, Silas took her with him in most of his journeys to the farm-houses, unwilling to leave her behind at Dolly Winthrop's, who was always ready to take care of her: and little curly-headed Eppie, the weaver's child, became an object of interest at several outlying homesteads, as well as in the village. Hitherto he had been treated very much as if he had been a useful gnome or brownie—a queer and unaccountable creature, who must necessarily be looked at with wondering curiosity and repulsion, and with whom one would be glad to make all greetings and bargains as brief as possible, but who must be dealt with in a propitiatory way, and occasionally have a present of pork or garden-stuff to carry home with him, seeing that without him there was no getting the yarn woven. But now Silas met with open smiling faces and cheerful questionings, as a person whose satisfactions and difficulties could be understood. Everywhere he must sit a little and talk about the child, and words of interest were always ready for him: "Ah, Master Marner, you'll be lucky if she takes the measles soon and easy!"—or, "Why, there isn't many lone men 'ud ha' been wishing to take up with a little un like that: but I reckon the weaving makes you handier than men as do out-door work—you're partly as handy as a woman, for weaving comes next to spinning." Elderly masters and mistresses, seated observantly in large kitchen arm-chairs, shook their heads over the difficulties attendant on rearing children, felt Eppie's round arms and legs, and pronounced them remarkably firm, and told Silas that, if she turned out well (which, however, there was no telling), it would be a fine thing for him to have a steady lass to do for him when he got helpless. Servant maidens were fond of carrying her out to look at the hens and chickens, or to see if any cherries could be shaken down in the orchard; and the small boys and girls approached her slowly, with cautious movement and steady gaze, like little dogs face to face with one of their own kind, till attraction had reached the point at which the soft lips were put out for a kiss. No child was afraid of approaching Silas when Eppie was near him: there was no repulsion around him now, either for young or old; for the little child had come to link him once more with the whole world. There was love between him and the child that blent them into one, and there was love between the child and the world—from men and women with parental looks and tones, to the red lady-birds and the round pebbles.

Silas began now to think of Raveloe life entirely in relation to Eppie: she must have every thing that was a good in Raveloe; and he listened docilely, that he might come to understand better what this life was, from which, for fifteen years, he had stood aloof as from a strange thing, wherewith he could have no communion: as some man who has a precious plant to which he would give a nurturing home in a new soil, thinks of the rain, and the sunshine, and all influences, in relation to his nursling, and asks industriously for all knowledge that will help him to satisfy the wants of the searching roots, or to guard leaf and bud from invading harm. The disposition to hoard had been utterly crushed at the very first by the loss of his long-stored gold: the coins he earned afterwards seemed as irrelevant as stones brought to complete a house suddenly buried by an earthquake; the sense of bereavement was too heavy upon him for the old thrill of satisfaction to rise again at the touch of the newly-earned coin. And now something had come to replace his hoard which gave a growing purpose to the earnings, drawing his hope and joy continually onward beyond the money.

In old days there were angels who came and took men by the hand and led them away from the city of destruction. We see no white-winged angels now. But yet men are led away from threatening destruction: a hand is put into theirs, which leads them forth gently towards a calm and bright land, so that they look no more backward; and the hand may be a little child's.

CHAPTER XV.

There was one person, as you will believe, who watched with keener though more hidden interest than any other, the prosperous growth of Eppie under the weaver's care. He dared not do any thing that would imply a stronger interest in a poor man's adopted child than could be expected from the kindliness of the young Squire, when a chance meeting suggested a little present to a simple old fellow whom others noticed with good-will; but he told himself that the time would come when he might do something towards furthering the welfare of his daughter without incurring suspicions. Was he very uneasy in the mean time at his inability to give his daughter her birthright? I can not say that he was. The child was being taken care of, and would very likely be happy, as people in humble stations often were—happier, perhaps, than those who are brought up in luxury.

That famous ring that pricked its owner when he forgot duty and followed desire—I wonder if it pricked very hard when he set out on the chase, or whether it pricked but lightly then, and only pierced to the quick when the chase had long been ended, and hope, folding her wings, looked backward and became regret?

Godfrey Cass's cheek and eye were brighter than ever now. He was so undivided in his aims, that he seemed like a man of firmness. No Dunsey had come back: people had made up their minds that he was gone for a soldier or gone "out of the country," and no one cared to be specific in their inquiries on a subject delicate to a respectable family. Godfrey had ceased to see the shadow of Dunsey across his path; and the path now lay straight forward to the accomplishment of his best, longest-cherished wishes. Every body said Mr. Godfrey had taken the right turn; and it was pretty clear what would be the end of things, for there were not many days in the week that he was not seen riding to the Warrens. Godfrey himself, when he was asked jocosely if the day had been fixed, smiled with the pleasant consciousness of a lover who could say "yes," if he liked. He felt a reformed man, delivered from temptation; and the vision of his future life seemed to him as a promised land for which he had no cause to fight. He saw himself with all his happiness centred on his own hearth, while Nancy would smile on him as he played with the children.

And that other child not on the hearth—he would not forget it; he would see that it was well provided for. That was a father's duty.

PART II.

CHAPTER XVI.

It was a bright autumn Sunday, sixteen years after Silas Marner had found his new treasure on the hearth. The bells of the old Raveloe church were ringing the cheerful peal which told that the morning service was ended; and out of the arched doorway in the tower came slowly, retarded by friendly greetings and questions, the richer parishioners who had chosen this bright Sunday morning as eligible for church-going. It was the rural fashion of that time for the more important members of the congregation to depart first, while their humbler neighbors waited and looked on, stroking their bent heads or dropping their courtesies to any large ratepayer who turned to notice them.

Foremost among these advancing groups of well-clad people, there are some whom we shall recognize, in spite of Time, who has laid his hand on them all. The tall blond man of forty is not much changed in feature from the Godfrey Cass of six-and-twenty: he is only fuller in flesh, and has only lost the indefinable look of youth— a loss which is marked even when the eye is undulled and the wrinkles are not yet come. Perhaps the pretty woman, not much younger than he, who is leaning on his arm, is more changed than her husband: the lovely bloom that used to be always on her cheek now comes but fitfully, with the fresh morning air or with some strong surprise; yet to all who love human faces best for what they tell of human experience, Nancy's beauty has a heightened interest. Often the soul is ripened into fuller goodness while age has spread an ugly film, so that mere glances can never divine the preciousness of the fruit. But the years have not been so cruel to Nancy. The firm yet placid mouth, the clear veracious glance of the brown eyes, speak now of a nature that has been tested and has kept its highest qualities; and even the costume, with its dainty neatness and purity, has more significance now the coquetries of youth car have nothing to do with it.

Mr. and Mrs. Godfrey Cass (any higher title has died away from Raveloe lips since the old Squire was gathered to his fathers and his inheritance was divided) have turned round to look for the tall aged man and the plainly dressed woman who are a little behind—Nancy having observed that they must wait for "father and Priscilla"—and now they all turn into a narrower path leading across the churchyard to a small gate opposite the Red House. We will not follow them now; for may there not be some others in this departing congregation whom we should like to see again—some of those who are not likely to be handsomely clad, and whom we may not recognize so easily as the master and mistress of the Red House?

But it is impossible to mistake Silas Marner. His large brown eyes seem to have gathered a longer vision, as is the way with eyes that have been short-sighted in early life, and they have a less vague, a more answering look; but in every thing else one sees signs of a frame much enfeebled by the lapse of the sixteen years. The weaver's bent shoulders and white hair give him almost the look of advanced age, though he is not more than five-and-fifty; but there is the freshest blossom of youth close by his side—a blonde dimpled girl of eighteen, who has vainly tried to chastise her curly auburn hair into smoothness under her brown bonnet: the hair ripples as obstinately as a brooklet under the March breeze, and the little ringlets burst away from the restraining comb behind and show themselves below the bonnet-crown. Eppie can not help being rather vexed about her hair, for there is no other girl in Raveloe who has hair at all like it, and she thinks hair ought to be smooth. She does not like to be blameworthy even in small things: you see how neatly her prayer-book is folded in her spotted handkerchief.

That good-looking young fellow, in a new fustian suit, who walks behind her, is not quite sure upon the question of hair in the abstract, when Eppie puts it to him, and thinks that perhaps straight hair is the best in general, but he doesn't want Eppie's hair to be different. She surely divines that there is some one behind her who is thinking about her very particularly, and mustering courage to come to her side as soon as they are out in the lane, else why should she look rather shy, and take care not to turn away her head from her father Silas, to whom she keeps murmuring little sentences as to who was at church, and who was not at church, and how pretty the red mountain-ash is over the Rectory wall?

"I wish we had a little garden, father, with double daisies in, like Mrs. Winthrop's," said Eppie, when they were out in the lane; "only they say it 'ud take a deal of digging and bringing fresh soil—and you couldn't do that, could you, father? Anyhow, I shouldn't like you to do it, for it 'ud be too hard work for you."

"Yes, I could do it, child, if you want a bit o' garden: these long evenings, I could work at taking in a little bit o' the waste, just enough for a root or two o' flowers for you; and again, i' the morning, I could have a turn wi' the spade before I sat down to the loom. Why didn't you tell me before as you wanted a bit o' garden?"

"*I* can dig it for you, Master Marner," said the young man in fustian, who was now by Eppie's side, entering into the conversation without the trouble of formalities. "It'll be play to me after I've done my day's work, or any odd bits o' time when the work's slack. And I'll bring you some soil from Mr. Cass's garden—he'll let me, and willing."

"Eh, Aaron, my lad, are you there?" said Silas; "I wasn't aware of you; for when Eppie's talking o' things, I see nothing but what she's a-saying. Well, if you could help me with the digging, we might get her a bit o' garden all the sooner."

"Then if you think well and good," said Aaron, "I'll come to the Stonepits this afternoon, and we'll settle what land's to be taken in, and I'll get up an hour earlier i' the morning, and begin on it."

"But not if you don't promise me not to work at the hard digging, father," said Eppie. "For I shouldn't ha' said any thing about it," she added, half-bashfully, half-roguishly, "only Mrs. Winthrop said as Aaron 'ud be so good, and—"

"And you might ha' known it without mother telling you," said Aaron. "And Master Marner knows too, I hope, as I'm able and willing to do a turn o' work for him, and he won't do me the unkindness to anyways take it out o' my hands."

"There now, father, you won't work in it till it's all easy," said Eppie, "and you and me can mark out the beds, and make holes and plant the roots. It'll be a deal livelier at the Stonepits when we've got some flowers, for I always think the flowers can see us and know what we're talking about. And I'll have a bit o' rosemary, and bergamot, and thyme, because they're so sweet-smelling; but there's no lavender only in the gentlefolks' gardens, I think."

"That's no reason why you shouldn't have some," said Aaron, "for I can bring you slips of any thing; I'm forced to cut no end of 'em when I'm gardening, and throw 'em away mostly. There's a big bed o' lavender at the Red House: the missis is very fond of it."

"Well," said Silas, gravely, "so as you don't make free for

us, or ask for any thing as is worth much at the Red House: for Mr. Cass's been so good to us, and built us up the new end o' the cottage, and given us beds and things, as I couldn't abide to be imposin' for garden-stuff or any thing else."

"No, no, there's no imposin'," said Aaron; "there's never a garden in all the parish but what there's endless waste in it for want o' somebody as could use every thing up. It's what I think to myself sometimes, as there need nobody run short o' victuals if the land was made the most on, and there was never a morsel but what could find its way to a mouth. It sets one thinking o' that—gardening does. But I must go back now, else mother ull' be in trouble as I aren't there."

"Bring her with you this afternoon, Aaron," said Eppie; "I shouldn't like to fix about the garden, and her not know every thing from the first—should *you*, father?"

"Ay, bring her if you can, Aaron," said Silas; "she's sure to have a word to say as'll help us to set things on their right end."

Aaron turned back up the village, while Silas and Eppie went on up the lonely sheltered lane.

"Oh, daddy!" she began, when they were in privacy, clasping and squeezing Silas's arm, and skipping round to give him an energetic kiss. "My little old daddy! I'm so glad. I don't think I shall want any thing else when we've got a little garden; and I knew Aaron would dig it for us," she went on with roguish triumph—"I knew that very well."

"You're a deep little puss, you are," said Silas, with the mild passive happiness of love-crowned age in his face; "but you'll make yourself fine and beholden to Aaron."

"Oh no, I sha'n't," said Eppie, laughing and frisking; "he likes it."

"Come, come, let me carry your prayer-book, else you'll be dropping it, jumping i' that way."

Eppie was now aware that her behavior was under observation, but it was only the observation of a friendly donkey, browsing with a log fastened to his foot—a meek donkey, not scornfully critical of human trivialities, but thankful to share in them, if possible, by getting his nose scratched; and Eppie did not fail to gratify him with her usual notice, though it was attended with the inconvenience of his following them, painfully, up to the very door of their home.

But the sound of a sharp bark inside, as Eppie put the key in the door, modified the donkey's views, and he limped away again without bidding. The sharp bark was the sign of an excited welcome that was awaiting them from a knowing brown terrier, who, after dancing at their legs in an hysterical manner, rushed with a worrying noise at a tortoise-snell kitten under the loom, and then rushed back with a sharp bark again, as much as to say, "I have done my duty by this feeble creature, you perceive;" while the lady-mother of the kitten sat sunning her white bosom in the window, and looked round with a sleepy air of expecting caresses, though she was not going to take any trouble for them.

The presence of this happy animal life was not the only change which had come over the interior of the stone cottage. There was no bed now in the living-room, and the small space was well filled with decent furniture, all bright and clean enough to satisfy Dolly Winthrop's eye. The oaken table and three-cornered oaken chair were hardly what was likely to be seen in so poor a cottage: they had come, with the beds and other things, from the Red House; for Mr. Godfrey Cass, as every one said in the village, did very kindly by the weaver; and it was nothing but right a man should be looked on and helped by those who could afford it, when he had brought up an orphan child, and been father and mother to her—and had lost his money too, so as he had nothing but what he worked for week by week, and when the weaving was going down too—for there was less and less flax spun—and Master Marner was none so young. Nobody was jealous of the weaver, for he was regarded as an exceptional person, whose claims on neighborly help were not to be matched in Raveloe. Any superstition that remained concerning him had taken an entirely new color; and Mr. Macey, now a very feeble old man of fourscore and six, never seen except in his chimney-corner or sitting in the sunshine at his door-sill, was of opinion that when a man had done what Silas had done by an orphan child, it was a sign that his money would come to light again, or leastwise that the robber would be made to answer for it—for, as Mr. Macey observed of himself, his faculties were as strong as ever.

Silas sat down now and watched Eppie with a satisfied gaze as she spread the clean cloth, and set on it the potato-pie, warmed up slowly in a safe Sunday fashion, by being put into a dry pot over a slowly-dying fire, as the best substitute for an oven. For Silas would not consent to have a grate and oven added to his conveniences: he loved the old brick hearth as he had loved his brown pot—and was it not there when he had found Eppie? The gods of the hearth exist for us still; and let all new faith be tolerant of that fetishism, lest it bruise its own roots.

Silas ate his dinner more silently than usual, soon laying down his knife and fork, and watching half-abstractedly Eppie's play with Snap and the cat, by which her own dining was made rather a lengthy business. Yet it was a sight that might well arrest wandering thoughts: Eppie, with the rippling radiance of her hair and the whiteness of her rounded chin and throat set off by the dark-blue cotton gown, laughing merrily as the kitten held on with her four claws to one shoulder, like a design for a jug-handle, while Snap on the right hand and Puss on the other put up their paws towards a morsel which she held out of the reach of both—Snap occasionally desisting in order to remonstrate with the cat by a cogent worrying growl on the greediness and futility of her conduct; till Eppie relented, caressed them both, and divided the morsel between them.

But at last Eppie, glancing at the clock, checked the play, and said, "Oh, daddy, you're wanting to go into the sunshine to smoke your pipe. But I must clear away first, so as the house may be tidy when godmother comes. I'll make haste —I won't be long."

Silas had taken to smoking a pipe daily during the last two years, having been strongly urged to it by the sages of Raveloe, as a practice "good for the fits;" and this advice was sanctioned by Dr. Kimble, on the ground that it was as well to try what could do no harm—a principle which was made to answer for a great deal of work in that gentleman's medical practice. Silas did not highly enjoy smoking, and often wondered how his neighbors could be so fond of it; but a humble sort of acquiescence in what was held to be good, had become a strong habit of that new self which had been developed in him since he had found Eppie on his hearth: it had been the only clue his bewildered mind could hold by in cherishing this young life that had been sent to him out of the darkness into which his gold had departed. By seeking what was needful for Eppie, by sharing the effect that every thing produced on her, he had himself come to appropriate the forms of custom and belief which were the mould of Raveloe life; and as, with re-awakening sensibilities, memory also reawakened, he had begun to ponder over the elements of his old faith, and blend them with his new impressions, till he recovered a consciousness of unity between his past and present. The sense of presiding goodness and the human trust which come with all pure peace and joy, had given him a dim impression that there had been some error, some mistake, which had thrown that dark shadow over the days of his best years; and as it grew more and more easy to him to open his mind to Dolly Winthrop, he gradually communicated to her all he could describe of his early life. The communication was necessarily a slow and difficult process, for Silas's meagre power of explanation was not aided by any readiness of interpretation in Dolly, whose narrow outward experience gave her no key to strange customs, and made every novelty a source of wonder that arrested them at every step of the narrative. It was only by fragments, and at intervals which left Dolly time to revolve what she had heard till it acquired some familiarity for her, that Silas at last arrived at the climax of the sad story—the drawing of lots, and its false testimony concerning him; and this had to be repeated in several interviews, under new questions on her part as to the nature of this plan for detecting the guilty and clearing the innocent.

"And yourn's the same Bible, you're sure o' that, Master Marner—the Bible as you brought wi' you from that country—it's the same as what they've got at church, and what Eppie's a-learning to read in?"

"Yes," said Silas, "every bit the same; and there's drawing o' lots in the Bible, mind you," he added in a lower tone.

"Oh dear, dear," said Dolly in a grieved voice, as if she were hearing an unfavorable report of a sick man's case. She was silent for some minutes; at last she said—

"There's wise folks, happen, as know how it all is; the parson knows, I'll be bound; but it takes big words to tell them things, and such as poor folks can't make much out on. I can never rightly know the meaning o' what I hear at church, only a bit here and there, but I know it's good words—I do. But what lies upo' your mind—it's this, Master Marner: as, if Them above had done the right thing by you, They'd never ha' let you be turned out for a wicked thief when you was innicent."

"Ah!" said Silas, who had now come to understand Dolly's phraseology, "that was what fell on me like as if it had been red-hot iron; because, you see, there was nobody as cared for me or clave to me above nor below. And him as I'd gone out and in wi' for ten year and more, since when we was lads and went halves—mine own famil'ar friend, in whom I trusted, and lifted up his heel again' me, and worked to ruin me."

"Eh, but he was a bad un—I can't think as there's another such," said Dolly. "But I'm o'ercome, Master Marner; I'm like as if I'd waked and didn't know whether it was night or morning. I feel somehow as sure as I do when I've laid something up though I can't justly put my hand on it, as there was a rights in what happened to you, if one could but make it out; and you'd no call to lose heart as you did. But we'll talk on it again; for sometimes things come into my head when I'm leeching or poulticing, or such, as I could never think on when I was sitting still."

Dolly was too useful a woman not to have many opportunities of illumination of the kind she alluded to, and she was not long before she recurred to the subject.

"Master Marner," she said, one day that she came to bring home Eppie's washing, "I've been sore puzzled for a good bit wi' that trouble o' yourn and the drawing o' lots; and it got twisted back'ards and for'ards, as I didn't know which end to lay hold on. But it come to me all clear like, that night when I was sitting up wi' poor Bessy Fawkes, as is dead and left her children behind, God help 'em—it come to me as clear as daylight: but whether I've got hold on it now, or can anyways bring it to my tongue's end, that I don't know. For I've often a deal inside me as 'll niver come out; and for what you talk o' your folks in your old country niver saying prayers by heart nor saying 'em out of a book, they must be wonderful cliver; for if I didn't know 'Our Father,' and little bits o' good words as I can carry out o' church wi' me, I might down o' my knees every night, but nothing could I say."

"But you can mostly say something as I can make sense on, Mrs. Winthrop," said Silas.

"Well, then, Master Marner, it come to me summat like this: I can make nothing o' the drawing o' lots and the answer coming wrong; it 'ud mayhap take the parson to tell that, and he could only tell us i' big words. But what come to me as clear as the daylight, it was when I was troubling over poor Bessy Fawkes, and it allays comes into my head when I'm sorry for folks, and feel as I can't do a power to help 'em, not if I was to get up i' the middle o' the night—it comes into my head as Them above has got a deal tenderer heart nor what I've got—for I can't be anyways better nor Them as made me; and if any thing looks hard to me, it's because there's things I don't know on; and for the matter o' that, there may be plenty o' things I don't know on, for it's little as I know—that it is. And so, while I was thinking o' that, you come into my mind, Master Marner, and it all come pouring in:—if *I* felt i' my inside what was the right and just thing by you, and them as prayed and drawed the lots, all but that wicked un, if *they*'d ha' done the right thing by you if they could, isn't there Them as was at the making on us, and knows better and has a better will? And that's all as ever I can be sure on, and every thing else is a big puzzle to me when I think on it. For there was the fever come and took off them as were full-growed, and left the helpless children;

and there's the breaking o' limbs; and them as 'ud do right and be sober have to suffer by them as are contrairy—eh, there's trouble i' this world, and there's things as we can niver make out the rights on. And all as we've got to do is to trusten, Master Marner—to do the right thing as fur as we know, and to trusten. For if us as knows so little can see a bit o' good and rights, we may be sure as there's a good and a rights bigger nor what we can know—I feel it i' my own inside as it must be so. And if you could but ha' gone on trustening, Master Marner, you wouldn't ha' run away from your fellow-creaturs and been so lone."

"Ah, but that 'ud ha' been hard," said Silas, in an undertone; "it 'ud ha' been hard to trusten then."

"And so it would," said Dolly, almost with compunction; "them things are easier said nor done; and I'm partly ashamed o' talking."

"Nay, nay," said Silas, "you're i' the right, Mrs. Winthrop—you're i' the right. There's good i' this world—I've a feeling o' that now; and it makes a man feel as there's a good more nor he can see, i' spite o' the trouble and the wickedness. That drawing o' the lots is dark; but the child was sent to me: there's dealings with us—there's dealings."

This dialogue took place in Eppie's earlier years, when Silas had to part with her for two hours every day, that she might learn to read at the dame school, after he had vainly tried himself to guide her in that first step to learning. Now that she was grown up, Silas had often been led, in those moments of quiet outpouring which come to people who live together in perfect love, to talk with *her* too of the past, and how and why he had lived a lonely man until she had been sent to him. For it would have been impossible for him to hide from Eppie that she was not his own child: even if the most delicate reticence on the point could have been expected from Raveloe gossips in her presence, her own questions about her mother could not have been parried, as she grew up, without that complete shrouding of the past which would have made a painful barrier between their minds. So Eppie had long known how her mother had died on the snowy ground, and how she herself had been found on the hearth by father Silas, who had taken her golden curls for his lost guineas brought back to him. The tender and peculiar love with which Silas had reared her in almost inseparable companionship with himself, aided by the seclusion of their dwelling, had preserved her from the lowering influences of the village talk and habits, and had kept her mind in that freshness which is sometimes falsely supposed to be an invariable attribute of rusticity. Perfect love has a breath of poetry which can exalt the relations of the least-instructed human beings; and this breath of poetry had surrounded Eppie from the time when she had followed the bright gleam that beckoned her to Silas's hearth; so that it is not surprising if, in other things besides her delicate prettiness, she was not quite a common village maiden, but had a touch of refinement and fervor which came from no other teaching than that of tenderly-nurtured unvitiated feeling. She was too childish and simple for her imagination to rove into questions about her unknown father; for a long while it did not even occur to her that she must have had a father; and the first time that the idea of her mother having had a husband presented itself to her, was when Silas showed her the wedding-ring which had been taken from the wasted finger, and had been carefully preserved by him in a little lacquered box shaped like a shoe. He delivered this box into Eppie's charge when she had grown up, and she often opened it to look at the ring: but still she thought hardly at all about the father of whom it was the symbol. Had she not a father very close to her, who loved her better than any real fathers in the village seemed to love their daughters? On the contrary, who her mother was, and how she came to die in that forlornness, were questions that often pressed on Eppie's mind. Her knowledge of Mrs. Winthrop, who was her nearest friend next to Silas, made her feel that a mother must be very precious; and she had again and again asked Silas to tell her how her mother looked, whom she was like, and how he had found her against the furze bush, led towards it by the little footsteps and the outstretched arms. The furze-bush was there still; and this afternoon, when Eppie came out with Silas into the sunshine, it was the first object that arrested her eyes and thoughts.

"Father," she said, in a tone of gentle gravity, which sometimes came like a sadder, slower cadence across her playfulness, "we shall take the furze-bush into the garden; it'll come into the corner, and just against it I'll put snowdrops and crocuses, 'cause Aaron says they won't die out, but 'll always get more and more."

"Ah, child," said Silas, always ready to talk when he had his pipe in his hand, apparently enjoying the pauses more than the puffs, "it wouldn't do to leave out the furze-bush; and there's nothing prettier, to my thinking, when it's yallow with flowers. But it's just come into my head what we're to do for a fence—mayhap Aaron can help us to a thought; but a fence we must have, else the donkeys and things 'ull come and trample every thing down. And fencing's hard to be got at, by what I can make out."

"Oh, I'll tell you, daddy," said Eppie, clasping her hands suddenly, after a minute's thought. "There's lots o' loose stones about, some of 'em not big, and we might lay 'em atop of one another, and make a wall. You and me could carry the smallest, and Aaron 'ud carry the rest—I know he would."

"Eh, my precious 'un," said Silas, "there isn't enough stones to go all round; and as for you carrying, wi' your little arms you couldn't carry a stone no bigger than a turnip. You're dillicate made, my dear," he added, with a tender intonation—"that's what Mrs. Winthrop says."

"Oh, I'm stronger than you think, daddy," said Eppie; "and if there wasn't stones enough to go all round, why they'll go part o' the way, and then it'll be easier to get sticks and things for the rest. See here, round the big pit, what a many stones!"

She skipped forward to the pit, meaning to lift one of the stones and exhibit her strength, but she started back in surprise.

"Oh, father, just come and look here," she exclaimed—"come and see how the water's gone down since yesterday. Why, yesterday the pit was ever so full!"

"Well, to be sure," said Silas, coming to her side. "Why, that's the draining they've begun on, since harvest, i' Mr. Osgood's fields, I reckon. The foreman said to me the other day, when I passed by 'em, 'Master Marner,' he said, 'I shouldn't wonder if we lay your bit o' waste as dry as a bone.' It was Mr. Godfrey Cass, he said, had gone into the draining: he'd been taking these fields o' Mr. Osgood."

"How odd it'll seem to have the old pit dried up!" said Eppie, turning away, and stooping to lift rather a large stone. "See, daddy, I can carry this quite well," she said, going along with much energy for a few steps, but presently letting it fall.

"Ah, you're fine and strong, arn't you?" said Silas, while Eppie shook her aching arms and laughed. "Come, come, let us go and sit down on the bank against the stile there, and have no more lifting. You might hurt yourself, child. You'd need have somebody to work for you—and my arm isn't over strong."

Silas uttered the last sentence slowly, as if it implied more than met the ear; and Eppie, when they sat down on the bank, nestled close to his side, and, taking hold caressingly of the arm that was not over strong, held it on her lap, while Silas puffed again dutifully at the pipe, which occupied his other arm. An ash in the hedgerow behind made a fretted screen from the sun, and threw happy playful shadows all about them.

"Father," said Eppie, very gently, after they had been sitting in silence a little while, "if I was to be married, ought I to be married with my mother's ring?"

Silas gave an almost imperceptible start, though the question fell in with the under-current of thought in his own mind, and then said, in a subdued tone, "Why, Eppie, have you been a-thinking on it?"

"Only this last week, father," said Eppie, ingenuously, "since Aaron talked to me about it."

"And what did he say?" said Silas, still in the same subdued way, as if he were anxious lest he should fall into the slightest tone that was not for Eppie's good.

"He said he should like to be married, because he was a-going in four-and-twenty, and had got a deal of gardening work, now Mr. Mott's given up; and he goes twice a-week regular to Mr. Cass's and once to Mr. Osgood's, and they're going to take him on at the Rectory."

"And who is it as he's wanting to marry?" said Silas, with rather a sad smile.

"Why, me, to be sure, daddy," said Eppie, with dimpling laughter, kissing her father's cheek; "as if he'd want to marry any body else!"

"And you mean to have him, do you?" said Silas.

"Yes, some time," said Eppie, "I don't know when. Every body's married some time, Aaron says. But I told him that wasn't true: for, I said, look at father—he's never been married."

"No, child," said Silas, "your father was a lone man till you was sent to him."

"But you'll never be lone again, father," said Eppie tenderly. "That was what Aaron said—'I could never think o' taking you away from Master Marner, Eppie.' And I said, 'It 'ud be no use if you did, Aaron.' And he wants us all to live together, so as you needn't work a bit, father, only what's for your own pleasure; and he'd be as good as a son to you—that was what he said."

"And should you like that, Eppie?" said Silas, looking at her.

"I shouldn't mind it, father," said Eppie, quite simply. "And I should like things to be so as you needn't work much. But if it wasn't for that, I'd sooner things didn't change. I'm very happy: I like Aaron to be fond of me, and come and see us often, and behave pretty to you—he always *does* behave pretty to you, doesn't he, father?"

"Yes, child, nobody could behave better," said Silas, emphatically. "He's his mother's lad."

"But I don't want any change," said Eppie. "I should like to go on a long, long while, just as we are. Only Aaron does want a change: and he made me cry a bit—only a bit—because he said I didn't care for him, for if I cared for him I should want us to be married, as he did."

"Eh, my blessed child," said Silas, laying down his pipe as if it were useless to pretend to smoke any longer, "you're o'er young to be married. We'll ask Mrs. Winthrop—we'll ask Aaron's mother what *she* thinks; if there's a right thing to do, she'll come at it. But there's this to be thought on, Eppie: things *will* change, whether we like it or no; things won't go on for a long while just as they are and no difference. I shall get older and helplesser, and be a burden on you, belike, if I don't go away from you altogether. Not as I mean you'd think me a burden—I know you wouldn't—but it 'ud be hard upon you; and when I look for'ard to that, I like to think as you'd have somebody else besides me—somebody young and strong, as'll outlast your own life, and take care on you to the end." Silas paused, and, resting his wrists on his knees, lifted his hands up and down meditatively as he looked on the ground.

"Then, would you like me to be married, father?" said Eppie, with a little trembling in her voice.

"I'll not be the man to say no, Eppie," said Silas, emphatically; "but we'll ask your godmother. She'll wish the right thing by you and her son too."

"There they come, then," said Eppie. "Let us go and meet 'em. Oh, the pipe! won't you have it lit again, father?" said Eppie, lifting that medicinal appliance from the ground.

"Nay, child," said Silas, "I've done enough for to-day. I think, mayhap, a little of it does me more good than so much at once."

CHAPTER XVII.

While Silas and Eppie were seated on the bank discoursing in the fleckered shade of the ash-tree, Miss Priscilla Lammeter was resisting her sister's arguments, that it would be better to stay tea at the Red House, and let her father have a long nap, than drive home to the Warrens so soon after dinner. The family party (of four only) were seated round the table in the dark wainscoted parlor, with the Sunday dessert before them, of fresh filberts, apples, and pears, duly ornamented with leaves by Nancy's own hand before the bells had rung for church.

A great change has come over the dark wainscoted parlor since we saw it in Godfrey's bachelor days, and under the wifeless reign of the old Squire. Now all is polish, on which no yesterday's dust is ever allowed to rest, from the yard's width of oaken boards round the carpet, to the old Squire's gun and whips and walking-sticks, ranged on the stag's antlers above the mantel-piece. All other signs of sporting and out-door occupation Nancy has removed to another room; but she has brought into the Red House the habit of filial reverence, and preserves sacredly in a place of honor these relics of her husband's departed father. The tankards are on the side-table still, but the bossed silver is undimmed by handling, and there are no dregs to send forth unpleasant suggestions: the only prevailing scent is of the lavender and rose-leaves that fill the vases of Derbyshire spar. All is purity and order in this once dreary room, for, fifteen years ago, it was entered by a new presiding spirit.

"Now, father," said Nancy, "*is* there any call for you to go home to tea? Mayn't you just as well stay with us?—such a beautiful evening as it's likely to be."

The old gentleman had been talking with Godfrey about the increasing poor-rate and the ruinous times, and had not heard the dialogue between his daughters.

"My dear, you must ask Priscilla," he said, in the once firm voice, now become rather broken. "She manages me and the farm too."

"And reason good as I should manage you, father," said Priscilla, "else you'd be giving yourself your death with rheumatism. And as for the farm, if any thing turns out wrong, as it can't but do in these times, there's nothing kills a man so soon as having nobody to find fault with but himself. It's a deal the best way o' being master, to let somebody else do the ordering, and keep the blaming in your own hands. It 'ud save many a man a stroke, *I* believe."

"Well, well, my dear," said her father, with a quiet laugh, "I didn't say you don't manage for every body's good."

"Then manage so as you may stay tea, Priscilla," said Nancy, putting her hand on her sister's arm affectionately. "Come now; and we'll go round the garden while father has his nap."

"My dear child, he'll have a beautiful nap in the gig, for I shall drive. And as for staying tea, I can't hear of it; for there's this dairymaid, now she knows she's to be married, turned Michaelmas, she'd as lief pour the new milk into the pig-trough as into the pans. That's the way with 'em all: it's as if they thought the world 'ud be new-made because they're to be married. So come and let me put my bonnet on, and there'll be time for us to walk round the garden while the horse is being put in."

When the sisters were treading the neatly swept garden-walks, between the bright turf that contrasted pleasantly with the dark cones and arches and wall-like hedges of yew, Priscilla said—

"I'm as glad as any thing at your husband's making that exchange o' land with cousin Osgood, and beginning the dairying. It's a thousand pities you didn't do it before; for it'll give you something to fill your mind. There's nothing like a dairy if folks want a bit o' worrit to make the days pass. For as for rubbing furniture, when you can once see your face in a table there's nothing else to look for; but there's always something fresh with the dairy; for even in the depths o' winter there's some pleasure in conquering the butter, and making it come whether or no. My dear," added Priscilla, pressing her sister's hand affectionately as they walked side by side, "you'll never be low when you've got a dairy."

"Ah, Priscilla," said Nancy, returning the pressure with a grateful glance of her clear eyes, "but it won't make up to Godfrey: a dairy's not so much to a man. And it's only what he cares for that ever makes me low. I'm contented with the blessings we have, if he could be contented."

"It drives me past patience," said Priscilla, impetuously, "that way o' the men—always wanting and wanting, and never easy with what they've got: they can't sit comfortable in their chairs when they've neither ache nor pain, but either they must stick a pipe in their mouths, to make 'em better than well, or else they must be swallowing something strong, though they're forced to make haste before the next meal comes in. But joyful be it spoken, our father was never that sort o' man. And if it had pleased God to make you ugly, like me, so as the men wouldn't ha' run after you, we might have kept to our own family, and had nothing to do with folks as have got uneasy blood in their veins."

"Oh, don't say so, Priscilla," said Nancy, repenting that she had called forth this outburst; "nobody has any occasion to find fault with Godfrey. It's natural he should be disappointed at not having any children: every man likes to have somebody to work for and lay by for, and he always counted so on making a fuss with them when they were little. There's many another man 'ud hanker more than he does. He's the best of husbands."

"Oh, I know," said Priscilla, smiling sarcastically, "I know the way o' wives; they set one on to abuse their husbands, and then they turn round on one and praise 'em as if they wanted to sell 'em. But father'll be waiting for me; we must turn now."

The large gig with the steady old gray was at the front door, and Mr. Lammeter was already on the stone steps, passing the time in recalling to Godfrey what very fine points Speckle had when his master used to ride him.

"I always *would* have a good horse, you know," said the old gentleman, not liking that spirited time to be quite effaced from the memory of his juniors.

"Mind you bring Nancy to the Warrens before the week's out, Mr. Cass," was Priscilla's parting injunction, as she took the reins, and shook them gently, by way of friendly incitement to Speckle.

"I shall just take a turn to the fields against the Stone-pits, Nancy, and look at the draining," said Godfrey.

"You'll be in again by tea-time, dear?"

"Oh yes, I shall be back in an hour."

It was Godfrey's custom on a Sunday afternoon to do a little contemplative farming in a leisurely walk. Nancy seldom accompanied him; for the women of her generation—unless, like Priscilla, they took to outdoor management—were not given to much walking beyond their own house and garden, finding sufficient exercise in domestic duties. So, when Priscilla was not with her, she usually sat with Mant's Bible before her, and after following the text with her eyes for a little while, she would gradually permit them to wander as her thoughts had already insisted on wandering.

But Nancy's Sunday thoughts were rarely quite out of keeping with the devout and reverential intention implied by the book spread open before her. She was not theologically instructed enough to discern very clearly the relation between the sacred documents of the past which she opened without method, and her own obscure, simple life; but the spirit of rectitude, and the sense of responsibility for the effect of her conduct on others, which were strong elements in Nancy's character, had made it a habit with her to scrutinize her past feelings and actions with self-questioning solicitude. Her mind not being courted by a great variety of subjects, she filled the vacant moments by living inwardly, again and again, through all her remembered experience, especially through the fifteen years of her married time, in which her life and its significance had been doubled. She recalled the small details, the words, tones, and looks, in the critical scenes which had opened a new epoch for her, by giving her a deeper insight into the relations and trials of life, or which had called on her for some little effort of forbearance, or of painful adherence to an imagined or real duty—asking herself continually whether she had been in any respect blamable. This excessive rumination and self-questioning is perhaps a morbid habit inevitable to a mind of much moral sensibility when shut out from its due share of outward activity and of practical claims on its affections—inevitable to a noble-hearted, childless woman, when her lot is narrow. "I can do so little—have I done it all well?" is the perpetually recurring thought; and there are no voices calling her away from that soliloquy, no peremptory demands to divert energy from vain regret or superfluous scruple.

There was one main thread of painful experience in Nancy's married life, and on it hung certain deeply-felt scenes, which were the oftenest revived in retrospect. The short dialogue with Priscilla in the garden had determined the current of retrospect in that frequent direction this particular Sunday afternoon. The first wandering of her thought from the text, which she still attempted dutifully to follow with her eyes and silent lips, was into an imaginary enlargement of the defense she had set up for her husband against Priscilla's implied blame. The vindication of the loved object is the best balm affection can find for its wounds:—"A man must have so much on his mind," is the belief by which a wife often supports a cheerful face under rough answers and unfeeling words. And Nancy's deepest wounds had all come from the perception that the absence of children from their hearth was dwelt on in her husband's mind as a privation to which he could not reconcile himself.

Yet sweet Nancy might have been expected to feel still more keenly the denial of a blessing to which she had looked forward with all the varied expectations and preparations, solemn and prettily trivial, which fill the mind of a loving woman when she expects to become a mother. Was there not a drawer filled with the neat work of her hands, all unworn and untouched, just as she had arranged it there fourteen years ago—just, but for one little dress, which had been made the burial-dress? But under this immediate personal trial Nancy was so firmly unmurmuring, that years ago she had suddenly renounced the habit of visiting this drawer, lest she should in this way be cherishing a longing for what was not given.

Perhaps it was this very severity towards any indulgence of what she held to be sinful regret in herself, that made her shrink from applying her own standard to her husband. "It was very different—it was much worse for a man to be disappointed in that way: a woman could always be satisfied with devoting herself to her husband, but a man wanted something that would make him look forward more—and sitting by the fire was so much duller to him than to a woman." And always, when Nancy reached this point in her meditations—trying, with predetermined sympathy, to see every thing as Godfrey saw it—there came a renewal of self-questioning. *Had* she done every thing in her power to lighten Godfrey's privation? Had she really been right in the resistance which had cost her so much pain six years ago, and again four years ago—the resistance to her husband's wish that they should adopt a child? Adoption was more remote from the ideas and habits of that time than of our own; still Nancy had her opinion on it. It was as necessary to her mind to have an opinion on all topics, not exclusively masculine, that had come under her notice, as for her to have a precisely marked place for every article of her personal property: and her opinions were always principles to be unwaveringly acted on. They were firm, not because of their basis, but because she held them with a tenacity inseparable from her mental action. On all the duties and proprieties of life, from filial behavior to the arrangements of the evening toilette, pretty Nancy Lammeter, by the time she was three-and-twenty, had her unalterable little code, and had formed every one of her habits in strict accordance with that code. She carried these decided judgments within her in the most unobtrusive way: they rooted themselves in her mind, and grew there as quietly as grass. Years ago, we know, she insisted on dressing like Priscilla, because "it was right for sisters to dress alike," and because "she would do what was right if she wore a gown dyed with cheese-coloring." That was a trivial but typical instance of the mode in which Nancy's life was regulated.

It was one of those rigid principles, and no petty egoistic feeling, which had been the ground of Nancy's difficult resistance to her husband's wish. To adopt a child, because children of your own had been denied you, was to try and choose your lot in spite of Providence: the adopted child, she was convinced, would never turn out well, and would be a curse to those who had willfully and rebelliously sought what it was clear that, for some high reason, they were better without. When you saw a thing was not meant to be, said Nancy, it was a bounden duty to leave off so much as wishing for it. And so far, perhaps, the wisest of men could scarcely make more than a verbal improvement in her principle. But the conditions under which she held it apparent that a thing was not meant to be, depended on a more peculiar mode of thinking. She would have given up making a purchase at a particular place if, on three successive times, rain, or some other cause of Heaven's sending, had formed an obstacle; and she would have anticipated a broken limb or other heavy misfortune to any one who persisted in spite of such indications.

"But why should you think the child would turn out ill?" said Godfrey, in his remonstrances. "She has thriven as well as child can do with the weaver; and *he* adopted her. There isn't such a pretty little girl anywhere else in the parish, or one fitter for the station we could give her. Where can be the likelihood of her being a curse to any body?"

"Yes, my dear Godfrey," said Nancy, who was sitting with her hands tightly clasped together, and with yearning, regretful affection in her eyes. "The child may not turn out ill with the weaver. But, then, he didn't go to seek her, as we should be doing. It will be wrong: I feel sure it will. Don't you remember what that lady we met at the Royston Baths told us about the child her sister adopted? That was the only adopting I ever heard of: and the child was transported when it was twenty-three. Dear Godfrey, don't ask me to do what I know is wrong: I should never be happy again. I know it's very hard for *you*—it's easier for me—but it's the will of Providence."

It might seem singular that Nancy—with her religious theory pieced together out of narrow social traditions, fragments of church doctrine imperfectly understood, and girlish reasonings on her small experience—should have arrived by herself at a way of thinking so nearly akin to that of many devout people, whose beliefs are held in the shape of a system quite remote from her knowledge—singular, if we did not know that human beliefs, like all other natural growths, elude the barriers of system.

Godfrey had from the first specified Eppie, then about twelve years old, as a child suitable for them to adopt. It had never occurred to him that Silas would rather part with his life than with Eppie. Surely the weaver would wish the best to the child he had taken so much trouble with, and would be glad that such good fortune should happen to her: she would always be very grateful to him, and he would be well provided for to the end of his life—provided for as the excellent part he had done by the child deserved. Was it not an appropriate thing for people in a higher station to take a charge off the hands of a man in a lower? It seemed an eminently appropriate thing to Godfrey, for reasons that were known only to himself; and, by a common fallacy, he imagined the measure would be easy because he had private motives for desiring it. This was rather a coarse mode of estimating Silas's relation to Eppie; but we must remember that many of the impressions which Godfrey was likely to gather concerning the laboring people around him would favor the idea that deep affections can hardly go along with callous palms and scant means; and he had not had the opportunity, even if he had had the power, of entering intimately into all that was exceptional in the weaver's experience. It was only the want of adequate knowledge that could have made it possible for Godfrey deliberately to entertain an unfeeling project; his natural kindness had outlived that blighting time of cruel wishes, and Nancy's praise of him as a husband was not founded entirely on a willful illusion.

"I was right," she said to herself, when she had recalled all their scenes of discussion—"I feel I was right to say him nay, though it hurt me more than any thing; but how good Godfrey has been about it? Many men would have been very angry with me for standing out against their wishes; and they might have thrown out that they'd had ill-luck in marrying me; but Godfrey has never been the man to say me an unkind word. It's only what he can't hide; every thing seems so blank to him, I know; and the land—what a difference it 'ud make to him, when he goes to see after things, if he'd children growing up that he was doing it all for! But I won't murmur; and perhaps if he'd married a woman who'd have had children, she'd have vexed him in other ways.

This possibility was Nancy's chief comfort; and to give it greater strength, she labored to make it impossible that any other wife should have had more perfect tenderness. She had been *forced* to vex him by that one denial. Godfrey was not insensible to her loving effort, and did Nancy no injustice as to the motives of her obstinacy. It was impossible to have lived with her fifteen years and not be aware that an unselfish clinging to the right, and a sincerity clear as the flower-born dew, were her main characteristics; indeed, Godfrey felt this so strongly, that his own more wavering nature, too averse to facing difficulty to be unvaryingly simple and truthful, was kept in a certain awe of this gentle wife who watched his looks with a yearning to obey them. It seemed to him impossible that he should ever confess to her the truth about Eppie: she would never recover from the repulsion the story of his earlier marriage would create, told to her now, after that long concealment. And the child, too, he thought, must become an object of repulsion: the very sight of her would be painful. The shock to Nancy's mingled pride and ignorance of the world's evil might be even too much for her delicate frame. Since he had married her with that secret on his heart, he must keep it there to the last. Whatever else he did, he could not make an irreparable breach between himself and this long-loved wife.

Meanwhile, why could he not make up his mind to the absence of children from the hearth brightened by such a wife? Why did his mind fly uneasily to that void, as if it were the sole reason why life was not thoroughly joyous to him? I suppose it is the way with all men and women who reach middle age without the clear perception that life never *can* be thoroughly joyous: under the vague dullness of the gray hours, dissatisfaction seeks a definite object, and finds it in the privation of an untried good. Dissatisfaction, seated musingly on a childless hearth, thinks with envy of the father whose return is greeted by young voices—seated at the meal where the little heads rise one above the other like nursery plants, it sees a black care hovering behind every one of them, and thinks the impulses by which men abandon freedom, and seek for ties, are surely nothing but a brief madness. In Godfrey's case there were further reasons why his thoughts should be continually solicited by this one point in his lot: his conscience, never thoroughly easy about Eppie, now gave his childless home the aspect of a retribution; and as the time passed on, under Nancy's refusal to adopt her, any retrieval of his error became more and more difficult.

On this Sunday afternoon it was already four years since there had been any allusion to the subject between them, and Nancy supposed that it was forever buried.

"I wonder if he'll mind it less or more as he gets older," she thought; "I'm afraid more. Aged people feel the miss of children: what would father do without Priscilla? And if I die, Godfrey will be very lonely—not holding together with his brothers much. But I won't be over-anxious, and trying to make things out beforehand: I must do my best for the present."

With that last thought Nancy roused herself from her reverie, and turned her eyes again towards the forsaken page. It had been forsaken longer than she imagined, for she was presently surprised by the appearance of the servant with the tea-things. It was, in fact, a little before the usual time for tea; but Jane had her reasons.

"Is your master come into the yard, Jane?"

"No 'm, he isn't," said Jane, with a slight emphasis, of which, however, her mistress took no notice.

"I don't know whether you've seen 'em, 'm," continued Jane, after a pause, "but there's folks making haste all one way, afore the front window. I doubt something's happened. There's niver a man to be seen i' the yard, else I'd send and see. I've been up into the top attic, but there's no seeing any thing for trees. I hope nobody's hurt, that's all."

"Oh, no, I daresay there's nothing much the matter," said Nancy. "It's perhaps Mr. Snell's bull got out again, as he did before."

"I wish he mayn't gore any body, then, that's all," said Jane, not altogether despising an hypothesis which covered a few imaginary calamities.

"That girl is always terrifying me," thought Nancy; "I wish Godfrey would come in."

She went to the front window and looked as far as she could see along the road, with an uneasiness which she felt to be childish, for there were now no such signs of excitement as Jane had spoken of, and Godfrey would not be likely to return by the village road, but by the fields. She continued to stand, however, looking at the placid churchyard with the long shadows of the gravestones across the bright green hillocks, and at the glowing autumn colors of the Rectory trees beyond. Before such calm external beauty the presence of a vague fear is more distinctly felt—like a raven flapping its slow wing across the sunny air. Nancy wished more and more that Godfrey would come in.

CHAPTER XVIII.

Some one opened the door at the other end of the room, and Nancy felt that it was her husband. She turned from the window with gladness in her eyes, for the wife's chief dread was stilled.

"Dear, I'm so thankful you're come," she said, going towards him. "I began to get—"

She paused abruptly, for Godfrey was laying down his hat with trembling hands, and turned towards her with a pale face and a strange unanswering glance, as if he saw her indeed, but saw her as part of a scene invisible to herself. She laid her hand on his arm, not daring to speak again; but he left the touch unnoticed, and threw himself into his chair.

Jane was already at the door with the hissing urn. "Tell her to keep away, will you?" said Godfrey; and when the door was closed again he exerted himself to speak more distinctly.

"Sit down, Nancy—there," he said, pointing to a chair opposite him. "I came back as soon as I could, to hinder any body's telling you but me. I've had a great shock—but I care most about the shock it'll be to you."

"It isn't father and Priscilla?" said Nancy, with quivering lips, clasping her hands together tightly on her lap.

"No, it's nobody living," said Godfrey, unequal to the considerate skill with which he would have wished to make his revelation. "It's Dunstan—my brother Dunstan, that we lost sight of sixteen years ago. We've found him—found his body—his skeleton."

The deep dread Godfrey's look had created in Nancy made her feel these words a relief. She sat in comparative calmness to hear what else he had to tell. He went on:

"The Stone-pit has gone dry suddenly—from the draining, I suppose; and there he lies—has lain for sixteen years, wedged between two great stones. There's his watch and seals, and there's my gold-handled hunting-whip, with my name on: he took it away, without my knowing, the day he went hunting on Wildfire, the last time he was seen."

Godfrey paused: it was not so easy to say what came next. "Do you think he drowned himself?" said Nancy, almost wondering that her husband should be so deeply shaken by what had happened all those years ago to an unloved brother, of whom worse things had been augured.

"No, he fell in," said Godfrey, in a low but distinct voice, as if he felt some deep meaning in the fact. Presently he added: "Dunstan was the man that robbed Silas Marner."

The blood rushed to Nancy's face and neck at this surprise and shame, for she had been bred up to regard even a distant kinship with crime as a dishonor.

"Oh Godfrey!" she said, with compassion in her tone, for she had immediately reflected that the dishonor must be felt still more keenly by her husband.

"There was the money in the pit," he continued—"all the weaver's money. Every thing's been gathered up, and they're taking the skeleton to the Rainbow. But I came back to tell you: there was no hindering it; you must know."

He was silent, looking on the ground for two long minutes. Nancy would have said some words of comfort under this disgrace, but she refrained, from an instinctive sense that there was something behind—that Godfrey had something else to tell her. Presently he lifted his eyes to her face, and kept them fixed on her, as he said—

"Every thing comes to light, Nancy, sooner or later. When God Almighty wills it, our secrets are found out. I've lived with a secret on my mind, but I'll keep it from you no longer. I wouldn't have you know it by some body else, and not by me —I wouldn't have you find it out after I'm dead. I'll tell you now. It's been 'I will' and 'I won't' with me all my life—I'll make sure of myself now."

Nancy's utmost dread had returned. The eyes of the husband and wife met with awe in them, as at a crisis which suspended affection.

"Nancy," said Godfrey, slowly, "when I married you, I hid something from you—something I ought to have told you. That woman Marner found dead in the snow—Eppie's mother —that wretched woman—was my wife: Eppie is my child."

He paused, dreading the effect of his confession. But Nancy sat quite still, only that her eyes dropped and ceased to meet his. She was pale and quiet as a meditative statue, clasping her hands on her lap.

"You'll never think the same of me again," said Godfrey, after a little while, with some tremor in his voice.

She was silent.

"I oughtn't to have left the child unowned: I oughtn't to have kept it from you. But I couldn't bear to give you up, Nancy. I was led away into marrying her—I suffered for it."

Still Nancy was silent, looking down; and he almost expected that she would presently get up and say she would go to her father's. How could she have any mercy for faults that must seem so black to her, with her simple, severe notions?

But at last she lifted up her eyes to his again and spoke. There was no indignation in her voice—only deep regret.

"Godfrey, if you had but told me this six years ago, we could have done some of our duty by the child. Do you think I'd have refused to take her in, if I'd known she was yours?"

At that moment Godfrey felt all the bitterness of an error that was not simply futile, but had defeated its own end. He had not measured this wife with whom he had lived so long. But she spoke again, with more agitation.

"And—Oh, Godfrey—if we'd had her from the first, if you'd taken to her as you ought, she'd have loved me for her mother—and you'd have been happier with me: I could better have bore my little baby dying, and our life might have been more like what we used to think it 'ud be."

The tears fell, and Nancy ceased to speak.

"But you wouldn't have married me then, Nancy, if I'd told you," said Godfrey, urged, in the bitterness of his self-reproach, to prove to himself that his conduct had not been utter folly. "You may think you would now, but you wouldn't then. With your pride and your father's, you'd have hated having any thing to do with me after the talk there'd have been."

"I can't say what I should have done about that, Godfrey. I should never have married any body else. But I wasn't worth doing wrong for—nothing is in this world. Nothing is so good as it seems beforehand—not even our marrying wasn't, you see." There was a faint sad smile on Nancy's face as she said the last words.

"I'm a worse man than you thought I was, Nancy," said Godfrey, rather tremulously. "Can you forgive me ever?"

"The wrong to me is but little, Godfrey: you've made it up to me—you've been good to me for fifteen years. It's another you did the wrong to; and I doubt it can never be all made up for."

"But we can take Eppie now," said Godfrey. "I won't mind the world knowing at last. I'll be plain and open for the rest o' my life."

"It'll be different coming to us, now she's grown up," said Nancy, shaking her head sadly. "But it's your duty to acknowledge her and provide for her; and I'll do my part by her, and pray to God Almighty to make her love me."

"Then we'll go together to Silas Marner's this very night, as soon as every thing's quiet at the Stone-pits."

CHAPTER XIX.

Between eight and nine o'clock that evening, Eppie and Silas were seated alone in the cottage. After the great excitement the weaver had undergone from the events of the afternoon, he had felt a longing for this quietude, and had even begged Mrs. Winthrop and Aaron, who had naturally lingered behind every one else, to leave him alone with his child. The excitement had not passed away: it had only reached the stage when the keenness of the susceptibility makes external stimulus intolerable—when there is no sense of weariness, but rather an intensity of inward life, under which sleep is an impossibility. Any one who has watched such moments in other men remembers the brightness of the eyes and the strange definiteness that comes over coarse features from that transient influence. It is as if a new fineness of ear for all spiritual voices had sent wonder-working vibrations through the heavy mortal frame—as if "beauty born of murmuring sound" had passed into the face of the listener.

Silas's face showed that sort of transfiguration, as he sat in his arm-chair and looked at Eppie. She had drawn her own chair towards his knees, and leaned forward, holding both his hands, while she looked up at him. On the table near them, lit by a candle, lay the recovered gold—the old long-loved gold, ranged in orderly heaps, as Silas used to range it in the days when it was his only joy. He had been telling her how he used to count it every night, and how his soul was utterly desolate till she was sent to him.

"At first, I'd a sort o' feeling come across me now and then," he was saying in a subdued tone, "as if you might be changed into the gold again; for sometimes, turn my head which way I would, I seemed to see the gold; and I thought I should be glad if I could feel it, and find it was come back. But that didn't last long. After a bit, I should have thought it was a curse come again, if it had drove you from me, for I'd got to feel the need o' your looks and your voice and the touch o' your little fingers. You didn't know then, Eppie, when you were such a little un—you didn't know what your old father Silas felt for you."

"But I know now, father," said Eppie. "If it hadn't been for you, they'd have taken me to the workhouse, and there'd have been nobody to love me."

"Eh, my precious child, the blessing was mine. If you hadn't been sent to save me, I should ha' gone to the grave in my misery. The money was taken away from me in time; and you see it's been kept—kept till it was wanted for you. It's wonderful—our life is wonderful."

Silas sat in silence a few minutes, looking at the money. "It takes no hold of me now," he said, ponderingly—"the money doesn't. I wonder if it ever could again—I doubt it might, if I lost you, Eppie. I might come to think I was forsaken again, and lose the feeling that God was good to me."

At that moment there was a knocking at the door; and Eppie was obliged to rise without answering Silas. Beautiful she looked, with the tenderness of gathering tears in her eyes and a slight flush on her cheeks, as she stepped to open the door. The flush deepened when she saw Mr. and Mrs. Godfrey Cass. She made her little rustic courtesy, and held the door wide for them to enter.

"We're disturbing you very late, my dear," said Mrs. Cass, taking Eppie's hand, and looking in her face with an expression of anxious interest and admiration. Nancy herself was pale and tremulous.

Eppie, after placing chairs for Mr. and Mrs. Cass, went to stand against Silas, opposite to them.

"Well, Marner," said Godfrey, trying to speak with perfect firmness, "it's a great comfort to me to see you with your money again, that you've been deprived of so many years. It was one of my family did you the wrong—the more grief to me—and I feel bound to make up to you for it in every way. Whatever I can do for you will be nothing but paying a debt, even if I looked no farther than the robbery. But there are other things I'm beholden—shall be beholden to you for, Marner."

Godfrey checked himself. It had been agreed between him and his wife that the subject of his fatherhood should be approached very carefully, and that, if possible, the disclosure should be reserved for the future, so that it might be made to Eppie gradually. Nancy had urged this, because she felt strongly the painful light in which Eppie must inevitably see the relation between her father and mother.

Silas, always ill at ease when he was being spoken to by "betters," such as Mr. Cass—tall, powerful, florid men, seen chiefly on horseback—answered with some constraint,

"Sir, I've a deal to thank you for a'ready. As for the robbery, I count it no loss to me. And if I did, you couldn't help it: you aren't answerable for it."

"You may look at it in that way, Marner, but I never can: and I hope you'll let me act according to my own feeling of what's just. I know you're easily contented: you've been a hard-working man all your life."

"Yes, sir, yes," said Marner, meditatively. "I should ha' been bad off without my work: it was what I held by when every thing else was gone from me."

"Ah," said Godfrey, applying Marner's words simply to his bodily wants, "it was a good trade for you in this country, because there's been a great deal of linen-weaving to be done. But you're getting rather past such close work, Marner: it's time you laid by and had some rest. You look a good deal pulled down, though you're not an old man, *are* you?"

"Fifty-five, as near as I can say, sir," said Silas.

"Oh, why, you may live thirty years longer—look at old Macey! And that money on the table, after all, is but little. It won't go far either way—whether it's put out to interest, or you were to live on it as long as it would last: it wouldn't go far if you'd nobody to keep but yourself, and you've had two to keep for a good many years now."

"Eh, sir," said Silas, unaffected by any thing Godfrey was saying, "I'm in no fear o' want. We shall do very well—Eppie and me 'ull do well enough. There's few working-folks have got so much laid by as that. I don't know what it is to gentlefolks, but I look upon it as a deal—almost too much. And as for us, it's little we want."

"Only the garden, father," said Eppie, blushing up to the ears the moment after.

"You love a garden, do you my dear?" said Nancy, thinking that this turn in the point of view might help her husband. "We should agree in that: I give a deal of time to the garden."

"Ah, there's plenty of gardening at the Red House," said Godfrey, surprised at the difficulty he found in approaching a proposition which had seemed so easy to him in the distance. "You've done a good part by Eppie, Marner, for sixteen years. It 'ud be a great comfort to you to see her well provided for, wouldn't it? She looks blooming and healthy, but not fit for any hardships: she doesn't look like a strapping girl come of working parents. You'd like to see her taken care of by those who can leave her well off, and make a lady of her; she's more fit for it than for a rough life, such as she might come to have in a few years' time."

A slight flush came over Marner's face, and disappeared, like a passing gleam. Eppie was simply wondering Mr. Cass should talk so about things that seemed to have nothing to do with reality; but Silas was hurt and uneasy.

"I don't take your meaning, sir," he answered, not having words at command to express the mingled feelings with which he had heard Mr. Cass's words.

"Well, my meaning is this, Marner," said Godfrey, determined to come to the point. "Mrs. Cass and I, you know, have no children—nobody to benefit by our good home and every thing else we have—more than enough for ourselves. And we should like to have somebody in the place of a daughter to us—we should like to have Eppie, and treat her in every way as our own child. It would be a great comfort to you in your old age, I hope, to see her fortune made in that way, after you have been at the trouble of bringing her up so well. And it's right you should have every reward for that. And Eppie, I'm sure, will always love you and be grateful to you: she'd come and see you very often, and we should all be on the look-out to do every thing we could towards making you comfortable."

A plain man like Godfrey Cass, speaking under some embarrassment, necessarily blunders on words that are coarser than his intentions, and that are likely to fall gratingly on susceptible feelings. While he had been speaking, Eppie had quietly passed her arm behind Silas's head, and let her hand rest against it caressingly; she felt him trembling violently. He was silent for some moments when Mr. Cass had ended—powerless under the conflict of emotions, all alike painful. Eppie's heart was swelling at the sense that her father was in distress; and she was just going to lean down and speak to him, when one struggling dread at last gained the mastery over every other in Silas, and he said, faintly—

"Eppie, my child, speak. I won't stand in your way. Thank Mr. and Mrs. Cass."

Eppie took her hand from her father's head, and came forward a step. Her cheeks were flushed, but not with shyness this time: the sense that her father was in doubt and suffering banished that sort of self-consciousness. She dropped a low courtesy, first to Mrs. Cass and then to Mr. Cass, and said—

"Thank you, ma'am—thank you, sir. But I can't leave my father, nor own any body nearer than him. And I don't want to be a lady—thank you all the same" (here Eppie dropped another courtesy). "I couldn't give up the folks I've been used to."

Eppie's lip began to tremble a little at the last words. She retreated to her father's chair again, and held him round the neck: while Silas, with a subdued sob, put up his hand to grasp hers.

The tears were in Nancy's eyes, but her sympathy with Eppie was, naturally, divided with distress on her husband's account. She dared not speak, wondering what was going on in her husband's mind.

Godfrey felt an irritation inevitable to almost all of us when we encounter an unexpected obstacle. He had been full of his own penitence and resolution to retrieve his error as far as the time was left to him; he was possessed with all-important feelings, that were to lead to a predetermined course of action which he had fixed on as the right, and he was not prepared to enter with lively appreciation into other people's feelings counteracting his virtuous resolves. The

"*She retreated to her father's chair again, and held him round the neck.*"—
Page 484.

agitation with which he spoke again was not quite unmixed with anger.

"But I have a claim on you, Eppie—the strongest of all claims. It is my duty, Marner, to own Eppie as my child, and provide for her. She is my own child—her mother was my wife. I have a natural claim on her that must stand before every other."

Eppie had given a violent start, and turned quite pale. Silas, on the contrary, who had been relieved, by Eppie's answer, from the dread lest his mind should be in opposition to hers, felt the spirit of resistance in him set free, not without a touch of parental fierceness. "Then, sir," he answered, with an accent of bitterness that had been silent in him since the memorable day when his youthful hope had perished—"then, sir, why didn't you say so sixteen year ago, and claim her before I'd come to love her, i'stead o' coming to take her from me now, when you might as well take the heart out o' my body? God gave her to me because you turned your back upon her, and He looks upon her as mine: you've no right to her! When a man turns a blessing from his door it falls to them as take it in."

"I know that, Marner. I was wrong. I've repented of my conduct in that matter," said Godfrey, who could not help feeling the edge of Silas's words.

"I'm glad to hear it, sir," said Marner, with gathering excitement; "but repentance doesn't alter what's been going on for sixteen year. Your coming now and saying 'I'm her father' doesn't alter the feelings inside us. It's me she's been calling her father ever since she could say the word."

"But I think you might look at the thing more reasonably, Marner," said Godfrey, unexpectedly awed by the weaver's direct truth-speaking. "It isn't as if she was to be taken quite away from you, so that you'd never see her again. She'll be very near you, and come to see you very often. See'll feel just the same towards you."

"Just the same?" said Marner, more bitterly than ever. "How'll she feel just the same for me as she does now, when we eat o' the same bit, and drink o' the same cup, and think o' the same things from one day's end to another? Just the same? that's idle talk. You'd cut us i' two."

Godfrey, unqualified by experience to discern the pregnancy of Marner's simple words, felt rather angry again. It seemed to him that the weaver was very selfish (a judgment readily passed by those who have never tested their own power of sacrifice) to oppose what was undoubtedly for Eppie's welfare; and he felt himself called upon, for her sake, to assert his authority.

"I should have thought, Marner," he said, severely—"I should have thought your affection for Eppie would have made you rejoice in what was for her good, even if it did call upon you to give up something. You ought to remember that your own life is uncertain, and that she's at an age now when her lot may soon be fixed in a way very different from what it would be in her father's home: she may marry some low working-man, and then, whatever I might do for her, I couldn't make her well-off. You're putting yourself in the way of her welfare; and though I'm sorry to hurt you after what you've done, and what I've left undone, I feel now it's my duty to insist on taking care of my own daughter. I want to do my duty."

It would be difficult to say whether it were Silas or Eppie that was most deeply stirred by this last speech of Godfrey's. Thought had been very busy in Eppie as she listened to the contest between her old long-loved father and this new unfamiliar father who had suddenly come to fill the place of that black featureless shadow which had held the ring and placed it on her mother's finger. Her imagination had darted backward in conjectures, and forward in previsions, of what this revealed fatherhood implied: and there were words in Godfrey's last speech which helped to make the previsions especially definite. Not that these thoughts, either of past or future, determined her resolution—that was determined by the feelings which vibrated to every word Silas had uttered; but they raised, even apart from these feelings, a repulsion towards the offered lot and the newly-revealed father.

Silas, on the other hand, was again stricken in conscience, and alarmed lest Godfrey's accusation should be true—lest he should be raising his own will as an obstacle to Eppie's good. For many moments he was mute, struggling for the self-conquest necessary to the uttering of the difficult words. They came out tremulously.

"I'll say no more. Let it be as you will. Speak to the child. I'll hinder nothing."

Even Nancy, with all the acute sensibility of her own affections, shared her husband's view, that Marner was not justifiable in his wish to retain Eppie, after her real father had avowed himself. She felt that it was a very hard trial for the poor weaver, but her code allowed no question that a father by blood must have a claim above that of any foster-father. Besides, Nancy, used all her life to plenteous circumstances and the privileges of "respectability," could not enter into the pleasures which early nurture and habit connect with all the little aims and efforts of the poor who are born poor: to her mind, Eppie, in being restored to her birthright, was entering on a too-long withheld but unquestionable good. Hence she heard Silas's last words with relief, and thought, as Godfrey did, that their wish was achieved.

"Eppie, my dear," said Godfrey, looking at his daughter, not without some embarrassment, under the sense that she was old enough to judge him, "it'll always be our wish that you should show your love and gratitude to one who has been a father to you so many years, and we shall want to help you to make him comfortable in every way. But we hope you'll come to love us as well; and though I haven't been what a father should have been to you all these years, I wish to do the utmost in my power for you for the rest of my life, and provide for you as my only child. And you'll have the best of mothers in my wife—that'll be a blessing you haven't known since you were old enough to know it."

"My dear, you'll be a treasure to me," said Nancy, in her gentle voice. "We shall want for nothing when we have our daughter."

Eppie did not come forward and courtesy, as she had done before. She held Silas's hand in hers, and grasped it firmly —it was a weaver's hand, with a palm and finger-tips that were sensitive to such pressure—while she spoke with colder decision than before.

"Thank you, ma'am—thank you, sir, for your offers— they're very great, and far above my wish. For I should have no delight i' life any more if I was forced to go away from my father, and knew he was sitting at home a-thinking of me and feeling lone. We've been used to be happy together every day, and I can't think o' no happiness without him. And he says he'd nobody i' the world till I was sent to him, and he'd have nothing when I was gone. And he's took care of me and loved me from the first, and I'll cleave to him as long as he lives, and nobody shall ever come between him and me."

"But you must make sure, Eppie," said Silas, in a low voice—"you must make sure as you won't ever be sorry, because you've made your choice to stay among poor folks, and with poor clothes and things, when you might ha' had every thing o' the best."

His sensitiveness on this point had increased as he listened to Eppie's words of faithful affection.

"I can never be sorry, father," said Eppie. "I shouldn't know what to think on or to wish for with fine things about me, as I haven't been used to. And it 'ud be poor work for me to put on things, and ride in a gig, and sit in a place at church, as 'ud make them as I'm fond of think me unfitting company for 'em. What could *I* care for then?"

Nancy looked at Godfrey with a pained questioning glance. But his eyes were fixed on the floor, where he was moving the end of his stick, as if he were pondering on something absently. She thought there was a word which might perhaps come better from her lips then from his.

"What you say is natural, my dear child—it's natural you should cling to those who've brought you up," she said mildly; "but there's a duty you owe to your lawful father. There's perhaps something to be given up on more sides than one. When your father opens his home to you, I think it's right you shouldn't turn your back on it."

"I can't feel as I've got any father but one," said Eppie, impetuously, while the tears gathered. "I've always thought of a little home where he'd sit i' the corner, and I should fend and do every thing for him: I can't think o' no other home. I wasn't brought up to be a lady, and I can't turn my mind to it. I like the working-folks, and their victuals, and their ways. And," she ended passionately, while the tears fell, "I'm promised to marry a working-man, as 'll live with father, and help me to take care of him."

Godfrey looked up at Nancy with a flushed face and a smarting dilation of the eyes. This frustration of a purpose towards which he had set out under the exalted consciousness that he was about to compensate in some degree for the greatest demerit of his life, made him feel the air of the room stifling.

"Let us go," he said, in an under-tone.

"We won't talk of this any longer now," said Nancy, rising. "We're your well-wishers, my dear—and yours too, Marner. We shall come and see you again. It's getting late now."

In this way she covered her husband's abrupt departure, for Godfrey had gone straight to the door, unable to say more.

CHAPTER XX.

NANCY and Godfrey walked home under the starlight in silence. When they entered the oaken parlor, Godfrey threw himself into his chair, while Nancy laid down her bonnet and shawl, and stood on the hearth near her husband, unwilling to leave him even for a few minutes, and yet fearing to utter any word lest it might jar on his feeling. At last Godfrey turned his head towards her, and their eyes met, dwelling in that meeting without any movement on either side. That quiet mutual gaze of a trusting husband and wife is like the first moment of rest or refuge from a great weariness or a great danger—not to be interfered with by speech or action which would distract the sensations from the fresh enjoyment of repose.

But presently he put out his hand, and as Nancy placed hers within it, he drew her towards him, and said,

"That's ended!"

She bent to kiss him, and then said, as she stood by his side, "Yes, I'm afraid we must give up the hope of having her for a daughter. It wouldn't be right to want to force her to come to us against her will. We can't alter her bringing up and what's come of it."

"No," said Godfrey, with a keen decisiveness of tone, in contrast with his usually careless and unemphatic speech—"there's debts we can't pay like money debts, by paying extra for the years that have slipped by. While I've been putting off and putting off, the trees have been growing—it's too late now. Marner was in the right in what he said about a man's turning away a blessing from his door: it falls to somebody else. I wanted to pass for childless once, Nancy—I shall pass for childless now against my wish."

Nancy did not speak immediately, but after a little while she asked—"You won't make it known, then, about Eppie's being your daughter?"

"No—where would be the good to any body? only harm. I must do what I can for her in the state of life she chooses. I must see who it is she's thinking of marrying."

"If it won't do any good to make the thing known," said Nancy, who thought she might now allow herself the relief of entertaining a feeling which she had tried to silence before, "I should be very thankful for father and Priscilla never to be troubled with knowing what was done in the past, more than about Dunsey: it can't be helped, their knowing that."

"I shall put it in my will—I think I shall put it in my will. I shouldn't like to leave any thing to be found out, like this of Dunsey," said Godfrey, meditatively. "But I can't see any thing but difficulties that 'ud come from telling it now. I must do what I can to make her happy in her own way. I've a notion," he added, after a moment's pause, "it's Aaron Winthrop she meant she was engaged to. I remember seeing him with her and Marner going away from church."

"Well, he's very sober and industrious," said Nancy, trying to view the matter as cheerfully as possible.

Godfrey fell into thoughtfulness again. Presently he looked up at Nancy sorrowfully, and said,

"She's a very pretty, nice girl, isn't she, Nancy?"

"Yes, dear; and with just your hair and eyes: I wondered it had never struck me before."

"I think she took a dislike to me at the thought of my being her father: I could see a change in her manner after that."

"She couldn't bear to think of not looking on Marner as her father," said Nancy, not wishing to confirm her husband's painful impression.

"She thinks I did wrong by her mother as well as by her. She thinks me worse than I am. But she *must* think it: she can never know all. It's part of my punishment, Nancy, for my daughter to dislike me. I should never have got into that trouble if I'd been true to you—if I hadn't been a fool. I'd no right to expect any thing but evil could come of that marriage—and when I shirked doing a father's part, too."

Nancy was silent; her spirit of rectitude would not let her try to soften the edge of what she felt to be a just compunction. He spoke again after a little while, but the tone was rather changed: there was tenderness mingled with the previous self-reproach.

"And I got *you*, Nancy, in spite of all; and yet I've been grumbling and uneasy because I hadn't something else—as if I deserved it."

"You've never been wanting to me, Godfrey," said Nancy, with quiet sincerity. "My only trouble would be gone if you resigned yourself to the lot that's been given us."

"Well, perhaps it isn't too late to mend a bit there. Though it *is* too late to mend some things, say what they will."

CHAPTER XXI.

The next morning, when Silas and Eppie were seated at their breakfast, he said to her,

"Eppie, there's a thing I've had on my mind to do this two year, and now the money's been brought back to us, we can do it. I've been turning it over and over in the night, and I think we'll set out to-morrow, while the fine days last. We'll leave the house and every thing for your godmother to take care on, and we'll make a little bundle o' things and set out."

"Where to go, daddy?" said Eppie, in much surprise.

"To my old country—to the town where I was born—up Lantern Yard. I want to see Mr. Paston, the minister: something may ha' come out to make 'em know I was innicent o' the robbery. And Mr. Paston was a man with a deal o' light—I want to speak to him about the drawing o' the lots. And I should like to talk to him about the religion o' this country-side, for I partly think he doesn't know on it."

Eppie was very joyful, for there was the prospect not only of wonder and delight at seeing a strange country, but also of coming back to tell Aaron all about it. Aaron was so much wiser than she was about most things—it would be rather pleasant to have this little advantage over him. Mrs. Winthrop, though possessed with a dim fear of dangers attendant on so long a journey, and requiring many assurances that it would not take them out of the region of carriers' carts and slow wagons, was nevertheless well pleased that Silas should revisit his own country, and find out if he had been cleared from that false accusation.

"You'd be easier in your mind for the rest o' your life, Master Marner," said Dolly—"that you would. And if there's any light to be got up the yard as you talk on, we've need of it i' this world, and I'd be glad on it myself, if you could bring it back."

So on the fourth day from that time, Silas and Eppie, in their Sunday clothes, with a small bundle tied in a blue linen handkerchief, were making their way through the streets of a great manufacturing town. Silas, bewildered by the changes thirty years had brought over his native place, had stopped several persons in succession to ask them the name of this town, that he might be sure he was not under a mistake about it.

"Ask for Lantern Yard, father—ask this gentleman with the tassels on his shoulders a-standing at the shop door; he isn't in a hurry like the rest," said Eppie, in some distress at her father's bewilderment, and ill at ease, besides, amidst the noise, the movement, and the multitude of strange indifferent faces.

"Eh, my child, he won't know any thing about it," said Silas; "gentlefolks didn't ever go up the Yard. But happen somebody can tell me which is the way to Prison Street, where the jail is. I know the way out o' that as if I'd seen it yesterday."

With some difficulty, after many turnings and new inquiries, they reached Prison Street; and the grim walls of the jail, the first object that answered to any image in Silas's memory, cheered him with the certitude, which no assurance of the town's name had hitherto given him, that he was in his native place.

"Ah," he said, drawing a long breath, "there's the jail, Eppie; that's just the same: I aren't afraid now. It's the third turning on the left hand from the jail doors, that's the way we must go."

"Oh, what a dark, ugly place!" said Eppie. "How it hides the sky! It's worse than the Workhouse. I'm glad you don't live in this town now, father. Is Lantern Yard like this street?"

"My precious child," said Silas, smiling, "it isn't a big street like this. I never was easy i' this street myself, but I was fond o' Lantern Yard. The shops here are all altered, I think—I can't make 'em out; but I shall know the turning, because it's the third.

"Here it is," he said, in a tone of satisfaction, as they came to a narrow alley. "And then we must go to the left again, and then straight for'ard for a bit, up Shoe Lane: and then we shall be at the entry next to the o'erhanging window, where there's the nick in the road for the water to run. Eh, I can see it all."

"Oh, father, I'm like as if I was stifled," said Eppie. "I couldn't ha' thought as any folks lived i' this way, so close together. How pretty the Stone-pits 'ull look when we get back!"

"It looks comical to *me*, child, now—and smells bad. I can't think as it usened to smell so."

Here and there a sallow, begrimed face looked out from a gloomy doorway at the strangers, and increased Eppie's uneasiness, so that it was a longed-for relief when they issued from the alleys into Shoe Lane, where there was a broader strip of sky.

"Dear heart!" said Silas, "why, there's people coming out o' the Yard as if they'd been to chapel at this time o' day—a weekday noon!"

Suddenly he started and stood still with a look of distressed amazement, that alarmed Eppie. They were before an opening in front of a large factory, from which men and women were streaming for their mid-day meal.

"Father," said Eppie, clasping his arm, "what's the matter?"

But she had to speak again and again before Silas could answer her.

"It's gone, child," he said, at last, in strong agitation,—"Lantern Yard's gone. It must ha' been here, because here's the house with the o'erhanging window—I know that—it's just the same; but they've made this new opening; and see that big factory! It's all gone—chapel and all."

"Come into that little brush-shop and sit down, father—they'll let you sit down," said Eppie, always on the watch lest one of her father's strange attacks should come on. "Perhaps the people can tell you all about it."

But neither from the brush-maker, who had come to Shoe Lane only ten years ago, when the factory was already built, nor from any other source within his reach, could Silas learn any thing of the old Lantern Yard friends, or of Mr. Paston, the minister.

"The old place is all swep' away," Silas said to Dolly Winthrop on the night of his return—"the little graveyard and every thing. The old home's gone; I've no home but this now. I shall never know whether they got at the truth o' the robbery, nor whether Mr. Paston could ha' given me any light about the drawing o' the lots. It's dark to me, Mrs. Winthrop, that is; I doubt it'll be dark to the last."

"Well, yes, Master Marner," said Dolly, who sat with a placid listening face, now bordered by gray hairs; "I doubt it may. It's the will o' Them above as a many things should be dark to us; but there's some things as I've never felt i' the dark about, and they're mostly what comes i' the day's work. You were hard done by that once, Master Marner, and it seems as you'll never know the rights of it; but that doesn't hinder there *being* a rights, Master Marner, for all it's dark to you and me."

"No," said Silas, "no: that doesn't hinder. Since the time the child was sent to me, and I've come to love her as myself, I've had light enough to trusten by; and now she says she'll never leave me, I think I shall trusten till I die."

CONCLUSION.

There was one time of the year which was held in Raveloe to be especially suitable for a wedding. It was when the great lilacs and laburnums in the old-fashioned gardens showed their golden and purple wealth above the lichen-tinted walls, and when there were calves still young enough to want bucketfuls of fragrant milk. People were not so busy then as they must become when the full cheese-making and the mowing had set in; and besides, it was a time when a light bridal dress could be worn with comfort and seen to advantage.

Happily the sunshine fell more warmly than usual on the lilac tufts the morning that Eppie was married, for her dress was a very light one. She had often thought, though with a feeling of renunciatiou, that the perfection of a wedding-dress would be a white cotton, with the tiniest pink sprig at wide intervals; so that when Mrs. Godfrey Cass begged to provide one, and asked Eppie to choose what it should be, previous meditation had enabled her to give a decided answer at once.

Seen at a little distance as she walked across the churchyard and down the village, she seemed to be attired in pure white, and her hair looked like the dash of gold on a lily. One hand was on her husband's arm, and with the other she clasped the hand of her father Silas.

"You won't be giving me away, father," she had said before they went to church; "you'll only be taking Aaron to be a son to you."

Dolly Winthrop walked behind with her husband; and there ended the little bridal procession.

There were many eyes to look at it, and Miss Priscilla Lammeter was glad that she and her father had happened to drive up to the door of the Red House just in time to see this pretty sight. They had come to keep Nancy company to-day, because Mr. Cass had had to go away to Lytherley, for special reasons. That seemed to be a pity, for otherwise he might have gone, as Mr. Crackenthorp and Mr. Osgood certainly would, to look on at the wedding-feast which he had ordered at the Rainbow, naturally feeling a great interest in the weaver who had been wronged by one of his own family.

"I could ha' wished Nancy had had the luck to find a

child like that and bring her up," said Priscilla to her father, as they sat in the gig; "I should ha' had something young to think of then, besides the lambs and the calves."

"Yes, my dear, yes," said Mr. Lammeter; "one feels that as one gets older. Things look dim to old folks: they'd need have some young eyes about 'em, to let 'em know the world's the same as it used to be."

Nancy came out now to welcome her father and sister, and the wedding group had passed on beyond the Red House to the humbler part of the village.

Dolly Winthrop was the first to divine that old Mr. Macey, who had been set in his arm-chair outside his own door, would expect some special notice as they passed, since he was too old to be at the wedding-feast.

"Mr. Macey's looking for a word from us," said Dolly; "he'll be hurt if we pass him and say nothing—and him so racked with rheumatiz."

So they turned aside to shake hands with the old man. He had looked forward to the occasion, and had his premeditated speech.

"Well, Master Marner," he said, in a voice that quavered a good deal, "I've lived to see my words come true. I was the first to say there was no harm in you, though your looks might be again' you; and I was the first to say you'd get your money back. And it's nothing but rightful as you should. And I'd ha' said the 'Amens,' and willing, at the holy matrimony; but Tookey's done it a good while now, and I hope you'll have none the worse luck."

In the open yard before the Rainbow the party of guests were already assembled, though it was still nearly an hour before the appointed feast-time. But by this means they could not only enjoy the slow advent of their pleasure; they had also ample leisure to talk of Silas Marner's strange history, and arrive by due degrees at the conclusion that he had brought a blessing on himself by acting like a father to a lone motherless child. Even the farrier did not negative this sentiment: on the contrary, he took it up as peculiarly his own, and invited any hardy person present to contradict him. But he met with no contradiction; and all differences among the company were merged in a general agreement with Mr. Snell's sentiment, that when a man had deserved his good luck, it was the part of his neighbors to wish him joy.

As the bridal group approached, a hearty cheer was raised in the Rainbow yard; and Ben Winthrop, whose jokes had retained their acceptable flavor, found it agreeable to turn in there and receive congratulations; not requiring the proposed interval of quiet at the Stone-pits before joining the company.

Eppie had a larger garden than she had ever expected there now; and in other ways there had been alterations at the expense of Mr. Cass, the landlord, to suit Silas's larger family. For he and Eppie had declared that they would rather stay at the Stone-pits than go to any new home. The garden was fenced with stones on two sides, but in front there was an open fence, through which the flowers shone with answering gladness, as the four united people came within sight of them.

"Oh, father," said Eppie, "what a pretty home ours is! I think nobody could be happier than we are."

THE END.

www.ingramcontent.com/pod-product-compliance
Lightning Source LLC
LaVergne TN
LVHW021321110826
845150LV00003B/639

9781425556594